20 062 686 86

AF744905

WITHDRAWN

THE LAW OF MERGER CONTROL IN THE EC AND THE UK

This text introduces the reader to the principles and practice of merger control in the EC and the UK. It deals clearly with both of the new regimes, providing a discussion of the policy and the relevant legislation, clarified through an analysis of pertinent cases and decisions. The aim is to provide the non-expert reader with a thorough and accessible introduction to the subject. The book deals first with matters common to both regimes, including relevant economics, and then focuses on the EC and UK systems as separate entities. In each case the text covers qualifying mergers, including principles of territorial jurisdiction, substantive tests, procedures, appeals, and third party rights, as well as the link between the UK and EC regimes. The book is up to date to 31 July 2006. Substantial appendices provide most of the relevant core legislation in one convenient place.

The Law of Merger Control in the EC and the UK

Mark Furse

·HART·
PUBLISHING
OXFORD AND PORTLAND, OREGON
2007

Published in North America (US and Canada) by
Hart Publishing
c/o International Specialized Book Services
920 NE 58th Avenue, Suite 300
Portland, OR 97213-3786
USA
Tel: +1 503 287 3093 or toll-free: (1) 800 944 6190
Fax: +1 503 280 8832
E-mail: orders@isbs.com
Website: www.isbs.com

© Mark Furse, 2007

Mark Furse has asserted his right under the Copyright, Designs and Patents Act 1988, to be identified as the author of this work.

All rights reserved. No part of this publication may be reproduced, stored in a retrieval system, or transmitted, in any form or by any mean, without the prior permission of Hart Publishing, or as expressly permitted by law or under the terms agreed with the appropriate reprographic rights organisation. Enquiries concerning reproduction which may not be covered by the above should be addressed to Hart Publishing at the address below.

Hart Publishing, 16C Worcester Place, OX1 2JW
Telephone: +44 (0)1865 517530 Fax: +44 (0)1865 510710
E-mail: mail@hartpub.co.uk
Website: http://www.hartpub.co.uk

British Library Cataloguing in Publication Data
Data Available

ISBN-13: 978-1-84113-575-0 (paperback)
ISBN-10: 1-84113-525-9 (paperback)

Typeset by Hope Services, Abingdon
Printed and bound in Great Britain by
TJ International Ltd, Padstow, Cornwall

NORTHUMBRIA UNIVERSITY
LIBRARY
ITEM No. 2006268686
CLASS No. 346.0662094 FUR

Preface

Merger control is an area which is simultaneously fascinating and complex. Individual cases are in fact so complex that Derek Bok once commented that 'consideration of all relevant factors may actually detract from the accuracy' of the decision taken.[1] It is an area that is hardly touched on in the process of formal legal education, and is left instead to be learnt in the process of practice. Where taught it is usually as a small component of a wider competition law programme, although it is assuming increasing prominence in such programmes. It is also an area in which practitioners may assert, with some justification, that only with practice can knowledge of the area be complete, and unfortunately practitioners may be unwilling to divulge know-how to those outside their firm. For the last two years at the University of Glasgow I have turned students away from an LLM option dealing with 'international merger control' due to the popularity of the subject.

While it may be presumptuous of an academic to attempt to write a book dealing with an area so grounded in practice, I want it to be clear what the aim of this book is. This is to provide an introduction to merger control in the EC and UK, in both of which 'new' regimes, albeit heavily based on earlier systems, of merger control have come into effect in the recent past. In the case of the UK the merger control system set out in the Enterprise Act 2002 offers a total restatement of the regime of the Fair Trading Act 1973, although many provisions of the new law are drawn directly from the old. In the EC, Regulation 139/2004 may be seen as an amendment of Regulation 4064/89, but it is a substantial amendment. In particular the substantive test under which a merger is to be assessed has been rewritten, although the Commission has indicated that it expects the majority of cases to continue to be determined on the basis of criteria applied under the older regime.

This book is intended to be appropriate and useful to those coming to merger control either as advanced students of competition law generally, or merger control specifically, or as lawyers who are not yet experienced in the application of merger control law in the EC and UK, but who are involved in their first cases, perhaps as part of a larger team. It is my hope that those embarking on case work in the area may find it useful to have available an introduction to the subject that goes beyond the few chapters found in general competition texts, but which is not steeped in the comprehensive detail of the large practitioner texts that are available in respect of both regimes (these are referenced in the bibliography). I am well aware, as the reader must be too, that there is virtually no

[1] DC Bok, 'Section 7 of the Clayton Act and the Merging of Law and Economics' (1960) 74 *Harvard Law Review* 226 at 228.

point at which any one paragraph in this text could not be expanded dramatically to take into account all the relevant legislation and practice.

In this book I deal first with the general outline of the merger control regimes in the UK and the EC, and then with the broad economic theories on which these regimes are predicated. In the case of both regimes the emphasis is on jurisdiction, notification, the substantive test to be applied, procedures and appeals. The relevant legislation and the mass of guidance published by DG Competition, the OFT and the CC is set out in what I hope is a clear structure, supported by reference to decisions and cases, and comment, as well as consideration of the views of commentators and those working with the regime where these clarify the position, or where they point to tensions or problems in the operation of the regime.

As anyone who has worked in the area of merger control will be aware the amount of literature it generates is vast. This is produced by the relevant authorities and their officials, the practitioner community, academics and industry commentators, and adopts both legal and economic perspectives. I have attempted in these 325 pages to analyse and present this wide body of work as clearly as possible. There is a bias in this book towards the law of the EC. This reflects the fact that there is a much more extensive literature in respect of the operation of EC merger control than there is in relation to the UK. Given that the EC regime applies only to the very largest of mergers this is perhaps understandable, but it does not fairly reflect the fact that even at the lower level at which the UK regime applies the transactions under consideration may be a matter of commercial life or death for the parties involved. It is the case, however, that many of the principles employed in the application of the law at the EC level are pertinent at the national level.

I owe thanks to a number of people. First, and most importantly, to Kimberley Goh, who has provided sterling research assistance in the collation of a vast range of material. Jennifer Hendry, a research student at the EUI, also provided assistance in the summer of 2006. The school of law of the University of Glasgow has been supportive of my work, and provided an excellent environment in which to pursue it. Students of international commercial law and international competition law and policy have formed a critical and intelligent audience over recent years, and have helped me to clarify points which at first appeared opaque. A number of practitioners, both lawyers and economists, have contributed to improving this book, and I am grateful to them. My publishers have been conscientious and helpful in the preparation of this text, and I am as grateful for their decision to accept this book for publication as I am for their commitment to publish it at a price within the reach of individual purchasers. Any errors or omissions remain my sole responsibility, and I would be grateful for any comments on the text. My email address is: m.furse@law.gla.ac.uk.

The law in this book is intended to be up to date as at 31 July 2006.

Mark Furse
University of Glasgow

Contents

List of Abbreviations

CA 03	Communications Act 2003
CAT	Competition Appeals Tribunal
CBI	Confederation of British Industry
CC	Competition Commission
CFI	Court of First Instance of the European Community
DG Comp	EC Commission, Competition Directorate (formerly DG IV)
DGFT	Director General of Fair Trading
DGES	Director General of Electricity Supply
DTI	Department of Trade and Industry
DWL	Deadweight welfare loss
EA 02	Enterprise Act 2002
EC	European Community
ECA	European Competition Authorities
ECJ	European Court of Justice
ECMR	EC Merger Regulation (Regulation 139/2004)
ECN	European Competition Network
ECSC	European Coal and Steel Community
EEA	European Economic Area
EEC	European Economic Community
FTA 73	Fair Trading Act 1973
FTC	Federal Trade Commission
HHI	Herfindahl–Hirschman Index
IT	Information technology
JV	Joint venture
MMC	Monopolies and Mergers Commission
NCA	National Competition Authority
Ofcom	Office of Communications
OFT	Office of Fair Trading
OFWAT	Office of the Water Regulator
OJ	Official Journal of the European Communities
R & D	Research and development
SIEC	Significantly impede effective competition
SLC	Substantial lessening of effective competition
SO	Statement of Objections
SSNIP	Small, but significant, non-transitory increase in price
WIA 91	Water Industry Act 1991
WSRA	Water Services Regulation Authority

Table of Cases

EC Commission Decisions

European Court of Justice and Court of First Instance

Alphabetical

Numerical

Italy

United Kingdom

Merger Decisions and Reports

United States

FTC

Table of Legislation

European Community

Decisions

Directives

Regulations

International

United Kingdom

Statutory Instruments

1

Introduction

THIS TEXT DEALS with the control of mergers at the point at which they are evaluated by the appropriate administrative body—the Commission in the case of the EC, and the Office of Fair Trading and Competition Commission in the case of the UK—in the light of the competitive impact of the merger. Other regulatory aspects that may impact on the merger process, such as financial rules, will not be considered here. This chapter provides a very broad outline of the respective regimes. In the second chapter there is an introduction to the economic arguments underpinning, and employed in the application of, the relevant law. Chapter 3 outlines the relationship between the two regimes, which is more fractured than is the case in respect of competition law generally. Chapters 4–9 deal with the relevant law of the EC, and Chapters 10–18 with the position in the UK. It should be stressed at the outset that merger control is a uniquely complex area of competition law (final decisions are often extremely lengthy and are based on a forecast of likely competitive scenarios rather than an analysis of an existing competitive environment), and that this text is intended as an introduction only—albeit a clear and accurate one—to the area. The emphasis throughout the text will be on the mergers that fall within the general regimes set out in Regulation 139/2004[1] and the Enterprise Act 2002 in the case of the EC and UK respectively. In the case of the UK there are special arrangements in place for some categories of mergers, and these are discussed separately in Chapters 16 and 17. In the EC regime the law applies, strictly, to 'concentrations'. Throughout this text, unless it is necessary for the purposes of precision, the term 'merger', which is more widely understood, shall be used. The term 'concentration' is defined in Chapter 4.

SOURCES AND REFERENCING

There are a number of bodies that are responsible for the application of merger control in the EC and the UK. This means inevitably that resources are not concentrated in one place, and there is no regular reporting system that covers this

[1] Council Regulation (EC) 139/2004 on the control of concentrations between undertakings [2004] OJ L 24/1 (hereinafter the ECMR).

area. Table 1.1 sets out the most direct route to the material emanating from the relevant authorities. However, this may change from time to time, and the references here are up to date as at 1 July 2006.

In the majority of merger cases decisions are made early on in the process, and the majority of these confirm only that the merger either does not fall within the necessary thresholds to be reviewed, or that it raises no competitive concern. However, where proceedings continue to a final decision on the competitive merits of the merger there may, along the way, be a number of decisions made, although these will for the most part be encapsulated in the final decision. EC Commission proceedings in respect of mergers are referenced separately from decisions taken in respect of the other areas of competition law, and a case carries with it the same reference number throughout the totality of these proceedings. Thus, for example, the *Airtours/First Choice* merger is consistently referenced as Case IV/M.1524. When the final Decision blocking the merger was published it appeared as Commission Decision (EC) 2000/276 [2000] OJ L 93/1. Throughout this book the only number given will be that allocated to the case at the outset, and stages of the procedure will, where necessary, be distinguished by the date on which the relevant decision was made or document was published. References to the Official Journal will not normally be given, save occasionally in footnotes, as by far the easier route to find the materials is via the EC Commission website, which presents a nearly comprehensive set of materials. Articles of the EC Treaty are throughout given their 'new' numbering unless the historical context demands otherwise. Where numbering is changed in quotations the numbers are placed in square brackets: thus 'Article 86' becomes 'Article [82]'.

Table of sources

Body	Type of material	Source
EC Commission	Legislation, guidance, speeches, all decisions through to final	http://europa.eu.int/comm/competition/index_en.html
Court of First Instance	First appeals from Commission actions	http://curia.eu.int/ Judgments are also reported in the ECR and CMLR series
Court of Justice	Appeals from judgments of the CFI	http://curia.eu.int/ Judgments are also reported in the ECR and CMLR series
Office of Fair Trading	Guidance, all decisions through to referral	www.oft.gov.uk Decisions are also reported in the UKCLR

Body	Type of material	Source
Competition Commission	Guidance, all decisions following referral by OFT	www.competition-commission.org.uk
Competition Appeals Tribunal	Judgments following appeals against OFT or CC actions and decisions	www.catribunal.org.uk Judgments are also comprehensively reported in Competition Appeal Reports (CompAR)

There are a large number of reference works that deal with merger control in the relevant jurisdictions, and some of these are listed in the bibliography at the end of this book. The literature in the area is vast, and the bibliography is not a comprehensive one, but refers to all the material relied on in the writing of this book, and may serve as a first point for further research. A number of relevant journals are published, of which the most useful is the *European Competition Law Review* published by Sweet & Maxwell. The appendices to this book reproduce the core legislative instruments of the ECMR and its implementing regulation, and the relevant sections and schedules of the Enterprise Act 2002. While there are a number of other relevant materials the selection here has been driven by the economics of publishing, and all guidelines and notices are referred to throughout this text as appropriate. All are available on the various websites referred to above.

MERGER CONTROL IN THE EC

The development of the law

As originally drafted the Treaty of Rome, following on from the ECSC Treaty, contained provisions relating to the control of anti-competitive agreements and the conduct of undertakings holding a dominant position, but did not contain, unlike the ECSC Treaty, any express provisions relating to merger control. Given that such a power had been written into the ECSC Treaty it appeared to be evident that its omission from the EEC Treaty was deliberate. Thus it has been noted that:

> there seems little doubt that those responsible for drafting articles 81 and 82 did not intend that this should give control over mergers to the Commission. Neither the actual wording of the [articles] nor the evidence of those who participated in the negotiations leading up to the Treaty or in its early administration support any contrary argument.[2]

[2] D G Goyder, *EC Competition Law* (4th edn, Oxford, OUP 2003), 335.

As the application of Articles 81 and 82 EC became more important, and eventually assumed a leading role in the development of EC law, this lacuna became a matter of some frustration to the EC Commission. There had been speculation that Articles 81 and 82 themselves could be applicable to merger situations, but this was a matter of concern to industry, which feared resulting legal uncertainty. The argument in essence was that it might be an abuse of a dominant position for an already dominant undertaking to acquire a competitor, and that the agreements inevitably made in a merger process might fall foul of Article 81. Were this established to be the position there would indeed have been grounds for serious concern. Merger control is largely a prophylactic process, whereas Articles 81 and 82 EC are enforced retrospectively (albeit that they are intended to deter anti-competitive conduct). Even were companies to notify their 'agreements' to merge to the Commission seeking clearance under the rules relating to the application of Article 81 EC the process was not structured to deal with the furnace of a merger. It was not uncommon for the Commission to take several years to respond to requests to examine standard agreements. Any informal response by the Commission would not provide the legal certainty that is essential to those contemplating large-, or even small-scale mergers. Nevertheless while case law was developing apace under Articles 81 and 82, and the primacy of EC competition law over the law of the Member States was being asserted, merger control remained in the hands of a patchwork of Member States. In 1966 the Commission accepted, erroneously, that Article 81 could not apply to merger control, arguing that the Article would no longer have any application to a situation which went beyond one of cooperation between independent enterprises.[3] This was based on the assumption that the wording of Article 81 EC limited its application to the situation in which there were 'two or more' *independent* undertakings.

In 1972 the Commission applied Article 82 to a situation in which a takeover bid was made by a dominant undertaking for a smaller competitor. The Commission first intervened in the deal, which took the form of a takeover bid made for Tomassen & Drijver Verblifa (TDV) by Europemballage Corp, itself a subsidiary of a much larger American company, Continental Can, which had substantial interests in the EEC. The Commission took the view that such an arrangement might be an abuse of Article 82 EC in that it would adversely affect the structure of competition in a market which was already weakened by a lack of competition. When the takeover proceeded the Commission made a Decision ordering that steps be taken to bring the 'infringement' to an end.[4] The parties appealed, and the Commission decision was annulled on the grounds that the Commission had failed adequately to define the relevant market (see Chapter 2, below). The European Court of Justice (ECJ) confirmed, however, that the Article could be applied to situations in which a dominant undertaking sought

[3] 'Le problème de la concentration dans le Marchè Commun', Etudes CEE (Series Concurrence No 3, 24 (1966)), cited in Goyder, above n 2, at 335.

[4] *Re Continental Can Co. Inc.* Dec 72/71, [1972] OJ L 7/25.

further to reduce competition through a process of takeover or acquisition. In particular the Court rejected the argument that because express provision had been made for merger control in the ECSC Treaty, but not in the EC Treaty, no such powers were available to the EC Commission in the application of EEC competition law.[5] Following the judgment of the Court, which alarmed many, the Commission, at the request of the Member States, prepared a draft legislative instrument for merger control. This needed to be unanimously approved by the Member States in order to be adopted, and unanimity was not forthcoming.

In 1988 a more significant development, with potentially far wider ramifications, saw the ECJ reviewing the application by the EC Commission of Article 81 EC to an agreement between cigarette manufacturers including Rembrandt Group, which had a controlling interest in Rothmans, and Philip Morris which would have given Philip Morris a strong degree of control over the Rembrandt tobacco division. The two parties notified their agreement to the Commission, and following negotiations between the parties, the agreement was given the Commission's seal of approval. However, the very fact that the parties had chosen to notify this agreement, and the fact that the Commission chose to examine it, was evidence of the possibility that Article 81 could be applied to agreements leading to mergers. This position therefore ran counter to that set out in the 1966 memorandum. BAT and Reynolds, two large undertakings competing with the notifying parties, brought an action on the basis of Article 230 EC seeking an annulment of the Commission decision to clear the arrangement. The ECJ rejected the applicants' argument, holding that it could not be demonstrated that the agreements actually infringed Article 81 EC in that it could not be established that they had the object or effect of preventing, restricting or distorting competition.[6] At the same time the Court held that agreements leading to concentrations in the market could be reviewed in the light of the application of Article 81 EC, and could fall within the prohibition set out in Article 81(1).

The combined effect of these two cases therefore was to demonstrate that both Articles 81 and 82 EC could be applied to mergers where the jurisdictional requirements of the Articles were satisfied. This led to the prospect that mergers could be reviewed by national authorities, yet still fall foul of Articles 81 and 82 EC. Particular fears were raised that private parties could, on the basis of the direct effect of these provisions, challenge consummated mergers, leading to commercial chaos. It was also recognised that to rely purely on the application of Articles 81 and 82 EC, with their formal limitations, would be unequal to the task of operating a rational and effective merger policy. Recital (7) of the ECMR

[5] Case 6/72, *Europemballage Corp. and Continental Can Co. v Commission*, [1973] CMLR 199. Goyder, above n 2, notes that: '[t]here is no better example of the difference between the approach adopted by the [ECJ] to the interpretation of the Treaty of Rome and that which would have been adopted by any English Court than this decision, whose outcome was a surprise to many, though received gratefully by the Commission' (at 337).

[6] Cases 142 and 156/84, *BAT Ltd and RJ Reynolds Industries Inc v Commission* [1988] 4 CMLR 24.

reflects this position, as well as the fact that by themselves Articles 81 and 82 would not provide an adequate basis for a coherent system of merger control:

> Articles 81 and 82, while applicable according to the case-law of the Court of Justice, to certain concentrations, are not sufficient to control all operations which may prove to be incompatible with the system of undistorted competition envisaged in the Treaty.

The EC Commission then brought forward proposals to introduce an effective merger control regime, relying also on Article 308 of the Treaty, under which the EC may give itself the power to perform tasks necessary to the attainment of the objectives of the EC, when the express power to do so is not otherwise given in the Treaty. After intense negotiations with the Member States the proposal resulted in the enactment of Council Regulation (EEC) 4064/89 on the control of concentrations between undertakings.[7] This Regulation entered into force on 21 September 1990, and set the shape for the EC merger regime which remains in place following subsequent amendments, and the enactment of Regulation 139/2004, which replaced the earlier Regulation.

Regulation 4064/89 provided that, save with certain defined exceptions, the EC Commission was to have exclusive competence to review mergers having a 'Community dimension'. Thresholds were established above which mergers would no longer fall to be reviewed under the terms of any Member State's merger regime.[8] In 1997 the merger was subject to some significant amendment,[9] and the thresholds at which it applied were amended, although the amendment was not as radical as the EC Commission had advocated.[10] At the end of 2001 the Commission launched a major review of the Regulation, designed in part to provoke a discussion on the extent to which the regime should be aligned with that of the US, given the increasing number of mergers that were being reviewed by both authorities.[11] In addition three judgments of the CFI overturning decisions taken by the EC Commission to block mergers had focussed attention on limitations in the substantive test.[12] Under Regulation 4064/89 the test of a merger's acceptance was linked to the law of dominance set out in Article 82 EC. The US, on the other hand, along with a number of significant jurisdictions (including now the UK) operates a test of whether the merger would tend to 'substantially

[7] First published at [1989] OJ L 395/1. However, the presence of an unacceptably high number of textual errors lead to a revised publication at [1990] OJ L 257/13.

[8] The Regulation cannot exclude the operation of non-member states' merger laws to qualifying mergers.

[9] Council Regulation 1310/97 [1997] OJ L 180/1.

[10] See RA Kassamali, 'From Fiction to Fallacy: Reviewing the EC Merger Regulation's Community-Dimension Thresholds in the Light of Economics and Experience in Merger Control' *EL Rev* (1996) 21 Supp (Competition).

[11] *Green Paper on the Review of Council Regulation (EEC) No 4064/89*, COM(2001)745/6 final, 11 Dec 2001.

[12] See Chaps 8 and 9, below.

lessen competition' (hereinafter the 'SLC' test).[13] The Commission Green Paper suggested that to align the test would:

> Facilitate merger parties' global assessment of possible competition issues arising from contemplated transactions, by obviating the need to argue their case according to differently formulated tests. This would in turn provide competition agencies with a better basis on which to build effective cooperation in cases that are notified in several jurisdictions.[14]

In the event there was disagreement between the Member States, with Germany resisting any change from the existing dominance test, and the UK favouring a move to an SLC test.[15] However:

> a large majority of delegations supports a compromise solution which combines the Dominance Test with the 'significant impediment of effective competition' (SIEC test) in a way that any possible gap with regard to non-collusive oligopolies is closed[16] and therefore providing a maximum certainty for business while persevering existing case-law by the Court of Justice by maintaining the threshold of 'significant impediment of effective competition'.[17]

[13] The case of Australia is interesting in this respect. Goldberg writes that:

> 'The experience of Australia, which has gone from a substantial lessening of competition test, to a market dominance test, and back again, is instructive. According to former ACCC Chairman, Allan Fels, Australia changed from a substantial lessening of competition test to a dominance test in 1977 to allow more mergers to take place. However, with the emergence of anti-competitive market structures in a number of industries whilst the market dominance test was employed, Australia reverted back to the substantial lessening of competition test, believing that it offered a more stringent standard and was better able to prevent mergers that gave rise to coordinated conduct, as well as single firm dominance'.

AH Goldberg, 'Merger Control: A Complex Trade-off' [2005] *Comp Law* 171, at 179.

[14] Para 160.

[15] See generally G Drauz and M Reynolds (eds), *EC Merger Control: A Major Reform in Progress* (Richmond, Surrey, Richmond Law and Tax, 2003); John Vickers, Chairman of the OFT at the time, was particularly scathing in his criticism of the dominance test. See, eg, 'How to Reform the EC Merger Test', 8 Nov 2002 available at www.oft.gov.uk, and J Vickers, 'Competition Economics and Policy' [2003] *ECLR* 95. See also Z Biro and D Parker, 'A New EC Merger Test? Dominance v Substantial Lessening of Competition' [2002] *Comp Law* 157; J Schmidt, 'The New ECMR: "Significant Impediment" or "Significant Improvement"?' (2004) 41 *CML Rev* 1555; U Böge and E Müller, 'From the Market Dominance Test to the SLC Test: Are There Any Reasons for a Change?' [2002] *ECLR* 495; S Baxter and F Dethmers, 'Unilateral Effects Under the European Merger Regulation: How Big is the Gap?' [2005] *ECLR* 380; K Fountoukakos and S Ryan, 'A New Substantive Test for EU Merger Control' [2005] *ECLR* 277; I Kokkoris, 'The Reform of the European Control Merger Regulation in the Aftermath of the *Airtours* Case—the Eagerly Expected Debate: SLC v Dominance Test', [2005] *ECLR* 37; S Bishop and D Ridyard, 'Prometheus Unbound: Increasing the Scope for Intervention in EC Merger Control' [2003] *ECLR* 357; W Berg and P Ostendorf, 'The Reform of EC Merger Control: Substance and Impact of the Proposed New Procedural Rules' [2003] *ECLR* 594; and SB Völcker 'Mind the Gap: Unilateral Effects Analysis Arrives in EC Merger Control' [2004] *ECLR* 395. See also T Soames and S Maudhuit, 'Changes in EU Merger Control' [2005] *ECLR* 57, at 75 and 144 (3 parts).

[16] See further Chap 7, below.

[17] COREPER Report to the Council of the European Union, *Proposal for a Council Regulation on the control of concentrations between undertakings ('The EC Merger Regulation')*, 15122/03 RC, 21 Nov 2003.

At the same time as raising discussion about the nature of the test to be adopted the Commission again sought to reduce the thresholds at which a concentration would have a Community dimension. Again the Commission failed in this objective, although Article 1(4) of Regulation 139/2004 incorporates a commitment to report on the operation of the present thresholds by 1 July 2009, and provides that the Commission *may* bring forward proposals to have these amended. Other procedural amendments were also made in the Regulation, and the discussion in this text ignores earlier procedures, and is based entirely on the new text.

Outline of the regime of the ECMR

This section provides an overview of the operation of the EC merger regime, and all the following points are made more fully in Chapters 3–9 as appropriate.

The institutions involved

The primary institution charged with the enforcement of the ECMR is the EC Commission, Competition Directorate (DG Comp). Article 85 EC gives the Commission the leading role in the enforcement of EC competition law generally, and the ECMR confers exclusive jurisdiction upon the Commission in the case of concentrations having a 'Community dimension'. The Commission generally is governed by Articles 211–219 EC, with Article 211 specifying that the Commission should ensure compliance with EC law, and must exercise the specific powers given to it by the Council of Ministers. In the case of merger control these specific powers are set out in the ECMR and in the implementing regulation.[18] The jurisdiction assigned to the Commission under the ECMR is exclusive. Individuals aggrieved by mergers falling within the ECMR have no right to challenge the merger under either EC or domestic law, although they may be involved in the Commission proceedings, and may, in some circumstances, have the right to challenge Commission decisions before the CFI.

At certain specific points in the procedure the Commission is obliged to consult an Advisory Committee on concentrations. Article 19(4) of the ECMR provides that this 'shall consist of representatives of the competent authorities of the Member States. Each Member State shall appoint one or two representatives'. The Advisory Committee is also consulted before the enactment of further secondary legislation.

National competition authorities do not, directly, play a role in the enforcement of the ECMR. The link between the EC and national merger control

[18] Commission Regulation 802/2004 implementing Council Regulation (EC) No 139/2004 on the control of concentrations between undertakings [2004] OJ L 133/1. The provisions of this regulation are extensively referred to in Chap 5, below.

regimes is discussed in Chapter 3. In essence Member States may refer mergers not having a Community dimension to the EC Commission for consideration under the ECMR if the Commission agrees to the request, and in certain defined cases mergers with a Community dimension, or parts of the transactions, may be referred back to the Member States for consideration under their national procedures. Member States do *not* apply the terms of the ECMR, but work exclusively on the basis of their relevant national law, although there may be some limitations imposed through the terms of the ECMR.

Acts of the Commission may, in certain circumstances (discussed in Chapter 9), be challenged before the Court of First Instance (CFI), and further appeals, on points of law only, may be made to the European Court of Justice (ECJ). Article 230 EC provides for a procedure akin to judicial review, which may be invoked by, inter alia, those to whom decisions are addressed, and in addition those to whom they are of direct and individual concern. Article 232 EC permits judicial review in the case of failures to act. Article 288 EC provides in part that:

> In the case of non-contractual liability, the Community shall, in accordance with the principles common to the laws of the Member States, make good any damage caused by its institutions or by its servants in the performance of their duties.

This procedure is only rarely invoked, although there is speculation that it may apply where mergers are wrongly blocked or approved.

Article 220 EC allocates to the ECJ the role of ensuring 'that in the interpretation and application of this Treaty the law is observed'. In 1988 the CFI was created by Council Decision 88/591 with the purpose of speeding up the judicial procedures within the EC, and the CFI is now governed by Article 225 EC, which provides in part that the Court has 'jurisdiction to hear and determine at first instance, subject to a right of appeal to the Court of Justice on points of law only . . . certain classes of action'. Cases brought on the basis of Article 230 EC are included within these classes of action, with the effect that the CFI is now the first port of call for challenges to competition decisions, including merger decisions, made by the Commission. Article 51 of the Protocol on the Statute of the ECJ sets out the grounds for further appeal from the CFI as being: (a) lack of competence of the CFI; (b) breach of procedure before the CFI; and (c) breach of Community law by the CFI.

ECMR procedures

Under the terms of the ECMR all qualifying concentrations must be notified to the EC Commission. Failure to notify is a breach of the ECMR and may attract penalties, as well as carrying with it the risk that the Commission may later require the consummated merger to be untangled.[19] The definition of 'concentration' is set out in Article 3 ECMR, and in essence is one of a 'change of

[19] See Art 8(4) ECMR.

control on a lasting basis'.[20] Such a change may occur through the merger of previously independent undertakings, or the acquisition by a controller of one undertaking of control of another. The concept of 'acquisition' is given a wide meaning, and includes any direct financial purchase, a purchase of shares, or any other means (including, for example, asset swaps). Control may flow either from ownership or from the ability to exercise certain rights if these confer a 'decisive influence' over the business strategy of the undertaking(s) concerned. The question whether there is a decisive influence is to be determined on a case by case basis in the light of all the relevant circumstances.[21] Thus, for example, control has been found in the case where a share of only 19 per cent of the company was held, given that the remaining shares were held by an investment bank whose approval was not always required in respect of important decisions.[22]

For the purposes of the ECMR concentrations must take place between 'undertakings'. This term is the one generally used in EC competition law, and is nowhere defined in the legislation.[23] For the purposes of competition law generally, as well as for merger control in particular, it is important that the legal and economic analysis focuses on the competitive impact of the entities concerned, rather than on the legal status of the relevant entities. The ECJ has thus held that 'the concept of an undertaking encompasses every entity engaged in economic activity, regardless of the legal status of the entity and the way in which it is financed'.[24] Parent and subsidiary companies may be held to be the same undertaking, the test being that of the extent to which the parent controls, or may control, the subsidiary.[25] State owned businesses may also be held to be undertakings for the purposes of competition law and merger control,[26] although this does not extend to those that merely purchase goods on the market place to use in the provision of services which are not commercially offered.[27] The ECMR makes express reference to 'persons', and where an individual acquires an undertaking that individual may, by virtue of other commercial interests held, be considered to be an undertaking for the purposes of the ECMR.[28]

The ECMR applies where concentrations have a Community dimension.[29] The relevant thresholds are set out in Article 1 ECMR, and are discussed in full

[20] A fuller discussion of this is given in Chap 4, below.

[21] See, eg, Case T–102/96, *Gencor Ltd v Commission* [1999] 4 CMLR 971, at paras 167–194.

[22] Case IV/M.258 *CCIE/GTE* (1992) [1992] OJ C 258/10.

[23] Although see the Commission *Notice on the concept of undertakings concerned under Council Regulation (EEC) 4064/89 on the control of concentrations between undertakings* [1998] OJ C 66/3.

[24] Case C–41/90, *Hofner and Elser v Macrotron GmbH* [1993] 4 CMLR 306, at para 21.

[25] See, eg, Case T–102/92, *Viho Europe BV v Commission* [1995] 4 CMLR 299.

[26] Case IV/M.157 *Air France/Sabena* (1992). Here the Commission held that the application of the ECMR 'cannot be called into question by the fact that the Belgian state is not an undertaking' (at para 11).

[27] Case T–319/99, *FENIN v Commission* [2003] 5 CMLR 1.

[28] See Case IV/M.82 *Asko/Jacobs/Adia* (1991).

[29] Although it may apply to concentrations without a Community dimension where referrals are accepted from Member States (see Chap 3, below).

in Chapter 4, below. There are two separate thresholds. The first catches the very largest of transactions where the combined turnover of the parties is in excess of €5,000 million, and where at least two of the relevant undertakings have turnovers in the EC in excess of €250 million, provided that not all of the undertakings concerned have two thirds of their turnover in the same EC Member State, in which case the matter is considered to be one best dealt with by that state, subject to its own procedures. The second set of thresholds applies to mergers where the combined turnover of the parties is in excess of €2,500 million, and requires a more diffuse EC wide turnover, again subject to the two-thirds rule. The Commission may also, with the consent of the Member States, assume jurisdiction where a merger would fall to be considered in at least three of the Member States and the parties request that the Commission take over the case.[30] For the purposes of establishing jurisdiction no distinction is made between mergers involving EC-based undertakings and those involving foreign-based undertakings.

Undertakings engaged in a merger with a Community dimension are required to notify the merger to the EC Commission, 'following the conclusion of the agreement, the announcement of the public bid or the acquisition of the controlling interest'.[31] Once a concentration has been notified, and even where it has not been, but does in fact have a Community dimension, Article 7(1) ECMR requires that 'it shall not be implemented . . . until it has been declared compatible with the common market'. The substantive test against which these mergers will be assessed is set out in Article 2 ECMR, which was amended with the enactment of Regulation 139/2004, as discussed above. The test now is whether the merger would 'significantly impede effective competition in the common market or in a substantial part of it, in particular as a result of the creation or strengthening of a dominant position'. The application of this test forms the subject of Chapters 6 and 7, below.

The Commission procedure is divided into two stages: Phase I and Phase II. Phase I applies to the procedures leading to a first decision, and Phase II to the procedures which apply should the Commission determine at the end of Phase I that a more thorough review of the notified concentration is necessary. Strict time limits are imposed on the Commission, and on the parties, at both stages. Article 6(1) ECMR provides that the Commission is obliged to examine the notification as soon as it is received, and the Commission has 25 working days to take a decision under Article 6(1). There are three possible decisions which may be taken at this stage: (1) the concentration does not have a Community dimension, in which case the proceedings shall be terminated at this stage; (2) the concentration, while having a Community dimension, 'does not raise serious doubts as to its compatibility with the common market',[32] in which case

[30] Art 4(5) ECMR. See further Chap 3, below.
[31] Recital (34) ECMR. See also Art 4(1), ECMR.
[32] Art 6(1)(b) ECMR.

the Commission shall issue a decision declaring the concentration to be compatible with the common market; and (3) that the concentration both has a Community dimension and does raise 'serious doubts as to its compatibility with the common market'.[33] In this case the Commission will initiate a Phase II procedure. In order to make a decision of compatibility with the common market in the case of concentration having a Community dimension, the Commission may accept commitments from the parties, and may attach conditions and obligations to the decision to ensure that these commitments are observed. In the event that commitments are not adhered to the Commission may revoke the compatibility decision.[34]

Phase II proceedings must conclude in a decision taken on the basis of Article 8 ECMR. Phase II decisions are to be taken within 90 working days of the opening of the Phase II procedure, although this period may be extended where the notifying parties offer commitments after the first 55 days, or where they request an extension. The decisions that may be taken are the following: (1) the notified concentration is compatible with the common market;[35] the concentration is compatible with the common market following the offering of commitments;[36] and the concentration is incompatible with the common market (ie, that the merger is blocked).[37] In any case where a concentration has been wrongly implemented the Commission has a wide choice of available remedies, including full divestiture and conduct requirements.

In the application of the ECMR the Commission has been given powers of investigation and enforcement which lie outwith the general competition law regime, but which mirror those powers. Thus Article 11 ECMR gives the Commission the authority to gather information, Article 13 to carry out investigations at the premises of undertakings in the Member States, and Article 12 to request the relevant authorities of Member States to carry out such investigations on its behalf. Financial penalties may be imposed for both procedural and substantive breaches of the ECMR.[38] The rights of undertakings are protected both by the specific terms of the ECMR and by the application of the general principles of EC law. As indicated above, appeals may be made to the CFI against any applicable act taken by the EC Commission in its application of the ECMR.

Figure 1.1 sets out a greatly simplified schema of the route through the ECMR, and does not take into account referrals from, or to, Member States.

[33] Art 6(1)(c) ECMR.
[34] Art 6(3) ECMR.
[35] Art 8(1) ECMR.
[36] Art 8(2) ECMR.
[37] Art 8(3) ECMR. Art 8 decisions are discussed more fully in Chap 9, below.
[38] Art 14 ECMR.

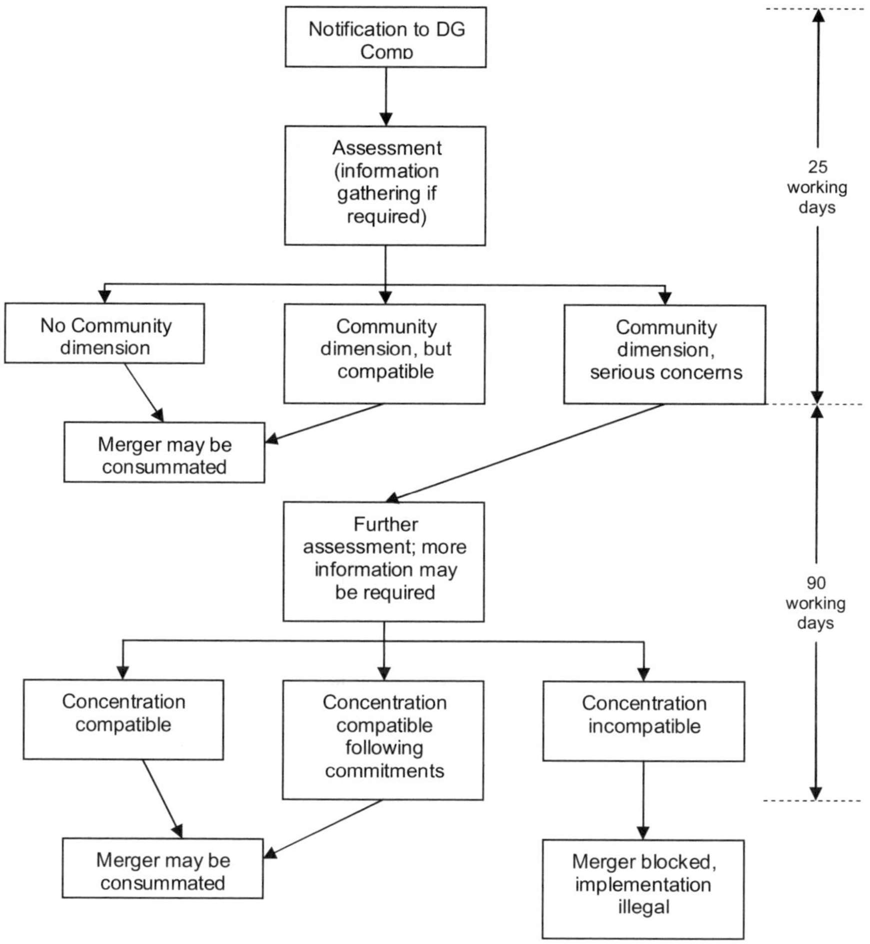

Figure 1.1 Simplified schema of merger control procedures in the EC Commission

MERGER CONTROL IN THE UK

The development of the law

The modern law of competition in the UK post-dates the Second World War and represents a clean break with older laws which, in a patchwork fashion, dealt with various anti-competitive practices. At no point did earlier laws regulate mergers. The first piece of post-war legislation to deal with competition policy was the Monopolies and Restrictive Practices (Inquiry and Control) Act 1948. This placed the Secretary of State for Trade and Industry at the apex of the regime, and created a Monopolies and Restrictive Practices Commission to investigate certain situations, against the yardstick of a 'public interest' test. Merger control was not covered in this Act, and it was not until the 1965 Monopolies and Mergers Act that a power to control mergers in the UK was created. This retained the public interest test of the 1948 Act, which was also carried through to the Fair Trading Act 1973 (FTA 73), which created a merger regime that is still recognisable in its new form as set out in the Enterprise Act 2002, although crucially the institutional arrangements and responsibilities have been fundamentally altered.

The regime as set out in the FTA 73, sections 63–75K[39] involved a tripartite structure: the Director General of Fair Trading (DGFT), heading the OFT, would undertake a provisional assessment of a qualifying merger, and make a recommendation to the Secretary of State on whether a fuller investigation was justified. The Secretary of State was not bound to accept the advice of the DGFT, and was free to decide whether or not a reference was justified. The Monopolies and Mergers Commission (MMC) would make any such investigation as was required of it, and would make recommendations to the Secretary of State, who again was not bound by these. If the Secretary of State decided that action was necessary it would be the responsibility of the DGFT to ensure that this was taken. There were no requirements to notify mergers, and no suspensory provisions applied. This cumbersome procedure attracted a great deal of criticism. First it was argued that too many players were involved; secondly, the politicisation of the process was condemned by many (although when he was Secretary of State, Norman Tebbit instituted a clear policy of following DGFT recommendations and making decisions on the basis of competition grounds); thirdly, the test itself was condemned, even by those charged with operating the system, as being vague.[40]

While the Competition Act 1998 modernised the UK law relating to anti-competitive agreements and monopoly conduct (abuse of dominant position),

[39] As amended by the Companies Act 1989. Newspaper mergers were subject to a separate regime set out in ss 52–62.

[40] The public interest test was enshrined in s 84, FTA 73, which was in the following terms:

> '(1) In determining for any purposes the extent to which this section applies whether any particular matter operates, or may be expected to operate, against the public interest, the Commission shall take into account all matters which appear to them in the particular circumstances to be relevant and, among other things, shall have regard to the desirability—
>
> (a) of maintaining and promoting effective competition between persons supplying goods and services in the United Kingdom;
>
> (b) of promoting the interests of consumers, purchasers and other users of goods and services in the United Kingdom in respect of the prices charged for them and in respect of their quality and the variety of goods and services supplied;
>
> (c) of promoting, through competition, the reduction of costs and the development and use of new techniques and new products, and of facilitating the entry of new competitors into existing markets;
>
> (d) of maintaining and promoting the balanced distribution of industry and employment in the United Kingdom; and

cont./

the merger provisions of the FTA 73 were left intact until 2002 when the Enterprise Act 2002 (EA 02) was brought forward.

The merger control provisions of the EA 02 replaced those set out in the FTA 73,[41] although the bones of the old regime are clearly visible, and many terms in the new legislation may be defined and explained by reference to decisions taken under the earlier regime. In the White Paper[42] published preparatory to the Act the Government indicated its main concerns about the 1973 regime:

> Government policy in recent years has been to take merger decisions primarily on competition grounds. Practice has been for the Government to follow the advice of the competition authorities in most cases. The reform proposals build on these developments. They have two central elements. Firstly, decisions on the vast majority of mergers will be transferred from Ministers to the OFT and the Competition Commission. Secondly, the test against which mergers are to be assessed will be changed from a broad-based 'public interest' test to a new competition-based test. The Government is also committed to procedural and other improvements, such as the introduction of maximum statutory timetables for investigations, and building more transparency into the process.[43]

These proposals were broadly welcomed, particularly by groups representative of industry, and in Committee it was recognised that 'the principles involved in changes to the [merger regime] are broadly supported by the whole gamut of organisations, and by Opposition members'.[44]

All of the aspects so heavily criticised in the FTA 73 were addressed when the Enterprise Bill was brought forward. First, it was proposed to amend the substantive test to bring it into line with that of the US and a number of Commonwealth jurisdictions. The test set out in the EA 02 is whether a merger may substantially lessen competition. The Government labelled this change 'one of the cornerstones of the new regime',[45] and in Committee it was argued by the Under Secretary of State that the introduction of the new test would 'ensure that the new regime is predictable, transparent and streamlined'.[46] The turnover test set out in the EA 02 replaces an asset test found in the FTA 73, and is set at £70 million in the case of the turnover of the enterprise being taken over in the UK. This figure is substantially higher than the £45 million that was in the

> (e) of maintaining and promoting competitive activity in markets outside the Untied Kingdom on the part of producers of goods, and of suppliers of goods and services, in the United Kingdom.'

The leading work on the FTA 73 was JP Cunningham, *The Fair Trading Act 1973: Consumer Protection and Competition Law* (London, Sweet & Maxwell, 1974).

[41] Although the FTA 73 remained in force in respect of newspaper mergers, until these provisions too were repealed. See further Chap 16, below.

[42] *A World Class Competition Regime*, Cm 5233 (London, DTI, 2001).

[43] Para 5.2. The reform process actually began well before the White Paper was published, with the Government publishing *Mergers: A consultation document on proposals for reform* in Aug 1999, and *Mergers: The response to the consultation on proposals for reform* in Oct 2000.

[44] HC Debs, Standing Committee B, 25 Apr 2002, col 253.

[45] HC Debs, 13 June 2002, vol 386, col 109.

[46] HC Debs, Standing Committee B, 25 Apr 2002, col 258.

Bill until Third Reading. The House of Lords was insisting on a figure of £100 million, and the final figure was that first suggested by the CBI.[47]

The new regime is also greatly streamlined. In all save a few specified exceptions (discussed in Chapter 17), the Secretary of State has no role to play.[48] The OFT has the role of making an initial consideration of relevant merger situations, and references are made, when it is appropriate to do so, to the Competition Commission (CC). The CC determines the outcome of the reference, and makes decisions on what remedies, if any, are appropriate, and acts accordingly.

Outline of the regime of the EA 02

This section provides an overview of the merger regime as set out in the EA 02. This is developed more fully in Chapters 11–18, below.

The institutions involved

The UK regime involves one more institution than is the case in the EC. The Office of Fair Trading (OFT) has the initial role of determining whether a relevant merger situation should be referred for further consideration to the CC. The OFT is the primary body charged with the implementation of competition law in the UK, and has responsibility under the Competition Act 1998 for applying the domestic rules relating to anti-competitive agreements and abuse of dominant position. It is also the relevant national competition authority for the purposes of EC competition law, and so may also apply Articles 81 and 82 EC, as well as being required to assist the EC Commission in the performance of its tasks. The EA 02 put the OFT on a new footing, and its responsibilities are set out in sections 1–8 of and Schedule 1 to the EA 02. The OFT is a non-ministerial government department and a Crown body. It is governed by a Board, which replaces the Director General of Fair Trading. The OFT has a specific responsibility to review markets, and is expected to be aware when mergers are made

[47] The Government had argued that the £70m turnover test would be roughly equivalent to the £45m asset test set out in the FTA 73, and that therefore the new regime would catch as many mergers as the old. Lord Sainsbury therefore argued that:

> 'The £45 million figure was derived from data research we undertook in my department. Briefly, the figure is based on an analysis of the assets and turnover levels of 110,000 UK companies. Our intention was to find a figure that we believed would account for roughly the same number of companies as is currently the case under the assets test'.

HC Debs, 18 July 2002, vol 637, col 1454. The effect of the move from £45m to £70m was estimated to be that 50% fewer mergers would be caught by the provisions.

[48] Most commentators responded positively to the move to a pure competition test, and to the removal of the Secretary of State from most decisions. See, eg, S Goodman, 'Steady As She Goes: The Enterprise Act 2002 Charts a Familiar Course for UK Merger Control' [2003] *ECLR* 331. For another view however, see BJ Rodger, 'UK Merger Control: Politics, the Public Interest and Reform' [2000] *ECLR* 24.

public. It is also required to publish information and guidance relating to the performance of its tasks. At the time of writing the OFT is reviewing its merger guidance in the light of the practice over the first years of the operation of the new regime and judgments of the Competition Appeals Tribunal. It is anticipated that the revisions will be published at the start of the 2007–8 financial year. For the purposes of general merger control law in the UK the OFT is the only body able to make a reference to the CC, and there are no private rights to challenge a merger in a civil court. Individuals may be involved in the OFT and CC procedures, and may in some circumstances have the right to appeal OFT and CC decisions to the Competition Appeals Tribunal.

The Competition Commission was created by the Competition Act 1998, and replaces the old Monopolies and Mergers Commission. The CC rules of procedure set out the rules applicable to references under the EA 02. In the case of merger inquiries a reference group is established. Each group must consist of at least three persons. The Chairman of the CC or a Deputy Chairman may attend meetings of the group and offer advice, which the group is bound to have regard to. Decisions are taken by a vote, and provision is made for the inclusion of 'minority reports' in the final published report.

Appeals against certain decisions of the OFT and the CC may be made to the specialist Competition Appeals Tribunal (CAT). This took over the functions of the Competition Commission Appeals Tribunal established by the Competition Act 1998. The appeals process is discussed below at Chapter 18. A further appeal may be made to the Court of Appeal, or the Court of Session in Scotland, on points of law. The Court of Appeal has recognised that the CAT is 'an expert and specialist tribunal, specifically constituted by Parliament to make judgments in an area in which judges have no expertise'.[49] As such it falls into the category identified in *Cooke v Secretary of State for Social Security*[50] as being a body the judgments of which the Court of Appeal would be reluctant to interfere with.

The role of the Secretary of State is discussed in Chapter 17 below, and is limited to certain defined considerations.

EA 02 procedures

Unlike the position under the ECMR there is no requirement to notify mergers to the OFT, although the OFT does have a binding duty to refer certain completed mergers to the CC. This is the case where a relevant merger situation has been created which has resulted in, or may be expected to result in, an SLC.[51] References may not be made where 'relevant customer benefits' outweigh the SLC.[52] In order to be a relevant merger situation two or more

[49] *Napp Pharmaceutical Holdings Ltd v The Director General of Fair Trading* [2002] EWCA Civ 796, [2002] UKCLR 726, per Buxton LJ at para 34.
[50] [2002] 3 All ER 279.
[51] S 21(1), EA 02.
[52] S 22(2), EA 02.

enterprises must cease to be distinct, and the value in turnover in the UK of the enterprise being taken over must exceed £70 million, or at at least one-quarter of the supply of goods or services of any description in the UK or a part of it are affected.[53] Enterprises cease to be distinct when they come under common ownership or control, with three different levels of control being identified: material influence over policy; control over policy; and a controlling interest.[54] References must be made to the CC within four months of the merger situation becoming public or, if earlier, being brought to the attention of the OFT—a significantly longer period than the 25 working days that the EC Commission has in which to decide whether to move to Phase II of its procedure. The majority of references made are in relation to anticipated mergers, and it is clear that, notwithstanding the fact that notification is not compulsory in the UK, many parties prefer to notify and seek the approval of the authorities before consummating their mergers.

The OFT may, where it identifies that an SLC may be expected to flow from a relevant merger situation, accept undertakings from the parties involved in order to remedy the harms in lieu of making a reference.[55] It may also make orders or accept undertakings in the event that a reference is made in order to preserve the competitive environment,[56] or to prevent the parties in the case of a completed merger from taking further steps to make it difficult to impose a future remedy. Although there are no standstill provisions at the initial stages in the UK (ie, a merger may lawfully be completed without the authorisation of the OFT), once a reference has been made standstill provisions do apply.[57]

Where a reference is made to the CC it is required to determine whether a relevant merger situation exists, whether an SLC may be expected to flow and, if so, what actions it should take in order to prevent, mitigate or remedy the SLC. It is required in this respect to 'have regard to the need to achieve as comprehensive a solution as is reasonable and practicable to the [SLC] and any adverse effects arising from it'.[58] The CC is required to publish a report on a merger reference within 24 weeks from the date of the reference concerned.[59] The report is to contain the decision, the reasons for it,[60] and any information necessary to understand the decision. The CC has the power to accept final

[53] S 23, EA 02. There may be situations in which this rubric catches 'small' mergers. Eg, in Feb 2004 a relevant merger situation was identified in the case of Tesco plc and a Co-op store in Uxbridge Road, Slough (OFT press release 14/04, 2 Feb 2004).

[54] S 26, EA 02. See further Chap 10, below.

[55] S 71, EA 02. The OFT has a duty in these cases to make public its intention to accept undertakings, and to take account of representations made.

[56] S 22, EA 02.

[57] Ss 77 and 78 EA 02.

[58] S 35(4) EA 02.

[59] Ss 38(1) and 39(1) EA 02.

[60] The CAT has indicated that the report should contain sufficient reasoning to form the basis for the defence of the decision in the case of an appeal: *Somerfield plc v Competition Commission* [2006] CAT 4.

undertakings from parties to remedy SLC concerns[61] and may make orders where such undertakings are not fulfilled.[62] Schedule 8 to the EA 02, discussed in Chapter 15, sets out the matters that may be imposed in orders for the purpose of remedying the adverse effects of mergers.

Both the OFT and the CC have been given the necessary powers to investigate merger situations. Sections 109–117 EA 02 give the CC the power to require the presentation of evidence and documents needed, and to compel the attendance of witnesses. Penalties may be imposed on those who do not comply with these requirements, with appeals against any penalties being made to the CAT. An offence is committed if any person supplies the OFT or CC with information which is false or misleading in a material respect, knowing this to be the case.[63]

In some public interest cases relating to considerations specified in section 58 EA 02, the Secretary of State has the power to intervene in the merger process.[64] The OFT and CC have a duty to bring to the attention of the Secretary of State such considerations if they are identified as arising (see further Chapter 17).

Figure 1.2 provides a greatly simplified schema of the route through the merger process of the EA 02. It does not take into account any mergers involving the Secretary of State, or those where the ECMR interacts with the UK system (see further Chapter 3).

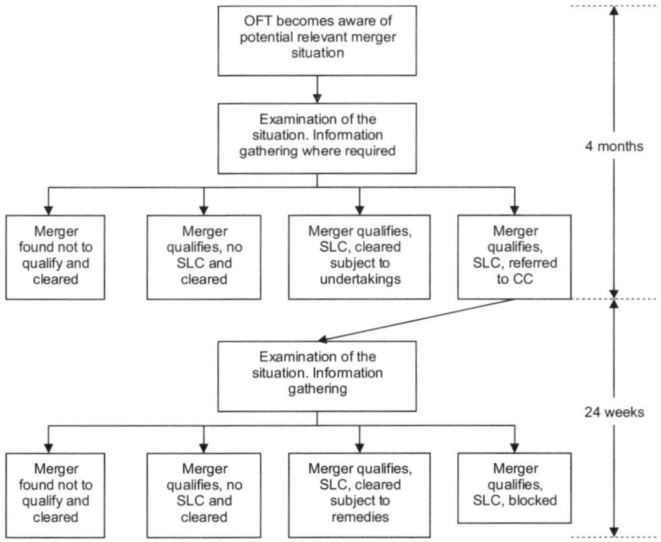

Figure 1.2 Simplified schema of merger control procedures under the EA 02

61 S 82 EA 02.
62 S 84 EA 02.
63 S 117 EA 02.
64 S 44 EA 02.

2

An Introduction to the Economics of Merger Control

INTRODUCTION

AS NOTED IN Chapter 1, merger control, for the most part, is the reserve of specialist agencies that apply a standard of review based around the prospective or actual competitive impact of the merger.[1] Notwithstanding that the test applied in the EC and the UK is somewhat different (although it is likely that the results in practice may be very similar), the same economic arguments and methods underpin the operation of both regimes, and it is these that are discussed in this chapter, although it should be noted at the outset that economists too struggle with mergers. Thus Mueller has noted that mergers 'have always been sort of an enigma in the theory of the firm'.[2] The EC Commission, the Office of Fair Trading (OFT), and the Competition Commission (CC), as well as reviewing courts, all apply the same basic approach to certain core issues, and to save repetition throughout this text these common principles are dealt with here, with any pertinent differences between the regimes highlighted. However, the application under the specific rules of each of the legal regimes and case examples is largely left to Chapters 6, 7 and 11 which deal with the substantive tests to be applied in each of the regimes.

It must, at the same time, be stressed—and particularly to economists—that whatever the general economic theories and specific tools relating to the understanding and analysis of competition, economics is used as a tool in the application of the relevant *law* in the area of merger control. To put it colloquially, law trumps economics. There are aspects of merger control law in both the EC and the UK with which some economists would disagree, and results in particular cases are often debated ex post in the academic and professional communities. It is important to bear in mind when considering the economic issues pertinent to a specific case, and the more general theories relevant to merger

[1] The position is somewhat different in the US, where the courts are more actively involved in the application of the regime. See generally R S Schlossberg (ed), *Mergers and Acquisitions: Understanding the Antitrust Issues* (2nd edn, Chicago, Ill, American Bar Association, 2004).

[2] DC Mueller, 'A Theory of Conglomerate Mergers' (1982) 82 *Quarterly Journal of Economics* 643.

control as a whole, to what use these arguments are being put. In this respect the tests set by the relevant legislation, as clarified by the relevant courts in particular cannot be ignored or shrugged aside on the ground that they are 'bad' economics, although efforts may be, and often are, made to persuade those charged with enforcement of the merits of different positions. In the meantime, and partly in response to the requirements of rigour that the law imposes, increasingly sophisticated economic tools are being developed to forecast the likely effects of mergers.[3]

It is necessary, in order to understand merger control, to have an understanding of at least a core of the economic concepts and terms that are applied in the analysis. As for this book as a whole the caveat must be given that, while the economics of mergers is not widely taught or studied within economics curricula, it is not possible to provide here more than an introduction to the subject, which may form the basis for further research or study as appropriate. In particular the bibliography given for this area is not exhaustive, as a full review of the economic literature would demonstrate. The leading work dealing exclusively with the application of economics in the wider arena of competition policy generally is S Bishop and M Walker, *The Economics of EC Competition Law*.[4]

The test to be applied to a relevant merger under the ECMR is whether the concentration:

> would significantly impede effective competition, in the common market or in a substantial part of it, in particular as a result of the creation or strengthening of a dominant position . . .[5]

The fact that this test is largely an economic one is made clear in Article 2(1)(a) and (b), which set out a list of the economic factors that the Commission is to have account of. These are as follows:

[3] See, eg, RBB Economics, 'The Emperor's New Clothes?—the Role of Merger Simulation Models', RBB Brief 12 (Jan 2004). The EC Commission has published a report analysing various tools used in the assessment of mergers involving differentiated products, including simulation models (RJ Epstein and DL Rubinfeld, 'Technical Report: Effects of Mergers Involving Differentiated Products' (2003) COMP/B1/2003/07). See also RJ Epstein and DL Rubinfeld, 'Merger Simulation: A Simplified Approach with New Applications' (2001) 69 *Antitrust Law Journal* 883; and PAG van Bergeijk and E Kloosterhuis (eds), *Modelling European Mergers: Theory, Competition Policy and Case Studies* (Cheltenham, Edward Elgar, 2005).

[4] (2nd edn, London, Sweet and Maxwell, 2002). See also D Hildebrand, *The Role of Economic Analysis in the EC Competition Rules* The Hague, Kluwer Law International, 2nd edn (2002), and MA Utton, *Market Dominance and Antitrust Policy* (2nd edn, Cheltenham, Edward Elgar, 2003). Few general industrial economics or strategy texts deal in great detail with the economics of mergers. See, however, DW Carlton and JM Perloff, *Modern Industrial Orgnanization* (4th edn, Boston, Mass, Addison Wesley, 2005), L Pepall, DJ Richards and G Norman, *Industrial Organization: Contemporary Theory and Practice* (2nd edn, Mason Ohio, South-Western, 2002), chap 8; J Church and R Ware, *Industrial Organization: A Strategic Approach* (Boston, Mass, Irwin McGraw Hill, 2000), chaps 22 and 23; and WK Viscusi, JE Harrington and JM Vernon, *Economics of Regulation and Antitrust* (4th edn, Cambridge Mass, The MIT Press, 2005), chaps 7 and 8. All of these texts also discuss the more basic economic issues that are relevant to merger control. See also R Van den Bergh, 'Modern Industrial Organisation versus Old-fashioned European Competition Law' [1996] *ECLR* 75.

[5] Art 2(3) ECMR.

(a) the need to maintain and develop effective competition within the common market in view of, among other things, the structure of all the markets concerned and the actual or potential competition from undertakings located either within or outwith the Community;
(b) the market position of the undertakings concerned and their economic and financial power, the alternatives available to suppliers and users, their access to supplies or markets, any legal or other barriers to entry, supply and demand trends for the relevant goods and services, the interests of the immediate and ultimate consumers, and the development of technical and economic progress provided that it is to consumers' advantage and does not form an obstacle to competition.

In the UK the formulation of the basic test is whether the merger concerned:

> has resulted or may be expected to result, in a substantial lessening of competition within any market or markets in the United Kingdom for goods or services.[6]

The obvious difference between these two formulations is the emphasis in the ECMR on the 'dominant position', although it is made clear now, unlike the position in Regulation 4064/89, that this is not a necessary condition for a merger to be found to fall within the prohibition. Although one of the UK threshold tests is based around a market share of 'at least one-quarter of all the goods of that description'[7] this does not approach the size of market share required for the establishment of dominance in the EC regime, where a figure of 40 per cent may be taken as a general threshold (see further below).

In both jurisdictions there is some scope for the examining authority to consider the benefits that would be likely to flow from the merger along with the detriments, although the framework within which such a balancing exercise is to be conducted differs, with the UK providing a clearer legislative route. Both the EC Commission and the OFT and CC within the UK have provided guidance on various aspects relating to the assessment exercise, and a number of economic papers and studies (some of them extremely lengthy and thorough) have been published. These are referred to in this chapter, and throughout the book, as appropriate.

THE GENERAL CASE FOR MERGER CONTROL

At its broadest level the economic case that may be made for merger control is the same as that which may be made for competition law generally. Political arguments, based around the accumulation of power, and social concerns raised by factors such as an unequal distribution of income are better left to one side, even though such factors have played a role in the development of competition

[6] See, eg, s 22(1)(b) EA 02.
[7] S 23(3) EA 02, and for services s 23(4) EA 02. The 'one-quarter' test is to be determined by reference to such criteria 'as the decision-making authority considers appropriate' (s 23(5)).

policy throughout the twentieth century.[8] In respect of these broad general arguments the first case for merger control is that a merger may produce 'unilateral effects', leading to an increase in market power for the merged entity. These arguments are thus closely aligned to that for the control of monopolies or 'dominant' undertakings, but clearly there are strong links too to the case made for the control of anti-competitive agreements. It is clear, for example, that if there were five firms in an industry which together determined that a price and output fixing cartel was profitable, but were faced with the illegality of such an arrangement and the credible threat of sanctioning, a merger between the firms would achieve exactly the same end, and might also provide efficiencies that an agreement would not provide. The second argument is that the merger may raise the prospects of coordinated effects arising in which a reduction in the number of industry participants increases the threat of tacit coordination. This principle is discussed further below.

Even where a state (or, in the case of the EC, a supra-national organisation) makes the decision to operate a merger control regime it would not make sense to block all mergers. Something that must be considered early on when examining merger control is the reason firms choose to merge. As a general principle, it is reasonable to suppose that the main motive for a merger is to increase profits.[9] Increased profits may flow from a number of factors. The one most likely to be stressed by merging parties (particularly where they may be answerable to an authority or court charged with merger control powers) is that the merger leads to efficiencies. Efficiencies may in turn arise in a number of ways, of which the most obvious are increases in economies of scale[10] or of scope.[11] Reductions in transaction costs and uncertainties may also generate efficiencies. For example, it may be efficient for a manufacturer to enter into a vertical merger with a component supplier, giving the supplier a permanent guaranteed customer and the manufacturer a secure source of supply without the need to contract for this.[12] An acquirer may also believe that by purchasing an enterprise that it

[8] This is particularly the case with respect to the German Ordo-Liberal movement, although at various times most regimes have been influenced by non-competition concerns. For a discussion of the development of European competition policy see DJ Gerber, *Law and Competition in Twentieth Century Europe: Protecting Prometheus* (Oxford, Clarendon Press, 1998).

[9] See, eg, Carlton and Perloff, above n 4 at 20: 'There are many explanations for mergers. The main motive is usually to increase profitability.' In practice empirical research based on US data suggests that efficiency gains do arise, with total shareholding values in the combined companies rising by between 2%–7.5% post-merger. Importantly for merger control '[t]he increased value of a consolidated firm is not typically due to the creation of market power' (ibid, at 28, summarising a number of studies).

[10] An economy of scale arises when the marginal cost of production falls as output increases. Eg, a product or service which requires a high level of fixed assets to produce it in relation to variable costs will rapidly generate economies of scale as production increases. Typically economies of scale will tail off as production increases.

[11] An economy of scope arises where it is cheaper on average to produce ranges of products or services than a single product.

[12] Typically such vertical mergers, unless they foreclose markets to others (eg, if there was only a single supplier of the component, but a number of manufacturers reliant on that component), are

believes to be badly run it can, by improving management, increase efficiencies in the target. The evaluation of an 'efficiency defence' advanced by merging parties faced with a merger investigation is considered further below.[13] Any merger in respect of which it can be clearly demonstrated that efficiencies of the types referred to above will be achieved will, *ceteris paribus* (all other things being equal), be 'efficiency enhancing', and should not be blocked. However, not all mergers will generate such efficiencies, although they may still lead to increased profitability, and in merger cases all other things are rarely equal. At the same time it has been argued that a merger is simply a way to dispose of a competitor, more effectively and more cheaply than by engaging in (potentially illegal) predation.[14] It also appears to be the case that market integration, which is fostered so strongly by the EC, encourages merger activity.[15] Of key importance to the theory of merger control is that profits may be increased due to an increase in market power flowing from a reduction in competition. If a post-merger enterprise has the ability to raise prices above the pre-merger level the merger may be attractive to the parties even where no efficiencies are identified. Even if efficiencies can be achieved it may be the case that the benefits of these are more than outweighed by the price increases. A simple reduction in the numbers of participants in a market following a merger may also lead to increased prices if the undertakings are able to interact to achieve this, again creating the possibility that a merger may be profitable even in the absence of efficiency gains.

While dominance and monopolies are not themselves condemned the position taken in competition law regimes is that dominant firms have an ability to act to the detriment of the competitive environment, and that they are therefore to be curbed to the extent necessary to mitigate against this. Thus in the EC the position is taken that an undertaking in a dominant position has a 'special responsibility'[16] not to allow its already abnormal position further to damage competition. This approach was imported into UK competition law in the Competition Act 1998 (CA 98). It is accepted by almost all that the natural emergence of monopolies through fair competition should not be prevented or

likely to be viewed more favourably by competition authorities than are horizontal mergers. Vertical integration is usually attributed to this desire to reduce transaction costs and uncertainty, and to negate the threat of strategic 'hold-outs' (see further Church and Ware, above n 4, chap 22). Vertical integration may also overcome the problem of 'double-marginalisation', in which the successive seeking of profit maximisation through a production/distribution chain may result in lower collective profits and output than would be the case were the successive entities vertically integrated.

[13] See, generally, F Ilzkovitz and R Meikeljohn (eds), *European Merger Control: Do we Need an Efficiency Defence?* (Cheltenham, Edward Elgar, 2006).

[14] See, eg, L Persson, 'Predation and Mergers: Is Merger Law Counterproductive?' (2004) 48 *European Economic Review* 239 and the references therein.

[15] K Bjorvatn, 'Economic integration and the profitability of cross-border mergers and acquisitions', (2004) 48 *European Economic Review* 1211. See also KE Lommerud, OR Straume and L Sørgard, 'Downstream Merger with Upstream Market Power' (2005) 49 *European Economic Review* 717.

[16] Case 322/81, *Nederlandsche Banden-Industrie Michelin NV v Commission* [1985] 1 CMLR 282, at 327.

condemned, and that to attempt to do so would lead to far greater harm than benefit. Indeed, it is often pointed out that the area of intellectual property demonstrates clearly that there are situations in which monopolies are to be expressly sanctioned, as the prospect of monopoly profits provides an incentive to invest in research and development and the creation of intellectual property. In the US, for example, it has been held that for the offence of 'monopolisation' to be condemned it is necessary to show, inter alia, 'the *wilful* acquisition or maintenance of [monopoly] power as distinguished from growth or development as a consequence of superior product, business acumen, or historical accident'.[17] In the case of merger control, however, the situation is typically that two viable enterprises that may be competitors (although this is not necessarily the case) are seeking to increase profitability by combining their operations, and one of the sources of this increased profitability may be an increase in market power. In this case a distinction may be drawn from the growth of the company through competitive means, and there may be situations in which the emergence of market power may be prevented and where the harm of doing so is outweighed by the benefits. If this position is not accepted merger control has no justifiable foundation.

The most common practice is to divide the analysis of mergers into three categories: horizontal; vertical; and conglomerate. The competitive effects produced by these mergers may be either unilateral or coordinated. This standard approach is followed below, once the most basic economic terms and analytical tools have been introduced.

ECONOMIC FUNDAMENTALS

The most basic building blocks of industrial economics, within which the study of competition lies, are the concepts of supply and demand, and the effect that they have on price and output. In a free market economy the price of any product or service is set by the relationship between the demand for and the supply of that product or service. *Ceteris paribus* the greater the supply and the lower the demand the lower the price. The demand for any product is the sum of the demands of individual consumers, and in all save exceptional cases the demand for a product will be inversely related to its price, such that a higher price results in lower demand. On a standard economic diagrammatic representation of this function the demand curve slopes downward from left to right, and the degree of the slope reflects the responsiveness of demand to price. More formally, the relationship between demand and price is termed 'elasticity'. A product is demand inelastic when a change in price produces a less than proportionate change in demand, and is demand elastic when the reverse is true. Thus, for example, the demand for petrol is inelastic, whereas the demand for Mars Bars

[17] *United States v Grinnell Corp* 384 US 563 (1966) (emphasis added).

may be presumed to be elastic. Elasticity is determined largely by the presence of available substitutes for the product, or the willingness of the consumer to forego consumption on the product altogether. A merger between two producers of a product that has an inelastic demand curve may be likely to raise more competitive concerns than a merger between two producers of a product with an elastic demand curve. Supply curves in most cases slope upwards from left to right, such that they intersect with demand curves, the point of intersection determining the output and price of the product or service in question. *Ceteris paribus* the higher the price that can be got the higher the level of supply. Elasticity of supply may also reflect issues such as the ease with which the supply of the product can be expanded or restricted.

As suggested above the demand for any given product will be affected by the prices of *other* products and the extent to which these serve as substitutes for the product in question. Thus 'cross elasticity of demand' measures the extent to which the demand for one product is affected by the change in the price of another. A high cross elasticity of demand implies that the products are close substitutes, and cross elasticity of demand may be seen as a statistically rigorous application of the concept of substitutability.

The concept of the relevant market

In the EC the concept of 'dominant position' is emphasised in the substantive test for the assessment of mergers, although the broader threshold is that of whether the merger may substantially impede effective competition, while in the UK the emphasis is on the ability of the merger to 'substantially lessen competition'. In the application of both tests it may be necessary to establish the degree of market power that will be held by the merged entity. Market power can be assessed only in relation to a relevant market. Both the EC Commission and the OFT have published guidelines relating to to market definition.[18] The OFT guidance 'follows a similar approach to the European Commission's',[19] and the emphasis here is therefore on the former, although there are some parts of the OFT guidance which go further than does the EC Commission's. Relevant markets may be defined in terms of the product, the geographical area, and, on

[18] EC Commission, *Notice on the definition of the relevant market for the purpose of Community competition law* [1997] OJ C372/5; OFT, *Market Definition*, Dec 2004. See also OFT, *Mergers: Substantive Assessment Guidance*, May 2003, paras 3.11–3.22, and Competition Commission, *Merger References: Competition Commission Guidelines*, June 2003, Part 2. For a substantial discussion of some of the issues relating to market definition, albeit in the US context, see R Pitofsky, 'New Definitions of Relevant Market and the Assault on Antitrust' (1990) 90 *Columbia Law Review* 1805. See also I Kokkoris, 'The Concept of Market Definition and the SSNIP Test in the Merger Appraisal' [2005] *ECLR* 209.

[19] OFT, *Market Definition*, above n 18, para 1.2.

occasion, the relevant time period. The techniques used to identify the product and geographic markets are substantially the same.[20]

The assessment of the competitive power of any merging entities is crucially dependant on a clear analysis of the market in which the relevant product or service is located—that is to say a determination of which other products and services serve as a realistic competitive constraint on those provided by the merging parties. As the EC Commission puts it, '[t]he definition of the relevant market in both its product and geographic dimensions often has a decisive influence on the assessment of a competition case'.[21] Failure adequately to identify the relevant market—which may be taken to imply a failure to assess properly the competitive conditions—may be fatal to the validity of a merger decision. For example, in the *iSOFT/Torex* merger, considered by the OFT, the CAT quashed a decision taken by the OFT not to refer the merger. On appeal by a third party the CAT held that the OFT had failed to conduct a proper analysis:

> In this case the description of the market is so scanty, and expressed at such a level of generality, that it is extremely difficult for the Tribunal to be satisfied that all material considerations have been taken into account and all material facts ascertained.[22]

At paragraph 246 of the same judgment the CAT held that:

> The present matter is a case of a direct merger between two companies who compete horizontally and who are identified in the decision as numbers 1 and 2 in the market, with combined market shares in the 45%/55% range. A decision by the OFT to the effect that on no reasonable view could such a merger be expected to lead to a substantial reduction of competition in our view needs a proper factual basis and exceptional clarity of analysis.

The Commission *Notice on the definition of the relevant market* emphasises in particular the importance of this analysis to the determination of cases in the light of the ECMR.[23] In this analysis the term 'market' has a precise meaning that may differ from the use of that word in a normal business context. According to the ECJ:

[20] Thus the OFT notes that: 'geographic markets are defined using the same process as that used to define product markets': para 4.1. For the EC a standard formulation to describe the geographic market is the following:

> A relevant geographic market comprises the area in which the undertakings concerned are involved in the supply and demand of products and services, in which the conditions of competition are sufficiently homogenous and which can be distinguished from neighbouring areas because the conditions of competition are appreciably different in those areas. (see, eg, Case COMP/M.2097, *SCA/Metsa Tissue*, para 47, discussed briefly in Chap 9, below).

[21] *Notice on the definition of the relevant market*, above n 18, para 4. There are a number of other examples of the Commission placing strong emphasis on market definition. Thus, eg, in the *Commission Notice on a simplified procedure for treatment of certain concentrations under Council Regulation (EC) No 139/2004* (discussed in Chap 6, below), the Commission states at para 6 that 'market definitions are likely to be a key element' in the relevant assessment.

[22] *IBA Health Ltd v OFT, supported by iSOFT plc and Torex plc* [2003] CAT 27, [2004] CompAR 235, at para 243.

[23] At para 1.

> The concept of the relevant market in fact implies that there can be effective competition between the products which form part of it and this presupposes that there is a sufficient degree of interchangeability between all the products forming part of the same market insofar as a specific use of such products is concerned.[24]

The SSNIP test[25]

There are a number of different ways by which it may be possible to reach a conclusion on what a relevant market is: for example producers and/or consumers could be asked what products and services compete with those which they are selling or buying; the characteristics of the product or service could be compared with those of other products or services; other methods might include analysing sales data, and in particular comparing the comparative sales of different products. The EC Commission states that it 'follows an open approach to empirical evidence, aimed at making an effective use of all available information which may be relevant in individual cases'.[26] While all of these, and other, methods may be of some use there is a consistency in the approach taken in the EC and in the UK in that the EC Commission, the OFT and the CC all place the SSNIP test at the heart of the exercise, although it may not always be appropriate to rely on this. If it is possible to carry out a SSNIP analysis this should take account of all relevant factors in determining the bounds of the market, including the possibilities of substitution on both the demand and supply sides, and the role of barriers to entry. For the sake of clarity these factors are further individually discussed below.

The methodology encompassed in the SSNIP test is to posit what would be the effect of a small, but significant, non-transitory increase in price on the profitability of the product at the heart of the exercise. Thus the SSNIP test asks whether it would be profitable for a monopoly supplier of A to raise price by 5–10 per cent, all else being equal.[27] If such a step would not be profitable then it is unlikely that a relevant product market for A may be deemed to exist. While the most likely reason that a price rise would not be profitable would be that enough consumers were defecting to product B, it may also be the case that some consumers would simply stop buying the product, or may switch to products C–Z. In practice these factors might be hard to measure, whereas significant defections to

[24] Case 85/76, *Hoffmann-La Roche v Commission* [1979] ECR 461, [1979] 3 CMLR 211, at para 28.

[25] Also referred to as 'the hypothetical monopolist test'. The test was first developed in the US for the purpose of the DOJ/FTC *Horizontal Merger Guidelines* (1982). The current version of the guidelines was published in 1992, and revised in 1997. See generally G Niels, 'The SSNIP Test: Some Common Misconceptions' [2004] *Comp Law* 267.

[26] *Notice on the definition of the relevant market*, above n 18, para 25.

[27] The CC is clear in preferring a 5% figure, 'because in many instances an increase in the price of a product of around [5%] might reasonably be judged to have a significant effect on customers' expenditure on that product and so provides an appropriate level at which to consider the test' (*Merger References: Competition Commission Guidelines*, above n 18, para 2.8).

B would be more readily observable.[28] The process is clearly explained at paragraphs 17–19 of the Notice on the definition of the relevant market:

> 17 The question to be answered is whether the parties' customers would switch to readily available substitutes or to suppliers located elsewhere in response to a hypothetical small (in the range of 5 per cent to 10 per cent) but permanent relative price increase in the products and areas being considered. If substitution were enough to make the price increase unprofitable because of the resulting loss of sales, additional substitutes and areas are included in the relevant market. This would be done until the set of products and geographical areas is such that small, permanent increases in relative prices would be profitable. The equivalent analysis is applicable in cases concerning the concentration of buying power, where the starting point would then be the supplier and the price test serves to identify the alternative distribution channels or outlets for the supplier's products . . .
>
> 18 A practical example of this test can be provided by its application to a merger of, for instance, soft-drink bottlers. An issue to examine in such a case would be to decide whether different flavours of soft drinks belong to the same market. In practice the question to be address would be whether consumers of flavour A would switch to other flavours when confronted with a permanent price increase of 5 per cent to 10 per cent for flavour A. If a sufficient number of consumers would switch to, say, flavour B, to such an extent that the price increase for flavour A would not be profitable owing to the resultant loss of sales, then the market would comprise at least flavours A and B. The process would have to be extended in addition to other available flavours until a set of products is identified for which a price rise would not induce a sufficient substitution of demand.
>
> 19 Generally, and in particular for the analysis of merger cases, the price to take into account will be the prevailing market price. This may not be the case where the prevailing price has been determined in the absence of sufficient competition. . . .

To put it another way, 'a relevant market is something worth monopolising'.[29]

One of the strengths of the SSNIP test is that its proper application should prevent markets being falsely identified in case of groups of consumers with inelastic demand patterns who would buy the product even if prices rose considerably. In *Chiquita*[30] the Commission took the view that bananas constituted a product market distinct from that for soft fruit in general. One of the factors was that it identified a group of customers for whom bananas could not be readily substituted with other fruits. Unless the seller has the ability to target this group of customers, imposing terms on them which are different from those set for other purchasers, the existence of such an infra-marginal group does not lead automatically to the existence of a separate product market. The correct question, and it is dealt with in the application of the SSNIP test, is whether this

[28] It should be noted that just because consumers will switch from product A to product B, it does not necessarily mean that they will likewise switch from product B to product A. This was found to be the case, eg, in Case COMP/M.2547 *Bayer/Aventis Crop Science* (2000), in which DG Comp found that there would be substitution from foliar and soil applications of fungicides and insecticides to seed treatments, but that seed treatments would not in turn be substituted by the former products.

[29] Bishop and Walker, above n 4, para 4.05. Although a more accurate wording might be 'a relevant market is the narrowest range of products or services worth monopolising'.

[30] Commission Decision 76/353, [1976] OJ L 95/1. On appeal Case 27/76, *United Brands Company and United Brands Continental v Commission* [1978] ECR 207, [1978] 1 CMLR 429.

customer group is protected from exploitation by those who would defect to substitutes in the event that price rises were imposed.

Paragraph 19 refers to the 'cellophane fallacy', under which there is a danger raised that were the output of a monopolist to be subjected to a forward looking SSNIP analysis the result would be to demonstrate that a price rise would not be profitable. Such a conclusion was reached by the Supreme Court of the United States in *DuPont*,[31] when the Court held that DuPont was not a monopolist in the market for cellophane, as there was no relevant product market for cellophane exclusively, as a price rise for cellophane would be unprofitable. To reach this conclusion, however, is to fall into a very obvious logical trap: the successful monopolist should *already* be pricing at the level where maximum profits are made, such that a further price rise would indeed be unprofitable. This problem, to which there is no easy solution, is well understood by competition authorities, and receives prominent mention in most of the relevant literature and guidance. In the OFT *Market Definition* guideline for example this is discussed at paragraphs 5.4–5.6, and the OFT notes at paragraph 5.6 that:

> The possibility that market conditions are distorted by the presence of market power (or other factors) will be accounted for when all the evidence on market definition is weighed in the round. For example, where prices are likely to differ substantially from their competitive levels, caution must be exercised when dealing with the evidence on switching patterns as such evidence may not be a reliable guide to what would occur in normal competitive conditions.

In practice there may be a lot of data which would provide evidence for the carrying out of the SSNIP test. However, as the EC Commission states at paragraph 19 of its market definition notice, there are particular reasons in merger control cases for adopting the prevailing market price as the appropriate one from which to run the SSNIP analysis. If the concern is that, post-merger, competition would be impaired, the presumption in most cases will be that competition is functioning pre-merger, and even if this is not the case the purpose of a merger control analysis should be to analyse the change effected by the merger, against the most appropriate alternative 'counterfactual', which in most, but not all, cases is likely to be the pre-merger status quo.

Past market definition exercises may be of some value in making present determinations, but the CFI has stressed the dangers of this practice. Competitive situations, technology and consumer tastes change over time, and may not be the same from place to place. In *Coca-Cola*[32] the CFI held that:

> in the course of any decision applying [art 82 EC] the Commission must define the relevant market again and make a fresh analysis of the conditions of competition

[31] *United States v El DuPont de Nemours & Co* 351 US 377 (1956).

[32] Cases T–125/97 and T–127/97, *The Coca-Cola Company and Coca-Cola Enterprises Inc v Commission* [2000] 5 CMLR 467. The facts in this case are unusual in that the appellants' merger had been cleared by the Commission. However, in the process the Commission set out views on market dominance that the appellants were concerned would have ramifications, if unchallenged, in other competition proceedings relating to the soft drinks industry.

which will not necessarily be based on the same considerations as those underlying the previous finding.[33]

Although the requirement here is framed in the context of the application of Article 82 EC, it is equally the case that the exercise should be carried out *de novo* in the case of the application of the ECMR, and similarly in the application of the EA 02, although in this respect there is no strict obligation to follow EC case law.

Demand and supply side substitution

Faced with a rise in prices of any product or service above the competitive level consumers will have an incentive to seek acceptable substitutes. In the case of almost all products as prices rise substitutes will become relatively more attractive, and what might be regarded as an unacceptable substitute following a 2 per cent price rise in the purchased product might be acceptable faced with a 10 or 20 per cent price rise. The SSNIP test, discussed above, is designed to test for the extent to which consumers are able to 'punish' the seller of a product who raises prices by substituting other products. Where it is not possible to carry out a SSNIP test, market definition may proceed by assessing consumer preferences and determining whether other products are reasonable substitutes for those produced or sold by the merging parties. The EC Commission has stated that '[t]here is a range of evidence permitting an assessment of the extent to which substitution would take place', and that the evidence that may be determinant will depend 'very much on the characteristics and specificity of the industry and products or services that are being examined'.[34] In order to be taken into account in determining the boundaries of the relevant market demand-side substitution must happen within a reasonably short period of time. A range of evidence may be relevant in assessing demand-side substitution: evidence from undertakings active in the market; evidence from customers and competitors, which may take the form of surveys[35] or interviews; the costs of switching; and product characteristics.[36]

According to DG Comp '[s]upply-side substitutability may also be taken into account when defining markets in those situations in which its effects are equiv-

[33] At para 82.

[34] *Notice on the definition of the relevant market*, above n 18, para 25.

[35] Surveys should be treated with care in the application of competition law. However, they are an important tool, and 'are generally recognised as an efficient and economical method of obtaining robust data from large populations': M Hughes and N Beale, 'Customer Surveys in UK Merger Cases—the Art and Science of Asking the Right People the Right Questions' [2005] *ECLR* 297.

[36] The OFT notes that care must be taken: 'first, even where products apparently have very similar characteristics and intended use, switching costs and brand loyalty may affect how substitutable they are in practice. Second, just because products display similar physical characteristics, this does not necessarily mean that customers would view them to be close substitutes. For example, peak customers may not view rail travel during off peak times to be a close substitute for rail travel at peak times. Third, products with very different physical characteristics may be close substitutes if, from a customer's point of view, they have a very similar use': OFT, *Market Definition*, above n 18, para 3.7, footnotes omitted.

alent to those of demand substitution in terms of effectiveness and immediacy'.[37] Supply-side substitution arises when a new supplier is tempted into a market by the perception that profits can be earned, as may happen if price rises. In order to be included within the market definition supply-side substitution must happen quickly, and this can be the case only where barriers to entry (see below) are limited. The example given by DG Comp is that of a paper producer which can readily switch the qualities of paper supplied in response to changes in relative prices.[38] DG Comp has stated that wherever 'supply-side substitutability would entail the need to adjust significantly existing tangible and intangible assets, additional investments, strategic decisions or time delays, it will not be considered at the stage of market definition'.[39] Supply-side substitution should therefore be distinguished from entry into the market,[40] which is a factor to be considered in relation to the assessment of market power, discussed below. The OFT therefore explains that supply-side substitution 'can be thought of as a special case of entry—entry that occurs quickly (eg less than one year), effectively (eg on a scale large enough to affect prices), and without the need for substantial sunk investments'.[41]

The assessment and effect of market power

Market power may be loosely defined as the ability of a supplier of goods or services to raise prices above the competitive level in a sustained and profitable manner.[42] Although the UK legislation does not make any explicit reference to market power in the carrying out of merger analysis, the EC legislation places dominance, or the attainment of dominance, in a prominent role, and in Regulation 4064/89 the dominance test was, as seen in Chapter 1, the sole test. In the UK there may always be discussion about what exactly constitutes a 'substantial lessening of competition', and in the EC there has for nearly 40 years been debate about what level of market power has to be attributed to any undertaking before a finding of dominance can be sustained. Following the enactment of Regulation 139/2004 there has been increased intention to the meaning of

[37] *Notice on the definition of the relevant market*, above n 18, para 20. See generally paras 20–23.

[38] The OFT imports this example at para 3.14 of its market definition guidance, above n 18. DG Comp relied on supply-side substitution in considering a merger in the markets for the supply of paper in Case IV/M.166 *Torras/Sarrio* (1992).

[39] *Notice on the definition of the relevant market*, above n 18, para 23. Supply-side substitution was rejected, eg in Case IV/M.53 *Aerospatiale/Alenia/De Havilland* (1991), in which the EC Commission found that aircraft manufacturers could not readily switch between the production of small and medium-sized planes just by adapting existing production lines. In fact it found that such changes would take 3 to 4 years to implement (para 14 of the Decision; this case is discussed briefly in Chap 9, below).

[40] Also referred to as 'potential competition'.

[41] OFT, *Market Definition*, above n 18, para 3.15.

[42] Or, in the case of a purchaser of goods or services, the ability to command selling prices from its suppliers below the competitive level. See generally Church and Ware, above n 4, chap 4; Bishop and Walker, above n 4, chap 3.

'substantial impediment to effective competition'. However, there is wide agreement on the factors that should be considered in an evaluation of market power. Market power is not synonymous with 'dominance', which may be better viewed as an extreme position of market power. The ECJ held, in the context of an Article 82 case which remains valid in respect of the application of the ECMR, that:

> The dominant position referred to in [Article 82] relates to a position of economic strength enjoyed by an undertaking which enables it to prevent effective competition being maintained on the relevant market by giving it the power to behave to an appreciable extent independently of its competitors, customers and ultimately of its consumers.[43]

The UK's Competition Commission has explained the concept of market power in the following terms:

> Market power may be described most simply as the ability to raise price consistently and profitably above competitive levels (or where a buyer has market power, the ability to obtain prices lower than their competitive levels). In the case of horizontal mergers . . . for instance, this might occur through the elimination of an effective source of competition thereby weakening the rivalry among the players left in the market after the merger. . . .
>
> Firms with market power may not raise price, but may instead simply opt not to compete as aggressively as they otherwise might, and, in so doing, allow costs to rise, reduce quality, restrict the diversity of choice and/or slow the rate of innovation.[44]

A useful analytical framework, but not one referred to expressly in any of the relevant guidelines or notices, is the five-forces model of competitive dynamics developed by Porter, which is widely referred to in strategic management and economics texts. This sets out the constraints on any undertaking operating in a market.[45] As noted above, the first step in any assessment of market power is

[43] Case 27/76, *United Brands Co v Commission* [1978] 1 CMLR 429, para 65.

[44] *Competition Commission, Merger References: Competition Commission Guidelines*, June 2003, para 1.24, boxed text.

[45] MP Porter, *Competitive Strategy: Techniques for Analyzing Industries and Competitors*, New York, The Free Press (1980). Although designed primarily to guide strategic choices made within firms, Porter's framework usefully outlines the pressures on firms:

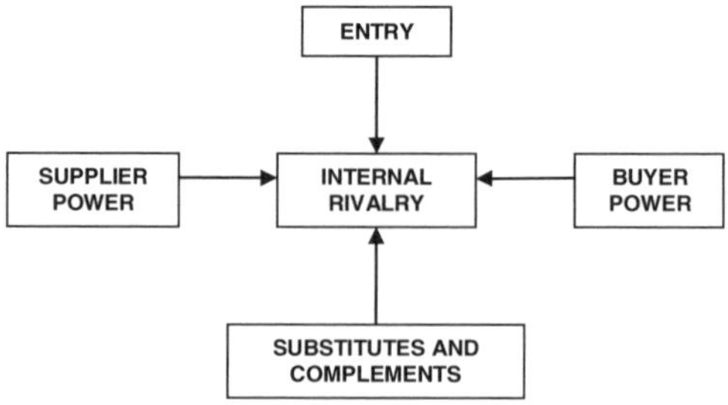

to define the relevant product market within which that power is to be determined. Having done this the most important factors to consider are: the market share of the undertaking; the market shares of competitors; the absolute and relative size and resources of the undertaking; the duration of market shares and size; and the existence of barriers to entry or exit.

Market shares, concentration ratios and the HHI

The most important single indicator of market power is the share of the (properly defined) relevant market held by the undertaking(s). Market shares may be measured in a number of different ways, but the most normal for the sake of merger investigations would be by sales revenue, although the OFT notes that other measures, 'such as production volumes, sales volumes, capacity or reserves, maybe used as appropriate'.[46] The necessary data will usually be readily available from a range of sources, including estimates made by companies or market studies, but where these are not available DG Comp has indicated that it 'will usually ask each supplier in the relevant market to provide its own sales in order to calculate total market size and market shares'.[47] Historically DG Comp was required to demonstrate that a merger might create or strengthen a dominant position, and in the EC the minimum threshold to establish dominance is generally considered to be around 40 per cent.[48] Market shares of 50 per cent or more are generally to be taken as evidence of the existence of a dominant position in the absence of evidence brought forward to rebut this presumption by the parties.[49] The classic statement relating to market shares in this context is that in *Hoffmann-La Roche*, where the ECJ held that:

> . . . although the importance of the market shares may vary from one market to another the view may legitimately be taken that very large shares are in themselves, and save in exceptional circumstances, evidence of the existence of a dominant position. An undertaking which has a very large market share and holds it for some time, by means of the volume of production and the scale of the supply which it stands for—without those having much smaller market shares being able to meet rapidly the demand from those who would like to break away from the undertaking which has the largest market share—is by virtue of that share in a position of strength which makes it an unavoidable trading partner and which already because of this secures for it, at the very last during relatively long periods, that freedom of action which is the special feature of a dominant position.[50]

[46] *Mergers: Substantive Assessment Guidance*, May 2003, para 4.3.

[47] *Notice on the definition of the relevant market*, above n 18, para 53.

[48] Exceptionally, in the Art 82 EC case of *Virgin/British Airways*, 2000/74 [2000] OJ L 30/1, dominance was found to exist with a market share of 39.7%. In this case however there were a number of other relevant factors indicative of dominance.

[49] See Case C–62/86, *AKZO Chemie BV v Commission* [1993] 5 CMLR 215. See also Case T–102/96, *Gencor Ltd v Commission* [1999] ECR II–753, [1999] 4 CMLR 971.

[50] Case 85/76, *Hoffmann-La Roche & Co AG v Commission* [1979] 3 CMLR 211, para 41.

The view of DG Comp is that, in the absence of exceptional factors, concentrations are unlikely to be found significantly to impede effective competition where the market shares of the undertakings do not, post-merger, exceed 25 per cent.[51] This would not necessarily be the case, however, in respect of a merger that created a position of collective dominance (see Chapter 7, below).

It is also necessary to consider the relative strength of the undertakings concerned, and this requires a consideration of the market shares of competitors. In this context one of the standard tools used by analysts is that of concentration ratios and the Herfindahl–Hirschman Index (HHI). Concentration ratios are very simple expressions that merely reflect in absolute terms the aggregate market share of a number of the largest suppliers in the market in question—typically three (C3) or four (C4) firms. Thus if a market consists of 12 firms, of which the largest three hold market shares of 18, 15 and 14 per cent respectively, the C3 for this market would be 47 per cent. This actually tells us very little about the market, and reveals nothing about the differences in the size of the firms that make up the group.

The HHI is more sensitive to the share of supply held by the larger firms, and is employed by the EC Commission and OFT in their assessment of certain horizontal agreements and by the US authorities in their assessment of certain mergers. Formally the HHI is the sum of the squared market shares of the companies on the relevant market, or $\Sigma s1^2 \ldots sn^2$, where sn is the market share of firm n. Thus, in a market with four firms, each of which have a 25 per cent market share, the HHI would be $25^2 + 25^2 + 25^2 + 25^2 = 2{,}500$. In a total monopoly market, the HHI would be 10,000 (100^2), and in a market of 100 firms, each with a 1 per cent market share, would be 100.

DG Comp is unlikely to be concerned about mergers with a post-merger HHI of less than 1,000. It:

> is also unlikely to identify horizontal competition concerns in a merger with a post-merger HHI between 1,000 and 2,000 and a delta below 250, or a merger with a post-merger HHI above 2,000 and a delta below 150, except where special circumstances . . . are present.[52]

The OFT has indicated that, when evaluating horizontal mergers, it:

> is likely to regard any market with a post-merger HHI in excess of 1,800 as highly concentrated, and any market with a post-merger HHI of 1,000 as concentrated. In a highly concentrated market, a merger with a delta in excess of 50 may give rise to potential competition concerns. In a concentrated market, a merger with a delta in excess of 100 may give rise to potential competition concerns.[53]

'Delta' in this context is the change in the HHI achieved by subtracting the pre-merger HHI from the post-merger HHI.

[51] Commission Notice, *Guidelines on the assessment of horizontal mergers under the Council Regulation on the control of concentrations between undertakings* [2004] OJ C 31/3, para 18.

[52] Ibid, para 20.

[53] *Mergers: Substantive Assessment Guidance*, above n 18, para 4.3.

The CC has indicated that it will have regard to the thresholds set out by the OFT, but it is likely to place less weight on these measures than the OFT, and in its guidance notes that it will consider HHI thresholds 'only as one factor in its wider assessment of competition'.[54]

Entry and barriers to entry

It was noted above that potential entry into a market should be distinguished from supply-side substitution, and that entry in anything other than the short term is not therefore a factor to be considered in relation to market definition.[55] It is, however, an important factor in assessing market power. It is also a matter that has been subject to intense discussion and debate amongst those involved with competition policy, and to some extent the approach taken to barriers to entry is a key factor separating the Harvard and Chicago schools of thought.[56] Market entry is dealt with at Part VI of the EC Commission's *Horizontal Merger Guidance*.[57] Entry is likely to take place into a market only where to do so is believed to be a profitable option within a reasonable period of time. Various barriers to entry exist, and there are different ways of categorising these. It is useful, however, to make a distinction between absolute, strategic and conduct barriers.[58] Absolute barriers are those which are generally outside the control of the undertaking itself, and include such elements as government regulation. Strategic barriers are those enjoyed by the undertaking as a result of its market position, and include such factors as first-mover advantage, distribution networks and so on. Conduct barriers would include active responses to competition, such as aggressive or predatory pricing strategies. A key factor determining ease of entry is the extent to which fixed sunk costs rise. Broadly, 'the higher sunk costs the less likely that entry will occur'.[59] These costs may be either exogenous (outside the control of the firm) or endogenous (within

[54] *Merger References: Competition Commission Guidelines*, above n 18, para 3.10. See also para 3.7.

[55] It is not therefore a factor which is discussed in the relevant guidance relating to market definition, save in the negative. The EC Commission, market definition notice addresses potential competition at para 24 in the following terms:

> 'The third source of competitive constraint, potential competition, is not taken into account when defining markets, since the conditions under which potential competition will actually represent an effective competitive constraint depend on the analysis of specific factors and circumstances related to the conditions of entry. If required, this analysis is only carried out at a subsequent stage, in general once the position of the companies involved in the relevant market has already been ascertained, and when such position gives rise to concerns from a competition point of view.'

[56] For an American perspective on the issue see J Baker, 'The Problem with *Baker Hughes* and *Syufy*: On the Role of Entry in Merger Analysis' (1997) 65 *Antitrust Law Journal* 353.

[57] Commission, *Guidelines on the assessment of horizontal mergers*, above n 51.

[58] In its guidance (ibid) the EC Commission adopts a slightly different threefold categorisation, although the same barriers are considered.

[59] M Motta, *Competition Policy: Theory and Practice* (Cambridge, Cambridge University Press, 2004) at 121.

the control of the firm). For example, the cost of land, buildings and machinery necessary to produce a product will, to a significant degree, be exogenous. The costs of advertising and product promotion may be regarded as determined by the firm as a matter of choice, although it may be the case that in some industries such outlays are regarded as essential. Where assets are highly specific—and nothing is more specific than brand advertising—the value cannot be recovered if the firm fails. Barriers to entry also play a role in analysing network industries, a feature of the 'new economy' that arises where the value of the product or service to one person rises as the numbers of users rise (for example a telecommunications system). This was a factor considered by the EC Commission in *MCI WorldCom/Sprint*,[60] discussed in Chapter 8, below.

The EC Commission, in the *Horizontal Merger Guidance*, recognises a wide range of factors as potentially raising barriers to entry. These include: regulatory hurdles; tariff and non-tariff trade barriers; preferential access held by the incumbent to, for example, essential facilities, natural resources, intellectual property rights, and innovation and R & D.[61] In addition the Commission recognises that the position of the incumbent firms in the market may raise barriers, and in this context refers to factors such as: experience and reputation; consumer brand loyalty; existing commercial relationships; promotion and advertising; the presence of excess capacity held by the incumbents; and customer switching costs.[62] Whether entry is likely may also depend on the nature of the market in question. Thus entry is more likely into a market that is in the early or growth stages of development than it is into one which is mature or declining.[63] Two conditions must be met in order for the Commission to consider that the threat of entry may counteract market power. The first is that entry 'should be sufficiently swift and sustained to deter or defeat the exercise of market power'.[64] Entry will normally be considered to be timely within this condition if it is expected to occur within two years post-merger.[65] The second is that entry 'must be of sufficient scope and magnitude to deter or defeat the anti-competitive effects of the merger. Small-scale entry, for instance into some market "niche", may not be considered sufficient'.[66] The OFT and CC take a similar approach.

[60] Case M.1741 *MCI WorldCom/Sprint*, 28 June 2000.

[61] These last two are particularly controversial, and the question would have to be whether the incumbent had unique access to, eg, poles of research that could not otherwise be replicated.

[62] In *Lloyds TSB Group and Abbey National plc: A Report on the Proposed Merger* (2001), the CC noted the role played by the fact that customers of banks find switching a difficult process: 'the existence of barriers to switching makes it difficult for entrants to acquire customers at a rapid rate' (at para 2.111). See RBB Economics, 'Switching Costs and Merger Assessment—Don't Move the Goalposts', RBB Brief 6, Nov 2002.

[63] At the same time mergers are more likely to occur in mature or declining markets as firms seek to rationalise existing (over)capacity.

[64] *Horizontal merger guidance*, above n 51, para 74.

[65] Ibid.

[66] Ibid, para 75.

Countervailing buyer power

Merging parties are likely often to point to the existence of countervailing buyer power to offset claims that the merger creates or enhances market power. Standard economics texts are likely to point out that where a monopoly exists the second-best outcome is generated by the existence of a single purchaser (a monopsony). In market situations countervailing buyer power can indeed serve to discipline a supplier with a large market share, and may effectively eliminate any market power that the seller has. However, this condition can arise only where the buyers can make a credible threat of taking their custom elsewhere. Faced with a monopoly supplier and no supply-side competition, a purchaser who requires the product will not be able to make such a threat.

The Horizontal Merger Guideline deals with countervailing buyer power at paragraphs 64–67. At paragraph 65 the Commission sets out the position in the following terms:

> The Commission considers, when relevant, to what extent customers will be in a position to counter the increase in market power that a merger would otherwise be likely to create. One source of countervailing buyer power would be if a customer could credibly threaten to resort, within a reasonable timeframe, to alternative sources of supply should the supplier decide to increase prices or to otherwise deteriorate quality or the conditions of delivery. This would be the case if the buyer could immediately switch to other suppliers, credibly threaten to vertically integrate into the upstream market or to sponsor upstream expansion or entry for instance by persuading a potential entrant to enter by committing to placing large orders with this company. It is more likely that large and sophisticated customers will possess this kind of countervailing buyer power than smaller firms in a fragmented industry. A buyer may also exercise countervailing buying power by refusing to buy other products produced by the supplier or, particularly in the case of durable goods, delaying purchases.[67]

A schema of the approach taken to the assessment of market power in the context of a relevant market, might be represented as Figure 2.1:[68]

HORIZONTAL, VERTICAL, AND CONGLOMERATE MERGERS

Horizontal mergers are more likely to raise competitive concerns than either vertical or conglomerate mergers, although the latter may exhibit characteristics of both horizontal and vertical situations. However, economists have at times been critical of the general approach taken by competition authorities under which horizontal mergers leading to increased market shares are deemed to raise concerns. The problem has been characterised as 'the merger paradox'.[69] The

[67] Internal footnotes omitted.

[68] I am indebted to Matthew Cherry, economist, who first developed this diagram.

[69] See SW Salant, S Switzer and RJ Reynolds, 'Losses from Horizontal Merger: The Effects of an Exogenous Change in Industry Structure on Cournot-Nash Equilibrium' (1983) 98 *Quarterly Journal of Economics* 185. It has been argued, however, that the model advanced by Salant *et al* *cont./*

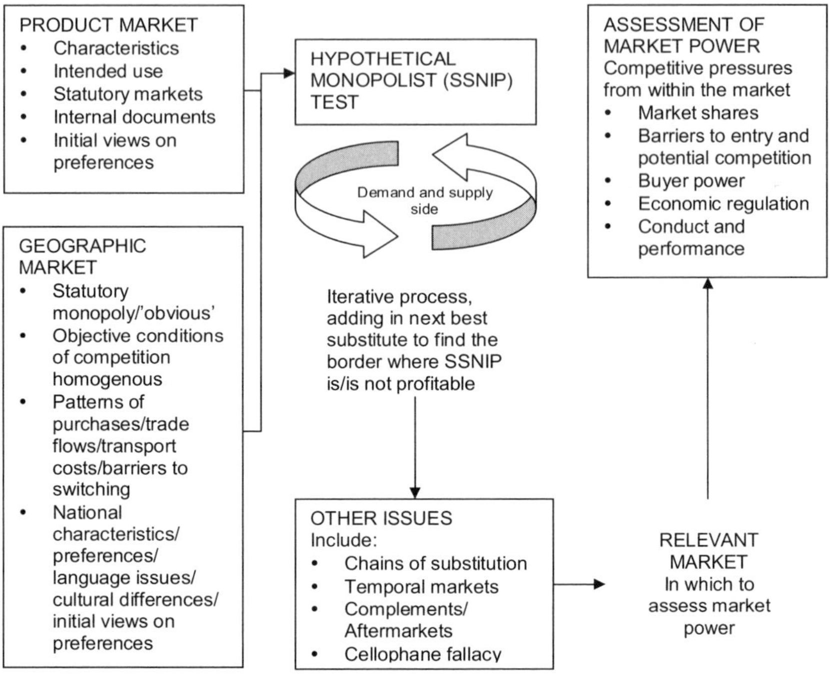

Figure 2.1: The Assessment of Market Power

argument made by those concerned about horizontal mergers is that each successive merger, *ceteris paribus*, increases the market power of the merging entities. However, 'the paradox is that it is, in fact, quite difficult to construct a simple economic model in which there are sizable profit gains for firms participating in a horizontal merger *that is not a merger to monopoly*'.[70] This result, which arises from an application of the Cournot model (see further below), is dependent upon treating all firms equally post-merger. However, 'what is miss-

'severely understates the incentive to merge'. See M Perry and R Porter, 'Oligopoly and the Incentive for Horizontal Merger' (1985) 75:1 *American Economic Review* 219.

[70] Pepall, Richards, and Norman, above n 4, 410 (emphasis in original); the proof is developed over the following pages. See also DJ Ravenscraft and FM Scherer, 'The Profitability of Mergers' [1989] *International Journal of Industrial Organization* Special Issue, 101 who found that in respect of mergers taking place in the US manufacturing sector between 1957 and 1977 the profitability of acquired companies declined post-merger in most cases. Pinske *et al*, however, demonstrate that, at least in the case of branded beers, mergers may be expected to result in price rises and brand disappearance: J Pinske and ME Slade, 'Mergers, Brand Competition, and the Price of a Pint' (2004) 48 *European Economic Review* 617. Barros *et al* derive a similar conclusion in respect of mergers in the Portuguese food retailing market: PP Barros, D Brito and Dd Lucena, 'Mergers in the Food Retailing Sector: An Empirical Investigation' (2006) 50 *European Economic Review* 447.

ing from the simple Cournot model is some credible means by which the merged firm can take advantage of its potential size'.[71]

Far less attention is paid to vertical mergers generally in merger regimes, and this is true of the EC and UK regimes.[72] This reflects the fact that vertical mergers give rise to far fewer concerns, and may not, axiomatically, be presumed to reduce competition. However, vertical mergers may give rise to market foreclosure[73] by, for example, depriving a rival producer of a distribution network if a producer merges with a retail chain. In such cases there may be concerns arising where rivals at the horizontal level lack a genuine alternative, either upstream or downstream, to the assets being acquired. In some cases vertical mergers may also give rise to concerns about coordinated conduct. This may be the position, for example, where there is a degree of vertical integration into the retail market in which prices are more transparent than in the wholesale market, facilitating coordination. In such cases the analysis may be similar to that for horizontal mergers.

There is also generally less concern regarding conglomerate mergers, which are mergers between firms operating in different markets. Non-horizontal mergers bring together suppliers of unrelated or of complementary products. Therefore they do not, on the face of it, directly eliminate a competitor. Indeed, it is the case that where the products involved are complementary (ie, product A is used with product B, such that if the demand for A rises so too does the demand for B), such mergers 'generally provide an incentive for firms to lower prices . . . since a reduction in the price of one good will increase demand for the other'.[74] It has been argued in one study that a significant incentive for conglomerate mergers to take place is that, by increasing the diversity within the merged entity, they reduce risk, and that for the managers of these firms (although not necessarily for shareholders) this is a desirable outcome.[75] The OFT has recognised that 'such mergers rarely lead to a [SLC] as a result solely of their conglomerate effects.[76] There is, however, the possibility that in some cases a portfolio of products may be built up which is sufficiently large to deter

[71] Pepall, Richards, and Norman, above n 4, 414. See also National Economic Research Associates (NERA), 'Merger Appraisal in Oligopolistic Markets', OFT Research Paper 19 (1999).

[72] See J Church, 'The Impact of Vertical and Conglomerate Mergers on Competition: Final Report' (2004) (DG Comp website).

[73] See MA Salinger, 'Vertical Mergers and Market Foreclosure' (1988) 103 *Quarterly Journal of Economics* 345.

[74] RBB Economics, 'Turning the Tables: Why Vertical and Conglomerate Mergers are Different', RBB Brief 18, Mar 2006. Here it is argued that 'there should be an economic presumption that non-horizontal mergers are pro-competitive'.

[75] Y Amihud and B Lev, 'Risk Reduction as a Managerial Motive for Conglomerate Mergers' (1981) 12:2 *The Bell Journal of Economics*, 605. See also DC Mueller, 'A Theory of Conglomerate Mergers' (1982) 82 *Quarterly Journal of Economics* 643 who links conglomerate mergers to the desire for growth maximisation.

[76] *Mergers: Substantive Assessment Guidance*, above n 18, para 6.1.

entry, or to act to the detriment of existing competitors, in relation to particular products within that portfolio.[77]

The counterfactual

Merger control is the most complex and problematic area of competition law. Not only must the competition authority predict the outcome of the merger in advance of the fact,[78] it must also consider what would happen in the absence of the merger—the counterfactual. The selection of the counterfactual may itself be of crucial importance, and it is not necessarily the case that the counterfactual is simply the status quo ex ante. It is important that the counterfactual take into account the dynamics of the market. It might therefore be necessary for the relevant authority to consider questions such as: what would happen to the target firm in the absence of the merger?;[79] what tactics might the acquiring firm adopt if denied the opportunity to acquire the target?; how might other firms in the market react? The EC Commission thus notes that it is required to compare the competitive conditions that would result from the merger 'with the conditions that would have prevailed without the merger'.[80] DG Comp takes the view that in most cases the relevant counterfactual will be the conditions prevailing at the time of the merger, although states that it may take into account changes 'that can reasonably be predicted'.[81] The relevant OFT guidance is in the following terms:

> 3.23 . . . the core concept of the substantial lessening of competition test is a comparison of prospects for competition with and without the merger. The competitive situation without the merger is hereafter referred to as the 'counterfactual'.

[77] Portfolio effects are explained in the following terms in the ibid, at para 6.2:

> 'When the market power deriving from a portfolio of brands exceeds the sum of its parts, a firm may be said to have 'portfolio power'. This may enable the firm to exercise market power in individual markets more effectively, with the result that competition is substantially lessened. Portfolio effects may have anti-competitive effects where they directly affect market structure, increase the feasibility of entry deterrence strategies and/or eliminate the competitive constraint imposed by firms in neighbouring markets.'

For a discussion of the potential exclusionary effects of such mergers see T Käserberg, 'Are Merger Control and Art 82 EC in the Same Market?—The Assessment of Mergers Which Facilitate Exclusionary Conduct under EC Merger Control' [2006] *ECLR* 409.

[78] In Case C–12/03 P *Commission v Tetra Laval BV* [2005] ECR I–987 the ECJ set out the nature of the problem: '[a] prospective analysis of the kind necessary in merger control must be carried out with great care since it does not entail the examination of past events—for which often many items of evidence are available which makes it possible to understand the causes—or of current events, but rather a prediction of events which are more or less likely to occur in future if a decision prohibiting the planned concentration or laying down the conditions for it is not adopted' (at para 42).

[79] This is particularly important if the 'failing-firm defence' is advanced, ie, in the absence of the merger the firm would in any event exit the market.

[80] Commission Notice, *Guidelines on the assessment of horizontal mergers*, above n 51, para 9.

[81] Ibid.

3.24 In most cases, the best guide to the appropriate counterfactual will be prevailing conditions of competition. However, the OFT may need to take into account likely and imminent changes in the structure of competition in order to reflect as accurately as possible the nature of rivalry without the merger. Examples of such circumstances may include the following—

—where a firm is about to enter or exit the market. Similarly, the OFT may also take account of committed expansion plans by existing competitors

—where changes to the regulatory structure of the market, such as market liberalisation, or tighter environmental constraints, will change the nature of competition.[82]

Unilateral effects[83]

'In general terms, unilateral effects are the harm that can arise from a merger even where the merger does not significantly improve the ability of firms to co-operate with each other . . . eg, in raising prices'.[84] The essential argument made in support of merger control is that, *ceteris paribus*, prices are higher and output is restricted in markets which are more monopolistic than in markets in which there is perfect competition.[85] This results in a welfare loss and a non-

[82] *Mergers: Substantive Assessment Guidance*, above n 18.

[83] Both the EC Commission and the OFT refer to 'non-coordinated effects' rather than 'unilateral effects'. The OFT states in its *substantive assessment guidance*, above n 18, that: '[t]he term "unilateral effects" is sometimes misunderstood as referring to action by a single firm, in particular the merged entity. In fact it refers more generally to independent or non-coordinated action by market participants.' (note 21, at para 4.5). At para 4.10 the OFT explains the position further:

> 'Though the profits from non-coordinated effects are generally captured by the merging parties, rival firms can also benefit from reductions in competitive pressure as a reulst of a merger. Even if rival firms can pursue the same competitive strategies as they did prior to the merger, this can result in their increasing prices in the wake of a merger. In such cases, the firms in the marketplace are not coordinating their competitive behaviour (tacitly or explicitly); they are simply reacting independently to expected changes in each other's commercial behaviour. Such instances of anti-competitive effects are still termed 'unilateral' or non-coordinated by merger analysts since they are based on independent actions of firms. The change in the structure of the market may mean that other firms will behave differently and may react to an increase in prices by raising their own prices.'

[84] B Dubow, D Elliott and E Morrison, 'Unilateral Effects and Merger Simulation Models' [2004] *ECLR* 114. See M Ivaldi, B Jullien, P Rey, P Seabright and J Tirole, 'The Economics of Unilateral Effects: Interim Report for DG Competition, European Commission' (2003) (DG Comp website).

[85] In its competitive impact statement in *United States v Vail Resorts Inc*, 1997–2 Trade Cas (D Colo 1997) the US DOJ, in the context of a merger between two ski-resorts, explained unilateral effects in the following way:

> 'Before a merger, increases in price by two independent resorts are deterred by the loss of customers that would result from a price increase. If resorts are put under common ownership by a merger, however, they no longer constrain each other's prices in the same way. A merger can make a price increase profitable. In particular, before a merger, if two resorts are significant competitors to each other and one of these increases its prices, a significant proportion of this resort's customers would be 'lost' to the other resort. After merger between these two resorts, however, some customers who switch away from the resort that raises its price would no longer be lost, but rather would be 'recaptured' at the newly acquired resort. Price increases

cont./

optimal allocation of resources, as it sends the consumer false signals about the value of the products being purchased, and distorts spending. Less consumer demand is satisfied under these conditions, and money that might have been spent on the monopoly product at a competitive price is diverted to consumption on other products, pushing up their prices. Under most interpretations of the law in the UK and the EC as it relates to dominant firm conduct the monopolist is not to be attacked purely for exploiting its monopoly position in this way.[86] Further, the more entrenched a monopolist is and the greater its control over the market, the more it may be able to raise strategic and conduct barriers to entry, deterring future competition. There is a further complication in that monopolists *might* engage in conduct which would be deemed to be abusive under the standards of the relevant law. In the case of mergers taking the form of the creation of joint ventures there is the concern that this may lead to coordinated conduct between the parents in respect of other aspects of their businesses. It is a matter of some debate whether these issues should feed into the merger control process or not. On the one hand it may be argued that conduct that is identifiably 'anti-competitive' under the standards of competition law may be addressed under that law, and that a pre-emptive blocking of a contemplated merger on the ground that it *might* result in anti-competitive conduct would result in too much enforcement compared to the benefits of enforcement (not all monopolists 'abuse' their position, and not all competitors enter into cooperative agreements). On the other hand it may be argued that acting *after* a dominant position has been abused or an illegal agreement has been effected is less effective than acting to prevent the infringement occurring at all. In *Tetra Laval*[87] the ECJ held that the Commission should take account of the disciplining effect of competition law on the likely behaviour of the post-merger entity.

There is debate amongst economists about the true extent of the harms that arise from the existence of monopolised, rather than competitive, industries, and some would argue that it is not possible to demonstrate that there is any harm at all. The seminal work in this respect dates from 1954 when Harberger produced an estimate of the difference between the total demand satisfied under competitive conditions and the reduced demand satisfied under monopoly con-

> that would have been unprofitable to either firm alone, therefore, would become profitable to the merged entity.'

As a result of this recapture phenomenon, a merged firm, acting independently to earn the most profits it can, will choose higher prices than its two component firms did before the merger, if those firms were significant competitors to each other before the merger. The loss of competition that arises as a result of this effect is what is meant by a 'unilateral' anti-competitive effect, that is, an effect that does not depend on the firms in the market acting interdependently.

[86] This is a slightly contentious statement. Monopolists may be found to infringe where they have committed the sin of 'excessive pricing' or where supplies are refused. However, there is usually an additional element to such infringements, above and beyond the mere choice of a profit-maximising price/output position.

[87] Case C–12/03 P, *Commission v Tetra Laval BV* [2005] ECR I–987.

ditions. Harberger's figure was only 0.1 per cent of the total national income, which might lead one to question the utility of competition policy.[88] More recent studies have pointed to higher figures than this, typically lying between 4 per cent at the lower end and 20 per cent at the upper end. The broad consensus now is that Harberger's figure may be seen very much as a lower boundary.[89]

Coordinated effects[90]

Alongside concerns relating to unilateral effects there exists the danger that a merger may increase the risk of collusion in a market. In essence the argument is that, by reducing the number of parties amongst whom understanding must be reached, the likelihood of reaching such an understanding is increased. Stories told in relation to tacit collusion at the horizontal level in concentrated markets are much more complex than is the story told in relation to a merger's unilateral effects.[91] Thus:

[88] AC Harberger, 'Monopoly and Resource Allocation' (1954) 44 *American Economic Review* 77. Harberger's work led to the adoption of the term 'Harberger triangle' to denote the area of 'deadweight welfare loss' arising from the presence of a monopoly on any given market.

[89] A further complexity, which will not be discussed in any detail here, relates to the fact that economists argue about *which* welfare standard to adopt when assessing mergers. In essence there are two choices: the total welfare standard (TWS), in which the welfare of all members of society—including producers—is equally balanced. This means that losses to consumers arising from a merger may be offset by enhanced profits. This first measure is generally preferred by economists, but is not followed within the merger control regimes. A second choice is that of the consumer welfare standard (CWS) in which only benefits and costs to consumers are taken into account. See BR Lyons, 'Could Politicians be More Right than Economists? A Theory of Merger Standards', Centre for Competition and Regulation, Working paper CCR 02-1 (2002), available at www.ecp.uea.ac.uk.

[90] Chap 7, below, discusses the approach taken to collective dominance giving rise to coordinated effects under the ECMR.

[91] A number of oligopoly models have been developed over the years and it is not possible here to go into all of them. The most frequently discussed in the context of competition law and economics is the Cournot equilibrium, sometimes referred to as Nash–Cournot. Nash (played in the film *A Beautiful Mind* by Russell Crowe) demonstrated that in certain situations an equilibrium could be arrived at whereby no one player in a game could achieve a better result by unilaterally adopting a strategy while other players adhered to the strategies adopted by them (the classic example is the prisoners' dilemma, but other formulations are available): see A Dixit and S Skeath, *Games of Strategy* (2nd edn, New York, WW Norton and Company, 2004). Bishop and Walker summarise the position thus: '[a]n equilibrium is a Nash non-co-operative equilibrium when, given the behaviour of all other firms in the market, no firm wishes to change its behaviour (i.e. each firm maximises profit given the behaviour of all the other firms)': Bishop and Walker, above n 4, para 2.29. In 1838 the French economist Augustin Cournot constructed a two-firm model in which each made assumptions about the other's reaction to its output strategy. The outcome of this model is a non-cooperative Nash equilibrium, in that both firms are making profit maximising decisions given each other's anticipated reactions, and an equilibrium is achieved. However, in a two-firm Cournot model price will be higher than that of a perfectly competitive market, but lower than that of monopoly, and output will be less than in perfect competition. As the number of firms increases the closer will be the position that would arise in a competitive market. A second oligopoly model is that of Bertrand, who assumed that firms react not on output but on price, but whose model has in-built theoretical limitations. For a technical discussion of some relevant aspects see O Compte, F Jenny and P Rey, 'Capacity Constraints, Mergers and Collusion' (2002) 46 *European Economic Review* 1. See also M Ivaldi *et al* above n 84.

> In most industries, firms recognise that their competitive stance—eg pricing and marketing decisions—affects the competitive stance of rival firms and is in turn affected by the competitive stance of these firms. Recognition of this competitive interdependence raises the question of whether firms will seek to reduce the vigour with which they compete with one another.[92]

In the *horizontal merger guidelines*[93] the EC Commission explains the principle in these terms:

> In some markets the structure may be such that firms would consider it possible, economically rational, and hence preferable, to adopt on a sustainable basis a course of action on the market aimed at selling at increased prices. A merger in a concentrated market may significantly impede effective competition, through the creation or the strengthening of a dominant position, because it increases the likelihood that firms are able to coordinate their behaviour in this way and raise prices, even without entering into an agreement or resorting to a concerted practice within the meaning of Article 81 of the Treaty. A merger may also make coordination easier, more stable or more effective for firms, that were already coordinating before the merger, either by making the coordination more robust, or by permitting firms to coordinate on even higher prices.[94]

The US FTC provided an elegant description of the process by which coordinated effects may arise in 1988:

> The effective coordination of price and output strategies requires developing a consensus concerning price and output levels, and a means of enforcing its terms. The first step requires harmonizing the incentives of participating firms and mitigating firm uncertainty concerning rival firms, so that they can effectively coordinate their behaviour. The second step requires creating circumstances in which the prospective value to each participating firm of cheating on the consensus does not exceed the prospective loss from rival firm retaliation. In order to create and maintain these circumstances, participating firms must be able to monitor rival firm conduct; that is, they must be able to detect cheating on the consensus. They must also be able to retaliate effectively if and when cheating occurs.[95]

This issue was central to the *Airtours/First Choice* merger blocked by the EC Commission on the ground that increased concentration in the post-merger market would lead to a restriction of competition by means of coordinated effects.[96] On appeal[97] the CFI held that for tacit collusion to be likely three conditions must be met. These are, first, that the market conditions must be such that the firms have the ability to align their behaviour in the absence of an explicit agreement to do so. Secondly there must be a sufficient incentive for the

[92] S Bishop and M Walker, *The Economics of EC Competition Law: Concepts, Application and Measurement* (London, Sweet and Maxwell, 1999), para 2.59.

[93] Commission, *Guidelines on the assessment of horizontal mergers*, above n 51.

[94] At para 39.

[95] *BF Goodrich Co*, 110 FTC 207 (1988).

[96] Case IV/M.1524, Decision 2000/276 [2000] OJ L 93/1.

[97] Case T–342/99, *Airtours plc v Commission* [2002] ECR II-2585, [2002] 5 CMLR 7. This case is discussed at length in Chap 7, below.

firms to maintain this conduct, which in turn means that there must be available some mechanism whereby firms which 'deviate' from this conduct may be 'punished' by the others. Thirdly the coordination should be sustainable in the face of other market pressures, including the possibility of entry into the market by new firms which do not understand the 'rules'. Competition Commission guidelines develop this argument further, and indicate the dangers of concluding that a market may be characterised by tacit coordination where prices converge, as there may be situations in which 'similar or identical prices' can result from intense competition.[98] In such a case it may be necessary to consider also profit levels in the industry and compare these with appropriate similar industries to determine whether these are excessive and suggestive of a lack of competition. The history of price movements may also be revealing. In a competitive market, even where prices converge, there are likely to be points at which they are different. This will be the case, for example, where there is a shock to the market outside the control of the firms, such as exit or entry, or a change in the pattern of consumption. In a market characterised by tacit coordination prices are more likely to be in perpetual alignment than they are in a competitive, yet oligopolistic, market. Perhaps most important in this area is the issue of identifying, with a reasonable degree of precision, what it is about the merger which changes the market conditions to permit a cooperative solution to be achieved where it could not be achieved previously. This basic problem has been eloquently summed up in the following terms: 'for collective dominance to be created or strengthened, there must be some point at which a merger transforms a (relatively) competitive market into a (relatively) uncompetitive one'.[99] It was this requirement that the EC Commission fundamentally failed to fulfil in the *Airtours* decision.

It may even be the case that in a market where there is, pre-merger, a tendency to coordinated behaviour allowing a merger that further reduces the number of participants may be pro-competitive. Although this may seem counter-intuitive it has been pointed out that asymmetry in such markets hinders coordination, and may, from society's view, be beneficial. The question in such a case might be how destabilising the merger would be. If, for example, it created a firm which was significantly larger than other equally sized participants, this might make coordination difficult to maintain.[100]

EFFICIENCIES

It has been stated above that the prime rationale for mergers is that they are profitable to those engaged in them, and that one source of such profit may be

[98] *Merger References: Competition Commission Guidelines*, above n 18, para 3.43.

[99] RBB Economics, 'Airtours/First Choice: CFI Holds Commission to Account', RBB Brief 2, June 2002.

[100] See AF Daughety, 'Beneficial Concentration' (1990) 80:1 *American Economic Review* 1231.

an increase in the efficiency of the merged enterprise. In a seminal article written in 1968 Oliver Williamson argued that mergers should be permitted where the efficiency gains were greater than the deadweight welfare loss (the Harberger Triangle).[101] The argument may be illustrated in Figure 2.2:

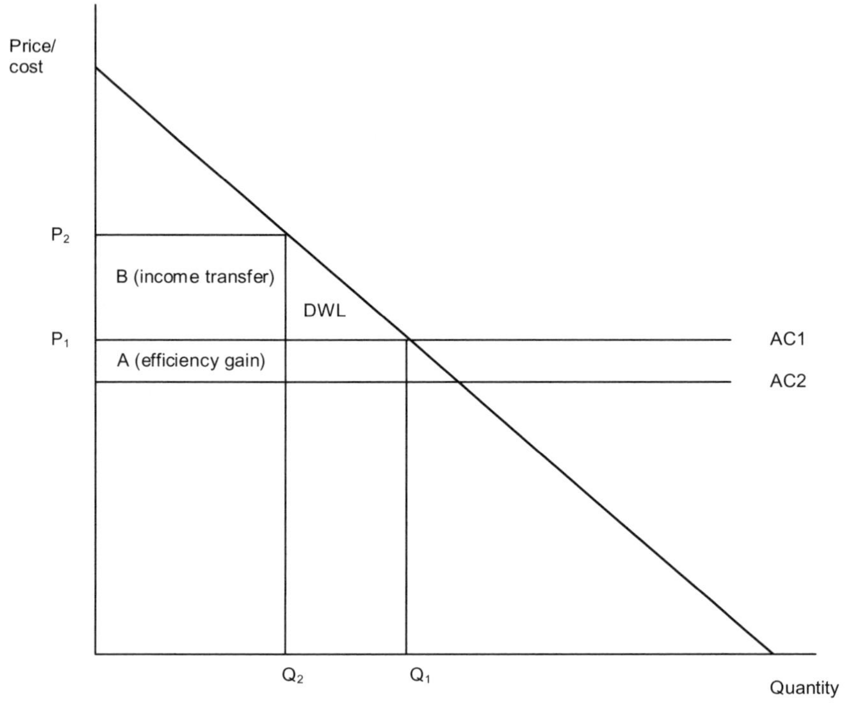

Figure 2.2: Merger welfare effects

In a long-run competitive situation the price, P_1 will be equal to the average cost of production, and the quantity produced will be Q_1. Following a merger, assuming market power has been created or increased, the price will rise to P_2, with the quantity produced falling to Q_2, with the result that price is now above cost. This has effected a transfer in wealth of B from the consumers to the merged entity. This may be of concern to politicians, and these concerns may be reflected in competition policy, but economists are unable to determine whether

[101] O Williamson, 'Economies as an Antitrust Defense: the Welfare Trade-offs' (1968) 58 *American Economic Review* 18. See generally D Gerard, 'Merger Control Policy: How to Give Meaningful Consideration to Efficiency Claims?' (2003) 40 *CML Rev* 1367. See also J Kattan, 'Efficiencies and Merger Analysis' (1994) 62 *Antitrust Law Journal* 513; D Yao and T Dahdouh, 'Information Problems in Merger Decision Making and Their Impact on Development of an Efficiencies Defense' (1993) 62 *Antitrust Law Journal* 23.

this is a harm—it may be the case that the merged entity is more deserving of this surplus than its customers. At the same time the area represented by the Harberger triangle (DWL) has simply disappeared from the equation. Thus far no benefits of the merger are assumed, but if at the same time the effect of the merger is to reduce average costs to AC_2 the position is different. There is now a cost saving, A. Williamson argued that the efficiency defence should be allowed where the area A is greater than the DWL. However, translating this straightforward argument into competition policy is not as easy as it may appear. A key issue is what the purpose of merger control actually is:

> If the objective is the protection of consumer interests, the central focus of merger analysis is on the price effects of mergers. On the other hand, if the objective is to enhance total surplus (generally defined as the sum of producer and consumer surplus), then the overall effects of the merger must be analysed.[102]

However, of greater concern is the practical issue of determining what the efficiencies are likely to be in advance of the merger being consummated, which 'accentuates the need to model competitive conditions in the relevant market more explicitly and precisely than has hitherto been thought necessary in European merger control'.[103] While it has been argued that it is important that merger regimes incorporate 'a recognition of the role that mergers play in the promotion of economic growth and development and the importance of taking merger efficiencies into account',[104] quite how this should be achieved is a matter that has led to substantial variance in competition authorities surveyed by the ICN. In the meantime economists have been developing merger simulation models which 'quantify the efficiency defence by allowing a number to be put on the competition detriment absent efficiencies and the extent to which efficiencies mitigate or overturn that effect'.[105]

It should come as no surprise then to learn that in some quarters scepticism has been expressed about the value of permitting an express 'efficiency' defence to a merger. The EC Commission's Green Paper produced as a preparation for the revision of the ECMR had suggested that such an approach could be adopted, but noted at the same time that there were concerns. The Irish Delegation agreed that the approach should be cautious:

[102] Ilzkovitz and Meikeljohn (eds), above n 13, at 50.

[103] Ibid.

[104] ICN Working Group: Analytical Framework Subgroup, 'Project on Merger Guidelines: Report for the third ICN annual conference in Seoul', Apr 2004, chap 6. This chap contains within it a survey of the approaches taken by various competition authorities in relation to the assessment of efficiencies in merger control.

[105] L Colley, 'From "Defence" to "Attack"? Quantifying Efficiency Arguments in Mergers' [2004] *ECLR* 342, at 342. These techniques were developed in the US, where the 1997 revision to the DOJ/FTC merger guidelines made explicit the fact that an efficiency defence could be made. The EC Commission has published a substantial report assessing efficiencies in the case of vertical and conglomerate mergers: (S Bishop, A Lofaro, F Rosati and J Young, *The Efficiency-Enhancing Effects of Non-Horizontal Mergers*, Brussels, Office for Official Publications of the European Communities 2005). See also M de la Mano, *For the Customer's Sake: The Competitive Effects of Efficiencies in European Merger Control* (Office for Official Publications of the European Communities, 2002).

> The Green paper seems to us to be inherently correct in expressing scepticism about efficiencies arising from mergers:
>
> —Empirical studies indicate that, on aggregate, the *ex post* performance of merged companies is, at best, mixed, suggesting that efficiencies may systematically fall below the parties' genuine expectations.
>
> —From an economic theory perspective, there is a fundamental doubt about efficiencies in mergers where market power increases. If we believe that competition is fundamental to driving cost reductions, then efficiencies are less likely to be attained precisely in the case where a merger creates market power . . .
>
> —It is not always obvious that a merger (involving market power) is necessary to achieve many efficiency benefits.
>
> —If an efficiency defence is allowed, then firms will have a strong incentive to exaggerate the efficiencies and it can be extremely difficult for a competition authority to verify them in advance. For this reason, the burden should likely lie on the parties to show the efficiencies, and a high standard of proof should be required.[106]

However, when the revised ECMR was promulgated it made explicit reference to efficiencies, albeit in the recitals and not in the substantive articles. Recital (29) notes that it 'is possible that the efficiencies brought about by the concentration counteract the effects on competition'. The wording of Article 2 is sufficiently open to admit an appraisal of efficiencies, and in the *Horizontal Guidance* the Commission deals with its approach to efficiencies at paragraphs 76–88. Its approach in specific cases is discussed further in Chapter 6.

The OFT has indicated that it will be cautious in evaluating claims of efficiencies made by merging parties. In *Phoenix Healthcare/EAP*[107] the OFT accepted that the case made by the parties relating to efficiencies was 'plausible', but then stated that 'due to the information asymmetries between the OFT and the merging parties in assessing efficiency claims, the OFT is generally sceptical about efficiency gains'.[108] The requirement that the OFT and the CC consider 'customer benefits' in evaluating mergers (see further Chapter 11) incorporates to an extent an efficiency defence into the EA 02, but the OFT has indicated that is likely to be only rarely that it will consider that efficiencies are sufficiently strong and proven to outweigh any SLC that it identifies,[109] and the CC argues that 'it would not normally be expected that a merger resulting in SLC would lead to benefits to customers'.[110]

[106] *Response of the Irish Delegation to the Merger Green Paper*, EC Commission website (no longer available) at time of merger review.

[107] *Anticipated acquisition by Phoenix Healthcare Distribution Limited of East Anglian Pharmaceuticals Limited*, OFT, 29 June 2005.

[108] At para 79.

[109] OFT, *Mergers: Substantive Assessment Guidelines*, above n 18, paras 7.7–7.10.

[110] *Merger References*, above n 18, para 4.35. Although the CC does not rule out the possibility that such benefits might arise.

3

EC and Member State merger control

INTRODUCTION[1]

THERE IS NOTHING in either the EC Treaty or the ECMR which precludes Member States from maintaining merger regimes that operate independently of the EC regime, as long as they do not purport to oust EC jurisdiction where the ECMR applies. The fundamental requirement of EC law is that Member States are not to frustrate its operation and are actively to cooperate in its application. This principle is enshrined in Article 10 EC, which requires that Member States shall:

> take all appropriate measures, whether general or particular, to ensure fulfilment of the obligations arising out of this Treaty, or resulting from action taken by the institutions of the Community. They shall facilitate the achievement of the Community's tasks.
>
> They shall abstain from any measure which could jeopardise the attainment of the objectives of this Treaty.

Clearly some demarcation between the regimes is necessary—it would defeat the objective of an EC merger regime to allow Member States to apply their laws to mergers that are subject to EC jurisdiction. As it is the EC legal regime which is superior to that of the Member States (in areas where the EC has competence), it is within this regime that the relationship between Community and Member States merger control is set out, although Member States are then free to frame their own response(s) to this within the parameters established by the EC.

Recitals (11)–(19) of the ECMR set out the broad principles governing the delimitation of jurisdiction. The most important of these is that 'member states should not be permitted to apply their national legislation on competition to concentrations with a Community dimension, unless this Regulation makes provision therefor'.[2] At the same time there is an emphasis in the ECMR on the principle of subsidiary, enshrined in Article 5 EC, which provides that:

[1] See generally LM Davison, 'The New EC Merger Control Regulation: Guaranteeing the Effectiveness of the Architecture of Separate Jurisdictional Zones?' [2005] *Intereconomics* (May/June) 148.

[2] Recital (18) ECMR.

> In areas which do not fall within its exclusive competence, the Community shall take action, in accordance with the principle of subsidiarity, only if and in so far as the objectives of the proposed action cannot be sufficiently achieved by the Member States and can, therefore by reason of the scale or effects of the proposed action, be better achieved by the Community.

Recital (8) of the ECMR applies this principle specifically to the area of merger control:

> The provisions to be adopted in this Regulation should apply to significant structural changes, the impact of which on the market goes beyond the national borders of any one Member State. Such concentrations should, as a general rule, be reviewed exclusively at Community level, in application of a 'one-stop shop' system and in compliance with the principle of subsidiarity. Concentrations not covered by this Regulation come, in principle, within the jurisdiction of the Member States.

At recital (14) the Commission makes reference to its partnership with the Member States 'in the light of the principle of subsidiarity'. More starkly, however, Article 21(3) ECMR sets out the principle that '[n]o member state shall apply its national legislation on competition to any concentration that has a Community dimension'.

At the outset it should be noted that there is a tension in the ECMR between the desire of the Commission to exercise control over those mergers whose 'impact goes beyond the national borders of any one Member State' and the very high thresholds that actually apply under Article 1 ECMR before a merger is deemed to have a Community dimension, and is thus subject to the 'one-stop shop'. There are thus provisions in the ECMR which apply to mergers falling below the Article 1 thresholds, but which nevertheless have the appearance of impacting on more than one Member State. However, these provisions, as will be seen below, lack force.

There are a number of provisions in the ECMR which govern the relationship between EC and national merger control more precisely, some the result of intense political discussion at the time of the enactment of Regulation 4064/89, and the Commission has published a *Notice on case referral in respect of concentrations*.[3] These provisions, and their operation, form the subject matter of this chapter.

Article 19 ECMR is addressed to the issue of liaison with the authorities of the Member States, and imposes on the Commission various obligations relating to the dissemination of information and consultation. In particular Article 19(2) provides in its first sentence that 'the Commission shall carry out the procedures set out in this Regulation in close and constant liaison with the competent authorities of the member states, which may express their views upon those procedures'. Although this does not make express mention of the European Competition Network (ECN) established as part of the modernised competition

[3] [2005] OJ C 56/2.

regime within the EC, it is to be presumed that this is the main forum within which this cooperation will take place. Recital (14) ECMR sets out the broad parameters of the relationship between the Commission and the Member States in relation to those situations in which concentrations may be referred from one to the other:

> The Commission and the competent authorities of the Member States should together form a network of public authorities, applying their respective competences in close cooperation, using efficient arrangements for information-sharing and consultation, with a view to ensuring that a case is dealt with by the most appropriate authority, in the light of the principle of subsidiarity and with a view to ensuring that multiple notifications of a given concentration are avoided to the greatest extent possible. Referrals of concentrations from the Commission to Member States and from Member States to the Commission should be made in an efficient manner avoiding, to the greatest extent possible, situations where a concentration is subject to a referral both before and after its notification.

ARTICLES 9 AND 4(4) ECMR

In the ECMR itself there are two clear exceptions to the general principle of exclusivity which work to concede authority to the Member States. Article 9 makes provision for 'referral to the competent authorities of the Member States'.[4] This provision is sometimes termed 'the German clause', as its insertion arose in part at the insistence of the German Government, which was reluctant to surrender merger control in all cases in which the thresholds were met. The Article may be invoked in situations in which, while having a Community dimension, the merger has an impact in one area which is specifically distinctive from its general impact. Acting either on its own initiative or at the request of the Commission (which may be rejected), authorities in Member States may request that the Commission refers to them cases in which:

> 9(2)(a) a concentration threatens to alter significantly competition in a market within that member state, which presents all the characteristics of a distinct market, or
> (b) a concentration affects competition in a market within that member state, which presents all the characteristics of a distinct market and which does not constitute a substantial part of the common market.

In the case of Article 9(2)(a) there are therefore two criterion that must be fulfilled in order for a concentration, or a part of it, to be referred back to the requesting Member States. The Member State is 'required to demonstrate that, based on a preliminary analysis, there is a real risk that the transaction may have a significant adverse impact on competition'.[5] The second requires the Member

[4] See M Pérez and R Burnley, 'The Article 9 Referral Back Procedure: A Solution to the Jurisdictional Dilemma of the European Merger Regulation? ' [2003] *ECLR* 364.

[5] *Notice on case referral in respect of concentrations*, para 35, avaiable at the DG Comp website.

State to show that a geographic market is affected which is national or narrower in scope. Clearly the question of what constitutes a 'distinct market' is of fundamental importance to the operation of this provision, although this question has not given rise to any reported litigation. Some further clarification of the meaning of this term is given in Article 2(7) ECMR. This requires that:

> The geographical reference market shall consist of the area in which the undertakings concerned are involved in the supply and demand of products or services, in which the conditions of competition are sufficiently homogeneous and which can be distinguished from neighbouring areas because, in particular, conditions of competition are appreciably different in those areas. This assessment should take account in particular of the nature and characteristics of the products or services concerned, of the existence of entry barriers or of consumer preferences, of appreciable differences of the undertakings' market shares between the area concerned and neighbouring areas or of substantial price differences.

In the case of Article 9(2)(b) the criteria are different. The first requires the Member State to show, based on a preliminary assessment, that the concentration may have an impact on competition in a market; the second requires that the geographic market in question is confined to a Member State, and is not a substantial part of the common market. The Commission states in the *Notice on case referral in respect of concentrations*, at paragraph 40, that 'based on past practice and case law, it appears that such situations are generally limited to markets with a narrow geographic scope'. Examples of markets deemed to satisfy, or not satisfy, the requirement of being a substantial part of the common market may be found in the decisions and case law relating to the application of Article 82 EC.[6] Only concentrations that fall within the ambit of relevant national merger control laws may be referred to Member States under Article 9(2).[7]

The distinction between Article 9(2)(a) and 9(2)(b) is important in determining the scope of the discretion left to the Commission under Article 9(3). Article 9(2) makes it clear that two situations can exist in respect of concentrations having a Community dimension.

In respect of Article 9(2)(a) where the relevant criteria are met, and where a Member State requests to the Commission that the merger be referred to it, it is not a requirement that the entire case be handed back. Indeed, it is clear from the wording of the Article that the Commission is not required to hand back any part of the case. Article 3(a) gives the Commission the power to continue to

[6] See, eg, J Faull and A Nikpay (eds), *The EC Law of Competition* (Oxford, Oxford University Press, 1999), at 3.112. In Case IV/M.1383 *Exxon/Mobil* (1999) the Commission accepted that Gatwick Airport was a substantial part of the common market. This is consistent with the approach taken in cases under Art 82 EC relating to the application of the essential facilities doctrine. Similarly in *Macquarie Airports Ltd/Ferrovial Aeropuertos SA* (2005) the EC Commission accepted an Art 9 request from the OFT in respect of a merger which related to Exeter and Bristol airports. A reference was made to the CC, and the merger was subsequently abandoned.

[7] *Notice on case referral in respect of concentrations*, above n 5, para 65.

determine the case itself. In the alternative 'it shall refer the whole *or part of the case*' (emphasis added). It is not uncommon for this latter option to be adopted, with the Member State having control over only that part of the case referred to it, although the Commission has stated that the one-stop shop principle mitigates in favour of a single authority dealing with the case wherever this is an effective approach (see further below). Where the Commission opts to review the merger itself this will not necessarily be a matter of contention. It may be that the purpose of the Member State in making the request is purely to bring to the attention of the Commission those characteristics of the merger which the Member State believes to be peculiar to it. For example in a case in 1999, *Exxon/Mobil*,[8] the DTI welcomed the EC Commission's 'resolution of competition detriments in the North West of Scotland, following which the Commission did not need to refer the case to the UK authorities as had been requested'.[9] There have been a small number of cases in which the CFI has considered the extent of the Commission's discretion under Article 9(2)(a). Two of these[10] related to the same merger, *SEB/Moulinex*.[11] The CFI in these cases confirmed that although the discretion of the EC Commission was substantial, it was not unfettered, and that a referral to a Member State could not be made when 'it is clear, on the basis of a body of precise and coherent evidence, that such a referral cannot safeguard or restore effective competition on the relevant markets'.[12] Cook and Kerse have argued that the scope of the discretion is sufficiently wide, even allowing for the comments of the CFI, that 'it will be difficult to succeed in challenging an Article 9 referral, except where the Commission has erred in law in judging whether the criteria are met'.[13]

Where the terms of Article 9(2)(b) are applicable Article 9(3)(b) leaves the Commission no discretion, and:

> where a member state informs the Commission pursuant to paragraph 2(b) that a concentration affects competition in a distinct market within its territory that does not form a substantial part of the common market, the Commission *shall* refer the whole or part of the case relating to the distinct market concerned, if it considers that such a distinct market is affected. (emphasis added)

The question what is a 'substantial part of the common market' has been considered extensively in the application of Article 82 EC, and it is not possible under this case law to give any firm predictive guidance. It is widely believed that any single Member State is a substantial part of the common market, although this presumption may lose some force in a Community of 25 Member States,

[8] Case IV/M.1383 (1999).

[9] DTI Press Release P/99/780, 29 Sept, 1999.

[10] Case T–119/02, *Royal Philips Electronics NV v Commission* [2003] ECR II-1433; Case T–114/02, *BaByliss SA and DeLonghi SpA v Commission* [2003] ECR II–1279.

[11] Case COMP/M.2621 (2002).

[12] Case T–119/02, *Royal Philips Electronics NV v Commission* [2003] ECR II-1433, para 343.

[13] CJ Cook and CS Kerse, *EC Merger Control* 4th edn London, Sweet & Maxwell, (2005), at 9–025.

and there have been a significant number of cases where areas smaller than individual states have been found to be substantial. The concept is not limited to a formalistic exercise based on the geographical area in question, but also takes into account the patterns of supply and demand, such that it is necessary to consider 'the pattern and volume of the production and consumption of the said product as well as the habits and economic opportunities of vendors and purchasers'.[14] The ECJ has thus held that, in respect of the market for sugar, the southern part of Germany constituted a substantial part of the common market. At the time the population of the area was some 22 million, and the production in that area was 800,000 tonnes, which the Court held 'to be sufficiently large, so far as sugar is concerned, to be considered a substantial part [of the EC]'.[15]

The Commission has stated at paragraph 9 of the *Notice on case referral* that:

> In principle, jurisdiction should only be re-attributed to another competition authority in circumstances where the latter is the more appropriate for dealing with a merger, having regard to the specific characteristics of the case as well as the tools and expertise available to the authority. Particular regard should be had to the likely locus of any impact on competition resulting from the merger. Regard may also be had to the implications, in terms of administrative effort, of any contemplated referral.

Where cases are referred back to Member State in part it is normal that this be done on the basis of a geographical determination. However, there have been rare incidents where cases are split on the basis of the sector of the industry affected. For example, in *BP/E.on*[16] the German competition authorities were able to examine the effect on downstream markets in Germany, while the EC Commission considered the wider upstream market throughout the EC as a whole.

If any Member States requests a referral under Article 9 ECMR the Commission has indicated that, even if it retains jurisdiction over the concentration, it will not apply the simplified procedure under which a short-form clearance decision is adopted within 25 days of the notification of the merger (see further Chapter 5).[17]

In the application of Article 9 the Commission may request information from the Member State's relevant authority.[18] In the UK provision is made for the OFT to gather necessary information by the EEC Merger Control (Distinct Market Investigations) Regulations 1990.[19] These give the OFT the power to compel persons to produce any documents or information relating to any relevant matter to the OFT in a manner specified by the OFT.

[14] Cases 40–48/73 etc, *Cooperative Vereniging 'Suiker Unie' UA v Commission* [1975] ECR 1663, [1976] 1 CMLR 295, at para 371.

[15] Ibid, at para 448.

[16] Case COMP/M.2533 (2001).

[17] *Commission Notice on a simplified procedure for treatment of certain concentrations under Council Regulation (EC) No 139/2004*, [2000] OJ C 217/32, para 13.

[18] Art 19(2) ECMR.

[19] SI 1990/1715, as amended by the Enterprise Act 2002 (Consequential and Supplemental Provisions) Order 2003, SI 2003/1398.

The first case to be referred to a Member State under Article 9 of Regulation 139/2004 was *The Coca-Cola Company/Coca-Cola Hellenic Bottling Company SA/Traficante*.[20] The acquisition involved a family-owned mineral water supplier active in southern Italy, and was referred back to the Italian Competition Authority (the AGCM). The request was interesting, given the very low market shares that were advanced by the AGCM, and the concerns arose in relation to portfolio effects.[21] The merger was cleared by the AGCM on 21 June 2006.[22] The question has been asked whether in future the Commission would be so generous as to accede to a request where the effect being alleged in the relevant Member State appeared to be so small, and it may be noted that in *Burda/Hachette*[23] the Commission rejected a request by Poland relating to the publishing market in which the horizontal overlaps between the two companies in Poland were limited.

Under the terms of Article 4(4) ECMR, which applies only at the pre-notification stage, the Commission may itself initiate this process, and parties engaged in concentrations with a Community dimension may, prior to making a full notification, alert the Commission to the fact that, in their opinion, the concentration should be examined, in whole or in part, by a Member State where the concentration affects competition in a distinct market. If following receipt of a Commission submission to this effect a Member State does not object within 15 working days the Commission may decide to refer the whole or part of the case to the Member State affected. In this case it will be deemed that no notification under the terms of the ECMR is made. Only concentrations that fall within the ambit of relevant national merger control laws may be referred to Member States under Article 4(4) ECMR.[24]

A merger may have effects in a number of markets, each of them having the characteristic of being distinct. However, the Commission recognises that the fragmentation of cases should, where possible, be avoided. Only if it 'appears that multiple authorities would be in a better position to ensure that competition in all markets affected by the transaction is effectively protected' should fragmentation be permitted.[25] The Commission includes itself in this rubric, and therefore takes the view that where a case falls under Article 9 or Article 4(4) ECMR, the case should, where possible, be referred back to the relevant Member State in its entirety. Thus at paragraph 22 of the notice the Commission states that:

[20] Case COMP/M.4174 (2006).

[21] See further Chap 2, above, and the discussion of *General Electric/Honeywell* in Chap 8, below.

[22] C 7668, *Coca Cola Hellenic Bottling/Fonti del Vulture* (provv n 15619).

[23] Case COMP/M.4122 (2006).

[24] *Notice on case referral in respect of concentrations*, above n 5, para 65. For a recent example involving the UK see *Boots/UniChem*, referred to the OFT for consideration under the UK regime on 30 November 2005. This case is discussed further in Chap 13, below. Two other cases were accepted by the OFT under this provision in 2005–6: *Southern Cross Healthcare Group Ltd/Cannon Capital Ventures Ltd* and *London and South Eastern Railway/Integrated Kent rail franchise*, available at the OFT website.

[25] *Notice on case referral in respect of concentrations*, above n 5, para 12.

> To the extent that a case may engender competition concerns in a number of Member States, and require coordinated investigations and remedial action, this may militate in favour of the Commission retaining jurisdiction over the entirety of the case in question. On the other hand, to the extent that the case gives rise to competition concerns which, despite involving national markets in more than one Member State, do not appear to require coordinated investigation and/or remedial action, a referral may be appropriate.

The Commission has, exceptionally, felt it necessary to refer a merger back to more than one Member State in the past.[26] The Commission may apply the simplified procedure to concentrations in respect of which an Article 4(4) referral request has been unsuccessful (see further Chapter 6).[27]

ARTICLE 21(4) ECMR

Article 21(4) sets out a second exception to the principle of Commission exclusivity, recognising the existence of certain 'legitimate interests' that lie outwith the ambit of the ECMR.[28] Article 21(4) is in the following terms:

> Notwithstanding paragraphs 2 and 3, Member States may take appropriate measures to protect legitimate interests other than those taken into consideration by this Regulation and compatible with the general principles and other provisions of Community law.
>
> Public security, plurality of the media and prudential rules shall be regarded as legitimate interests within the meaning of the first subparagraph.
>
> Any other public interest must be communicated to the Commission by the Member State concerned and shall be recognised by the Commission after an assessment of its compatibility with the general principles and other provisions of Community law before the measures referred to above may be taken. The Commission shall inform the Member State concerned of its decision within 25 working days of that communication.

Public security

The reference to 'public security' may be seen in part as a recognition of the impact of Article 296(b) EC which, even without the existence of Article 21(4) ECMR, provides for a further exception. This is in the following terms:

> Any member state may take such measures as it considers necessary for the protection of the essential interests of its security which are connected with the production of or

[26] The first case in which this was happened was *Leroy Merlin/Brico*, in which the Commission emphasised that the relevant markets were highly localised in character.

[27] *Commission Notice on a simplified procedure for treatment of certain concentrations under Council Regulation (EC) No 139/2004*, [2000] OJ C 217/32, para 14.

[28] See generally CM Borges, 'The Legitimate Interests of Member States in EC Merger Law' (2003) 9 *European Public Law* 345.

trade in arms, munitions and war material; such measures shall not adversely affect the conditions of competition in the common market regarding products which are not intended for specifically military purposes.

The operation of Article 296 EC is not in any way subject to limitations imposed by the terms of the ECMR, and acts independently of the merger regime.

The first case to be dealt with relating to public security under the terms of Article 21(4) ECMR was *IBM France/CGI*, in which the French Government was concerned by the fact that two of CGI's subsidiaries contracted for the Ministry of Defence.[29] These provisions are only rarely invoked, but, for example, in June 2000 the UK asserted jurisdiction over the public security aspects of Thomson CSF's proposed acquisition of Racal Electronics plc,[30] and again in November 2002 in *BAE System/Astrim/EADS*.[31] There has been no litigation dealing with the scope of the term 'public security' in this context, but it has been argued that were there to be so, the ECJ would be likely to take a restrictive approach to the exception, construing it narrowly, consistent with its general approach to exceptions set out in EC legislation.[32]

Plurality of the media

It is not unusual for merger regimes to treat media mergers differently from those taking place in other sectors.[33] While competition concerns may still be important, media ownership raises wider issues such as the maintenance of a plurality of views that may be jeopardised by concentrations in this sector. The EC Commission is not well placed to deal with such considerations, and it may be argued that subsidiarity principles dictate that such concerns should be resolved within affected Member States. Article 21(4) ECMR ensures that, even where a concentration would have a Community dimension, such mergers may be reviewed within Member States. The provision was relied upon by the UK in *Newspaper Publishing*,[34] in which an international consortium was formed to acquire *The Independent*, a UK national daily newspaper. The proposed merger was notified to both the EC and the UK authorities, and the UK authorities reviewed those elements of the transaction relating to non-competition factors only.

[29] EC Commission, *Twenty-Third Annual Report on Competition Policy* (Luxembourg, Office for Official Publications of the EC, 1993), para 321.

[30] DTI Press Release P/2000/401, 12 June 2000.

[31] DTI Press Release P/2002/732, 22 Nov 2002.

[32] See CJ Cook and CS Kerse, *EC Merger Control*, London, Sweet and Maxwell, 3rd edn (2000), para 8.4.2.1.

[33] In the case of the UK see Chap 16, below.

[34] Case IV/M.423 (1994).

Prudential rules

Prudential rules are rules relating to the supervision and control of companies in the financial services industry, and usually relate to the power of some public authority or other equivalent body, to regulate the ownership, control and financial stability of such companies. Although this is an area in which the EC is increasingly active in setting standards, it remains the case that Member States are free within the bounds of the ECMR to assert jurisdiction over mergers having a Community dimension when it is necessary to do so in order to comply with prudential rules within the Member States. The UK authorities were granted the right to review the *Sun Alliance/Royal Insurance* merger[35] on the ground that it was necessary for them to do so to protect the interests of the relevant insurees. However the EC Commission resisted an application by Portugal in relation to *BSCH/Champalimaud*.[36] Here the Portuguese authorities attempted to block the acquisition of an undertaking involved in the banking and insurance industry in Portugal by a Spanish bank. The Commission both doubted whether the claims made by Portugal could be deemed to fall within the Article 21(4) requirements, and also found that the claims were not substantiated. More recently, in March 2006, the EC Commission announced that it was taking action against Poland following the latter's requiring the Italian bank Unicredit to divest itself of its shares of the Polish bank BPH SA.[37] The Commission had previously cleared the *Unicredit/Bayerische Hypo-und Vereinsbank AG* merger on October 18 2005.[38] However, on 20 December 2005, the Polish Treasury instructed Unibank to sell its shares in BPH on the ground that when it had earlier acquired another Polish bank it had entered into a 'non-competition clause', the purpose of which, according to the Polish Government, was to ensure the 'protection of competition on the Polish market of financial and banking services'. The Commission pointed out in its Press Release that Article 21(4) did not allow Member States to act to protect competition interests.[39]

Any other public interest

The text of Article 21(4) reflects a compromise achieved at the time of the negotiations surrounding the introduction of the ECMR. Some Member States argued for the inclusion of a relatively long list of exceptions to the exclusive

[35] Case IV/M.759 (1996).

[36] Case IV/M.1616 (1999).

[37] EC Commission Press Release IP/06/277, 8 Mar 2006.

[38] 18 Oct 2005 (IP/05/1299).

[39] For the position with banking mergers generally see S Mohamed, 'National Interests Limiting EU Cross-Border Bank Mergers' [2000] *ECLR* 248. See also J Dermine, 'Bank Mergers in Europe: The Public Policy Issues' (2000) 38 *Journal of Common Market Studies* 409.

competence assigned to the EC Commission to review concentrations having a Community dimension. As is clear from the text of Article 21(4) in the end a short list was adopted, but the third element within that Article, relating to 'any other public interest', is intended to provide some flexibility. As with the other Article 21(4) exceptions this provision has not often been invoked. The Commission has the power to determine whether the interest raised by the Member State is in fact a relevant 'public interest', and this assessment is to take into account 'the general principles and other provisions of Community law'. This requirement means that Member States *cannot* rely on factors relating directly to competition, as these are encompassed within the ECMR itself. However, the provision may be invoked where regulatory concerns, which extend to wider issues than those which may fall to be determined within competition considerations, are applicable. This was the case, for example, in relation to a water merger within the UK, *Lyonnaise des Eaux SA/Northumbrian Water Group*,[40] discussed in Chapter 16, below. In *EdF/London Electricity*[41] the EC Commission rejected a request by the UK to be assigned jurisdiction based on the role of the Director General of Electricity Supply in regulating the electricity industry. The argument made by the Commission was that the role fulfilled by the DGES was not such as to require an intervention in the merger, but could be fulfilled by the exercise of his powers in a post-merger environment.

ARTICLE 22 ECMR

Under the terms of Article 22 the referral process may work in the other direction, with mergers without a Community dimension being notified to the Commission. This clause was originally inserted at the request of the Dutch, who lacked a merger control law at the time of the enactment of Regulation 4064/89, although this position has now been rectified. In the event of concentrations not meeting the requirements of Article 1 one or more Member States may request the Commission to conduct the examination where the concentration 'affects trade between Member States and threatens to significantly affect competition within the territory of the member state or states making the request' (art 22(1)). The provision is rarely used, and it was widely anticipated that as Member States adopted merger control regimes (if these were not already in place) it would fall into desuetude. However, some states that have merger control regimes have themselves made such requests. The UK, for example, asked the Commission to consider competition aspects of the proposed merger between GE Engine Services and Unison Industries in 2002,[42] and in 2005 it referred to the EC Commission the anticipated acquisition by the Dow Chemical Company of the divinylbenzene business of Total Petrochemicals

[40] Case IV/M.567 (1995), on reference in the UK, Cm 2936 (1995), available at the OFT website.
[41] Case IV/M.1346 (1999), [1999] 4 CMLR 374.
[42] DTI Press Release P/2002/134, 26 February 2002.

France SA.[43] If such a request is accepted by the Commission, and acceptance is not automatic, though may be presumed to be likely, the national authorities making the request lose control over the review process and cannot determine the scope of the Commission investigation.[44] Only concentrations within the meaning of Article 3 ECMR may be referred to the Commission under Article 22.[45] The Commission will not apply the simplified procedure to any concentration referred to it under this Article (see further Chapter 6).[46]

It is also possible to apply Article 22 in situations in which the same merger situation has been identified to a number of the members of the ECN. The OFT notes the application of this possibility in its procedural guidance,[47] in which it is noted that although this would allow for a one-stop consideration of the merger, and thus may be beneficial, 'few multi-jurisdictional mergers are suitable for reference to the Commission, and the application of [Article 22] is not automatic in these cases'. There have, however, been some rare examples of such an approach being taken.[48] Such an approach would also now more likely be replaced by the application of Article 4(5) ECMR, it being likely that the parties themselves would recognise the benefits that would flow from a single assessment of the merger (see below).

[43] OFT, *Office of Fair Trading Annual Report 2005–06* (2006) at 56.

[44] Case T–221/95, *Endemol Entertainment Holding BV v Commission* [1999] 5 CMLR 611, paras 37–47. In this case at the stage of making the decision, the parties had argued that the Commission was limited to examining the effects of the relevant concentrative JV in relation only to the market for TV advertising, as the request of the referring Dutch government was to examine this market. However, the Commission also considered the position in relation to TV broadcasting (Case IV/M.553, *RTL/Veronica/Endemol*, (1995); see further Chap 9, below).

[45] *Notice on case referral in respect of concentrations*, above n 5, para 65.

[46] *Commission Notice on a simplified procedure for treatment of certain concentrations under Council Regulation (EC) No 139/2004*, above n 17, para 13.

[47] OFT, *Mergers: Procedural Guidance*, May 2003, para 5.29, avaiable at the OFT website. See also paras 9.12–9.20. The OFT states, at para 9.13 that when determining whether a multi-jurisdictional merger should be referred to the Commission under Art 22(3) ECMR the NCAs would take into consideration, inter alia, whether: 'the merger is a concentration as defined in [Art 3 ECMR]; the concentration is subject to filing in several EU member states; a relevant geographic market affected by the concentration is wider than national; the concentration threatens to create or strengthen a dominant position as a result of which effective competition would be significantly impeded within the territory of the member states making the joint request; the concentration affects trade between member states'.

[48] See for example case COMP/M.2698 *Promatech/Sulzer* (2002), and case COMP/M.2738 *GEES/Unison* (2002). In the former case the complexity of the procedure when a number of member states are involved is clear. The following time-line is taken from C Bright and M Persson, 'Article 22 of the EC Merger Regulation: An Opportunity Not to be Missed?', [2003] *ECLR* 490:

Promatech/Sulzer timeline

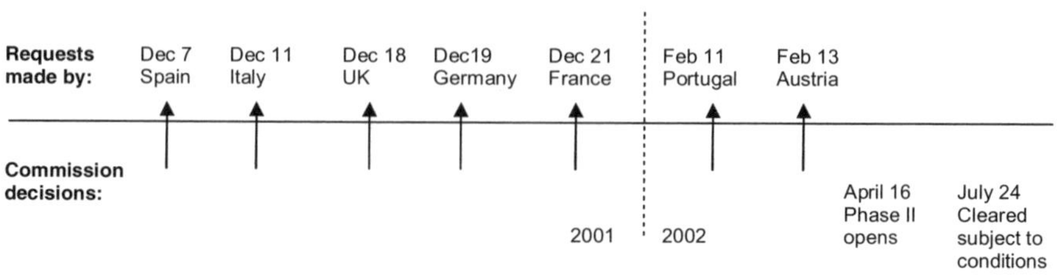

ARTICLE 4(5) ECMR

The EC Commission had hoped to extend its jurisdiction, increasing the numbers of qualifying mergers, when the ECMR was amended in 2004. In particular it sought jurisdiction over mergers falling to be notified in three or more Member States—a 'mandatory 3+ system'. Many of those who responded to the Green Paper[49] criticised this proposal on the ground that although the proposal was ostensibly simple it failed to take into account the true impacts of a merger. It was argued that some 3+ mergers would have little cross-border impact, while there could be mergers which would not need to be notified in three Member States that would have significant cross-border impact. A second criticism was that different jurisdictional tests operated in different states, complicating the issue.[50] In the event a compromise was reached, as reflected in Article 4(5), which grants the Commission jurisdiction where the parties to the merger themselves request it and where no Member State to which a referral would be required objects:

> With regard to a concentration as defined in Article 3 which does not have a Community dimension within the meaning of Article 1 and which is capable of being reviewed under the national competition laws of at least three Member States, the persons or undertakings referred to in paragraph 2 may, before any notification to the competent authorities, inform the Commission by means of a reasoned submission that the concentration should be examined by the Commission. The Commission shall transmit this submission to all Member States without delay.
>
> Any Member State competent to examine the concentration under its national competition law may, within 15 working days of receiving the reasoned submission, express its disagreement as regards the request to refer the case.
>
> Where at least one such Member State has expressed its disagreement in accordance with the third subparagraph within the period of 15 working days, the case shall not be referred. The Commission shall, without delay, inform all Member States and the persons or undertakings concerned of any such expression of disagreement.

When parties are contemplating making a request to the Commission on the basis of Article 4(5) the Commission *Notice on case referral in respect of concentrations* states that the parties should consider whether the referral is likely to be considered appropriate by the Commission.[51] At recital (16) of the ECMR it is suggested that a request for a pre-notification referral to the

[49] EC Commission, *Green Paper on the Review of Council Regulation (EEC) No 4064/89*, COM(2001)745 final, 11 Dec 2001.

[50] See generally G Drauz, 'Merger Review—Jurisdictional Issues' in G Drauz and M Reynolds (eds), *EC Merger Control: A Major Reform in Progress* (Richmond, Surrey, Richmond Law and Tax, 2003).

[51] Para 25.

Commission is 'particularly pertinent in situations where the concentration would affect competition beyond the territory of one member state'. At paragraph 28 of the *Notice* the Commission clarifies its likely approach to what concentrations it is likely to be minded to view as falling within Article 4(5) ECMR:

> Cases where the market(s) in which there may be a potential impact on competition is/are wider than national in geographic scope, or where some of the potentially affected markets are wider than national and the main economic impact of the concentration is connected to such markets, are the most appropriate candidate cases for referral to the Commission. In such cases, as the competitive dynamics extend over territories reaching beyond national boundaries, and may consequently require investigative efforts in several countries as well as appropriate enforcement powers, the Commission is likely to be in the best position to carry out the investigation.

Only concentrations within the meaning of Article 3 ECMR may be referred to the Commission under Article 4(5),[52] and the provision may only be invoked 'before any notification to the competent [national] authorities'.[53] The Commission may apply the simplified procedure, under which a short-form clearance decision is adopted within 25 days of the notification of the merger to mergers falling within Article 4(5) (see further Chapter 6).[54]

PROCEDURE

The procedures under which the referral systems set out above are to operate are set out in part III of the Commission's *Notice on case referral in respect of concentrations*. As discussed above, referrals may be made either pre- or post-notification, and from the Commission to the Member States, or from Member States to the Commission.

Pre-notification referrals

At the pre-notification stage[55] the undertakings concerned are the only parties who can request referral in either direction, and it is for the undertakings to demonstrate to the required standard that the relevant criteria are met. Requests

[52] *Notice on case referral in respect of concentrations*, above n 5, para 65.

[53] Ibid, para 69

[54] *Commission Notice on a simplified procedure for treatment of certain concentrations under Council Regulation (EC) No 139/2004*, above n 17, para 14.

[55] According to the *Notice on case referral in respect of concentrations*, above n 5, pre-filing requests for referrals 'must concern concentrations the plans for which are sufficiently concrete. In that regard, there must at least exist a good faith intention to merge on the part of the undertakings concerned, or, in the case of a public bid, at least a public announcement of an intention to make such a bid' (para 66).

may be made on Form RS, available from the Commission website.[56] In the application of Article 4(4) ECMR the Member States have 15 working days from the date on which they receive notice of the request from the Commission to agree or disagree with the request. Silence will be deemed to constitute agreement to accept the case. If the Member States agree, the Commission has a further period of up to a maximum of 25 days to decide whether to refer the case or not. If no decision is made within this time the case will be allocated to the Member States.

In the application of Article 4(5) ECMR Member States again have 15 days in which to respond to the request. At the end of that period the Commission will check whether any relevant Member State has expressed disagreement with the referral request made. In the event that there is no disagreement the concentration is deemed to acquire a Community dimension, and the Commission will therefore have exclusive jurisdiction. In this case the concentration must be notified to the Commission by the normal method, using Form CO. The objection of even one of the relevant Member States would frustrate the referral to the Commission, and the merger would fall to be considered under the relevant national merger laws, with no further Community involvement in the process.[57]

Post-notification referrals

Whereas pre-notification referrals are triggered by the requests of the undertakings concerned, post-notification referrals flow from Member States, either by their own initiative or at the invitation of the Commission. The procedures to be adopted under Articles 9(2) and 22(1) ECMR alter depending on whether the request is for the merger to be referred to, or from, the Commission. The elements of both provisions have been discussed above. Under Article 9 the Member

[56] The requirements for the satisfactory completion of Form RS are set out in part in the *Notice on case referral in respect of concentrations*, above n 5, at paras 59–63. Para 61 of the Notice states that:

> 'When providing information on Form RS or generally in making a request for a pre-notification referral, it is not envisaged or necessary for the undertakings concerned to show that their concentration will lead to detrimental effects on competition. They should, however, provide as much information as possible showing clearly in what way the concentration meets the relevant legal criteria set out in Art 4(4) and (5) and why the concentration would be most appropriately dealt with by the competition authority or authorities specified in the request. The Merger Regulation does not require publication of the fact that a Form RS has been lodged, and it is not intended to do so. A non-public transaction can consequently be the subject of a pre-notification referral request.'

[57] *Notice on case referral in respect of concentrations*, above n 5, para 72, and Art 4(5) ECMR. Although all Member States will be sent a copy of Form RS, only those competent to review the case may obstruct a referral to the EC Commission. One of the requirements of Form RS is that it is completed by the undertakings concerned in such a way as to permit all states to identify whether or not they are competent to review the merger in question. The possibility of disagreement on whether a Member State is competent to review the merger or not is contemplated in para 75 of ibid.

States have 15 days from the receipt by them of a copy of Form CO. The Commission will first verify whether the legal criteria for the application of Article 9(2) are met: in the case of Article 9(2)(a) it will then decide whether or not to refer the concentration, and in the case of Article 9(2)(b) it will have no choice. In either case, if a referral is made, the Member States then apply their own merger control laws, subject only to the limitations imposed by Article 9(6) and (8) ECMR. Article 9(6) provides that the Member State will 'decide upon the case without undue delay'. A time limit of 45 days is imposed within which the Member State concerned is to inform the undertakings of the result of its preliminary assessment of the competition concerns, and what further action, if any, it intends to take. Article 9(8) provides that 'in applying the provisions of this article, the Member State concerned may take only the measures strictly necessary to safeguard or restore effective competition on the market concerned'.

Under Article 22 ECMR Member States must make a request to the Commission that the latter take the case within 15 working days from the date of national notification, or when the concentration became known to them if there is no compulsory national notification procedure (as is the case in the UK). The Commission will send a copy of the request to all Member States, and any of these also have the right to join in with the original request within a further 15 day period. National time limits relating to relevant merger proceedings are to be suspended during this period. The Commission must decide, within 10 days of the closure of the second 15 day period, whether or not it wishes to accept the case. If the Commission does decide to accept the case proceedings in any state that requested it to do so are suspended, and jurisdiction passes to the Commission. However, Member States that had jurisdiction and that rejected the request for a referral to the Commission are entitled to continue to apply national law. In light of the Commission commitment to avoiding a multiplicity of actions wherever it is reasonable to do so, it may be presumed that in the unlikely event that a merger falls to be considered in more than one Member State, and that there is disagreement between these states on whether Article 22 ECMR should be invoked, the Commission may be likely to reject the request from those states seeking to remit jurisdiction to the Commission.

THE POSITION WITHIN THE UK

There are a large number of references in the Enterprise Act 2002 and relevant secondary legislation to procedural matters relating to situations in which mergers are referred to, or are received from, the EC Commission. These are dealt with as appropriate throughout this text. For the purposes of the interrelationship between EC and national merger control, the OFT is the UK competent authority, and is therefore the body which takes the decisions on whether to request the referral of a merger falling within the ECMR to the UK under Article 9, and whether to refer a UK merger to the EC Commission under Article 22

ECMR. The Secretary of State has responsibility for taking decisions relating to the protection of the UK's national security and other legitimate non-competition interests under Article 296 EC or Article 21(3) ECMR. The procedures to be adopted in situations falling under section 67 EA 02, which deals with intervention to protect legitimate interests in the case of 'European mergers', are considered further in Chapter 17.

In relation to the application of Article 9 the OFT will, when considering action, publish a notice seeking views on the implications for competition in the UK of the merger. If a request for a referral to the UK is made and accepted, the OFT will apply the procedures set out in Chapters 12–14 below to the merger as if it were a UK merger. The only difference is that the ECMR requires that a report on the assessment of the merger must be published within four months of the taking of the Article 9 decision by the EC Commission.

4

Qualifying Mergers in the EC

INTRODUCTION

THE MOST IMPORTANT question to ask of any merger control regime is which mergers fall within its jurisdiction. In the case of the EC the relevant criteria are a mix of turnover thresholds and the geographical area within which that turnover takes place. Recital (9) ECMR states that 'the scope of application of this Regulation should be defined according to the geographical area of activity of the undertakings concerned and be limited by quantitative thresholds in order to cover those concentrations which have a Community dimension'. Recital (10) states that 'a concentration with a Community dimension should be deemed to exist where the aggregate turnover of the undertakings concerned exceeds given thresholds'. It is irrelevant for the purposes of jurisdiction where the undertakings concerned have their seat or their principal fields of activity. It is however necessary that they have 'substantial operations' in the EC, as will automatically be the case where the turnover thresholds are met. In addition to the turnover and geographical requirements, the ECMR applies only where a relevant 'concentration' occurs. In this chapter turnover is addressed first, followed by the approach taken to 'concentration', and finally issues of territorial jurisdiction are considered.[1]

THE CONCEPT OF 'UNDERTAKINGS'

The Commission has published a *Notice on the concept of undertakings concerned under Council Regulation (EEC) No 4064/89 on the control of concentrations between undertakings*.[2] The purpose of this is to clarify the interpretation of the term 'undertaking' as used in Articles 1 and 5 of Regulation 4064/89, but this remains valid in relation to the application of Regulation 139/2004, and also clarifies the term 'undertaking' in so far as it is relevant to the

[1] The leading work on jurisdiction under the ECMR is MP Broberg, *The European Commission's Jurisdiction to Scrutinise Mergers* 2nd edn, The Hague, Kluwer Law International, 2003).

[2] [1998] OJ C 66/14. This Notice replaces an earlier *Notice on the notion of undertakings concerned* [1994] OJ C 385/12.

application of Article 3 ECMR.[3] In essence, mergers take place when previously independent undertakings come together to form a new entity, or when one undertaking is subsumed within another. It is irrelevant to EC merger control that the new entity may constitute legally separate and apparently distinct companies. There are many different ways in which it would be possible to frustrate the intent of the ECMR were it to focus on the legal entities involved in the relevant transactions, rather than the economic undertakings, and both the terminology of the ECMR and its interpretation are designed to avoid this. However, some of the reasoning adopted in the Commission's guidance may appear a little circular at first blush. Thus, in the *Notice on the concept of undertakings* the Commission states that in the case of a merger (as defined in Article 3(1)(a) ECMR) 'the undertakings concerned will be the undertakings that are merging'. In the case of the acquisition of control falling under Article 3(1)(b) ECMR 'it is the concept of "acquiring control" that will determine which are the undertakings concerned'.[4]

In the case of the acquisition of parts of one or more undertakings, as set out in Article 5(2) ECMR, it is only those parts which are the subject of the acquisition that are deemed to be the relevant undertaking as far as the seller is concerned.[5] This means that only the turnover attributable to those parts is relevant for the purposes of the calculation of turnover and the determination of whether the relevant thresholds set out in Article 1 ECMR are met. The *Notice on the concept of undertakings* defines 'parts' as being:

> one or more separate legal entities (such as subsidiaries), internal subdivisions within the seller (such as a division or unit), or specific assets which in themselves could constitute a business (eg in certain cases brands or licences) to which a market turnover can be clearly attributed. In this case, the undertakings concerned will be the acquirer and the acquired part(s) of the target company.[6]

The relevant date for the determination of the bounds of the relevant undertakings is that which triggers the notification to the EC Commission under the terms of Article 4(1) ECMR. Thus if the target company has divested itself of a business prior to the date of the agreement, the announcement of the public bid or the acquisition of a controlling interest, or where such a divestment is a condition of the concentration, then the turnover of the divested undertaking will not be included within the turnover of the acquired undertaking. The reverse is true in the case of a business being acquired.[7]

Where an acquisition is made by a subsidiary of a group of companies, the notification of the merger may be made by either the subsidiary or its parent. However, 'all the companies within a group . . . constitute a single economic

[3] See, eg, para 5 of the Notice, above n 2.
[4] Para 7 of ibid.
[5] Ibid, para 14.
[6] Ibid.
[7] Ibid, para 17.

entity, and therefore there can be only one undertaking concerned within the one group—ie, the subsidiary and the parent company cannot each be considered as separate undertakings concerned, either for the purposes of ensuring that the threshold requirements are fulfilled . . . or that they are not'.[8] In any event, Article 5(4) ECMR, discussed below, provides that the relevant turnover is to be that of the group to which the subsidiary belongs.

In the case of acquisition of joint control (see further below) the relevant considerations are set out at paragraphs 21–25 of the *Notice on the concept of undertakings*. Where the concentration relates to a newly set up JV there will be no turnover of the JV to assess at the time of the notification, and the relevant undertakings are those of the companies acquiring control of the newly set up entity. Where the acquisition is of an already established company, then the relevant undertakings are the companies acquiring control and the target company or business. Where, however, the target company was previously under the sole control of a parent and a number of new shareholders acquire joint control, while the initial parent remains, the relevant undertakings for the purposes of Article 1 ECMR are each of the jointly-acquiring companies, including the initial parent. In this case, the Commission indicates, the target company is not an undertaking concerned, and its turnover is to be assessed as the turnover of the initial parent.[9] Where an acquisition is carried out by several undertakings with the intention of immediately splitting the target between the acquiring parties, the Commission has stated that there is no concentration of economic power and that the merger may be deemed as existing only for an instant. Any such operation will therefore be treated by the Commission as being separated out into a number of transactions, each one relating to an acquiring company and that part of the target which it is acquiring, resulting in a treatment, in effect, of a series of sole acquisitions.[10]

A complication arises in cases in which a target is acquired by a JV. In such a case a determination needs to be made whether the relevant undertaking is the JV, or whether it is each of its separate parents. As the Commission has stated, 'the issue is whether or not to "lift the corporate veil" of the intermediate undertaking'.[11] Recognising the possibility that 'shell' companies may be set up as acquisition vehicles, with the intention of avoiding the turnover thresholds, the Commission 'will look at the economic reality of the operation to determine which are the undertakings concerned'.[12] Where the acquiring JV is 'full function', such that it has sufficient resources to carry out business independently on a lasting basis,[13] the Commission will normally consider that the relevant undertaking is the JV itself. However, where the JV is a vehicle created for the

[8] Ibid, para 19.
[9] Ibid, para 23.
[10] Ibid, para 24.
[11] Ibid, para 26.
[12] Ibid, para 26.
[13] See the *Commission Notice on the concept of full-function joint ventures* [1998] OJ C 66/1.

purpose of carrying out the acquisition, the Commission will consider that the relevant undertakings are the JV's parents.[14] In the *Notice* the Commission cites the example of *TNT/Canada Post, DBP Postdienst, La Poste, PTT Post and Sweden Post*,[15] (see Figure 3.1) a complex case in which joint control over a JV (JVC) was to be acquired by a JV entered into between five parent companies, and another acquiring company.

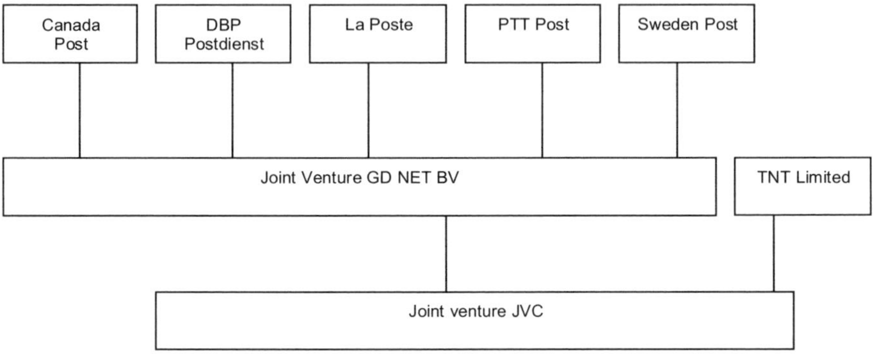

Figure 3.1: Joint Control Structure—Example

The Commission took the view that GD NET BV was established purely as a vehicle for the acquisition of JVC, and to act as a coordinating unit between the five parent companies, such that the five parents, and not a full-function JV, would exercise a decisive influence, along with TNT, over JVC. As such the relevant undertakings, and hence the turnover to be considered, were the five parent undertakings.

In the situation in which joint control is replaced by sole control, the exiting company, which has sold its stake to the company acquiring sole control, is irrelevant to the determination of the power of the new entity on the market, and thus the relevant undertakings are the existing JV over which sole control is now being exercised and the company exercising sole control.[16] Such a situation arose in *ICI/Tioxide*,[17] in which there was pre-merger joint 50/50 control, followed by sole control post-merger. The Commission found that the under-

[14] *Notice on the concept of undertakings*, above n 2, para 28. The Commission further states that '[t]his is the case in particular where the joint venture is set up especially for the purpose of acquiring the target company, where the joint venture has not yet started to operate, where an existing joint venture has no legal personality or full-function character as referred to above or where the joint venture is an association of undertakings.'

[15] Case IV/M.102 (1991).

[16] *Notice on the concept of undertakings*, above n 2, paras 30–32.

[17] Case IV/M.023 (1990).

takings concerned were the purchaser, ICI, the acquiree, Tioxide, but not the seller, Cookson.[18]

Where there are changes in shareholdings in the case of a jointly controlled JV the question to be asked is whether the change in shareholding leads to a change in control.[19] Complexities are raised by the range of factual circumstances which may arise. The Commission deals in the *Notice on the concept of undertakings* with a reduction in the number of shareholders leading to a change from joint control to sole control,[20] a reduction in the number of shareholders not leading to sole control,[21] and 'any other changes in the composition of the shareholder.[22]

The final sections of the *Notice on the concept of undertakings* deal with demergers and company break-ups,[23] the exchange of assets,[24] acquisitions of control by individual persons,[25] management buy-outs[26] and the acquisition of control by a state-owned company.[27] In demergers a number of possible scenarios arise, but typically there will be more than acquisition of control as joint control over assets is replaced by separate situations of sole control over assets. For a typical demerger the relevant undertakings will be the original parties to the merger and the assets that each is acquiring. A similar finding will lie in the case of a break up of a JV where the undertakings will be the original owners and each of the parts of the JV over which they separately retain sole control. In the case where parties exchange assets, each acquisition of control is a separate concentration, even where the parties regard the swaps as interdependent and constituting a single transaction.

Where an individual person acquires control over an asset or business, they may be regarded as an undertaking, and the other companies or businesses controlled by that person may be taken into account for the purpose of the calculation of turnover. This was the approach taken in *Asko/Jacobs/Adia*,[28] where a Swiss entrepreneur was held to be an undertaking because of his economic interests in various relevant sectors. Management buy-outs are also treated as acquisitions by individual persons, and will be treated in the same way. Where the management creates a jointly controlled vehicle to facilitate the

[18] *Notice on the concept of undertakings*, above n 2, para 32. The Commission held in its decision that: 'decisive influence exercised solely is substantially different to decisive influence exercised jointly, since the latter has to take into account the potentially different interests of the other party or parties concerned . . . By changing the quality of decisive influence exercised by ICI on Tioxide, the transaction will bring about a durable change of the structure of the concerned parties.'

[19] Ibid, para 33.

[20] Ibid, paras 35–37.

[21] Ibid, paras 38–39.

[22] Ibid, paras 40–45.

[23] Ibid, paras 46–48, Annex.

[24] Ibid, paras 49–50.

[25] Ibid, paras 51–52.

[26] Ibid, paras 53–54.

[27] Ibid, paras 55–56.

[28] Case IV/M.082 (1991).

buy-out this will be treated as if it were an acquisition by a JV. However, where the managers acted on the basis of their own resources and where investors did not have a controlling stake in the company, there would be no turnover attributable to the managers, such that the merger would not be a qualifying one under the terms of Article 1 ECMR. Further, there would be no change to the competitive structure of the market.

The issue of state-owned companies is considered below, but the general position is that the question is whether the acquisition of a state-owned or controlled company by another owned or controlled by the same state is to be seen as a matter of internal restructuring, or whether it is a concentration between independent entities. The ECMR should not discriminate in favour of state-owned enterprises,[29] and the question will be one of fact to be determined largely by reference to whether or not the companies are both part of the same industrial group, or operate and are owned separately.

TURNOVER THRESHOLDS

The relevant turnover thresholds are set out in Article 1 ECMR, which sets out two alternative formulations:

> 1. Without prejudice to Article 4(5) and Article 22, this Regulation shall apply to all concentrations with a Community dimension as defined in this Article.
> 2. A concentration has a Community dimension where:
>
> (a) the combined aggregate worldwide turnover of all the undertakings concerned is more than EUR 5 000 million; and
> (b) the aggregate Community-wide turnover of each of at least two of the undertakings concerned is more than EUR 250 million,
>
> unless each of the undertakings concerned achieves more than two-thirds of its aggregate Community-wide turnover within one and the same Member State.
>
> 3. A concentration that does not meet the thresholds laid down in paragraph 2 has a Community dimension where:
>
> (a) the combined aggregate worldwide turnover of all the undertakings concerned is more than EUR 2 500 million;
> (b) in each of at least three Member States, the combined aggregate turnover of all the undertakings concerned is more than EUR 100 million;
> (c) in each of at least three Member States included for the purpose of point (b), the aggregate turnover of each of at least two of the undertakings concerned is more than EUR 25 million; and
> (d) the aggregate Community-wide turnover of each of at least two of the undertakings concerned is more than EUR 100 million,

[29] See recital (22) of the ECMR.

unless each of the undertakings concerned achieves more than two-thirds of its aggregate Community-wide turnover within one and the same Member State.[30]

In the case of Article 1(2), therefore, the first requirement is that the concentration be a very large one, with a substantial worldwide turnover, and with at least two parties having turnover in the EC as a whole in excess of €250m. This ensures that as well as the transaction being large at the global level it is also one that is relevant for the EC to consider.[31] Thus a merger between two very large Japanese undertakings would only be subject to the jurisdiction of the ECMR only where each had at least a €250m turnover in the EC. Finally the two-thirds rule applies, under which turnover of all relevant parties must not be substantially within the same Member State, in which case it may be presumed under the principle of subsidiarity that the EC is not best placed to deal with the merger, although the Member State may make a request to the EC Commission that jurisdiction be assigned to it (see Chapter 3, above).

In the case of Article 1(3), which was introduced into the ECMR by the 1997 revisions,[32] the required worldwide turnover is halved, but at the same time a more precisely defined dispersal of turnover throughout the EC is required, and the two-thirds rule again applies. Article 1(3) can be applied only where the Article 1(2) criteria are not met, and the two thresholds may not be combined to assert jurisdiction over a merger which meets neither criterion individually. In essence therefore the requirements of Article 1(2) and (3) are relatively straightforward. In practice however difficulties may be encountered.

Figure 4.2 illustrates the relationship between turnover thresholds and jurisdiction.[33]

Calculation of turnover

The first important issue, dealt with in Article 5 ECMR is that of the calculation of turnover. The Commission has also published a *Notice on calculation of turnover under Council Regulation (EEC) No 4064/89 on the control of*

[30] Sects 3.3 and 3.4 of Form CO require notifying parties to provide information relevant to turnover at the time of notification.

[31] The Commission has stated that 'Article 1(2) sets out the thresholds which must first be checked in order to establish whether the transaction has a Community dimension. In this respect, the worldwide turnover threshold is intended to measure the overall dimension of the undertakings concerned; the Community turnover threshold seeks to determine whether the concentration involves a minimum level of activities in the Community; and the two-thirds rule aims to exclude purely domestic transactions from Community jurisdiction': *Commission Notice on calculation of turnover under Council Regulation (EEC) No 4064/89 on the control of concentrations between undertakings*, [1998] OJ C 66/25, para 3.

[32] Regulation 1310/97 [1997] OJ L 180/1.

[33] Adapted from I Sinan and J Lomax, 'Transatlantic Mergers and Merger Control' (2001) 20 *International Financial Law Review* Supp, 71. See further R Burnley, 'The EC Merger Regulation and the Meaning of "Community Dimension"' [2003] *European Business Law Review* 819.

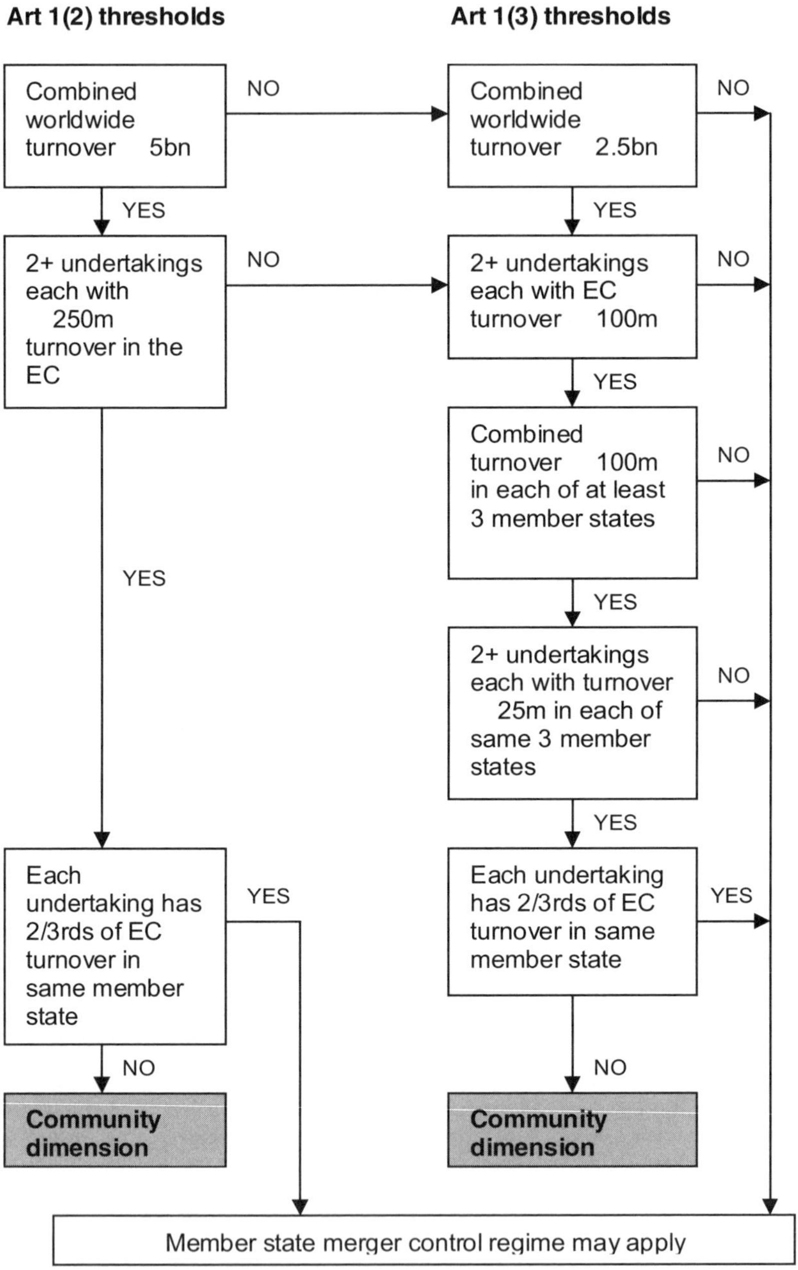

Figure 4.2: Turnover thresholds and jurisdiction

concentrations between undertakings (hereinafter, *Notice on turnover*).[34] The calculation of turnover is a technical matter, and the treatment here is not a full one, but introduces the core concepts and applicable rules.

Aggregate turnover, referred to in Article 1 ECMR, is defined in Article 5(1) ECMR as 'the amounts derived by the undertakings concerned in the preceding financial year from the sale of products and the provision of services falling within the undertakings' ordinary activities after deduction of sales rebates and of value added taxes, and other taxes directly related to turnover'. It will be noted that Article 5(1) refers to 'ordinary activities'. Aid given to the undertaking by the state is included within turnover only if it is intended to support these 'ordinary activities' and is reflected in the price of the products sold or services supplied.[35] In *Cereol/Continentale Italiana*,[36] for example, the Commission did not include in turnover aid given by the EC because the aid was given to support the producers of the raw material used by the undertakings, and not the products supplied by the undertakings. Sales from the preceding year are used, as there are usually no accounts available for the year in which the merger transaction is to take place, and the Commission considers that 'the closest representation of a whole year of activity of the company in question is the one given by the turnover figures for the most recent financial year'.[37] However, account should be taken of any acquisitions or divestments made since the last accounting period. The part of turnover attributed to any disposed of component of the undertaking(s) may be subtracted from the turnover figures, and the turnover of components acquired since the last financial year must be added in.[38] The Commission will normally base its assessment on the audited accounts of the undertakings in question. However, the Commission has indicated that 'in cases where major differences between the Community's accounting standards and those of a non-member country are observed, the Commission may consider it necessary to restate those accounts in accordance with Community standards in respect of turnover'.[39] The Commission will be reluctant to base its assessment on either provisional or management accounts in any but the most exceptional circumstances.[40]

Article 5(2) ECMR, second indent, provides that where transactions take place over a two-year period between the same persons or undertakings these shall be treated as one and the same transaction. Although the Commission recognises that in some cases the staggering of transactions is entirely legitimate,

[34] [1998] OJ C 66/25. This notice replaced an earlier *Notice on calculation of turnover* [1994] OJ C 385/21.

[35] *Notice on turnover*, above n 31, para 16.

[36] Case IV/M.156 (1991).

[37] *Notice on turnover*, above n 31, para 25. Where the proposed concentration is to take place early in the financial year, and last year's accounts are not yet available, the Commission will look at the figures from the year before: ibid, para 26.

[38] Ibid, para 27.

[39] Ibid, para 26.

[40] Ibid, para 26.

and best serves the interests of the relevant parties, it also recognises the danger that some parties may stagger transactions in an attempt to avoid the jurisdiction of the ECMR.[41] This means that where a series of transactions takes place no one of which would be individually notifiable, notification must take place with the transaction which lifts the overall series into the relevant thresholds.

Sales made between any of the undertakings specified in Article 5(4) ECMR shall not be included as relevant turnover, on the basis that the aim of turnover calculation 'is to exclude the proceeds of business dealings within a group so as to take account of the real economic weight of each entity'.[42] Where the acquisition is not of an entire undertaking, but of a part or parts of it only, only the turnover directly related to those relevant parts shall be included as being relevant turnover. This reflects the fact that although the seller of the assets being transferred is necessary to the transaction, its remaining assets are independent of the transaction, and will not in the future be related to the impact that the transaction has on the competitive environment in the market.[43]

In the case of financial and insurance undertakings where sales are not an appropriate measure of turnover, other measures are specified. In the case of financial undertakings these are set out at Article 5(3)(a)[44] and in the case of insurance undertakings these are set out at Article 5(3)(b).[45]

Article 5(4) ECMR sets out the scope of the undertaking as regards the turnover to be included. This is in the following terms:

> 4. Without prejudice to paragraph 2, the aggregate turnover of an undertaking concerned within the meaning of this Regulation shall be calculated by adding together the respective turnovers of the following:

[41] At para 34 of ibid the Commission sets out the position clearly: 'In practical terms, this provision means that if company A buys a subsidiary of company B that represents 50% of the overall activity of B and one year later it acquires the other subsidiary (the remaining 50% of B), both transactions will be taken as one. Assuming that each of the subsidiaries attained a turnover in the Community of only ECU 200 million, the first transaction would not be notifiable unless the operation fulfilled the conditions set out in Art 1(3). However, since the second transaction takes place within the two-year period, both have to be notified as a single transaction when the second occurs.'

[42] Ibid, para 23. Ie, 'the "amounts" taken into account by the Merger Regulation reflect only the transactions which take place between the group of undertakings on the one hand and third parties on the other'.

[43] Ibid, paras 30–31.

[44] The relevant turnover will be determined by the sum of the income derived from items defined in Council Directive 86/635/EEC on the annual accounts and consolidated accounts of banks and other financial institutions [1988] OJ L 316/51, after deductions of relevant taxes, as being: (i) interest income and similar income; (ii) income from securities; (iii) commissions receivable; (iv) net profit on financial operations; and (v) other operating income.

[45] Defined as being: 'the value of gross premiums written which shall comprise all amounts received and receivable in respect of insurance contracts issued by or on behalf of the insurance undertakings, including also outgoing reinsurance premiums, and after deduction of taxes and parafiscal contributions or levies charged by reference to the amounts of individual premiums or the total value of premiums'. For further detail on the approach to be taken to the turnover of financial or insurance undertakings see part III of the *Notice on turnover*, above n 31.

(a) the undertaking concerned;
(b) those undertakings in which the undertaking concerned, directly or indirectly:

   (i) owns more than half the capital or business assets, or
   (ii) has the power to exercise more than half the voting rights, or
   (iii) has the power to appoint more than half the members of the supervisory board, the administrative board or bodies legally representing the undertakings, or
   (iv) has the right to manage the undertakings' affairs;

(c) those undertakings which have in the undertaking concerned the rights or powers listed in (b);
(d) those undertakings in which an undertaking as referred to in (c) has the rights or powers listed in (b);
(e) those undertakings in which two or more undertakings as referred to in (a) to (d) jointly have the rights or powers listed in (b).[46]

Finally Article 5(5) ECMR relates to joint rights or powers held by the undertakings concerned in the concentration, and provides that in calculating aggregate turnover:

(a) no account shall be taken of the turnover resulting from the sale of products or the provision of services between the joint undertaking and each of the undertakings concerned or any other undertaking connected with any one of them, as set out in paragraph 4(b) to (e);
(b) account shall be taken of the turnover resulting from the sale of products and the provision of services between the joint undertaking and any third undertakings. This turnover shall be apportioned equally amongst the undertakings concerned.

Part 3.4 of the *Notice on turnover* deals with the turnover of groups. Where an undertaking involved in a concentration is part of a group it is the turnover of the group that is to be taken into account in assessing whether the thresholds apply. Were this not the case any large undertaking would be able to avoid jurisdiction by simply creating a vehicle with low or no turnover to engage in the acquisition. As the *Notice* indicates, the aim is 'to capture the total volume of the economic resources that are being combined through the operation'.[47] The definition of the group is dependent 'on whether the companies have the right to manage the undertaking's affairs as the yardstick to determine which of the companies that

[46] Ibid, para 38, states:

> 'This means that the turnover of the company directly involved in the transaction (point (a)) should include its subsidiaries (point (b)), its parent companies (point (c)), the other subsidiaries of its parent companies (point (d)) and any other undertaking jointly controlled by two or more of the companies belonging to the group (point (e)).'

The Commission further points out at para 42 that: 'since the aim of this provision is simply to identify the companies belonging to the existing groups for the purposes of turnover calculation, the test of having the right to manage the undertaking's affairs in article 5(4) is somewhat different from the test of control set out in article 3(3)'. The test of control is a more demanding one, and is discussed in more detail below.

[47] Ibid, para 36.

have some direct or indirect links with an undertaking concerned should be regarded as part of its group'.[48] It is important to note that the groups are defined as existing before the relevant concentration takes place, such that the parameters of each group should be identified as existing before any restructuring that might take place as a result of the concentration proceeding.[49]

Recital (22) makes some reference to the turnover of state undertakings. It states that:

> The arrangements to be introduced for the control of concentrations should, without prejudice to Article 86(2) of the Treaty, respect the principle of non-discrimination between the public and the private sectors. In the public sector, calculation of the turnover of an undertaking concerned in a concentration needs, therefore, to take account of undertakings making up an economic unit with an independent power of decision, irrespective of the way in which their capital is held or of the rules of administrative supervision applicable to them.

The *Notice on turnover* at paragraph 43 specifies that in accordance with the principle set out above, Article 5(4) should be read in conjunction with the recital in respect of state-owned enterprises. The implication of this is that the fact that two undertakings involved in a concentration are both owned by the same state does not imply that they are necessarily part of the same group. The question is rather whether each undertaking constitutes a separate entity.[50]

Geographical allocation of turnover[51]

Part II of the *Notice on turnover* deals with the geographical allocation of turnover, which may be an important issue in determining whether a concentration has a Community dimension within the terms of Articles 1(2) or (3) ECMR. In order to determine whether the thresholds are met turnover needs to be allocated geographically. The last sentence of Article 5(1) ECMR provides that: '[t]urnover, in the Community or in a Member State, shall comprise products sold and services provided to undertakings or consumers, in the Community or in that Member State, as the case may be'. In the case of both goods and services the Commission states in the *Notice on turnover* that 'turnover should be attributed to the place where the customer is located because that is, in most circumstances, where a deal was made, where the turnover for the supplier in question was generated and where competition with alternative suppliers took place'.[52] Where goods or services are supplied to the customer in one place, but billed to another, it is the place of supply which is the relevant one for the purposes of the

[48] *Commission Notice on calculation of turnover under Council Regulation (EEC) No 4064/89 on the control of concentrations between undertakings, [1998] OJ C 66/25, note 31 above*, para 37.

[49] Ibid, para 41.

[50] See also para 44 of ibid.

[51] See MP Broberg, 'The Geographic Allocation of Turnover under the Merger Regulation' [1997] *ECLR* 103.

[52] Above n 31, at para 46.

geographical allocation of turnover. Finally, where turnover is generated in currencies other than the euro the notice specifies that the annual turnover should be converted at the average rate for the 12 months' accounting period, and should not be broken down into component quarterly, monthly or weekly figures which are individually converted.[53]

The meaning of 'concentration'

The ECMR applies only to 'concentrations' which fall within its scope. A 'concentration consists of contractual arrangements and agreements establishing control within the meaning of Article 3(2) of the [ECMR]'.[54] The concept of 'concentration' is first defined in recital (20) ECMR 'to cover operations bringing about a lasting change in the control of the undertakings concerned and therefore in the structure of the market'. A fuller definition is given in Article 3 ECMR, which states in part that:

> 1. A concentration shall be deemed to arise where a change of control on a lasting basis results from:
>
> (a) the merger of two or more previously independent undertakings or parts of undertakings, or
> (b) the acquisition, by one or more persons already controlling at least one undertaking, or by one or more undertakings, whether by purchase of securities or assets, by contract or by any other means, of direct or indirect control of the whole or parts of one or more other undertakings.
>
> 2. Control shall be constituted by rights, contracts or any other means which, either separately or in combination and having regard to the considerations of fact or law involved, confer the possibility of exercising decisive influence on an undertaking, in particular by:
>
> (a) ownership or the right to use all or part of the assets of an undertaking;
> (b) rights or contracts which confer decisive influence on the composition, voting or decisions of the organs of an undertaking.
>
> 3. Control is acquired by persons or undertakings which:
>
> (a) are holders of the rights or entitled to rights under the contracts concerned; or
> (b) while not being holders of such rights or entitled to rights under such contracts, have the power to exercise the rights deriving therefrom.
>
> 4. The creation of a joint venture performing on a lasting basis all the functions of an autonomous economic entity shall constitute a concentration within the meaning of paragraph 1(b).

[53] Ibid, para 49.
[54] *Notice on restrictions directly related and necessary to concentrations* [2001] OJ C 188/5, para 10.

The Commission has published a *Notice on the concept of concentration*[55] which provides guidance on the way in which the Commission interprets the term 'concentration' used in Article 3 ECMR.

In the *Concentration Notice* it is made clear that the determination whether or not a concentration has been effected is one of qualitative, rather than quantitative criteria. The relevant criteria therefore contain matters both of law and of fact, and 'it follows, therefore, that a concentration may occur on a legal or a *de facto* basis'.[56] As is clear from the text of Article 3 ECMR there are two situations in which concentrations may take place. The first arises where previously independent undertakings have merged,[57] and the second in situations in which control of another undertaking is acquired.[58] The notice therefore treats these two situations separately in its explanation of the terms.

Previously independent undertakings

Mergers within the meaning of Article 3(1)(a) ECMR may occur in two circumstances. First two or more independent undertakings may join together in a new undertaking, such that they cease to exist as legal entities. This may include the absorption of one undertaking into another, with one ceasing to exist and the other retaining its legal identity. The second situation may arise where, 'in the absence of a legal merger, the combining of the activities of previously independent undertakings results in the creation of a single economic unit'.[59] This will be considered to be a merger when it leads to the de facto existence of a common economic unit. Such a situation may occur, for example, where undertakings arrange for common management through a contractual arrangement, even if they retain their legal personalities. The Commission has stated that for this to apply 'a prerequisite . . . is the existence of a permanent, single economic management'.[60] Cross shareholdings between the group may reinforce a finding that a single economic entity may exist, as may arrangements relating to, for example, internal profit and loss compensation within the group. The concept of control may be important in determining whether undertakings have previously been independent, and there is no single formula by which control may be established. For example, minority shareholders may have control over an undertaking if history shows that they have obtained a majority of votes on

[55] [1998] OJ C 66/5. Although published in relation to the application of Regulation 4064/89 this has not been updated in the light of the entry into force of Regulation 139/2004, and may for the time being be considered as an accurate statement of the Commission's practice. The notice replaced an earlier *Notice on the notion of concentration* [1994] OJ C 385/5.

[56] *Notice on the concept of a concentration*, [1998] OJ C 66/5, para 4.

[57] Art 3(2(a) ECMR.

[58] Art 3(2)(b) ECMR.

[59] *Notice on the concept of a concentration*, above n 56, para 7.

[60] Ibid, para 7.

major decisions at shareholder meetings over the previous three years. The issue of control is considered further below.

Acquisition of control

The acquisition of control raises more complex issues than the merging of previously autonomous undertakings. Paragraph 9 of the Commission *Notice* provides that:

> Whether an operation gives rise to an acquisition of control depends on a number of legal and/or factual elements. The acquisition of property rights and shareholders' agreements are important, but are not the only elements involved: purely economic relationships may also play a decisive role. Therefore, in exceptional circumstances, a situation of economic dependence may lead to control on a *de facto* basis where, for example, very important long-term supply agreements or credits provided by suppliers or customers, coupled with structural links, confer decisive influence.[61]

Control may be acquired by one or more undertakings acting either individually or collectively, or by a person where that person already controls at least one other undertaking.[62] Article 3(3) ECMR provides that:

> Control is acquired by persons or undertakings which:
>
> (a) are holders of the rights or entitled to rights under the contracts concerned; or
> (b) while not being holders of such rights or entitled to rights under such contracts, have the power to exercise the rights deriving therefrom.

In the *Notice on the concept of concentration* the Commission recognises that the above position will be the one most normally encountered, although there may be exceptional cases in which the formal holder of a controlling interest is not the same person as the one who in fact has the real power to exercise the rights arising from this interest. In this situation control will be deemed to be held by the person or undertaking who in reality enjoys the power to control the target undertaking.[63] It is not necessary for the purposes of Article 3(3) ECMR that control over an entire pre-existing legal entity is acquired in order for a concentration to be deemed to exist. It is sufficient that assets, which may include brands or licences, be transferred, although these 'must constitute a business to which a market turnover can be clearly attributed'.[64] Whether control is acquired solely or jointly, it remains defined as the ability to exercise decisive influence on an undertaking.

[61] See, eg, Case IV/M.258 *CCIE/GTE* (1992).

[62] The term 'person' includes public bodies, private entities and individuals. Public bodies may be the state, as was the case, eg in Case IV/M.157 *Air France/Sabena* (1992) where the Belgian State was the relevant person.

[63] As provided in Art 3(3)(b) ECMR.

[64] *Notice on the concept of a concentration*, above n 56, para 12.

The meaning of 'control'[65]

Control may be acquired either solely or jointly.[66] The primary way in which sole control of an undertaking may be acquired is the situation in which an undertaking acquires the majority of the voting rights of a company. It is the voting rights which are important, and not the simple acquisition of shares.[67] However, sole control may also be acquired when a qualified minority is held, on either a legal or de facto basis. Control may be acquired on a legal basis where the minority shareholding held carries with it specific rights, as would be the case where the shares were preferential and allowed the minority shareholder 'to determine the strategic commercial behaviour of the target company'.[68] This would be the case, for example, were the shareholder in a position to appoint more than half the members of the board. On a de facto basis a minority shareholder may be deemed to exercise control where, for example, the remaining shares are very widely dispersed, enabling the minority shareholder to be likely to achieve a majority of votes at any shareholders' meetings.[69] Whether this is the case or not will be determined on the basis of a consideration of the attendance at shareholders' meetings in the previous years.[70] Where a minority shareholder has the right to manage the business affairs of the undertaking and to determine its business policy, sole control may also be found to exist.[71] Options to purchase shares or to convert shares in the future are unlikely to be the basis of a finding of control, unless the option 'will be exercised in the near future according to legally binding commitments'.[72]

Joint control can also be established on both legal and de facto bases. For example, joint control will exist if the parent company shareholders are bound to reach agreement on major decisions relating to the management of the controlled undertaking (the JV). As with sole control the key factor is that the relevant parties are able to exercise decisive influence over another undertaking. However, the fact that control is being assessed in the context of two or more undertakings exercising it changes the analysis somewhat. Paragraph 19 of the *Notice on the concept of a concentration* provides that:

[65] See generally MP Broberg 'The Concept of Control in the Merger Control Regulation' [2004] *ECLR* 741.

[66] Para 16 of the *Notice on the concept of a concentration*, states that above n 56 'A change from joint to sole control of an undertaking is deemed to be a concentration within the meaning of the [ECMR] because decisive influence exercised alone is substantially different from decisive influence exercised jointly. For the same reason, an operation involving the acquisition of joint control over one part of an undertaking and sole control of another part is in principle regarded as two separate concentrations under the [ECMR]'.

[67] Ibid, para 13.

[68] Ibid, para 14.

[69] See, eg, Case IV/M.025 *Arjomari/Wiggins Teape* (1990).

[70] *Notice on the concept of a concentration*, above n 56, para 14.

[71] See, eg, Case IV/M.343 *Societe Generale de Belgique/Generale de Banque* (1993).

[72] *Notice on the concept of a concentration*, above n 56, para 15.

> Decisive influence in this sense normally means the power to block actions which determine the strategic commercial behaviour of an undertaking. Unlike sole control, which confers the power upon a specific shareholder to determine the strategic decisions in an undertaking, joint control is characterised by the possibility of a deadlock situation resulting from the power of two or more parent companies to reject proposed strategic decisions. It follows, therefore, that these shareholders must reach a common understanding in determining the commercial policy of the joint venture.

Most obviously this position may arise where two parents have equal voting rights in the JV, and where this situation arises joint control will be found to exist even in the absence of an agreement between the parents. In order for joint control to be established on the basis of an agreement, it must be the case that the agreement is 'consistent with the principle of equality between the parent companies'.[73] Joint control may also exist where minority shareholders have the right to veto decisions 'which are essential for the strategic commercial behaviour of the joint venture'.[74] Any such veto rights must go beyond the normal rights relating to the protection of minority shareholders, which are usually related 'to decisions on the essence of the joint venture, such as changes in the statute, an increase or decrease in the capital or liquidation'.[75] Veto rights over issues such as 'the budget,[76] the business plan,[77] major investments,[78] or the appointment of senior management'[79] may lead to a finding of joint control. The powers that are sufficient to establish joint control do not have to be available to the acquirer on a day-to-day basis, and it is not necessary to demonstrate that the holder of the rights will actually make use of the decisive influence granted to them. It is, the Commission states, merely the possibility that the rights will be used which is sufficient to sustain a finding of joint control.[80] It is not necessary for a minority shareholder to have all of the veto rights set out in paragraph 23, and it may be the case that the existence of even one may confer

[73] Ibid, para 20. This would be the case, eg, where each is entitled to the same number of representatives in the management bodies, and where neither has a casting vote.

[74] Ibid, para 21.

[75] Ibid, para 22. The Commission further states that '[a] veto right, for example, which prevents the sale or winding-up of the joint venture does not confer joint control on the minority shareholder concerned'.

[76] At para 25 of ibid, the Commission states that control over the budget and the appointment of the management constitute the most important veto rights.

[77] At para 26 of ibid, the Commission states:'The business plan normally provides details of the aims of the company together with the measures to be taken in order to achieve those aims. A veto right over this type of business plan may be sufficient to confer joint control even in the absence of any other veto right. In contrast, where the business plan contains merely general declarations concerning the business aims of the joint venture, the existence of a veto right will be only one element in the general assessment of joint control but will not, on its own, be sufficient to confer joint control.'

[78] The importance of the right to veto investment plans depends on two factors: the level of the investment(s) which are subject to the approval of the parent companies; and the extent to which the investments are an essential feature of the market in which the joint venture is active: ibid, para 27.

[79] Ibid, para 23.

[80] Ibid, para 23.

decisive influence.[81] In some rare cases the right of a veto over such issues as the technology to be used by a JV may be enough to constitute control where the matter is one which is important in the context of a particular market.[82]

Control may also be established where two or more undertakings acquire minority shareholdings in another undertaking. In order for this to be the case the minority shareholdings must be able, together, to have a majority of voting rights, but need also to act together in the exercise of those rights. This may be the case, for example, where they act under a legally binding agreement,[83] although this may also be established purely on a de facto basis.[84] The latter situation however is an exceptional one, and would arise in situations in which 'strong common interests exist between the minority shareholders to the effect that they would not act against each other in exercising their rights in relation to the joint venture'.[85] In the case of the establishment of JVs the greater the number of parents the less likely it is that control by minority shareholders will be found to exist. However, where the number of parents is limited, and where each parent company provides a vital contribution to the JV which is essential for its success (for example, technology or know-how), the possibility exists that it may be necessary for the parents to work in cooperation with each other, even in the absence of any provision relating to veto rights.[86] Where factors such as these do not exist it is unlikely that joint minority interests will be found to constitute control, and the Commission recognises at paragraph 35 of the *Notice on the concept of a concentration* that 'changing coalitions between minority shareholders' will operate so as to exclude the possibility of control being found to exist.

Joint control may be found to exist even where there is an asymmetry in the power held by each of the relevant undertakings or persons. The fact that one of the parent companies holds specific experience or knowledge relating to the JV does not exclude the possibility that the other parent has the 'real possibility of contesting decisions taken by the other parent company'. If it does not have this real possibility and plays only a minor role in the management of the JV, then the dominant undertaking in the relationship is likely to be found to be in sole control.[87] Where joint control exists only for a limited period during the starting-up of a new undertaking, but will, by virtue of legally binding agreements, be converted to sole control the Commission will normally consider the

[81] *Notice on the concept of a concentration*, above n 56, para 24.

[82] Ibid, para 28.

[83] Legal means to establish the joint exercise of voting rights could either be by way of a pooling agreement in which the undertakings agree to act in the same way, or by way of the formation of a holding company to which the minority rights are transferred: ibid, para 31.)

[84] Ibid, para 30.

[85] Ibid, para 32. The existence of prior links between the minority shareholders, or a concerted action leading to a purchase of the shares, would be a factor that might indicate the existence of common interests: ibid, para 33.

[86] Ibid, para 34.

[87] Ibid, para 36.

entire acquisition to be one of sole control.[88] Such a start-up period must not exceed three years.[89]

Concentrations can also occur when there is a change in control from sole to joint control, or vice versa. The *Notice on the concept of undertakings concerned* deals with this situation at paragraphs 30–48.

ARTICLE 3(5) ECMR—EXCEPTIONS

Article 3(5) ECMR sets out three exceptions to the general rule in which concentrations shall not be deemed to arise. The first of these relates to the holding of securities by credit, financial or similar institutions where these are held only temporarily with a view to being resold, provided that the holding institution does not seek to exercise any voting rights it benefits from in such a way as to determine the competitive conduct of the undertaking in which the rights are held.[90] Any disposal of the securities must take place within one year of the acquisition, although this period may be extended by the Commission at the request of the holding institutions where they are able to show that it was not possible to dispose reasonably of the securities within the time limit. The second exception arises where 'control is acquired by an office-holder according to the law of a Member State relating to liquidation, winding up, insolvency, cessation of payments, compositions or analogous proceedings'.[91] The third and final exception arises where the operations described in the second exception are carried out by financial holding companies as defined in Article 5(3) of Directive 78/660/EEC,[92] again provided that any voting rights are not exercised so as to determine the competitive conduct of the undertakings in which the rights are held. In the *Notice on the concept of undertakings concerned* the Commission notes that the operation of Article 3(5) ECMR may raise the question 'of whether a rescue operation constitutes a concentration under the [ECMR]'.[93] Rescue operations typically arise where existing debt is converted into a new company, such that a consortium of banks may acquire joint control of the undertaking concerned. In situations in which this leads to joint control being exercised a concentration may have occurred within the meaning of the ECMR.[94]

[88] Ibid, para 38.
[89] See, eg, Case IV/M.425 *British Telecom/Banco Santander* (1994).
[90] Art 3(5)(a) ECMR.
[91] Art 3(5)(b) ECMR.
[92] [1978] OJ L 222/11.
[93] *Notice on the concept of undertakings*, above n 2, para 45.
[94] This is so because 'the restructuring programme normally requires the controlling banks to determine the strategic commercial behaviour of the rescued undertaking. Furthermore, it is not normally a realistic proposition to transform a rescued company into a commercially viable entity and to resell it within the permitted one-year period. Moreover, the length of time needed to achieve this aim may be so uncertain that it would be difficult to grant an extension of the disposal period': *Notice on the concept of a concentration*, above n 56, para 45. It should also be noted that in such cases it is likely that the failing firm defence (see Chap 6) would be applicable. Further, any such

TERRITORIAL JURISDICTION

The issue of the extent to which one territory may assert jurisdiction over subjects of another territory or actions undertaken in another territory is a matter of much interest to those involved in mergers, many of which are international in either scope or effect.[95] As we have seen, it is a fundamental requirement of the ECMR that mergers must have some relationship with more than one state within the EC in order to be subject to the ECMR. While it is clear that a merger between a large German and a large British based undertaking may, subject to the relevant thresholds applying, be subject to EC scrutiny, what would be the position were the merger instead between a large US and a large Japanese undertaking, or if it were between two US undertakings? As is evident from even a quick survey of merger decisions there are situations in which the EC may assert, and has asserted, jurisdiction over such cases. For example, in *Gencor/Lonhro*,[96] it blocked a merger between the South African mining interests of two undertakings, where the transaction involved no physical assets in the EC.

A broad outline of the position is given in recitals (9) and (10) of Regulation 139/2004, where it is stated that:

> (9) The scope of application of this Regulation should be defined according to the geographical area of activity of the undertakings concerned and be limited by quantitative thresholds in order to cover those concentrations which have a Community dimension . . .
> (10) A concentration with a Community dimension should be deemed to exist where the aggregate turnover of the undertakings concerned exceeds given thresholds; that is the case irrespective of whether or not the undertakings effecting the concentration have their seat or their principal fields of activity in the Community, provided they have substantial operations there.

Article 1 of the ECMR makes no reference to territorial limitations, providing only that a concentration shall have a Community dimension where the relevant turnover thresholds are met. Once these thresholds are satisfied the requirements of notification are applicable and the concentration is subject to EC jurisdiction. This position is not without its international critics, and the possibility of conflict is clearly evident. This is particularly the case where a merger may also fall within the jurisdiction of another state or states, and there remains the threat to the merging undertakings that they may satisfy one state

merger is unlikely to raise serious competition concerns unless the banks or undertakings concerned also exercise control over other companies in related markets.

[95] See generally DJ Neven and L-H Röller, 'The Allocation of Jurisdiction in International Antitrust' (2000) 44 *European Economic Review* 845. For a US perspective see JP Griffin, 'Antitrust Aspects of Cross-Border Mergers and Acquisitions' [1998] *ECLR* 12.

[96] Case IV/M.619 (1996). See also *General Electric/Honeywell* (below n 97).

of the acceptability of the merger, but not another. This was the position reached in *General Electric/Honeywell*,[97] where the merger, between two large US undertakings, was cleared by the US authorities but blocked by the EC Commission.[98] The extent to which jurisdiction in the EC is determined in accordance with Article 1 ECMR, irrespective of the location of the merging parties, is made clear at Article 7 of the Decision:

> The undertakings concerned have a combined aggregate worldwide turnover of more than EUR 5,000 million . . . both GE and Honeywell have a Community-wide turnover in excess of EUR 250 million . . ., but they do not achieve more than two-thirds of their aggregate Community-wide turnover within one and the same Member State. The notified operation therefore has a Community dimension.

In this case (discussed in more detail in Chapter 9) the Commission held that the merger would create or strengthen several dominant positions in markets for aero-engines, avionics systems and other aircraft components, and found that remedies suggested by General Electric were insufficient to address the competitive concerns. In a press release the Commission addressed the concerns of international commentators and the business community:

> The European Commission and the US Department of Justice have worked in close cooperation during this investigation. It is unfortunate that, in the end, we reached different conclusions, but each authority has to perform its own assessment and the risk of dissenting views, although regrettable, can never be totally excluded. This does not mean that one authority is doing a technical analysis and the other pursuing a political goal, as some might pretend, but simply that we might interpret facts differently and forecast the effects of an operation in different ways. The GE/Honeywell [merger] is a rare case where the transatlantic competition authorities have disagreed.[99]

Perhaps the most contentious case to have arisen to date is *Boeing/McDonnell Douglas*,[100] which was susceptible to charges of political interference in the regulatory process, although on both sides of the Atlantic such charges were rebutted vigorously. The merger between the two parties reduced from three to two the numbers of manufacturers of large commercial aircraft, and as a result of this Airbus Industrie, a European consortium owned by governments of some of the EC Member States, was left facing a single dominant competitor, with a

[97] Case COMP/M.2220 (2001). See also Commission press releases IP/01/855, 18 June, 2001, and IP/01/939, 3 July 2001. See further Chap 8.

[98] There have been a significant number of cases in which 'foreign' mergers have been subject to the terms of the ECMR. Eg, in Case IV/M.24 *Mitsubishi/UCAR* (1991) Mitsubishi of Japan agreed to take a 50% interest in the carbon business of Union Carbide Corporation of the US. Although less than 10% of the turnover of the parties was within the EC this was sufficient to bring the merger within the scope of the ECMR. The Commission cleared the merger on the ground that there was likely to be no significant impact on competition within the EC. Similarly, in Case IV/M.37 *Matsushita/MCA* (1991) the Commission cleared a joint venture entered into outside the EC where the parties had less than 10% of their turnover within the EC.

[99] Press Release IP/01/939, above n 97.

[100] Case IV/M.877 (1997); Commission Decision 97/816 [1997] OJ L 336/16.

post-merger market share of some 60 per cent in respect of commercial aircraft with more than 100 seats. The FTC in the US publicly acknowledged that this level of restriction in the market was a matter of concern, but cleared the merger on the ground that there was no effective competition between the two merging parties to be snuffed out. The FTC denied that its decision was influenced by the desire to create a 'national champion', although press reports emphasised this function of the new merged entity.[101] The EC Commission did clear the merger, but only after being given various assurances by Boeing relating to its future commercial conduct. United States commentators have argued that the concessions had little to do with the merger itself, but that the Commission was exploiting its regulatory power to the advantage of Airbus Industrie.[102]

The most substantial discussion of the scope of extra-territorial jurisdiction in the area of merger control at the EC level is that which arose in *Gencor/Lonhro*. Here the parties appealed to the CFI,[103] arguing, inter alia, that the EC Commission lacked the competence to review the merger. Although this debate arose in the context of Regulation 4064/89 it is equally valid to the application of Regulation 139/2004. At paragraph 82 of the judgment the CFI held that:

> The legal basis for the Regulation, namely articles [83] and [308] of the Treaty, and more particularly the provisions to which they are intended to give effect, that is to say articles 3(g) and [81] and [82] of the Treaty, as well as the first to fifth, ninth and eleventh recitals in the preamble to the Regulation, merely point to the need to ensure that competition is not distorted in the common market, in particular by concentrations which result in the creation or strengthening of a dominant position. They in no way exclude from the Regulation's field of application concentrations which, while relating to mining and/or production activities outside the Community, have the effect of creating or strengthening a dominant position as a result of which effective competition in the common market is significantly impeded.

[101] See, eg, *New York Times*, 17 December 1996.

[102] See also A Schaub, who argued that 'diverging approaches of the competition authorities in Brussels and Washington made it impossible to reach commonly accepted solutions', (1998) 1 *Competition Policy Newsletter* 4. A further discussion of this case is given in B Zanettin, *Cooperation between Antitrust Agencies at the International Level* (Oxford, Hart Publishing, 2002), 93–8. Zanettin describes this case as 'a politicised conflict'. See also EC Commission, *27th Annual Report on Competition Policy* 1997 (Luxembourg Office of Official Publications of the EC, 1997), paras 169–172. See also P Karacan, 'Differences in Merger Analysis Between the United States and the European Union, Highlighted in the Context of the Boeing/McDonnell Douglas and GE/Honeywell Mergers' (2004) 17 *Transnational Law* 209; JD Banks, 'The Development of the Concept of Extraterritoriality under European Merger Law and its Effectiveness under the Merger Regulation following the Boeing/McDonnell Douglas Decision' [1998] *ECLR* 306; and AF Bavasso, 'Boeing/McDonnell Douglas: Did the Commission Fly Too High?' [1998] *ECLR* 243. See also the substantial comment on the GE/Honeywell merger, referred to in Chap 8, below.

[103] Case T–102/96, *Gencor Ltd v EC Commission* [1999] ECR II–753, [1999] 4 CMLR 971. See EM Fox, 'The Merger Regulation and its Territorial Reach: Gencor Ltd v Commission' [1999] *ECLR* 334, and PJ Slot, 'Case T–102/96, *Gencor Ltd v Commission*' (2001) 38 *CML Rev* 1573.

Gencor sought to rely on the earlier judgment given by the ECJ in the Article 81 EC case of *Wood pulp*[104] and to argue that as a merger between mining interests in South Africa was not 'implemented' in the EC it could not be caught by Article 1 of the ECMR, notwithstanding the operation of the thresholds. The CFI rejected this argument, holding, at paragraph 87, that:

> The applicant cannot, by reference to the judgment in *Wood pulp*, rely on the criterion as to the implementation of an agreement to support its interpretation of the territorial scope of the Regulation. Far from supporting the applicant's view, that criterion for assessing the link between an agreement and Community territory in fact precludes it. According to *Wood pulp*, *the criterion as to the implementation of an agreement is satisfied by mere sale within the Community*, irrespective of the location of the sources of supply and the production plant. It is not disputed that Gencor and Lonhro carried out sales in the Community before the concentration and would have continued to do so thereafter. (emphasis added)

The approach of the CFI is to draw a distinction between the territorial reach of the Regulation, which appears from the above passages to be unfettered subject only to the requirements of Article 1 ECMR, and the approach to be taken by the Commission once jurisdiction is established. The territorial reach of the Regulation is to be established by reference to the implementation criteria set out in *Wood pulp*, and this is given a wide definition in that 'mere sale' in the EC suffices. Once jurisdiction is established the question becomes whether it is appropriate to block a merger. Here the CFI makes reference to the 'effect' of the concentration in question. The position taken in this respect by the CFI is that the application of the Regulation 'is justified under public international law

[104] Case 114/85 etc, *A Ahlström Oy v Commission* [1988] ECR 5193, [1988] 4 CMLR 901. Here the ECJ dealt with the extent to which Art 81 EC and, by implication, Art 82 EC applied extraterritorially. The court avoided a full acceptance of the effects doctrine, but instead adopted a formula for the assertion of jurisdiction which made reference to the 'implementation' of the practice considered in the contested decision. The relevant passages of the judgment are as follows:

> '[16] It should be observed that an infringement of Article [81], such as the conclusion of an agreement which has had the effect of restricting competition within the Common Market, consists of conduct made up of two elements, the formation of the agreement, decision or concerted practice and the implementation thereof. If the applicability of prohibitions laid down under competition law were made to depend on the place where the agreement, decision or concerted practice was formed, the result would obviously be to give undertakings an easy means of evading those prohibitions. The decisive factor is therefore the place where it is implemented.
>
> [17] The producers in this case implemented their agreement within the Common Market. It is immaterial in that respect whether or not they had recourse to subsidiaries, agents, sub-agents, or branches within the Community in order to make their contacts with purchasers within the Community.
>
> [18] Accordingly the Commission's jurisdiction to apply its competition rules to such conduct is governed by the territoriality principle as universally recognised in public international law . . .
>
> [22] As regards the argument relating to disregard of international comity, it suffices to observe that it amounts to calling in question the Community's jurisdiction to apply its competition rules to conduct such as that found to exist in this case and that, as such, that argument has already been rejected.'

when it is foreseeable that a proposed concentration will have an immediate and substantial effect in the Community'.[105] The CFI then refines this formulation slightly and sets the criterion as being that of an 'immediate, substantial and foreseeable effect'.[106] This language is very similar to that adopted by the US courts when applying the effects doctrine to the application of antitrust law, but it should not be taken to mean that the EC courts have embraced the effects doctrine in the application of the EC merger control law. Although the distinction may appear to be a moot one, it is important to note that there is, in the application of the ECMR to 'foreign' mergers, a two-stage test: (1) is the merger implemented in the EC; (2) is enforcement justified by reference to the criteria set out in *Gencor*?.[107]

Just as 'foreign' mergers may fall within the ambit of the ECMR, so too may mergers entered into between EC undertakings and non-EC undertakings. A number of such concentrations have been notified under the ECMR. For example, in *BNP/Dresdner Bank (Czechoslovakia)*[108] the two credit institutions formed a joint venture in Budapest, which would be involved in credit transactions and in the balancing of import and export trade. The JV was found to be full-function and therefore subject to the terms of the ECMR, and the turnover thresholds were met, such that the concentration had a Community dimension. In this case the merger was cleared on the ground that it was unlikely to have a serious effect on competition within the EC.

The question how the ECMR is to be enforced in respect of undertakings not having a presence in the EC is not addressed directly by the ECMR. Various powers are conferred on the Commission, including the collection of information, the suspending and blocking of mergers, and the imposition of penalties in the event of breaches of the requirements of the ECMR. The question of the extent to which these may be enforced against foreign parties is a matter of general EC law. In practice this issue has not arisen, and it may be presumed that where parties are contemplating a merger that is likely to fall within the terms of Article 1 ECMR they may be reluctant to place themselves in the position of facing the legal uncertainty that a refusal to comply with the Commission's powers would entail. Where the parties have a presence in the EC, either directly or through a subsidiary, the Commission would be able to exercise powers against them directly through the territoriality principle, and would be able to rely also on the economic entity doctrine recognised in the case of *ICI*.[109]

[105] Case 114/85 etc *A Ahlström Oy v Commission* [1988] ECR 5193, [1988] 4 CMLR 90, n 103 above at para 90.

[106] Ibid, at para 92.

[107] See, generally, A Ezrachi, 'Limitations on the Extraterritorial Reach of the European Merger Regulation' [2001] *ECLR* 137, and AR Fiebig, 'International Law Limits on the Extraterritorial Application of the European Merger Control Regulation and Suggestions for Reform', [1998] *ECLR* 323.

[108] Case IV/M.124 (1991).

[109] Case 48/69, *ICI v Commission* [1972] ECR 619, [1972] CMLR 557.

The simplified procedure established by the Commission for the treatment of certain concentrations[110] reduces the burden of notification in respect of some categories of concentrations. These include JVs where 'the joint venture has no, or negligible, actual or foreseen activities within the territory of the European Economic Area'.[111] In restricted circumstances the *Notice* may be pertinent to other mergers involving parties outside the EC, but draws no further distinctions based on the location of the parties.

A number of steps, of varying degrees of formality, have been taken to address concerns relating to conflicts in the operation of merger control. Two agreements have been entered into between the EC and the US in relation to the application of their competition laws. The most important of these in respect of merger control is the *Agreement between the Government of the United States of America and the Commission of the European Communities regarding the application of their competition laws*.[112] The purpose of the agreement is to promote cooperation and coordination and to lessen the possibility or impact of differences between the US and the EC in the application of their competition laws, including those relating to merger control, and the agreement enshrines the principle of comity. The EC and US have also entered into an agreement regarding *EU–US Best Practices on cooperation in merger investigations*.[113] It is also the case that, even without formal agreement on alignment of their respective regimes the EC and US merger control regimes have moved closer together, in both substance and procedure, since the introduction of the ECMR, although important differences do remain.[114]

Although the principle of comity does not yet have the full force of law it is important in the application of competition law, and requires, in essence, that one state respect the interests of another in the application of its law. The majority of cases notified under the agreement have related to merger control, and the Commission has emphasised the value of cooperation in this area. In *Guinness/Grand Metropolitan*,[115] for example, there was a significant amount of cooperation between the EC Commission and the US FTC, with the FTC sending observers to the public hearings held under the ECMR. The parties to the merger permitted discussions between the regulators on the proposed remedies, ensuring a level of coordination that would not otherwise have been possible.[116] Similar

[110] Commission *Notice on a simplified procedure for treatment of certain concentrations under Council Regulation (EC) No 139/2004* [2000] OJ C 217/32.

[111] Ibid, Art 5(a).

[112] 95/145/EC, ECSC [1995] OJ L 95/45. The second agreement entered into in 1998 on the application of positive comity principles specifically excludes its application to the area of merger control.

[113] Avaliable at http://europa.eu.int/comm/competition/mergers/others/eu_us.pdf.

[114] See generally S Megregian and D Garrod, 'EU and US Merger Control: Transatlantic Convergence Rolls On' [2005] *Comp Law* 124.

[115] Case IV/M.938 (1997).

[116] *27th Annual Report on Competition Policy 1997*, above n 102, para 326.

benefits were clear in *WorldCom/MCI*.[117] In *Gencor* the CFI was asked to address the issue of comity as Gencor argued that 'by virtue of the principle of non-interference the Commission should have refrained from prohibiting the concentration in order to avoid a conflict of interest with the South African authorities'. The CFI was dismissive of this argument, while appearing to recognise the value of comity principles, holding that 'there was no conflict between the course of action required by the South African Government and that required by the Community'.[118] The EC has also entered into agreements with Canada[119] and Japan[120] on terms similar to the first EC/US agreement.

In March 2005 the OECD Council adopted a *Recommendation on Merger Review*.[121] The recommendation does not suggest that in every case cooperation will be necessary or advisable, but does encourage members to cooperate when they are investigating the same merger, and to consider action, including legislation, to facilitate such cooperation and coordination. Particular emphasis is placed on the adoption of remedies, and it is suggested that remedies should, as far as possible, be domestic (ie, they should not be more than is necessary to remedy the competition concerns identified within the jurisdiction, and should not, wherever possible, have effect extraterritorially). The recommendation has no binding legal effect, but other OECD recommendations in the area of competition law have been influential in the development of the approaches of member states.

ARTICLE 24 ECMR

Article 24 ECMR deals with 'relations with third countries', and requires Member States to 'inform the Commission of any general difficulties encountered by their undertakings . . . in a third country'.[122] The Commission is required periodically to draw up reports examining the treatment accorded by

[117] *28th Annual Report on Competition Policy 1998* (Luxembourg, Office of Official Publications of the EC, 1998), para 311, Case COMP/M.1741, see paras 13–15 of the Decision. At para 14 the Commission states that:

> 'In the course of the investigation and analysis of the merger proposal there was a considerable degree of cooperation between the two agencies, involving preliminary exchanges of views on the analytical framework, coordinated requests for information, attendance of [DOJ] observers at the Oral Hearing and Commission officials at a 'Pitch Meeting' at the [DOJ], and joint meetings with the notifying parties.'

[118] *Gencor v Commission*, above n 103, at para 103.

[119] Competition Laws Cooperation Agreement 1999 (EC/ECSC/Canada) 1999/445 [1999] OJ L 175/1.

[120] Decision Concluding the Agreement between the European Community and Japan concerning cooperation on anti-competitive activities (Decision 2003/250/EC, [2003] OJ L 183).

[121] Available at *www.oecd.org/competition*. See also (2005) 7(3) OECD Journal of Competition Law and Policy, 7.

[122] Art 24(1) ECMR.

third countries to undertakings having their seat in the EC. Where it appears that the treatment is not comparable to that set out in the ECMR (ie, where there are fears that discriminatory measures or measures lacking in rigour are being applied) the Commission may seek a mandate to negotiate agreements seeking comparable treatment.

5

ECMR Procedures

INTRODUCTION

THIS CHAPTER DEALS with the procedures to be followed during the application of the ECMR where these are not otherwise dealt with elsewhere in this text.[1] Both of the stages of merger review, Phases I and II, are considered here, as it is not possible to separate out discussion of matters such as information gathering powers and the rights of the undertakings. Where necessary the distinction is made between these stages. Decisions taken at the end of Phase II are discussed more fully in Chapter 8, and rights of appeal and third party rights are discussed in Chapter 9.

Alongside the requirements of the ECMR itself the leading instrument dealing with procedures is Commission Regulation (EC) 802/2004 implementing Council Regulation (EC) No 139/2004 on the control of concentrations between undertakings (hereinafter 'the implementing regulation').[2] This deals with notification requirements, time limits, the right to be heard and access to file and the treatment of confidential information, and commitments. In 2004 the Commission published a revised version of its *Best practices on the conduct of EC merger control proceedings* (hereinafter '*Best Practice*'), which replaced an earlier version published in 1999. This incorporates the experience of the Commission earned in the application of the ECMR since 1990, and sheds further light on certain procedures, particularly those relating to pre-notification contacts, fact-finding, communication between the Commission, notifying parties and third parties, and procedural rights.[3] During the course of all the proceedings discussed here the Commission is required to respect the fundamental rights of all parties, and is in particular required to observe the principles recognised in the Charter of Fundamental Rights of the European Union.[4]

[1] Procedures relating to the referral of cases between the Commission and the Member States are, eg, dealt with in Chap 3. See generally HCH Hofmann, 'Good Governance in European Merger Control: Due Process and Checks and Balances under Review' [2003] *ECLR* 114.

[2] [2004] OJ L 133/1.

[3] The best practices 'should not be taken as a full or comprehensive account of the relevant legislative, interpretative and administrative measures which govern Community merger control' (para 3), and they 'do not create or alter any rights or obligations as set out in the Treaty . . . the Merger Regulation, its Implementing Regulation . . . and as interpreted by the case-law of the Community Courts' (para 4).

[4] [2003] OJ C 20/4. See ECMR, recital (36).

PROCEDURAL STAGES IN MERGER CASES

Introduction

Procedures before the EC Commission are defined in terms of whether they are Phase I or Phase II. The Phase I procedure runs from the point at which a notification of a concentration is made to the Commission, and concludes with one of three decisions: that there is no concentration with a Community dimension; that there is such a concentration but no significant impediment to effective competition (SIEC), which may be the case where necessary commitments are given; or that the merger should proceed to fuller examination under Phase II. The Commission has 25 working days to make one of these decisions, assuming that no extensions apply (see below). If Phase II is opened the Commission has a further 90 days in which to make a final decision. These decisions are discussed in Chapter 8, below. All time periods are set in terms of working days, as defined in Article 24 of the implementing regulation.[5]

Pre-notification contacts

Any pre-notification contacts with the Commission are entirely voluntary, as there is no legal requirement to approach it save for the notification requirement set out in the ECMR. However, the Commission emphasises at a number of places in its merger notices that pre-notification contacts with it are of great value, particularly in clarifying the issues and the range of information that the notifying parties will have to supply in order to conform to the requirements of Form CO.[6] The Commission argues that the best approach to pre-notification contacts is for both legal and business advisors to be available, and that a good understanding of the relevant markets is important even at this early stage. Paragraphs 5–15 of *Best Practice* discuss the conditions in which pre-notification contacts are held. In *Best Practice* the Commission makes the point that it is its experience 'that in cases in which notifications have been declared incomplete, usually there were no or very limited pre-notification contacts'.[7] The Commission urges the notifying parties to hold any pre-notification discussions 'in an open and cooperative atmosphere, where all potential issues are addressed in a constructive way' if the parties hope to maximise the benefits of

[5] Art 24 provides that '[t]he expression working days . . . means all days other than Saturdays, Sundays, and Commission holidays as published in the *Official Journal of the European Union* before the beginning of each year'. A working day is deemed to expire at the end of that day.

[6] Recital (11) of Regulation 802/2004 states in part that: 'The Commission should give the notifying parties and other parties involved in the proposed concentration, if they so request, an opportunity to discuss the intended concentration informally and in strict confidence'.

[7] *Best Practice*, para 7, available at the DG Comp website.

the discussions.[8] Given the commercial sensitivity which may surround a merger situation it is particularly necessary that early discussions with the regulatory authorities are confidential, and the Commission indicates at paragraph 8 of *Best Practice* that such discussions are 'held in strict confidence'.

Paragraph 10 of *Best Practice* requests that pre-notification contacts be made at least two weeks before the expected date of notification—anything less would not allow much time to revise a Form CO notification in the light of feedback from the Commission. Even at this early stage it is anticipated that some substantial work will have been done towards completing the notification process, and the Commission requests that it be given a submission that at least permits it to select the appropriate case management team. However, such a submission does not need to be detailed, and can take the form of providing a brief background to the transaction, a brief description of the relevant markets or sectors involved, and the likely competitive impact of the transaction. In complex cases the Commission may suggest that a meeting is necessary to discuss the issues raised, whereas in more straightforward cases it may be sufficient for the Commission to comment orally or in writing.[9] If a meeting is to be held the Commission requests that it be given further information, perhaps amounting to a draft Form CO. Further clarification of the information to be provided at the pre-notification stage, and the timing of any such submissions, is given at paragraphs 16–19 of *Best Practice*.[10]

Alongside formalised pre-notification discussions the Commission is also prepared to enter into informal discussion giving guidance on such issues as jurisdiction. However, informal guidance will only be given if the questions are related to 'an actual, planned transaction' and if sufficient information is given to allow the Commission properly to assess the issue.[11]

[8] Ibid, para 8.

[9] Ibid, para 12.

[10] In particular notifying parties are asked 'to fully and frankly disclose [*sic*] information relating to all potentially affected markets and possible competition concerns, even if they may ultimately consider that they are not affected and notwithstanding that they may take a particular view in relation, to for example, the issue of market definition' (para 16). Paras 17–18 are in the following terms:

> '17. In addition, DG Competition recommends that notifying parties should, as early as possible in pre-notification, submit internal documents such as board presentations, surveys, analyses, reports and studies discussing the proposed concentration, the economic rationale for the concentration and competitive significance or the market context in which it takes place. Such documents provide DG Competition with an early and informed view of the transaction and its potential competitive impact and can thus allow for a productive discussion and finalisation of the Form CO.
>
> 18. Where appropriate, it is also recommended that notifying parties put forward, already at the pre-notification stage, any elements demonstrating that the merger leads to efficiency gains that they would like the Commission to take into account for the purposes of its competitive assessment of the proposed transaction. Such claims are likely to require extensive analysis. It is thus in the interests of the notifying parties to present these claims as early as possible to allow sufficient time for DG Competition to appropriately consider these elements in its assessment of a proposed transaction.'

[11] *Best Practice*, above n 7, para 25.

Phase I

Notification

Notification of qualifying concentrations is compulsory in the EC regime. The failure to notify would lay the undertaking(s) concerned open to the imposition of penalties and, more importantly, to the prospect of the merger being declared illegal in the future. Article 14(2)(a) ECMR provides that the Commission may impose a penalty of up to 10 per cent of the aggregate turnover of the undertakings concerned where they fail to notify a concentration when they are required to do so. In determining the size of the fine 'regard shall be had to the nature, gravity, and duration of the infringement'.[12]

Recital (34) ECMR sets out clearly the position with respect to notification:

> To ensure effective control, undertakings should be obliged to give prior notification of concentrations with a Community dimension following the conclusion of the agreement, the announcement of the public bid or the acquisition of a controlling interest. Notification should also be possible where the undertakings concerned satisfy the Commission of their intention to enter into an agreement for a proposed concentration and demonstrate to the Commission that their plan for that proposed concentration is sufficiently concrete, for example on the basis of an agreement in principle, a memorandum of understanding, or a letter of intent signed by all undertakings concerned, or, in the case of a public bid, where they have publicly announced an intention to make such a bid, provided that the intended agreement or bid would result in a concentration with a Community dimension.

Article 4 ECMR makes provision for the prior notification of concentrations, Article 4(1) specifying that:

> Concentrations with a Community dimension . . . shall be notified to the Commission prior to their implementation and following the conclusion of the agreement, the announcement of the bid, or the acquisition of a controlling interest.

The second paragraph of the Article permits concentrations to be notified prior to the above conditions being fulfilled as long as there is a 'good faith intention to conclude an agreement' or where a public bid has been announced, provided that the agreement or bid would lead to the conclusion of a concentration with a Community dimension. Notification is to be made jointly by the parties to the merger, or by those acquiring control of an undertaking,[13] or by the person acquiring control in all other cases.[14] The Commission will publish the basic

[12] Art 14(3) ECMR. 'Gun jumping' (the practice of implementing a merger earlier than is permitted under relevant law) is rare in the context of the application of the ECMR, although partial gun-jumping was an issue in Case COMP/M.993 *Bertelsmann/Kirch/Premiere* (1998), discussed in Chap 8, below. For a discussion of the approaches to this practice in the US and EC see JR Modrall and S Ciullo, 'Gun-Jumping and EU Merger Control' [2003] *ECLR* 424.

[13] As defined in Art 3(1)(a) and (b) ECMR.

[14] Art 4(2) ECMR.

facts relating to the concentration, having regard to any business secrets brought to its attention.[15] Article 4(4) ECMR provides that the undertakings making the notification may inform the Commission that the concentration meets the criteria to be examined, either in whole or in part, by a Member State. This procedure is discussed more fully in Chapter 3, above, as is the procedure under Article 4(5). The implementing regulation sets out procedures and duties relevant to notification in Chapter II, at Articles 2–6.

Notifications are to be made on Form CO, attached as an Annex to the implementing regulation. Those responsible for notifying are required to submit one original copy of Form CO and the supporting documentation, along with an additional 35 copies. A short form may be used in respect of those concentrations subject to the simplified procedure discussed in Chapter 6, below.[16] Notifications are to be made in one of the official languages of the EC, and this language shall become the language used for the case throughout its progress.[17] The Commission has stated elsewhere that parties may note that it might be beneficial to choose a widely understood language. The information and documentation to be provided are set out in Form CO, and are further clarified at Articles 16–19 of *Best Practice*,[18] but the Commission may dispense with any of these requirements if it considers that the information or documentation is not necessary for the proper consideration of the case.[19] This is one area in which pre-notification contacts, discussed above, may be useful in reducing the burdens imposed on the notifying parties.

The Commission is required to acknowledge the notification 'without delay',[20] and notifications become valid from the day on which they are received by the Commission. This is the date at which the strict time limits imposed by the ECMR and the implementing regulation become effective.[21] Where the information is deemed by the Commission to be incomplete in any material respect notification is not considered to have taken place until the complete documentation is received.[22] Notification shall also be deemed not to have taken place where information provided is incorrect or misleading.[23] To this end the

[15] Art 4(3) ECMR.

[16] See also Annex II to the implementing regulation [2004] OJ L 133/1.

[17] Ibid, Art 3(4).

[18] These paras are set out above, and discussed in the context of pre-notification. Although these paragraphs are framed in the context of pre-notification contacts they remain pertinent to the completion of Form CO, and particularly so in situations in which pre-notification contacts have been minimal or non-existent.

[19] Implementing regulation, above 16 n, Art 4(2).

[20] Ibid, Art 4(3).

[21] Ibid, Art 5(1).

[22] Ibid, Art 5(2).

[23] Ibid, Art 5(4). At para 23 of *Best Practice*, above n 7, the Commission indicates that where it discovers omissions in Form CO 'the notifying parties may be given an opportunity to urgently put right such omissions before a declaration of incompleteness is adopted . . . the time for such rectification is normally limited to 1 or 2 days. This opportunity will not be granted, however, in cases where DG Competition finds that the omissions immediately hinder the proper investigation of the proposed transaction.'

notifying parties are requested in particular to 'take special care that the appropriate contact details are provided for customers, suppliers and competitors'.[24] The Commission warns that failure to comply with this obligation may 'significantly delay the investigation and therefore may lead to a declaration of incompleteness'.[25]

As regards the position of third parties who might object to the proposed concentration, the first two sentences of paragraph 37 of *Best Practice* are pertinent:

> If third parties wish to express competition concerns as regards the transaction in question or to put forward views on key market data or characteristics that deviate from the notifying parties' position, it is essential that they are communicated as early as possible to DG Competition, so that they can be considered, verified and taken into account properly. Any point raised should be substantiated and supported by examples, documents and other factual evidence.

A Short Form Notification process was introduced in 1994, and was modified in 2004 in an attempt to make the procedure more widely applicable. The Short Form, also attached as an appendix to the implementing regulation, may be used in situations in which the activities of the merging parties do not overlap, or do so only in areas in which there is likely to be no realistic prospect of competition concerns flowing from the concentration.

Suspension of concentrations

Article 7 ECMR sets out the rules relating to the suspension of notified concentrations during the process of their consideration. This requirement is first discussed at recital (34) ECMR:

> The implementation of concentrations should be suspended until a final decision of the Commission has been taken. However, it should be possible to derogate from this suspension at the request of the undertakings concerned, where appropriate. In deciding whether or not to grant a derogation, the Commission should take account of all pertinent factors, such as the nature and gravity of damage to the undertakings concerned or to third parties, and the threat to competition posed by the concentration. In the interest of legal certainty, the validity of transactions must nevertheless be protected as much as necessary.

Given that it may be impossible to disentangle a completed concentration it is, of course, entirely reasonable that undertakings should be precluded from continuing with the transaction until the Commission has had an opportunity to deliver its decision. Article 7(1) ECMR therefore provides that:

> A concentration with a Community dimension as defined in Article 1, or which is to be examined by the Commission pursuant to Article 4(5), shall not be implemented either before its notification or until it has been declared compatible with the common

[24] Implementing regulation, above para 20.
[25] Ibid.

> market pursuant to a decision under Articles 6(1)(b), 8(1) or 8(2), or on the basis of a presumption according to Article 10(6).[26]

This provision shall not operate to prevent a public bid being implemented or a series of transactions in securities taking place as long as: (a) the concentration has been notified to the Commission without delay; and (b) the acquirer does not exercise any voting rights acquired along with the securities, 'or does so only to maintain the full value of its investments based on a derogation granted by the Commission'.[27] The Commission may grant derogations from the obligations imposed by Article 7(1) ECMR in response to a reasoned request.[28] Article 7(3) further provides that:

> In deciding on the request, the Commission shall take into account inter alia the effects of the suspension on one or more of the undertakings concerned by the concentration or on a third party and the threat to competition posed by the concentration. Such a derogation may be made subject to conditions and obligations in order to ensure conditions of effective competition. A derogation may be applied for and granted at any time, but it before notification or after the transaction.

When the Commission intends taking a decision under Article 7(3) ECMR that adversely affects any of the parties it is required to inform the notifying parties and other parties involved in writing of its objections, and shall set a time limit under which they may make their views known.[29] In the alternative it may make a provisional decision, and then is required to send them the text of the provisional decision without delay, and again to set a time limit within which their views may be made known.[30] If there is no response within the time limit set by the Commission its provisional decision shall become final. In the alternative, where the parties do make their views known, the Commission will make a final decision, which may be the same as that envisaged, or which can annul, or amend the provisional decision.[31] In practice the application of the Article 7(3) procedure is rare. Cook and Kerse estimate that since 1990 the Commission has granted derogations in only about 2 per cent of cases.[32] Derogations are most likely to be granted where the target undertaking is facing bankruptcy or is in severe financial difficulties and requires support to continue in existence. This was the case for example in *ING/Barings*.[33]

Where any transaction is carried out in contravention of Article 7(1) ECMR, Article 7(4) states that its validity is dependent on a relevant decision taken by

[26] A presumption arises under Art 10(6) when the Commission has not taken an Art 6 decision within the time limits specified.
[27] Art 7(2), ECMR.
[28] Art 7(3), ECMR.
[29] Implementing regulation, above n 16, Art 12(1).
[30] Ibid, Art 12(2). In setting the time limit 'the Commission shall have regard to the time required for the preparation of statements and the urgency of the case': ibid, Art 22.
[31] Ibid, Art 12(2).
[32] CJ Cook and CS Kerse, *EC Merger Control* (4th edn, London, Sweet & Maxwell, 2005) at 5–022.
[33] Case IV/M.573 (1995).

the Commission under Article 6 or 8 ECMR.[34] The second sentence of Article 7(4) provides that this does not apply to:

> the validity of transactions in securities including those convertible into other securities admitted to trading on a market such as a stock exchange, unless the buyer and seller knew or ought to have known that the transaction was carried out in contravention of paragraph 1.

Further, Article 14(1)(c) provides for a fine of up to 10 per cent of the aggregate turnover of the undertakings concerned in such a case. The effect of this 'invalidity' may, to an extent, depend on the jurisdiction in respect of which the question is asked. If the transaction was simply void, third parties could be placed in the unfortunate position of innocently contracting with an entity against which they would be unable to enforce any rights. The final sentence of recital (34) provides that '[i]n the interests of legal certainty, the validity of transactions must nevertheless be protected as much as necessary'. However, the position under English law is that any transaction which is carried out in contravention of the ECMR is void. If it arose, and it has not yet done so, this provision could lead to severe complexities, stretching the limits of the courts to deal with the resultant chaos under the traditional principles of common law. It has been noted that the 'Commission's powers under [the ECMR] are likely to prove more flexible in unscrambling a transaction than the traditional remedies of English common law dealing with illegality'.[35] In practice any such arrangements are usually made conditional upon the appropriate regulatory approvals being obtained.

Abandonment

Anticipated concentrations may be abandoned at any stage during the ECMR proceedings, and no legal detriment flows from this. The most common scenario is that the parties take the view that the concentration is likely to progress to the Phase II proceedings, withdraw the concentration, modify it, and re-notify, or abandon it altogether. This may in many cases be preferable to defending the notified concentration as it stands at Phase II, and is a procedure which has often been employed. Once the Commission has been satisfied that the concentration as notified has been abandoned any new proposal between the parties will be treated as a new notification.

[34] Art 7(4) ECMR. The presumption set out in Art 10(6) ECMR may also apply where the Commission fails to take a decision within the time limits specified. Art 7 has 'no effect on the validity of transactions in securities . . . unless the buyer or seller knew, or ought to have known that the transaction was carried out in contravention of paragraph 1': Art 7(4) ECMR.

[35] Cook and Kerse, above n 32, at 5-025.

Phase I decisions—Article 6 ECMR

Article 6 ECMR relates to the 'examination of the notification and initiation of proceedings'. Under Article 6(1) three decisions are possible: Article 6(1)(a)—a decision finding that the concentration notified 'does not fall within the scope of this Regulation'; Article 6(1)(b)—a decision finding that a concentration does fall within the terms of the Regulation, but does not raise serious doubts about its compatibility with the common market. In this case the Commission 'shall decide not to oppose it and shall declare that it is compatible with the common market'; and Article 6(1)(c)—an initiation of proceedings where the concentration does fall within the terms of the ECMR and does raise serious doubts about its compatibility with the common market. The third scenario is somewhat modified by Article 6(2), which allows the Commission to declare the concentration compatible with the common market where the parties modify the arrangement, which is usually effected by offering commitments to the Commission (see further below). Conditions and obligations may be attached to decisions to ensure that undertakings comply with any commitments that have been made.[36] A decision taken in accordance with Articles 6(1)(a) or (b) may be revoked by the Commission where: (a) it is based on incorrect information supplied by one of the parties or is obtained by deceit; or (b) the undertakings commit a breach of an obligation attached to the decision.[37] No time limits apply in the case of any such decision.[38]

The vast majority of decisions made under Article 6(1) are those confirming that a relevant concentration has occurred, but that there are no serious doubts about its compatibility with the common market. In 2004, for example, only eight Phase II Procedures were initiated. Article 6(1)(a) decisions are also rare, as the ECMR is now sufficiently well understood, and the burdens of notification are so onerous, that unnecessary notifications are rarely made. Pre-notification contacts may also serve to reduce this likelihood arising.

Commitments[39]

Articles 6(2) and 8(2) ECMR recognise the validity of procedures under which the notifying parties to a concentration may make modifications to the transaction to address concerns raised by the Commission. In both cases if the Commission is satisfied that the commitments offered address the concerns it shall issue decisions declaring the concentration to be compatible with the common market. There are, however, differences between the precise requirements

[36] Art 6(2) ECMR.
[37] Art 6(3) ECMR.
[38] Art 6(4) ECMR.
[39] See MP Broberg, 'Commitments in Phase One merger proceedings: the Commission's power to accept and enforce Phase One commitments' (1997) 34 *CML Rev* 845.

of commitments offered in Phase I and those offered after Phase II proceedings have opened. Commitments generally 'should be proportionate to the competition problem and entirely eliminate it'.[40] However, before a Phase II proceeding has opened recital (30) states that it is only appropriate to accept commitments 'where the competition problem is readily identifiable and can easily be remedied'. The CFI held in *Royal Philips Electronics v Commission*[41] that:

> the specific purpose of the commitments entered into during the Phase I procedure, which, contrary to the commitments entered into during the Phase II procedure, are not intended to prevent the creation or strengthening of a dominant position but, rather to dispel any serious doubts in that regard. It follows that commitments entered into during the Phase I procedure must constitute a direct and sufficient response capable of clearly excluding the serious doubts experienced.[42]

Cook and Kerse identify three situations in which Phase I commitments are most suitable: (1) those where there exist clearly defined product and geographic markets, such that competition issues may be identified at a very early stage; (2) those where the notifying parties acknowledge the problem early on and cooperate with the Commission in finding a solution (a process which may be facilitated by extensive pre-notification contacts); and (3) those where the parties quickly identify, and are prepared to implement, an effective remedy.[43] Although the general treatment of remedies is discussed in Chapter 8, below, it is worth noting here some of the specific requirements for Phase I commitments, which are discussed at paragraphs 33–38 of the *Commission notice on remedies*.[44] In order to consider accepting Phase I commitments the Commission requires that proposals meet three key requirements: (1) they must be submitted in time; (2) the commitments entered into must be specified in sufficient detail to allow a full assessment to be carried out; and (3) they must explain how the commitments offered address the competition concerns identified by the Commission.

The decision made by the Commission may have attached to it conditions and obligations which are legally enforceable to ensure that the undertakings comply with the commitments they make.[45] Any commitments offered must be made within 20 working days of the notification of the concentration in the case of Article 6(2),[46] or within 65 working days in the case of Article 8(2).[47] The

[40] ECMR, recital (30).

[41] Case T–119/02, [2003] ECR II–1433.

[42] At para 79.

[43] Cook and Kerse, above n 32, at 8-003.

[44] *Commission notice on remedies acceptable under Council Regulation (EEC) No 4064/89 and under Commission Regulation (EC) No 447/98* [2001] OJ C 68/3.

[45] The decision may be revoked where the parties breach any obligation attached to the decision (Art 6(3)(a) ECMR or under Art 8(6)(b) as appropriate).

[46] Implementing regulation, above n 16, Art 19(1).

[47] Ibid, Art 19(2). In exceptional circumstances the Commission may permit the parties to offer commitments after the expiry of the time limit. See also Art 20 for the relevant procedure for making commitments.

issue of remedies, and the Commission approach to them, is also discussed in Chapter 8, below.

Phase II

The Commission has 90 working days in which to make a final Article 8 decision following the opening of Phase II proceedings. As noted above, these proceedings may only be opened where the Commission has 'serious doubts' about the compatibility of the merger with the common market. The decision to move to Phase II may have serious, or even fatal, consequences for a merger. It may therefore be regretted that the Regulation does not clarify the meaning of 'serious doubts', and it is not possible to appeal an Article 6(1)(c) decision to the CFI as this is regarded as an interim stage of the proceedings, and is not therefore an appealable act (see further Chapter 9, below). There is little guidance in the literature on how high this hurdle is, although it may be noted that in practice the vast majority of cases are *not* referred to Phase II. Navarro *et al* state that '"[s]erious doubts" are characterised by the presence of a series of factors and/or indicators that reasonably allow it to be argued that the notified concentration is capable of significantly impeding effective competition'.[48]

Within two weeks of taking a decision under Article 6(1)(c) a 'state of play' meeting will be held between the Commission and the parties at which there will be an attempt to map out the course to be followed during the Phase II stage. These meetings and the rights to hearings are discussed below.[49] If, following the necessary information gathering (see below), the Commission continues to maintain the position that the merger is likely to be incompatible with the common market, it is required to issue a Statement of Objections (SO) to the notifying parties. The content of this assumes fundamental importance if the Commission proceeds to a decision declaring the concentration to be incompatible with the common market (Article 8(3) ECMR), as, under the terms of Article 18(3) ECMR, '[t]he Commission shall base its decision only on the objections on which the parties have been able to submit their observations'.[50]

At the same time the relationship between the SO and the final decision should not be over-emphasised. In a final decision the Commission is 'not obliged to explain any differences by comparison with the [SO]', as the latter is 'is a preparatory document containing assessments which are purely provisional'.[51] At the same time, where there is a difference between the argument made in the SO and that made in the final decision the Commission 'must be in

[48] E Navarro, A Font, J Folguera and J Briones, *Merger Control in the EU* (2nd edn, Oxford, OUP, 2005), at 13.31.

[49] *Best Practice*, above n 7, para 43.

[50] See M Kekelekis, 'The "Statement of Objections" as an Inherent Part of the Right to be Heard in EC Merger Proceedings: Issues of Concern' [2004] *ECLR* 518.

[51] Case T–464/04 *Independent Music Publishers and Labels Association (Impala, international association) v Commission*, judgment of 13 July 2006, para 284.

a position to explain . . . at least in the context of the proceedings before the Court, its reasons for considering that its provisional findings were incorrect'.[52]

Article 13(2) of the Implementing Regulation further requires the Commission to 'inform other involved parties in writing of these objections'. The Commission will set a time limit within which the notifying parties must reply to the SO. The reply should be a thorough response, containing all the relevant facts, any documents which establish the proof of those facts and and they may suggest persons whom the Commission should call to a hearing in order to corroborate these facts.[53] There is no time limit within which the Commission is required to send the SO to the parties, although this is likely to be around 30–45 days after the commencement of Phase II.

Time limits

Article 10 ECMR sets out the time limits for initiating proceedings and for making decisions. These have already been referred to at the relevant points at which they apply. However, one further element should be noted. This is the ability of either the parties or the Commission to 'stop the clock' on the proceedings. Article 10(3), paragraph 2, provides that after proceedings have been initiated under Article 6(1)(c) either the parties or the Commission may request an extension of up to 20 days.[54]

INFORMATION GATHERING AND THE ASSESSMENT PROCESS

The powers referred to here apply equally to Phase I and Phase II in so far as they relate to the gathering of information. Under the ECMR the Commission is given the powers necessary to enable it to gather all necessary information for the purposes of the application of the Regulation. These powers operate independently of those set out in Regulation 1/2003 in respect of investigations for the purposes of the application of Articles 81 and 82 EC, although the same general principles of law are applicable to both sets of powers. Recital (38) thus provides, in part, that:

> In order properly to appraise concentrations, the Commission should have the right to request all necessary information and to conduct all necessary inspections throughout the Community. . . . The Commission should, in particular, have the right to interview any persons who may be in possession of useful information and to record the statements made.

[52] Case T–464/04 *Independent Music Publishers and Labels Association (Impala international association) v Commission*, judgment of 13 July, 2006, para 335.

[53] Implementing Regulation, above n 16, Art 13(3).

[54] See A Andreangeli, 'Fairness and Timing in Merger Control Proceedings: Will the "Stop-the-Clock" Clause Work?' [2005] *ECLR* 403.

It will be noted at the outset that this recognises a practical limitation on the powers of the Commission, in that it is not able to conduct inspections outside the Community. Although the application of the ECMR should be less contentious than investigations into alleged anti-competitive conduct carried out in relation to the enforcement of Articles 81 and 82, the relevant Articles of the ECMR do provide the Commission with the necessary enforcement powers, and in particular with the right to require the cooperation of relevant authorities of the Member States, including the courts. The Commission's powers relating to information gathering are set out at Articles 11–13 ECMR, and these are backed up with the power to impose fines or periodic penalty payments on undertakings which obstruct the application of these powers.[55] Such information gathering will not normally start until after the notification of the proposed concentration, although the Commission 'may exceptionally decide that, in the interest of its investigation, market contacts could be initiated informally prior to notification'.[56]

Requests for information

Although undertakings are required to submit substantial amounts of information in the notification process it is quite likely that more will be sought by the Commission. In particular the notifying undertakings will approach the merger from the perspective of seeking to persuade the Commission of its legitimacy, and may downplay factors which might mitigate against this, although they are also asked to identify problems.[57]

Article 11 entitles the Commission to request information from both the notifying parties, as well as from 'undertakings or associations of undertakings'.[58] This means that unless a natural person is one of the notifying parties the Commission cannot request information from natural persons, unless it does so under the powers granted it under Article 11(7).[59] Under the terms of this Article information may be either requested or demanded by decision. In the first case the Commission is required to state the legal basis for the request, to identify the information required, and to fix a time limit within which it is to be provided.[60] Although there is no obligation on the parties to whom such requests are addressed to respond to them, any response that is made must be full and accurate, and Article 14 ECMR provides that a fine of up to 1 per cent of turnover

[55] Arts 14 and 15, ECMR. Under Art 229 EC the ECJ has unlimited jurisdiction to review any decision under which the EC Commission imposes a fine or periodic penalty payment. See also Art 16 ECMR.

[56] *Best Practice*, above n 7, para 26.

[57] See, eg, Art 16 of ibid.

[58] In ibid, at para 35, the Commission states that 'the primary way for third parties to contribute to the Commission's investigation is by means of replies to requests for information'.

[59] Although Arts 11(2) and (3) makes reference to 'persons' this should be read alongside Art 11(1) which defines 'persons' as being those 'referred to in Art 3(1)(b)'.

[60] Art 11(2) ECMR.

may be imposed where incorrect or misleading information is supplied in response to an Article 11(2) request.[61] Article 11(3) gives the Commission power to order the supply of information by decision.[62] In this case, in addition to the above criteria it is required to indicate that penalties may also be imposed under Article 15 ECMR, and that any such decision may be appealed to the CFI. Article 14(1)(c) ECMR provides that penalties may also be applied in this case for failure to supply complete information. Article 15 ECMR gives the Commission the additional power to impose periodic penalty payments of up to 5 per cent of the average aggregate daily turnover of the undertaking(s) on those who fail to comply with an Article 11(3) decision within the time limit set out in the decision. The information requested is to be supplied by 'the owners of the undertakings or their representatives', or in other cases by persons authorised to represent the undertakings by law or by their constitution.[63] It is the undertakings that remain liable for the quality of the information supplied.[64] Any decision taken under Article 11(3) shall also be forwarded to the competent authorities of the Member State in whose territory the seat of the addressee is located.[65] The Commission may also request information from governments or competent authorities of the Member States. It does not need to be given the power to demand this information by decision, first because it is unlikely that such bodies would not cooperate with a legitimate Commission request, and secondly because the provisions of Article 10 EC would apply in the event that there was a failure to cooperate.

Article 11(7) gives the Commission the power to interview natural or legal persons, but only where those persons consent to the interview, and no penalties may be imposed on those who consent to interview, even if the information they provide is inaccurate or misleading.

[61] Art 14(1)(b) ECMR.

[62] It is uncommon, but not rare, for undertakings to fail to supply information under the operation of the ECMR, probably in part because it is in the best interests of the undertakings concerned to keep the process cooperative rather than contentious. However, there have been instances on which proceedings have been suspended where parties have failed to comply with time limits imposed by the Commission. Eg, in Case COMP/M.1672 *Volvo/Scania*, the Commission had imposed a time limit of 7 Dec 1999 for the supply of certain specified information. This was not forthcoming until 20 Dec 1999, and the proceedings were therefore suspended for a period of 13 days. The period of review was also extended in Case COMP/M.1741 *MCI WorldCom/Sprint*, where a request was made for information to be supplied, and following the expiry of the time limit specified in the request a decision was made requiring its provision. The parties fully complied three days after the deadline specified in the decision, resulting in a total extension of 8 days to the Commission's timetable. The substantive issues of both these cases are discussed briefly in Chap 9.

[63] Art 11(4) ECMR.

[64] Art 11(5) ECMR.

[65] Art 11(6) ECMR.

Inspections

Inspections of undertakings or associations of undertakings may be carried out either by the Commission or, at its request and authorisation, by the competent authorities of Member States.[66] The Commission's powers of inspection are set out in Article 13 ECMR. Recital (40) ECMR states in part that 'in the course of an inspection, officials authorised by the Commission should have the right to ask for any information relevant to the subject matter and purpose of the inspection'. The Commission also has the right to affix seals, particularly in circumstances where the Commission has reasonable grounds to suspect that the undertaking is not fully compliant with the requests of the Commission. The core powers of the Commission in relation to the carrying out of inspections are set out in Article 13(2) ECMR, which is in the following terms:

> The officials and other accompanying persons authorised by the Commission to conduct an inspection shall have the power:
>
> (a) to enter any premises, land and means of transport of undertakings and associations of undertakings;
> (b) to examine the books and other records related to the business, irrespective of the medium on which they are stored;
> (c) to take or obtain in any form copies of or extracts from such books or records;
> (d) to seal any business premises and books or records for the period and to the extent necessary for the inspection;
> (e) to ask any representative or member of staff of the undertaking or association of undertakings for explanations on facts or documents relating to the subject matter and purpose of the inspection and to record the answers.

Seals should be affixed only in the circumstances referred to in recital (39) ECMR, and should, 'in any event . . . only be used in exceptional circumstances, for the period of time strictly necessary fro the inspection, normally not for more than 48 hours'. Inspections may proceed without a formal decision compelling compliance being taken,[67] or on the basis of a decision, in which case undertakings are obliged to comply with these.[68] In the first case the Commission is to give notice of the inspection to the competent authority of the relevant Member State 'in good time before the inspection'.[69] Undertakings are not obliged to comply with inspections not authorised by decision, but if they do choose to comply they have the obligation when giving information or answers to questions not to give incorrect or misleading information or responses, and in the case of the supply of information it must be complete. Any breach of this obligation may leave the undertaking liable to penalties of up to 5 per cent of turnover under Article 14(1)(d) or (e).

[66] Arts 12 and 13 ECMR.
[67] Art 13(3) ECMR.
[68] Art 13(4) ECMR.
[69] Art 13(3) ECMR.

Under Article 13(4) ECMR undertakings are required to submit to inspections carried out under the authority of a formal decision. Such decisions shall be taken only after consultation with the competent authority of the Member State in whose territory the inspection is to be conducted. Failure to comply with a decision leaves the undertaking vulnerable both to fines where it complies in a manner which is inaccurate, incomplete or misleading, and to periodic penalty payments under Article 15(1)(b). The Commission may require the assistance of officials of the competent authority of the relevant Member State when carrying out such inspections,[70] and these will enjoy the same powers as those held by the Commission under Article 13(2). The Commission may also, where necessary, require the authorisation of a national court for the inspection process, and may do so in interlocutory proceedings as a precautionary measure.[71] National courts may not call into question the necessity for the inspection, and their authority is limited to determining the authenticity of the decision, and the fact that the 'coercive measures envisaged are neither arbitrary nor excessive having regard to the subject matter of the decision'.[72]

Recital (41) of the ECMR clarifies the rights of undertakings as regard self-incrimination. There has been substantial discussion of this matter in the case law of the ECJ,[73] and the position as set out in the recital is consistent with the approach of the ECJ in its attempt to balance the needs of the Commission in enforcing competition policy with the rights of undertakings. Recital (41) therefore provides that:

> When complying with decisions of the Commission, the undertakings and persons concerned cannot be forced to admit that they have committed infringements, but they are in any event obliged to answer factual questions and to provide documents, even if this information may be used to establish against themselves or against others the existence of such infringements.

The advisory committee

Under the terms of the ECMR 'an Advisory Committee on concentrations shall be consulted before any decision is taken pursuant to Article 8(1) to (6), and Articles 14 or 15 with the exception of provisional decisions taken in accordance with Article 18(2)'.[74] The Advisory Committee consists of at least one and not more than two representatives of the national competition authorities. The

[70] Art 13(5) ECMR.

[71] Art 13(7) ECMR.

[72] Art 13(8)ECMR. See also recital (40) ECMR.

[73] See, eg Case 374/87 *Orkem SA v Commission*, [1991] 4 CMLR 502; Case T–112/98, *Mannesmannrohren-Werke AG v Commission* [2001] 5 CMLR 1; and Case C-60/92 *Otto v Postbank* [1993] ECR I–5683. None of these cases arose from the application of the ECMR, and the procedures under Arts 81 and 82 EC are by nature more contentious than those arising under the ECMR, but the principles are the same.

[74] Art 19(3) ECMR.

Commission is responsible for convening and chairing the meeting, and the Commission shall present to the meeting a summary of the case, along with indications of the most important documents considered and a preliminary draft of the decision to be taken. The Advisory Committee shall deliver an opinion on the Commission's draft decision, and the Commission is required to 'take the utmost account' of the opinion.[75] The opinions are to be made public and are to be communicated to the addressees of the decision.[76] However, beyond this persuasive consultancy role the Advisory Committee has no formal powers.

Meetings and hearings

The Commission *Best Practice* notice sets out some of the principles relating to communication between the Commission and relevant parties. Paragraphs 30–33 relate to state of play meetings which are aimed at improving the transparency of proceedings. Paragraph 30 states that 'the objective of State of Play meetings is to contribute to the quality and efficiency of the decision-making process and to ensure transparency and communication between DG Competition and the notifying parties'. Such meetings are entirely voluntary in nature.[77] There is no restriction on the matters that may be discussed at state of play meetings, including key issues such as remedies proposed by the notifying parties in the event that the Commission expresses concerns. The Commission has indicated that it will normally offer parties the possibility of attending state of play meetings at five different points during the total Phase I and II procedure: (a) 'where it appears that "serious doubts" within the meaning of article 6(1)(c)' ECMR; (b) 'normally within 2 weeks following the adoption of the article 6(1)(c) decision'; (c) 'before the issuing of a Statement of Objections'; (d) following the reply to the SO and the Oral Hearing' (see below); (e) 'before the Advisory Committee meets'.[78] The primary purpose of each of these potential meetings is set out in *Best Practice*. Although it is envisaged that most meetings will be bilateral the possibility remains that some may be triangular where 'it is desirable, in the interests of the fact-finding investigation, to hear the views of the notifying parties and such third parties in a single forum'.[79]

In addition to state of play meetings, under some circumstances parties are entitled to the benefit of a formal hearing. Articles 14–16 of the implementing regulation set out the core rules relating to hearings during the proceedings. These will be conducted by the Hearing Officer, who is an independent

[75] Art 19(6) ECMR.

[76] Art 19(7) ECMR.

[77] *Best Practice*, above n 7, para 30.

[78] Ibid, para 33.

[79] Ibid, para 38. Such meetings 'should ideally be held as early in the investigation as possible in order to enable DG Competition to reach a more informed conclusion as to the relevant market characteristics and to clarify issues of substance before deciding on the issuing of an SO'.

official.[80] There are a number of decisions before taking which the Commission is required to allow the relevant parties to present their views at a hearing. These are substantive decisions taken under Articles 6(3) and 8(2)–(6) ECMR, and Articles 14 and 15 in relation to the imposition of fines or periodic penalty payments. In the case of the substantive decisions notifying parties and 'other involved parties' who have so requested will be given the right to develop their arguments orally.[81] In the case of hearings relating to the imposition of fines or periodic penalty payments the persons on whom the Commission intends to impose these shall be entitled to an oral hearing.[82] The competent authorities of the Member States shall also be invited to take part in any formal oral hearings. Persons attending formal hearings may be, and usually will be, assisted by their lawyers or other duly qualified persons admitted as such by the Hearing Officer. Hearings are not held in public, although where it is appropriate several parties may be invited to attend the same hearing.[83] Third parties, as defined in Article 11(c) of the implementing regulation,[84] may apply in writing to be heard. Although they have no right to be heard, Article 16(2) of the implementing regulation states that the Commission 'may, where appropriate, afford such third parties who have so requested in their written comments the opportunity to participate in a formal hearing'. The Commission may also 'invite any other natural or legal person to express its views, in writing as well as orally, including at a formal hearing'.[85]

The publication of decisions

Recital (42) ECMR states that, 'for the sake of transparency, all decisions of the Commission which are not of a merely procedural nature should be widely publicised'. Decisions taken in accordance with Article 8(1) to (6), 14 or 15, with the exception of provisional decisions taken in accordance with Article 18(2), shall be published in the Official Journal. The Commission shall 'have regard to the legitimate interest of undertakings in the protection of their business secrets'.[86]

[80] See Commission Decision 2001/462/EC/ECSC [2001] OJ L 162/21. Recital (6) of the Decision states that '[i]n order to ensure the independence of the hearing officer, he should be attached, for administrative purposes, to the member of the Commission with special responsibility for competition.' See also Art 2 of the Decision.

[81] Implementing regulation, above n 16, Art 14(1) and (2).

[82] Ibid, Art 14(3).

[83] Ibid, Art 15(6).

[84] Defined as 'natural or legal persons, including customers, suppliers and competitors, provided they demonstrate a sufficient interest within the meaning of article 18(4) [ECMR]'. Art 18(4) ECMR does not define 'sufficient interest'. The second sentence of that article reads as follows: '[n]atural or legal persons showing a sufficient interest and especially members of the administrative or management bodies of the undertakings concerned or the recognised representatives of their employees shall be entitled, upon application, to be heard.'

[85] Implementing regulation, above n 16, Art 16(3).

[86] Art 20 ECMR.

However, no time period is given within which decisions are to be published, and in some cases a considerable period of time has elapsed between the making of a decision and its communication to the parties, and the publication of the decision in the OJ.

Professional secrecy

A number of provisions, as well as the general principles of Community law, relate to the protection of confidentiality and business secrets in the application of the ECMR.[87] Article 17 ECMR provides first that the information supplied as a result of the application of the ECMR 'shall be used only for the purposes of the relevant request, investigation or hearing'. This implies, inter alia, that the Commission or other NCAs may not use information supplied under the terms of the ECMR in the context of other competition law proceedings. Article 18 of the implementing regulation provides in its first paragraph that:

> Information, including documents, shall not be communicated or made accessible by the Commission in so far as it contains business secrets or other confidential information the disclosure of which is not considered necessary by the Commission for the purpose of the procedure.

The onus is very much on the parties submitting information to the Commission, whether they be the notifying undertakings or any third party, to make known at the time of the submission which information they consider to be confidential.[88] The professional secrecy provisions apply not only to the Commission, but also to members of the NCAs, including their 'officials and other servants, and other persons working under the supervision of those authorities as well as officials and civil servants of other authorities of the member states'.[89] The Commission may, however, publish general information or surveys which do not contain information relating to particular undertakings.[90]

[87] See, eg, Regulation (EC) No 45/2001 of the European Parliament and of the Council of 18 December 2000 on the protection of individuals with regard to the processing of personal data by the Community institutions and bodies and on the free movement of such data [2001] OJ L 8/1.

[88] Implementing regulation, above n 16, Art 18(2). See also Art 18(3). In *Best Practice*, above n 7, the Commission states at para 47 that 'In accordance with Art 287 of the EC Treaty and Art 17(1) of the Implementing Regulation, the Commission will, throughout its investigation, protect confidential information and business secrets contained in submissions provided by all parties involved in EC merger proceedings. Given the short legal deadlines of EC merger procedures, parties are encouraged to clarify as soon as possible any queries related to confidentiality claims with members of the case team. Guidance on what is considered to be business secrets or other confidential information is provided in the Commission's *Notice on Access to file*' (see below).

[89] *Commission notice on case referral in respect of concentrations*, para 57; see also Art 17(2) ECMR.

[90] Art 17(3), ECMR. Where notifying parties seek the review of 'key documents' under para 45 of *Best Practice*, DG Comp 'will respect justified requests by third parties for non-disclosure of their submissions prior to the issuing of the SO relating to genuine concerns regarding confidentiality, including fears of retaliation and the protection of business secrets': *Best Practice*, para 46 above n 7.

Access to file

The right of parties to proceedings under the ECMR to have access to the documents held by the Commission on the basis of which it has taken its decisions is verified in the implementing regulation, at Article 17.[91] However, recital (16) provides that the Commission should ensure the protection of business secrets and other confidential information.[92] Article 17 is in the following terms:

> 1. If so requested, thc Commission shall grant access to the file to the parties to whom it has addressed a statement of objections, for the purpose of enabling them to exercise their rights of defence. Access shall be granted after the notification of the statement of objections.
> 2. The Commission shall, upon request, also give the other involved parties who have been informed of the objections access to the file in so far as this is necessary for the purposes of preparing their comments.
> 3. The right of access to the file shall not extend to confidential information, or to internal documents of the Commission or of the competent authorities of the Member States. The right of access to the file shall equally not extend to correspondence between the Commission and the competent authorities of the Member States or between the latter.
> 4. Documents obtained through access to the file pursuant to this Article may only be used for the purposes of the relevant proceeding pursuant to Regulation (EC) No 139/2004.

The Commission will also allow parties to have access to documents received after the issuing of the SO and up until the consultation of the advisory committee, but not after this point.[93] Notifying parties will also be given the opportunity to review and comment on any 'key documents' obtained by the Commission.[94] In December 2005 the Commission published a revised version of its *Notice* relating to access to file.[95] This states at paragraph 10 that relevant parties:

> must be able to acquaint themselves with the information in the Commission's file, so that, on the basis of this information, they can effectively express their views on the preliminary conclusions reached by the Commission in its objections. For this purpose they will be granted access to all documents making up the Commission file, as defined in para 8, with the exception of internal documents, business secrets of other undertakings, or other confidential information.

[91] Further information relating to access to file is given in ibid, at paras 42–44.

[92] See generally CS Kerse and N Khan, *EC Antitrust Procedure* (5th edn, London, Sweet & Maxwell 2005), 4.III.

[93] *Best Practice*, above n 7, para 43.

[94] Ibid, para 45. Key documents 'would comprise substantiated submissions of third parties running counter to the notifying parties' own contentions received during Phase I and thereafter, including key submissions to which specific reference is made in the Art 6(1)(c) decision and market studies'.

[95] *Commission Notice on the rules for access to the Commission file in cases pursuant to Arts 81 and 82 EC, Arts 53, 54 and 57 EEA and Council Regulation 139/2004* [2005] OJ C 325/7.

The documents referred to in paragraph 8 are a wide set, as the Commission file is defined as consisting 'of all documents, which have been obtained, produced and/or assembled by [DG Comp], during the investigation'.[96] Documents originating from Member States may also be disclosed. The Commission notes that in the area of merger control this may apply in particular to submissions made by Member States under Article 9(2) ECMR. In the course of merger proceedings access to the file will be granted 'at every stage of the procedure following the notification of the Commission's objections up to the consultation of the Advisory Committee'.[97] Any person who submits information or comments in the circumstances set out in paragraph 35(b) of the *Access to file notice* is required to identify any documents or parts of documents which that person considers to contain business secrets or other confidential information belonging to them.[98]

[96] The parties will not be granted access to 'internal documents', which include 'drafts, opinions, memos or notes from the Commission departments or other public authorities concerned': para 12, and internal fn 14.

[97] *Access to file notice*, above n 95, para 28.

[98] In merger proceedings the following are the relevant situations:

> '—notifying parties or other involved parties making known their views on Commission objections adopted with a view to take a decision with regard to a request for a derogation from suspension of a concentration and which adversely affects one or more of those parties, or on a provisional decision adopted in the matter;
>
> —notifying parties to whom the Commission has addressed a statement of objections, other involved parties who have been informed of those objections or parties to whom the Commission has addressed objections with a view to inflict a fine or a periodic penalty payment, submitting their comments on the objections;
>
> —any person which supplies information pursuant to Art 11 of the [ECMR].' (*Access to file notice*, above n 95, para 35(b)).

6

The Substantive Test Under the ECMR

INTRODUCTION

THE MOST FUNDAMENTAL question facing anyone contemplating a merger, apart from whether the merger falls to be examined under any regime, is what test will be applied by the regimes under which it falls. In the EC the test is linked to, but is not exactly the same as, that of the dominance threshold applying to Article 82 EC. As indicated in Chapter 1 the lack of a specific provision in the Treaty relating to merger control meant that it was necessary to establish the regime in part on the basis of other competition law provisions. It is for this reason that Regulation 4064/89 applied a test of dominance. In Regulation 139/2004 this was amended, although the Commission still expects most mergers to be analysed under this rubric.[1] The process of amendment of the ECMR, and the options that were considered, has been discussed in Chapter 1. This chapter sets out the application of the substantive test applied to the analysis of concentrations in the EC, considering first the general terms of the test, and then some specific factors in its application. The treatment of restrictions ancillary to concentrations is also dealt with here. This chapter concludes with a discussion of the *Commission Notice on a simplified procedure for treatment of certain concentrations under Council Regulation (EC) No 139/2004*.[2]

The recital to the ECMR appears to place some emphasis on the wider objectives of the EC Treaty in the evaluation of mergers, even though it gives primacy to competition objectives. Recital (23) thus provides that:

> It is necessary to establish whether or not concentrations with a Community dimension are compatible with the common market in terms of the need to maintain and develop effective competition in the common market. In so doing, the Commission must place its appraisal within the general framework of the achievement of the fundamental objectives referred to in Article 2 of the Treaty establishing the European Community and Article 2 of the Treaty on European Union.

In practice it is to be hoped that the emphasis will be on competition factors, and indeed the words of the substantive provisions of the ECMR require that

[1] See para 4 of the Horizontal Merger Guidance [2004] OJ C 31/5.
[2] [2000] OJ C 217/32.

this be the case.[3] Further support for the proposition that economic considerations should, and do, dominate, may be found in recital 28, ECMR, which states that:

> In order to clarify and explain the Commission's appraisal of concentrations under this Regulation, it is appropriate for the Commission to publish guidance which should provide a sound economic framework for the assessment of concentrations with a view to determining whether or not they may be declared compatible with the common market.

The guidance that has been published to date is discussed in this chapter, and has already been referred to in Chapter 2 in so far as it clarifies the general economic approach taken to the assessment of mergers. As has been stressed before the ECMR creates a strongly centralised system, unlike that which operates in relation to the application of Articles 81 and 82. This implies that there is less likelihood of 'policy contamination' of competition decisions in the application of the tests. In a slightly different context Navarro *et al* point out that save for a small set of social objectives, including the reinforcing of the economic and social cohesion of the EC, and the recognition of the fact that nothing in the ECMR operates to the detriment of the collective rights of workers, the emphasis whenever the ECMR is being applied is 'strictly economic'.[4]

The core substantive provision of the ECMR is Article 2, which given its importance is set out here in its entirety. The analysis of this article, and the practice in its application, will form the basis of this chapter.

[3] Eg, in the context of mergers referred back to Member State authorities under the provisions of Art 9 ECMR, it should be noted that there exists a requirement at Art 9(8) that '[i]n applying the provisions of this article, the member state concerned may take only the measures strictly necessary to safeguard or restore effective competition on the market concerned'.

[4] E Navarro *et al*, *Merger Control in the EU* (2nd edn, Oxford, OUP, 2005), para 11.36. An analysis of the debates that took place at the time of the enactment of Regulation 4064/89 also demonstrates that competition considerations are to the fore in the assessment of mergers. It has been pointed out that this competition emphasis does 'not totally exclude other considerations, in particular technical and economic progress': CJ Cook and CS Kerse, *EC Merger Control* (3rd edn, London, Sweet and Maxwell 2000), 126. Although some still argue that EC competition law has to be read very much against a wider context of EC policy, including economic, industrial, social, environmental and, crucially, market integration factors, the dominant belief, supported in the application of the ECMR, is that only rarely, if ever, will competition factors be marginalised in favour of other considerations in the assessment of mergers. While other provisions in the EC Treaty point to additional considerations at a wider policy level there is evidence even here that competition considerations are not to be pushed aside in order to support these considerations. For example, Art 130 EC makes provision for the development of Community industrial policy. In the Article however it is stated that 'it shall not provide a basis for the introduction by the Commission of any measures which could lead to a distortion of competition'. The most important case in which other considerations appear to have played a role is that of *Perrier* in which the CFI placed some emphasis on employment and social factors: Case T–96/92, *Comite Central d'Enterprise de la Societe Generale des Grandes Sources v Commission* [1992] ECR II–2579. This case is discussed further below. See also D Banks, 'Non-Competition Factors and their Future Relevance under European Merger Law' [1997] *ECLR* 182.

(2) **Appraisal of concentrations**

1. Concentrations within the scope of this Regulation shall be appraised in accordance with the objectives of this Regulation and the following provisions with a view to establishing whether or not they are compatible with the common market. In making this appraisal, the Commission shall take into account:

(a) the need to maintain and develop effective competition within the common market in view of, among other things, the structure of all the markets concerned and the actual or potential competition from undertakings located either within or outwith the Community;

(b) the market position of the undertakings concerned and their economic and financial power, the alternatives available to suppliers and users, their access to supplies or markets, any legal or other barriers to entry, supply and demand trends for the relevant goods and services, the interests of the intermediate and ultimate consumers, and the development of technical and economic progress provided that it is to consumers' advantage and does not form an obstacle to competition.

2. A concentration which would not significantly impede effective competition in the common market or in a substantial part of it, in particular as a result of the creation or strengthening of a dominant position, shall be declared compatible with the common market.

3. A concentration which would significantly impede effective competition, in the common market or in a substantial part of it, in particular as a result of the creation or strengthening of a dominant position, shall be declared incompatible with the common market.

4. To the extent that the creation of a joint venture constituting a concentration pursuant to Article 3 has as its object or effect the coordination of the competitive behaviour of undertakings that remain independent, such coordination shall be appraised in accordance with the criteria of Article 81(1) and (3) of the Treaty, with a view to establishing whether or not the operation is compatible with the common market.

5. In making this appraisal, the Commission shall take into account in particular:

—whether two or more parent companies retain, to a significant extent, activities in the same market as the joint venture or in a market which is downstream or upstream from that of the joint venture or in a neighbouring market closely related to this market,

—whether the coordination which is the direct consequence of the creation of the joint venture affords the undertakings concerned the possibility of eliminating competition in respect of a substantial part of the products or services in question.

The key ingredient here is that the concentration will be assessed on the basis of whether or not it 'would significantly impede effective competition, in the common market or in a substantial part of it, in particular as a result of the creation or strengthening of a dominant position'. During the debates surrounding the revisions to the ECMR there was considerable discussion on what form the revised test should take, and indeed on whether or not it should be revised at all.

The Commission took the view that to abandon the dominance test of Regulation 4064/89 in its entirety would result in also jettisoning useful precedent built up in its application. At the same time the difficulties encountered in applying the dominance test in oligopolistic markets meant that some revision was necessary. The particular problems relating to oligopoly and merger control in the context of the EC are discussed further in the next chapter.

In shifting the emphasis of the test away from one of dominance exclusively towards a wider SIEC rubric the Commission has been at pains to point out that this is not to be seen as a radical change which will result in a great many more mergers being condemned. This is made clear at a number of points in the recitals. Thus, for example, recital (25), which refers to the problems encountered in oligopolistic markets concludes:

> The notion of 'significant impediment to effective competition' in article 2(2) and (3) should be interpreted as extending, beyond the concept of dominance, only to the anticompetitive effects of a concentration resulting from non-coordinated behaviour of undertakings which would not have a dominant position on the market concerned.

Further, recital (26) states that a 'significant impediment to effective competition generally results from the creation or strengthening of a dominant position'. Further indication that the most important element of the test remains that of dominance is found in the *Guidelines on the assessment of horizontal mergers under the Council Regulation on the control of concentrations between undertakings*[5] (hereinafter the 'Horizontal merger guidance'[6]) at paragraphs 2–4:

> 2. Accordingly, the Commission must take into account any significant impediment to effective competition likely to be caused by a concentration. The creation or the strengthening of a dominant position is a primary form of such competitive harm. The concept of dominance was defined in the context of Council Regulation (EEC) No 4064/89 of 21 December 1989 on the control of concentrations between undertakings (hereinafter 'Regulation No 4064/89') as: 'a situation where one or more undertakings wield economic power which would enable them to prevent effective competition from being maintained in the relevant market by giving them the opportunity to act to a considerable extent independently of their competitors, their customers and, ultimately, of consumers'.
>
> 3. For the purpose of interpreting the concept of dominance in the context of Regulation No 4064/89, the Court of Justice referred to the fact that it 'is intended to apply to all concentrations with a Community dimension insofar as they are likely, because of their effect on the structure of competition within the Community, to prove incompatible with the system of undistorted competition envisaged by the Treaty'.

[5] [2004] OJ C 31/3.

[6] See RBB Economics, 'Full Marks? The Draft EC Notice on the Appraisal of Horizontal Mergers', RBB Brief 7, 2003, which, albeit raising some criticisms, generally praises the economic approach taken by the Commission in the notice. See also S Voigt and A Schmidt, 'The Commission's Guidelines on Horizontal Mergers: Improvement or Deterioration?' (2004) 41 *CML Rev* 1583.

4. The creation or strengthening of a dominant position held by a single firm as a result of a merger has been the most common basis for finding that a concentration would result in a significant impediment to effective competition. Furthermore, the concept of dominance has also been applied in an oligopolistic setting to cases of collective dominance. As a consequence, it is expected that most cases of incompatibility of a concentration with the common market will continue to be based upon a finding of dominance. That concept therefore provides an important indication as to the standard of competitive harm that is applicable when determining whether a concentration is likely to impede effective competition to a significant degree, and hence, as to the likelihood of intervention. . . .[7]

Some concerns have been expressed, however, about the role to be played by 'dominance' in the application of the revised ECMR. Thompson, for example, argues that 'the amendment to the ECMR seems to be intended precisely to make it clear that it is not, any longer, *necessary* for a dominant position to be created or strengthened for a merger to be declared incompatible with the common market'.[8]

A merger which would normally be regarded as leading to the creation or strengthening of a dominant position may be regarded as not giving rise to such a market position if it is clearly the case that, even without the merger taking place, the acquirer would inevitably achieve the same position.[9]

The process that is to be gone through in assessing a merger under the ECMR is set out in para 10 of the *horizontal merger guidance*:

10. The Commission's assessment of mergers normally entails:

(a) definition of the relevant product and geographic markets;
(b) competitive assessment of the merger. The main purpose of market definition is to identify in a systematic way the immediate competitive constraints facing the merged entity. Guidance on this issue can be found in the Commission's Notice on the definition of the relevant market for the purposes of Community competition law. Various considerations leading to the delineation of the relevant markets may also be of importance for the competitive assessment of the merger.

The issue of market definition has been considered already in Chapter 2. Once the process has moved beyond the evaluation of the relevant market and the determination of market shares the *horizontal merger guidance* indicates that the Commission will work through the following phases in determining the competitive effects of a merger: (1) the likelihood that a merger would have

[7] Internal footnotes omitted.

[8] R Thompson, 'Goodbye to "the Dominance Test"? Substantive Appraisal Under the New UK and EC Merger Regimes' [2003] *Comp Law* 332, at 337 (emphasis in original).

[9] This principle has been discussed in Chap 2 in relation to the failing-firm defence. However, it might also apply were the acquirer clearly in the ascendancy in any event, although in this case the counterfactual would at least have to recognise the existence of the acquired firm as exercising some competitive constraint on the acquirer. See Commission Decision 94/449/EC, *Kali + Salz* [1994] OJ L 186/38, paras 70 ff; confirmed on appeal, Joined Cases C–68/94 and C–30/95, *France v Commission* [1998] ECR I–1375.

anti-competitive effects in the relevant markets in the absence of countervailing factors; (2) the likelihood that a buyer would act as a countervailing factor to an increase in market power; (3) the likelihood that entry would maintain effective competition; (4) the likelihood that efficiencies would act as a factor counteracting the harmful effects on competition; and (5) the conditions for a failing firm defence.[10] It is only in 'exceptional circumstances' that the Commission will consider whether the failing firm defence is met.[11] This approach will be followed in the remainder of this chapter. The Commission stresses that 'these factors are not a "checklist" to be mechanically applied in each and every case', and that 'the competitive analysis in a particular case will be based on an overall assessment of the foreseeable impact of the merger in the light of the relevant factors and conditions'.[12] It may, for example, become clear early on that there is no countervailing buyer power, or that the relevant market is one in which entry would be relatively straightforward and would likely be triggered by any signals being sent as to higher profitability.

It will be noted that any SLC identified must lie in the common market 'or a substantial part of it'. The meaning of 'substantial part' has been discussed briefly in Chapter 3, above. In *Schneider*[13] the CFI cited Articles 81 and 82 EC case law to support its conclusions on the meaning of 'substantial part'.[14]

THE ANALYSIS OF THE EFFECTS OF A MERGER

The broad arguments relating to the possible anti-competitive effects of mergers have been discussed already in Chapter 2. This and the following sections of this chapter consider the application of the law to these general principles in greater detail, drawing in part on the considerable body of decisions taken by the EC Commission in the application of the ECMR since 1990. The analysis in this chapter will focus on unilateral anti-competitive effects, tied in to the dominance test. Coordinated effects are also considered here, but a fuller discussion is found in the following chapter.[15]

[10] *Horizontal merger guidance*, above n 1, para 11.

[11] Ibid, para 12.

[12] Ibid, para 13.

[13] Cases T–310/01 and T–77/02, *Schneider Electric SA v Commission* [2003] 4 CMLR 17 (discussed further in Chap 8).

[14] It has been noted that this judgment 'has the potential to synchronise the interpretation of the notion of substantial part of the common market in both merger cases and [art 82 EC] infringements': LM Davison, 'EU Merger Control and the Compatibility Test: A Review of Recent Developments' (2004) 25 *Liverpool Law Review* 195 at 202.

[15] For a survey of more recent application of the substantive test see ibid.

Market share and concentration levels

The general economic approach to the definition of a relevant market and the determination of the power held by an undertaking in that market has been discussed in Chapter 2, above. The analysis of the relevant market and concentration levels 'provide useful first indications of the market structure and of the competitive importance of both the merging parties and their competitors'.[16] *The Horizontal merger guidance* continues to place the focus on dominance when discussing market shares and power. The Commission notes the general position taken under EC competition law that a market share in excess of 50 per cent will generally be taken as evidence of the existence of a dominant position, but notes too that where a market share remains below 50 per cent post-merger competitive concerns may still be raised 'in view of other factors such as the strength and number of competitors, the presence of capacity constraints or the extent to which the products of the merging parties are close substitutes'.[17] There have been a number of cases in which the Commission has held that mergers resulting in market shares of between 40 and 50 per cent lead to the creation or strengthening of a dominant position, and in some cases the Commission has found this to be the case at shares of below 40 per cent.[18] Unless exceptional circumstances apply a post-merger market share of less than 25 per cent will *not* be expected to result in an anti-competitive effect.[19] It is *not* the case that a share of above 25 per cent will be presumed to lead to the creation of a dominant position. Reliance should not, normally, be placed exclusively on market shares to determine dominance (as made clear in Chapter 2). The Commission has stated that a share as high as 90 per cent may still not, on the facts of the case, be determinative of the existence of a dominant position:

> in certain rare circumstances even such a high market share may not necessarily result in dominance. In particular, if sufficient active competitors are present on the market, the company with the large market share may be prevented from acting to an appreciable extent independently of the pressures typical of a competitive market.[20]

The approach taken to HHI concentration ratios and the relevant bands and movements which give rise to concerns are discussed in Chapter 2, above.

Unilateral (non-coordinated) effects

As noted in Chapter 2, unilateral anti-competitive effects are deemed to arise by virtue of the relative growth in market share of the merged entity over the

[16] *Horizontal merger guidance*, above n 1, para 14.
[17] Ibid, para 17.
[18] See, eg, Case COMP/M.2337 *Nestle/Ralston Purina* (2001).
[19] *Horizontal merger guidance*, above n 1, para 18.
[20] Case IV/M.68 *Tetra Pak/Alfa Laval* (1991), para 33.

market share previously held by the larger of the undertakings, and by the fact that a competitor has been eliminated from the market place, and with that elimination a competitive constraint on the acquirer has been removed. This analysis is typically applicable to horizontal mergers, although unilateral effects may also be found to exist in relation to vertical mergers. In the *horizontal merger guidance* unilateral effects are referred to as 'non-coordinated effects', and are discussed at paragraphs 24–38.

The introduction to the approach to non-coordinated effects in the *Horizontal merger guidance* restates the broad case for merger control, stating that the 'most direct effect of the merger will be the loss of competition between the competing firms'.[21] Other firms in the same market may, the Commission points out, also benefit from the reduced competition, since, if the merging firm raises its prices, customers may switch to competing firms which may raise their prices. Of course, if enough customers appear likely to switch from the merging firm if prices rise then in fact prices will *not*, or should not, rise, so the spill-over effects of the merger in this regard should not be overstated. The Commission states, at paragraph 46 of the *Horizontal merger guidance* that:

> A number of factors, which taken separately are not necessarily decisive, may influence whether significant non-coordinated effects are likely to result from a merger. Not all of these factors need to be present for such effects to be likely. Nor should this be considered an exhaustive list.

The factors that the Commission sets out are: (1) merging firms have large market shares; (2) merging firms are close competitors; (3) customers have limited possibilities of switching supplier; (4) competitors are unlikely to increase supply if prices increase; (5) the merged entity is able to hinder expansion by competitors; and (6) the merger eliminates an important competitive force.

As regards market shares the position has already been stated above that, *ceteris paribus*, the larger the post-merger market share the more likely it is that the undertaking will have market power. The more closely the products of the merging entities are related the more likely it is that market power will be increased, and 'the fact that rivalry between the parties has been an important source of competition may be a central factor in the analysis'.[22] In *Volvo/Scania*[23] for example, an Article 8(3) decision was taken blocking the merger in which there was substantial overlap and pre-merger competition between the parties in respect of trucks, buses and engines. The evidence that may be relied on in determining the degree of substitutability between the products affected is set out in paragraph 29, and includes 'customer preference surveys, analysis of purchasing patterns, estimation of the cross-price elasticities

[21] Para 24 of the Horizontal Merger Guidance, above n 1.
[22] *Horizontal merger guidance*, above n 1, para 28.
[23] Case IV/M.1672 (2000); see further Chap 8.

of the products involved, or diversion ratios'.[24] Customer preference surveys should be treated with caution, the most important factor being for whom and under what circumstances the survey was carried out. Greater credence will be given to independent surveys produced by market analysts such as AC Nielsen, than in-house surveys, which may be somewhat self-serving.

The extent to which customers can switch suppliers in the event that the merged entity attempts to exploit an increase in market power will depend in part on the costs of switching. In some industries, such as network industries, these are going to be substantial. In other industries for fungible homogenous products switching will be far easier. Particular problems may arise in relation to 'aftermarkets'—those where consumables are purchased for continuing use with a durable product (for example photocopier toner). It may be the case that customers are 'locked-in' by virtue of their commitment to the durable product, and that the switching costs would be substantial as they would be required to change the durable product in order to change the consumable. However, this will not always be the case, and in markets which are subject to rapid technological progress switching costs will be reduced. It may also be easier for customers to switch where competitors of the merged entity are able to expand production to meet any increase in demand. Thus the Commission notes, at paragraph 33 that:

> when market conditions are such that rival firms have enough capacity and find it profitable to expand output sufficiently, the Commission is unlikely to find that the merger will create or strengthen a dominant position or otherwise significantly impede effective competition.

A further complication arises if by some means the merged entity is itself able to restrict the ability of competitors to respond by increasing supply. This may be the case if the merged firm has significant power in relation to inputs or distribution channels. In particular 'a merger may give the merged entity the ability and incentive to raise the costs or decrease the quality of service, of its rivals'.[25] The issue of vertical foreclosure was discussed by the EC Commission in its assessment of the *Telia/Sonera* merger.[26] Here the Commission stated that in assessing the likelihood of vertical foreclosure 'it is necessary to establish not only that the merged entity will have the incentive to foreclose, but also whether

[24] Diversion ratios are frequently used in the US to estimate the extent to which price rises may be expected following a merger involving differentiated products. 'The diversion ratio between two products is the proportion of the sales lost by one product, when its price rises, that go to the other product. . . . Under special circumstances, the diversion ratio can be used to estimate quickly the likely effect on prices of a merger': S Bishop and M Walker, *The Economics of EC Competition Law: Concepts, Application and Measurement* (2nd edn, London, Sweet & Maxwell, 2002) at 10.39–10.40. See also A Lindsay, *The EC Merger Regulation: Substantive Issues* (2nd edn, London, Sweet & Maxwell, 2006) at 7-006.

[25] *Horizontal merger guidance*, above n 1, para 36.

[26] Case COMP/M.2803 (2002).

it has the ability to do so, and whether it will have any significant effect on competition on the market in question'.[27]

The final factor discussed by the Commission at this point is whether the merger eliminates an 'important competitive force'. Such a situation may arise either where the merger involves two close competitors or where it involves the take over of a 'maverick' firm that competes in a way which is unusual in that market—and perhaps is more innovative than others in its approach.[28] In *CVC/Lenzing*,[29] for example, which was blocked, the Commission was concerned about the fact that the merger involved the only company in the relevant market which had significantly increased its capacity in the recent past.[30]

Coordinated effects

The consideration of coordinated effects in merger control is, as has been suggested in Chapter 2, a complex matter, and was complicated further in the case of the ECMR by the wording of Regulation 4064/89 in its exclusive reliance on the dominance test. The approach taken under Regulation 4064/89 is discussed in the following chapter. The test as set out in the revised Article 2 ECMR makes clear that the EC Commission may prohibit mergers which do not create or strengthen a dominant position, but which do otherwise lead to an SIFC. The problem to be dealt with is set out at recital (25):

> In view of the consequences that concentrations in oligopolistic market structures may have, it is all the more necessary to maintain effective competition in such markets. Many oligopolistic markets exhibit a healthy degree of competition. However, under certain circumstances, concentrations involving the elimination of important competitive constraints that the merging parties had exerted upon each other, as well as a reduction of competitive pressure on the remaining competitors, may, even in the absence of a likelihood of coordination between the members of the oligopoly, result in a significant impediment to effective competition. The Community courts have,

[27] *Horizontal Merger Guidance* [2004] OJ C 31/5, above n 1, at para 91. Lindsay identifies a four stage analysis in this respect: (1) identify the leveraging conduct; (2) analyse whether the merged entity will have an incentive and the ability to pursue such conduct; (3) identify the foreclosure effect, if any, arising from the leveraging conduct; and (4) assess whether there is a causal link between any foreclosure effect and the merger: Lindsay, above n 24, at 11.011, and see the discussion following.

[28] It is often asserted that maverick firms exercise a competitive constraint on a market out of proportion to their size, and that in particular they may prevent the emergence of tacit collusion (coordinated effects). It has been noted however that it is necessary 'to identify carefully the origin of the "maverick" character, in order to determine whether it is an inherent, long lasting characteristic, or only reflects a transitory situation': (M Ivaldi, B Jullien, P Rey, P Seabright and J Tirole, 'The Economics of Tacit Collusion: Final Report for DG Competition, European Commission' (2003) at 55, available at the DG Comp website).

[29] Case COMP/M.2187 (2001), [2004] OJ L 82/20.

[30] In Case COMP/M.3314 *Air Liquide/Messer Targets* (2004) the evidence showed that Air Liquide had committed to an expansionary policy, and the Commission found that were it to purchase an incumbent as an alternative to developing its own capacity it would lose the incentive to expand.

however, not to date expressly interpreted Regulation (EEC) No 4064/89 as requiring concentrations giving rise to such non-coordinated effects to be declared incompatible with the common market. Therefore, in the interests of legal certainty, it should be made clear that this Regulation permits effective control of all such concentrations by providing that any concentration which would significantly impede effective competition, in the common market or in a substantial part of it, should be declared incompatible with the common market. The notion of 'significant impediment to effective competition' in Article 2(2) and (3) should be interpreted as extending, beyond the concept of dominance, only to the anti-competitive effects of a concentration resulting from the non-coordinated behaviour of undertakings which would not have a dominant position on the market concerned.

It will be noted at the outset that the issue here is not whether the merger might lead those parties left in the market post-merger explicitly to coordinate their activities, as any such explicit arrangement could be condemned on the basis of the application of Article 81 EC.[31] Rather the issue is the much more complex one, which cannot adequately be dealt with under either Articles 81 or 82 EC, of parties in a presumably narrow oligopoly aligning their conduct to each other's independently on the ground that to do so is entirely a rational profit maximising strategy. The competition provisions of the Treaty do not prohibit independent action, even if this means following the conduct of others.

The treatment of coordinated effects is discussed in the next chapter in some detail.

Countervailing buyer power

Countervailing buyer power is often considered by DG Comp as merging parties, particularly those with significant market shares, often claim that they are constrained by their customers. A leading case is *Enso/Stora*.[32] Here the relevant product market was liquid packaging board, used to make cartons containing milk and juices. Post-merger the parties would have a market share of between 50 per cent and 70 per cent, and there were high barriers to entry (in part created by strong reputation effects). However, countervailing buyer power was significant, with Tetra Pak alone accounting for some 60 per cent and 80 per cent of purchases. The Commission held that Tetra Pak could credibly threaten to go elsewhere, in part because it 'would have the option of developing new capacity with other existing or new suppliers should the parties attempt to exercise market power'.[33] In some cases, even where buyers are relatively large and

[31] See, eg, Case C–12/03 P, *Commission v Tetra Laval BV*, [2005] ECR I–987 in which the ECJ held that, where the Commission's case was developed in part on an expectation of future anti-competitive conduct it was to take into account the disciplining effect of the operation of general competition law: at para 75; see further Chap 8, below.

[32] Case IV/M.1225 (1998). See S Baker and A Lofaro, 'Buyer Power and the Enso/Stora Decision' [2000] *ECLR* 187.

[33] Above n 31, at para 91.

powerful organisations they will have little choice but to purchase the product in question from the merged entity. The Commission has found this to be the case, for example, in respect of leading brands of consumer products, which are supplied to supermarkets with substantial resources, but where the item in question is a 'must-stock' item.[34] In its *Horizontal merger guidance* the Commission states that 'countervailing buyer power cannot be found to sufficiently off-set potential adverse effects of a merger if it only ensures that a particular segment of customers, with particular bargaining strength, is shielded'.[35]

Entry

The starting point in the *Horizontal merger guidance* with respect to entry is set out at paragraph 68:

> When entering a market is sufficiently easy, a merger is unlikely to pose any significant anti-competitive risk. Therefore, entry analysis constitutes an important element of the overall competitive assessment. For entry to be considered a sufficient competitive constraint on the merging parties, it must be shown to be likely, timely and sufficient to deter or defeat any potential anti-competitive effects of the merger.[36]

Entry will be considered in almost any competitive assessment, although Bishop and Walker stress that analysis of entry should be placed in its correct context, and that 'the consideration of entry is necessary only if one considers that the merger may give rise to competition concerns in the absence of entry'.[37] Entry is discussed at reasonable length in Chapter 2. There have been a number of cases in which the Commission has found the prospect of entry decisive in clearing a merger that otherwise would have raised significant competitive concerns. This was the case, for example, in *Mercedes-Benz/Kassbohrer*[38] where the Commission held that the merger affected the bus market in Germany, but that the threat of entry from foreign suppliers was of 'decisive importance' to constrain the merged entity in the future. In *HP/Compaq*[39] the merger would have led to a market share of up to 95 per cent for personal digital organisers, but the

[34] See, eg, Case IV/M.190 *Nestle/Perrier* (1992) and Case IV/M.938 *Guinness/Grand Metropolitan* (1997).

[35] Above n 1, at para 67.

[36] In *Nestle/Perrier* (above, n 34) the Commission put the matter this way:'[t]o address the question of potential competition it needs to be examined whether there exists competitively meaningful and effective entry that could and would be likely to take place so that such entry would be capable of constraining the market power [of the merged entity]. The question is not whether new local water suppliers or foreign firms can merely enter by producing and selling bottled water but whether they are likely to enter and whether they would enter on a volume and price basis which would quickly and effectively constrain a price increase or prevent the maintenance of a supra-competitive price. The entry would have to occur within a time period short enough to deter the company(ies) concerned from exploiting their market power': at para 91.

[37] Bishop and Walker, above n 24, at 7.82.

[38] Case IV/M.477 (1995).

[39] Case COMP/M.2609 (2002).

evidence showed clearly that barriers to entry were low and that other firms had plans in place to enter this market.

Efficiencies

As noted in Chapter 2 there are reasons to be cautious about accepting efficiency claims in respect of mergers, and the Commission has been accused of 'adopt[ing] a hostile stance towards the claimed efficiency benefits of mergers'.[40] While the driving force behind most, if not all, mergers will be a desire on the part of the merging parties to rationalise operations and save costs, in practice the available evidence suggests that in many cases such efficiencies are not achieved. It is an irony of merger control that the situation in which competitors of the merging entities are likely to complain most vociferously is that in which the merger leaves the new undertaking in a more efficient situation, better able to compete than previously.[41] In Regulation 4064/89 there was no explicit recognition of an 'efficiency defence', but the Commission took the view that it was legitimate for it to consider efficiencies claimed by the merging parties under the test as set out in Article 2 of the Regulation.[42] There is also no explicit recognition of an efficiency defence in Regulation 139/2004 although the Commission

[40] Bishop and Walker, above n 24, at 301. The authors accept that it is the case that 'firms often claim efficiencies but rarely deliver them post-merger': ibid.

[41] In *GE/Honeywell* in particular the Commission appears to have been concerned about the impact of the merger on competitors, which may be a misplaced concern in the framework of merger control. However, following this criticism Mario Monti, in a speech given in 2001, robustly responded to charges that the Commission was operating a doctrine of 'efficiency offence'. Mr Monti argued that:

> 'we distinguish clearly between—on the one hand—mergers leading to price reductions that are the result of strategic behaviour on the part of a dominant firm, the purpose of which is to eliminate or marginalise competitors with a view to exploiting consumers in the medium term, and—on the other—mergers which will objectively lead to significant and durable efficiency gains that are likely to be passed on to the consumer. By 'efficiency gain' I do not refer to any cost reduction resulting from the merger, but the types of efficiencies which are relevant for antitrust authorities; that is a long-term and structural reduction in the marginal cost of production and distribution, which comes as a direct and immediate result of the merger, which cannot be achieved by less restrictive means and which reasonably will be passed on to the consumer on a permanent basis, in terms of lower prices or increased quality. When the merging parties do not provide a clearly articulated and quantified defence in terms of efficiencies . . . it is much harder for an antitrust authority to clear a transaction that is likely to lead to foreclosure effects, because if foreclosure takes place and competitors are marginalised, there is no guarantee that prices are going to be maintained at least over the medium and longer term, at the low level that the merged entity might strategically set them in order to foreclose competition'

('Antitrust in the US and Europe: A History of Convergence', 14 Nov 2001, available at www.europa.eu.int/comm/competition/speeches/index_2001.html).

[42] See P-E Noël, 'Efficiency Considerations in the Assessment of Horizontal Mergers under European and US Antitrust Law' [1997] *ECLR* 498; PD Camesasca, 'The Explicit Efficiency Defence in Merger Control: Does it Make the Difference' [1999] *ECLR* 14; and C Luescher, 'Efficiency Considerations in European Merger Control—Just Another Battle Ground for the European Commission, Economists and Competition Lawyers? ' [2004] *ECLR* 72.

did invite comment on whether one should be included in the Green Paper. However, recital (29) sets out the position of the Commission in this regard:

> In order to determine the impact of a concentration on competition in the common market, it is appropriate to take account of any substantiated and likely efficiencies put forward by the undertakings concerned. It is possible that the efficiencies brought about by the concentration counteract the effects on competition, and in particular the potential harm to consumers, that it might otherwise have and that, as a consequence, the concentration would not significantly impede effective competition, in the common market or in a substantial part of it, in particular as a result of the creation or strengthening of a dominant position. The Commission should publish guidance on the conditions under which it may take efficiencies into account in the assessment of a concentration.[43]

The *Horizontal merger guidance* provides that the Commission may conclude that a merger is compatible with the common market as a consequence of efficiencies generated where

> the Commission is in a position to conclude on the basis of sufficient evidence that the efficiencies generated by the merger are likely to enhance the ability and incentive of the merged entity to act pro-competitively for the benefit of consumers, thereby counteracting the adverse effects on competition which the merger might otherwise have.[44]

This implies that in the absence of any competitive constraint on the merged entity an efficiency defence is unlikely to be successful. In such a case the only beneficiary of the efficiencies will be the monopolist, who will be able still to charge monopoly prices but at lower costs, thereby benefiting from increased profits with no countervailing consumer benefit. The key factor indicated by the Commission is that 'consumers will not be worse off as a result of the merger' such that 'efficiencies should be substantial and timely, and should, in principle, benefit consumers in those relevant markets where it is otherwise likely that competition concerns would occur'.[45] The Commission has the following to say about reductions in costs as a result of the merger:

> cost savings in production or distribution may give the merged entity the ability and incentive to charge lower prices following the merger. In line with the need to ascertain whether efficiencies will lead to a net benefit to consumers, cost efficiencies that lead to reductions in variable or marginal costs are more likely to be relevant to the assessment of efficiencies than reductions in fixed costs; the former are, in principle, more likely to result in lower prices for consumers. Cost reductions, which merely result from anti-competitive reductions in output, cannot be considered as efficiencies benefiting consumers.[46]

[43] The Commission has not yet published guidance exclusively directed to efficiencies, and these are dealt with generally in the *Horizontal merger guidance*, above n 1.

[44] Ibid, at para 77.

[45] Ibid, at para 79.

[46] Ibid, para 80.

The Commission also recognises that efficiency gains may accrue in areas other than cost, as would be the case, for example, where R & D was facilitated by a merger which led to the throwing together of complementary research assets, skills or technologies.[47]

In the case of coordinated effects (discussed above) the Commission accepts that efficiency savings as a result of a horizontal merger may make coordinated anti-competitive effects less likely, as the merger may provide an incentive for the more efficient post-merger undertaking to compete on price, quantity or quality, when it might not otherwise have done so.[48] This would not however be likely to be the case where a chain of mergers in an industry led to an overall reduction in competitors, with those remaining retaining competitive parity with one another.

Two further conditions are important to the operation of an efficiency defence. The first is that the efficiencies must arise specifically from the merger, and would not otherwise be achieved:

> Efficiencies are relevant to the competitive assessment when they are a direct consequence of the notified merger and cannot be achieved to a similar extent by less anti-competitive alternatives. In these circumstances, the efficiencies are deemed to be caused by the merger and thus, merger-specific. It is for the merging parties to provide in due time all the relevant information necessary to demonstrate that there are no less anticompetitive, realistic and attainable alternatives of a non-concentrative nature (e.g. a licensing agreement, or a cooperative joint venture) or of a concentrative nature (e.g. a concentrative joint venture, or a differently structured merger) than the notified merger which preserve the claimed efficiencies. The Commission only considers alternatives that are reasonably practical in the business situation faced by the merging parties having regard to established business practices in the industry concerned.[49]

Secondly, and perhaps most importantly of all, the efficiencies that are claimed for the merger must be *verifiable*:

> Efficiencies have to be verifiable such that the Commission can be reasonably certain that the efficiencies are likely to materialise, and be substantial enough to counteract a merger's potential harm to consumers. The more precise and convincing the efficiency claims are, the better the Commission can evaluate the claims. Where reasonably possible, efficiencies and the resulting benefit to consumers should therefore be quantified. When the necessary data are not available to allow for a precise quantitative analysis, it must be possible to foresee a clearly identifiable positive impact on consumers, not a marginal one. In general, the longer the start of the efficiencies is projected into the future, the less probability the Commission may be able to assign to the efficiencies actually being brought about.[50]

[47] Ibid, para 81.
[48] Ibid, para 82.
[49] Ibid, para 85.
[50] Ibid, para 86.

The efficiency defence was carefully considered by the Commission in *Aerospatiale-Alenia/de Havilland*,[51] the first decision taken under the ECMR in which a merger was blocked.[52] Although there appeared to be cost savings arising out of the merger the Commission took the view that these were likely to be small in relation to the scale of the merger, and found that any such savings were not likely to be passed on to the customers. The Commission has been criticised for not considering as efficiencies the fact that as a result of the merger a single undertaking would offer a full range of models, allowing customers to purchase all their requirements from the one customer.[53]

The failing firm defence

The failing firm defence may apply in situations where, but for the merger, one of the parties would exit the market and its assets would be lost to the market. The essential argument is that in such a case the merger might not in fact lead to an increase in the market share of the acquiring undertaking, as the market share would rise in any event (or, to put it another way, the acquirer gains capacity but does not gain market share). Further the merger allows the assets of the failing firm to remain in the industry, avoiding a reduction in capacity, and may in some cases lead to the retention of some employment. In effect in such a case the merger itself is not the cause of any harm which is, rather, the result of the failure.[54] In *Kali und Salz/MdK/Treuhand*[55] the EC Commission set three conditions for the application of the 'defence'. These are that: (1) in the absence of the merger the company would exit the market in a reasonably short space of time; (2) the proposed merger would be less harmful than an alternative merger; and (3) if the alleged failing firm left the market its share of the customers would pass to the acquiring undertaking. In *Kali + Salz/MdK/Treuhand* the Commission found that the conditions were satisfied:

> the Commission has come to the conclusion that after the proposed merger a dominant position on the German market for agricultural potash will be strengthened. However, it has also concluded that K+S's dominant position would be reinforced even in the absence of the merger, because MdK would withdraw from the market in the foreseeable future if it was not acquired by an undertaking other than K+S; it can be practically ruled out that an undertaking other than K+S would acquire all or a substantial part of MdK.[56]

[51] Case IV/M.53 (1991).

[52] This case is discussed further in Chap 8, below.

[53] Navarro *et al*, above n 4, para 11.09.

[54] See para 91 of the *Horizontal Merger Guidance*, above n 1, quoted below. See E Rousseva and G Monti, 'Failing Firms in the Framework of the EC Merger Control Regulation' [1999] *EL Rev* 38, who argue that failing firms require special treatment under the ECMR. See also V Baccaro, 'Failing Firm Defence and Lack of Causality: Doctrine and Practice in Europe of Two Closely Related Concepts' [2004] *ECLR* 11.

[55] Case IV/M.308 [1994] OJ L 136/38.

[56] Ibid, at para 95.

On appeal the decision was upheld by the ECJ, which set out its view of the conditions necessary for the defence to operate.[57] The test formulated by the court was wider than that set out by the EC Commission, and the Court held that the defence would apply where 'the competitive structure resulting from the concentration would deteriorate in similar fashion even if the concentration did not proceed'.[58] Following this decision the Commission revisited the issue in *BASF/Eurodiol/Pantochim*.[59] In this case the second two parties had already entered into the protective regime provided for under Belgian bankruptcy law. BASF was not able to fulfil the *Kali + Salz* test as set out by the Commission as it could not demonstrate that it would necessarily attract the customers of the failing firms were they to exit the market. However, following the judgment of the ECJ in *France v Commission*, the Commission refined its test to a new four stage criterion: (1) the acquired undertaking would exit the market if not acquired by any other undertaking; (2) there was no other purchaser leading to a less harmful purchase; (3) the assets of the acquired undertaking would be forced out of the market if the acquisition were not to proceed; and (4) the competitive structure of the market would be no less bad following the acquisition than it would following exit of the failing firm.

By the time the *Horizontal merger guidance* was published the test was again set out as being threefold, in terminology that brought it close to the ECJ's formulation in *Commission v France*, although the third condition is, as has been pointed out, slightly easier to meet in the new formulation:[60]

> The Commission considers the following three criteria to be especially relevant for the application of a 'failing firm defence'. First, the allegedly failing firm would in the near future be forced out of the market because of financial difficulties if not taken over by another undertaking. Second, there is no less anti-competitive alternative purchase than the notified merger. Third, in the absence of a merger, the assets of the failing firm would inevitably exit the market.[61]

[57] Cases C–68/94 and C–30/94, *France v Commission* [1998] ECR I–1375, paras 112–116.

[58] Ibid, at para 114.

[59] Case COMP/M.2314 [2002] OJ L 132/45. This principle was also discussed in Case IV/M.993, *Bertelsmann/Kirch/Premiere*, (discussed in Chap 8). Here DG Comp stated that:

> 'normally there would be a presumption that a concentration which results in the creation or strengthening of a dominant position is the cause of this deterioration in the competitive structure. Consequently, the burden of proof of a missing linki of causality lies with the merging firms (at para 70).

In this case the Commission considered an argument relating not to a failing undertaking, but to a division within that undertaking, and raised the barrier even higher:

> 'Where the "failing division defence" and not the "failing company defence" is invoked, particularly high standards must be set for establishing that the conditions for a defence on the grounds of lack of a causal link have been met. If this were not so, any concentration involving the disposal of an allegedly unprofitable area of a business could be justified for merger-control purposes by a declaration on the part of the seller that, without the merger, it would be necessary to close down the seller's business in that area' (at para 71).

[60] See Navarro *et al*, above n 4, para 11.33.

[61] *Horizontal merger guidance*, above n 1, para 90.

As this test amply demonstrates the EC Commission is clearly prepared to permit a failing firm to exit the market if the purchase would create greater competitive harm than the exit. Indeed the general approach to the failing firm defence is to treat it with some scepticism. It is of course an easy claim for merging parties to make, but the fact that the Commission will accept the defence only in 'exceptional' cases demonstrates that the onus is on the parties to establish that the necessary criteria are met. Thus paragraph 91 of the *Horizontal merger guidance* provides that 'it is for the notifying parties to provide . . . all the relevant information necessary to demonstrate that the deterioration of the competitive structure that follows the merger is not caused by the merger'. There have been cases in which the EC Commission explicitly rejected the failing firm defence when it was raised by the parties. This was the case, for example, in *Aerospatiale-Alenia/de Havilland*,[62] in which the EC Commission accepted the argument neither that de Havilland would exit the market were the merger not to proceed, nor that no alternative purchaser could be found. In the case of *NewsCorp/Telempiù*,[63] however, the Commission cleared a merger leading to near monopoly on the ground in part that the target *would* exit the market. This case is discussed further in Chapter 8.

TECHNICAL AND ECONOMIC PROGRESS

Although the primary test of the ECMR is, as has been set out above, whether the merger may significantly impede effective competition, and this is the basis on which the *Horizontal merger guidance* is framed, there is, in Article 2(1)(b) ECMR reference to 'the development of technical and economic progress provided it is to the consumer's advantage and does not form an obstacle to competition'. This rubric has been considered in a number of mergers, although a reasonable approach is to be sceptical as to its value. Thus Cook and Kerse note first that this provision is somewhat illogical, and then explain that:

> Since, by definition, a proposed concentration will, in most cases, be held incompatible with the Common Market only if it leads to dominance which hinders effective competition there seems little scope to take account of the benefits of a market dominating merger or acquisition. The reference to 'technical and economic progress' in Article 2(1)(b) seems, therefore, to create false hopes. This is borne out by Commission merger decisions.[64]

It has also been recognised that there is 'considerable confusion'[65] about the extent to which this relates to the efficiency defence. Two leading cases are *MSG*

[62] Case IV/M.53 (1991).
[63] Case IV/M.2876.
[64] Cook and Kerse, above n 4, at 273.
[65] Noël, above n 42.

Media Service[66] and *Bertelsmann/Kirch/Premiere*,[67] in which the Commission blocked mergers in relation to digital broadcasting systems notwithstanding the fact that the parties advanced substantial arguments relating to the fact that the mergers would advance technical progress (see further Chapter 8).

COMMITMENTS

Where the Commission finds in Phase I or in Phase II that the concentration as notified either raises serious doubts about its compatibility with the common market or is likely significantly to impede effective competition, the parties may offer commitments aimed at redressing these concerns. These and the relevant procedures are discussed in Chapter 5, above.

RESTRICTIONS ANCILLARY TO CONCENTRATIONS

Mergers, particularly those taking effect at the large scale required for jurisdiction under the ECMR to be established, necessarily entail a large range of contractual arrangements. A potential concern is that those that are not at the core of the merger itself might fall to be examined under Article 81 EC, raising the prospect of legal complexity, uncertainty and delay. In practice this should not be an issue in respect of those restrictions which are necessary to give effect to the concentration. At recital (21) ECMR it is therefore stated that:

> This Regulation should also apply where the undertakings concerned accept restrictions directly related to, and necessary for, the implementation of the concentration. Commission decisions declaring concentrations compatible with the common market in application of this Regulation should automatically cover such restrictions, without the Commission having to assess such restrictions in individual cases. At the request of the undertakings concerned, however, the Commission should, in cases presenting novel or unresolved questions giving rise to genuine uncertainty, expressly assess whether or not any restriction is directly related to, and necessary for, the implementation of the concentration. A case presents a novel or unresolved question giving rise to genuine uncertainty if the question is not covered by the relevant Commission notice in force or a published Commission decision.[68]

[66] Commission Decision 94/922/EC.

[67] Case IV/M.993 (1998).

[68] The *Notice on restrictions directly related and necessary to concentrations* (see below) states that '[t]o the extent that cases involving exceptional circumstances have been previously addressed by the Commission in its published decisions, they do not constitute "novel or unresolved questions" within the meaning of recital 21 of the [ECMR]' (para 5). Restrictions falling under the safe harbour provided by the ECMR analysis do not fall under the terms of Regulation 1/2003, 1017/68 or 4056/86. This also excludes national courts from hearing disputes related to the legality of these restrictions on the basis either of Art 81 EC, or through the principles of the supremacy of EC law, on the basis of national competition laws relating to agreements. See G Metaxas and H Armengod, 'EC Merger Regulation and the Status of Ancillary Restrictions: Evolution of the European Commission's Policy' [2005] *ECLR* 500.

At three separate places in the ECMR itself it is declared that 'a decision declaring a concentration compatible shall be deemed to cover restrictions directly related and necessary to the implementation of the concentration'.[69] In order to provide further clarity on what provisions may fall within this rubric, and may therefore benefit directly from the clearance of the concentration itself, the EC Commission has published a *Notice on restrictions directly related and necessary to concentrations*.[70] Restrictions that are deemed *not* to be ancillary to the concentration remain subject to the potential application of Article 81 EC and of national competition law, and no inferences may be drawn from the fact that they may have been entered into in the wider context of a concentration that has been cleared by the EC Commission. Likewise where a concentration has been found not to fall within the jurisdiction conferred by the ECMR the status of any restrictions remains to be determined. Where the notifying undertakings expressly request that the EC Commission consider the status of ancillary restraints the simplified procedure, discussed below, is unlikely to be used.[71]

The EC Commission makes it clear that 'just because the parties regard them as such'[72] it does not mean that restrictions are ancillary to a concentration. The standard to be applied is an objective one. The purpose of the notice, read alongside previous Commission decisions, is 'to provide legal certainty to the undertakings concerned'.[73] The general principles relevant to the assessment of ancillary restrictions are set out in paragraphs 10–16 of the notice. Paragraph 10 provides in part that:

> All agreements which carry out the main object of the concentration, such as those relating to the sale of shares or assets of an undertaking, are integral parts of the concentration. In addition to these arrangements and agreements, the parties to the concentration may enter into other agreements which do not form an integral part of the concentration but can restrict the parties' freedom of action in the market. If such agreements contain ancillary restraints, these are automatically covered by the decision declaring the concentration compatible with the Common Market.

The essential requirements to a finding that a restriction is ancillary to a concentration are that the restriction is both directly related and necessary to the concentration.[74] In order for these criteria to apply the restrictions 'must be closely linked to the concentration itself',[75] and it is not sufficient simply that the

[69] See Arts 6(1)(b), 8(1) and 8(2).

[70] [2001] OJ C 188/5. The application of the Commission's procedure set out in this notice was cast into doubt by the CFI in Case T–251/00, *Lagardere SCA v Commission* [2002] ECR II–4825, [2003] 4 CMLR 20, but is, post-modernisation of the application of Arts 81 and 82 EC, consistent with the new law. See D Sinclair, 'Ancillary Restraints Under the Merger Regulation: The Commission's Approach Cast into Doubt by the Court of First Instance' [2003] *ECLR* 315.

[71] *Commission Notice on a simplified procedure for treatment of certain concentrations under Council Regulation (EC) No 139/2004*, [2000] OJ C 217/32, para 19.

[72] *Notice on restrictions directly related and necessary to concentrations*, para 11.

[73] Ibid, para 4.

[74] Ibid, para 11.

[75] Ibid, para 12.

restriction be entered into at the same time as the agreements effecting the concentration are entered into. Restrictions directly related to the concentration are those which 'are economically related to the main transaction and intended to allow a smooth transition to the changed company structure after the concentration'.[76] Restrictions are 'necessary' to the concentration when 'in the absence of those agreements, the concentration could not be implemented or could only be implemented under considerably more uncertain conditions, at substantially higher cost, over an appreciably longer period or with considerably greater difficulty'.[77] Such restrictions may include those aimed at: (1) protecting the value transferred; (2) maintaining commercial continuity; or (3) enabling the start up of a new entity.[78] Again it should be stressed that simply because the parties assert that the conditions are satisfied it does not mean that they will be found to be so. Thus the Commission states that:

> In determining whether a restriction is necessary, it is appropriate not only to take account of its nature, but also to ensure that its duration, subject matter and geographical field of application does not exceed what the implementation of the concentration reasonably requires. If equally effective alternatives are available for attaining the legitimate aim pursued, the undertakings must choose the one which is objectively the least restrictive of competition.[79]

Where a concentration is put into place by stages, restrictions relating to stages which fall short of the establishment of control required for the concentration to fall within Article 3 ECMR will not typically be ancillary to the concentration. An exception may be made for an agreement which preserves the structure of the target business during the acquisition process. Similarly an agreement between joint purchasers that neither will individually bid for the target company would be found to be an ancillary restriction.[80] Agreements aimed at facilitating the division of a company's assets following a joint purchase are also likely to be regarded as ancillary restrictions,[81] as are those that make the break up of a pre-existing economic entity proceed under reasonable conditions.[82]

Paragraphs 17–35 deal with three common types of restrictions: (1) noncompetition clauses; (2) licence agreements; and (3) purchase and supply obligations.

As regards non-competition clauses the Commission recognises that in order to obtain the full value of the asset transferred 'the acquirer must be able to benefit from some protection against competition from the vendor in order to

[76] Ibid, para 12.
[77] Ibid, para 13.
[78] Ibid, para 13.
[79] Ibid, para 13.
[80] Ibid, para 14.
[81] Ibid, para 15.
[82] Ibid, para 16.

gain the loyalty of customers and to assimilate and exploit the know-how'.[83] While restrictions which achieve this object are recognised to be necessary to the concentration, the safe-harbour is not an unlimited one. Such clauses will be valid only for periods of up to three years in cases in which the assets transferred include both know-how and goodwill, but only up to two years when goodwill alone is transferred.[84] When the only assets that are transferred are physical ones non-competition clauses will not be regarded as ancillary.[85] Non-competition clauses may be applied only in the geographical territory in which the vendor has offered the services or goods prior to the concentration, as the purchaser would not have been protected from competition outside this territory prior to the concentration.[86] For the same reasons the subject matter of the non-competition clauses must be limited to those goods and services offered by the vendor prior to the concentration.[87]

Intellectual property rights may be transferred as part of a concentration, but there may be situations in which some rights are retained by the original holder, in which case licences may be used as a vehicle to achieve the correct division of rights. Paragraph 28 of the notice provides that:

> Licences of patents, of similar rights,[88] or of know-how, can be considered necessary to the implementation of the concentration. They may equally be considered an integral part of the concentration and, in any event, need not be limited in time. These licences can be simple or exclusive and may be limited to certain fields of use, to the extent that they correspond to the activities of the undertaking transferred.

The Commission does not consider that it is necessary to impose territorial limitations on manufacture matching the territory of the transferred activity, although a licence granted by a seller to a buyer can contain the same territorial restrictions as would be permitted in the case of a non-competition obligation.[89]

Purchase and supply obligations may be necessary to prevent the disruption to a business that could follow its transfer, and obligations may be imposed on either the purchaser or the vendor as appropriate.[90] Such obligations may be imposed only for the length of time that is necessary to replace 'the relationship of dependency by autonomy in the market', and the Commission considers the limit to be five years.[91] Such obligations may be imposed in relation to fixed quantities, but may not be imposed for unlimited quantities, and may not confer exclusivity or preferred supplier or purchaser status.[92]

[83] *Notice on restrictions directly related and necessary to concentrations*, para 18.
[84] Ibid, para 20.
[85] Ibid, para 21.
[86] Ibid, para 22.
[87] Ibid, para 23.
[88] At para 31 the Commission includes rights in: trade marks, business names, design rights, copyrights and other similar rights.
[89] *Notice on restrictions directly related and necessary to concentrations*, above n 72, para 29.
[90] Ibid, para 32.
[91] Ibid, para 33.
[92] Ibid, para 34.

Part IV of the notice deals with the principles that are applicable to commonly encountered restrictions in the case of joint ventures falling within the ECMR, and modify slightly the above conditions to take into account the difference in market structure.[93]

THE SIMPLIFIED PROCEDURE

The Commission has published a *Notice on a simplified procedure for treatment of certain concentrations under Council Regulation (EC) No 139/2004*[94] which establishes a simplified procedure to be adopted in the case of concentrations 'on the basis that they do not raise competition concerns'.[95] Under the terms of the notice the Commission will adopt a short form decision within 25 working days of the date of notification, under the terms of Article 6(1)(b) ECMR.[96]

The first condition for the application of the simplified procedure is that two or more undertakings acquire joint control of a joint venture, provided that the latter has no or negligible activities within the EEA.[97] The second condition is that the merger is such that none of the parties is 'engaged in business activities in the same product or geographical market, or in a product market which is upstream or downstream of a product market in which any other party to the concentration is engaged'.[98] The third condition arises where the merger falls below certain market share thresholds. Where there is a horizontal merger resulting in a combined market share of less than 15 per cent,[99] or where vertical relationships of the merging parties arise such that no individual or combined market share is 25 per cent or more,[100] the simplified procedure will be applied. The final condition arises where a party acquires sole control over an undertaking over which it already has joint control.[101] Because the definition of

[93] See ibid, paras 36–44.

[94] [2000] OJ C 217/32.

[95] *Commission Notice on a simplified procedure for treatment of certain concentrations under Council Regulation (EC) No 139/2004*, above n 71, para 1.

[96] This is in the following terms:

> 'Where [the Commission] finds that the concentration notified, although falling within the scope of this Regulation, does not raise serious doubts as to its compatibility with the common market, it shall decide not to oppose it and shall declare that it is compatible with the common market.'

[97] *Commission Notice on a simplified procedure for treatment of certain concentrations under Council Regulation (EC) No 139/2004*, above n 71, para 5(a). This condition is met where the turnover of the JV and/or of the contributed activities is less than ?100m in the EEA *and* the total value of the assets transferred to the JV is less than ?100m in the EEA.

[98] Ibid, para 5(b).

[99] Ibid, para 5(c)(i).

[100] Ibid, para 5(c)(ii).

[101] Ibid, para 5(d). In some circumstances the Commission experience has shown that such mergers may still raise competition concerns, and may not qualify for the application of the simplified procedure. This may be the case, eg, 'where the former joint venture is integrated into the group or

the relevant market is crucial to the first three of these conditions the notifying parties are asked to 'provide information on all plausible alternative market definitions during the pre-notification phase'.[102] The simplified procedure will *not* be applied where the Commission finds it difficult to define the relevant markets or to determine the parties' shares within markets. The procedure is also unlikely to be applied to situations which raise novel legal issues of a general interest. At paragraph 8 of the Notice the Commission indicates that some cases may be excluded from the simplified procedure:

> Certain types of concentrations may increase the parties' market power, for instance by combining technological, financial or other resources, even if the parties to the concentration do not operate in the same market. Concentrations where at least two parties to the concentration are present in closely related neighbouring markets may also be unsuitable for the simplified procedure, in particular, where one or more of the parties to the concentration holds individually a market share of 25% or more in any product market in which there is no horizontal or vertical relationship between the parties but which is a neighbouring market to a market where another party is active. In other cases, it may not be possible to determine the parties' precise market shares. This is often the case when the parties operate in new or little developed markets. Concentrations in markets with high entry barriers, with a high degree of concentration or other known competition problems may also be unsuitable.[103]

If either a Member State or a third party expresses concerns about the merger which are substantiated within the time-limits laid down for comments the Commission will also adopt a full decision.[104] The application of the simplified procedure to mergers referred to or from the Commission under the provisions of Articles 4(4), 4(5), 9 or 22 ECMR are discussed in brief in Chapter 3 above.

The mechanisms relating to the simplified procedure are set out at paragraphs 15–18 of the Notice. First, the Commission points out at paragraph 15 that even in cases which are apparently unproblematic pre-notification contacts between the Commission and the parties are useful, and that certain issues, such as market definition, are better resolved, where possible, at the pre-notification stage. The remaining three paragraphs relate to the publication of the notification, the timing of the short-form decision, and its publication.

network of its remaining single controlling shareholder, whereby the disciplining constraints exercised by the potentially diverging incentives of the different controlling shareholders are removed and its strategic market position could be strengthened' (para 9). The Commission may also apply the normal Phase I procedure in cases where the prior acquisition of joint control of the undertaking in question has not been reviewed by itself or by a competent authority of a Member State (para 10).

[102] Ibid, para 6.

[103] The Commission may also revert to the standard Phase I procedure where concerns are raised in relation to the application of Art 2(4) ECMR (see Chap 5, above).

[104] *Commission Notice on a simplified procedure for treatment of certain concentrations under Council Regulation (EC) No 139/2004*, above n 71, para 12.

7

Collective Dominance and Coordinated Effects

INTRODUCTION

PRIOR TO THE entry into force of Regulation 139/2004 any text dealing with the EC merger control regime would, by force of necessity, have included a substantial section dealing with 'collective dominance'.[1] It will be recalled that the test to be applied under Regulation 4064/89 was whether a concentration would 'create or strengthen a dominant position as a result of which competition would be significantly impeded'.[2] This flowed from the fact that the legal basis of the ECMR was derived in part from Article 82 EC, and was broadly consistent with a theory of economic harm in which the focus lies on the 'unilateral effects' of a merger on the competitive environment.[3] As has been discussed in Chapter 2, however, not all detrimental effects of a merger may be characterised as unilateral. One potential harm might flow from the fact that in a more concentrated market (as might arise, for example, in the case of a four to three merger) the situation might arise in which firms were able to recognise their mutual interdependence, and to adjust their behaviour accordingly so as to create a situation in which *in the absence of any agreement* the firms act cooperatively rather than competitively. This situation of 'coordinated effects' is well-known to economists and is subject to a considerable amount of economic literature and debate.[4] There is a limit to which such conduct can be attacked post-merger under the application of rules relating to the control of anti-competitive agreements—Article 81 in the case of the EC, and the Chapter I Prohibition of the CA 98 in the case of the UK—as co-operation in such a situation is not necessarily dependent upon anything other than independently

[1] The terms 'joint dominance' and 'oligopolistic dominance' are sometimes also used in this context. The term 'collective dominance' will be used throughout this text unless an alternative formulation is used in a direct quotation.

[2] Art 2(2), (3) of Regulation 4064/89 [1990] OJ L 257/13.

[3] See Chap 2, above.

[4] The EC Commission Notice, *Guidelines on the assessment of horizontal mergers under the Council Regulation on the control of concentrations between undertakings* [2004] OJ C 31/3 (hereinafter the *horizontal merger guidance*), deals with the treatment of coordinated effects at paras 39–48. For a comprehensive treatment of the area see S Stroux, *US and EC Oligopoly Control* (The Hague, Kluwer Law International, 2004).

derived, intelligent responses to the realities of the market. It is generally recognised by those charged with the application of competition law that these oligopolistic markets present the greatest problems in terms of competition law enforcement. Steps may be taken, for example, to reduce the extent to which information may be exchanged between the undertakings on the market, but it is neither desirable nor practical to 'punish' undertakings for merely recognising that their conduct has an impact on their competitors who may respond with conduct which has an impact on them. In the UK this is precisely the argument which supported the retention in the EA 2002 of the ability to undertake a competition inquiry in relation to a market in which there may be no individual wrongdoing, but in which the market characteristics lead to an undesirable outcome.[5] In the context of the dominance test of the ECMR Stroux has noted that 'the dividing line between the natural functioning of a tightly oligopolistic market and oligopolistic dominance is a very subtle one, and is extremely hard to define'.[6]

The question arose early on in the application of EC competition law whether Article 82 EC could be applied to situations of abuse of collective dominance, and, the answer being in the affirmative,[7] the question then arose whether the approach to collective dominance could be read across to the ECMR. In the context of the ECMR in 1991 the EC Commission expressed the concern that a duopoly situation could give rise to an alignment in the behaviour of both competitors.[8] In a chain of cases the EC Commission and the ECJ dealt with this question, and the complex arguments of fact which were raised in the application of the principle in practice. This chain ended with the unsatisfactory result in *Airtours*,[9] which may reasonably be argued to be one of the more important factors leading to a change in the substantive test in Regulation 139/2004. It is unfortunate that the wording of the test set out in Regulation 4064/89 required the approach to these markets to be framed within the context of an approach to dominance. However, the removal of the exclusive reliance on this rubric within the application of Regulation 139/2004 does not remove the concerns relating to coordinated effects and their evaluation.[10] There are a number of

[5] See Part 4, EA 02, which replaced the monopoly provisions of the FTA 73.

[6] S Stroux, 'Collective Dominance under the Merger Regulation: A serious evidentiary reprimand for the Commission' [2002] *European Law Review* 736 at 744. See also O Black, 'Collusion and Co-ordination in EC Merger Control' [2003] *ECLR* 408.

[7] See, eg, the approach taken by the CFI in Joined Cases T–68, 77 and 78/89, *Società Italiana Vetro SpA v Commission* [1992] ECR II–1403.

[8] Case IV/M.12 *Varta/Bosch* (1991).

[9] Commission Decision 2000/276 *Airtours/First Choice* [2000] OJ L 93/1, on appeal Case T–342/99 *Airtours plc v Commission* [2002] ECR II-2585, [2002] 5 CMLR 7.

[10] It should be noted that the EC is not alone in applying merger control in situations giving rise to coordinated effects. Perhaps the most-discussed case is *H J Heinz/Beech-Nut* (US FTC, *In the Matter of H J Heinz Company; Milnot Holding Corporation; and Madison Dearborn Partners Capital LP*, Docket No 9295, 28 Nov 2000). Here a merger in the baby food market would have resulted in the post-merger company having a market share of 32%, while its leading competitor held a share of 65%, a combined share held by the two largest firms of 97%. The FTC found that 'no environment could be more conducive to coordinated interaction than a duopoloy and because

problematic issues arising in this area, but the dominant concern is how to identify correctly situations in which such coordinated effects may be expected to arise.[11]

CASE LAW

The first case in which there was substantial debate about the approach to collective dominance to be taken under the ECMR was *Nestlé/Perrier*.[12] In this case the proposed merger gave rise to the three largest suppliers of mineral water in France holding a joint market share of 82.3 per cent by value and 74 per cent by volume.[13] A number of factors led to concerns about the likelihood of coordinated conduct arising. However the Commission permitted a merger subject to obligations and conditions, but the available documentation, including the opinion of the Advisory Committee on Concentrations,[14] shows that there was in existence at the time the merger was being considered a range of views on whether the ECMR could be applied to mergers which might create a situation of collective dominance. In part confusion was created by the judgment of the CFI in *Società Italiana Vetro SpA v Commission*,[15] in which the CFI had discussed collective dominance as arising when there were 'economic links' between the undertakings concerned, but had not clarified whether the doctrine could be applied to situations in which there were no such links. Although the *Nestlé/Perrier* decision was appealed by employees' representatives the CFI found that the appeal was inadmissible,[16] and the approach taken by the Commission was not therefore subjected to judicial scrutiny.

of the substantial entry barriers in this market, it is without doubt that this duopoly is forever'. On appeal a request for an interim injunction was granted and the merger was abandoned (*FTC v H. J. Heinz Co*, 116 F Supp 2d 190 (DDC 2000), reversed in *FTC v H. J. Heinz Co*, 246 F 3d 708 (DC Cir 2001)). See J Baker, 'Efficiencies and High Concentration: Heinz Proposes to Acquire Beech-Nut' in JE Kwoka, Jr and LJ White (eds), *The Antitrust Revolution: Economics, Competition and Policy* (4th edn, New York, OUP, 2004). For an analysis of the approach taken in the US towards coordinated effects in merger control see R S Schlossberg (ed), *Mergers and Acquisitions: Understanding the Antitrust Issues* (2nd edn, Chicago, Ill, American Bar Association 2004), 116–26. A leading example in the UK is *BASF AG/Takeda Chemical Industries Limited*, Cm 5209 (July 2001). In its inquiry into this merger in the vitamins industry the CC was concerned by a past history of collusion in the industry, and discussed the issue of coordinated effects at some length. However, it also noted that: '[w]e expect that there would be a considerable degree of competitive pressure after the merger . . . We also believe that, while it is possible for tacit collusion to exist, any such situation would exist independently of, and would not be affected by, the merger'. For a discussion of the treatment of coordinated effects in UK merger control see N Parr, R Finbow and M Hughes, *UK Merger Control: Law and Practice* (2nd edn, London, Sweet & Maxwell 2005), paras 6.128–6.160.

[11] See, eg, D Parker, 'A Screening Device for Tacit Collusion Concerns' [2006] *ECLR* 424.

[12] Case COMP/M.190 [1992] OJ L 365/1.

[13] Para 48 of the decision.

[14] [1992] OJ C 319/3.

[15] Joined Cases T–68, 77 and 78/89, [1992] ECR II–1403.

[16] Case T–96/92, *Comité Central d'Entreprise de la Société Générale des Grandes Sources v Commission* [1992] ECR II-2579.

The second decision taken by the Commission in this area was *Kali + Salz/MDK/Treuhand*.[17] This case related to a full-function joint venture between two producers of potash and rock salt. The Commission found that the concentration would result in there being only two producers in a relevant geographic market, and at paragraph 57 of its decision argued that 'the record of the past behaviour of K+S and SCPA would lead to a situation of oligopolistic dominance'. The Commission pointed in part to a number of links between the relevant undertakings in the market, and also drew attention to the fact that it had previously made an infringement decision in respect of an export cartel operated by them.[18] Appeals against the decision were made, and the ECJ was obliged to consider whether the ECMR could be applied to situations of collective dominance.[19] The French government argued that the application of the ECMR to collective dominant situations was not authorised on the terms of the ECMR,[20] but its arguments were rejected by the ECJ, which noted that although the Regulation was silent on the issue it would be inconsistent with the intention of the Regulation not to extend its application to such situations. In a decision taken very shortly after this judgment the Commission seemed to indicate that it would find it difficult to satisfy the conditions the Court set out to establish that a position of collective dominance existed.[21]

[17] Case IV/M.308 [1994] OJ L 186/38.

[18] Commission Decision 73/212/EEC *Société Commerciale des Potasses et de l'Azote and Kali und Salz (formerly VDK)*, [1973] OJ L 217/3. The question of the extent to which past conduct should be relevant to a present merger inquiry has been discussed by G Robert and C Hudson, 'Past Co-ordination and the Commission Notice on the Appraisal of Horizontal Mergers' [2004] *ECLR* 163.

[19] Joined Cases C–68/94 and C–30/95, *French Republic v Commission; Société Commerciale des Potasses et de l'Azote (SCPA) and Entreprise Minière et Chimique (EMC) v Commission* [1998] ECR I–1375. At para 221 the ECJ made its first attempt to define collective dominance, focusing on: analysis of the market; factors which would encourage the undertakings to coordinate their activity; and the ability of the undertakings to adopt common behaviour, taking into account the actions of any remaining competitors and their customers. See further MGP Pérez, 'Collective Dominance Under the Merger Regulation' [1998] *EL Rev* 475, who argues that the result of the case was unsatisfactory in that it 'limited the discretion of the Commission in the economic assessment of the case, but without establishing clear rules'; J Ysewyn and C Caffarra, 'Two's Company, Three's a Crowd: The Future of Collective Dominance After the Kali & Salz Judgment' [1998] *ECLR* 468; S Bishop, 'Power and Responsibility: The ECJ's Kali-Salz Judgment' [1999] *ECLR* 37; and JS Venit, 'Two Steps Forward and No Steps Back: Economic Analysis and Oligopolistic Dominance after *Kali&Salz*' (1998) 35 *CML Rev* 1101.

[20] It relied on two arguments in particular: first, that Art 2 of Regulation 4064/89 did not import the words 'one or more undertakings' found in Art 82; and secondly upon the terms of recital (15) of the Regulation which suggested that a concentration would not be found to impede effective competition 'where the market share of the undertakings concerned does not exceed 25% . . .'. The AG also questioned the applicability of the ECMR to situations of collective dominance, arguing in particular that limited third party rights in the application of the ECMR procedures would limit the ability of other members of the 'oligopoly' to participate in the proceedings.

[21] Case IV/M.1016, *Price Waterhouse/Coopers & Lybrand*, Decision 1999/152 [1999] OJ L 50/27. The Commission noted that the Court 'emphasised that there is a strong burden of proof on the Commission in the case of an oligopolistic market which the Commission holds to be subject to collective dominance' (at para 104). In para 105 the Commission further pointed to the fact that 'in addition, the Court's judgment implies that evidence of the lack of effective competition between a group of suppliers held to be collectively dominant must be very strong, as must evidence of the

The approach taken by the ECJ in *Kali + Salz* was confirmed in *Gencor v Commission*[22] which followed a Commission decision to block a merger between two producers of platinum and rhodium. The merger would have reduced the number of producers from three to two, and the Commission found that the resulting duopoly would fulfil the conditions required to constitute a position of collective dominance. The Commission made clear in this decision its view of collective dominance, arguing that it:

> can occur where a mere adaptation by members of the oligopoly to market conditions causes anti-competitive parallel behaviour whereby the oligopoly becomes dominant. Active collusion would therefore not be required for members of the oligopoly to become dominant and to behave to an appreciable extent independently of their remaining competitors, their customers and, ultimately their consumers.[23]

On appeal the parties argued that the Commission had not demonstrated that the necessary economic links were in place to support a finding of collective dominance. The CFI again confirmed the approach taken by the EC Commission, and, at paragraphs 104–105 of its judgment, held that:

> there is no reason whatsoever in legal or economic terms to exclude from the notion of economic links the relationship of interdependence existing between the parties to a tight oligopoly within which, in a market with the appropriate characteristics, in particular in terms of market concentration, transparency and product homogeneity, those parties are in a position to anticipate one another's behaviour and are therefore strongly encouraged to align their conduct in the market, in particular in such a way as to maximise their joint profits by restricting production with a view to increasing prices. In such a context, each trader is aware that highly competitive action on its part designed to increase its market share (for example a price cut) would provoke identical action by the others, so that it would derive no benefit from its initiative.

It has been pointed out that, given the nature of the market in *Gencor*, once the CFI had removed the need to rely on structural links 'it became very easy to find collective dominance'.[24]

This recognition that collective dominance could be established purely on the basis of 'interdependence' has thrown the test open to economic analysis, rather

weakness of competitive pressure from other suppliers'. In this case the Commission found that some of the factors referred to in *Gencor/Lonhro* (see below) were also factors in the accountancy market. However, post-merger there would have been five competitors in the relevant market, and the Commission stated that '[f]rom a general viewpoint, collective dominance involving more than three or four suppliers is unlikely simply because of the complexity of the interrelationships involved, and the consequent temptation to deviate; such a situation is unstable and untenable in the long term' (at para 103).

[22] Case T–102/96, *Gencor Ltd v Commission* [1999] ECR II–753, [1999] 4 CMLR 971, an appeal from Case IV/M.619, Decision 97/26, *Gencor/Lonhro* [1997] OJ L 11/30.

[23] Ibid, at para 140.

[24] GP Elliott, 'The Gencor Judgment: Collective dominance, remedies and extraterritoriality under the Merger Regulation' [1999] *EL Rev* 638 at 645. See also C Caffarra and K-U Kühn, 'Joint Dominance: The CFI Judgment on Gencor/Lonrho' [1999] *ECLR* 355; and V Korah, 'Gencor v Commission: Collective Dominance' [1999] *ECLR* 337.

than to an elaborate exercise of attempting to establish the existence of links in practice between the relevant parties. However, although this approach is to be welcomed, it is not in practice an easy area in which to demonstrate, ex ante, that the necessary interdependence will exist and is sustainable. The problems were clearly demonstrated in the course of the application of the ECMR to the *Airtours/First Choice*[25] merger. This case was the first in which the Commission blocked a merger that would, it argued, have led to collective dominance held by three undertakings which would together have held approximately 80 per cent of the relevant market, and in which a number of significant fringe competitors existed. The relevant undertakings operated in the UK market for short-haul foreign package holidays, travel agency services, and the supply to tour operators of seats on charter flights to short-haul destinations. The Commission set out at paragraph 87 of the decision the conditions that it argued needed to be satisfied to sustain a finding of collective dominance. These included: product homogeneity; low demand growth; low price sensitivity of demand; similar cost structures of the main suppliers; substantial barriers to entry such that any coordination would not be subject to shocks; and insignificant countervailing buyer power'. The Commission also stressed, in the face of protests from Airtours, that a finding of collective dominance did not require that there be any active collusion between the parties alleged to be holding the position. Thus it stated at paragraph 53 that 'active collusive conduct of any kind is not a prerequisite for collective dominance to occur. It is sufficient that adaptation to market conditions causes an anti-competitive outcome'.[26] The argument the Commission made was that collective dominance would not be achieved by permitting a cooperative solution to price-setting,[27] but by encouraging a cooperative solution to the problem of setting capacities (supply) at the point at which the companies purchased the necessary inputs to their package holidays that would be offered in the following season. These decisions would be taken some 18 months prior to the sales, a factor that further complicated the analysis. The Commission also argued that the collectively dominant undertakings would be in a position effectively and swiftly to retaliate against any member of the oligopoly which departed from this common strategy. Finally the Commission took the position that those participants in the industry who would not share the collective dominance and new entrants would not be in a position to undermine the stability of the mechanism it outlined.

The approach taken by the Commission was criticised by a number of commentators, and was subject to strong rebuff by the CFI. Thus it has been argued that '[i]n this decision it appeared that the Commission was struggling to

[25] Case IV/M.1524, Decision 2000/276 [2000] OJ L 93/1.

[26] It will be noted that here the Commission is largely parroting the statement made in this respect in *Gencor/Lonhro*, above n 22, at para 140.

[27] A particular hurdle to such a strategy lay in the significant amount of product differentiation in this market, which would make price comparisons, and hence detection of divergence from any cooperative solution, difficult.

impose a model on a market that did not really fit it', and that in order to achieve this fit 'the Commission focussed its assessment almost exclusively on a discussion of the "rational incentives" that existed for members of the oligopoly to collude in terms of higher profits'.[28] Writing before the appeal against the decision was heard, Cook and Kerse sounded a note of alarm: '[t]he decision represents the most significant development in EC merger control since the adoption of the Regulation itself. Companies and their advisers will need to consider their acquisition strategies carefully and anticipate where he Commission might have concerns about oligopolies emerging'.[29] NERA argued that:

> the real element of surprise in the *Airtours* case concerns the nature of the industry involved. Unlike platinum or potash, package holidays are differentiated, branded consumer products. Furthermore, a brief look at the history of the industry indicates a market in which there has been a huge variability in supplier shares and profitability and in which high profile exits (such as the collapse of the industry number two ILG in the early 1990s) have been counterbalanced by instances of equally dramatic entry and growth.[30]

However, even before the outcome of the appeal was known DG Comp appeared to moderate its position in two cases, *MAN/Auwärter*[31] and *UPM-Kymmene/Haindl*,[32] taking a more restrictive approach to the analysis of collective dominance than it had in *Airtours*.

The Commission decision was overturned on appeal, and the CFI was strongly critical of the conclusions reached by the Commission and the evidence on which this capacity setting was based.[33] The CFI, reaching very different conclusions from the Commission, found that the market conditions were not conducive to the parties determining a common strategy in respect of capacity setting, on the ground that capacity was at least as heterogeneous as prices, and that it would be quite difficult even by formal agreement to reach a communal solution to this problem. Secondly, the Court held that if it *were* possible to reach a cooperative solution to capacity setting there would be incentives for each individual member of the oligopoly to cheat, and that, contrary to the argument made by the Commission, no robust mechanism existed to punish this. Given that past evidence showed that the companies had at times failed significantly to anticipate forward demand for their packages, it was unlikely that a punishment mechanism which relied on an 18 month time-lag would be effective. Finally the CFI argued that the smaller companies in the industry,

[28] E Navarro, A Font, J Folguera and J Briones, *Merger Control in the EU* (2nd edn, Oxford, OUP, 2005), para 7.04.

[29] CJ Cook and CS Kerse, *EC Merger Control* (3rd edn, London, Sweet and Maxwell 2000), para 5.7.6.

[30] NERA, Newsletter (2000) (no longer available).

[31] Case COMP/M.2201 (2001).

[32] Case COMP/M.2498 (2001).

[33] At para 294 of its judgment, eg, the CFI held that the Commission decision: 'far from basing its prospective analysis on cogent evidence, is vitiated by a series of errors of assessment as to factors fundamental to any assessment of whether a collective dominant position might be created'.

excluded by the Commission from the collective dominant position and dismissed as being unable to undermine any cooperative solution, were in fact sufficiently active, with access to distribution sources for their products, to discipline any attempt by the larger parties collectively to control supply.

At paragraph 62 of its decision the CFI set out the three conditions that it required to be fulfilled for a finding of collective dominance to be sustained:

> —first, each member of the dominant oligopoly must have the ability to know how the other members are behaving in order to monitor whether or not they are adopting the common policy. As the Commission specifically acknowledges, it is not enough for each member of the dominant oligopoly to be aware that interdependent market conduct is profitable for all of them but each member must also have a means of knowing whether the other operators are adopting the same strategy and whether they are maintaining it. There must, therefore, be sufficient market transparency for all members of the dominant oligopoly to be aware, sufficiently precisely and quickly, of the way in which the other members' market conduct is evolving;
>
> —secondly, the situation of tacit co-ordination must be sustainable over time, that is to say, there must be an incentive not to depart from the common policy on the market. As the Commission observes, it is only if all the members of the dominant oligopoly maintain the parallel conduct that all can benefit. The notion of retaliation in respect of conduct deviating from the common policy is thus inherent in this condition. In this instance, the parties concur that, for a situation of collective dominance to be viable, there must be adequate deterrents to ensure that there is a long-term incentive in not departing from the common policy, which means that each member of the dominant oligopoly must be aware that highly competitive action on its part designed to increase its market share would provoke identical action by the others, so that it would derive no benefit from its initiative . . .;
>
> —thirdly, to prove the existence of a collective dominant position to the requisite legal standard, the Commission must also establish that the foreseeable reaction of current and future competitors, as well as of consumers, would not jeopardise the results expected from the common policy.

This judgment was welcomed in a number of quarters, and it has been argued that it 'articulates a useful analytical framework for assessing collective dominance concerns. . . . The three-step procedure identified by the CFI—assessment of transparency, retaliation possibilities and external constraints—represent an important improvement on the checklist approach commonly used by the Commission.'[34] The position following the judgment was that in order to show

[34] RBB Economics, 'Airtours/First Choice: CFI Holds Commission to Account', RBB Brief 2, June 2002. See also F Montag and A Bonin, 'Collective Dominance in Merger Cases after Airtours' in G Drauz and M Reynolds (eds), *EC Merger Control: A Major Reform in Progress* (Richmond, Richmond Law and Tax, 2003), at 323–42; B Etter, 'The Assessment of Mergers in the EC under the Concept of Collective Dominance: An Analysis of the Recent Decisions and Judgments by an Economic Approach' (2000) 23(3) *Journal of World Competition* 103; M Motta, 'EC Merger Policy and the Airtours Case', [2000] *ECLR* 199; S Stroux, 'Collective Dominance under the Merger Regulation: A Serious Evidentiary Reprimand for the Commission' [2002] *EL Review* 736; L Farrell, 'Airtours plc v Commission' [2002] *Comp Law* 207; J Langer, 'The *Airtours* Judgment: a Welcome Lecture on Oligopolies, Economics and Joint Dominance' (2003) 10 *Columbia Journal of European Law* 105; R O'Donoghue and C Feddersen, 'Case T–342/99, *Airtours plc v Commission*' (2002) 39

that a position of collective dominance would be achieved by the merger DG Comp would have to demonstrate first that, pre-merger, the position was a competitive one, or that any equilibrium was 'non-cooperative',[35] and secondly that, post-merger, the members of the oligopoly would be able to achieve a coordinated solution *because* of the merger.

Following the *Airtours* judgment the next substantial action taken by the EC Commission in this area was in *MCI WorldCom/Sprint*,[36] in which the Commission stated that the position it took in earlier cases was merely one possible approach, and that other approaches were also possible. The Commission argued that the fundamental questions to be asked in the application of merger control in oligopoly situations were the following: did the structure of the market create incentives for undertakings to engage in parallel behaviour?; would it be possible for competitors to monitor others' behaviour?; would there be disincentives (punishment mechanisms) to persuade competitors not to deviate from a cooperative solution?; and would customers be able to prevent parallel conduct? It has been argued that this formulation:

> seems to ignore the fact that [the first three questions] are inextricably linked with each other, in so far as it may be inferred that [the third question] implicitly refers to punishment and retaliation. It is unclear how the question of incentives can be raised on its own, as a distinct question from the issue of monitoring and retaliation. These questions do not address either of the fundamental issues concerning oligopolies, the sustainability or the stability of parallel behaviour.[37]

Even following the damning *Airtours* judgment it was clear that the EC Commission had not abandoned its efforts to regulate mergers which gave rise to narrow oligopolies, and it was right not to do so. However, had the substantive test set out in the ECMR not been amended it is likely that its efforts to do so may have been continued to be frustrated by the complexities of making the necessary evaluations ex ante within the framework of a dominance test.[38] The new substantive test, although it has not yet been significantly tested in this area, appears to make the control of such mergers easier, as the Commission no longer has to demonstrate that a dominant position has been created.

CML Rev 1171; and H Haupt, 'Collective Dominance Under Article 82 EC and EC Merger Control in the Light of the *Airtours* Judgment' [2002] *ECLR* 434. For a different view, arguing that 'the judgment is no more than a distillation and summation of the status of the law as established in *Gencor v Commission*', see A Nikpay and F Houwen, 'Tour de Force or a Little Local Turbulence? A Heretical View on the *Airtours* Judgment' [2003] *ECLR* 193.

[35] Para 63 of the *Airtours* judgment, above n 9.

[36] Case COMP/M.1741 [2003] OJ L 300/1. See further Chap 8, below.

[37] Navarro *et al*, above n 28 para 7.24.

[38] See generally J Fingleton, 'Does Collective Dominance Provide Suitable Housing for All Anti-competitive Oligopolistic Mergers?' in G Drauz and M Reynolds (eds), *EC Merger Control: A Major Reform in Progress* (Richmond, Richmond Law and Tax, 2003), at 343–57.

At the time of writing the most recent case in which the CFI has discussed the approach to collective dominance is *Impala*.[39] Here the Commission cleared the Sony/BMG merger,[40] having raised concerns in the SO that it would lead to the creation of a collective dominant position in two music markets. Following a challenge by a third party the CFI examined in some detail the evidence relating to collective dominance available in the markets in question. The approach set out in *Airtours* was followed. However, the CFI indicated that a flexible approach could be taken to the establishment of those criteria:

> although the three conditions . . . are indeed also necessary, they may, however, in the appropriate circumstances, be established indirectly on the basis of what may be a very mixed series of indicia and items of evidence relating to the signs, manifestations and phenomena inherent in the presence of a collective dominant position.
>
> Thus, in particular, close alignment of prices over a long period, especially if they are above a competitive level, together with other factors typical of a collective dominant position, might, in the absence of an alternative reasonable explanation, suffice to demonstrate the existence of a collective dominant position, even where there is no firm direct evidence of strong market transparency, as such transparency may be presumed in such circumstances.[41]

In this case prices had been aligned over the previous six years, even though the products were differentiated (as each CD album is different), and prices were held at a stable level even though demand had fallen. The CFI held that in the absence of evidence to the contrary this would indicate the existence of a collective dominant position when combined with an oligopolistic market and stable market shares.[42]

THE APPROACH SET OUT IN THE HORIZONTAL MERGER GUIDANCE

The economic approach, including some comment on the approach taken in the *Horizontal merger guidance*, has been briefly introduced in Chapter 2. The guidelines first introduce the general principles of coordinated effects[43] and stress that coordination 'is more likely to emerge in markets where it is relatively simple to reach a common understanding on the terms of coordination'.[44] Then, following the approach set out by the CFI in *Airtours*, the Commission states that three further conditions need to be satisfied in order for any such coordination to be sustainable. These are that: (1) the coordinating firms need to be able to monitor adherence to the cooperative strategy; (2) there must be some

[39] Case T–464/04, *Independent Music Publishers and Labels Association (Impala, international association) v Commission* judgment of 13 July 2006 (this case is also discussed in Chap 8, below).

[40] Case COMP/M.3333 *Sony/BMG* (2004).

[41] Above n 39, paras 251–252.

[42] Ibid, para 253.

[43] Ibid, paras 39–43.

[44] Ibid, para 41.

credible deterrent mechanism that can be adopted if the strategy is not adhered to;[45] and (3) the reaction of outsiders, including potential entrants into the market, and customers, should not be capable of undermining the cooperatively achieved solution.

The determination of a coordinated strategy will be facilitated where firms can 'easily arrive at a common perception as to how the coordination should work'.[46] For this to be likely it is necessary that the firms would take roughly similar views on similar situations. The presence of industry mavericks in particular would work against the achievement of a coordinated strategy. As the Commission recognises, such an 'agreement' is more likely in markets which are relatively simple and stable, where there are a limited number of industry participants, and where the product is homogeneous. It is no surprise, then, that the case examples dealt with above include potash and platinum. However, the foreign package holiday business does not, at first sight, seem to fit this pattern.[47] In particular the guidelines state that:

> Firms may find it easier to reach a common understanding on the terms of coordination if they are relatively symmetric, especially in terms of cost structures, market shares, capacity levels and levels of vertical integration. Structural links such as

[45] A deterrent mechanism in this context does not require that the other members of the oligopoly agree on a punishment strategy, as might be the case in a cartel arrangement, but rather that, having detected defection from the profit-maximising common strategy, other members of the oligopoly respond competitively in a way that brings detriment to the rogue member, but which maximises their position given that defection has taken place. If the rogue was able to maximise their profits in the long term by departing from a cooperative solution then in fact the cooperative solution does not exist. In Case T–464/04 *Independent Music Publishers and Labels Association (Impala, international association) v Commission*, judgment of 13 July 2006 (discussed above) the CFI held that: '[t]he mere existence of effective deterrent mechanisms is sufficient, in principle, since if the members of the oligopoly conform with the common policy, there is no need to resort to the exercise of a sanction' (at para 466).

[46] *Horizontal merger guidance*, [2004] OJ C 31/5, para 44. Any explicit contact between firms to facilitate the determination of the coordinating points and mechanism would likely be an infringement of Art 81 EC. However, the Commission notes at para 51 that more informal mechanisms may be used which could be lawful:

> 'In some markets where the general conditions may seem to make monitoring of deviations difficult, firms may nevertheless engage in practices which have the effect of easing the monitoring task, even when these practices are not necessarily entered into for such purposes. These practices, such as meeting-competition or most-favoured-customer clauses, voluntary publication of information, announcements, or exchange of information through trade associations, may increase transparency or help competitors interpret the choices made.'

Although these comments are made in the context of monitoring, rather than determining, a coordinated strategy, they may also hold true in relation to the first problem. Thus, eg, a speech at a trade association meeting or a comment to the media may send a signal to other industry participants as to the terms on which coordination could be reached. It is almost impossible to apply competition law to curtail such situations, unless a clear pattern of behaviour indicates the existence of a concerted practice.

[47] Indeed, in its 1997 report, *Foreign Package Holidays: a report on the supply in the UK of tour operators' services and travel agents' services in relation to foreign package holidays* Cm 3813, the MMC had found that the industry was dynamic and competitive, although it expressed concerns about the degree of vertical integration amongst the larger players in the industry.

cross-shareholding or participation in joint ventures may also help in aligning incentives among the coordinating firms.[48]

The fact that a firm which is coordinating with others has an incentive to 'cheat' on the arrangement is well understood.[49] However, cheating is an optimal strategy only where the other oligopoly participants do not deviate from the coordinated strategy in response. The first condition to be fulfilled in this respect to maintain coordination is that the market be a transparent one, such that the participants are able to determine if one of their cohort is not adhering to the agreed strategy. As the Commission states, 'when evaluating the level of transparency in the market, the key element is to identify what firms can infer about the actions of other firms from the available information'.[50] The ability of firms to discern the actions of others will be hindered where the competitive environment is generally unstable, or where transactions are negotiated individually and the details remain confidential. The second, related, criterion is that 'the consequences of [detected] deviation are sufficiently severe to convince coordinating firms that it is in their best interest to adhere to the terms of coordination'.[51] Retaliation is most likely where it may be swiftly carried out, and where it is of little cost to those retaliating. However, even where retaliation carries a cost this does not mean that it will not take place, the question being whether the cost is outweighed by the long-term benefits of securing general compliance to the coordinated strategy.

Finally in its guidelines the Commission points to the de-stabilising effect that 'outsiders' may have on the ability to reach and adhere to a coordinated solution. This may flow typically from two sources: other competitors (or entrants) who are able to respond with lower prices or increased capacity; and customers who are able to apply buyer power to constrain the actions of the oligopoly.

REGULATION 139/2004

The very fact that the EC Commission pays such attention to coordinated effects in its horizontal merger guidance is itself evidence of the fact that the oligopoly problem has not been eliminated by the change in the wording of the substantive test. Although the need to establish 'collective dominance' is no longer present, as the Commission is no longer shoe-horned into framing its

[48] Note 46 above, at para 48 (footnotes omitted).

[49] Arguments derived from the early application of game theory suggested that firms will always have an incentive to cheat, and that cooperative oligopoly outcomes cannot be sustained. However, in the case of any game played in stages—as is the case in a market where transactions regularly take place – such that players can learn from past events, and where the end-date of the game is not known, this argument does not hold, and long-term cooperation may be both rational and achievable (see Chapter 2, above).

[50] Ibid, para 50 (footnotes omitted).

[51] Ibid, para 52.

arguments within the 'dominance' restriction, it remains the case that where the Commission objects to a merger on the ground that the substantial impediment to effective competition arises from a coordinated, rather than a unilateral, effect, it must demonstrate that this coordinated effect is likely. The case law analysed in this chapter and the response set out in the guidelines go directly to this point, and remain applicable within the new system.

8

Final Decisions and Remedies

INTRODUCTION

AT THE OUTSET of this chapter it should be noted that the designation 'final decision' applies here to a decision taken where the merging parties have pressed the Commission to the end, and have sought approval of the merger without abandoning it at an earlier stage. In practice earlier stages in the process may in fact be 'final' if it becomes clear to the parties that there is little likelihood of the merger being approved. Article 8, however, must be used in any case in which Article 6(1)(c) ECMR has been applied—a procedure which itself is unusual—unless the parties abandon the proposal.[1] Article 8 of the ECMR sets out the 'powers of decision of the Commission' in relation to the substantive assessment of qualifying concentrations, and makes provision for the taking of a number of different decisions relating to the acceptability of a concentration. These decisions are the following:

> ECMR, Article 8(1): the Commission may issue a decision declaring a concentration compatible with the common market, where the conditions set out in Articles 2(2) and (4) are applicable.[2]
>
> ECMR, Article 8(2): the Commission may issue decisions as for Article 8(1) where the parties have offered commitments or modifications to the merger which render it compatible with the common market. Such conditions and commitments may be attached to the decision and are enforceable.
>
> ECMR, Article 8(3): the Commission may issue a decision declaring a concentration incompatible with the common market, where the conditions set out in Articles 2(3) or (4) apply.[3]
>
> ECMR, Article 8(4): where concentrations have been implemented in contravention of the terms of the ECMR, or in contravention of conditions or commitments attached to decisions taken under Article 8(2) the Commission

[1] Art 6(1)(c) ECMR.

[2] Art 2(2) ECMR relates to concentrations 'which would not significantly impede effective competition in the common market'. Art 2(4) ECMR relates to JVs which coordinate the competitive behaviour of undertakings which remain competitive.

[3] Art 2(3) ECMR applies to concentrations 'which would significantly impede effective competition, in the common market or in a substantial part of it'. Decisions taken on the basis of Art 8(3) are discussed in more detail below.

may: (i) require the undertakings concerned to dissolve the concentration;[4] or may 'order any other appropriate measure to ensure that the undertakings concerned dissolve the concentration or take other restorative measures as required in its decision'.[5]

ECMR, Article 8(5): interim measures 'appropriate to restore or maintain conditions of effective competition' where concentrations have been implemented in contravention of the ECMR, or of a condition attached to a decision.

In the case of decisions taken under Articles 8(1) or (2) ECMR the EC Commission may revoke the decision where it is based on incorrect information supplied by one of the relevant undertakings, or where the decision has been obtained by deceit.[6] All decisions taken shall be notified to the undertakings concerned, and to the competent authorities of the Member States.[7]

ARTICLE 8(1) ECMR—COMPATIBILITY

Where a compatibility decision has been made the parties are protected from all further legal action in the EC in relation to the merger as cleared. This safety does not, however, apply where the decision was obtained on the basis of 'incorrect' information provided by the parties,[8] or where the parties breach an obligation attached to the Decision.[9] The Commission has only twice used this power, and on the second occasion its revocation decision was overturned on appeal to the CFI. In the first case, *Sanofi/Synthelabo*,[10] the Commission revoked its compatibility decision after holding that the parties had failed properly to describe their activities in the original notification.[11] In the second case the Commission itself made a mistake when it dealt with two JV cases, having treated as ancillary restraints terms that it later identified as being central to the transactions. On appeal the CFI held that the legitimate expectations of the parties had been breached as it was not they who had infringed the ECMR procedures.[12]

[4] Art 8(4)(b) first indent ECMR.
[5] Art 8(4)(b) second indent ECMR.
[6] Art 8(6) ECMR.
[7] Art 8(8)ECMR.
[8] Art 8(6)(a) ECMR.
[9] Art 8(6)(b) ECMR.
[10] Case IV/M.1397 (1999).
[11] The merger was later cleared following a re-notification and the opening of a new procedure.
[12] Cases COMP/JV.40 *Canal+/Lagardere/Canalsatellite* (2000) and COMP/JV.47 *Canal+/Lagardere/Liberty Media* (2000); on appeal Case T–251/00, *Lagardere and Canal+ v Commission* [2002] ECR II-4825.

ARTICLE 8(2) ECMR—REMEDIES AND MODIFICATION

In October 2005 Neelie Kroes, the Competition Commissioner, stated that the Commission 'should only accept remedies that clearly and unambiguously eliminate the identified threats to competition'.[13] At the same time commentators point to the fact that conditional clearances are increasingly complicated, with the Commission accepting complex remedies packages that may include both divestiture and behavioural commitments.[14] Regulation 139/2004 does not give the Commission the power to impose conditions unilaterally on the merging parties so as to render a concentration compatible with the Common Market. In the case of concentrations which have already been implemented the Commission may initiate steps to render the concentration compatible with the common market.[15] However, in the case of a notified contemplated concentration it is for the parties to suggest modifications or to offer divestiture commitments, although the extent to which such suggestions may be necessary is likely to emerge during the course of pre- and post-notification contacts with the Commission.[16] The powers of decision are those set out in Article 8 ECMR, and paragraph (2) provides that:

> The Commission may attach to its decision conditions and obligations intended to ensure that the undertakings concerned comply with the commitments they have entered into vis-à-vis the Commission with a view to rendering the concentration compatible with the Common Market.

Conditions and obligations are to be distinguished, in that conditions are commitments to change the market structurally, while obligations are the

[13] Commission Press release, IP/05/1327, 'Mergers: Commission analysis of past merger remedies provides guidance for future cases', 21 Oct 2005. This statement is consistent with the requirements of the ECMR (see below). The *Merger Remedy Study* (2005), is discussed below.

[14] See, eg, S Holmes and S Turnbull, 'Remedies in Merger Cases: Recent Developments' [2002] *ECLR* 499.

[15] Art 8(4) ECMR. See, eg, Case COMP/M.2416 *Tetra Laval/Sidel II* (2001), discussed below.

[16] The following figures give some indication of the extent to which commitments are offered and accepted:

	2000	2001	2002	2003
Notifications	345	335	277	212
Final decisions	345	340	275	231
Article 8(2) decisions	15	15	7	8
Article 8(3) decisions (prohibition)	2	5	0	0

Source: EC Commission, *Thirty-Third Annual Report on Competition Policy* (Luxembourg, Office for Official Publications of the EC, 2003), pp 92 and 301.

implementing steps necessary to fulfil the commitments made.[17] The procedure relating to the offering of commitments by the parties to the Commission has been addressed in Chapter 5. In this part of the text the attention is purely on the nature of the conditions and obligations attached to decisions.[18] The major Commission instruments in this area are the *Notice on remedies* (hereinafter *Remedies Notice*),[19] and the *Best Practice Guidelines: The Commission's Model texts for Divestiture Commitments and the Trustee Mandate under the EC Merger Regulation* (hereinafter *Divestiture Best Practice*). Both of these are, as of mid-2006, open for consultation as part of a revision process. The *Notice on remedies* was published in December 2000, reflecting a perceived need for transparency in an area which had become increasingly important.[20] Remedies need not be offered to the Commission unless it has first demonstrated that the concentration as notified raises competition concerns, but it is the responsibility of the relevant parties to demonstrate to a satisfactory standard that the remedies, if adopted, would ease these competition concerns. In the *Remedies Notice* the Commission states that 'the parties are required to show clearly, to the Commission's satisfaction in accordance with its obligations under the [ECMR] that the remedy restores conditions of effective competition in the common market on a permanent basis'.[21] At paragraph 7 of the *Remedies Notice* the Commission explains that:

> In assessing whether or not a remedy will restore effective competition the Commission will consider all relevant factors relating to the remedy itself, including *inter alia* the type, scale and scope of the remedy proposed, together with the likelihood of its successful, full and timely implementation by the parties. Moreover, these

[17] 'It is important to note that there are different legal consequences for breaches of conditions as opposed to obligations, and the aim of drawing the distinction between conditions and obligations in the decisions is to ensure that there can be no doubt about the implications of failure to comply with the different parts of the commitments. In the case of a breach of a condition (ie, the commitment to divest a certain asset), the Commission's decision will automatically be void. If one of the implementing steps should not be fulfilled (ie, a deadline not respected), the Commission, if required, will make full use of its power to withdraw the decision and to impose fines and penalty payments': M Monti, 'The Commission Notice on Merger Remedies—One Year After', Speech, Paris, 18 Jan 2002, available at the DG Comp website.

[18] See, generally, F Leveque and H Shelanski, *Merger Remedies in American and European Union Competition Law* (Cheltenham, Edward Elgar, 2003), and in particular M Motta, M Polo and H Vasconcelos, 'Merger Remedies in the European Union: An Overview', at 106–28. See also D Went, 'The Acceptability of Remedies Under the EC Merger Regulation: Structural Versus Behavioural' [2006] *ECLR* 455; NC Ersbøll, 'Commitments under the Merger Regulation', [2001] *ECLR* 357; and G Alpa, 'Mergers: Remedies and Freedom of Contract' [2004] *EBLR* 129.

[19] *Commission Notice on remedies acceptable under Council Regulation (EEC) No 4064/89 and under Commission Regulation (EC) No 447/98* [2001] OJ C 68/3.

[20] Speaking in 2002 Mario Monti acknowledged that 'the Commission's approach to remedies as set out in the Notice was influenced by the FTC's previous study on the divestiture process, which demonstrated that some remedies secured by the FTC had proved less effective than intended. Furthermore the EU and US antitrust authorities discussed their respective approaches to remedies within the framework of a working group on merger control': Monti, above n 17.

[21] *Remedies Notice*, above n 19, para 7. The CFI confirmed in Case T–102/96, *Gencor v Commission* [1999] ECR II–753, at para 316 that the fundamental aim of remedies is to ensure that market structures are competitive.

> factors have to be judged by reference to the structure and particular characteristics of the market in which the competition concerns arise, including of course the position of the parties and other players on the market. It follows that it is incumbent on the parties from the outset to remove any uncertainties as to any of these factors which might cause the Commission to reject the remedy proposed.

Remedies should not need monitoring once they are implemented. This therefore reflects a bias in favour of structural, as opposed to conduct, remedies.[22] In the leading case of *Gencor v Commission*[23] the CFI stated, at paragraph 319, that structural remedies:

> prevent once and for all, or at least for some time, the emergence or strengthening of the dominant position previously identified by the Commission and do not, moreover, require medium or long-term monitoring measures.[24]

The leading statement from the Court on the role of remedies or commitments generally also appears in this case, at paragraph 316 of *Gencor*. The Court held that where the Commission:

> concludes that the concentration is such as to create or strengthen a dominant position, it is required to prohibit it, even if the undertakings concerned by the proposed concentrations pledge themselves vis-à-vis the Commission not to abuse that position. Since the purpose of the [ECMR] is to prevent the creation or strengthening of market structures which are liable to impede significantly effective competition in the common market, situations of that kind cannot be allowed to come about on the basis that the undertakings concerned enter into a commitment not to abuse their dominant position, even where it is easy to check whether those commitments have been complied with.

The Commission has relied on this authority, perhaps erroneously, to reject commitments that are in effect a promise of future good conduct. The key point that emerges from the CFI judgment is that remedies *must* deal with the creation or strengthening of a dominant position. It is therefore inevitable that structural remedies will be preferred, although if they are fully supported by an effective framework it may be the case that behavioural remedies achieve the same end.

[22] It was noted at the time of promulgation that 'the Notice clearly shows the Commission's reluctance to accept behavioural remedies . . . such remedies are considered less effective, for they require continued monitoring by the Commission': Vanderelest Wijckmans Everaert Witters & Vennoten, *European Law Update*, Feb/Mar 2001, available at www.vwew.be). See also the comments of the CFI in Case T–102/96, *Gencor v Commission* [1999] ECR II–753 (below). However, at para 9 of the *Remedies Notice*, above n 19, the Commission has stated that 'the possibility cannot be automatically ruled out that other types of commitments may themselves also be capable of preventing the emergence or strengthening of a dominant position. However, whether such commitments can be accepted has to be determined on a case-by-case basis'.

[23] Case T–102/96, *Gencor Ltd v Commission* [1999] ECR II–753, [1999] 4 CMLR 971. See GP Elliott, 'The Gencor Judgment: Collective Dominance, Remedies and Extraterritoriality under the Merger Regulation' [1999] *EL Rev* 638 at 648ff.

[24] It has been noted, therefore, that 'the Court appears to be saying that structural remedies are those that cause an immediate and permanent or at least long-term change in the structure of the relevant market such that, once implemented, a dominant position is not created or strengthened, and require at most short-term monitoring': D Went, 'The Acceptability of Remedies Under the EC Merger Regulation: Structural Versus Behavioural' [2006] *ECLR* 455 at 455.

In April 2001 a dedicated enforcement unit was established within DG Comp to advise on the acceptability and the implementation of remedies in merger cases.[25] Although the *Remedies Notice* is being reviewed by the Commission it remains the best source of guidance in this area.

The majority of remedies involve divestiture, and a principle set out at paragraph 13 of the *Remedies Notice* is that the most effective way to restore competition is to create the conditions for either the emergence of new competition or the strengthening of existing competition.[26] In 2001, for example, of the 13 cases cleared conditionally at Phase I, eight involved divestment of some sort, and in Phase II divestment of a controlled business was the most common remedy adopted.[27] In order to be accepted by the Commission a commitment to divest must relate to a viable business that would be capable of competing effectively with the merged entity on a long-term basis. For this condition to be met the business being divested must be capable of operating viably on a stand-alone basis, at least as regards the merging entities, and must not be dependent on them for either supplies or for distribution outlets.[28] It is in the case of horizontal mergers that competitive problems are most likely to be identified, and that divestiture is most likely to be the appropriate remedy, although divestiture may also be required in the case of vertical mergers which lead, for example, to market foreclosure. In such a case the Commission has indicated that it is necessary that the most appropriate business be divested, and there could be

[25] As explained by Mario Monti, above n 17:

> 'The Enforcement Unit's core objective is to develop and ensure a consistent policy for remedies in merger cases. Members of the Unit join the case-teams of merger cases where remedies may be required or even just discussed, and do so at the earliest possible moment. Their role is to ensure that the general principles set out in the Commission's Remedies Notice are applied in a coherent manner whilst taking account of the specific requirements of each case. The unit's main function is thus to provide guidance for and ensure consistency in both the negotiation phase [prior to the taking of a decision] and the implementation phase post decision until full compliance of the parties with the commitments given.'

[26] Para 13 of the *Remedies Notice*, above n 19, states that:

> 'Where a proposed merger threatens to create or strengthen a dominant position which would impede effective competition, the most effective way to restore effective competition, apart from prohibition, is to create the conditions for the emergence of a new competitive entity or for the strengthening of existing competitors via divestiture.'

While the attraction of divestiture as a remedy in horizontal mergers is obvious, it may be the case that divestitures are not appropriate in the case of vertical mergers. Where competition concerns are identified in the latter it may be more appropriate to accept a behavioural remedy, as the concern is typically exclusion of a third party from a market. In this case a commitment to supply might be the best solution. This issue arose in Case COMP/M.2050 *Vivendi/Canal+/Seagram* (2000) where the issue related to vertical relationships in the broadcasting industry when Canal+ had privileged access to content. The concentration was cleared following a commitment not to grant Canal+ more than 50% of 'first window' rights to Universal motion pictures for a period of 5 years from the expiration of arrangements existing at the time of the merger.

[27] Monti, above n 17. See, eg, *Allianz/Dresdner* (Case COMP/M.2431 (2001)) in which the parties agreed to reduce their combined shareholdings in a competitor. In *United Airlines/US Airways* (Case COMP/M.2041 (2001)) the commitment was to divest two landing slots.

[28] *Remedies Notice*, above n 19, para 14.

circumstances in which this would be the business of the acquiring rather than the target company—particularly in hostile bids where the acquirer's knowledge of the target company may not be as good as its knowledge of its own business.[29] While the Commission has accepted divestitures involving assets of the both the acquiring and the target companies,[30] the Commission is concerned that such a divestment raises great risks and will be examined very carefully.[31] Usually divestment commitments take the form of agreeing to sell a part of the relevant undertaking within an agreed period. However, occasionally it has been the case that undertakings have agreed to find a purchaser for a part of the target company before completing the merger transaction.[32] The first such example of a 'fix it first' remedy being applied was that in *Bosch/Rexroth*.[33] In this case there was a series of transactions leading to the transfer of the engineering and automotive businesses of Mannesmann. The Commission was in doubt about the compatibility of the last transaction with the common market, and Bosch offered to divest one of Rexroth's components. The Commission's inquiries revealed that it would be difficult to find a purchaser post-merger, and Bosch agreed to suspend the merger until such time as a purchaser could be found. A further problem, identified by Motta *et al*, was that Bosch maintained very strong customer relations in the relevant market, and might have been able to persuade its former customers to make the switch from the radial piston pumps, the business of which was to be divested, to axial piston pumps, the business for which was to be retained.[34] In the US such fix-it-first remedies are relatively common, and it is to be expected that they will be increasingly common in the application of the ECMR where concerns are raised about the compatibility of a merger with the common market.

In addition to the requirement that the divested business must be viable, in order to make a clearance decision the Commission requires that the business is transferred to a suitable purchaser within a specific deadline.[35] It is for the parties to the merger to find a suitable purchaser for the business once a conditional clearance requires divestiture. Where the parties are unable to be certain that this will take place within the required period, it is for them to suggest an alternative remedy or remedies 'which has to be at least equal if not better than suited to restore effective competition, as well as a clear timetable as to how and when the other alternative will be implemented'.[36]

[29] Ibid, para 16.

[30] See, eg, Case IV/M.603 *Crown Cork & Seal/Carnaud/Metalbox* (1996).

[31] *Remedies Notice*, above n 19 para 18.

[32] See, eg Case COMP/M.1915 *The Post Office/TPG/SPPL* (2001). And see also *Remedies Notice*, above n 19, para 20.

[33] Case COMP/M.2060 (2000).

[34] M Motta, M Polo and H Vasconcelos, 'Merger Remedies in the European Union: An Overview' in Leveque and Shelanski, above n 18, 111.

[35] *Remedies Notice*, above n 19, para 19.

[36] Ibid, para 23.

The standard model texts set out in *Divestiture Best Practice*[37] are applicable to all remedy proceedings in both Phase I and Phase II, and deal specifically with divestiture commitments on the ground that the *Remedies Notice* states that these are the preferred form of merger remedies. The main purpose of the standard models is to increase the speed at which commitments may be offered and considered by reducing the negotiation burdens in relation to standard terms and provisions. As provided in the standard commitments it may be necessary to appoint both a monitoring and divestiture trustee, although the same person may serve in both roles.[38] The trustee is appointed on the basis that the Commission cannot supervise every element of the divestiture process, and considers it appropriate to have appointed a trustee with responsibilities for overseeing the implementation of the divestment.[39]

It will not always be possible to implement divestitures, and the Commission has indicated its willingness to consider alternate remedies.[40] Occasionally the Commission has accepted a package of remedies that offer alternatives to divestiture, with the possibility that divestiture will take place where the alternative remedies fail. For example, in *Nestlé/Ralston Purina*[41] two alternative remedies were put forward. Under the first Nestlé was to license its Friskies brand in Spain. However, if this was not implemented, a second alternative of a divestiture of the 50 per cent shareholding of Ralston Purina in a Spanish JV would be required. The Commission recognises that 'competition problems can also result from specific features, such as the use of exclusive agreements, the combination of networks ("network effects") or the combination of key patents'.[42] Thus, for example, it suggests that in some cases it may be necessary to terminate exclusive supply agreements.[43] Remedies may also aim at easing access to a necessary infrastructure or a vital technology, where barriers to entry result from control being held over these by the merged entity.[44] This was the case, for example, in

[37] Available at the DG Comp website. This guideline was published to accompany Regulation 4064/89, and as at mid-2006 is under review.

[38] Trustees are to be independent, and 'the absence of conflicts of interest of the trustee are of great importance to the Commission in deciding on the approval of the Trustee and the respective mandate': *Divestiture Best Practice*, para 40, available at the DG Comp website.

[39] *Remedies Notice*, above n 19, para 53. See generally part 3 of the Notice.

[40] In Case IV/M.877 *Boeing/McDonnell Douglas* (1997), eg, the Commission found that there was no company which was willing to purchase Douglas Aircraft Company from Boeing. Motta *et al* note the many problems of behavioural remedies, of which the most significant is the monitoring cost:

> 'Most of these remedies by their nature require some type of ongoing regulation or monitoring, and they are therefore likely to engage the resources of a [competition authority] long after the merger has been cleared and carried out. Some of these measures are relatively easy to evade unless there is careful monitoring and the regulatory knows the industry very well, which is not likely to be the case for a [competition authority].'

Motta, Polo and Vasconcelos, above n 34, at 118.

[41] Case COMP/M.2337 (2001).

[42] *Remedies Notice*, above n 19, para 26.

[43] Ibid, para 27. See, eg, Case IV/M.1467 *Rohm and Haas/Morton* (1999).

[44] *Remedies Notice*, above n 19, para 28.

Vivendi/Canal+/Seagram,[45] in which the Commission accepted a series of commitments which included granting competitors access to films released through Universal (see above). In *Vodafone/Airtouch/Mannesmann*[46] the Commission was satisfied by a commitment to grant competitors access to roaming tariffs and wholesale services. On occasion the Commission has indicated that it may be necessary for the parties to offer a remedies package, including elements both of divestiture and other commitments, where competition problems are raised by the merger in several markets.[47]

In some cases it will simply not be possible to craft remedies that address the concerns identified by the Commission in its analysis of the merger. The Commission has stated in the *Remedies Notice* that parties cannot expect to resolve every situation by way of identifying an appropriate remedy:

> The Commission is willing to explore solutions to the competition problems raised by a concentration, provided that these solutions are convincing and effective. There are however, concentrations where remedies adequate to eliminate competition concerns within the common market cannot be found. In such circumstances the only possibility is prohibition.
>
> Where the parties submit proposed remedies that are so extensive and complex that it is not possible for the Commission to determine with the required degree of certainty that effective competition will be restored to the market, an authorisation decision cannot be granted.[48]

In October 2005 the Commission published a study analysing the design, implementation and effectiveness of 96 remedies imposed in 40 cases under the ECMR from 1996 to 2000.[49] It is a matter of concern that, although it is generally acctepted that divestiture remedies are the most effective form of relief in the case of anti-competitive mergers, in practice they are often shown to have been ineffective. Thus in 44 per cent of cases divestiture (or transfer) remedies were found not to have solved the competition concern, although in 25 per cent of cases remedies were found to be partially effective. The assessment of whether a remedy was effective was based on whether the divested entity remained on the market as a viable competitor three to five years post-divestment. Divestiture remedies were nevertheless more effective than remedies requiring access, which were found to be ineffective in 60 per cent of cases.[50]

[45] Case COMP/M.2050 (2000).

[46] Case IV/M.1430 (1999).

[47] *Remedies Notice*, above n 19, para 30.

[48] Ibid, paras 31–32.

[49] EC Commission, 'Merger Remedy Study' (2005), available at the DG Comp website. See also Commission Press Release, IP/05/1327, 'Mergers: Commission analysis of past merger remedies provides guidance for future cases', 21 Oct 2005; P Papandropoulos and A Tajana, 'The Merger Remedies Study—In Divestiture We Trust?' [2006] *ECLR* 443; and A Kopke, 'Merger Remedies Study' [2005] *Competition Policy Newsletter*, Autumn, 3. The sample of 96 remedies imposed was drawn from the total of 227 remedies adopted by the Commission over the relevant period.

[50] Although this group was based on a small sample of only 5 cases out of the total of 96.

The study will feed through into the review process under way at the time of writing in respect of the EC Commission approach to remedies.

Impala v Commission[51]

In July 2006, for the first time, the Commission lost an appeal against a clearance decision taken under Article 8(2) ECMR.[52] The importance of this development cannot be overstated. The relevant concentration was notified to the Commission on 9 January 2004. It was to be effected between Bertelsmann AG and Sony Corporation of America, and would involve a merger of the respective parties' global recorded music businesses. On 12 February 2004 the Commission made a decision under Article 6(1)(c) ECMR, and on 24 May 2004 the Commission sent an SO to the parties, indicating that it believed the concentration to be incompatible with the common market, in that it would strengthen a collective dominant position in the recorded music market and in the wholesale market for licences for online music. However, the parties submitted substantial further economic evidence to the Commission which on 19 July 2004, made its Article 8(2) decision, although the case was one of only 22 per cent[53] of cases cleared without any commitments being made. The applicants lodged their action on 3 December 2004, and the CFI agreed to the use of the expedited procedure (see Chapter 9, below). The applicants relied on five grounds, all of which went to the substance of the decision in that they relied upon the fact that the Commission erred in finding that the concentration, as amended by the parties, would not create or strengthen either individual or coordinated dominant positions.[54] The arguments of the applicant are summed up by the CFI at paragraph 243 of its judgment:

> The applicant maintains that the considerations relating to product homogeneity, market transparency, deterrence and the absence of constraints, which served as the basis for a finding that the majors did not have a collective dominant position on the markets for recorded music before the proposed concentration, are vitiated by insufficient reasoning, a manifest error of assessment and an error of law.[55]

[51] Case T–464/04, *Independent Music Publishers and Labels Association (Impala, international association) v Commission*, judgment of 13 July 2006; an appeal against case COMP/M.3333 *Sony/BMG* (2004).

[52] This was the first time *any* clearance decision taken by the Commission had been annulled. See, for example, T Buck, 'Watchdog reels at Sony/BMG ruling', *Financial Times*, July 13, 2006. The *Financial Times* reported that the case 'present[ed] a real challenge for the EC Commission, and 'shattered' the confidence of officials.

[53] See CJ Cook and CS Kerse, *EC Merger Control* (4th edn London, Sweet & Maxwell, 2005), at 288, n 21.

[54] See above n 51, para 31.

[55] The approach taken to collective dominance in this case is discussed briefly in Chap 7 above.

Although the CFI stressed that the Commission was not obliged to explain its decision 'by comparison with the [SO]',[56] it did state that the 'fundamental U-turn in the Commission's position may indeed appear surprising, particularly in view of the late stage at which it was made'.[57] The relevant question, however, was not the extent to which the final decision differed from the SO, but whether the final decision was sufficiently reasoned. The CFI found that the part of the decision dealing with transparency in the market (a requirement for a finding of collective dominance) was 'insufficient',[58] and that there was inconsistency between the arguments relied on in court and those advanced in the decision itself. The CFI further pointed to 'numerous sources of transparency on the market', although the Commission had not found that the market was sufficiently transparent to permit a collective dominant position to exist.[59] In this respect, 'the evidence, as mentioned in the decision, does not support the conclusions drawn from it'.[60] The CFI annulled the Decision. The immediate commercial effect of the judgment was to throw the global music industry 'into turmoil', and to wipe just over 9 per cent off the value of EMI, and 15 per cent off the value of Warner Music, which were in merger talks.[61] It has been suggested that the judgment will make life exceptionally difficult for the EC Commission, and may force a rethink as to whether the timetables set out in the ECMR are realistic, given the standard to which the merger review is to be conducted. The immediate legal effect of the judgment was, of course, to require the Commission to reconsider the Sony/BMG merger. At the time of writing that process was under way.[62] It should be noted that actions such as the one here can lay the merging parties open to considerable uncertainty. The application of Article 230 EC (see further Chapter 9) does not serve to invalidate or suspend the contested decision. Although the CFI may grant interim measures,

56 Above n 51, para 284.

57 Ibid, para 283.

58 Ibid, para 325.

59 Ibid, para 364.

60 Ibid, para 377. There are similar damning criticisms of the decision throughout the judgment. The following are merely some extracts: '[t]he Commission's argument cannot be followed' (para 380); 'those responses do not support the conclusions which the Commission drew from them' (para 386); 'the Commission's assessment of the retailers' responses is vitiated by a manifest error' (para 387); '[n]one of those three sources can support the conclusions drawn by the Commission' (para 389); 'it is surprising that the Commission should rely on' (para 395); 'it is not apparent that the Commission undertook a serious examination' (para 398); 'merely justified its conclusions by reference solely to the data provided by the parties to the concentration' (para 410); 'the Commission clearly cannot maintain' (para 413); 'it cannot . . . go so far as to delegate, without supervision, responsibility for conducting certain parts of the investigation to the parties to the concentration' (para 415); 'the new evidence submitted by the Commission does not appear to be sufficiently reliable, relevant or cogent' (para 435); '[a]t the very least, the Commission ought to have examined and explained' (para 436); 'the decision does not contain the slightest information capable of showing the effect of' (para 447); 'these few observations, which are so superficial, indeed purely formal, cannot satisfy the Commission's obligation' (para 528).

61 A Edgecliffe-Johnson, 'Sony BMG Ruling Rocks Music Industry', FT.com, 13 July 2006.

62 Art 10(5) ECMR provides that where the ECJ annuls a decision 'the concentration shall be re-examined by the Commission with a view to adopting a decision pursuant to Article 6(1)'.

including, for example, the suspension of a contemplated concentration, no such application was made in this case.[63] The effect of this is that: (1) a merger could, lawfully, take place; (2) the Commission decision could be annulled; (3) a re-opened procedure could end in an Article 8(3) decision blocking the now-consummated merger; (4) the parties could be compelled to a full divestiture, having to bear all the expense of this. Whether the Commission could be found to be liable under Article 288 EC for the resultant damage is a matter of speculation, although public policy requirements might suggest that to impose such liability, which could apply equally in the case of wrongfully blocked mergers, would have a highly detrimental impact on the operations of the EC Commission. It should be noted that most transactions are structured in such a way that debt is drawn down immediately on clearance of the merger or the end of Phase I. The parties could not be held to be at fault for pursuing the transaction at this point, and could not be expected reasonably to delay further in the absence of a preliminary order to do so by the CFI. However, the risk that clearance decisions will be overturned on appeal goes some way to undermining a system based on compulsory pre-merger notification and review.

International cooperation with respect to remedies

It is in the interests both of merging parties and of relevant authorities to coordinate, where possible, on the imposition of remedies. In the case of the EC and the US such cooperation is particularly strong, although it is not the only jurisdiction with which the EC has cooperated on such matters. For example, in *Metso/Svedala*[64] the Commission and the FTC cooperated in obtaining very similar undertakings by which various rock-crushing businesses were to be divested. In *Nestlé/Ralston Purina*[65] the cooperation was tri-partite, involving the Commission, the FTC and the Canadian authorities, although the markets considered were national in character. The acquisition was cleared by the Commission, subject to the divestiture of certain plants and brands in Spain, Italy and Greece. Divestitures were also required in the US, the difference being that the US imposed a permanent divestiture, whereas in the EC the Commission accepted a licensing of the brand for a limited period of time, combined with some re-branding.

[63] Sony and BMG merged to create Sony BMG, on August 5, 2004. On July 23, 2006 Rolf Schmidt-Holtz, Chief Executive of Sony BMG told *Der Speigel* that the company was confident that divestiture would not be ordered by the Commission on a re-examination of the merger ('*Die zeit der Egos ist vorbei*', *Der Speigel*, 23 July 2006).

[64] Case COMP/M.2033.

[65] Case COMP/M.2337 (2001).

ARTICLE 8(3) DECISIONS—INCOMPATIBILITY WITH THE COMMON MARKET

The most stark decision that can be made by the Commission is that Article 8(3) ECMR applies. It will be recalled that Article 8(3) provides that:

> Where the Commission finds that a concentration fulfils the criterion defined in article 2(3) or, in the cases referred to in article 2(4), does not fulfil the criteria laid down in article 81(3) of the Treaty, it shall issue a decision declaring that the concentration is incompatible with the common market.

Of the 2827 relevant notifications made to the Commission between 21 September 1990 and 31 July 2005, only 19 resulted in an Article 8(3) incompatibility decision.[66] The full list is as follows:

M.53 *Aérospatiale-Alenia/De Havilland*, 2 October 1991
M.469 *MSG Media Service*, 9 November 1994
M.490 *Nordic Satellite Distribution*, 19 July 1995
M.553 *RTL/Veronica/Endemol ('HMG')*, 20 September 1995
M.619 *Gencor/Lonhro*, 24 April 1996[67]
M.774 *Saint Gobin/Wacker Chemie/NOM*, 4 December 1996
M.784 *Kesko/Tuko*, 20 November 1996
M.890 *Blokker/Toys "R" Us (II)*, 26 June 1997
M.993 *Bertelsmann/Kirch/Premiere*, 27 May 1998
M.1027 *Deutsche Telekom/Betaresearch*, 27 May 1998
M.1524 *Airtours/First Choice*, 22 September 1990[68]
M.1672 *Volvo/Scania*, 14 March 2001
M.1741 *MCI WorldCom/Sprint*, 28 June 2000
M.2097 *SCA/Metsa Tissue*, 31 January 2001
M.2187 *CVC/Lenzing*, 17 October 2001
M.2220 *General Electric/Honeywell*, 3 July 2001
M.2283 *Schneider/Legrand*, 10 October 2001
M.2416, *Tetra Laval/Sidel*, 30 October 2001
M.3440, *ENI/EDP/GDP*, 9 December 2004

It is not possible in a work of this length to go into detail in respect of all 19 cases, but some further detail will be given in respect of a sample of these. In particular attention will be paid to those cases where the parties were successful on appeal to the CFI. Three of these cases in particular, *Airtours/First Choice, Schneider/Legrand* and *Tetra Laval/Sidel*, have been credited with spurring on

[66] European Merger Control—Council Regulation 4064/89 and—Statistics, available at http://europa.eu.int/comm/competition/mergers/cases/stats.html.
[67] This case is discussed in Chap 7, above.
[68] This case is discussed in some detail in Chap 7, above.

the moves towards reform of Regulation 4064/89,[69] and in the latter two cases parties benefited from the 'fast track' appeals process discussed in the next chapter.[70] In all cases dealt with below it must be emphasised that a wealth of detail and analysis presented in the decision underlies the very short treatment accorded to these cases here.

Aerospatiale-Alenia/De Havilland

This was the first case in which the Commission blocked a merger under the ECMR. It was also politically contentious, in that the concentrative JV involved a 'national champion' of France. The prospective merger was between producers of commuter aircraft, with the market being defined by reference to the number of seats of each type of aircraft. Market shares were calculated on the basis of orders rather than products already delivered, but excluded aircraft no longer in production, as they could not operate as competitive constraints on the parties in the future. The merger would give Avions de Transport Régional (ATR), controlled by Aérospatiale and Alenia, an increase in market share in one of the relevant markets from 46 to 64 per cent. The Commission found that the merger would give the parties a range of products across each of the three relevant markets, and held that parties that were active in a number of related markets operated at an advantage against those more specialised. The Commission argued that:

> This logic flows from the fixed costs borne by the carrier for each aircraft manufacturer dealt with by that carrier. These costs include the fixed costs of pilot and mechanic training as well as the costs of maintaining different in-house inventories of parts and the fixed costs of dealing with several manufacturers when ordering parts stocked only by the individual manufacturers themselves.[71]

One of the key features of this case is the treatment accorded to a failing firm defence argument. The Commission was faced with the argument that de Havilland faced liquidation if it was not taken over. At first DG Comp appeared to question whether that consideration, if true, was even pertinent under the

[69] Mario Monti recognised the damage done to the Commission's standing by these cases, accepting that 'the Commission has faced unprecedented criticism in the wake of three judgments of the Court of First Instance overturning on appeal the prohibition decisions [of *Airtours/First Choice, Schneider/Legrand,* and *Tetra Laval/Sidel*]. . . . These judgments, no matter how painful, came at the right moment' (M Monti, 'Merger Control in the European Union: a radical reform', Speech, 7 Nov 2002). See also: J Temple Lang, 'Two Important Merger Regulation Judgments: The Implications of *Schneider-Legrand* and *Tetra Laval-Sidel*' [2003] *EL Rev* 259; C Ahlborn and J Ysewyn, 'EC Merger Control Regulation—Problems and Solutions' [2002] *Comp Law* 301; P Lowe, 'The Future of EU Merger Control' [2002] *Comp Law* 310; Editorial, 'The Next Step in Reform of EC Competition Law: Merger control' (2003) 40 *CML Rev* 1.

[70] See A Nucara, '*Schneider/Legrand* and *Tetra Laval/Sidel*: Fast Track Towards Merger Reform?' [2003] *European Business Law Review* 193.

[71] Case IV/M.53 (1991), para 32.

ECMR.[72] It has been noted that '[t]his seems a dubious position to have adopted'.[73] It has been argued in Chapter 2 above, and is now generally accepted, that the question whether a firm will, absent the merger, exit the market in any case is an important one in assessing the competitive effects of the merger itself. In the final analysis DG Comp expressly rejected the application of the failing-firm defence, arguing that it was not inevitable that de Havilland would exit the market, and that even if it were to do so there were other potential purchasers.

The parties also argued that the merger would generate efficiencies, but the Commission was not prepared to take into account efficiencies which were not 'merger specific', and in particular rejected arguments relating to cost savings flowing from better management on the ground that these could be achieved by improvements in de Havilland itself, irrespective of the merger.

MSG Media Service and *Bertelsmann/Kirch/Premiere*

This first case related to a JV established in relation to digital pay-TV in Germany by three established media and telecommunications groups. Pay-TV was held to constitute a relevant product market separate from other forms of television broadcasting. The case turned in part on the treatment to be given to alleged improvements to technical and economic progress. It was clear that the JV would have the potential to contribute to such development, but the Commission also feared that it would establish a dominant position which would have the longer term effect of hindering the development of the medium.[74] At paragraph 91 of its decision the Commission thus argued that '[i]n view of the considerable competitive advantages that are involved for Bertlesmann and Kirch in MSG and the possible adverse effect on future competitors, it is to be expected that the proposed concentration will create a durable dominant position'. An effect of this would be that any party in the future seeking to enter the pay-TV market in Germany would have no choice but to rely on the platforms and distribution services developed by MSG. Undertakings were offered by the

[72] [1991] OJ L 334/42, at para 31.

[73] Cook and Kerse, above n 53, at 279.

[74] At para 100 of its decision in Case IV/M.469 (1994) the Commission stated:

> 'The reference to [technical and economic progress] in Art 2(1)(b) of the Merger Regulation is subject to the reservation that no obstacle is formed to competition. . . . however the foreseeable effects of the proposed concentration suggest that it will lead to a sealing-off of, and early creation of, a dominant position on the future markets for technical and administrative services and to a substantial hindering of effective competition on the future market for pay-TV.'

At para 101 the Commission went further, and stated that '[t]his hindering of effective competition does in fact make even the achievement of technical and economic progress questionable. It is extremely doubtful whether, under the conditions given, the establishment of a digital infrastructure for pay-TV by MSG will actually contribute in a positive manner to the development of technical and economic progress'.

parties under which, inter alia, decoders developed by the JV would not be blocked from preventing reception of programmes not handled by MSG. DG Comp however held that the undertakings were insufficient to address the concerns raised, and that they were 'partly subject to conditions and reservations which put their enforceability into question'.[75]

Bertelsmann/Kirch/Premiere was notified to DG Comp on 1 December 1997, and in many ways, including the identity of the parties involved and the relevant markets, was very similar to *MSG Media Service*.[76] It related to a proposed transaction, by way of share purchase, under which CLT–UFA SA and Taurus Beteiligungs-GmbH & Co KG would acquire joint control over three undertakings involved in the digital pay-TV market in Germany, which would be brought within a general umbrella undertaking, Premiere, which would be run as a JV by the two parents.[77] The German government informed the Commission on 22 December 1997, pursuant to Article 9(2) ECMR, that the concentration would lead to significant impediment of competition on six markets in Germany, each of which it argued constituted a separate geographic market within the meaning of Article 9(7) ECMR. Following *MSG Media Service* (see above), the Commission held that pay-TV constituted a separate product market from that of free-access TV. It also found that a separate market existed in respect of the provision of technical services necessary to operate pay-TV systems. The relevant geographic market was identified as being the German-speaking region of Germany, Austria and the German-speaking parts of Belgium and Switzerland, along with Luxembourg. In respect of the pay-TV market the effect of the concentration would be to eliminate what was characterised as 'intense competition':[78] 'this competition will cease and for all practical purposes there will be only one pay-TV supplier, which will combine the programme resources of [the relevant two undertakings]'.[79] Given the position of the two parent companies Premiere would have 'access to programme resources unparalleled in Germany'.[80] The parties themselves accepted that Premiere would have a very strong position on the market over at least the five years following the concentration, and that it would not be significantly constrained by the existence of public TV suppliers. The Commission found, however, that dominance could be expected to last even longer than this, and

[75] *MSG Media Service* (Case IV/M.469)(1994), (Dec 94/922/EC) above n 74, para 95. See generally T Usher, 'EU Mergers and Strategic Alliances in the Broadcasting Industry' [2002] *Comp Law* 15; PD Camesasca, 'Mayday or Heyday? Dynamic Competition Meets Media Ownership Rules after Premiere' [2000] *ECLR* 76; and N Nikolinakos 'Mergers and Strategic Alliances in the Emerging Multi-Media Sector: The EU Competition Policy' [2004] *ECLR* 625.

[76] A second merger, *Deutsche Telekom/Beta Research* (case IV/M.1027) was notified to the Commission on Dec 8 1997 as part of the same chain of transactions. This merger too was blocked.

[77] The structure of the transaction, and the relationship between the parties are somewhat complicated, and have been simplified greatly here. See paras 8–15 of Case IV/M.993 (1998).

[78] Ibid, para 30. Note however that this competition had lead to the two competitors 'each running separate decoder projects'.

[79] Ibid, para 30.

[80] Ibid, para 34.

indeed that it would 'be established on a lasting basis',[81] particularly because no potential entrant would have access to the necessary programming content. The control over programming, a subscriber base and the decoder infrastructure which would arise were the concentration to be consummated were ultimately fatal to the parties. A 'failing division' defence advanced by the parties was rejected,[82] in part because, even if the pay-TV operations that were being shut down as part of the transaction were to fail within the existing structure, the resource would be available to others.

It was also 'to be expected that the proposed concentration will give BetaDigital a dominant position on a lasting basis on the market in technical services for satellite pay-TV'.[83]

As with *MSG Media Service* the parties argued that the merger would give rise to technical and economic progress, as the parties argued that it was only by combining their respective resources that the infrastructure necessary for the breakthrough of digital TV could be established. As with the earlier case, this argument was rejected. The Commission held that these claims gave 'rise to considerable doubt in practical terms',[84] and that by creating a sustainable dominant position it would be 'impossible for the market to develop on a competitive basis . . . it should be stressed that the criterion of technical and economic progress contained in article 2(1)(b) [ECMR] is subject to the proviso that it does not form an obstacle to competition'.[85] A first set of undertakings advanced by the parties designed to address these concerns was rejected, along with an expanded set brought forward later.

It may be worth noting that in a more recent case, *NewsCorp/Telempiù*,[86] the EC Commission cleared a merger in the Italian market for pay-TV services which would create a near total monopolist in that market,[87] although significant remedies were put forward by the parties at the Phase II stage of the process. There was, however, in this case a genuine prospect that the firm being acquired was failing, and the Commission appears to have accepted that the alternative of a single monopolist, limited by the remedies offered, was better than the alternative scenario under which the target would exit the market, causing disruption to its suppliers and customers, and a monopoly would in any event be created.

[81] Ibid, para 47.
[82] See Chap 6, above.
[83] Above n 77, para 118.
[84] Ibid, para 120.
[85] Ibid, para 122.
[86] Case IV/M.2876 (2002).
[87] For a discussion of this case, and the economic incentives underpinning consolidation in the pay-TV sector, see C Caffarra and A Coscelli, 'Merger to Monopoly: *NewsCorp/Telepiù*' [2003] *ECLR* 625.

RTL/Veronica/Endemol

The case of *RTL/Veronica/Endemol* is unusual in part because it came before the EC Commission by way of an Article 22 ECMR request made by the Dutch government, and was a completed transaction, as the standstill provisions of the ECMR did not apply under this procedure. The concentrative JV took place in the broadcasting market, with effects in the TV broadcasting and TV advertising markets, and led to the creation of a new company, HMG, the purpose of which was to package and supply TV and radio programmes to the Netherlands and Luxembourg. The Commission rejected the argument of the parties to the effect that its review should be limited to the market for TV advertising, given that the Dutch authorities had couched the referral request in these terms. The view of the Commission was that, given the interconnections between the two markets, along with a third market for TV production, 'the combination of the strengths of the partners within HMG confers upon the [JV] itself and also Endemol a very strong position vis-à-vis their respective competitors'.[88] The public broadcasters active in the market would not be able to react effectively to the JV, and the prospects of any private broadcaster gaining a significant position on the Dutch market were considered to be difficult in any event, and made more difficult following the concentration. Following the concentration the market share of the three HMG channels would be around 42–43 per cent. Although this figure lies very much at the lower bound of the size required for dominance to be established, the Commission pointed to the fact that it would be a higher market share than that of the three public channels combined. In the event the Commission did not feel it necessary to make a final determination in this respect, as it took the view that 'the prime significance of the audience share is that it is the most important parameter for determining market power in the TV advertising market'.[89] In the TV advertising market HMG would have been the clear leader and would 'be in a position to counteract all active attempts to compete from existing players [rendering] the entrance of newcomers to this market very difficult'.[90] Finally the Commission found that the position of Endemol on the independent Dutch TV production market would be increased as a result of its participation in the JV. The Commission declared the concentration incompatible with the common market, and set out in the Decision its intention to adopt a separate decision under Article 8(4) to restore effective competition having heard representations from the parties on what these measures should be. The case was concluded when one of the parties subsequently withdrew from the JV, and a commitment was also given that resulted in the Commission holding that the concentration had been modified and was compatible with the common market.

[88] Case IV/M.553 (1995), para 30.
[89] Above n 88, para 64.
[90] Ibid, para 87.

Blokker/Toys "R" Us

Like *RTL/Veronica/Endemol* this case came before the EC Commission following an Article 22 ECMR referral request made by the Dutch government. The transaction in question was the acquisition of the Dutch operations of Toys "R" Us by Blokker, agreed on 24 December 1997, and notified on 13 January 1997. Prior to the transaction Blokker operated some 147 wholly owned toy shops under the 'Bart Smit' trade mark, and a further 196 toy shops under the 'Intertoys' trade mark. It also sold toys in its household articles stores. Toys "R" Us was one of the largest toys retailers in the world, and the Dutch subsidiary was wholly owned by the US parent. However, in the Dutch market the Commission accepted that 'Toys "R" Us suffered from structural weaknesses and made marketing errors which severely limited its ability to compete strongly on the Dutch market. . . . [It] did not develop into a significant competitive force on the Dutch market'.[91] The agreement took the form of a franchising agreement, and the parties argued that this was not a concentration within the meaning of the ECMR. The Commission however relied upon the meaning of 'control' under the ECMR, and held that 'acquisition of control is not limited to cases where a legal entity is taken over, but can also happen through the acquisition of assets'.[92] The product market was defined as the retail of toys through specialised toy retail outlets. Prior to the concentration Blokker already held a dominant position on this market. The effect of the concentration was to increase this market share, and additional factors 'demonstrate[d] that the potential of the acquired business [was] much greater than [was] reflected in its actual market share'.[93] The acquisition of the Toys "R" Us assets gave Blokker a fourth selling formula which was distinct from the existing outlets it operated, namely megastores with substantial floor space located outside the city centres and easily accessible by car. This type of outlet was considered to be particularly important for the future development of retailing and gave Blokker a significant 'first mover advantage'. The acquisition also gave Blokker, according to the Commission, the opportunity to 'ensure the greatest complementarity between the four formulas with respect to product ranges and prices'.[94] Dealing with the point that Toys "R" Us was, in effect, struggling in the Dutch market prior to the transfer, the Commission noted that 'the formula and stores still have a considerable market potential, particularly in the hands of Blokker, which has the necessary knowledge of the Dutch market'.[95]

As with the *Aérospatiale-Alenia/De Havilland* merger the issue of the failing company defence was also important. Toys "R" Us argued that its Dutch operations were not financially viable, and that it would close its Dutch operations

[91] Ibid, para 76.
[92] Ibid, para 13.
[93] Ibid, para 88.
[94] Ibid, para 94.
[95] Ibid, para 95.

if the transaction was not permitted, in which case its market share would inevitably go to Blokker. The Commission summed up its position in relation to the failing firm defence, recognising that:

> The Commission has decided in earlier cases that a merger is generally not regarded as leading to a deterioration in the competitive structure if it is clear that the acquired undertaking would in the near future be forced out of the market, the acquiring undertaking would take over the market share of the acquired undertaking if the latter were forced out of the market, and that there is no less anti-competitive alternative purchaser in the market. The burden of proof in this respect is on the parties themselves.
>
> The failing-company doctrine as developed in these cases . . . is based on the lack of causality between the concentration and the creation or strengthening of a dominant position. This means that it is the disappearance of the failing company, which is unavoidable whether or not the concentration takes place, and not the concentration itself, which creates or strengthens the dominant position.[96]

In this case however the Commission found that the causality referred to above had not been established, and that it was not clear that, even if Toys "R" Us exited the market, its market share would go to Blokker. Further the Commission's concerns went partly to the fact that it believed that it was the *potential* of Toys "R" Us as part of the Blokker group that raised concerns. The parties offered measures, basically consisting of the divestiture of Toys "R" Us from the Blokker group, that would restore effective conditions of competition on the common market, and an order was made to set this in place. In the event that Blokker was unable to divest the Toys "R" Us assets to a third party before a date specified by the Commission,[97] Blokker was ordered to 'transfer all rights, obligations and assets acquired pursuant to the Letter Agreement of 24 December 1996 to Toys "R" Us'.

Volvo/Scania

The notified concentration in this case related to the purchase by AB Volvo of the whole of Scania AB, the notification being received by the Commission on 22 September 1999. Both parties were engaged in the manufacture and sale of, inter alia, heavy trucks, buses[98] and marine and industrial engines, although Volvo's interests were wider than those of Scania. The merger was thus a relatively straightforward horizontal concentration.[99] The analysis was compli-

[96] Above n 88, paras 110–111 (footnote omitted).

[97] The date was redacted from the published decision.

[98] For the purposes of the decision the market for buses was further divided into three separate product markets: touring coaches, inter-city buses and city buses (see Case IV/M.1672 (2001), para 230).

[99] The justification for the merger advanced by Volvo was summarised by the Commission at para 7 of its Art 8(3) decision:

> 'Volvo has explained that its rationale for the proposed concentration is to support Volvo's efforts to compete in large, emerging markets for heavy trucks and buses in Asia, Central

cated, however, by the range of different geographic markets identified in the decision, each of which had to be analysed separately, and DG Comp had commissioned an econometric report to attempt to measure what the effects of the merger would be on each of these separate markets.[100] The Commission found that the proposed concentration would lead to the creation of dominant positions in the market for heavy trucks in Sweden, Norway, Finland and Ireland, and that there were 'strong indications' that this would also be the position in Denmark.[101] In respect of the various bus markets it was found that dominant positions would be created in the UK and Finland in respect of touring coaches; in Sweden, Finland, Norway and Denmark for city and inter-city buses; and in Ireland for city buses.

Volvo offered undertakings which had the aim of opening up certain distribution networks and easing barriers to entry posed by a Swedish safety test, along with offering access to body-building capacity in respect of the bus market in Finland. The Commission accepted that these undertakings 'could, if properly implemented, have some beneficial effect on the competitive situation in the relevant markets', but came to the conclusion that they were insufficient to address the competitive concerns identified.[102] The concentration was therefore blocked.

MCI WorldCom/Sprint

MCI WorldCom and Sprint, both US-based companies engaged in providing communications systems to business customers, notified their intention to merge by way of an exchange of shares to the Commission on 11 January 2000.[103] The merger was also notified to the DOJ, and the two agencies cooperated during the course of the investigation, exchanging information where appropriate to do so, as the parties had granted waivers permitting this. In an

Europe, the former Soviet Republics, and in South America. According to Volvo, substantial investments will be required to take advantage of opportunities in those regions. Volvo's ability to expand in those emerging markets is stated to be a critical requirement if it is to operate efficiently and remain competitive with the world's leading truck and bus manufacturers, and, particularly, with DaimlerChrysler and the large North American engine producers.'

[100] The report was based on a 'nested logit model where certain parameters relating to the pricing decisions of firms and to the buying decisions of customers are estimated from prices, market shares and other variables' (above n 98, para 73). Although the results generated pointed to serious competition problems arising from the merger, the Commission recognised that the reliance on this type of study was a new development in EC merger control, and given that Volvo contested fundamental elements of the study the Commission chose not to rely on it in making its decision (see ibid, para 75).

[101] See ibid, para 213.

[102] Ibid, paras 338–362.

[103] AG Abbamonte and V Rabassa, 'Foreclosure and Vertical Mergers—The Commission's Review of Vertical Effects in the Last Wave of Media and Internet Mergers: AOL/Time Warner, Vivendi/Seagram, MCI Worldcom/Sprint' [2001] *ECLR* 214.

earlier decision which permitted the merger of MCI and WorldCom,[104] DG Comp had identified three relevant product markets in the provision of internet services: provision of host to point of presence connectivity; provision of internet access services; and provision of top-level or universal connectivity. For the purpose of the present transaction DG Comp identified that the focus should be on the last of these markets. As with the previous investigation DG Comp concluded that the geographic market was a global one. A second relevant, global, market was identified in respect of global telecommunications services. It was accepted by all that there was some difficulty in assessing market shares in relation to the first of these markets, but the Commission estimated that the merged entity's market share would be between 37 and 51 per cent based on traffic exchanged, and 30 and 65 per cent based on revenue. The next largest competitor, under any of the assumptions made, had a market share of no higher than 15 per cent.[105] The Commission also argued that the merger would 'lead to the creation of a top-level network provider that through its sheer size would be able to behave to an appreciable extent independently of its competitors and customers'.[106] The resultant power would give the merged entity the ability to control technical developments, raise prices and 'discipline the market'.

In the market for global telecommunications services there were, pre-merger, three main suppliers: the Concert Alliance, MCI WorldCom and the Global One Alliance, of which Sprint was a member.[107] At the same time as the concentration was notified to the Commission, the Global One Alliance had lost two other members, and it was expected that it would be severely undermined by the withdrawal of Sprint, leaving a situation in which only two significant competitors would operate in this market. The Commission argued in its statement of objections that the duopoly that would emerge would give rise to a situation in which the market was prone to tacit collusion but, following arguments made by the parties, accepted that 'one of the key factors to examine when proving the creation of a collective dominant position, i.e. the absence of possibility for the demand to counterbalance the position of the possible oligopolists, could not be shown'.[108] This line of argument was not therefore pursued by the Commission.

An undertaking to divest the public internet activities of Sprint was rejected on six grounds: (1) the scope of the divested services was too narrow; (2) the

[104] Case IV/M.1069 (1998). See N Nikolinakos, 'The Importance of Maintaining Competition in the Internet Market: the WorldCom/MCI Case' [2000] *ECLR* 393. For an American perspective see MD Pelcovits, 'The Long-Distance Industry: One Merger Too Many? MCI WorldCom and Sprint' in JE Kwoka, Jr and LJ White (eds), *The Antitrust Revolution: Economics, Competition and Policy* (4th edn, New York, OUP 2004).

[105] Case IV/M. 1741 (2000), para 123.

[106] Ibid, at para 145. It will be recalled that this is the standard formulation for the dominance test adopted by the ECJ.

[107] This market had previously been analysed by the Commission in Case IV/JV.15 *BT/AT&T* (1999).

[108] Ibid, para 302.

divested entity would not be able to retain its customer basis; (3) there were many uncertainties relating to the personnel to be transferred with the divestiture; (4) the entity would remain dependent on MCI WorldCom/Sprint for its continued existence;[109] (5) it would be very difficult to monitor the situation; and (6) there was uncertainty as to which assets would be transferred.

SCA/Metsa Tissue

The Commission blocked the *SCA/Metsa Tissue* merger, notified on 11 August 2000, on the ground that it would create or strengthen a dominant position in a number of markets in the Scandinavian countries and Denmark in respect of various paper tissue products. The contemplated merger was between SCA, a company that manufactured and distributed a variety of tissue-based hygiene products throughout the EEA, and Metsa Tissue ('MT'), active in the production of tissue products, baking and cooking papers. In some of the relevant markets SCA was found by the Commission to be the best placed competitor to MT and the other large incumbent. Were the concentration to proceed a collective dominant position would be created in the markets for branded consumer toilet tissue and kitchen towels in Finland.

The notified concentration was part of a complicated wider set of transactions, three of which fell to be notified.[110] A number of relevant markets were identified, and the Commission was able to draw in part on analysis carried out in an earlier case, *Kimberly-Clark/Scott*.[111] One issue pertinent to this case was whether branded and private-label[112] products were in the same markets. Although evidence was presented to show that many consumers were prepared to switch between branded and private-label products, the Commission had found in *Kimberly-Clark/Scott* that for many retail chains leading brands were essential stock-items, used in part to lure customers into the stores, in part to provide an adequate range, and in part to provide consumers with a price point against which to compare private-label products. Further the evidence from the merging parties was that there was a substantial difference in the way that supermarkets purchased branded and private-label products. The Commission therefore drew a distinction between the wholesale and retail level, concluding that at the former the markets were separate.[113] It was clear that for 'converted products' (products in their final packaged form), the geographic markets were

[109] The vice-chairman of MCI WorldCom had stated before the decision was made that: 'if you own the network, you have better control of cost *and* quality and we get to decide when to implement new products and services' (quoted at para 400 of the decision, emphasis in original).

[110] See also Case COMP/M.2020 (2000), *Metsa-Serla/Modo* and Case COMP/M.2032 (2000) *SCA Packaging/Metsa Corrugated*. Neither of these cases proceeded to a prohibition decision.

[111] Case IV/M.623 (1996), Commission Decision 96/435/EC [1996] OJ L 183/1. See also N Levy, 'Kimberly-Clark/Scott and the Power of Brands' [1996] *ECLR* 403.

[112] Ie, own-label products marketed by retail chains alongside branded products.

[113] See paras 20–28 of the Decision in Case COMP/M.2097(2001).

smaller than in the case of 'parent reels', in respect of which the market was at least as wide as the EEA. The ratio of transport costs to value was much smaller in respect of the latter, which were much more compact, leading to a more expansive geographic market.

General Electric/Honeywell[114]

General Electric/Honeywell is one of the more controversial decisions taken by DG Comp, in part because the merger, under the agreed terms of which Honeywell would become a 100 per cent owned subsidiary of GE, involved two US industrial giants and was cleared by the US authorities with only minor conditions being imposed.[115] A second reason for the intense discussion generated by the case lay in the fact that it was a rare example of a conglomerate merger being blocked. The merger was notified to DG Comp in February 2001, and an

[114] Case COMP/M.2220, [2004] OJ L 48/1.

[115] The DOJ required divestiture in markets relating to US military helicopter engines and heavy maintenance, repair and overhaul services for certain aircraft engines. See DOJ Press Release, *Justice Department Requires Divestitures in Merger Between General Electric and Honeywell*, 2 May 2 2001. Zanettin argues that:

> 'the divergent results of the EC and the US analyses cannot be attributed to a lack of bilateral cooperation between the agencies involved . . . but from a clear divergence of views on both the theoretical and empirical analysis of the effects of this merger. . . . the DOJ disagreed with the European Commission on essential points: the definition of dominance, the level of protection to be given to competitors, and the respective importance of the short-term efficiencies versus more uncertain long-term anti-competitive effects . . . it is still clear that the *GE/Honeywell* case will have a more lasting and negative impact on bilateral cooperation between [DG Comp] and its US counterparts than the *Boeing/McDonnell Douglas* case.'

(B Zanettin, *Cooperation Between Antitrust Agencies at the International Level* (Oxford, Hart Publishing, 2002), 100–2. See also C Canenbley and M Rosenthal, 'Cooperation between Antitrust Authorities in and outside the EU: What Does it Mean for Multinational Corporations?' (Part 2) [2005] *ECLR* 178; A Burnside, 'GE, Honey, I Sunk the Merger' [2002] *ECLR* 107; E S Hochstadt, 'The *Brown Shoe* of European Union Competition Law' [2002] *Cardozo Law Review* 287; J Grant and D J Neven, 'The Attempted Merger Between General Electric and Honeywell: A Case Study of Transatlantic Conflict' [2005] 1 *Journal of Competition Law and Economics* 595; D Giotakos, 'GE/Honeywell: A Theoretic Bundle Assessing Conglomerate Mergers Across the Atlantic' (2002) 23 *University of Pennsylvania Journal of International Economic Law* 469; S Schmitz, 'How dare They? European Merger Control and the European Commission's Blocking of the General Electric/Honeywell Merger' (2002) 23 *University of Pennsylvania Journal of International Economic Law* 325; DK Schnell, 'All Bundled Up: Bringing the Failed GE/Honeywell Merger in from the Cold' (2004) 37 *Cornell International Law Journal* 217; and LM Davison, 'The GE/Honeywell Merger Controversy and the Path to Analytical Convergence in International Merger Assessment: A Critical Commentary' (2002) 24 *Liverpool Law Review*, 89. Davison notes that the differences between the two approaches in the EC and the US were of a fundamental nature:

> 'A worrying concern here is that when both the [DOJ] and the [EC] Commission sought to gauge the market power that a merged GE/Honeywell would command—a key element in their respective SLC test and the [ECMR] dominance test—they reached the opposite conclusion. Just as worrying is the fact that the two competition authorities were at loggerheads as to the contribution made by factors—individually and when combined together—to the merged entity's market power' (at 92).

SO was issued in May 2001. The case was a complicated one, but 'the essence of the theory against the merger lies in the fact that it brought together a series of businesses that were complements in the economic sense'.[116] The primary markets concerned were those for engines for large commercial aircraft, avionics[117] and non-avionics.[118]

In relation to the market for engines there was some debate on how market shares could be best assessed, but based on the installed base of engines competitor shares were: GE 52.5 per cent; Pratt & Whitney 26.5 per cent; and Rolls Royce 21 per cent. On a second analysis of backlog market shares, which included unfulfilled orders, the evidence showed that GE was gaining market share at the expense of its competitors. There was little prospect of entry into a market with such high technical, scale and reputation barriers. By itself this market share would be regarded as indicative of dominance, but perhaps not conclusive, and the merger would not directly increase horizontal market shares. However, DG Comp relied on additional factors in concluding that GE was dominant. GE had a very substantial financial strength, as manifested in particular through its subsidiary GE-Capital, which, inter alia, allowed it to take risks above those of its competitors, allowing it to compensate for product and strategic failures.[119] Further GE's subsidiary in the area of aircraft purchasing, financing and leasing ('GECAS'), accounted for some 10 per cent of the purchase of new aircraft, making it the world's single largest purchaser of the product. DG Comp argued that GECAS was able to support smaller airlines with GE engines, creating fleet commonality, and erecting further barriers to entry,[120] and that the combined effect of GECAS and GE-Capital was such as to enable GE to negotiate exclusivity arrangements for GE engines on new airframes.[121]

The markets for avionics and non-avionics are complex, and every individual product may be a separate market. Honeywell is unique in that it manufactures a broad range of products in both markets. The Decision went into great detail in relation to market shares in different avionics products, and distinguished between two broad categories: buyer furnished equipment (BFE), and supplier furnished equipment (SFE).[122] DG Comp's analysis of the non-avionics market was much more superficial, and did not go into the same level of detail.

[116] RBB Economics, 'A Bridge Too Far?—Complements, Substitutes and Theories of Exclusion in EC Merger Control', RBB Brief 1, May 2002. See also M Pflanz and C Caffarra, 'The Economics of GE/Honeywell' [2002] *ECLR* 115.

[117] Avionics are devices necessary for the navigation of aircraft, and include radar, radio and GPS systems.

[118] Non-avionics are all the other equipment found on an aircraft, and include brakes, tyres, and air-conditioning systems.

[119] Para 110 of the Decision, above n 114.

[120] Ibid, paras 124 and 146 ff. The Commission noted at para 151, eg, that economies arose from operating a fleet with only one type of engines in terms of engineers' training.

[121] Ibid, paras 115 ff.

[122] Ibid, paras 244 ff. SFE is put onto the platform by the airframer, and BFE is put onto the platform by the end-user.

DG Comp took the view that the merger would have the effect of strengthening GE's dominant position in the markets for engines, and that it would help Honeywell to achieve dominance in the market for avionics and non-avionics.

General Electric appealed DG Comp's decision to the CFI, which substantially upheld the Decision, but was in parts critical of the approach taken by DG Comp.[123] In a judgment which is at points difficult the CFI argued that GECAS's market share was small, and that DG Comp had not proved any causal link between GECAS's actions and a significant increase in sales of engines.[124] However, the CFI argued that GE deliberately exploited its position and that DG Comp was correct to ascribe a number of sales to GECAS' machinations and GE-Capital's financial strength.[125] The CFI did not share the reasoning adopted by DG Comp in relation to its arguments to the effect that the sale of SFE products would be boosted by GE's strength and tactics. The CFI relied upon the tests set out in *Tetra Laval*,[126] arguing that in the case of conglomerate effects and vertical integration DG Comp had to show that post-merger GE would have the ability to transfer its conduct to Honeywell, that it was likely that this would actually happen, and that, in the short term, this would create a dominant position where none existed at present.[127] In this respect DG Comp failed, as it had not shown that such a strategy would be profitable in the medium term.[128] The CFI rejected DG Comp's market definitions in respect of avionic and non-avionic products, as the Decision had failed to take into consideration the fact that the markets might be divided by aircraft type. In the absence of an accurate market definition it was impossible for the CFI to take a clear view on the nature of the market pre-merger, and it could not therefore compare the pre- and post-merger positions.[129]

A central plank of DG Comp's argument was that a strategy of mixed bundling engaged in by the merged entity could be successful, and it relied in part on evidence that, it argued, showed that Honeywell had a history of offering bundled products to airframers and airlines.[130] The CFI was unconvinced that evidence of bundling in avionics and non-avionics was predictive of bundling in these and engines.[131]

The CFI was more supportive of DG Comp's arguments relating to an enhanced dominant position arising from vertical integration in the market for

[123] Case T–210/01 *General Electric Company v Commission* [2006] 4 CMLR 14.

[124] Ibid, paras 238–239.

[125] Ibid, para 242.

[126] Case T–5/02 *Tetra Laval BV v Commission (I)* [2002] ECR II-4381, [2002] 5 CMLR 28, appealed to the ECJ as Case C–12/03 P *Commission v Tetra Laval BV* [2005] ECR I–987. See above.

[127] Ibid, para 325 of the judgment, above n 123.

[128] Ibid, paras 337 ff.

[129] Ibid, paras 361 ff.

[130] A different approach had been reached in the earlier case *Allied Signal/Honeywell* (Case COMP/M.1601, see paras 103 ff). The CFI was unconvinced by DG Comp's arguments, finding that some of the alleged earlier bundling episodes were simply examples of *attempts* to bundle: ibid, para 440.

[131] See, eg, n 123, para 239.

engine starters. Honeywell was the leading supplier of these, and was also active in the production of other devices necessary to control jet engines. Technological barriers to entry were high. DG Comp therefore argued that there existed in this respect a direct relationship between the activities of GE and Honeywell, such that post-merger integration, to the exclusion of others, was likely. In particular DG Comp argued that post-merger there would be 'an incentive to delay or disrupt the supply of . . . engine starters to competing engine manufacturers'.[132] In respect of this argument the CFI found that, 'even in the absence of economic studies'[133] 'the simple economic and commercial realities of the particular case . . . constitute[d] the convincing evidence required',[134] and that DG Comp's argument was 'persuasive'.[135] However, the CFI then progressed to an analysis of whether such conduct could be restrained by a post-merger application of Article 82 EC, and held that DG Comp had failed to take into account adequately the constraint that competition law would exercise on the parties' post-merger conduct.[136]

It was noted above that this case has generated substantial comment. There appears to be some inconsistency in the CFI judgment, in that it applied a different standard of review to the conglomerate and vertical aspects of the merger. In respect of the former the CFI held that DG Comp was required to establish to the required standard that there existed economically rational reasons to behave in accordance with DG Comp's predictions, and that there were economic data to support this proposition. It will be noted though that in the case of the vertical aspects of the merger the CFI expressly held that the arguments made sense, even where there were no economic studies to support them. In part this difference in approach may be attributed to the dynamics of the appeal process. In *Tetra Laval* the ECJ had not expressly rejected its approach to conglomerate effects, and in *General Electric Company v Commission* the CFI relied on its view that the arguments for and against the likelihood of any particular post-merger outcome were to be weighed up and supported with reference to detailed evidence.[137] When it came to vertical integration the standard adopted was that set out by the ECJ in *Tetra Laval* (discussed below).

Tetra Laval/Sidel

In this case, which may be best analysed as a conglomerate merger, the undertakings had already put into effect a concentration by the time at which the Article 8(3) decision was made. The parties notified their concentration to the

[132] Para 420 of the Decision, above n 114.
[133] Para 299 of the judgment, above n 123.
[134] Ibid, para 297.
[135] Ibid, para 299.
[136] Ibid, paras 301–304, 309.
[137] Case T–210/01, *General Electric Company v Commission*, above n 123, at paras 327, 405.

Commission on 18 May 2001. The Commission then identified three main horizontal overlaps in relevant markets in relation to packaging systems for foodstuffs and liquids. The two undertakings were active in the markets for plastic and carton packaging. Plastic bottle products are made with specialised Stretch Blow Moulding (SBM) machines and may either be purchased ready made, or made by the user themselves with an in-house SBM machine. This was the market in which Sidel specialised. Tetra Laval's main activities were in the markets for carton packaging machines and cartons. DG Comp argued that it was dominant in this market, although Sidel was not considered to be dominant in the plastic packaging market. The case is discussed by Bishop *et al*, from whom Figure 8.1 is taken:[138]

The undertakings claimed that the merger would enable them to provide the leading producers of liquid foods with cutting-edge plastics equipment, but the EC Commission was concerned about the creation of a vertically integrated entity with a strong position in the markets both for carton and plastic packaging. In particular the Commission believed that in the future carton packaging

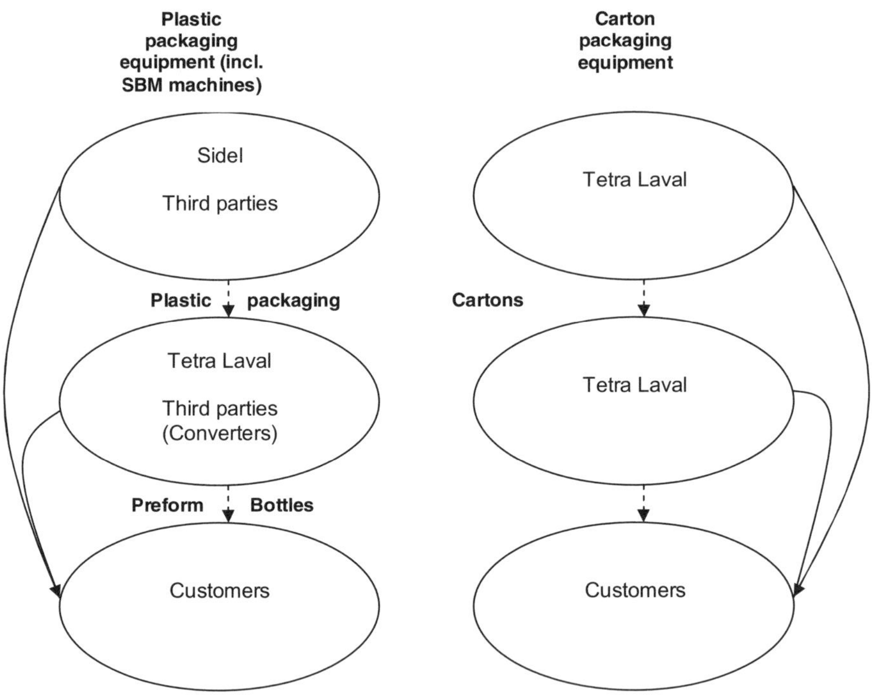

Figure 8.1 Simplified representation of relevant Tetra Laval and Sidel businesses

[138] S Bishop, A Lofaro, F Rosati and J Young, *The Efficiency-Enhancing Effects of Non-Horizontal Mergers*, Luxembourg, Office for Official Publications of the European Communities, 2005), figure 6–5, p 144.

would compete with plastic packaging systems,[139] and that Tetra Laval would be able to use its dominant position in the former market to leverage a dominant position in the plastic packaging market. The fact that the Commission appeared here to base its case not on an immediate assumption of dominance post-merger but on a foreseeable creation of dominance has raised some comment, and this was the first time at which a merger had been blocked in part on this basis.[140] Commitments were offered by the undertakings to address the concerns raised by the Commission, but these were rejected as being insufficient. It appeared to be the case that the merger offered clear efficiency gains. Thus, Bishop *et al* note that:

> The merged entity could derive efficiency benefits from operating in separate but closely related markets of plastic and carton packaging. For example, Tetra Laval enjoyed a good reputation in aseptic cartons, which it could transfer to the market for PET packaging. Indeed, the European Commission decision concluded that reputation and proven ability were the most important factors in the market for aseptic machinery and packaging. Tetra also had a number of very successful selling strategies which could be applied to Sidel's products. Finally, the merged entity could be expected to have a number of common customers who may benefit from reduced transaction and marketing costs.[141]

By the time the Commission made its final Article 8(3) decision Tetra Laval had acquired some 95 per cent of Sidel's shares by way of a public bid. The Commission then presented proposals on the basis of Article 8(4) ECMR to rectify the harm it had identified, which required the divestiture of the two undertakings in a short space of time. While Tetra Laval did not fundamentally object to the divestiture it did argue that the time period set by the Commission was unreasonable and unnecessary and suggested that there was 'virtually no competition at present between the two businesses'. The Commission did not agree and expressed strongly its concerns about the effect of current investment and product development decisions on future competition between the parties. The Commission insisted at paragraph 22 that:

> An effective and final divestiture should consist of the sale of Sidel as a going concern without any change in its status, or in the scope or current range of its activities, which

[139] Cartons are not gas permeable and do not admit light into the product, so are suitable for products that must be protected from these elements, but are not as strong as plastic bottles. However, changes in bottle technologies suggested that they would be suitable in the future for sensitive products.

[140] See, eg, LM Davison, 'EU Merger Control and the Compatibility Test: A Review of Recent Developments' (2004) 25 *Liverpool Law Review* 195 at 203.

[141] Bishop *et al*, above n 138 at 146. In an analysis critical of the Commission's decision the authors conclude that '[i]n particular, the lack of convergence in the two markets and the non-existence of a distinct market for consumers of "sensitive" products suggest that competitors are unlikely to have been marginalized by any bundling or tying': ibid. See also RBB Economics, 'A Bridge Too Far?—Complements, Substitutes and Theories of Exclusion in EC Merger Control', RBB Brief 1, May 2002; and SB Völcker, 'Leveraging as a Theory of Competitive Harm in EU Merger Control' (2003) 40 *CML Rev* 581.

> might weaken its viability and effectiveness as a competitor on the markets in question. paragraph 22.

As long as the basic objective of maintaining the viability of Sidel was met, Tetra Laval would have the freedom to choose the method of divestiture. Tetra Laval was also banned from holding a minority stake or other financial interest in Sidel which might have the effect of impeding the restoration of competition. Both decisions taken by the Commission were appealed to the CFI, which annulled the Article 8(3) decision, and found, as an inevitable consequence of this, that the divestiture decision was also invalid.[142]

In making its judgment the CFI found that the Commission had 'committed manifest errors of assessment in relying on the horizontal and vertical effects of the modified merger to support its analysis of the creation of a dominant position'.[143] Further, the Court found that the Commission had overstated the conglomerate effects of the merger, and had wrongly disregarded the commitments offered by Tetra Laval. On 13 January 2003 the Commission lodged its appeal against the CFI judgments as Cases C–12 and 13/03 P *Commission v Tetra Laval BV*.[144] However, DG Comp also re-decided the matter, and withdrew its opposition to the merger, making a second decision on 13 January 2003.

The ECJ gave judgment on 15 February 2005, rejecting the Commission's appeal.[145] Two aspects of the final judgment are particularly worthy of attention. In relation to the standard of review to be applied to conglomerate mergers DG Comp argued that the CFI set a standard under which they should be presumed to be legal, whereas DG Comp has always argued that anti-competitive effects may flow depending on the facts.[146] The ECJ did not find that the CFI had adopted a specific presumption in this regard, but that it was necessary to examine the relevant facts closely. Thus at paragraph 41 of its judgment the ECJ held that:

> Although the [CFI] stated, in paragraph 155, that proof of anti-competitive conglomerate effects of a merger of the kind notified calls for a precise examination, supported by convincing evidence, of the circumstances which allegedly produce those effects, it by no means added a condition relating to the requisite standard of proof but merely

[142] Case T–5/02, *Tetra Laval BV v Commission (I)* [2002] 5 CMLR 28; Case T–80/02, *Tetra Laval BV v Commission (II)* [2002] 5 CMLR 29.

[143] Case T–5/02, *Tetra Laval BV v Commission (I)* [2002] 5 CMLR 28, para 141.

[144] The Commission appealed on 5 grounds: (1) the CFI wrongly required DG Comp to bring forward 'convincing evidence', and did not adequately respect the Commission's discretion when making decisions based on complex facts; (2) the CFI overstated the duty of the Commission to take into account the fact that Arts 81 and 82 EC would have in deterring future anti-competitive conduct; (3) the CFI drew the boundaries of its judicial review powers too widely; (4) the CFI distorted the facts; and (4) the CFI erred when it rejected DG Comp's findings in relation to the creation of a dominant position on the market for stretch blow moulding machines.

[145] Case C–12/03 P, *Commission v Tetra Laval BV* [2005] ECR I–987. See generally MM Dabbah, 'Opinion: *Tetra Laval v European Commission*' [2004] *Comp Law* 234; A Nucara, '*Schneider/Legrand* and *Tetra Laval/Sidel*: Fast Track Towards Merger Reform?' [2003] *European Business Law Review* 193.

[146] See the short discussion of conglomerate mergers in Chap 2, above.

drew attention to the essential function of evidence, which is to establish convincingly the merits of an argument or, as in the present case, of a decision on a merger.

At paragraph 44 the ECJ dealt expressly with the difficulties of analysing 'conglomerate-type' concentrations:

> The analysis of a 'conglomerate-type' concentration is a prospective analysis in which, first, the consideration of a lengthy period of time in the future and, secondly, the leveraging necessary to give rise to a significant impediment to effective competition, mean that the chains of cause and effect are dimly discernible, uncertain and difficult to establish. That being so, the quality of the evidence produced by the EC Commission in order to establish that it is necessary to adopt a decision declaring the concentration incompatible with the common market is particularly important, since that evidence must support the EC Commission's conclusion that, if such a decision were not adopted, the economic development envisaged by it would be plausible.[147]

The Commission also argued that the CFI erred in holding that the Commission should have taken into account the disciplining effect of the general law of competition on the conduct of the post-merger undertaking. Here the ECJ again sided with the CFI, holding that as the Commission had built an argument based in part on the conduct likely to be adopted by the merged entity, it was obliged to consider all relevant factors impacting on that conduct, including the role of competition law in disciplining conduct. At the same time the ECJ held that the Commission could not be required, in each and every case, to consider 'the extent to which such incentives would be reduced, or even eliminated, as a result of the unlawfulness of the conduct in question'.[148] It was of course the case that the purpose of the ECMR was to prevent the 'creation' or 'strengthening' of a dominant position, and not any subsequent abuse of that dominant position.

It is unclear whether, under the SIEC test of the revised ECMR, the Commission's task would have been any easier, although Dabbah suggests that, 'arguably [the case] could have been stronger'.[149] Irrespective of the change in the ECMR the case remains an important benchmark in establishing the standards to be applied in relation to conglomerate mergers, and was considered further in *General Electric/Honeywell,* discussed above.

[147] Howarth has argued that '[a] more economic approach would acknowledge that the uncertainty and information imperfections exist in reality and would then seek to structure the decision-making by applying probability and/or discount factors to possible results, or designing decision rules that minimise the total expected error costs over all cases where the uncertainty arises, thereby maximising total welfare. This sort of weighted probability approach better reflects what happens in real markets. The competitive effect of a merger is determined partly by what happens tomorrow, but also by what firms do today in expectation of what will happen tomorrow. This expectation is usually based on rough probabilities adjusted in the light of what happened yesterday': D Howarth, '*Tetra Laval/Sidel*: Microeconomics or Microlaw?' [2005] *ECLR* 369, at 371.

[148] Above n 145, at para 75.

[149] Dabbah, above n 145, at 237.

Schneider/Legrand

In this case DG Comp blocked a merger between two French electrical equipment manufacturers which were both active worldwide, holding that the merger would create or strengthen a dominant position in various sectors of the market, and that commitments proposed by Schneider were not sufficient to remedy the harm identified. A number of relevant product markets were identified in the general area of individual components, or of particular types of switchboard and other built products, and the Commission found that the geographic markets were national in scope. Brand loyalty was a strong feature of the market, with some electricians working with the same brands for their entire careers, with the effect that branding was very important and that manufacturers sought to develop as wide a range of products as possible. This in turn raised a substantial barrier to entry, as any new entrant would have to establish a brand reputation from scratch. Further, there was a lack of price sensitivity. Prior to the merger both parties had very wide ranges of products, and following the merger there would be only two countries in the EEA in which the combined entity would not occupy a leading position. DG Comp also found that there was little countervailing buyer power as, given the fragmented nature of the market at the purchaser level coupled with the brand loyalty, no buyers would be in a position to exercise a significant competitive constraint on the producer. In conclusion the Commission found that the merged entity would be able to raise the price of its product for its own benefit, and declared the merger to be incompatible with the common market.

Schneider launched a successful appeal against the decision.[150] On 22 October 2002, the CFI found that the Commission had failed properly to evaluate the geographic market, noting that there were different national geographic markets, but referring to the European-wide coverage of the merged entity to show that a dominant position would be created. While the CFI did not rule that the Commission could not undertake such an exercise it did require that, were the Commission to do so, it was obliged to demonstrate clearly the link between the two different geographic situations, and had failed in this case to do so. The Court further found that the Commission had failed adequately to consider the role of wholesalers and had not clearly demonstrated that they would be unable to exercise a restraint on the merged entity. Finally, the CFI held that the Commission had infringed the parties' procedural rights, finding that the Commission had made one allegation in the statement of objections, but had relied on a different ground in making its final decision, and had therefore deprived Schneider of its guaranteed rights of defence, and denied it the opportunity to offer appropriate commitments to the Commission to mitigate the latter's concern.[151]

[150] Cases T–310/01 and T–77/02, *Schneider Electric SA v Commission* [2003] 4 CMLR 17.

[151] Notwithstanding their victory, the parties withdrew the merger notification on 11 Dec 2002. See F Ragolle, '*Schneider Electric v Commission*: The CFI's Response to the Green Paper on Merger Review' [2003] *ECLR* 176.

ENI/EDP/GDP

As of July 2006 the most recent merger to be blocked is that of *ENI/EDP/GDP*, on 9 December 2004. This was notified to the Commission on 9 July 2004 and involved a transaction whereby Energias de Portugal SA (EDP) and Eni Spa (Eni), through a subsidiary, would acquire joint control over Gas de Portugal SGPS SA (GDP) by way of a purchase of shares. Notwithstanding the fact that the parties were offering commitments the Commission took the view that the merger would lead to the strengthening of the respective dominant positions of EDP and GDP in the electricity and gas markets in Portugal. Unusually this is a case in which a vertical relationship was central in the development of the Commission's argument.

The market definition in this case was relatively straightforward, adhering to an approach adopted in previous cases in which the Commission separated markets by reference to the type of energy being supplied,[152] with an overwhelming majority of customers indicating that they would not consider switching from gas to electricity or vice versa, even in the face of significant relative price rises given the high costs of switching. At the same time the Commission found that undertakings able to offer supplies of both gas and electricity through 'dual offers' possessed a competitive advantage over undertakings being able to offer only a single product.

EDP held a dominant position in the market for electricity in Portugal, accounting for some 70–80 per cent of generation and generation capacity, and was also the largest importer of electricity into Portugal, accounting for some 50–60 per cent of total imports from Spain. As a result of the merger this dominance would be strengthened through both horizontal and vertical effects. At the horizontal level GDP would be eliminated as a significant potential competitor, with an analysis of the way in which the industry was developing suggesting that GDP would, in the light of the experience in other Member States, 'be a natural competitor to EDP'.[153] Respondents on the supply side were strongly of the view that this was a likely scenario, and there was, according to the Commission, a strong economic rationale for such entry taking place. On the vertical side it was noted that gas was the most effective and common input to generate more electricity in Europe using gas-based power generators, and the Commission argued that by allowing EDP 'to integrate upstream with the only supplier of natural gas in Portugal, the operation is likely to change immediately and in the near

[152] Further divisions existed within each form of energy. Thus for electricity the Commission distinguished between: generation and wholesale supply of electricity; transmission; distribution; retail supply; and, 'possibly' the provision of regulating/balancing power services (see para 31 of the Decision, Case COMP/M.2416(2001)). In relation to the supply of natural gas the relevant markets were deemed to be: supply to gas-based power plants; supply to local distribution companies; supply to large industrial customers; and supply to smaller customers including domestic users: ibid, para 270.

[153] Ibid, para 337.

future, the conditions of competition on the wholesale market',[154] resulting in further strengthening of the already existing dominant position. If EDP became a supplier of gas to its competitors in the electricity market it would be placed in the unusual position of knowing the key input costs of its main competitor, giving it 'a very important advantage'.[155] It would also have the ability to raise the input costs of its rivals.[156] The Commission further argued that the merger would give EDP the ability to 'maintain a privileged and preferential access to natural gas to the detriment of companies actually or potentially involved in electricity generation'.[157] EDP's dominant position in relation to the retail supply of electricity in Portugal would also be strengthened by its elimination of the potential competition flowing from GDP.

In relation to the supply of natural gas in Portugal the Commission found GDP to be in a dominant position, and that it possessed significant advantages through its incumbency. In particular: (1) it had gained a strong experience and knowledge of the market at every level; (2) it had a large customer base and significant sales volumes throughout the country; (3) it had developed strong brand recognition; (4) it had acquired a unique knowledge of the profile of its customers; and (5) it controlled the distribution system operators.[158] Entry barriers were also very high, arising in particular from GDP's control over all the entry points in Portugal and the only storage facility in the country, as well as from the high economies of scale in the industry, giving rise to the need for entrants to achieve a crucial size in order to operate effectively. The parties argued that there was evidence that increased demand for gas would lead to the development of new facilities, and that steps were already in place to achieve this. However, the Commission noted that the realisation of the new projects was doubtful, and that EDP could itself threaten these developments either by taking direct action to delay them, or by anticipating its competitors' moves by speeding up a new project of its own.

The parties offered various remedies on 28 October 2004 to divest various assets to competitors; to offer certain supply guarantees based on transparent and non-discriminatory criteria; not to book further capacity on certain pipelines; and not to make dual offers until the market was liberalised. Further remedies were offered, after the deadline, on 26 November 2004. None of these was sufficient, according to the Commission, to remove the competitive concerns identified, and the merger was blocked.

In September 2005 the CFI upheld the Commission's decision.[159]

[154] *Tetra Laval/Sidell II* (Case COMP/M.2416)(2001), above n 152, para 366.
[155] Ibid, para 368.
[156] Ibid, para 411.
[157] Ibid, para 380.
[158] Ibid, para 481.
[159] Case T-87/05 *EDP-Energias de Portugal SA v Commission* [2005] CMLR 4.

9

Appeals and Third Party Rights

INTRODUCTION

THE ONLY COURTS able to review decisions of the EC Commission taken in the application of the ECMR are the CFI and, on further appeal, the ECJ. Article 220 EC charges the ECJ, of which the CFI is part, with ensuring that 'in the interpretation and application of the Treaty the law is obeyed'. Article 21(1) ECMR provides simply that, '[s]ubject to review by the [ECJ] the Commission shall have sole jurisdiction to take the decisions provided for in this Regulation'. Article 16 makes specific reference to the right of parties to seek a review of any decision in which a penalty has been imposed under the ECMR.

The general right to appeal against actions of the Commission is set out in Article 230 EC, which provides, in part, that:

> The Court of Justice shall review the legality of acts . . . of the Commission, other than recommendations and opinions . . .
>
> It shall for this purpose have jurisdiction . . . on grounds of lack of competence, infringement of an essential procedural requirement, infringement of this Treaty or of any rule of law relating to its application, or misuse of powers.
>
> . . .
>
> Any natural or legal person may . . . institute proceedings against a decision addressed to that person . . .
>
> The proceedings provided for in this article shall be instituted within two months of the publication of the measure, or of its notification to the plaintiff . . .

Article 232 EC establishes the right to bring an action in the case of a failure of one of the EC institutions to act when required to do so, and Article 229 EC gives the ECJ competence to review sanctions imposed under any provision of EC law. The large number of cases being brought before the ECJ challenging the Commission's actions in the application of Articles 81 and 82 EC, and the attendant delays before the Court, was one reason behind the creation in 1998[1] of the CFI, which was given jurisdiction over acts relating to the application of the EC competition rules by any Community institution. Appeals may be made from the CFI to the ECJ exclusively on points of law, and the ECJ is bound by the

[1] Council Decision 88/591 creating the CFI [1988] OJ L 319/1.

facts as determined by the CFI. Although the CFI and ECJ are to have regard to the discretion conferred on the Commission in their review of Commission acts, the ECJ held in *Tetra Laval*[2] that:

> Whilst the Court recognises that the Commission has a margin of discretion with regard to economic matters, that does not mean that the Community Courts must refrain from reviewing the Commission's interpretation of information of an economic nature. Not only must the Community Courts, inter alia, establish whether the evidence relied on is factually accurate, reliable and consistent, but also whether that evidence contains all the information which must be taken into account in order to assess a complex analysis and whether it is capable of sustaining the conclusions drawn from it.[3]

Third party rights are generally most noticeable by their absence in the application of the ECMR. It is certainly right that third parties are precluded from challenging mergers on their own initiative. Some involvement for third parties is provided for under the ECMR and the implementing regulation, as well as in *Best Practice*. Where these have not been expressly dealt with elsewhere in the preceding chapters these are briefly dealt with below. The rights of third parties to challenge Commission acts before the CFI/ECJ are dealt with in the immediate following section.

APPEALS

What may be challenged

Article 230 makes reference to 'acts' of the Commission, and excludes from this rubric only opinions and recommendations. While it is clear that some of the formal decisions taken under the various relevant provisions of the ECMR may be appealed, it is not clear that all can, and it is less clear what else may fall within the term 'act'. In a different context the ECJ held that the key factor determining whether any particular act was capable of being appealed was whether it produced legal effects on the applicant such that its legal situation was changed.[4] Thus in *IBM* the ECJ stated that:

> Any measure the legal effects of which are binding on, and capable of affecting the interests of, the applicant by bringing about a distinct change in his legal position is an

[2] Case C–12/03 P, *Commission v Tetra Laval BV* [2005] ECR I–987.

[3] Ibid, para 39. Bailey has noted that in the leading three cases in which the CFI overturned Commission decisions that although the 'cases were remarkable in the publicity they attracted [they were] of far greater significance [in] the rigorous way in which the CFI exercised its jurisdiction. Where the Commission's decision lacked convincing evidence, the CFI did not hesitate to depart from the Commission's findings': D Bailey, 'Standard of Proof in EC Merger Proceedings: a Common Law Perspective' (2003) 40 *CML Rev* 845 at 845.

[4] See, eg, Case 22/70, *Commission v Council (ERTA)* [1971] ECR 263; Case T–3/93, *Air France v Commission* [1994] ECR II-121.

act or decision which may be the object of an action under [art 230] for a declaration that it is void.[5]

In *Air France*, for example, which flowed from the acquisition of Dan Air by British Airways, a public statement was made by an official of the EC Commission stating that the merger did not fall within the jurisdiction of the ECMR as it lay below the appropriate thresholds. Air France sought to appeal, arguing that the effect of this public announcement, along with a letter in similar terms sent to British Airways, was to determine that the relevant state to review the merger was the UK. The CFI held that the Commission action in this case did amount to an 'act' capable of being reviewed, as it was determinative of the legal position—in effect absolving the parties from notifying the merger under the ECMR.[6]

In the context of the general application of EC competition law it has been held that acts which are preparatory to a final act, which may itself be reviewed, are not generally capable of being appealed. This applies, for example, to requests for information or to formal decisions requiring the submission of information. These do not determine the parties' legal positions, although any penalties imposed for a failure to comply may be appealed on the basis of Article 229 EC.[7] An Article 9 ECMR referral to a Member State may be challenged,[8] but the ECJ has no jurisdiction over the actions of Member States, and a referral request from a Member State to the Commission under Article 22 ECMR may *not* be challenged.[9] In respect of cases in which the Commission has made a decision that the notified concentration is not blocked under the ECMR two different results may be contrasted. In *Assicurazioni*[10] the CFI held that the decision to terminate proceedings under Article 6(1)(a) of Regulation 4064/89 was capable of being challenged. In this case the arrangements in place were designed to create a JV, and the Commission took the view that it was not a concentrative JV, and therefore fell to be analysed under the terms of Article 81 EC. The CFI held that it was this aspect of the case which entitled the parties to seek annulment. On the other hand, in *Coca-Cola*[11] the Commission cleared a merger, but Coca-Cola sought to challenge aspects of the reasoning published

[5] Case 60/81, *IBM v Commission* [1981] 3 CMLR 635, para 9.

[6] *Air France v Commission,* above n 4.

[7] The CFI has held that '[o]nly measures immediately and irreversibly affecting the legal situation of the undertakings concerned would be of such a nature as to justify before completion of the administrative procedure, the admissibility of an action for annulment': Cases T–10–12 & 14–15/92, *Cimenteries CBR SA v Commission* [1993] 4 CMLR 243 at para 42. The leading work on procedures and rights in the application of EC competition law generally is CS Kerse and N Khan, *EC Antitrust Procedure* (5th edn, London, Sweet & Maxwell, 2005), although this does not deal with ECMR procedures.

[8] See, eg, Case T–119/02, *Royal Philips NV v Commission* [2003] ECR II–1433.

[9] See, eg, Case T–221/95, *Endemol Entertainment Holding BV v Commission* [1999] ECR II–1299.

[10] Case T–87/96, *Assicurazioni Generali SpA and Unicredito SpA* [1999] ECR II–203.

[11] Cases T–125/97 and T–127/97, *The Coca-Cola Company and Coca-Cola Enterprises Inc v Commission* [2000] 5 CMLR 467.

in the decision. In particular the Commission had found that Coca-Cola occupied a dominant position in the market for cola-flavoured carbonated soft drinks in the UK, and it was argued by Coca-Cola that this would prejudice their position in possible future mergers or competition law actions. The CFI in this case held that there was no appealable decision capable of being challenged, as there was nothing in this statement of findings which was operative on the parties. The fact that Coca-Cola had offered undertakings was found to be irrelevant, as these did not affect the decision taken by the Commission.

Penalties

Article 16 ECMR provides that:

> The Court of Justice shall have unlimited jurisdiction within the meaning of article 229 of the Treaty to review decisions whereby the Commission has fixed a fine or periodic penalty payments; it may cancel, reduce or increase the fine or periodic penalty payment imposed.

Permitted appeals are heard by the CFI, and a further appeal on a point of law may lie to the ECJ.

Locus standi

Certain parties have privileged standing in relation to the application of Article 230 EC, and may in any circumstances bring an action for judicial review, provided that a relevant act has taken place. These are the Member States, the Council of Ministers, the Commission and, in certain cases, the European Parliament, the Court of Auditors and the European Central Bank, although it is unlikely that this latter group would be able to invoke its rights in relation to the application of the ECMR.

The primary parties that may bring an action are those concerned directly by the relevant decision—typically the merging undertakings in the case of the application of the ECMR. Appeals may also be brought by other natural or legal persons where they are not the addressees of decisions, but are individually and directly affected by them. In order to fall within this class it is not enough that the person be one of a general category affected by the decision, but rather that in some way they are distinctly affected as a result of certain attributes that set them apart from the generality.[12] Four categories of applicants may be identified in the case of merger control: those to whom the decision is addressed (ie, the undertakings themselves); shareholders in those undertakings; competitors; and employees, including trade unions representing them.

[12] Case 25/62, *Plaumann v Commission* [1963] ECR 95.

Undertakings to whom decisions are addressed

Those to whom decisions are addressed—the parties to the concentration in respect of which the decision is made—are axiomatically entitled to appeal against the decision. In *Gencor* the CFI rejected an argument of the Commission that would have limited this principle. The merger was made subject to certain contractual limitations, including the requirement of sanction from relevant regulatory authorities. Therefore, when the Commission blocked the merger it collapsed, and the Commission argued that the parties therefore had no legitimate interest in pursuing an appeal. While the logic of this argument may be doubted and appears to be spurious, the CFI held that the right to appeal of the parties to the concentration was protected by the Treaty, and could not be circumvented by any such argument.[13]

Shareholders

The first appeal to be brought before the CFI in relation to the ECMR was that by a group of shareholders in one of the relevant undertakings, none of whose shareholdings exceeded 0.5 per cent.[14] The Commission had found that an increase in a shareholding in Assicurazioni Generali (AG), acquired by Mediobanca did not constitute a concentration for the purposes of the ECMR as it did not, given the pattern of shareholdings, confer an ability on Mediobanca to exercise control or decisive influence over AG. The shareholders argued that the Commission had not been made aware of crucial facts, and sought the right to appeal. The CFI held that no one shareholder was individually affected by the decision in such a way as to confer locus standi, and refused to hear the appeal. There was a further appeal to the ECJ.[15] The Advocate General reasoned that the shareholders were *directly* affected by the decision, but were not, given that they were members of a huge class of 140,000 minority shareholders, *individually* affected by the decision, and argued further that shareholders should not generally have the right to appeal in such cases. It is perhaps to be regretted that the ECJ neither followed nor rejected this reasoning, finding in favour of the Commission instead on the ground that it had not in the present case taken an actionable measure, as it had merely confirmed a position it had previously taken.

[13] Case T–102/96, *Gencor Ltd v Commission* [1999] ECR II–753, [1999] 4 CMLR 971.

[14] Case T–83/92, *Zunis Holding and others v Commission* [1993] ECR II-1169; an appeal against the Commission's decision in Case IV/M.159 *Mediobanca/Generali* (1991).

[15] Case C–480/93P, *Zunis v Commission* [1996] ECR I–1.

Competitors

The CFI has found that competitors have locus standi to challenge merger decisions taken by the EC Commission.[16] The leading case is *Dan Air* (discussed briefly above).[17] Here the CFI held that:

> the contested decision is to be regarded as of direct concern to the undertakings engaged in the international civil aviation market or markets who could, on the date of the contested act, be certain of an immediate or imminent change in the market.

In another case involving Air France[18] the appellant was permitted to challenge a Commission decision in relation to *British Airways/TAT*.[19] Here different, more specific grounds were given in permitting the appeal, amongst which was the fact that Air France had participated in the Commission proceedings prior to the taking of the decision. Cook and Kerse note that 'whilst that criterion should not be determinative, competitor undertakings need to bear it in mind if their position on a market is likely to be adversely affected by a notified concentration. They need to act quickly to make representations.'[20] Such action may have assisted BaByliss in its challenge when the Commission argued that it was not a direct competitor of the undertakings subject to the decision, and had not even brought forward convincing evidence that it was a likely potential competitor. The CFI however admitted the appeal, basing its decision in part on the fact that BaByliss had participated in the proceedings at Phase I, and was active in relevant general markets.[21] In the recent case of *easyJet*[22] the complainant sought an annulment of the Commission's decision in *Air France/KLM*[23] which cleared the merger subject to the fulfilment of various commitments. easyJet had submitted comments on the proposed commitments

[16] It should be noted that the grounds of appeal are different from the rights granted to third parties in the US. In the latter jurisdiction actions may be brought by those suffering 'antitrust injury'. It may be generally presumed that competitors are most likely to seek to challenge a merger which threatens them. Although a threat may arise, eg, through foreclosure of markets, it may also arise through an enhancement of the ability of the post-merger entity to offer effective competition on the relevant market. In the latter case a challenge under the US system will not be accepted. The leading case in this respect is *Brunswick Corporation v Pueblo Bowl-O-Mat, Inc* 429 US 477 (1977), in which the Supreme Court held that third parties were protected under the antitrust laws only from 'injury of the type the antitrust laws were intended to prevent and that flows from that which makes the defendants' acts unlawful' (at 489). In the EC parties may challenge a decision on the grounds set out in Art 230, which may include that the Commission erred in its findings of fact and its analysis of the merger, but which do not go directly to the effect of the merger on the parties.

[17] Case T–3/93, *Air France v Commission* [1994] ECR II–121.

[18] Case T–2/93, *Air France v Commission* [1994] ECR II–323.

[19] Case IV/M.259.

[20] CJ Cook and CS Kerse, *EC Merger Control* (4th edn, London, Sweet & Maxwell, 2005), at 10-011.

[21] Case T–114/02, *BaByliss SA and DeLonghi SpA v Commission* [2003] ECR II–1279.

[22] Case T–177/04, *easyJet Airline Co Ltd v Commission*, judgment of 4 July 2006.

[23] Case COMP/M.3280 (2004). See O Stehmann and JR Aguado, 'The Air France—KLM Merger: a First Step Towards the Consolidation of the European Aviation Industry' [2005] *ECLR* 258 and J Parker, 'Air France/KLM: an Assessment of the Commission's Approach to Consolidation in the Air Transport Sector' [2005] *ECLR* 128.

on two occasions during the Phase I procedure. easyJet failed on the substance of the case, but was granted locus standi to mount the challenge. The CFI found that easyJet was directly concerned by the contested decision as the effect of the decision was to permit the merger, which was 'capable of bringing about an immediate change in the state of the relevant markets'.[24] The question then arose whether the applicant was also individually concerned by the decision. Again the CFI pointed to the 'active' involvement of easyJet in the Commission's procedure, noting that:

> Whilst mere participation in the procedure is not sufficient to establish that the decision is of individual concern to the applicant, particularly in the field of merger control, the careful examination of which requires regular contact with numerous undertakings, active participation in the administrative procedure is a factor regularly taken into account in the case-law on competition.[25]

Employees and their representatives

Paragraph (4) of Article 18 ECMR, which sets out the rights of third parties to be heard in the application of the ECMR, provides that 'the recognised representatives of [the undertakings'] employees shall be entitled, upon application, to be heard'. The Regulation does not however set out any specific rights in relation to appeals, although, as discussed above, participation in proceedings is a relevant factor in determining whether an appellant is directly and individually affected by the decision. In the *Perrier* cases employees' representatives and trade unions sought to challenge the Commission's decision taken in *Nestlé/Perrier*[26] approving the acquisition of Source Perrier by Nestlé. The Commission opposed the application, but the CFI drew attention to Article 18(4) ECMR, recital (19) of Regulation 4064/89, which makes reference to this Article, and the factors referred to in Article 2(1)(b) ECMR which, although they do not make explicit reference to employment, do refer to some wider considerations.[27] However, the CFI found that the workers being represented by these bodies were not in the present cases directly affected by the outcome of the decision, in part because it was not inevitable that deleterious effects on employees would flow from the merger. However, the CFI found that the effect of Article 18(4) ECMR was such as to guarantee representative bodies the right to challenge Commission merger decisions specifically to protect the recognition of their rights in the procedures, the effect of which is somewhat different from admitting challenges based on substantive considerations.

[24] Above n 22, para 32.
[25] Ibid, para 35.
[26] Case COMP/M.190 (1992).
[27] Case T–96/92, *Comité Central d'Entreprise de la Société Générale de Grandes Sources v Commission* [1995] ECR II–1213, and Case T–12/93, *Comité Central d'Entreprise de la Société Anonyme Vittel v Commission* [1995] ECR II–1247.

Interim effects of appeals

It is expressly provided in Article 242 EC that appeals brought before the ECJ (and hence the CFI) do not have suspensory effect on the action being contested. Given the nature of the appeal process and the length of time required to hear cases, this is a necessary provision to ensure the smooth operation of the Community procedures. It would be particularly exasperating to merging parties if a Commission decision permitting a merger were suspended during the course of proceedings brought by a third party with locus standi to challenge that decision. However, Article 243 EC does give the ECJ the power to order interim measures where it is appropriate to do so.[28] It has been noted that 'interim protection is particularly relevant in cases brought under [the ECMR], particularly where the undertakings affected have brought annulment proceedings against Commission decisions ordering the break-up of undertakings or assets'.[29]

Requests for interim suspension of decisions must be made separately from the main pleadings in the case, and the President of the CFI has indicated that the parties seeking interim relief must make a prima facie case that serious and irreparable loss will flow should the decision not be suspended. There have been few applications made in respect of the ECMR, and only one at the time of writing in which interim measures have been granted.[30] It is relevant that the existence of the fast track procedure, discussed below, may greatly speed up the process in relation to merger cases, limiting the necessity for interim measures. The one case in which an application for interim suspension of a merger decision was granted related to the decision taken in *Kali + Salz/MDK/Treuhand*.[31] Here the President of the CFI ordered the suspension of the decision clearing the merger, which required that divestments be made.[32] One of the commitments required Kali + Salz to withdraw from a JV in which the Société Commerciale

[28] See, eg, Case T–24/93, *Compagnie Maritime Belge Transports NV v Commission* [1993] ECR I–543, where the CFI stated at para 18 that: '[b]y virtue of the combined provisions of Arts 185 and 186 of the EEC Treaty and Art 4 of the Council Decision of 24 October 1998 establishing [the CFI], the [CFI] may, if it considers that circumstances so require, order that application of the contested act be suspended or prescribe any necessary interim measure.'

See generally E Navarro Varona and H Gonzalez Durantez, 'Interim Measures in Competition Cases Before the European Commission and Courts' [2002] *ECLR* 512.

[29] E Navarro, A Font, J Folguera and J Briones, *Merger Control in the EU* (2nd edn, Oxford, OUP, 2005), para 15.48.

[30] Unsuccessful applications include *Union Carbide v Commission* Case T–322/94, [1994] ECR II–1159, in which the interests of the merging parties were placed ahead of those of the applicant, and Case T–96/92 *Comité Central d'Entreprise de la Société Générale de Grandes Sources v Commission* [1995] ECR II–1213, and *Comité Central d'Enterprise de la Société Anonyme Vittel v Commission* case T–12/93, [1995] ECR II–1247 in which the President of the CFI held that the applicants were unable to show an immediate risk of serious and irreparable harm were the merger to proceed.

[31] Case IV/M.308 [1994] OJ L 186/86 (see Chap 7).

[32] Case T–88/94R, *Société Commerciale des Potasses et de l'Azote and Entreprise Minière et Chimique v Commission* [1994] ECR II–403.

des Potasses et de l'Azote (SCPA) held a 25 per cent stake. SCPA was able to persuade the President that if Kali + Salz were to withdraw the JV would collapse, and that it would be difficult to re-establish it.

The fast-track procedure[33]

It is a matter of some frustration to competition lawyers generally that the procedures before the CFI and ECJ are slow, and in the case of merger control time is clearly of the essence. In *Airtours/First Choice*,[34] for example, the Court victory overturning the Commission's decision came nearly three years after the parties first attempted to merge. Accordingly, from 1 February 2001, a 'fast track', or expedited, appeal procedure was introduced into the CFI. Article 76(a) of the CFI Rules of Procedure states that the CFI 'may, on application by the applicant or the defendant, after hearing the other parties and the Advocate General, decide, having regard to the particular urgency and the circumstances of the case to adjudicate under an expedited procedure'. Either the applicant or the defendant may request that this procedure be invoked. The aim was to reduce the period of appeal to 12 months, and this appears to have been met. In *Schneider*, for example, the judgment was delivered only 10 months after the appeal was lodged.[35] It should be evident that, where mergers have not been abandoned, the test of urgency is axiomatically met. However, the second requirement for the application of the fast-track procedure is the circumstances of the case, which are taken to include its complexity and the extent of the pleadings. In this respect merger cases may face a hurdle, and it has been pointed out that 'most of the merger cases need the review of very complex economic reasoning and factual backgrounds'.[36] The importance of this procedure for the dynamics of the merger control process cannot be overstated, and has been explained clearly by Nucara, referring to the high proportion of merger cases before the CFI proceeding under the fast-track procedure:

> This shows something that was not difficult to foresee: as soon as private parties had an efficient and quick (or at least quicker) way of challenging merger control decisions, they used it. In merger cases, in fact, it is of little use and would be a pyrrhic victory for the companies to obtain a judgment annulling a Commission's decision two years after the merger has been prohibited. Now that private parties have the possibility to obtain judicial review within a reasonable time, they have an incentive to keep the deal 'alive' and challenge the Commission's decision. The same is true for third parties' interest in challenging a deal that has been cleared by the Commission.[37]

[33] See, generally, C Chibnall, 'Expedited Treatment of Appeals against EC Commission Decisions under the EC Merger Regulation' [2002] *Comp Law* 327.

[34] Case IV/M.1524, Decision 2000/276, [2000] OJ L 93/1.

[35] Cases T–310/01 and T–77/02, *Schneider Electric SA v Commission* [2003] 4 CMLR 17.

[36] A Nucara, '*Schneider/Legrand* and *Tetra Laval/Sidel*: Fast Track Towards Merger Reform?' [2003] *European Business Law Review* 193, at 197.

[37] Ibid, at 198.

Some commentators however remain concerned that even the reduced delay to the merger process that applies in the case of the fast-track system is still excessive.[38] Most recently the fast track procedure was used in the *Impala* case,[39] in which the CFI made the first annulment of a Commission decision clearing a merger (see Chapter 8, above).

Re-examining the case—Article 10(5) ECMR

Article 10(5) ECMR sets out the obligations in the event that the CFI or ECJ annuls, in whole or in part, a relevant Commission decision.[40] In such a case the concentration is to be re-examined by the Commission as if a Phase I proceeding were under way with a view to reaching a decision under Article 6(1) (ie, a Phase I decision). This examination is to be conducted 'in the light of current market conditions', and, where there have been changes since the original notification was made, the parties are required to re-notify the merger, or to supplement the original notification, or in the alternative are required to certify that the original notification remains valid. The normal time periods commence from the working day following that on which this obligation is fulfilled. Parties may, of course, withdraw their notification where the merger has been abandoned, or may reconstitute the arrangement and submit a new notification.

THIRD PARTY RIGHTS

It was noted in the introduction to this chapter that third party rights are not to the fore in the application of the ECMR, although there are points at which such rights are recognised in the Regulation.[41] In particular, the Commission is the only body authorised to apply the ECMR, and the fact that the application of Articles 81 and 82 EC is precluded, along with equivalent provisions of national law, means that third parties are not able to challenge mergers independently of the EC Commission. Third parties are entitled to participate in the Commission's proceedings to the extent set out in the ECMR, in particular by virtue of Article 18(4), which provides that '[n]atural or legal persons showing a sufficient interest . . . shall be entitled, upon application, to be heard'. Article 11(c) of the Implementing Regulation states that this rubric includes customers, suppliers and competitors, again provided that they show a sufficient interest.

[38] See, eg, A Overd, 'After the Airtours Appeal', [2002] *ECLR* 375 at 377: 'The new "fast track" procedure is little better: this still involves a significant delay, is not automatically granted and requires significant limitations on the areas to be investigated by the Court.'

[39] Case T–464/04, *Independent Music Publishers and Labels Association (Impala, international association) v Commission* judgment of 13 July 2006.

[40] For the purposes of this Art these are decisions subject to a time-limit set by Art 10.

[41] See in particular M Kekelekis, 'The Rights of Notifying Parties and Third Parties During the Preliminary Investigation Procedures under the ECMR' [2003] *European Business Law Review* 429.

Article 16 of the Implementing Regulation sets out provisions relating to the hearing of third persons. Where the Commission considers it to be appropriate it *may* 'afford such parties who have so requested in their written comments the opportunity to participate in a formal hearing'.[42] However, there are no other avenues by which third parties can participate in the proceedings. Rights of appeal are set out above.

Where actions which are unlawful under the terms of the ECMR are taken, such as, for example, the consummation of a merger subject to the ECMR without the authorisation of the Commission, or the breach of any commitments entered into to secure approval, third parties may bring actions before national courts on the basis of the general application of EC law. No such actions have been reported at the time of writing.

[42] Art 16(2), Implementing Regulation [2004] OJ L 133/1.

10

UK Qualifying Mergers

INTRODUCTION

THE PROVISIONS OF the EA 02, with only specified exceptions, relate to mergers insofar as 'a relevant merger situation has been created', and where this has resulted, or may be expected to result, in a substantial lessening of competition within any market in the UK[1] for goods or services.[2] The primary role in determining whether a relevant merger situation exists belongs to the Office of Fair Trading (OFT), which has a duty to make references in respect of such mergers unless certain conditions apply (see further Chapter 14, below). The Competition Commission (CC) however is also required, once a reference has been made to it, to determine that a relevant merger situation exists.[3]

It is not necessarily the case that every 'relevant merger situation' will be referred to the CC, as the OFT is given the power to make an assessment of the likely impact of the merger, and no reference need be made where the markets concerned are of insufficient importance to justify the reference.[4] The procedures applied to relevant mergers and the tests to be employed in their evaluation are discussed in the following chapters. This short chapter is concerned solely with the question of what constitutes a 'relevant merger situation'.

The primary requirements of establishing that a relevant merger situation exists are set out in section 23 EA 02 and in essence are that:

—Two or more enterprises cease to be distinct; *and*
—The value of the turnover in the UK of the enterprise being taken over exceeds £70million; *or*
—In relation to the supply of goods or services of any description, at least one-quarter of all the goods or services of that description which are supplied in the UK, or a substantial part of it, are supplied by or to one and the same person.

[1] A reference to the UK includes any part of the UK, and extends to markets which operate in the UK as well as in other countries (s 22(6), EA 02).

[2] S 128(2) EA 02 provides that '[t]he supply of services does not include the provision of services under a contract of service or apprenticeship whether it is express or implied and (if it is express) whether it is oral in writing'.

[3] Thus, eg, s 35 EA 02 'questions to be decided in relation to completed mergers', requires the CC to 'decide the following questions—(a) whether a relevant merger situation has been created . . .'.

[4] S 22(2)(a).

'Enterprise' is defined in section 129, and 'means the activities, or part of the activities, of a business'.[5] Business, in turn:

> includes a professional practice and includes any other undertaking which is carried on for gain or reward or which is an undertaking in the course of which goods or services are supplied otherwise than free of charge.

Finally in order for a relevant merger situation to exist either the merger must not have taken place (ie, it is an anticipated merger) or it has taken place within the last four months. The four month time limit does not apply where the merger was neither made public nor brought to the attention of the OFT. The four month limit applies only from the point at which the first of these two conditions is met. The OFT guidance, *Mergers: Substantive assessment guidance*,[6] provides some clarification of the ways in which it will be determined whether a relevant merger situation exists.[7]

'CEASE TO BE DISTINCT'

Enterprises cease to be distinct where 'they are brought under common ownership or common control (whether or not the business to which either of them formerly belonged continues to be carried on under the same or different ownership or control)'.[8] The provisions in this respect are based on those of section 65 FTA 73, with a minor modification allowing for the operation of the CA 98. The effect of section 26(2)–(4) EA 02 is the same as that of section 65(2)–(4) FTA 73, and in this respect decisions taken under the earlier Act may reasonably be relied on in relation to the application of the new rules.[9]

Three levels of control may be distinguished: material influence over policy; control over policy; and a controlling interest in the relevant enterprise. One effect of this is that enterprises may cease to be distinct when there is a change in the level of control. Section 26(4)(a), for example, would cover the situation in which there was a change from a 'material influence' to 'control' (see further below). It has been pointed out that this means that it may be possible to refer a merger which proceeds over time at any one of three points. Section 29[10] provides, however, that in situations where control is achieved by a 'series of transactions' these may be treated as having occurred simultaneously on the date on which the last of them occurred, thus obviating the need to examine the transactions individually, consolidating the process into one of a single refer-

[5] In *The Government of Kuwait/British Petroleum Company plc*, Cm 477 (1988), it was confirmed that 'enterprise' includes the investment activities of states.

[6] (London, OFT, May 2003).

[7] See Chap 2 of ibid.

[8] S 26(1) EA 02.

[9] For a commentary on the merger provisions of the FTA 73 see D Livingston, *Competition Law and Practice* (London, FT Law and Tax, 1995), chaps 33 and 37.

[10] This reproduces s 66A of the FTA 73.

ence only. This also has an effect on the timetables under which the OFT may proceed to make a reference (see Chapter 12). Section 29 EA 02 applies only in the event that the relevant transactions take place within a two year period.

Section 27 EA 02 deals with the time when enterprises cease to be distinct.[11] The effect of this section is to allow the authorities to treat any incremental changes in control achieved through a series of transactions ('successive events') as having all taken effect on the date of the last transaction, and there is, in this case, no need to determine which precise transaction lead to the increase in control necessary to qualify as a merger situation. The difference between this section and section 29 EA 02 is that section 27 applies to what might appear to be a single transaction (for example a series of acquisitions of individual share holdings over a short period of time), whereas section 29 applies to a series of discrete transactions, albeit one having the same effect as the single transaction broken up over time to which section 27 applies.[12]

There are various ways in which 'common control' may be found to exist. Section 26(2) provides that enterprises may be treated as being under common control if they are: (a) enterprises of interconnected bodies corporate; (b) enterprises carried on by two or more bodies corporate of which one and the same person has control; and (c) an enterprise carried on by a body corporate and an enterprise carried on by a person or group of persons having control of that body corporate.

'Interconnecting bodies corporate' is defined in section 129(2) EA 02 to apply to situations in which:

> (a) one of them is a body corporate or which the other body is a subsidiary; or (b) both of them are subsidiaries of one and the same body corporate.

Section 127 EA 02 provides that for the purposes of the merger provisions '[a]ssociated persons, and any bodies corporate which they or any of them control shall be treated as one person'. Thus the OFT may consider when a number of persons acquire a target whether they are in fact to be treated as acting together. The Act in particular makes reference to family members;[13] trustees and settlors;[14] and 'two or more persons acting together'.[15] The OFT has stated that:

> This situation will most commonly arise where the acquiring persons are related or have signed an agreement to act jointly to make an acquisition. It is also possible that separate entities may be considered to be "associated persons" where they appear to

[11] This reproduces s 66 of the FTA 73.

[12] The application of s 27, EA 02 was considered in *Archant Limited/London Newspapers of Independent News and Media Ltd*, Sept 2004, in which the question arose whether a transaction fell within the terms of a merger reference or was time-barred (see Chap 14, below). The CC concluded that the two agreements of 11 Dec 2003 and 30 Dec 2003 were 'successive transactions between the same parties by virtue of which each of two enterprises ceased to be distinct' (Appendix C, para 22).

[13] S 127(4)(a) and (c) EA 02.

[14] S 127(4)(b) EA 02.

[15] S 127(4)(d) EA 02.

> have common incentives to act together for the purpose of gaining control over the acquired enterprise.[16]

Control

There are three different ways in which 'control' may be found to exist. The first is that there exists an ability by the acquirer to influence the policy of the target materially; the second is that the acquirer may have the ability to control the policy of the target (de facto control); and the third is that the acquirer may have a controlling interest in the target (de jure control). The control or material influence may be wielded directly or indirectly.[17]

Material influence

The ability materially to influence policy is not a matter which is capable of being reduced to any precise formula. The OFT states that the approach to whether an ability materially to influence policy exists will proceed on a case by case basis in which all the circumstances of the case will be considered.[18] Four factors are indicated to be of paramount importance: the size of the shareholding; the distribution of shares and exercise of shareholding rights; the level of board representation; and any other additional agreements. In relation to the size of the shareholding a 25 per cent stake will, in most cases, be sufficient to establish that the holder has the ability materially to influence policy:

> A shareholding conferring on the holder 25 per cent or more of the voting rights in a company generally enables the holder to block special resolutions; consequently, a 25 per cent share of voting rights is likely to be seen as presumptively conferring the ability to materially influence policy—even when all the remaining shares are held by only one person. The OFT may examine any case where there is a shareholding of 15 per cent or more in order to see whether the holder might be able materially to influence the company's policy. Occasionally, a holding of less than 15 per cent might attract scrutiny where other factors indicating the ability to exercise influence over policy are present.[19]

The OFT will also consider the distribution of the remaining shareholdings, and the way in which the rights attached to these are used. Where the shareholding in question carries with it special provisions relating to the constitution of the company this may be a significant factor depending on the nature of the rights. It is also possible, for example, that the ability materially to influence the company's policy would be more likely to be found where the major part of

[16] OFT, above n 6, para 2.17.
[17] S 26(3), EA 02.
[18] OFT, above n 6, para 2.10.
[19] Ibid, para 2.10.

the remaining shareholding was held by investment groups or pension funds, with little active interest in the day-to-day affairs of the company.

There have been a number of reports in relation to the regime as set out in the FTA 73 in which a shareholding of more than, but close to, 20 per cent has been found to confer the ability materially to influence policy. This was the case, for example, in *Stora Koppargergs Bergslags AB/Swedish Match NV/The Gillette Company*.[20] Gillette had taken a 22 per cent holding of the equity of Swedish Match NV in the form of non-voting convertible loan stock, and also held certain pre-emption rights. The MMC concluded in part that:

> in our view a prudent Wilkinson Sword management would be bound constantly to take into account the fact that Gillette was a major shareholder in its parent company, Swedish Match NV, was its parent company's largest creditor and had important rights in relation to significant decisions affecting the future of the company, notwithstanding the limits to Gillette's rights.[21]

The MMC also concluded in *The Peninsular and Oriental Steam Navigation Company and European Ferries Group plc*[22] that a shareholding of 20.8%, which carried 16.1% of the voting rights, conferred on the holder of the shares a material influence over the policy of the target. The MMC noted that '[t]here have been only a few cases in which the Commission have had to consider ability to materially influence the policy of a company rather than to control it. In all the cases in which the Commission have found ability to materially influence policy the voting rights have been in excess of 20%'.[23] In the present case however the MMC found that there were circumstances peculiar to the case such that, even at the low level of voting rights held, P&O was able to materially influence the policy of EFG. Where a low shareholding is combined with other factors, such as the apparent preparedness of the target to take advice from the acquirer, an ability to materially influence policy may also be found to exist.[24]

De facto control

There are also 'no precise criteria for determining when an acquirer gains "de facto" control of a company's policy',[25] and the OFT will again take a case-by-case approach. In practice there has been only a very small number of cases in which de facto control has been of central importance. Generally 'the OFT is likely to reach a belief that merger arrangements give rise to a position of "de facto" control when an entity is clearly the controller of a company, notwithstanding that it holds less than a 50.1 per cent stake in the target'.[26] The OFT

[20] Cm 1473 (1991).
[21] Ibid, para 1.6.
[22] Cm 31 (1986).
[23] Ibid, at para 8.4.
[24] See, eg, *Stagecoach Holdings plc and Mainline Partnership Limited*, Cm 2782 (1995).
[25] OFT, above n 6, May 2003, para 2.11.
[26] Ibid, para 2.11.

indicates that this may be the case, for example, where the acquirer's advice is followed in nearly all cases,[27] or where there is an ability to veto any resolution requiring a supra-majority. In two cases the MMC has determined that the pattern of share ownership was such as to give control to the holder of the largest stake.[28] There is, in the *Lonrho plc and House of Fraser plc* report,[29] a discussion of whether a situation of being able materially to influence policy had become one of control. Here Lonrho proposed making changes to the way in which the House of Fraser was managed, and at the same time nominated 12 new members to the Board. Although these proposals were subsequently abandoned, a reference had been made on the basis that it was likely that these moves would in fact confer control.

De jure control

In order to establish that a controlling interest exists it is normally necessary to show that the stake of the acquirer is in excess of 50 per cent of the target. Thus only one person can have a controlling interest in a company.

Acquisition of control by stages

As indicated above, it is possible for control to be acquired by stages, and more than one merger situation may flow in respect of A increasing a stake in B. This may be the case, for example, where a shareholding which confers the ability materially to influence policy increases to one which gives de facto control over the company. Equally there could be a move from de facto control to a controlling interest. Once a controlling interest has been acquired there can be no further merger situations arising in relation to that company unless control is transferred from A to B, which would constitute a new merger situation. It is clearly inappropriate to examine each of these situations as a separate merger, save in exceptional circumstances. As discussed above, as long as these situations occur within the same two-year period, the transactions are to be treated as having occurred simultaneously, obviating the need for more than one reference to be made.

[27] In *Stagecoach Holdings*, above n 24, the MMC found that a shareholding of 20% was, by itself, insufficient for Stagecoach to exercise material influence over Mainline, but that Mainline's management appeared willing to take advice from Stagecoach.

[28] See *Eurocanadian Shipholdings Limited and Furness, Withy & Company Ltd and Manchester Lines Ltd*, HC 369 (1975–76), and *Amalgamated Industrials Ltd and Herbert Morris Ltd*, HC 434 (1975–76). In the first of these it was found that a holding of just under 30% would confer control in the absence of other large holdings. In the second case an increase in the holding from 33.44% to 37.96% constituted a move from the ability to materially influence policy to control, again following an analysis of the other voting blocks.

[29] Cmnd 9458 (1985).

TURNOVER EXCEEDS £70 M

Compared to the EC thresholds the turnover test in the UK is set at a very small threshold, but it hardly needs pointing out that the economy of the UK is much smaller than that of the EC as a whole, and, as we have seen, it was the aim of the EC only to catch the very largest mergers. The turnover test set out in section 23(1)(b) EA 02 and expanded on in section 28 replaced the asset test of the FTA 73. The level at which the turnover test was set was a matter of considerable contention in Parliament, with the Government giving way at third reading. The Government had argued for a turnover test of £45m, and the House of Lords insisted on £100m. The £70m figure was originally suggested by the CBI. For the Government it was argued that the £45m figure would equate roughly to assets of £70m, one of the tests enshrined in the FTA 73, and would therefore catch as many mergers as were caught under the FTA 73. Thus Lord Sainsbury argued that:

> The £45 million figure was derived from data research we undertook in my department. Briefly, the figure is based on an analysis of the assets and turnover levels of 110,000 UK companies. Our intention was to find a figure that we believed would account for roughly the same number of companies as is currently the case under the assets test.[30]

Further research showed that the number of UK companies with assets of £70m or more was 7,473 and the total number with a turnover of more than £45m was 7,057.[31] The effect of the move from £45m to £70m was estimated to be that 50 per cent fewer mergers would be caught by the provisions. In 2000–1 there were only 5,350 companies registered on the Fame database with turnover in excess of more than £70m.[32]

The value of the turnover, which must be turnover in the UK, of the enterprise being taken over is to be determined in accordance with such rules as are made by the Secretary of State.[33] The OFT is to keep the threshold figure under review, and is to advise the Secretary of State from time to time on whether the figure remains appropriate.[34]

It should be clear that there will be circumstances in which a company with a turnover in excess of £70m may be acquired by another in situations where there would be little impact on competition. This might be the case in particular if the companies were not competitors (in the case of a vertical or conglomerate merger), or where the size of the industry in question was very large, such that

[30] HL Debs, vol 651, col 1454, 18 July 2002.
[31] HL Debs, vol 653, col 792, 15 Oct 2002.
[32] Vol 391, col 937, 30 Oct 2002.
[33] S 28(2). See Enterprise Act 2002 (Merger Fees and Determination of Turnover) Order 2003, SI 2003/1370.
[34] S 28(5).

the acquired company held only a relatively small position in the market. The operation of such circumstances would not serve to remove the merger from being a 'relevant merger' for the purposes of the Act, but it could mean that no reference was made by the OFT to the CC on the ground that it was not likely that there would be an SLC.

Section 28(1) EA 02 provides that:

> For the purposes of section 23 the value of the turnover in the United Kingdom of the enterprise being taken over shall be determined by taking the total value of the turnover in the United Kingdom of the enterprises which cease to be distinct enterprises and deducting—
>
> (a) the turnover in the United Kingdom of any enterprise which continues to be carried on under the same ownership and control; or
> (b) if no enterprise continues to be carried on under the same ownership and control, the turnover in the United Kingdom which, of all the turnovers concerned, is the turnover of the highest value.

Part 3 of the Enterprise Act 2002 (Merger Fees and Determination of Turnover) Order 2003[35], makes further provision in relation to the determination of turnover. Relevant turnover is that for the business year preceding the date on which the enterprises concerned in the relevant merger situation ceased to be distinct, or, in respect of an anticipated merger, the business year preceding the date when the reference decision is to be made. In the event that the enterprise the turnover of which is to be calculated has made an acquisition or a divestment in the preceding year that will have a significant impact on the turnover of the enterprise this may be taken into account if the OFT considers it appropriate to do so. The Schedule to the Order makes yet more detailed provision in respect of credit institutions, financial institutions, insurance undertakings and aid granted to businesses.

25 PER CENT OF RELEVANT GOODS OR SERVICES

Section 23(3) EA 02 provides that:

> The condition mentioned in this subsection is that, in relation to the supply of goods of any description, at least one-quarter of all the goods of that description which are supplied in the United Kingdom, or in a substantial part of the United Kingdom—
>
> (a) are supplied by one and the same person or are supplied to one and the same person; or
> (b) are supplied by the person by whom the enterprises concerned are carried on, or are supplied to those persons.

Section 23(4) EA 02 matches section 23(3), save that it relates to the supply of services.

[35] SI 2003/1370, above n 33, reg 11(2).

This share-of-supply test is taken directly from the FTA 73. A relevant merger situation is created where, in conjunction with the first part of the test, a merger creates or enhances a share of the market, however defined, of 25 per cent or above.[36] Section 23 allows the person making the reference to determine what the reference framework is in terms of the relevant goods or services, as well as the appropriate benchmark by which the 25 per cent figure is determined. The OFT has indicated that in its analysis of a merger and in the making of any reference it:

> will have regard to the narrowest reasonable description of a set of goods or services to determine whether the share of supply test is met. This practice is intended to make it easier for companies and their advisers to determine whether the Act applies to a particular merger situation.[37]

It is not necessarily the case, however, that the share of supply considered will be that which equates exactly to the relevant market assessed by either the OFT or the CC for the purposes of determining the impact on competition. The CC, which must in the case of a reference made to it determine that a relevant merger situation exists,[38] points in its guidance to the considerable discretion left to it under the Act in determining the relevant supply.[39] Thus it notes that it 'may apply such criteria (including value, cost, price, quantity, capacity, number of workers) as it considers appropriate'. This is a straightforward restatement of section 23(5) EA 02.[40] Section 23(6) EA 02 provides that references to the supply of goods or services which take different forms of supply may be treated by the OFT or the CC as being references to the separate forms of supply, or the forms of supply taken together, or any groups of the forms of supply. A different form of supply may be determined to exist whenever 'the transactions concerned differ as to their nature, their parties, their terms or their surrounding circumstances',[41] and this difference is one which, in the opinion of the decision-making authority, is a material one.[42] Such a difference may exist, for example, in relation to wholesale and retail supplies of goods, or in services supplied to commercial and domestic users, or perhaps in high-street and internet retailing.

The lack of a robust market based criterion in relation to the establishment of the share of supply test may cause some concern. However, it remains the case that this threshold exists purely in order to establish jurisdiction, and does not

[36] There is some debate whether this would apply were an undertaking with a 25% or greater market share to merge with an undertaking with no market share. The orthodox view is that it does not, as such a merger neither creates nor enhances the 25% share. However, see O Black, 'The Fair Trading Act's Market Share Test: A Heresy' [1996] *ECLR* 414.

[37] OFT, *Mergers*, above n 16, para 2.19.

[38] The exception to this is in relation to mergers referred to it in the context of a public special interest notice—see further Chap 17, below.

[39] CC, *Merger References: Competition Commission Guidelines*, June 2003, paras 1.17–1.18, available at the CC website.

[40] This reflects the provisions in the earlier FTA 73.

[41] S 23(7)(a) EA 02.

[42] S 23(7)(b) EA 02.

relate to the SLC analysis. If an economically inappropriate supply criterion is used at this stage this should be mitigated by a proper market analysis necessary to determine whether an SLC may be identified.

It will be noted that the enhancement of a 25 per cent market share constitutes a relevant merger situation. In other words the merger 'must result in an increment to the share of supply or consumption and the resulting share must be at least 25%'.[43] This is to say that a merger resulting in a move from 25 per cent to 26 per cent of supply would be caught.

The reference to a 'substantial part' of the UK in section 23(3) and (4) is not expanded on in the legislation. In *R v MMC, ex parte South Yorkshire Transport Ltd*[44] the House of Lords was asked to determine whether the market occupied by South Yorkshire Transport Ltd was a 'substantial part' of the UK.[45] Their Lordships held that it was not possible to provide a fixed definition of 'substantial part', but that the area considered must be of sufficient importance, size or character to make it worthy of the application of merger control. The OFT indicates that it will consider factors such as 'the size, population, social, political, economic, financial and geographic significance of the specified area or areas, and whether it is (or they are) significant in some way'.[46]

TERRITORIAL JURISDICTION

The EA 02 does not explicitly set out a territorial restriction on the application of the domestic merger control regime. However, as the OFT notes:

> It is implicit in [the] criteria that at least one of the enterprises must be active within the UK. Where the turnover test is met, this will by definition be because the target generates turnover from sales to UK customers. For the share of supply test, both of the enterprises ceasing to be distinct must be active in supplying or acquiring goods or services within the UK or a substantial part of the UK. These principles apply equally to non-UK companies that sell to (or acquire from) UK customers or suppliers. In assessing whether a firm is active in the UK, the OFT will have regard to whether its sales are made directly or indirectly (via agents or traders) and the extent to which a firm is active at each level of trade.[47]

There have been a number of cases arising in which two foreign businesses have merged when they have held interests in the UK. Examples have been provided under the mergers regime of the FTA 1973. In *Stora Kopparbergs Bergslags AB/Swedish Match NV and Stora Kopparbergs Bergslags AB/The*

[43] OFT, *Mergers*, above n 16, para 2.2.

[44] [1993] 1 WLR 23.

[45] This was in the context of an action for judicial review brought under the FTA 73. The principles remain relevant to the operation of the EA 02.

[46] OFT, above n 6, para 2.24.

[47] Ibid, para 2.4.

Gillette Company,[48] for example, the MMC investigated a merger affecting the wet-shaving market in the UK. The MMC concluded that Gillette's control over a Dutch company could operate against the public interest by reducing competition in the UK, and recommended divestiture by Gillette UK of its interest in the Dutch company, although subsequent events rendered this recommendation irrelevant.[49] In 2000 the CC report on *Air Canada and Canadian Airlines Corpn*[50] dealt with a merger between Canadian companies which traded in the UK. Here the CC both noted the fundamental interests of the Canadian authorities and found in any event that there was no substantial detriment to the public interest within the terms of the Act, and thus did not consider the question of remedies.

The OFT has considered that a relevant merger situation arose under the FTA 73 when a UK company acquired the interests of a US company.[51] However, it would be unlikely that an SLC would be identified in such a case. Various provisions in the Act limit the ability to act of the OFT and CC to those situations in which they are able to effect a remedy. Although it may not be possible to impose a structural remedy on enterprises which are located outside the UK's jurisdiction, it may be possible to impose conduct remedies in situations in which they act within the UK.[52] There is also the possibility that the OFT may not become aware of a foreign merger, even when it affects enterprises in the UK and has been well-publicised.[53]

[48] Cm 1473 (1991).

[49] The CC stated, at para 8.2 of the report, that '[t]he assets are partly situated in the United Kingdom where they include businesses involved in the manufacture and distribution of shaving equipment . . . We are satisfied that these business include at least one "enterprise" within the meaning of the Act. In practice the investigation has been concerned with the effect of the merger so far as businesses within the United Kingdom are concerned.'

[50] Cm 4838 (2000).

[51] *Dee Corporation* (1986).

[52] The CC has indicated that where it is dealing with a part of a supranational merger 'it will seek to cooperate with competition authorities in other jurisdictions to adopt a consistent approach to remedies where this is feasible and effective': CC, *Application of Divestiture Remedies in Merger Inquiries: Competition Commission Guidelines*, Dec 2004. See further Chap 15, below.

[53] Livingston eg, notes that: 'a possible example is mentioned in *Book Club Associates and The Leisure Circle* [Cm 277 (1988)]. In that case Book Club Associates (BCA), the largest UK book club business, was originally controlled 50 per cent by W.H. Smith & Son (Holding) PLC (WHS) and 50 per cent by Doubleday, the American publishing house. Doubleday was acquired by the German publishing house, Bertelsmann AG, at the end of 1986. At this time Bertelsmann already controlled Leisure Circle, BCA's largest competitor: this situation seems to have gone unnoticed until clearance was sought in the latter part of 1987 for Bertelsmann's purchase of WHS's interest in BCA' (D Livingston, *Competition Law and Practice*, London, FT Law and Tax (1995), para 33.13). Livingston notes that it is quite possible that the first merger situation was identified, but considered not to be significant in competition terms.

11

The Substantive Test under the Enterprise Act 2002

INTRODUCTION

THE STANDARD TEST to be applied during the evaluation of mergers in the UK regime is whether the merger results in, or may be expected to result in, a substantial lessening of competition (SLC).[1] This 'competition' test is different from the test set out in the FTA 73 which was based on an analysis of 'the public interest'.[2] At first sight it may then appear as if the change made to the test in the EA 02 is fundamental. In fact this is not the case, although the change is to be welcomed as raising to the statutory level what had become a principle in practice. At the time of the enactment of the EA 02 the adoption of the SLC test was described as 'one of the cornerstones of the new merger regime',[3] which would 'ensure that the new regime is predictable, transparent and streamlined'.[4] At the same time it was recognised that 'in practice competition has been the principal factor in UK merger policy for many years . . . legislating for a competition test is not likely to make a large difference to the way in which mergers are regulated'.[5] In adopting the SLC test the UK aligned itself with a number of significant merger regimes, including the United States, but the test is notably different from that employed under the ECMR.[6] That the test is an economic one is made clear in the DTI's *Explanatory Notes* to the EA 02, at paragraph 126:

[1] This test is modified in cases in which a public interest consideration intervention is made by the Secretary of State (see Chaps 16 for the position in relation to newspaper and media mergers, and 17 generally), and in water mergers (see Chap 16). For an excellent and thorough discussion of the approach to SLC in the UK see N Parr, R Finbow and M Hughes, *UK Merger Control: Law and Practice* (2nd edn, London, Sweet & Maxwell, 2005), chap 6.

[2] S 69(1)(b) required the MMC to investigate and report on whether the creation of a merger situation 'operates, or may be expected to operate, against the public interest'.

[3] Standing Committee B, HC, vol 386, col 109, 13 June 2002.

[4] Standing Committee B, HC, vol 384, col 258.

[5] Ibid, col 296. The OFT has itself argued that 'the change to the [SLC] test is expected to make little difference to how mergers are assessed. For some years, the effect of a merger on competition has been the primary consideration in decisions on whether to refer a merger to the CC, and in the CC's conclusions on mergers referred to it. Consequently, the [OFT's] published advice on reference decisions, and the CC's reports on merger references, under the FTA regime provide useful insights into how the new test is likely to be applied': OFT, *Mergers: Substantive Guidance*, summary.

[6] See Chap 6, above.

> Similar language is used in the legislation controlling mergers in a number of other major jurisdictions, including the US, Canada, Australia and New Zealand. The concept is an economic one, best understood by reference to the question of whether a merger will increase or facilitate the exercise of market power (whether unilateral, or through coordinated behaviour), leading to reduced output, higher prices, less innovation or lower quality of choice. A number of matters may be potentially relevant to the assessment of whether a merger will result in a substantial lessening of competition. These matters include, but are not limited to:
>
> —market shares and concentration;
> —extent of effective competition before and after the merger;
> —efficiency and financial performance of firms in the market;
> —barriers to entry and expansion in the relevant market;
> —availability of substitute products and the scope for supply- or demand-side substitution;
> —extent of change and innovation in a market;
> —whether in the absence of the merger one of the firms would fail and, if so,
> —whether its failure would cause the assets of that firm to exit the market;
> —the conduct of customers or of suppliers to those in the market.

The test is set out on the face of the legislation, at sections 22(1)(b),[7] 33(1)(b),[8] 35(1)(b)[9] and 36(1)(b).[10] Section 22(1)(b) therefore provides that in the appropriate circumstances the OFT shall make a reference to the CC where a relevant merger situation has been created and:

> the creation of that situation has resulted in, or may be expected to result, in a substantial lessening of competition within any market or markets in the United Kingdom for goods or services.

The Act also makes reference to 'customer benefits', which equate to efficiencies. Section 22(2)(b) EA 02 provides, for example, that the OFT may decide not to make a reference to the CC where it believes that 'any relevant customer benefits in relation to the creation of the relevant merger situation concerned outweigh the [SLC] concerned and any adverse effects of the [SLC] concerned'. Section 30 provides that a benefit is a relevant customer benefit if:

> (a) it is a benefit to relevant customers in the form of—
>
> (i) lower prices, higher quality or greater choice of goods or services in any market in the United Kingdom . . .; or
> (ii) greater innovation in relation to such goods or services.

The relationship between such customer benefits and the power of the OFT to accept undertakings or make orders is discussed in Chapter 13. In this chapter the discussion of customer benefits is dealt with in the context of efficiencies

[7] OFT's duty to refer in relation to completed mergers.
[8] OFT's duty to refer in relation to anticipated mergers.
[9] CC's duty to report in relation to completed mergers.
[10] CC's duty to report in relation to anticipated mergers.

(below). There is little evidence in decisions taken since the entry into force of the merger provisions of the EA 02 that an analysis of customer benefits has had a significant effect on the outcome of cases—and indeed the opposite appears to be true. Thus, for example, the CC found in *H+H Celcom Limited and Marley Building Materials Limited*[11] that, although the parties had claimed that cost reductions would flow from the merger, the resulting 66 per cent market share meant that they would be under no competitive pressure to pass these benefits on to customers.

The record of the OFT and CC in evaluating mergers has been considered in a report published in 2005,[12] which focussed on 10 of the 29 mergers cleared by the CC between 1991 and 2000 without remedies being required. In all the cases studied there appeared to be effective competition, with one possible exception in respect of which not enough time had passed to draw firm conclusions. Further the competitive constraints identified were 'for the most part, very similar to those identified by the CC'.[13] The CC was also praised for having 'a generally good record at predicting where entry is likely to act as a significant competitive constraint'.[14] While this report is encouraging, it is not possible to know whether the generally positive result arose because of an over-conservative approach on the part of the CC, clearing only those mergers which presented no problems. It is unfortunately impossible to test for the effects of blocking a merger.

THE APPROACH OF THE OFT

The OFT has set out its approach to the assessment of SLC in its relevant guidance.[15] The relevant advice runs to 29 pages, and can only be summarised here. Many of the general economic principles dealt with in this respect have been considered in Chapter 2, and there is little need in this chapter to discuss the general principles underpinning merger control or the place of horizontal, vertical and conglomerate mergers.[16] The OFT notes that six broad analytical elements will be reviewed in determining which mergers may be expected to give rise to SLC, although stresses that these should not be regarded as giving rise to a mechanistic process. The elements set out are: definition of the relevant product and geographic markets; the nature and extent of pre- and post-merger competition; the prospect of entry into the market post-merger; other factors such as buyer power which may constrain the post-merger firm; efficiency gains; and

[11] Cm 5540 (2002).

[12] PricewaterhouseCoopers LLP, 'Ex post Evaluation of Mergers' (2005), available at the OFT website.

[13] Ibid, para 1.10.

[14] Ibid, para 1.11.

[15] OFT, *Mergers: Substantive assessment guidance*, May 2003, above n 5.

[16] Dealt with in Part 3 of ibid.

whether the failing firm defence may be applicable. All of these factors have been discussed in general terms in Chapter 2, and reference may also be made to the treatment of these by the EC Commission discussed in Chapter 6. The OFT's *Substantive assessment guidance* treats horizontal, vertical and conglomerate mergers separately, although clearly some of the factors set out above are common to all.

The relevant market and its structure

The OFT has published guidance under the Competition Act 1998 in relation to the definition of the relevant market,[17] and notes in its *Substantive assessment guidance* that reference should be made to that. The approach is consistent with that set out in Chapter 2, and with the EC Commission's guidance. Although there is no legal requirement to follow EC practice in the merger regime some coordination arises by virtue of the fact that the relevant market definition guidance applies equally to the application of the Competition Act 1998, in which there *is* a harmonisation requirement set out on the face of the legislation. Thus the hypothetical monopolist test (the SSNIP test) is placed at the heart of the analysis,[18] and may be employed in respect of the determination of both the product and geographic market. The key issue, the OFT states, is 'whether the undertaking could *sustain* prices sufficiently above competitive levels . . . As a rule of thumb, if substitution would take longer than one year, the products to which customers eventually switched would not be included in the same market as the focal product'.[19]

The OFT will consider evidence from a number of sources, including: the undertakings active in the market; customers and competitors who may be interviewed; switching costs; product characteristics; patterns in price changes; own or cross price elasticities of demand; critical loss analysis;[20] and the price—concentration relationship. Supply side substitution is not factored into the

[17] OFT 403, *Market Definition* (2004), available at the OFT website.
[18] Ibid, at paras 2.5–2.13.
[19] Ibid, at para 3.6.
[20] Critical loss analysis is explained in the following terms by Bishop and Walker:

> 'This asks the question: based on current prices and margins, how many sales could a hypothetical monopolist afford to lose before a five per cent (or x per cent) price increase became unprofitable? This amount is termed the *critical loss*. Once the analyst has answered this question, the next step is to find out how many sales a hypothetical monopolist would actually lose in response to a five per cent (or x per cent) price increase. If the answer is that it would lose more than the critical loss amount, then the price increase would not be profitable for the hypothetical monopolist and so the market should be widened. This form of analysis can clearly be adapted to simulate the effect of a merger directly: how many sales would the merged firm lose if it raised prices by x per cent and would this amount make the price unprofitable?'

S Bishop and M Walker, *The Economics of EC Competition Law: Concepts, Application and Measurement* (2nd edn, London, Sweet & Maxwell, 2002) at 10.18A.

process of market definition unless 'it is reasonably likely to take place, and already has an impact by constraining the supplier of the product or group of products in question'.[21] In the *Substantive assessment guidance* the OFT stresses that when it has the data to run the SSNIP test it will use prevailing prices prior to the merger. This is because 'a merger investigation focuses on whether prices could be raised above current levels, rather than whether current prices are too high'.[22]

The OFT uses three principal, standard, measures to examine market concentration. These are the market shares (usually, but not exclusively, measured by sales revenue), concentration ratios, and the Herfindahl-Hirschman Index (HHI), all of which are discussed in Chapter 2. The approach to HHI ratios (which is matched by the CC) is as shown in Figure 11.1:

Table 11.1: OFT and CC Approach to HHI Changes

	HHI	Δ leading to concern
Highly concentrated	>1800	>50
Concentrated	>1000	>100

Competition pre- and post-merger

Following standard analysis the *Substantive assessment guidance* notes that there are two ways in which a horizontal merger may give rise to an SLC: non-coordinated (unilateral) effects and coordinated effects. The OFT states that the following factors are likely to give rise to non-coordinated effects: there are few firms in the market; the parties to the merger are close competitors; customers have little choice of alternative suppliers; rivals cannot react quickly; there is little spare capacity in the hands of competitors; there is no strong competitive fringe; one of the merging firms is a 'maverick'; one of the merging firms is a recent new entrant or a strong potential entrant. However, these factors are not to be considered as a checklist, but 'are intended simply as a broad indication of the circumstances in which the OFT may consider the risk of such anti-competitive effects to be high'.[23]

The treatment accorded to coordinated anti-competitive effects is consistent with the approach set out by the CFI in the *Airtours* case,[24] although there is no

[21] OFT 403, above n 17, para 3.18.
[22] Ibid, para 3.20.
[23] Ibid, para 4.9.
[24] Case T–342/99, *Airtours plc v Commission* [2002] ECR II–2585, [2002] 5 CMLR 7, an appeal from Commission Decision 2000/276 *Airtours/First Choice* [2000] OJ L 93/1. See further Chap 7, above.

legal requirement for the OFT to follow EC law in the approach to merger control. Thus the focus is on the three conditions that need to be met in order for coordinated anti-competitive effects to arise: the participants in the market post-merger must have the ability to align their conduct in the market; there must be incentives for this alignment to be maintained, including detection and punishment mechanisms; and the behaviour should be sustainable in the face of other competitive pressures.[25]

Entry

In order for entry into a market to be considered a sufficient competitive constraint to mitigate any apparent anti-competitive increase in market power flowing from a merger three conditions must be satisfied according to the OFT. These are, first, that entry may be expected to occur in the event that the merging parties seek to exercise their market power. Secondly, 'any new entry should be of sufficient scope to constrain any attempt to exploit greater post merger market power'.[26] Thirdly, any entry would need to be 'sufficiently timely and sustainable to provide lasting and effective post merger competition'.[27] For the OFT, entry should take place within two years in order to count as being 'timely'. The OFT will also consider whether incumbents are able to expand their capacity in response to any price increases imposed by the merging parties.[28]

Buyer power

As is the case with the application of the ECMR the OFT recognises that countervailing buyer power may constrain seller power, but only in situations in which the purchaser(s) can credibly threaten to switch. Sellers may also be constrained by other strategic actions on the part of buyers, such as refusing to buy other products produced by them, or by delaying orders, and they may be able to enter the market themselves. However, the ability of a seller to discriminate post-merger against customers who are not faced with a credible alternative may mitigate against the situation in which some customers have choice or power.

In a report prepared for the OFT, CC and DTI the authors noted that 'buyer power is a much richer and more complex notion than that which is often

[25] OFT 403, *Mergers: Substantive assessment guidance* (2004), available at the OFT website, para 4.12.

[26] Ibid, para 4.22.

[27] Ibid, para 4.23.

[28] Ibid, para 4.26.

reflected in competition assessments . . . [and] is hard to pin down'.[29] In a number of cases it was found that mergers had reduced buyer power, despite the expectation that this would not be the case. Elsewhere buyer power had remained unimpaired.

Efficiencies and 'customer benefits'

Although the EA 02 makes reference to 'customer benefits', the OFT *Substantive assessment guidance* discusses 'efficiencies' and customer benefits in separate terms.[30] The ICN's examination of merger control frames the UK approach to efficiencies within the context of these 'customer benefits',[31] and the factors referred to in section 30—lower prices, higher quality, choice and innovation—are more generally treated in other regimes and in economic literature as efficiencies. Further, the OFT guidance itself draws the link, although it recognises the formal separation flowing from the shape of the legislation. Thus at paragraph 7.10 of the *Substantive assessment guidance* it states that 'efficiency claims may fall for consideration in the [SLC] test and/or subsequently in relation to the customer benefits test'. If there is a difference in the analysis it is not, on the face of it, a substantial one, although in the part of the guidance dealing with efficiencies somewhat more factors are invoked. Thus the OFT states that:

> possible efficiencies may include cost savings (fixed or variable)[32], more intensive use of existing capacity, economies of scale or scope, or demand-side efficiencies such as increased network size or product quality. Efficiencies might also encompass pro-competitive changes in the merged entity's incentives, for example by capturing complementarities in, eg, R&D activity, which in turn might increase incentives to invest in product development in innovation markets.[33]

Like the EC Commission the OFT maintains three conditions which must be met in order for efficiency gains to be taken into account. These are that they must be: demonstrable; a direct consequence of the merger; and that there be sufficient post-merger competition to ensure that the gains are, to a reasonable

[29] PricewaterhouseCoopers LLP, above n 12, at 5.44. The conclusions in this regard were that 'first it is not straightforward to determine whether a buyer will have sufficient alternative (and credible) sources of supply after the merger, particularly where buyers experience high switching costs. . . . factors other than the number of credible suppliers also appear to be important. . . . buyers appeared to be able to exercise buyer power through a number of means including the collection of information, incentive-based contracts, and the level of effort devoted to the bargaining process': ibid, paras 1.13–1.14.

[30] Ibid n 25, at paras 7.7–7.10.

[31] ICN Working Group: Analytical Framework Subgroup, 'Project on Merger Guidelines: Report for the third ICN annual conference in Seoul', Apr 2004, chap 6, available at the ICN webite.

[32] The OFT indicates elsewhere that efficiency claims are more likely to be upheld in relation to marginal or variable costs, in which case savings are more likely to be passed on to the consumer than they are in relation to fixed costs. See OFT, above n 15, para 4.33, n 27.

[33] Ibid, para 4.33, internal footnotes omitted.

extent, passed on to the consumers.[34] In the absence of compelling evidence relating to efficiencies the OFT will remain sceptical that they will be achieved, or if achieved, that they will be passed on. The fact that there is an information asymmetry between the merging parties and the OFT is clearly a matter of some concern to the OFT, which makes clear the onus on the parties claiming efficiencies at paragraph 4.35 of the guidance:

> All of the information relating to such claims is in the hands of the merging parties, so it is for them to demonstrate their case on the basis of the information available to them. Such evidence might, for example, include estimates and origin of likely cost-savings as evidence in pre-merger planning and strategy documents, coupled with objective factual and accounting information needed to verify proposed cost saving claims. External consultancy reports pre-dating the merger might also be helpful in this context.

In its specific discussion of customer benefits the OFT focuses on the three areas set out in the legislation: lower prices; greater quality; and greater innovation. The normal expectation is that these benefits will accrue in the market where the SLC is identified, although as usual there is the problem that if the merger truly does lead to an SLC then the pressures to pass such benefits on to customers may be reduced. However, even in the case of a merger tending to monopoly, the OFT notes that some cost savings (if these are achieved) may be passed on to consumers.

Failing firm defence

It was noted in Chapter 2 that one of the key tasks in the analysis of mergers is to select the appropriate counterfactual against which to assess the effects of the merger. This may be of particular significance where it is argued that the target firm would exit the market even absent the merger, whether it be a failing firm or for some other reason. The OFT states at paragraph 4.37 of its *Substantive assessment guidance* that in order for the failing firm defence to apply three conditions need to be met. The first is that the target is in a 'parlous' state, and that it and its assets would exit the market in the near future. This criteria may be met by firms which are on the verge of administration, but will not be met in the event that a profitable firm is seeking to dispose of a loss-making subsidiary. The second criterion is that 'there must be no serious prospect of reorganising the business', although the OFT recognises that it can be exceptionally difficult in these cases to identify the correct counterfactual, as it is often very hard to anticipate what the future of a struggling firm will be. The third criterion is that 'there should be no less anti-competitive alternative to the merger'.

All of these criteria were met in *First West Yorkshire Ltd and Black Prince Buses Ltd*.[35] Here the OFT cleared the anticipated acquisition of Black Prince

[34] OFT, above n 15, para 4.34.
[35] OFT, 8 June 2005, above n 5.

Buses Ltd by a rival operator, First West Yorkshire Ltd, which had been the main competitor of Black Prince for bids on urban out of hours contracts. It was clear that the loss of Black Prince would have a significant impact on competition, given the lack of competitors in relation to such services. This was true for a number of market sectors. However, Black Prince told the OFT that the owning family had in any event determined to sell the business, had marketed it to a number of potential purchasers, and that First West Yorkshire was the only credible purchaser. This evidence was convincing, and the OFT concluded that there was no counterfactual position against which the merger could be judged which would produce any better outcome, such that, although competition was being substantially lessened, this could not be attributed to the merger itself.

The OFT may require the following evidence in order to determine whether the failing firm defence applies: that the company is about to fail immediately under current ownership; that all re-financing options have been exhausted; that there are no other credible bidders; and how the acquiring firm intends to use the assets in the future.[36]

Vertical mergers

The assessment of vertical mergers is discussed in the *Substantive assessment guidance* at paragraphs 5.1–5.6. The main concern here relates to the threat of market foreclosure, which may arise in situations in which the merged entity is either an important downstream customer or an upstream supplier of an input, or controls a means of distribution to downstream customers. In any of these situations the OFT will be concerned where 'rivals lack a reasonable alternative to the vertically integrated firm'.[37] The OFT notes here that it is in the process of developing financial modelling and simulation techniques to establish whether firms have an incentive and the ability to foreclose markets in the way predicted.

The risk of vertical integration giving rise to collusion, as may be the case where suppliers are better able to monitor retail prices, is also acknowledged here, although it is recognised that any such cases would be rare.

Conglomerate mergers

Conglomerate mergers, the OFT recognises, 'rarely lead to a [SLC] as a result solely of their conglomerate effects'.[38] However, it may exceptionally be the case that portfolio power is created.[39]

[36] OFT, above n 15, para 4.39.
[37] Ibid, para 5.3.
[38] Ibid, para 6.1.
[39] See the discussion of this in the *GE/Honeywell* and *Tetra Laval/Sidel* cases in Chap 8.

THE APPROACH OF THE CC

The CC has set out its views in relation to the SLC test in its publication *Merger References: Competition Commission Guidelines*.[40] At the outset it sets out the 'burden of proof', stating that:

> it will not be sufficient for the Commission to believe that an SLC is possible: for the Commission to reach an adverse decision either the merger must have resulted in an SLC or the Commission must expect such a result. The Commission will usually have such an expectation if it considers that it is more likely than not that the SLC will result.[41]

The focus of the CC will be 'on the effects that the merger has on competition. Competition concerns that do not result from the merger under consideration are outside the Commission's remit in merger references'.[42] At paragraph 1.22 of its guidance the CC states that, in applying the SLC test, it will:

> evaluate the competitive constraints on firms with the merger compared to the situation that would have been expected to prevail without the merger (sometimes referred to as the 'counterfactual'). The counterfactual will be that situation which the Commission expects to arise in the absence of the merger under consideration and will, in many cases, relate to the existing, pre-merger, competitive conditions. However, in certain circumstances the Commission may need to take account of other factors, such as expected changes in the structure of the market or alternative developments that may be expected in the absence of the merger. This is in order to reflect as accurately as possible the Commission's expectation of the rivalry which will occur in the absence of the merger.

The CC's approach to SLC 'is framed in terms of two related issues':[43] the first is the relevant market definition,[44] and the second is the CC's assessment of whether the merger would increase the market power of firms in the market.[45] In practice, the CC recognises, these issues may substantially overlap, such that 'market definition and competition assessment should not be viewed as two distinct, chronological stages—rather they should be viewed as two overlapping analyses'.[46] The CC's approach to SLC analysis will here be dealt with somewhat briefly—the issues are the same as for the OFT (discussed above), and although the UK and EC merger regimes are discrete the EC Commission's approach is also similar, and the general issues have been discussed in Chapter 2. Part 2 of the relevant guidance deals with market definition, and Part 3 with the assessment of the competitive effects of the merger. Part 3 examines inter-

[40] CC2, June 2003, available at the CC website.

[41] Ibid, para 1.19.

[42] Competition Commission, *Merger References: Competition Commission Guidelines*, June 2003, para 1.23, available at the CC website.

[43] Ibid, para 1.24

[44] Ibid, Part 2.

[45] Ibid, Part 3.

[46] Ibid, para 1.25.

market rivalry (the market structure), horizontal mergers, failing firms, vertical mergers, and 'other types of mergers'.

The relevant market

Market definition is dealt with at Part 2 of the CC *Merger references* guidance—the CC does not, unlike the OFT, have a role in the enforcement of competition law extending to agreements or abuse of dominance in the UK, and does not therefore produce general guidelines. Like the OFT and the EC Commission the CC places the SSNIP test at the heart of its market definition assessment. The CC has indicated that it will usually employ the 5 per cent figure for the SSNIP test, as this may, in most cases, be presumed to have a significant effect on consumers' expenditure, and an appreciable effect on a firm's profit margin.[47] Demand and supply-side substitution will both be considered, and both relate back to the SSNIP analysis. Exactly the same process will be applied to the determination of the relevant geographic market. The fact that the process by which market definition is carried out—at least in theory—is widely employed and understood does not mean that market definition will raise no problems. For example, in *P&O Princess and Royal Caribbean Cruises Ltd*[48] the CC appeared to struggle with defining the market, and stated in the report that it 'was not able to come to a single view'.[49] In analysing the effects of the *Somerfield plc and Wm Morrison Supermarkets plc* merger[50] the CC relied on 'diversion ratios' in reaching its conclusion that in 12 local areas the merger might be expected to lead to an SLC.[51] These measure the extent to which customers for A will switch

[47] Ibid, para 2.8.

[48] (2002).

[49] Ibid, at para 2.64. See also RBB Economics, 'Goldilocks and the Three Bears—the Story of Market Definition and the Cruise Mergers', RBB Brief 11, Oct 2003.

[50] *Somerfield plc and Wm Morrison Supermarkets plc, a report on the acquisition by Somerfield plc of 115 stores from Wm Morrison Supermarkets plc*, September 2005.

[51] 'When firm A loses sales as a result of any given price increase, the diversion ratio from A to B measures the proportion of those lost sales that are capture by B. Following a merger between A and B, the merged firm takes account of the fact that B recaptures a part of the sales lost by A, and this relaxes the constraints on the pricing decision of the firm. The higher the rate of diversion between A and B, the stronger is the pre-merger constraint that the firms exert on one another and, thereby, the greater the risk of [an SLC].

> In principle, a reliable diversion ratio approach dispenses with any need to measure the relevant market because it measures directly the extent of the competitive constraints that disappear due to the merger'

RBB Economics, 'Lost in Translation: The Use and Abuse of Diversion Ratios in Unilateral Effects Analysis', RBB Brief 19, June 2006. RBB point out that '[t]he fact that in one store the CC's model predicted Somerfield would seek to charge £8.00 for a can of Coca-Cola that had previously been on offer for 50p ought to suggest an immediate need for some kind of reality check'. See also BC Harris and CG Veljanovski, 'Critical Loss Analysis: Its Growing Use in Competition Law' [2003] *ECLR* 212. See also S Baker, A Coscelli and TV Dijk, 'Unilateral Effects in Retail Chain Mergers: An Application to Supermarkets' [2002] *ECLR* 180 which discusses generally the issue of market definition in such cases.

to B in the face of a price rise, and do not therefore immediately measure the relevant market, but rather go straight to the competitive constraint and effects between A and B. In this report a large number of local markets were identified, a factor which arises in a number of inquiries in which horizontal mergers take place at the retail level. In *Vue Entertainment Holdings (UK) Ltd and A3 Cinema Limited*,[52] for example, the CC had to deal with both the national market for screen advertising, film distribution and the supply of food and drink at concession points, and local markets in respect of filmgoers. In the case of the latter the CC worked from a 20-minute drive-time isochrone.[53] This gave rise to highly localised markets, and an SLC was anticipated in Basingstoke, giving rise to a requirement of divestiture of just one cinema.[54]

Competitive effects

Intra-market rivalry

Market shares and the degree of concentration will be the two key factors considered in assessing the level of competition within the market. The CC 'will have regard to the combined market shares of the merging parties',[55] and stresses that there is no particular market share threshold which will be indicative of SLC. However, 'a combined market share of 25% or above . . . would normally be sufficient to raise potential concerns'. Of course, the corollary of this is that a merger which results in a post-merger market share of less than 25 per cent will, *ceteris paribus*, be unlikely to raise competition concerns.[56] It will be noted that this is the same level at which the EC Commission considers competition concerns to be unlikely to be raised.

The concentration ratio that the CC is likely to prefer is the HHI (discussed in Chapter 2). It follows the OFT in its approach to concerns raised by the levels of change (see Table 11.1). It is recognised here that in the case of markets characterised by network effects, in which case competition is *for* the market, rather than *within* the market, market shares and concentration ratios may be of little value in assessing the state of competition. It is not inevitable that increased concentration, even at high levels, will lead to a finding of SLC. In *HJ*

[52] *Vue Entertainment Holdings (UK) Ltd and A3 Cinema Limited: A report on the completed acquisition of A3 Cinema Limited by Vue Entertainment Holdings (UK) Limited*, Feb 2006.

[53] Simply, an area within which it was possible to drive to a cinema within the specified time (see para 4 of the report, above n 52).

[54] Local markets were also considered in *HMV Group plc and Ottakar's plc: Proposed acquisition of Ottakar's plc by HMV Group plc through Waterstone's Booksellers Ltd*, May 2006. Here the CC found no evidence that competition at a local level had an impact on service quality, and concluded that the merger would not result in an SLC at local level.

[55] Ibid n 42, para 3.4.

[56] Ibid, para 3.4.

Heinz and HP Foods[57] the acquisition brought the HP brands for baked beans and tinned pasta products under Heinz's control. The market was already 'highly concentrated', and became more so as a result of the merger. Table 11.2 sets out the position in relation to plain baked beans:[58]

Table 11.2 *Market Share 2005 (%)*

Heinz	67.7
Premier	6.7
HP beans	5.1
Crosse & Blackwell beans	0.9
Branston beans	0.7
Own label	25.3
Other branded	0.4
HP/Heinz combined	**72.8**
HHI pre-merger	5,251
HHI post-merger	5,941
Increase in HHI	(Δ) 691

The merger was cleared on the ground that the CC did not expect an SLC to arise. The result is at first surprising, but the CC found that there was 'some' buyer power, that barriers to entry were not increased, that competition between the two companies was not strong pre-merger, that there was no evidence of Heinz bundling or attempting to bundle its products pre-merger, and that there were low barriers to customers switching.[59]

Like the OFT the CC draws attention to the role played by switching costs,[60] but otherwise does not significantly discuss the concept of buyer power. In 2001 the CC recommended the blocking of a merger involving Lloyds TSB Group and Abbey National, notwithstanding the fact that the latter accounted for only 5 per cent of the market. The CC found that a position of collective dominance would arise, with the four leading players having a combined market share of some 77 per cent. The fact that customers rarely switch bank accounts, and find the process to be a difficult one, was a major factor behind the CC's decision.[61]

[57] *HJ Heinz and HP Foods: A report on the completed acquisition of the HP Foods companies by HJ Heinz Company and HJ Heinz Company Ltd*, Mar 2006.

[58] CC report, above n 57, para 5.128.

[59] For a summary of the argument see para 12 of the decision taken by the OFT on 26 Oct 2005.

[60] Ibid n 42, para 3.14.

[61] *Lloyds TSB Group and Abbey National plc: A report on the proposed merger*, Cm 5208 (2001). At para 4.62 the CC stated:

> 'Switching barriers may also raise the costs of entry and expansion: entrants will tend to incur large sunk costs of customer acquisition (generous terms have to be offered to attract customers and costs are incurred in providing a switcher service to deal with originators of direct debits and others). Furthermore, by constraining the rate of expansion, a low rate of switching makes it more difficult to take advantage of economies of scale. In this context [personal

Perhaps following the expertise it has gained in the course of market investigation references the CC draws particular attention to information asymmetries prevailing in the market in a way that the OFT does not. It notes that 'the competitive process can be significantly affected in some markets where sellers have more information than customers regarding the quality of the products'.[62] It does not, however, state exactly how the presence of such a factor will affect its merger analysis, although presumably any further restriction of choice, and therefore of competition, in a market already characterised by information asymmetry may be more likely to result in an SLC.

Conduct of firms

The CC recognises that market structure is not the only determinant of the degree of competition within a market, and that a number of factors relating to the conduct of firms may be relevant. These include: the ability and capacity to innovate; objectives and culture of firms; and pricing behaviour, including the extent of the transparency of prices within the market.[63]

Non-price factors in competition

The CC points to the fact that in some markets non-price competition will be more important than price competition.[64] This may in particular arise in situations in which there are incentives not to compete on price alone, or where there are incentives to raise barriers to entry. Where it is appropriate to do so the CC will have regard to: product development, product range and quality, marketing, servicing and R & D. In oligopolies undertakings may have incentives not to engage in either price or non-price competition, although a key factor will be the time within which other members of the oligopoly could respond to any move by the initiator.

Horizontal mergers

In the case of horizontal mergers the CC's approach is a standard one. The CC 'will evaluate the competitive constraints on firms with the merger, compared to

> customer accounts] entrants face both a low rate of switching and a low natural rate of account opening and closure compared with some other products such as mortgages'.

See A Lofaro and D Ridyard, 'Switching Costs and Merger Assessment—Don't Move the Goalposts' [2003] *ECLR* 268.

62 Above n 42, para 3.15.

63 Price transparency may be a double-edged sword. Where customers have good access to price information they may be better able to shop around; however, it may also be easier for sellers to coordinate their prices if transparency prevails.

64 Above n 42, paras 3.17–3.19.

the situation that would have been expected without the merger'.[65] It is unlikely, the CC states, that concerns will be raised where post-merger intra-market rivalry will still be substantial. The approach that the CC takes to efficiencies is similar to that of the OFT, in that any efficiencies claimed must be expected to arise in a short time, to be a direct consequence of the merger, and to be likely to 'increase rivalry among the remaining firms in the market'.[66]

The most common grounds on which mergers are blocked in the UK are that they give rise to unilateral effects by way of increasing concentration at the horizontal level. A recent example of such a case is *Emap plc and ABI Building Data Ltd*.[67] In this case the two largest suppliers, with a post-merger market share of 70 per cent, in the UK of project information and contact data to the construction industry merged. There were substantial barriers to entry, including the need to provide a similar range of coverage and accuracy and a very steep learning curve. All but one of the potential entrants identified by the parties considered the costs of entry to be unviable. The CC concluded that the merged entity was likely to raise prices, and to restrict product innovation and improvement, and ordered divestiture.

The CC states that non-coordinated (unilateral) effects may arise in the following circumstances: (1) where the merger results in a firm with a large market share; (2) where no competitor or competitors can apply sufficient pressure on the merged firm to constrain it; (3) where the merger itself eliminates an important competitive force on the market; (4) where customers have little option to switch; (5) where products are homogenous and competitors are capacity constrained; (6) where the merger affects differentiated products that are regarded by consumers as reasonable substitutes; (7) where the potential for entry is limited; and (8) where there is no, or limited, countervailing buyer power.

The treatment of coordinated effects in the CC guidance is relatively extensive, but in principle comes down to the same factors, albeit spelt out in more detail, as are at play in the OFT's and EC Commission's analysis. The CC states that in relation to coordinated effects its assessment will first consider whether these exist prior to the merger and, if they do, whether the merger will maintain or exacerbate coordinated effects. Where they do not the assessment is to determine whether they may exist after the merger, in which case SLC is likely to be found. In its *Lloyds TSB Group plc and Abbey National plc* report,[68] the CC considered the acquisition of a 'maverick' bank by one of the leading suppliers of banking services. The market as a whole was concentrated, with a C4 of 72 per cent in the personal current account market, and 85 per cent in the market for banking services for small and medium-sized enterprises. The CC recommended that the merger be prohibited in part because it believed that

[65] Ibid, para 3.20.
[66] Ibid, para 3.27.
[67] *Emap plc and ABI Building Data Ltd: A report on the acquisition of ABI Building Data Ltd by Emap plc*, Jan 2005.
[68] Cm 5208 (2001).

the personal customer account market was 'vulnerable to tacit collusion in pricing'.[69]

Entry and expansion

Entry and expansion is dealt with at paragraphs 3.45–3.57 of the CC guidance. A number of factors will be considered, including: (1) the history of past entry and expansion, and any evidence of plans in this respect; (2) the extent to which entrants in the past have succeeded in gaining market share, and the cost of this; (3) direct observations and statistical evidence; (4) the costs involved; (5) the likelihood that entry or expansion will happen in such a short frame of time as to impact on the incentives and strategies of the incumbents; (6) the cost of exit in the event of failed entry; (7) the affect of technological change and innovation; and (8) the likely response to entry by the incumbents.

As is the general position in relation to entry a number of factors may serve as barriers (see Chapter 2). There have been a number of cases in which the CC has found that strong brand recognition and reputation serves as a barrier. The CC has stated generally that possession of a 'widely recognised name is helpful for marketing purposes and confers a significant advantage upon its holder'.[70] In *Cendant Corporation and RAC Holdings*[71] the MMC pointed to the high barriers to entry into the market for vehicle breakdown services arising from the brand strength of the AA and the RAC. It noted that developing such a brand entailed a significant sunk cost which could not be recovered in the event of failure, and that Green Flag had incurred 'considerable' advertising and promotion expenditure, but had a public recognition factor of only around 35 per cent.

In some cases new entry may be actively encouraged by existing customers, and the analysis may become linked to that of buyer power. This was held to be the case for example in *CHC Helicopter Corporation and Helicopter Services Group ASA*,[72] in which the CC found that oil companies operating in the North Sea oil fields could 'encourage new entry without undue difficulty, and would do so if they felt that existing operators were charging too much or otherwise offering an unsatisfactory service'.[73]

[69] At 21. See the discussion of this case in F Montag and A von Bonin, 'Collective Dominance in Merger Cases after Airtours' in G Drauz and M Reynolds (eds), *EC Merger Control: A Major Reform in Progress* (Richmond, Surrey, Richmond Law and Tax, 2003) at 331.

[70] *Coloplast A/S and SSL International plc*, Cm 5522 (2002), at para 2.71.

[71] *Cendant Corporation and RAC Holdings Ltd: A report on the proposed acquisition by Cendant Corporation of RAC Holdings Ltd*, Cm 4196 (1999).

[72] *CHC Helicopter Corporation and Helicopter Services Group ASA*, Cm 4556 (2000)

[73] Ibid, para 2.82. Parr *et al* note that in an earlier report the CC had found the opposite to be the case: N Parr, R Finbow and M Hughes, *UK Merger Control: Law and Practice* (2nd edn, London, Sweet & Maxwell, 2005), at 355.

Countervailing buyer power

As with the other areas discussed here the CC's treatment of countervailing buyer power is consistent with that adopted by the OFT and the EC Commission. Factors that it considers to be important are: (1) the ability to find an alternative supplier; (2) the ease of switching; (3) the extent to which buyers may be able credibly to threaten setting up their own supply arrangements; (4) the extent to which buyers may threaten to stop purchasing other products from the supplier; and (5) the extent to which buyers can impose costs on suppliers. Although buyer power is often raised by the parties as a 'defence' to a merger, it is rare that mergers are cleared on the basis that countervailing buyer power does indeed protect against an expansion and exploitation of market power. This was however the case in the CC investigation into *Cott Beverages and Macaw*.[74] Here the relevant market was for the supply of own-label and tertiary-branded carbonated soft drinks in the UK. The parties were the two largest producers in the UK, and post-merger the market share of Cott would be around 50 per cent by capacity, or 65 per cent by sales. The CC found however that retailers possessed substantial bargaining power, and that this was backed up by spare capacity in the industry such that they could credibly threaten to withhold their custom.[75] In *Francisco Partners LP and G International, Inc*[76] the CC examined a horizontal merger in the market for electronic data interchange communications services, which would remove from the market one of three small competitors, and concluded that sufficient viable alternatives existed for core customers to resist any exploitation of the enhanced position enjoyed by the post-merger entity, although two of the inquiry group disagreed with this conclusion.

Failing firms

In order to accept the failing firm defence the CC needs to be satisfied that the firm will, in the near future, be unable to meet its financial obligations, and that it would be unable to restructure itself successfully. In addition the CC will consider whether other credible purchasers would exist in respect of whom a merger would raise less concern.[77] In *British Salt Ltd and New Cheshire Salt Works Ltd*[78] the CC cleared a merger between two producers of vacuum salt in a market characterised by high concentration, low buyer power and substantial barriers to entry on the ground that the target was not likely to remain a

[74] *Cott Beverages Limited and Macaw (Holdings) Limited: A report on the acquisition by Cott Beverages Limited of Macaw (Holdings) Limited*, 26 April 2006.

[75] Buyer power is analysed at paras 5.34–5.46 of ibid, and in Appendix C of the final report.

[76] *Francisco Partners LP and G International, Inc*, 2 Sept 2005.

[77] Ibid n 42, paras 3.61–3.63.

[78] *British Salt Ltd and New Cheshire Salt Works Ltd: A report on the acquisition of New Cheshire Salt Works Ltd by British Salt Ltd*, Nov 2005.

competitor in the market, being likely to close late in 2006 as it could not absorb price rises for gas.

Vertical mergers and other types of merger

The CC expresses the standard concern that vertical mergers may foreclose competition,[79] and also points to the fact that they may, where the acquisition involves a new or recent entrant or a particularly aggressive firm, 'be an effective means of preventing the development of competition in a downstream or upstream market'.[80] One case in which a vertical merger was blocked, and one which attracted more than its fair share of media attention, was that of the bid for Manchester United plc by the satellite broadcaster British Sky Broadcasting.[81] The Secretary of State, when following the recommendation, stated that the merger would:

—reduce competition for the broadcasting rights to Premier League matches, which would lead to less choice for the Premier League and less scope for innovation in the broadcasting of Premier League football;
—enhance BSkyB's ability to secure rights to Premier League matches and hence reduce competition in the market for sports premium TV channels, feeding through into reduced competition in the wider pay-TV market.

The primary concern was that BSkyB would be in a uniquely strong position when it came to bid for future rights packages as it would also, through its control of Manchester United, occupy a seat on the other side of the table. The MMC had previously approved, subject to some conditions, a bid by BT for a Canadian manufacturer of telecommunications equipment with a significant market share in the UK,[82] and it has been argued that the approach of the UK authorities—at least under the 'old' merger regime—has been a little inconsistent in relation to vertical mergers.[83]

In relation to conglomerate mergers the CC first briefly discusses the issue of portfolio power, noting that 'instances are likely to arise only when customers have a strong incentive to purchase from a single source rather than from many suppliers'.[84] This, the CC recognises, may happen—as was the case in the

[79] Ibid n 42, para 3.65.

[80] Ibid, para 3.66.

[81] *British Sky Broadcasting Group Plc and Manchester United Plc*, Cm 4305 (1999). See also DTI Press Release P/99/309, 9 Apr 1999.

[82] *British Telecommunications Plc and Mitel Corporation*, Cm 9715 (1986).

[83] See, eg, F Tassano, 'Are Vertical Mergers Harmful?' [1999] *ECLR* 395. See also JF Pickering, 'Competition Policy and Vertical Relationships: The Approach of the UK Monopolies and Mergers Commission' [1999] *ECLR* 225 which examines the stance taken in relation to vertical arrangements under the monopoly provisions of the FTA 73.

[84] Above n 42, para 3.69.

General Electric/Honeywell[85] merger discussed in Chapter 8—in sectors in which there is a high service component relating to the products. However, such cases are rare. Two further concerns relating to conglomerate mergers are raised by the CC. The first is that the merger may bring together products which are complements, in which case the incentive will be to *lower* prices, although it may also raise the prospect of anti-competitive bundling. The second is that the merger may relate to two separate product markets which are, nevertheless, the nearest to each other. The CC notes that this possibility is one reason why in merger analysis the SSNIP is best carried out at the prices prevailing at the time of the merger.[86]

[85] Case COMP/M.2220 (2001) 3 July 2001 [2004] OJ L 48/1.
[86] *Merger references*, above n 42, para 3.72.

12

Procedure Before the Making of a Reference

INTRODUCTION

THE OFFICE OF Fair Trading is the primary body charged with the enforcement of merger policy in the UK, and has a number of duties assigned to it in this respect under the terms of the EA 02. It evaluates approximately 230 mergers a year.[1] Generally the OFT, inter alia, 'has the function of obtaining, compiling and keeping under review information about matters relating to the carrying out of its functions'.[2] Given that notification of mergers falling within the jurisdictional thresholds set out in the EA 02 is not compulsory, this is an important responsibility of the OFT in relation to merger control. The OFT also has the responsibility of making proposals or giving advice to Ministers and public authorities relating to its functions.[3] The primary duty of the OFT in relation to mergers is that set out in sections 22 and 33, which give it a duty to make references to the CC in relation to completed and anticipated mergers respectively. However, as is discussed in Chapter 14, below, this duty is subject to various qualifications, and is not therefore absolute. The OFT may determine that a reference is unjustified where the merger in question takes place in a market which is not of sufficient importance to justify a reference,[4] or where the merger gives rise to relevant customer benefits which outweigh the SLC.[5] The OFT also has the power to accept undertakings from parties in lieu of making a reference,[6] and may make orders relating to these undertakings.[7] It may also make orders in respect of completed mergers where it is considering making a reference,[8] and has other interim powers[9] and enforcement powers.[10]

[1] OFT, *Interim arrangements for informal advice and pre-notification contacts,* Apr 2006, para 11, available at the OFT website.
[2] S 5(1) EA 02.
[3] S 7 EA 02.
[4] Ss 22(2)(a) and 33(2)(a) EA 02.
[5] Ss 22(2)(b) and 33(2)(c) EA 02.
[6] S 73 EA 02.
[7] S 75 EA 02.
[8] S 71 EA 02.
[9] S 76 EA 02.
[10] S 92 EA 02.

In this chapter the focus is on the OFT's procedure in relation to the assessment of mergers prior to the point at which a reference is made to the CC. The exercise of its powers in relation to the acceptance of undertakings and the making of orders, as well as their enforcement, is discussed in Chapter 13, below. The role of the OFT in relation to those mergers falling within the scope of the public interest or the special public interest provisions of the EA 02 is dealt with in Chapter 17, and its role in relation to media and water mergers is dealt with in Chapter 16.

Generally the OFT obtains information about merger activity from a wide range of sources, including the media. It may also be the case that concerned third parties may alert the OFT to relevant merger situations. The OFT has taken steps to encourage pre-merger contacts between relevant parties and itself, although by April 2006 it had withdrawn the provision of informal guidance. Paragraph 3.3 of *Mergers: Procedural Guidance*[11] indicates that there are a number of ways in which parties may ask the OFT to consider a merger: informal advice; confidential guidance; pre-notification discussions; statutory voluntary pre-notification; and informal submissions/common notification form. These are dealt with below. In the financial year 2005–6 the OFT examined 248 mergers and merger proposals. Thirty-six of these raised sufficient concern to be considered at a case review meeting (see below). Twenty-one (8.4 per cent) were referred to the CC.[12]

MERGER PRE-NOTIFICATION

Informal advice and pre-notification contacts

In April 2006 the OFT, following pressure from the legal community, withdrew its refusal to offer informal advice on proposed mergers. The OFT announced interim arrangements,[13] to apply until April 2007 at which time the position would again be reviewed,[14] under which it would consider applications for informal advice in situations in which there was a good faith intention to proceed, and where there was a genuine issue about whether the OFT would have a duty to refer the merger to the CC. The OFT is clearly concerned about its role in offering such advice, noting in the guidance that its role is substantially different from that under the FTA 73, in which such advice was given to Ministers, that the provision of 'non-statutory services' detracts from its statutory role, and that informal advice may, in practice, provide 'minimal added

[11] OFT, May 2003.

[12] OFT, *Office of Fair Trading Annual Report 2005–2006* (London, OFT, 2006), at 51, available at the OFT website.

[13] OFT, above n 1.

[14] The OFT is committed to a general review of its guidance and enforcement procedures, leading to the publication of new guidance by March 2007.

value' to the parties' own assessment.[15] At the same time the OFT accepts that 'its advice may assist business in a way that the parties' legal and economic advisers cannot'.[16] The OFT's record on informal advice under the EA 02 is one that must raise concerns: in *Emap/ABI Building Data Ltd* it gave 'favourable' advice in respect of a merger which was subsequently blocked by the CC,[17] and in *Phoenix/EAP* it gave 'unfavourable' confidential guidance in respect of a merger that was cleared by the CC.[18]

The interim arrangements announced in April 2006 are therefore conservative in nature, and are based around a number of 'screening principles'. The first of these is that informal advice is available only in respect of transactions which are 'neither hypothetical', 'nor in the public domain'.[19] In order to recognise that a good faith intention to proceed exists the OFT will have regard to evidence such as financing, heads of agreement, and evidence of board-level consideration within the acquirer. The second principle is that there must be a genuine issue, and the advisers will be 'expected to articulate a theory of harm that the OFT might reasonably rely upon as a credible candidate case for reference'.[20] The standard by which the OFT judges this is that of whether the case would likely be subject to the OFT's Case Review Meeting procedure (see below). The OFT stresses that self-incrimination should not be a matter of concern for the parties, noting that it has a record of dealing with parties' arguments on a without-prejudice basis. The OFT will limit its informal advice to that which 'would most assist business in the circumstances',[21] and may restrict itself to making clear that its officials have no greater insight, in the light of the facts disclosed, than would be possessed by the parties and their advisers. Even in this case, however, the OFT may offer advice relating to any formal notification, including evidence which may be appropriate in order to assist in the evaluation of the competition concerns raised by the case.

Where interim advice is sought, the application should be addressed to the Director of Mergers, and should be in a concise and clear format. The OFT will in most cases make a decision within five working days on whether it will accept or reject such an application, although urgent cases may be dealt with more swiftly. A number of caveats apply where advice is given: the advice does not bind the OFT; both the content of the advice and the fact that it has been applied

15 OFT, above n 1, paras 5–7.

16 Ibid, para 3.

17 Jan 2005. In this case the merger involved two direct competitors. The CC found that had it not been for the merger ABI Building Data Ltd would have remained in the market as a viable and profitable competitor, and that the only remedy was divestiture.

18 *Anticipated acquisition by Phoenix Healthcare Distribution Limited of East Anglian Pharmaceuticals Limited,* OFT, 29 June 2005. The OFT found that a proposed merger between two pharmaceutical wholesalers in East Anglia would result in an SLC, which was not outweighed by a plausible case in relation to efficiencies which would be achieved by the merger.

19 OFT, above n 1, para 11.

20 Ibid.

21 Ibid.

for are to be strictly confidential; advice given is based on the evidence submitted by the parties, which will not be tested by the OFT; and the process is a 'one-shot', although pre-notification contacts may be encouraged. The revised approach to informal advice replaces the relevant section of *Mergers: Procedural Guidance*, and therefore also removes from that guidance the provisions relating to confidential guidance.[22]

Although its approach to informal advice is a cautious one, the OFT, like DG Comp, is keen to encourage good use of pre-notification contacts. The benefits of such contact, as set out by the OFT in *Interim arrangements for informal advice and pre-notification contacts,* paragraph 19, are such as to:

—educate the case team where markets are complex and/or unfamiliar
—frame the transaction, including its rationale and efficiencies, in a realistic context early on
—clarify what information and evidence the OFT will require to deem a submission satisfactory or a Merger Notice complete, or will request early in the review procedure
—identify useful items of evidence that may assist the parties' case
—potentially avoid or minimise burdensome information requests
—be an additional forum for informal dialogue on the OFT's likely approach to a novel issue or on competition concerns, if the parties wish
—promote agreement on pragmatic methodological solutions to tackling issues . . .

Requests for pre-notification discussions will normally be dealt with within five to 10 working days of the receipt of the request. Meetings may be held if appropriate, but more normally it may be expected that communications will be by way of telephone, email or formal written contacts.[23]

Statutory pre-notification

The arrangements relating to formal merger pre-notifications in the UK are based on the Enterprise Act 2002 (Merger Prenotification) Regulations 2003,[24] which are made on the basis of the authority set out in section 101(2) EA 02. Sections 96–102 EA 02 establish the legislative framework.[25] The relevant procedures can be used only in respect of anticipated mergers which have been

[22] OFT, *Mergers: Procedural* guidance, May 2003, paras 3.11–3.18, available at the OFT website.
[23] OFT, above n 1, para 21.
[24] SI 2003/1369. Merger pre-notification was first introduced into the UK regime by the Companies Act 1989.
[25] Fees will be charged whenever a merger pre-notification is made. These are based on the Enterprise Act 2002 (Merger Fees and Determination of Turnover) Order 2003, SI 2003/1370. The fees were raised from 6 April 2006. They are loosely based on the value of the turnover of the enterprise being acquired. Where the value is £20m or less the fee is £15,000; for enterprises with turnovers in excess of £20m, but less than £70m, the fee is £30,000; for enterprises with turnover in excess of £70m the fee is £45,000. These are substantially higher than the fees applicable up to 5 April 2006: see OFT, *Mergers fee information*, Feb 2006.

made public,[26] and are entirely voluntary, although if notification is made there is an obligation to do so honestly and with full disclosure of relevant information. Notification takes the form of a 'merger notice', and shall be in the form set out by the OFT and available on its website.[27] The procedure provides that the OFT may consider an anticipated public merger within 20 working days, subject to a maximum extension of 10 working days. Where a merger notice is accepted by the OFT as being complete, if the OFT does not make a reference in relation to the anticipated merger within that time limit then no reference can subsequently be made, subject to certain exceptions set out in section 100.[28] A merger notice may be made to the OFT by a person authorised to make one,[29] who must be a person 'carrying on an enterprise to which the notified arrangements relate'.[30] This means that a notification cannot be made by any third party, although third parties are invited elsewhere to bring relevant merger situations to the attention of the OFT. The person making the merger notice can withdraw it at any time before the end of the consideration period,[31] although the fee will not be refunded unless the merger falls within the ECMR. The merger notice requires a great deal of information to be supplied, and this in itself should ensure that applications are not frivolously made. Point 14, for example, requires:

> copies of analyses, reports, studies and surveys submitted to or prepared for any member(s) of the board of directors, the supervisory board, or the shareholders' meeting, for the purpose of assessing or analysing the proposed transaction with respect to competitive conditions, competitors (actual and potential), and market conditions . . .[32]

The pre-notification period begins at 09:00 on the first working day after the receipt of the merger notice,[33] and the relevant period expires at 17:00

[26] The OFT is obliged by virtue of s 99(1) EA 02 to, 'so far as practicable . . . bring [the relevant information] to the attention of those whom the OFT considers would be affected if the arrangements were carried into effect'.

[27] S 96(2), EA 02. See OFT, *Merger notice under section 96 of the Enterprise Act 2002*, June 2003. See also OFT, *Prior notice of publicly proposed mergers*, June 2003. Both are available at the OFT website.

[28] The exceptions apply: where the merger notice is rejected; where the merger is in fact consummated before the end of the 20 day period; where relevant information known to the person making the notice is not disclosed; where either of the parties merges with another party during the period; the parties do not merge within 6 months of the end of the period; the merger notice is withdrawn; or any information given is false or misleading.

[29] Enterprise Act 2002 (Merger Prenotification) Regulations 2003, SI 2003/1369, reg 3. This happened, eg, in *Greene King plc/Laurel Pub Holdings Limited* (OFT decision of 6 Oct 2004) in which the parties notified a transaction to the OFT on 9 July 2004, but withdrew it before completing the relevant transaction on 6 Aug 2004. The OFT announced its intention to make a reference, but subsequently accepted divestiture undertakings (see Chap 13).

[30] The person may appoint a representative to complete the notice and to act on their behalf. This is most likely to be a firm of solicitors. See also SI 2003/1369, above n 29, reg 14.

[31] Ibid, reg 7.

[32] The notice also requires the parties to have considered carefully market shares held by the relevant parties, and the impact of the merger on both horizontal and vertical links.

[33] Assuming the appropriate fee has been paid to the OFT.

20 working days later. Where the notice throws up issues which are complex or where it appears that there are areas that the OFT needs to consider further, the OFT may extend the period by a further 10 working days. The OFT may also extend the period by notice if it is contemplating seeking undertakings under section 73 EA 02.[34] The position in respect of cases in which an intervention notice is made is dealt with in Chapter 17, below. The OFT is sensitive to the need to comply with the City Code on Takeovers and Mergers, but states that it is the responsibility of the parties making the notice to submit it in good time to allow the OFT's decision to coincide with the relevant first closing date. The OFT warns that it cannot be bound by the offer timetable, and that it may, where necessary, extend the consideration period.[35]

The OFT can reject a merger notice for five reasons: it suspects that information given is false or misleading; it suspects that the merger will not, in fact, take place; information is not supplied on time; it suspects that the merger would fall within the jurisdiction of the ECMR; and the fee is not paid. Such a rejection may occur at any time during the consideration period, and the fact that a notice is acknowledged and is being considered does not preclude subsequent rejection. Section 99(2) EA 02 provides that the OFT may request further information from the parties once it has entered the period of consideration. Any such request shall be made by way of a notice, which is to state the information required, the period within which it must be required, and the possible consequences of not providing the information in the required manner.[36] It is an offence knowingly or recklessly to supply false or misleading information to the OFT in connection with the exercise of its merger powers.[37]

INFORMATION GATHERING POWERS

A number of statutory provisions give the OFT the power it needs to secure information and carry out investigations necessary to the performance of its functions. Where a statutory pre-merger notification is made or the parties make an informal pre-notification the most important hurdle, that of becoming aware of the merger's existence, has obviously been overcome. Further, the requirements set out in respect of information to be provided in the merger notice form and in part 4 of the OFT's *Mergers: Procedural Guidance*[38] are substantial, and are backed up by an obligation in respect of the statutory notification neither knowingly nor recklessly to provide the OFT with false or

[34] S 97(7) EA 02. This section may also apply where the Secretary of State is seeking undertakings in respect of a merger in which an intervention notice is in force (see Chap 18, below). The period may also be extended if the EC Commission is considering an Art 22(1) ECMR request (see Chap 3, above).

[35] See OFT, *Prior notice of publicly proposed mergers*, June 2003.

[36] S 99(3) EA 02.

[37] S 117 EA 02.

[38] May 2003.

misleading information.[39] In the case of the formal pre-notification process the OFT has the power to request further information, and will not be held to the strict time limits when this is not forthcoming. However, as has been noted above, companies are under no obligation to notify the OFT of a merger, and there is evidence to suggest that some advisers may, in exceptional circumstances, be prepared to recommend consummation ahead of notification, although it should be recognised that such a strategy has a high risk.

Section 31 EA 02 sets out the powers of the OFT to gather information in respect of completed mergers.[40] It provides that:

> (1) The OFT may by notice to any of the persons carrying on the enterprises which have or may have ceased to be distinct enterprises request him to provide the OFT with such information as the OFT may require for the purpose of deciding whether to make a reference under s 22.
> (2) The notice shall state—
>
> (a) the information required;
> (b) the period within which the information is to be provided; and
> (c) the possible consequences of not providing the information within the stated period and in the authorised or required manner.

The section 31 power may also be used in situations in which an informal pre-merger notification has been made (there being no other power under which the OFT could act in this respect), and in situations in which neither of the merging parties has made any approach to the OFT. It should be noted that, under section 25(2) EA 02, the OFT can unilaterally extend the four-month period within which a decision to refer can be made where any person subject to a section 31 notice has failed to provide the information requested. Any such extension may run until the information *is* provided to the satisfaction of the OFT.[41] Where a merger has been referred to the OFT under the ECMR Articles 4(4) or (9), identical powers are given to the OFT.[42]

The OFT recognises that it may on occasion be difficult for the parties to supply it with the information it requests in the form in which it requests it. At paragraph 5.4 of its procedural guidance the OFT urges parties in receipt of requests for information to discuss with the OFT any difficulties that might arise, and the OFT indicates that it may 'vary the information request or the stipulated response date'.[43]

[39] S 117 EA 02.

[40] Note, too that the OFT may when it is considering imposing an initial enforcement order (see Chap 13, below) make use of the power to obtain information set out in Sched 8, para 19, EA 02.

[41] S 25(3) EA 02.

[42] S 34B EA 02, inserted by the EC Merger Control (Consequential Amendments) Regulations 2004, SI 2004/1079, reg 2, Sched, para 2(1), (9).

[43] OFT, *Mergers: Procedural guidance*, May 2003, above n 22.

Confidentiality of information

It is obviously the case that much of the information that will be given to the OFT, in particular but not exclusively that relating to future strategic plans which may impact on the competitive environment, will be commercially sensitive. Part 9 of the Enterprise Act 2002 contains provisions designed to secure the confidentiality of information obtained by a relevant public authority in relation to the carrying out of its functions under the EA 02.[44] Section 237 sets out a general restriction under which information relating to the affairs of an individual or an undertaking must not be disclosed either during the lifetime of that individual or while the undertaking continues in existence, unless the disclosure is authorised by Part 9 EA 02. This does not apply in respect of information which has already been made public in a circumstance which does not breach any relevant law.[45]

Information covered by Part 9 may be disclosed only in limited circumstances. These are: where consent is obtained;[46] where the disclosure is necessary in order to fulfil an obligation arising under EC law, which is most likely to take place in relation to the operation of the ECMR;[47] where the disclosure is necessary in order for the public authority to fulfil a statutory function;[48] in connection with criminal proceedings;[49] and in some circumstances to relevant overseas public authorities.[50] Wherever information is disclosed the relevant public authority must have regard to certain considerations set out in section 244. These are, first, the need to exclude from the disclosure, so far as practicable, any information in respect of which the authority believes disclosure would be contrary to the public interest;[51] secondly, the need to exclude from the disclosure any information which may significantly harm the legitimate business interests of the relevant undertakings,[52] and any information relating to the private affairs of a person where the disclosure may significantly harm that person's interests;[53] and, thirdly, the need to balance the interests referred to in the second point with the extent to which such information may be necessary for the purpose for which the authority is permitted to make the disclosure.[54]

It is likely that, in the fulfilment of its statutory function, the OFT may disclose information relating to specific mergers to government departments or

[44] See also The Enterprise Act 2002 (Part 9 Restrictions on Disclosure of Information) (Specification) Order 2004, SI 2004/693. The provisions of Part 9 do not affect the Competition Appeals Tribunal.

[45] S 237(3) EA 02.

[46] S 239(1) EA 02.

[47] S 240 EA 02.

[48] S 241 EA 02.

[49] S 242 EA 02.

[50] S 243 EA 02.

[51] S 244(2) EA 02.

[52] S 244(3)(a) EA 02.

[53] S 244(3)(b) EA 02.

[54] S 244(4) EA 02.

regulators with expertise in the sector. Any such disclosure will be confidential, and the purpose is to allow the OFT to take account of the views of those with relevant expertise about the competitive impact of the merger.[55] It is also likely that all relevant information obtained by the OFT during the course of its initial examination of the merger will be passed on to the CC in the event that a merger reference is made. Given that the CC has its own powers, which match those of the OFT, to obtain information, this transmission of information should raise no concerns. The only restriction that may apply here is where the OFT is precluded from passing on such information by other legislation, for example, the ECMR. In some circumstances information will be exchanged between the members of the ECN. This will be the case where parties to a merger indicate that the merger has also been notified to other authorities within the ECA. In this case the members of the ECN have agreed that they will communicate with relevant officials in the other ECAs and exchange views on the case. However, unless the parties consent or national legislation permits it, confidential information will not be exchanged. The OFT has indicated that it may seek permission from the parties to exchange such information when 'the analysis will demonstrate a competition problem worthy of further investigation or, potentially, of remedy, and an exchange of confidential information will benefit the analysis of the case or make it easier to identify an appropriate remedy'.[56]

The OFT is required to publish all its decisions save those relating to non-public mergers. Before any decision is published it will be circulated to the parties or relevant advisers, and they will be given the opportunity to request the excision of business secrets from the text.[57]

THE DECISION MAKING PROCESS WITHIN THE OFT

The OFT sets out the shape that its internal procedures take in *Mergers: Procedural Guidance*. The OFT starts by noting that approximately 80 per cent of the cases that it deals with each year raise no competition concerns. In these cases the decision to clear the merger will be made within the Mergers Branch of the OFT. The Branch will prepare a clearance decision paper which will be circulated to a review group within the OFT.[58] A case review meeting may be held where members of the review group either disagree with the suggested

[55] OFT, *Mergers: Procedural guidance*, May 2003, para 5.10, available at the OFT website.

[56] Ibid, para 5.28.

[57] Ibid, para 5.24. The same statutory restrictions apply to the activities of the CC. Reference should also be made to the *Chairman's Guidance on Disclosure of Information in Merger and Market Inquiries*, CC, June 2003, available at the CC website. See further Chap 14.

[58] This includes: the Chairman, Executive Director, Director Competition Enforcement Division, a representative of OFT Legal Division, representatives of the Branch and the director of the relevant OFT sectoral branch if appropriate: OFT, *Mergers: Procedural guidance*, May 2003, para 5.16.

decision or believe that the case raises issues which should be subject to further review. Where there is neither dissent nor calls for a case review meeting the decision will be made known to the parties, and, where the case is a public one, announced.

In more complex cases or cases which raise material competition issues a different procedure will be followed. In these cases the parties will be invited to attend an issues meeting with the Branch, and will be sent an issues letter setting out the core arguments and evidence. An issues letter will 'set out the arguments in favour of a reference so that parties have an opportunity to respond to the reasons why a reference, if it follows, has been made'.[59] It may not be the case that a reference is made in all cases in which an issues letter is sent out, but the approach taken by the OFT does mean that the parties will have a clear indication of the concerns raised, and the chance to address these either by persuading the OFT to change its stance or perhaps by offering undertakings to address the harm identified. It was stressed by the CAT in *UniChem Limited v OFT* that it was incumbent on the OFT to give parties an opportunity to comment on evidence that it intended to rely upon in taking a decision.[60] Responses to the issues letter may be made orally at an issues meeting, or in writing, or both. At this point in the procedure the time limits are somewhat tight, and the OFT 'envisages an interval of around two to three days between receipt of the "issues" letter and the date of the issues meeting to allow the parties time to prepare'.[61] An outline decision summarising the arguments for and against a reference will be circulated after the issues meeting, along with the issues letter and the Branch's economic analysis. The Branch may, but is not committed to, set out the recommendations on whether or not a reference should be made. There will then be a case review meeting, with a member of the review group being appointed to play the role of 'devil's advocate' in relation to any recommendation made by the case team. A separate decision meeting will be held following that case review meeting at which the decision maker[62] will be given a report on the debate, along with specific criticisms of the outline decision if these exist. Once the decision has been taken a case officer will draft the final decision, which will be communicated to the parties and, in the case of a public merger, announced.

[59] OFT, *Mergers: Procedural guidance*, May 2003, para 5.17.

[60] [2005] CAT 8. This was particularly the case where the information emanated from a competitor and was contestable.

[61] Ibid, para 5.18.

[62] This 'may be the Chairman, another member of the Board, or a duly authorised officer acting on behalf of the OFT': OFT, *Mergers: Procedural guidance*, May 2003, para 5.19. In cases which are particularly complex or where time is pressing, the decision maker may also chair the case review meeting.

13

Undertakings and Orders at the OFT

INTRODUCTION

THE PREVIOUS CHAPTER has considered the procedures to be adopted when relevant mergers come to the attention of the OFT, and the next chapter examines the procedures to be applied when references are made to the CC and the approach that the CC will take. This short chapter examines the powers of the OFT to remedy situations in which an SLC has been identified and a reference to the CC has not yet been made, or to accept undertakings in lieu of making a reference where these will address the concerns raised by the OFT. This chapter does not deal with the use of these powers in situations in which the Secretary of State has intervened, or in respect of media and water mergers, which are considered in Chapters 17 and 16 respectively. The relevant powers of the CC are dealt with in Chapters 14 and 15.

The OFT's powers are set out in Chapter 4 of the EA 02, and address both completed and anticipated mergers, with appropriate differences in procedures. Section 71 relates to situations in which undertakings may be sought in relation to completed mergers, where the OFT is considering making a reference to the CC. Section 72 relates to the making of 'initial enforcement orders' in respect of completed mergers, and section 73 to the acceptance of undertakings in lieu of the making of a reference. This is a power which is regularly used, and the OFT consults publicly before accepting such undertakings. Parts 7 of *Mergers: Procedural guidance*[1] and 8 of *Mergers: Substantive assessment guidance*[2] deal with the approach that the OFT takes to the acceptance of undertakings in lieu of a reference. Section 75 EA 02 gives the OFT the power to make orders where section 73 undertakings are not fulfilled. Section 76 provides a supplementary power to make interim orders in situations where it intends to make an order, and believes that the effect of this may be frustrated by pre-emptive action taken by the companies.

[1] OFT, May 2003, available at the OFT website.
[2] OFT, May 2003, available at the OFT website

INITIAL UNDERTAKINGS AND ORDERS

Initial undertakings in respect of completed mergers

Section 71 EA 02 provides that the OFT may, in respect of completed mergers, 'for the purpose of preventing pre-emptive action, accept from such of the parties concerned as it considers appropriate undertakings to take such action as it considers appropriate'.[3] This power applies only where the OFT is considering making a reference under section 22,[4] although it need not have determined that such a reference will in fact be made. The OFT must have 'reasonable grounds' for suspecting that a relevant merger situation has been created.[5] Pre-emptive action means 'action which might prejudice the reference concerned or impede the taking of any action under this Part which may be justified by the Commission's decisions on the reference'.[6] Undertakings made under this section come into force at the point at which they are accepted. They may be varied or superseded by another undertaking, and may be released by the OFT.[7] Further provisions relating to the termination of such undertakings are set out in section 71(5) and (6).

Initial enforcement orders in respect of completed mergers

Section 72 EA 02 makes provisions similar to those set out in section 71, save that in this case the power is to make orders. Orders can be made only where the OFT has reasonable grounds for suspecting that a relevant merger situation has been created, and that pre-emptive action by the parties is either in progress or under contemplation.[8] Enforcement orders made under this section can relate to conduct outside the UK only if the person against whom the order is made is a UK national or a body incorporated in the UK, or is a person carrying on business in the UK.[9] Such orders may contain any terms that the OFT believes to be necessary to restrict or prohibit the doing of things which would constitute pre-emptive action. For example, during the passage of the Act it was stated at the Committee stage that:

> If a merged entity makes staff redundant, sells off assets, integrates computer systems or takes any other similar action, it could be very difficult for the [CC] to effect a divestment of the merger business thereafter.

[3] S 71(2) EA 02.
[4] S 71(1) EA 02.
[5] S 71(3) EA 02.
[6] S 71(8) EA 02.
[7] S 71(4) EA 02.
[8] S 72(3) EA 02.
[9] S 86(1) EA 02.

> In the past, the authorities have sought to prevent such further integration by seeking voluntary undertakings from the parties or by imposing an interim order. It is clearer, simpler and more efficient to create a new prohibition that applies to all.[10]

At section 72(2)(a) reference is also made to Schedule 8, paragraph 19, which provides that orders may require any person to supply information to the relevant authority—in this case the OFT.

UNDERTAKINGS IN LIEU OF REFERENCES UNDER SECTIONS 22 AND 33

Section 73(2) EA 02 is in the following terms:

> The OFT may, instead of making such [a reference under ss 22 or 33] and for the purpose of remedying, mitigating or preventing the substantial lessening of competition concerned or any adverse effect which has or may have resulted from it or may be expected to result from it, accept from such of the parties concerned as it considers appropriate undertakings to take such action as it considers appropriate.

The OFT can accept undertakings in lieu of a reference only where it has already concluded that the merger should in fact be referred to the CC, and therefore cannot accept such undertakings in any situation in which it may determine that the merger should not be referred.[11] This has the consequence that undertakings cannot be designed to improve 'customer benefits', as these will have already been considered during the process of determining whether or not a reference should be made. However, section 73(4) provides that 'the OFT may, in particular, have regard to the effect of any action on any relevant customer benefits in relation to the creation of the relevant merger situation concerned'. The OFT interprets this to mean that it will 'seek to agree undertakings that preserve any merger-specific customer benefits'.[12] In the financial year 2005–6 the OFT accepted undertakings in lieu of a reference on four occasions.[13]

When deciding whether to accept such undertakings the OFT is obliged to 'have regard to the need to achieve as comprehensive a solution as is reasonable and practicable to the substantial lessening of competition and any adverse

[10] Standing Committee (HC) B, cols 371–372 1 May 2002.

[11] It has been argued that 'accordingly the OFT will only accept undertakings in lieu to address the underlying competition concerns and not to enhance any perceived customer benefits' (G Lindrup, *Butterworths Competition Law Handbook* (10th edn, London, LexisNexis, 2005), para [3324].

[12] OFT, above, n 2, para 8.2. The OFT further indicates that it 'will not accept undertakings in lieu of a reference that do not address the identified competition effects but which are designed instead to "lock in" sufficient customer benefits to outweigh the risks of a substantial lessening of competition arising': ibid.

[13] OFT, *Office of Fair Trading Annual Report 2005–2006* (2006), at 53, available at the OFT website.

effects resulting from it'.[14] The OFT has stated that it will accept undertakings only in situations in which it is 'confident' that the competition concerns identified can be resolved by the undertakings, and where a more extensive inquiry before the CC is not necessary.[15] Accordingly the OFT's guidance provides that such undertakings are 'appropriate only where the competition concerns raised by the merger and the remedies proposed to address them are clear cut, and those remedies are capable of ready implementation'.[16] Such a 'clear cut' situation would not be likely to arise in situations in which there was doubt about the precise identification of the SLC or about the efficacy of any proposed remedies.

The OFT has indicated that:

> An acquiring company can always take the initiative to propose suitable undertakings in its initial submission to the OFT if it thinks that they may be appropriate to meet any competition concerns that it foresees. Alternatively, the acquiring company may wish to offer undertakings at the issues meeting in cases where the OFT thinks that a merger raises competition issues that would require a case review meeting.[17]

The OFT may itself invite companies to offer undertakings where it appears to the OFT that competition concerns may be suitably addressed by the offering of undertakings in lieu of a reference.

Provisions contained in an undertaking are not limited to the matters specified in Schedule 8 (see below), and the attraction to the merging parties may lie in the flexibility available within undertakings.[18] Undertakings may be either structural or behavioural and, as is the case throughout the operation of merger control regimes, the preference will be for structural undertakings. These 'are more likely to be accepted as undertakings in lieu than behavioural undertakings because they clearly address the market structure issues that give rise to the competition concerns'.[19] A typical structural undertaking will offer the divestiture of either of the overlapping businesses the acquisition of which has given rise to the concern.[20] This 'should be a self-standing business, capable of being fully separated from the merging parties, and in most cases will be part of the acquired enterprise'.[21] Divestiture, to a purchaser approved by the OFT,

[14] S 73(3) EA 02.

[15] OFT, above n 2, para 8.2.

[16] Ibid, para 8.3.

[17] OFT, above n 1, para 7.5.

[18] S 89 EA 02.

[19] OFT, above n 2, para 8.6.

[20] This was the case, eg, in *iSOFT/Group plc/Torex plc* (29 Apr 2004), in which the OFT accepted an undertaking from iSOFT to divest part of the business of the target to address concerns that the merger would lead to an SLC in the supply of laboratory information management systems to NHS hospitals in the UK. See also: *Greene King plc/Laurel Pub Holdings Limited* (6 Oct 2004), where there was an undertaking by Greene King to divest itself of 13 pubs; *Blackstone Group/UGC Cinemas Holdings Limited* (28 Apr 2005), where there was an undertaking to make divestments in six geographic areas in which cinema holdings overlapped pre-merger; *Terra Firma Investments (GP) 2 Ltd/United Cinemas International (UK) Limited/Cinema International Corporation (UK) Limited* (7 Jan 2005), where there is divestment of cinemas in six geographic areas.

[21] OFT, above n2, para 8.7.

should be completed within six months, and the OFT may require that an independent trustee be appointed. The purchaser must be one who would be able to operate the divested entity as an effective competitor. The OFT might consider divestitures taking a form other than that suggested above, and gives as an example the possible divestment of the existing business held by the acquirer, although 'the OFT will also need to consider the competition implications of the asset swap'.[22]

In *Boots/Alliance UniChem*[23] the OFT decided not to refer the anticipated acquisition by Boots plc of Alliance UniChem plc to the CC subject to a satisfactory undertaking being made. The merger involved the acquisition of some 958 UK pharmacies, and although there was no national competition concern, there were concerns in some 100 local markets.[24] Boots agreed to divest stores in all of those areas, and the OFT accepted this undertaking. A third party, Celesio AG appealed this decision to the CAT, which gave judgment, rejecting the application, on 9 May 2006.[25] Following the practice in earlier merger inquiries in the pharmaceutical sector,[26] the OFT paid particular attention to a 'fascia reduction test', and worked on the basis that a one mile radius was appropriate for the purpose of ascertaining the relevant geographic market. Celesio argued that although it was generally appropriate to apply this test, this would not be the case where there were special features that impacted on competition. In the present case Celesio pointed to the reduction in the number of national competitors, the large market share it alleged that the merged entity would have, the strength of the Boots brand, and the post-merger strength of the

[22] Ibid, para 8.9. In *Capital Radio plc/GWR Group plc* (22 Dec 2004) the OFT accepted an undertaking from Capital Radio to divest itself of Century 106 FM, a radio station in the East Midlands already owned by Capital Radio. The OFT may also consider amendment to intellectual property licences. It may also be the case that structural remedies will need to be supported by behavioural remedies.

[23] 6 Feb 2006. This merger met the thresholds for the application of the ECMR, but an Art 4(4) ECMR request to refer the case to the OFT was accepted by the EC Commission on 30 Nov 2005.

[24] At para 82 of its decision the OFT stated that:

> The parties overlap in the provision of retail pharmacy services. In terms of national competition, no concerns arise. However, on a local level on the basis of a one mile radius around both Boots and UniChem pharmacies there are 38 areas where the merger would result in a two to one reduction in the number of competing pharmacies ('fascias') and a further 61 areas where it would result in a reduction in the number of fascias from three to two. The evidence considered during this assessment clearly shows that a reduction in pharmacy fascias from two to one in a local area is, despite the restrictive terms of the NHS contract, expected to result in a [SLC]. Such an SLC could take the form of reductions in quality or the level of service provided (over and above the levels stipulated in the contract.) There may also be an impact on pricing, particularly of [medicines that can only be dispensed by a doctor or pharmacist]. The evidence on whether an SLC would arise in the case of three to two overlaps is less conclusive but, on balance, the OFT takes the view that it may be the case that the merger may be expected to result in an SLC within these three to two overlap areas given the high barriers to entry present in this market as a result of the control of entry regulations.

[25] *Celesio AG v OFT, supported by Boots Group plc and Alliance UniChem plc* [2006] CAT 9.

[26] See *UniChem PLC/Lloyds Chemists plc and GEHE AG/Lloyds Chemists plc: A report on the proposed mergers*, Cm 3444 (1996).

entity's purchasing power and pricing power.[27] Before the CAT Celesio argued, inter alia, that the OFT relied too heavily on the fascia test,[28] was incorrect in finding that a reduction from four to three fascias did not give rise to competition concerns, and, given that it had erred in its assessment of the local markets, it had also erred in finding no national concerns. The CAT held that the decision taken by the OFT was supported by the evidence, and rejected Celesio's application.[29]

Behavioural undertakings will be considered only when 'divestment would be impractical, or disproportionate to the nature of the concerns identified'.[30] Given this restriction it is unlikely that these will be commonly employed, and the OFT notes that it 'is unlikely to consider generally that behavioural undertakings have sufficiently clear effects to address the identified competition concerns'.[31] There have, however, been cases in which behavioural undertakings have been accepted in lieu of a reference. It is noteworthy that one such case was the first time the OFT accepted undertakings in lieu of a merger under the EA 02. In *IVAX International GmbH/3M Company's distribution business for certain asthma products*, the OFT indicated an intention to refer following concerns relating to horizontal aspects of the merger in relation to two types of asthma inhalers. The OFT accepted undertakings from IVAX in which it agreed not to increase the price of the relevant products until an effective substitute neither manufactured nor distributed by IVAX became available in the UK.[32] A second example is *Arriva plc/Wales and Borders Rail Franchise*,[33] in which Arriva gave an undertaking that it would ensure that other bus operators were able to participate in any public transport multi-modal ticketing scheme run by Arriva on fair and reasonable terms, not less favourable than the terms applied to its own bus operators.

Orders in relation to undertakings in lieu of a reference

Where undertakings have been accepted under section 73 no relevant authority[34] shall make a reference in relation to the creation of that relevant merger situation.[35] However, a reference can still be made if material facts about the

[27] See para 26 of the judgment, above n 25.

[28] This ground of appeal was subsequently abandoned.

[29] The CAT also held that it was incorrect of Celesio to treat the OFT report in this case as if it were a statute to be subject to intensive linguistic scrutiny, noting that the report was in short form, and was prepared under strict time limits (above n 25, at para 188).

[30] OFT, above n 2, para 8.10.

[31] Ibid, para 8.10.

[32] OFT decision of 9 Jan 2004.

[33] OFT decision of 9 July 2004.

[34] The OFT or, in respect of cases in which there has been an intervention, the Secretary of State (s 74(5) EA 02).

[35] S 74(1) EA 02.

transaction were not notified to the OFT or made public[36] before the undertaking was accepted. Undertakings may be amended or revoked where the appropriate criteria are fulfilled, and the OFT is obliged to consult before doing so.

Where undertakings accepted under section 73 are not being, or will not be, fulfilled or false, or misleading information was given to the OFT by the person giving the undertaking before the undertaking was accepted the OFT has the power to make an order under section 75 EA 02. Any order made under section 75 may contain anything permitted by Schedule 8 to the EA 02 (see below), and 'such supplementary, consequential or incidental provision as the OFT considers appropriate'.[37] Where such an order is made the OFT is obliged to consider any representation made to it requesting a variation or revocation of the order.[38] Where the OFT has the power to make an order under section 75 and intends to make such an order, section 76 gives it an additional power to make any order necessary to prevent any party taking any action which might prejudice the making of such an order. The scope given to the OFT under this section is considerable in relation to the obligations it may impose.[39]

Schedule 10

Schedule 10 to the EA 02, sets out certain further requirements relating to section 73 undertakings and section 75 orders. Before accepting an undertaking in lieu of a reference or making a section 75 order the OFT is required to give notice of its intention, and to consider any representations made in relation to this.[40] Various information must be given in the notice, and a time limit must be indicated within which representations may be made. In every case the notice must be published,[41] and in the case of section 75 orders a copy of the notice must be served on the person against whom the order is to be made.[42]

SCHEDULE 8

Schedule 8 EA 02 to the sets out the provisions that may be contained in certain enforcement orders. As such it applies also to the orders made by the CC in the carrying out of its functions (see Chapter 15, below). As noted above, however, orders made under section 76 are not limited by the operation of Schedule 8, and

[36] 'Made public' means 'so publicised as to be generally known or readily ascertainable': s 74(4) EA 02.

[37] S 75(4)(b) EA 02.

[38] S 75(6) EA 02.

[39] See s 76(4) EA 02.

[40] Sched 10, para 2(1) EA 02.

[41] Sched 10, para 2(3)(b) EA 02.

[42] Sched 10, para 2(3)(a) EA 02.

even in the case of sections 72 and 77 where reference is made to Schedule 8, the OFT may also impose obligations not specified in that Schedule where these are required to remedy the concern. Schedule 8 is discussed more fully in Chapter 15, below.

PUBLICISING, MONITORING AND ENFORCING ORDERS AND UNDERTAKINGS

In addition to the publicity requirements in relation to undertakings set out in Schedule 10 to the EA 02, the OFT is required to maintain a register of undertakings and orders.[43] This must be available to the public.[44] The OFT has, under section 92 EA 02, a duty to monitor compliance with undertakings and orders accepted and made under this part of the Act. Section 92(2) therefore requires the OFT to 'from time to time consider—(a) whether an enforcement undertaking or order has been or is being complied with'. In addition it is to review undertakings and orders to determine whether they remain appropriate and, if not, whether parties should be released from them or they should be modified. In practice, given that the OFT is obliged to consider representations made in respect of undertakings and orders it is most likely that the initiative for such changes would come from the parties themselves.

Section 94(6) EA 02 gives the OFT the power to enforce compliance with orders and undertakings by way of civil proceedings brought for an injunction or for interdict, or any other appropriate relief or remedy. The application of this provision in no way prejudices the right of an injured third party to bring an independent action (see below).[45]

THIRD PARTY RIGHTS—SECTION 94, EA 02

Section 94 EA 02 is one of the few provisions expressly to allow for third party rights in the UK merger regime. Any person to whom an undertaking or order relates, whether the measure is an interim or final one, has a duty to comply with it.[46] This duty is owed to any person who may be affected by a breach of the order or undertaking,[47] and 'any breach of the duty which causes such a person to sustain loss or damage shall be actionable by him'.[48] At the time of writing no such cases have been reported.

[43] S 91(1) EA 02.
[44] S 91(6) EA 02.
[45] S 94(8) EA 02.
[46] S 94(2) EA 02.
[47] S 94(3) EA 02.
[48] S 94(4) EA 02.

14

References to the Competition Commission

INTRODUCTION

THE OFT HAS a duty to make a reference to the CC in respect of either completed mergers[1] or anticipated mergers[2] when the appropriate jurisdictional thresholds are satisfied, although this duty is ameliorated by the provisions of sections 22(2)–(3) and 33(2)–(3). The provisions relating to completed and anticipated mergers are largely identical, save for a recognition of the fact that it may not be appropriate to make references in the case of anticipated mergers which 'are not sufficiently far advanced, or are not sufficiently likely to proceed, to justify the making of a reference'.[3] Whether sections 22 or 33 applies the OFT has a general duty to 'have regard . . . to the need for making a decision as soon as reasonably practicable'.[4] The approach of the OFT to the SLC test is discussed in Chapter 11 above. In its 2005–6 annual report the OFT indicates that it expects to make between 10 and 25 merger references a year.[5]

COMPLETED MERGERS

Section 22 provides that the OFT 'shall' make a reference to the CC where a relevant merger situation has been created, and this 'has resulted, or may be expected to result, in a substantial lessening of competition'.[6] However, subsection (2) qualifies this seemingly inflexible obligation:

[1] S 22 EA 02.
[2] S 33 EA 02.
[3] S 33(2)(b) EA 02.
[4] S 103(1) EA 02.
[5] OFT, *Office of Fair Trading Annual Report 2005–06* (2006), at 57, available at the OFT website.
[6] The SLC test is dealt with in Chap 11, above.

The OFT may decide not to make a reference under this section if it believes that—

(a) the market concerned is not, or the markets concerned are not, of sufficient importance to justify the making of a reference to the Commission; or
(b) any relevant customer benefits in relation to the creation of the relevant merger situation concerned outweigh the substantial lessening of competition concerned and any adverse effects of the substantial lessening of competition concerned.

Sub-section (3) contains a further six qualifications to the duty to refer set out in s 22(1). These are: (a) if the OFT has accepted undertakings under section 73, EA 02 in relation to the merger situation[7] or a merger notice has been made in respect of the merger and the notice has expired without a reference being made,[8] or if the Secretary of State has accepted an undertaking in respect of a merger in which a public interest consideration intervention notice has been made;[9] (b) the OFT is considering whether to accept undertakings in lieu of a reference; (c) the relevant merger situation is already being dealt with under section 33; (d) a public interest intervention notice is in force or such a matter has finally been determined; (e) the EC Commission is considering a request made by the OFT under Article 22(1) ECMR;[10] or (f) a reasoned submission requesting referral to the EC Commission has been submitted under Article 4(5) ECMR.[11]

The important factors to be considered here therefore are: (1) has a relevant merger situation occurred?[12] (2) has this resulted, or may it be expected to result, in an SLC?[13] (3) is the market or are the markets not sufficiently important to justify a reference? (4) are there relevant customer benefits which outweigh the SLC and its adverse effects? and (5) can the OFT itself redress the harms identified by accepting undertakings from the parties?[14]

Importance of the markets

The provision giving the OFT the power not to make a reference in respect of markets which are not of sufficient importance 'is designed to avoid references being made where the costs involved would be disproportionate to the size of

[7] S 74(1) EA 02.
[8] S 96 EA 02. Merger notices are discussed in Chap 17, below.
[9] Sched 7, para 4, EA 02.
[10] See Chap 3, above.
[11] See Chap 3, above. S 22(3)(f) EA 02 ceases to apply where 'the OFT is informed that a Member State competent to examine the concentration under its national competition law has, within the time permitted by Art 4(5) of the [ECMR], expressed its disagreement as regards the request to refer the case to the European Commission': s 22(3A), as inserted by the EC Merger Control (Consequential Amendments) Regulations 2004, SI 2004/1079, reg 2, Sched, para 2(1), (4).
[12] See Chap 10, below.
[13] See Chap 12, above.
[14] See Chap 14, above.

the markets concerned'.[15] There has not yet been a case arising under the EA 02 where the OFT has determined that a market is so small as to not merit further action in relation to a relevant merger situation. To an extent such a conclusion is mitigated by the relatively high thresholds for jurisdiction set out in the legislation. In its first published guidance to the operation of the new regime the OFT indicated that the exception could be expected to be applied 'only very rarely'.[16] At the same time the OFT noted that there are some circumstances in which mergers in very small markets may still justify references being made. These include: those where the product is an important input into a larger market; where the market is growing quickly; where the market is one essential to vulnerable consumers; or where the market is one of many smaller or local markets that are together of significance.[17] The discretion in making a reference, once the thresholds are satisfied and an SLC is identified, lies with the OFT, although the exercise of this discretion is subject to appeal to the CAT.

Relevant customer benefits[18]

Relevant customer benefits are defined in section 30, which in part is in the following terms:

(1) For the purposes of this Part a benefit is a relevant customer[19] benefit if—

(a) it is a benefit to relevant customers in the form of—

(i) lower prices, higher quality or greater choice of goods or services in any market in the United Kingdom (whether or not the market or markets in which the substantial lessening of competition concerned has, or may have, occurred or (as the case may be) may occur); or

(ii) greater innovation in relation to such goods or services; and

(b) the decision-making authority believes—

. . .

(2) . . . that—

(a) the benefit has accrued as a result of the creation of the relevant merger situation concerned or may be expected to accrue within a reasonable period as a result of the creation of that situation; and

(b) the benefit was, or is, unlikely to accrue without the creation of that situation or a similar lessening of competition.

[15] OFT, *Mergers: Substantive Assessment*, may 2003, para 7.5, available at the OFT website.

[16] Ibid.

[17] Ibid, para 7.6.

[18] Relevant customer benefits are, in essence, efficiencies, although the Act forces an artificial separation between the two. See the discussion of this point in Chap 11 above.

[19] A 'relevant customer' is defined in s 30(4) EA 02 to mean a customer of the merged entity, customers of such a customer, and any other customer in a chain of customers. This includes future customers.

Any benefits identified as being likely to arise under this provision must, as stated, be likely to arise within a reasonable period of time, and can be considered only to the extent that they would not arise but for the merger. The OFT requires that benefits be 'clear and, in the case of cost savings, quantifiable'.[20] The OFT further states that:

> It is not sufficient to demonstrate that there are merely some theoretical benefits to customers: the merging parties must also show that the parties will have an incentive to pass benefits on to customers and that these benefits will be sufficient to outweigh the competition detriments caused by the merger.[21]

Examples of benefits set out in the guidance are: lower prices, greater innovation and greater choice or higher quality. It may be quite difficult to persuade the OFT that these are likely to arise in practice. In particular the fact that an SLC may be equated with an increase in market power means that the merged entity may not face significant competitive pressure compelling it to pass these benefits on to customers. If it does face substantial competitive pressure the argument could be reasonably made that no SLC has occurred.

It is not necessary that the benefits arise in the same market as the SLC takes place. The OFT's 'normal expectation is that these benefits will arise in the market where the competition concerns have been identified. To show that benefits in one market outweigh an expected [SLC] in another will require clear and compelling evidence'.[22]

TIME LIMITS

Section 24 EA 02 reproduces the time-limits of the FTA 73 governing the period in which a reference under section 22 can be made. These are four months from the date on which the merger was consummated, and either was notified to the OFT or the facts were made public. 'Made public' is defined as being 'so publicised as to be generally known or readily ascertainable'.[23] There is no reported instance in which the issue of 'being made public' was a key factor, and it has been suggested that 'the filing of documents at Companies House should be sufficient to place the information in the public domain and make it readily ascertainable'.[24] This period can be extended in accordance with section 25 where: (1) the parties agree to this;[25] (2) the parties fail to provide the OFT with information it has requested;[26] (3) the OFT is seeking undertakings from the

[20] OFT, above n 15, para 7.8.
[21] Ibid, para 7.8.
[22] Ibid, para 7.9.
[23] S 24(3) EA 02.
[24] D Livingston, *Competition Law and Practice* (London, FT Law and Tax, 1995), para 33.52.
[25] The maximum extension under this provision is 20 days.
[26] In which case the OFT must issue a notice to the parties informing them of the extension (s 25(2) EA 02). No time-limit is set for this period.

parties;[27] and (4) the EC Commission is considering a request made in relation to Article 22(1) ECMR.[28] More than one extension may be granted, with the exception that only one extension may be granted under section 25(1).[29]

There was some discussion of time-limits for the making of a reference in *Archant Limited/London Newspapers of Independent News and Media Ltd.*[30] In this case, the relevant acquisition was completed by a sale agreement of 30 December 2003, but a first agreement was entered into on 11 December 2003. The reference was made to the CC on 29 April 2004. The CC acknowledged that there was 'a degree of complexity' to the question whether the reference had been made in time.[31] The CC discussed the issue in the following terms at paragraphs 17–18:

> There are two ways in which the time limits for the making of a reference can be calculated. The first is by taking the time at which the reference is made and, working backwards, calculating whether the relevant enterprises ceased to be distinct 'before the day on which the reference relating to them is made and . . . not more than four months before that day'.
>
> The second is concerned with the time at which notice of material facts about the circumstances in which the relevant enterprises ceased to be distinct came to the attention of the OFT or were made public. If notice of material facts is not given to the OFT or made public prior to the entering into of the arrangements or transactions leading to the relevant enterprises ceasing to be distinct, the time at which material facts are given to the OFT or are made public becomes the relevant time for calculating the period in which the reference can be made. In this case a reference is invalid if notice was given or if facts became public 'more than four months before the date on which the reference is to be made'.

In the view of the OFT in this case the reference was made in time on whatever of the above two bases was used to make the calculation. The OFT and Archant were not agreed on which was the operative date, with the two candidates being 29 and 30 December 2003. Both fell within the period of four months necessary to comply with section 24 of the Act, although 29 December was the first day of that four-month period.

Where a reference is made to the CC the merging parties are required to pay a fee in respect of this, determined in accordance with the requirements set out in the Enterprise Act 2002 (Merger Fees and Determination of Turnover) Order 2003, SI 2003/1370.[32]

[27] In which case the OFT must issue a notice to the parties informing them of the extension (s 25(4) EA 02). No time-limit is set for this period.

[28] A notice must be issued to the parties (s 25(6) EA 02 and the OFT must inform the parties, again by notice, when the Commission has made its decision in response to the Art 22(1) request (s 25(8) EA 02).

[29] S 25(12) EA 02.

[30] *Archant Limited and the London Newspapers of Independent News and Media Limited: A report on the proposed acquisition by Archant Limited of the London Newspapers of Independent News and Media Limited*, Oct 2004.

[31] Ibid, App C, para 17.

[32] As amended by The Enterprise Act 2002 (Merger Fees and Determination of Turnover) Order 2004, SI 2004/3204.

ANTICIPATED MERGERS

The provisions relating to the making of references in the case of anticipated mergers are almost exactly the same as for those relating to completed mergers, with the necessary linguistic and procedural amendments to take account of the fact that the merger is not yet consummated, and that the procedure is therefore forward looking.

THE TEST FOR A REFERENCE

Following the judgment of the Court of Appeal in *IBA Health Ltd v OFT*[33] the OFT was obliged to revise its stance on the standard of the test to be met in respect of a reference, and revised guidance was published in October 2004.[34] The case itself is discussed in Chapter 18, below, in so far as it relates to the standard of review to be adopted by the CAT in appeals under this part of the EA 02. The applicant before the CAT[35] had applied under section 120 for a review of a decision by the OFT not to make a reference to the CC on an anticipated acquisition by iSOFT Group plc of Torex plc, both of which supplied IT applications to the health sector. It was common ground that the merger and the case related to the supply of software systems to hospitals. An issues letter was sent by the OFT to iSOFT and Torex in which it raised certain concerns, but it did not communicate these with any third parties. Following various meetings and communications with the parties the Chairman of the OFT gave guidance on the drafting of a decision to the effect that the merger should not be referred. The OFT found that the post-merger market shares of the parties were substantial, being either 39 per cent of contracts awarded over the past five years, or 44 per cent of the installed base of systems on an historic basis. However the OFT was persuaded to its view by the fact that a new procurement

[33] [2004] EWCA Civ 142. See also F Alese, 'UK Merger Review and S 33: Was the CAT Not Right?', [2004] *ECLR* 470.

[34] OFT, *Guidance note revising 'Mergers—substantive assessment guidance'*, OFT 516a, May 2003, available at the OFT website. The test as originally set out was described in the following terms:

> '3.2 The test for reference will be met if the OFT has a reasonably held belief that, on the basis of the evidence available to it, there is at least a significant prospect that a merger may be expected to [SLC] substantially. The OFT considers that this threshold is the same as that against which FTA references were prepared. It differs from that used by the CC in its merger enquiries, reflecting the fact that the OFT is a first-phase screen while the CC is determinative. Hence, the test for making a merger reference is lower than the CC's test for deciding that a merger may be expected to SLC.' (Footnote omitted)

[35] *IBA Health Ltd v OFT, supported by iSOFT plc and Torex plc* [2003] CAT 28, [2004] CompAR 294, para 66, on appeal *OFT v IBA Health Ltd* [2004] EWCA Civ 142, [2004] UKCLR 683. See also C Brown, 'IBA Health: The First Challenge Under the New UK Merger Regime' [2003] *Comp Law* 347.

system for healthcare IT in the public sector was being launched, and took the view that this would alter the likely pattern of future purchases such that past market shares were no indication of future power.

The CAT noted the presence of a two stage procedure split between the OFT and the CC, and that a key question in the case was to determine the correct balance between these two stages. The CAT was *not* being asked whether the OFT decided the matter correctly or incorrectly, but whether the decision was a lawful one. Section 33(1) carried within it three elements: 'the OFT believes'; 'that it is or may be the case'; and 'may be expected to result'. The CAT held that in order to prohibit a merger what was required by the Act was an 'expectation' which is more than a mere possibility. Thus at paragraph 182 of its judgment the CAT held that the words:

> reflect the fact that in a merger case one is looking at the future effects of a merger, as to which there can never be absolute certainty. In order to prohibit a merger, what is required by the statute is something less than a certainty, namely an 'expectation'. An expectation is, however, more than a possibility, as the MMC acknowledged in *S & W Berisford Ltd/British Sugar Corporation* (1981) CHP 241. A 'more than 50% chance' may be a crude way of expressing the idea of 'an expectation'.

The OFT's belief was not intended to be a subjective test, but rather meant that 'the OFT believes on reasonable grounds',[36] and the concept of a reasonable belief supposed that the OFT had sufficient material to support the grounds of the decision in question, which in turn presupposed that a sufficient investigation had been carried out. Under this formulation the CAT saw the role of the OFT as primarily that of a first stage screen to identify where competition concerns *may* arise. It was the third element of section 33(1) that the CAT believed to be central to the present proceedings. If there was genuine room for two views on the question whether there was at least a significant prospect that the merger might be expected to lead to a SLC then the requirement in section 33(1) would be satisfied.[37] In such a circumstance, the CAT held, the statutory duty on the OFT was not to decide definitively which of those two views the OFT preferred, but was to make a reference to the CC.[38] The CAT seemed to require that in 'grey' areas a reference be made, when it held at paragraph 195 that:

> Where, however, the situation is the other way round, and the OFT decides not to make a reference, it is deciding that the merger does not even reach the threshold of 'it may be the case'. In other words, in such circumstances the OFT decides that the merger does not even reach 'the grey area' where there may be room for more than one view. In its practical effect, a decision not to make a reference effectively decides the issue of substantial lessening of competition in the negative. It not only prejudges, but also excludes, any further investigation by the Commission.

[36] Above n 35, at para 184.
[37] Ibid, at para 191.

At paragraphs 197–198 the CAT set out clearly its view of the obligations on the OFT under the scheme of section 33 EA 02:

> What is the correct approach in cases in the 'grey area' in between? In a case where real issues as to the substantial lessening of competition potentially arise, it seems to us that the words 'it may be the case' imply a two-part test. In our view, the decision maker(s) at the OFT must satisfy themselves (i) that as far as the OFT is concerned there is no significant prospect of a substantial lessening of competition; and (ii) there is no significant prospect of an alternative view being taken in the context of a fuller investigation by the Commission. These two elements may resemble two sides of the same coin, but in our view they are analytically distinct.
>
> In our view it follows from our construction of s 33(1) that, where there is a real issue as to whether there is a substantial lessening of competition it is only in the exceptional case that the OFT should, under the Act, seek to resolve the matter itself rather than making a reference to the Commission. That is particularly so in cases with a complex factual matrix. In our view that approach is supported by the general scheme of the Act . . .

On further appeal the Court of Appeal upheld the decision of the CAT,[39] but at the same time held that the CAT's description of the role of the OFT was not the correct one, and that the OFT was able to work to a lower degree of likelihood than suggested by the CAT. Thus at paragraph 47 the Court held that:

> The [OFT] is a first screen, the [CC] decides the matter. Accordingly, although the word 'may' appears in the opening phrase of s 33(1) and in para (b) of both s 33(1) and 36(1), it is clear from the opening phrase 'believes that it . . . may be the case' imports a lower degree of likelihood than para (b) in ss 33(1) or 36(1) would by itself involve. That lower degree of likelihood might, for example, exist in circumstances where the work done by the OFT did not justify any positive view, but left some uncertainty, and where the OFT therefore believed that a SLC might prove to be likely on further and fuller examination of the position (which could only be undertaken by the Competition Commission).

The Vice Chancellor concluded that:

> it appears to me either the OFT applied too high a test of likelihood when forming their belief or they failed adequately to justify the belief they formed in accordance with the proper test. In either event, notwithstanding the fact that the Tribunal adopted a wrong test as to likelihood, their ultimate conclusion is right and should be upheld.[40]

It was this approach that led to the amendment to the OFT's guidance. The revised guidance states at the outset that:

> The test for reference will be met if the OFT has a reasonable belief, objectively justified by relevant facts, that there is a realistic prospect that the merger will lessen competition substantially. By the term 'realistic prospect' the OFT means not only

[38] Above n 35, at para 192.
[39] *OFT v IBA Health Ltd* [2004] EWCA Civ 142, [2004] UKCLR 683.
[40] Ibid, at para 75.

that a prospect has more than a 50 per cent chance of occurring, but also a prospect that is not fanciful but has less than a 50 per cent chance of occurring.[41]

Wherever the OFT's view is that there is a greater than 50 per cent chance of a merger resulting in an SLC the OFT *will* make a reference unless the exceptions set out above apply. However, no such exact formula may be given in respect of mergers where the likelihood of an SLC arising is less than 50 per cent, and in these cases the OFT has substantial discretion in judging 'whether it *may be* the case that the merger may be expected to result in [an SLC]'.[42] Of particular importance to advisers is the stance the OFT takes in relation to the degree of probability of harm and the amount of evidence on which this assessment is based. In essence the position of the OFT is that the greater the amount of evidence available (and hence the lower the degree of uncertainty), the further up the scale of probability must be the likelihood that an SLC will arise, subject always to the fact that a 50 per cent probability *will* trigger a reference.

PROCEDURE BEFORE THE CC

The CC does not have any jurisdiction in respect of mergers unless these are referred to it by the OFT or by the Secretary of State, as the case may be. Once a reference has been made it is the duty of the CC to determine certain questions, which are specified in section 35 EA 02 in respect of completed mergers, and section 36 in respect of anticipated mergers. Although the CC may cancel or vary a reference in the circumstances specified in section 37 EA 02, it will generally make a report, following an inquiry during the course of which the parties will be consulted and be given the opportunity to make observations and present evidence to the CC. Evidence will also be obtained from third parties, including relevant public authorities. Where the CC identifies SLC issues arising out of the merger situation it will communicate these to the parties, and give them the opportunity to make representations in respect of these concerns. If the CC identifies an SLC that it believes can and should be remedied it is its duty either to accept undertakings or to impose remedies to address the situation, again having given the parties the opportunity to comment on any proposed courses of action. The CC may also rely on interim powers to accept undertakings or impose orders to prevent a further deterioration of a situation until such time as it is able to craft a remedy or determines that there is in fact no SLC which needs remedying. The powers of the CC in relation to final merger remedies are considered in the next chapter, and its role in relation to mergers in respect of which a public interest intervention or special public interest intervention has been made is considered in Chapters 16 and 17. The workload of the CC in relation to merger inquiries in the year 2005–6 was as shown in Table 14.1:[43]

[41] OFT, above n 15, para 3.2, as revised.

[42] Ibid.

[43] Competition Commission, *Annual Report and Accounts 2005/2006* (2006), fig 4, available at the CC website.

Table 14.1

Work load	No of inquiries	Outcome
Merger inquiries received 2005/06	17	
Merger inquiries carried over to 2004/05	5	
Merger inquiries cancelled in 2005/06	6	
Merger inquiries completed in 2005/06	11	4 SLC found
Merger inquiries carried over into 2006/07	5	

Figure 14.1 outlines the procedures gone through before the CC during the course of a merger investigation.[44]

QUESTIONS TO BE DETERMINED BY THE CC

Section 35 EA 02 sets out the questions to be determined by the CC where a reference has been made to it by the OFT under section 22 EA 02. The first questions to be determined are:

(a) whether a relevant merger situation has been created;[45] and
(b) if so, whether the creation of that situation has resulted, or may be expected to result, in a substantial lessening of competition within any market or markets in the United Kingdom for goods or services.

Where the CC finds that the answer to both these questions is in the affirmative, and, in the words of the legislation, that there is 'an anti-competitive outcome',[46] it is required to consider further the question what action, if any, should be taken in order to remedy, mitigate or prevent the SLC, or any adverse effect arising from it.[47] The CC is, in deciding this second set of questions, to

[44] Competition Commission, *General Advice and Information*, June 2003, table 2.

[45] The CC may not be required to consider all the different formulations by which a relevant merger situation may be identified (s 35(6) EA 02), and references may be framed in such a way as to require the CC to consider a position only in relation to either goods or services (s 35(7) EA 02).

[46] S 35(2) EA 02 provides that there is an anti-competitive outcome where a relevant merger situation has been created, or where arrangements are in place which, if carried into effect, would result in the creation of a relevant merger situation, and where there is or may be expected to be an SLC.

[47] It is not inevitably the case that the CC will find that an SLC arises, or may be expected to arise, where a relevant merger situation exists. In *Heinz/HP Foods Group*, eg, the OFT referred the acquisition in part because the number of suppliers of branded ketchup to retail customers would drop from two to one. The merger would also bring together the two largest suppliers of branded tinned baked beans and pasta products. The CC found that the merger would not be expected to result in an SLC in any of the relevant markets: *HJ Heinz and HP Foods: A report on the completed acquisition of the HP Foods companies by HJ Heinz Company and HJ Heinz Company Ltd*, Mar 2006. See also Chap 11, above.

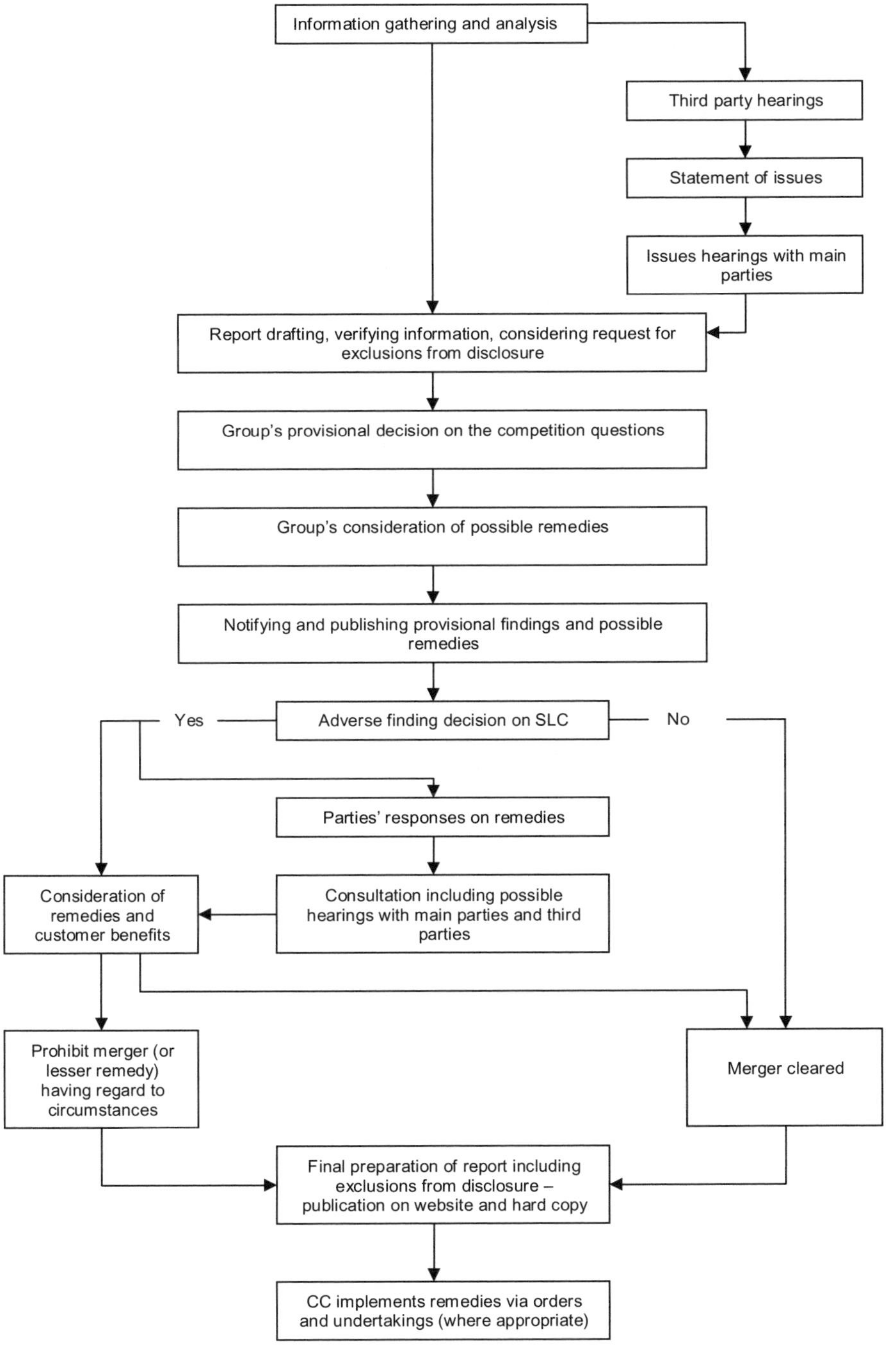

Figure 14.1: Typical Shape of a Merger Inquiry

'have regard to the need to achieve as comprehensive a solution as is reasonable and practicable to the [SLC] and any adverse effects arising from it'.[48] The CC 'may . . . have regard to the effect of any action on any relevant customer benefits in relation to the creation of the relevant merger situation concerned'.[49] The questions to be decided in relation to anticipated mergers are largely the same as in respect of completed mergers, save that the first question to be answered is whether a relevant merger situation will arise and, if it does, whether an SLC may be expected.[50]

The CC has been given the power to cancel a reference made under section 33 EA 02 where 'it considers that the proposal to make arrangements of the kind mentioned in the reference has been abandoned'.[51] It may also treat references made under section 22 EA 02 as if they were made under section 33 EA 02 and vice-versa.[52] Such a power would, it appears, be used only were the OFT to have made a mistake in its framing of the reference, treating an anticipated merger as if it were completed, and vice-versa. Both the CC *Rules of Procedure*[53] and its relevant guidelines[54] are silent on the circumstances in which this power may be used. The OFT may also, at any time, vary a section 22 or 33 reference once it has been made, although it must first consult the CC, and the CC may itself request a variation. Again, it is to be presumed that this power would be used in situations in which further evidence came to hand which altered the presumptions on which the reference was made.[55]

[48] S 35(4) EA 02.

[49] S 35(5) EA 02.

[50] S 36 EA 02.

[51] S 37 EA 02. The Act does not appear to give an express power to abandon references made under s 22 EA 02 were the CC to find that the relevant merger situation identified by the OFT had in fact been terminated. This was the situation that arose in *NTL Communications Corp and Newcastle United plc*, Cm 4411 (1999), in which a combined reference had been made by the Secretary of State in relation to two merger situations, involving both media companies and football teams. Although the NTL/Newcastle merger situation was only anticipated the reference was framed in such a way as to require it to be treated as if it were a completed merger, even though attempts to consummate the merger were abandoned after the CC's report into the other merger (*British Sky Broadcasting Group plc and Manchester United plc*, (Cm 4305 (1999)) was published. The CC subsequently produced a 3-page report—the shortest in its, or the MMC's, history—after a procedure described by Frazer as 'a pointless waste of time made necessary only by the absence of any provision in the Fair Trading Act 1973 for the laying aside of a merger reference in relation to an alleged completed merger situation': see T Frazer, 'NTL Communications Corp/Newcastle United plc', case note, [1999] UKCLR 252. The CC does have the power to treat a reference made under s 22 EA 02 'as if it had been made under section 33', and it may be the case that the CC would, faced with such an unlikely scenario in the future, be able to move through a two-step process that would have the result of the abandonment of the reference. It is also to be hoped that the OFT would not be as careless in its framing of a reference as was the Secretary of State in the 1999 cases.

[52] S 37(2) EA 02.

[53] June 2003.

[54] CC, *Merger References: Competition Commission Guidelines*, June 2003, available at the CC website.

[55] S 37(6)–(7) EA 02.

INFORMATION GATHERING POWERS

The OFT will pass on to the CC the information in its possession at the time of the making of the reference, but the CC, in order to fulfil its functions, must have access to further information. Section 109 EA 02 sets out the powers of the CC to require the attendance of witnesses, or the presentation of documents relevant to its investigation, and sections 110–117 EA 02 make further provision in respect of the enforcement of this power.

Under section 109 EA 02 the CC may: require any person to give evidence to the CC at a specified time and place;[56] require any person to produce any specified documents or documents falling within a specified category;[57] and require any person to provide 'estimates, forecasts, returns or other information as may be specified'.[58] When giving any notice under this section the CC must inform the person about the consequences of a failure to comply with the terms of the notice[59] (see further below). No person shall be obliged to give statements or produce evidence which could not be compelled from that person in civil proceedings before a court.[60]

Section 110(5) EA 02 makes it an offence for any person intentionally to alter, suppress or destroy any document which they are required to produce under a section 109 notice. The penalty on summary conviction is a fine not exceeding the statutory maximum, and on conviction on indictment to a prison term not exceeding two years, or a fine, or both.[61] The CC may itself impose penalties provided for in section 111 EA 02 where a person has 'without reasonable excuse, failed to comply with any requirement of a notice under [section 109 EA 02]'.[62] The penalties provided for in section 111 EA 02 'shall be of such amount as the [CC] considers appropriate'.[63] In this event the CC may impose a fixed penalty, a penalty calculated on a daily basis, or a combination of the two. The CC may also impose a penalty where any person has 'intentionally obstructed or delayed

[56] S 109(1) EA 02. Where witnesses are called to attend the CC evidence may be taken from them on oath: s 109(5) EA 02.

[57] S 109(2) EA 02.

[58] S 109(3) EA 02.

[59] S 109(4) EA 02.

[60] S 109(7) EA 02. In this section 'court' means the High Court or the Court of Session: s 109(10) EA 02.

[61] Where the offence is committed by a body corporate, but 'is proved to have been committed with the consent or connivance of, or to be attributable to any neglect' on the part of a director etc, that person may also be convicted of the offence, and punished accordingly: s 125 EA 02.

[62] S 110(1) EA 02.

[63] S 111(1) EA 02. However, no penalty may be greater than that provided for in an order made by the Secretary of State, and s 111(7) EA 02 sets out limits that may not be exceeded in any such order. These are fixed amounts of a maximum of £30,000, and daily amounts of a maximum of £15,000. Daily amounts may be levied until such time as the person complies with the s 109 requirement, such that, in theory, the amount that may be levied is unlimited. Daily penalties may not be imposed from the beginning of the day on which the s 109 requirement is satisfied (s 111(5)(b)(i) EA 02), or the latest day on which the report may be published (s 111(5)(b)(ii), EA 02).

another person in the exercise of his powers under s 109(6)'.[64] In this case the penalty imposed may only be a fixed amount.[65] Double jeopardy principles apply, such that the CC may not impose a penalty on a person who has been found guilty of an offence, and a person may not be found guilty of an offence if a penalty has already been imposed against them. Whenever the CC imposes any penalty it is required, as soon as practicable, to give notice of it in the form specified in section 112 EA 02. Anyone on whom a penalty has been imposed has a right of appeal to the CAT in relation to: the imposition or nature of the penalty; the amount of the penalty; and the date by which the penalty is to be paid.[66] Any such appeal must be made within 28 days from the date of notification of the penalty.[67] The CAT has the power to: quash the decision; alter the penalty to either a greater or lesser amount; or amend the date imposed by the CC.[68] A further appeal may be made to the Court of Appeal or the Court of Session either on a point of law or in relation to the amount of any penalty.[69] Penalties may be recovered as if they were civil debts in the event that they are not paid, and interest may be levied.[70]

The CC is required by virtue of section 116 EA 02 to publish a statement of policy in relation to penalties. The current version was published in June 2003.[71] In this the CC states that when determining whether to impose a penalty it will 'take into account all the relevant circumstances, including any relevant information brought to the [CC's] attention, including whether . . . the failure arose from circumstances outside the control of the person who has failed to comply'.[72] The CC has indicated that:

> The following factors may make the decision to impose a penalty more likely—
>
> (i) the failure, obstruction or delay adversely affected the efficient carrying out of the [CC's] functions. The [CC] might conclude that there was such an effect even though it had not extended the period in which to prepare and publish or deliver its report;
> (ii) the failure adversely affected other persons in relation to the carrying out of the [CC's] functions;
> (iii) the imposition of a penalty was likely to encourage compliance with the Act;
> (iv) the absence of good reason for the failure;
> (v) the person concerned attained or sought to attain some advantage or benefit from the failure.[73]

[64] S 110(3) EA 02.
[65] S 111(3) EA 02.
[66] S 114(1) EA 02.
[67] S 114(4) EA 02.
[68] S 114(5) EA 02.
[69] S 114(10) EA 02.
[70] S 115 EA 02.
[71] CC, *Statement of Policy on Penalties*, June 2003, available at the CC website. At points this does little more than state the obvious, and statements such as 'the amount of the penalty will be reasonable, appropriate and thus proportionate in the circumstances' (para 17), may be regarded as somewhat self-serving.
[72] Ibid, para 12.
[73] Ibid, para 13.

Following an assessment of these factors the CC will consider whether there exist any aggravating or mitigating factors that should impact on the level of the penalty imposed.[74] Aggravating factors may include: a number of failures to comply with the section 109 requirements; intention; continuing failure to comply; the involvement of senior management in the failure; the absence of any effective compliance mechanisms designed to correct this; and attempts to conceal the failure from the CC. Mitigating factors may include steps being taken to comply with the CC's request, and the fact that the person concerned has in the past complied with such requests in relation to the same inquiry.

It is also an offence, under section 117 EA 02, to provide false or misleading information to the CC (or to the OFT, Ofcom, or the Secretary of State) in connection with any of its functions in relation to merger references.

MERGER REPORTS

The CC has the duty to 'prepare and publish a report on a reference . . . within the period permitted by [section 39 EA 02]'.[75] The report is to contain: the decisions taken by the CC on the questions it was required to answer; the reasoning supporting these decisions; and 'such information as the [CC] considers appropriate for facilitating a proper understanding of those questions and of its reasons for its decisions'.[76] According to the CAT in *Somerfield plc v Competition Commission*[77] a merger report should contain all the main reasons, the principal considerations taken into account, and the principal facts found, although not necessarily all the supporting detail if such detail was not necessary for facilitating the reader's understanding under section 38(2)(c) EA 02.[78]

The relevant time limit within which a report should be concluded is 24 weeks from the date on which the reference was made.[79] However, the CC has a unilateral discretion to extend this period by a maximum period of eight weeks

[74] Ibid, para 18.

[75] S 38 EA 02.

[76] S 38(1)(c) EA 02.

[77] [2006] CAT 4.

[78] Ibid, at para 63. The case in question was an appeal against the imposition of a structural remedy (see below). The CAT argued, in effect, that only limited further evidence should be brought before the CAT in the context of defending such an appeal, suggesting that the report itself should provide the relevant argument to the required legal standard. At para 67 the CAT discussed the extent to which further evidence in the form of expert reports could be put before it by the CC in the course of an appeal:

> 'we would anticipate that in most cases such as this supplementary witness evidence from the CC should be kept to a minimum. As with judicial review generally, any witness statements that are necessary should be closely cross-referred to the report under consideration, with any appropriate explanation of the relevant of the additional evidence, bearing in mind that *it is the report, not the witness statement, that is the subject of the review*' (emphasis added).

[79] S 39(1) EA 02. The Secretary of State has the power to amend by Order this time limit, and the s 39(3) EA 02 time limit (see below) (s 40(8), EA 02).

where it believes that there are 'special reasons' justifying such an extension,[80] but may avail itself of this power only once in respect of any one inquiry.[81] Extensions may also be made in circumstances which relevant persons have failed to comply with obligations set out in section 109 EA 02, which relates to the information gathering powers of the CC (see above). Any such extension may run until the relevant information is supplied.[82]

Where any person or persons who are members of the relevant inquiry group disagree with the conclusion of the CC in relation to a merger reference the report must, if the member or members wish, include a 'minority report' within it, setting out a statement of disagreement, and the reasons for doing so.[83] While such minority reports are uncommon they have from time to time featured in past reports made under the FTA 73. It might, however, be expected that in a regime in which clearer rights of appeal are established the members of the inquiry group would have an incentive to come to a unanimous position, although no doubt minority reports will on occasion continue to appear.

INTERIM RESTRICTIONS AND POWERS AVAILABLE TO THE CC

Restrictions

Just as is the case with the OFT, the CC has the power to take interim action in relation to anticipated or completed mergers in cases in which a reference has been made, and where action taken by the parties may frustrate any outcome of the inquiry. Sections 77 and 78 EA 02 make provision in respect of restrictions on dealings in the case of completed and anticipated mergers respectively. Section 77 EA 02 provides that in situations in which a reference has been made, but not determined, and where neither undertakings nor orders are in force, no relevant person shall, without the consent of the CC:

(a) complete any outstanding matters in connection with any arrangements which have resulted in the enterprises concerned ceasing to be distinct enterprises;
(b) make any further arrangements in consequence of that result (other than arrangements which reverse that result); or
(c) transfer the ownership or control of any enterprise to which the reference relates.

Where consent is given this shall be published, such that it may be brought to the attention of any person affected by it. Conduct outside the UK can be subject to this rule only where the relevant person is a citizen of the UK or a UK body corporate, or is a person carrying on business in the UK.[84] In 2005, for

80 S 39(3) EA 02.
81 S 39(4) EA 02.
82 The CC may, at the same time as stopping the clock on the inquiry period, impose a penalty under s 111 EA 02 (s 110(2) EA 02).
83 S 119 EA 02.
84 S 77(7) EA 02.

example, a reference was made to the CC in *Bucher Industries AG and Johnston Sweepers Limited*. The merger, which affected the market for outdoor sweepers, had already taken place, and the CC obtained interim undertakings requiring Bucher and Johnston to act as separate undertakings until the completion of the inquiry. It became clear, however, that these undertakings were not being complied with, and on 13 July 2005 the CC issued written directions requiring Bucher to put in place a monitoring trustee[85] to ensure compliance. The merger was subsequently cleared.

Section 78 creates a similar regime in respect of anticipated mergers, preventing any relevant person without the consent of the CC from acquiring, whether directly or indirectly, any 'interest in shares in a company if any enterprise to which the reference relates is carried on by or under the control of that company'.[86]

Interim restrictions give rise to rights which may be relied upon by third parties.[87] The position in this respect is discussed in Chapter 18.

Undertakings and orders

Section 80 EA 02 gives the CC the power to accept undertakings from appropriate parties to take appropriate action 'for the purpose of preventing pre-emptive action'.[88] The CC may also adopt, and would be likely to do so, any such undertaking accepted by the OFT under section 71 EA 02 if this remains in force at the point at which the CC would adopt it.[89] Any such undertaking will cease to be in force when the reference is finally determined,[90] when any order comes into force,[91] or when the undertaking is released by the CC.[92] The CC is also obliged to consider any representations made relating to the variation or releasing of an undertaking.[93]

Interim orders may also be made by the CC under section 81 EA 02. The CC may:

> (a) prohibit or restrict the doing of things which the [CC] considers would constitute pre-emptive action;

[85] Para 6.1 of *Application of divestiture remedies in merger inquiries* (London, CC, 2004) provides that '[m]onitoring or divestiture trustees should be independent of the parties, have appropriate qualifications for the task and should not be subject to conflicts of interest'.

[86] S 78(2) EA 02.

[87] S 95 EA 02.

[88] S 80(2) EA 02. See Chap 13, above, and s 80(10) EA 02, which defines pre-emptive action as 'action which might prejudice the reference concerned or impede the taking of any action under this Part which might be justified by the [CC's] decisions on the reference'.

[89] S 80(3) EA 02.

[90] S 80(8) EA 02.

[91] S 80(7) EA 02.

[92] Ss 80(4)(c) and (5)(c) EA 02.

[93] S 80(9) EA 02.

(b) impose on any person concerned obligations as to the carrying on of any activities or the safeguarding of any assets;
(c) provide for the carrying on of any activities or the safeguarding of any assets either by the appointment of a person to conduct or supervise the conduct of any activities (on such terms and with such powers as may be specified or described in the order) or in any other manner;
(d) do anything which may be done by virtue of paragraph 19 of Schedule 8.[94]

An example of the application of this power arose in *British Salt and New Cheshire Salt Works Ltd*.[95] Here the CC adopted undertakings given by the acquirer to the OFT prior to the referral. The undertakings ensured that the integrity of the acquired business was maintained, with British Salt being prevented from taking any action leading to integration of the business with its own, and being required to run the acquired business under a different name from its own, and to maintain it as a going concern. The merger was subsequently cleared (see Chapter 11, above).

Any undertaking accepted by the CC under this provision may be varied or superseded by another undertaking,[96] or may be released by the CC,[97] which is obliged as soon as reasonably practicable to consider any representation made to it in this regard.[98]

Any 'enforcement order'—orders made under sections 72,[99] 75,[100] 76,[101] 81,[102] 83[103] and 84,[104] or under certain paragraphs of Schedule 7[105]—may *not* contain provisions which have the effect of cancelling or modifying conditions in licences granted under the Patents Act 1977,[106] or in respect of any design registered under the Registered Designs Act 1949.[107] Enforcement orders may, however, relate to agreements that are already in place,[108] and may, in appropriate circumstances, have the effect of modifying licence conditions in respect of regulated markets.[109]

The power of the CC to accept final undertakings and make final orders is discussed in the next chapter.

[94] Para 19 of Sched 8, EA 02, relates to the conditions that may be imposed on any person to supply any information to any relevant authority, including the CC.
[95] Nov 2005.
[96] S 82(2)(b) EA 02.
[97] S 82(2)(c) EA 02.
[98] S 82(5) EA 02.
[99] OFT initial enforcement orders (see Chap 13).
[100] OFT order making powers where initial undertakings are not fulfilled (see Chap 13).
[101] Supplementary interim orders (see Chap 13).
[102] CC interim orders (see above).
[103] CC order making powers where final undertakings are not fulfilled (see Chap 15).
[104] CC final orders (see Chap 15).
[105] Enforcement regime for public interest and special public interest mergers (see Chaps 16 and 17).
[106] Or a European Patent within the meaning of that Act: s 86(2)(a) EA 02.
[107] S 86(2)(b) EA 02.
[108] S 86(3) EA 02.
[109] See Sched 9, Pt 1, EA 02.

15

Final Decisions and Remedies

INTRODUCTION

WHEN DEALING WITH situations in which SLC has been identified and in respect of which remedies are believed to be appropriate the CC shall 'in particular, have regard to the need to achieve as comprehensive a solution as is reasonable and practicable to the [SLC] and any adverse effects resulting from it'.[1] In determining which remedies, if any, to impose, the CC 'will consider the effectiveness (including feasibility of implementation) of different remedies and their associated costs and will have regard to the principle of proportionality'.[2] Section 41 EA 02 imposes a duty on the CC to take appropriate action under its final powers[3] in cases in which it has identified an SLC. Any decision taken in this respect must 'be consistent with its decisions as included in its report . . . unless there has been a material change of circumstances since the preparation of the report or the [CC] otherwise has a special reason for deciding differently'.[4] As with the earlier requirements relating to the consideration of matters following the making of the reference the CC is to have regard to the need to achieve as comprehensive a solution as possible, and may have regard to any relevant customer benefits. As with the OFT the CC takes the view that structural remedies are to be preferred to behavioural remedies, but that the latter may be the remedy of choice in appropriate circumstances, and that in some cases a combination of the two may be necessary.

The CC will discuss remedy options with the merging parties at the time at which it publishes a notice of possible remedies. The *Rules of Procedure*[5] require groups to 'give as much notice as is practicable' of actions which may be taken by the CC to remedy the identified adverse effects. It is suggested here that a notice of those actions may be published at the same time as its provisional findings, but that if this is not the case 'the group shall notify the main parties as soon as practicable after it has notified them of its provisional findings'.[6] The

[1] Ss 35(4) and 36(3) EA 02.

[2] CC, *Application of divestiture remedies in merger inquiries: Competition Commission Guidelines*, Dec 2004, para 1.7.

[3] Set out in ss 82 and 84 EA 02 (see below).

[4] S 41(3) EA 02.

[5] CC, *Competition Commission Rules of Procedure*, June 2003.

[6] Ibid, para 11.2.

CC will also consult, as necessary, competitors, customers and other relevant parties in order to test whether remedy options are viable and effective.

The role of the inquiry group reporting into the merger usually ends with the acceptance of final undertakings, or the making of a final order in cases in which a remedy is required. Once this process has been completed it is the role of the Remedies Standing Group to monitor the implementation of any undertakings or orders, and to review the process, which may include, for example, approving any potential purchasers should divestment be required. It is the job of the OFT to monitor compliance with behavioural undertakings and with certain aspects of divestment remedies.

FINAL UNDERTAKINGS AND ORDERS

The powers of the CC to accept final undertakings and make final orders are discussed in the previous chapter. Sections 82 and 84 EA 02 give the CC the power to accept final undertakings and make final orders following the determination of the reference. Section 83 provides an additional power to make orders where final undertakings are not fulfilled.

Final undertakings may be accepted from appropriate persons in the fulfilment of the CC's duty to remedy the detrimental affects of completed or anticipated mergers.[7] Undertakings may contain provisions which go beyond those provided for in Schedule 8 to the EA 02 (see below).[8] They come into force on the date on which they are accepted,[9] may be varied or superseded by another undertaking,[10] and may be released by the CC.[11] Undertakings accepted under this section shall also cease to be in force if an order is subsequently made under sections 83 or 84 EA 02.

Where final undertakings are not fulfilled or where they are based on false or misleading information, the CC has the power to make orders under section 83 EA 02. Any such order may contain provisions different from those set out in the undertakings,[12] and may be revoked or varied by another order.[13] However, no order made under this section shall be revoked or varied unless the OFT, which has the duty of monitoring compliance with orders, advises that this would be appropriate.[14]

[7] See s 41 EA 02.
[8] S 89(1) EA 02.
[9] S 82(2)(a) EA 02.
[10] S 82(2)(b) EA 02.
[11] S 82(2)(c) EA 02.
[12] S 83(5)(b) EA 02.
[13] S 83(5)(c) EA 02.
[14] S 83(6) EA 02. Any order made on the basis of s 83 or 84 (see below) shall, either on its face or in accompanying explanatory material, state:

(a) the actions that the persons or description of persons to whom the order is addressed must do or (as the case may be) refrain from doing;
(b) the date on which the order comes into force; *cont./*

Final orders are those made on the basis of the power granted in section 84, EA 02. Orders may not be made where an undertaking has been accepted under section 82 EA 02.[15] Any order made under this section 'may contain—(a) anything permitted by Schedule 8; and (b) such supplementary, consequential or incidental provision as the [CC] considers appropriate'.[16] Orders come into force at the time determined,[17] and may be varied or revoked by another order.[18] Orders may be revoked or varied only where the OFT advises that it is appropriate to do so.[19]

Schedule 8

Reference has been made on a number of occasions to the matters set out in Schedule 8, to the EA 02. This is a list of 'provision that may be contained in certain enforcement orders', and sets out a comprehensive set of restrictions and obligations that may be imposed on the conduct of parties subject to the merger regime. In the relevant circumstances outlined in this book both the OFT and the CC may have regard to this. The first 19 paragraphs apply generally; paragraph 20 relates to national security; and paragraph 20A to newspaper mergers. In outline the contents of Schedule 8 are the following:

Paragraph 2	Orders may prohibit the making or performance of an agreement, or may require the termination of an agreement but the paragraph does not apply to contracts of employment.
Paragraph 3	Orders may prohibit refusals to supply goods or services.
Paragraph 4	Orders may prohibit the tying or bundling of goods or services.
Paragraph 5	Orders may prohibit discriminatory practices.
Paragraph 6	Orders may prohibit giving any preference in relation to the supply of goods or services.
Paragraph 7	Orders may prohibit the charging of prices different from published or list prices.
Paragraph 8	Orders may regulate prices to be charged, but this power is limited to situations in which 'the relevant report . . . identifies the prices charged for the goods or services as requiring remedial action'.
Paragraph 9	Orders may prohibit the exercise of any voting rights attributable to stocks, shares or securities
Paragraph 10	Orders may require the supply of goods or services.

(c) the possible consequences of not complying with the order; and
(d) the section of this Part under which a review can be sought in relation to the order.

15 S 84(5) EA 02.
16 S 84(2) EA 02.
17 S 84(3)(a) EA 02.
18 S 84(3)(b) EA 02.
19 S 84(4) EA 02.

Paragraph 11	Orders 'may require any activities to be carried on separately from any other activities'.
Paragraph 12	Orders may prohibit the acquisition of a whole or parts of an undertaking, or the doing of anything which would result in two or more bodies corporate becoming interconnected.
Paragraph 13	Orders may provide for the division of businesses, including (paragraph 14) separations of any assets or parts of enterprises under common control.
Paragraph 15	Orders may require the publication of lists of prices.
Paragraph 16	Orders may prohibit the recommending of resale prices.
Paragraph 17	Orders may require the publication of certain accounting information relating to the supply of goods and services, the quantities sold, and the areas in which they are sold, and (paragraph 18), may specify the manner in which publication is to be made.[20]
Paragraph 19	Orders may require any person to supply any information to the OFT or other relevant authority.
Paragraph 20	Any provision appropriate in the interests of national security[21] may be contained in an order.
Paragraph 20A	In relation to newspaper mergers orders may make 'such provision as the person making the order considers to be appropriate in all the circumstances of the case'.

Structural remedies

The CC published its guidance in relation to structural remedies in 2004.[22] It is stated here that the approach to be taken to completed and anticipated mergers will, in principle, be similar.[23] The guidance emphasises that in order to be effective 'a divestiture should involve the sale of an appropriate divestiture package to a suitable purchaser through an effective divestiture process'.[24] There are, however, risks inherent in the divestiture process. The CC classifies these as:

[20] To competition lawyers this requirement may at first blush appear anomalous, as the exchange of such information between undertakings which would be facilitated by public dissemination is likely to be prohibited under general competition law. However, merger control may be related to situations of dominance, and third-party enforcement of rights arising under undertakings and orders made under this Part of the Act may be assisted by the ready availability of information, which might suggest that patterns of sales are indicative of a failure to comply, or of failure of the undertakings and orders to achieve a desired solution.

[21] As defined in s 58 EA 02. See further Chap 17.

[22] CC, above n 2.

[23] Ibid, para 2.7.

[24] Ibid, para 2.2.

composition risks;[25] purchaser risks;[26] and asset risks.[27] At paragraph 2.5 of its guidance the CC notes that:

> The nature and magnitude of perceived risks will guide the type and extent of protective measures to be adopted by the CC in formulating and implementing an effective divestiture remedy. The CC may, of course, conclude that the perceived risks are such that, even with the adoption of protective measures, a divestiture would not be effective so that prohibition of the merger or other remedies may be appropriate.

In determining the appropriate 'package' to be divested the CC will attempt to identify the smallest possible operating unit of a business that contains within it the elements in which there is competitive overlap and that would be capable of competing on a stand-alone basis. In effect this means that the most likely component of a business to be divested would be a subsidiary or a division. In *Somerfield plc and Wm Morrison Supermarkets plc*[28] a number of individual supermarket stores were identified for divestiture (see below). The CC may be very prescriptive in the text of any undertakings or orders accepted or made in relation to divestiture as to precisely what it is that is to be divested.[29] Generally the CC will prefer that the divestiture be of an existing business, rather than one crafted by the merging parties for the purpose of divestiture, on the ground that this is 'less likely to be subject to purchaser and composition risk'.[30] For the same reason the CC is averse to packages which consist of a combination of assets held by different parties pre-merger.[31] Where a divestiture package is suggested that is not an existing unit capable of standing alone, as may be the case for example in respect of divestiture of assets such as intellectual property rights, the CC may require that the parties are able to establish that an up-front buyer exists in order to mitigate the risk.[32] In exceptional cases the CC may identify a 'crown jewels' package to be divested if an initial divestiture package is not not disposed of within the required period. Given the need to ensure an effective remedy in good time, the CC needs to be assured that, if delays occur in selling the initial package, any back-up package will be very attractive to

[25] '[T]hese are risks that the scope of the divestiture package may be too constrained or not appropriately configured to attract a suitable purchaser or may not allow a purchaser to operate effectively and viably in the market': para 2.4.

[26] '[T]hese are risks that a suitable purchaser is not available or that the merger parties will dispose to a weak or otherwise inappropriate purchaser': ibid.

[27] '[T]hese are risks that the competitive capability of a divestiture package will deteriorate prior to completion of divestment, for example through loss of customers or key members of staff': ibid.

[28] CC, *Somerfield plc and Wm Morrison Supermarkets plc, a report on the acquisition by Somerfield plc of 115 stores from Wm Morrison Supermarkets plc*, Sept 2005.

[29] Ibid, para 3.2.

[30] CC, above n 2, para 3.3.

[31] Ibid, para 3.5.

[32] Ibid, para 3.4.

prospective purchasers.[33] Any such package 'will include all the core assets necessary to remedy the SLC'.[34]

The identity of a prospective purchaser is of 'major importance' in determining the success of a divestiture remedy.[35] The CC has the right to require that any purchaser be approved by it, and to veto purchasers. The CC will consider, inter alia, the extent to which the purchaser is independent of the merging parties;[36] the capability of the purchaser to operate the divested business or assets on a competitive basis; and whether divestment to the identified purchaser would itself raise any SLC concerns.[37] Except for situations in which a divestiture trustee is in place, the responsibility is on the parties themselves to find a suitable purchaser.[38] In exceptional cases the CC may require the merger parties 'to identify a suitable purchaser that is contractually committed to the transaction before permitting a proposed merger to proceed or a completed merger to progress with integration'.[39]

Finally, having identified the package to be divested and the purchaser, the CC requires that the process of divestiture itself should be effective. Given that the purpose of a divestiture is to provide competition to the merging parties the CC recognises that 'the parties to a merger may have significant incentives to run down or neglect the business or assets of a divestment package in order to reduce future competitive impact'.[40] To protect against such eventualities the CC is likely to require undertakings from the relevant parties which create a duty of care to preserve the integrity and competitiveness of the package to be sold. Where the CC believes that there is a significant risk that the asset may be run down it may also require 'hold-separate' undertakings:

> These will require the divestiture package to be held and managed separately from the retained business. The appointment of a 'hold-separate' manager or management team may also be required to manage the assets/business to be divested so as to maintain their competitiveness and separation from the retained assets.[41]

The divestiture process may be enhanced by the appointment of an approved independent monitoring trustee who will have the duty to act in the best inter-

[33] The CC notes that '[f]or example, where a business is subject to major asset risks, speed of divestiture is likely to be a critical requirement. In such circumstances, prior identification of a crown jewels package may be the most effective means of facilitating rapid disposal if the initial package has failed to sell to suitable buyers within a specified period': ibid, para 3.7.

[34] Ibid, para 3.7.

[35] Ibid, para 4.1.

[36] The CC stresses that '[a] purchaser should not have continuing links with the merger parties after divestiture that may compromise the purchaser's incentives to compete with these parties, eg financial, ownership or management links. However, it is recognised that purchasers may require access to key inputs or services at appropriate terms from the merger parties, on an interim basis, in order to enable the divestiture to operate effectively': ibid para 4.4).

[37] Ibid, para 4.2.

[38] Ibid, para 4.3.

[39] Ibid, para 4.5.

[40] Ibid, para 5.2.

[41] Ibid, para 5.3.

ests of the package to be divested, and whose remuneration, whilst coming from the merging parties, must be arranged in such a way as not to compromise the ability to act independently.[42]

Any divestiture period will normally be limited to six months, and will be made clear to the parties, although the time limit may not be made public so as not to undermine the divestment process.[43] It should be clear that prospective purchasers may be in a stronger position in relation to the acquisition of divestment packages than in relation to normal commercial purchases, knowing that the holding undertakings have no choice but to sell the divestment packages. The risk of strategic behaviour arising, to the detriment of the process, where the prospective purchasers also know the date by which the assets must be sold should be evident.

The CC faced a challenge before the CAT after it imposed a structural remedy in *Somerfield plc and Wm Morrison Supermarkets plc*.[44] At the time of the inquiry Somerfield was the fifth largest supermarket group in the UK, and Morrison was the fourth. In part as a response to a requirement to divest itself of 52 Safeway stores following its acquisition of Safeway plc in March 2003,[45] Morrison determined to sell 115 of its stores to Somerfield. The CC followed a complex analysis in which it identified that all stores over 280 square metres competed in a market for 'secondary shopping', and determined that geographic markets should be delineated by isochrones of five-minute drive times in urban areas and ten-minute drive times in rural areas. It then adopted a four to three facia rule in order to identify markets in which acquisitions might be expected to lead to SLC. As a result of this analysis 36 problem stores were identified, and a further 12 were brought into the equation by virtue of the percentage of the local population that would be affected by a reduction in choice. The second stage of the report then assessed the effect, at the local level, of the acquisitions upon each of the 48 stores raising possible problems. In 12 cases the CC found that the acquisitions might be expected to lead to SLC in terms of higher prices, reduced product ranges, loss of choice and poorer service. Having ruled out the practicality of imposing any behavioural remedies the CC found that the only satisfactory remedy was the divestment of the 12 specified stores. It was unusual for the CC to be so prescriptive in identifying precisely which stores were to be divested. In its *Safeway* report, for example, the CC limited itself to identifying the areas within which stores had to be divested, but not the specific stores themselves.[46] Somerfield had argued that it should be permitted itself to make the

[42] Ibid, paras 5.4 and 6.1–6.3.

[43] Ibid, para 5.5.

[44] *Somerfield plc and Wm Morrison Supermarkets plc, a report on the acquisition by Somerfield plc of 115 stores from Wm Morrison Supermarkets plc*, Cm 5950 (2005).

[45] Ibid.

[46] Ibid.

choice of what stores to divest, and had expressed a clear preference for selling its existing stores and retaining the acquired stores.[47]

Somerfield appealed, arguing that the CC had erred in directing that the specific stores be sold, and argued exclusively on the ground that the CC had acted unlawfully in imposing the structural remedy; it was not disputed before the CAT that the acquisitions led to SLC.[48] The CAT held that it followed that the SLC was to be remedied as quickly and effectively as possible,[49] and ruled that the CC had a clear margin of appreciation to decide what reasonable action was appropriate for remedying, mitigating or preventing the SLC.[50] The CC had followed its own guidelines in preferring a structural remedy,[51] and it was reasonable, for reasons of practicality, to place the onus on the merging parties to provide evidence to the CC to persuade it to adopt an alternative remedy.[52] In this respect the CAT appeared to have been swayed, at least in part, by the limited time available to the CC to consider remedies. A criterion applied by the CC in determining precisely which stores should be divested was which would be an attractive prospect to potential purchasers. The CAT found that this was a perfectly lawful approach to adopt.[53] The CAT held further that the CC had a great deal of evidence before it, and that Somerfield advanced no detailed case to the effect that the CC's report was against the weight of, or unsupported by, the evidence.[54] Finally it is worth noting that in specifying that the purchasers should be approved by the CC and that some potential purchasers would be excluded, the CC acted reasonably, particularly as it indicated that this position would be adopted only during an initial phase of the divestiture period. It has been argued that this case:

> . . . will be of considerable importance for many merging parties in the future . . . companies will now need to consider in advance very carefully what divestment remedies might be required by the CC, rather than simply counting on being given the option to divest either their existing or their acquired assets.[55]

Following the loss of its appeal Somerfield Limited gave undertakings to the CC to divest itself of 12 stores. These undertaking were accepted on 9 March 2006.

[47] The CC had stated, at para 11.22 of ibid, that '[d]ivestment of the existing store would be significantly inferior to divestment of the acquired store in remedying the SLC as these have significantly greater risk of not attracting a suitable purchaser'.

[48] *Somerfield plc v Competition Commission* [2006] CAT 4.

[49] Ibid, para 86.

[50] Ibid, para 88.

[51] Ibid, para 98.

[52] Ibid, para 101. Para 1.9 of cc, above n 2, states, in part, that '[t]he onus will be on the parties to demonstrate that their proposed remedy options will address the expected SLC and the resulting adverse effects'.

[53] Above n 48, para 115.

[54] Ibid, para 130.

[55] N Beale, 'The *Somerfield* Decisions of the Competition Commission and Competition Appeal Tribunal and the Economics of Divestment Remedies' [2006] *Comp Law* 45, at 46. See also M Jephcott and M R Mahtani, 'The *Somerfield* Judgment: A Damp Squib?' [2006] *Comp Law* 56.

ENFORCEMENT FUNCTIONS OF THE OFT

The CC's role ceases with the acceptance or adoption of final undertakings and orders—and it is not involved in monitoring or enforcing them. Although the OFT has the responsibility for enforcing the measures accepted or implemented by the CC, this is a reasonable split of responsibilities, given the OFT's continuing responsibility to monitor markets and oversee competition in the UK. The position is certainly preferable to that arising under the FTA 73, under which the OFT had the role of effecting a remedy following a report made by the CC, which led to unreasonable duplication of effort and created the possibility of tensions arising within the regime.

Section 91 EA 02 obliges the OFT to compile and maintain a register of undertakings and orders, copies of which may be inspected or obtained by any person on payment of a reasonable fee. The register must contain the provisions of any enforcement undertaking or order, and details of any variation or revocation of these. The maintenance of the register may support the efforts of those third parties who seek to enforce undertakings and orders.[56]

Section 92 EA 02 imposes a duty on the OFT to monitor undertakings and orders. Thus section 92(1) EA 02 provides that:

The OFT shall keep under review—

(a) the carrying out of any enforcement undertaking or any enforcement order; and
(b) compliance with the prohibitions in sections 77(2) and (3) and 78(2)[57] . . .

The OFT is further obliged from time to time to consider whether enforcement orders or undertakings are being complied with,[58] and whether, as a result of a change of circumstances, an enforcement undertaking or order is appropriate, and should be either varied or released.[59] Wherever it believes that it is appropriate to do so, the OFT shall take action following its reviews, including notifying the Secretary of State or the CC that it should take action. More generally the OFT is obliged to keep under review the efficacy of enforcement undertakings and orders, and to publish a report on this, although there is no statutory deadline within which this exercise is to be carried out.

[56] See s 94 EA 02. Third party rights are discussed in Chap 19.
[57] Which relate to restrictions on dealings unless the CC's permission has been obtained (see Chap 15, above).
[58] S 92(2)(a) EA 02.
[59] S 92(2)(b) and (c) EA 02.

16

Mergers in the Media and Water Sectors

INTRODUCTION

IN TWO SECTORS, the media and the water industry, special merger rules apply in the UK. In the case of newspapers the regime is no longer as discrete as was the case prior to the entry into force of the Communications Act 2003,[1] section 373 of which repealed the relevant provisions of the FTA 73, which had remained in force notwithstanding the enactment of the EA 02. At the same time the Communications Act repealed, in section 374, section 69 of the EA 02, which had exempted newspapers from the operation of the merger regime set out in the EA 02. However, the Communications Act also amended section 58 EA 02 and introduced five special 'media public interest considerations' which serve to set the approach to media mergers apart from the general regime, although in the absence of the application of any of these special interest considerations the general regime applies. Under the old regime it was clear that those engaged in newspaper mergers were subject to substantial burdens, and many of the mergers considered by the MMC raised no significant concerns.

Water mergers[2] in England and Wales, where attempts have been made to open the industry to competition are governed by the provisions of the Water Industry Act 1991 sections 32–35.[3] The Act does not apply to Scotland, where the industry has not been opened up in any significant way. Section 32 WIA 91 requires the OFT, save in the case of 'small mergers',[4] to make references to the CC automatically, and the role of the CC is to determine whether the merger in question 'has prejudiced, or may be expected to prejudice, the ability of the Authority[5] in carrying out its functions by virtue of the 1991 Act, to make comparisons between different water enterprises'.[6] Both of these regimes are dealt

[1] The relevant provisions came into force on 29 Dec 2003. See Part V of the Communications Act. See generally A Pryor, 'The New Regime for the Regulation of Newspaper Mergers' [2004] *Comp Law* 63.

[2] Throughout this chap, unless otherwise indicated, 'water merger' is to be taken to include mergers involving water undertakings or sewerage undertakings.

[3] Replaced by s 70 of the EA 02. See also Sched 4ZA to the WIA 91.

[4] See s 33 WIA 91.

[5] The Water Services Regulation Authority, which in 2005 replaced the office of the Director General of Water Services.

[6] Ss 35(1)(b) and 36(1)(b) WIA 91, as amended by the Water Mergers (Modification of Enactments) Regulations 2004, SI 2004/3202, reg 11.

with in more detail in the remainder of this chapter. In all other sectors of the economy, which are not statutory monopolies, the general law of the EA 02, which may include the operation of the public interest considerations outlined in the next chapter, apply.

MEDIA MERGERS

Introduction

For many years the approach taken to mergers in the newspaper industry in the UK was more interventionist than was the case in respect of general mergers, and it was accepted that such mergers raised particularly strong public interest concerns, relating to plurality and diversity in the media.[7] Even as recently as 2002 the Government argued that a combination of market forces and competition law 'cannot necessarily provide the market-place of ideas that enables democracy to prosper'.[8] However, following the changes put into place by the Communications Act 2003 (CA 03), the default regime in relation to mergers within the media industry, and newspapers in particular, is the general merger regime of the EA 02. However, the amendment made to section 58 EA 02 by section 375 CA 03 introduced five new 'media public interest considerations' that may, in the appropriate circumstances, be invoked by the Secretary of State.

The new section 58(2A)–(2C) EA 02 is in the following terms:

> (2A) The need for—
>
> (a) accurate presentation of news; and
> (b) free expression of opinion;
>
> is specified in this section.
>
> (2B) The need for, to the extent that it is reasonable and practicable, a sufficient plurality of views in newspapers in each market for newspapers in the United Kingdom or a part of the United Kingdom is specified in this section.
>
> (2C) The following are specified in this section—
>
> (a) the need, in relation to every different audience in the United Kingdom or in a particular area of locality of the United Kingdom, for there to be a sufficient plurality of persons with control of the media enterprises serving that audience;
> (b) the need for the availability throughout the United Kingdom of a wide range of broadcasting which (taken as a whole) is both of high quality and calculated to appeal to a wide variety of tastes and interests; and

[7] See, eg, *Report of the Royal Commission on the Press 1961–1962*, Cmnd 1811 (London, HMSO, 1962). The Commission's proposals were partly incorporated in the Monopolies and Mergers Act 1965, ss 57–62.

[8] DTI, *Enterprise Act 2002: Public Interest Intervention in Media Mergers* (2004), para 2.6, available at the DTI website.

(c) the need for persons carrying on media enterprises, and for those with control of such enterprises, to have a genuine commitment to the attainment in relation to broadcasting of the standards objectives set out in section 319 of the Communications Act 2003.

A media enterprise is defined in section 58A(1) EA 02 as one that 'consists in or involves broadcasting'.[9] A newspaper enterprise is defined in section 58A(3) EA 02 as 'an enterprise consisting in or involving the supply of newspapers'.[10] Section 58A(2) provides that where a merger situation occurs in which at least one of the enterprises ceasing to be distinct consists in or involves broadcasting, the references in section 58(2C)(a) to media enterprises include references to newspaper enterprises, with the effect that plurality of the media becomes a matter that may be considered when there arises a merger between a media and a newspaper enterprise. Section 58(2A) and 58(2B) in effect reproduces the earlier regime relating to newspapers, referring as before to the accuracy of news and freedom of expression, but the remaining three considerations set out in section 58(2C) are new, flowing in part from a relaxation of various rules relating to cross-ownership of media, a recognition of the increased marketisation of the UK media industry, and a diversity of platforms on which broadcasts may be made.

Section 59(3C)–(3D) specifies that the usual thresholds of the EA 02 apply before a relevant merger situation is found to exist, and without there being a relevant merger situation the Secretary of State cannot issue a special intervention notice. However, an exception to the general rule applies in the introduction of a modified share of supply test, which permits the Secretary of State to intervene in cases in which either of the parties to a media merger has an existing share of supply of 25 per cent in the UK or in a substantial part of the UK.[11] In determining whether the 25 per cent share of supply test is met:

[9] S 44(9) EA 02 defines broadcasting as 'the provision of services the provision of which—(a) is required to be licensed under Part 1 or 3 of the Broadcasting Act 1990 or Part 1 or 2 of the Broadcasting Act 1996; or (b) would be required to be so licensed if provided by a person subject to licensing under the Part in question'.

[10] S 44(10) EA 02 defines a newspaper as 'a daily, Sunday or local (other than daily or Sunday) newspaper circulating wholly or mainly in the United Kingdom or in a part of the United Kingdom'. Livingston has argued that '[i]t is unfortunate that the definition of the concept which is central to the application of these provisions . . . is so opaque': D Livingston, *Competition Law and Practice* (London, FT Law and Tax, 1995), para 33.111. The DTI has stated that the definition includes free newspapers and that the definition applies only where the publication includes a significant proportion of news content: DTI, above n 8, paras 3.12–3.13. The MMC (as it then was) dealt with the definition of newspapers in a 1996 inquiry, *Northcliffe Newspapers Group Ltd/Aberdeen Journals Ltd*, Cm 3174, when the parties argued that certain publications were not, in fact, newspapers. Each contained an amount of editorial content, but none was published more frequently than monthly. The MMC opined that it was likely that such irregular publication meant that the publications in question were periodicals rather than newspapers. In *Johnston Press plc/Trinity Mirror plc*, Cm 5495 (2002), the CC recognised certain publications as newspapers, notwithstanding 'the relatively small proportion of editorial content' (para 1.10). In this case the publications were four local titles published weekly.

[11] S 59(3C) EA 02.

> the decision-making authority shall apply such criterion (whether value, cost, price, quantity, capacity, number of workers employed or some other criterion, of whatever nature), or such combination of criteria, as the decision-making authority considers appropriate.[12]

Although the relevant procedure to be applied in relation to media mergers in which public interest considerations are invoked is in general the standard regime, a complicating factor was introduced by the CA 03, which gave Ofcom a role to play alongside the OFT and the Secretary of State, who has a decision-making role in the procedure, although, as with other public interest cases, the Secretary of State is bound by the competition assessment made by the OFT and the CC as the case may be. While the addition of Ofcom to the list of those involved in making the decision appears to complicate the procedure, it has indicated that, where possible, parties will deal with a single body, and the roles assigned to the bodies are reasonably clearly set out.[13]

Procedure

Mergers in the media sector can, like other mergers, either be notified or not be notified to the OFT. In addition parties may seek informal guidance under the interim arrangements laid down in this respect by the OFT in April 2006. If the parties do choose to notify the merger—and this is an area in which, given the public interest considerations and the inherent risk, notification is likely to be the preferred strategy—the Ofcom guidance recommends that the parties include information which addresses the relevant public interest considerations.[14] This should include information relating to: ownership, the activities of the parties, audience shares, and any information relating to past audience complaints and compliance with the requirements imposed by relevant regulatory bodies. Where necessary either Ofcom or the DTI may seek further information relating to the parties' audiences, demographics, and their policies on editorial independence and any future plans.[15] If the parties seek informal guidance they are recommended to submit the relevant information also to the DTI if they believe that media public interest considerations may apply, and can also submit the same information to Ofcom.

As is the case with general mergers which raise public interest considerations,[16] the Secretary of State can issue an intervention notice as long as this is

[12] S 59(3C) EA 02, s 59A(1).

[13] Ofcom, *Guidance for the Public Interest Test for Media Mergers* (2004), para 27 (available at the Ofcom website): '[t]he OFT and Ofcom propose to offer media enterprises contemplating a merger a "one stop shop" service whereby they will receive competition advice from the OFT as well as Ofcom's advice on the media public interest issues raised by the merger together'.

[14] Ibid, App.

[15] Ibid.

[16] See Chap 18, below.

issued before the making of a reference to the CC by the OFT.[17] A special intervention notice can also be issued within four months of the date of the completion of the merger in the case of a merger which would not normally fall within the jurisdictional thresholds of the EA 02, but which meets the qualified criteria in respect of media mergers.[18] Any decision to intervene by the Secretary of State will normally be taken within 10 days of the notification of the merger to the OFT, or within 10 days of the merger coming to the attention of the Secretary of State.[19] If the Secretary of State chooses to intervene the parties will be notified of this fact and will have the opportunity to make submissions to the point.[20] If the decision is taken not to intervene the OFT will continue to examine the merger based exclusively on the competition criteria outlined in the EA 02.

Following the issue of an intervention notice both the OFT and Ofcom will provide a report to the DTI. The OFT report will focus on the competition aspects of the case (although it may also offer advice in relation to the media considerations), and Ofcom will report on the media public interest considerations. Where the case is a special merger situation the role of the OFT is purely to determine that the jurisdictional threshold has been met, and it will not carry out any competitive assessment. This reflects the principle that such mergers do not raise competition concerns, and are brought within the ambit of the merger regime purely to ensure that the special considerations set out in section 58(2A)–(2C) EA 02 are taken into account. The Ofcom guidance sets out the procedures that Ofcom will adopt in preparing its report. A case manager will be appointed, who may meet the parties, and consult more widely, including with members of the panel of newspaper industry experts and with interested third parties. Both the OFT and Ofcom reports must be published by the DTI in due course, although confidentiality requirements will be considered, and material may be redacted from the published version of the reports.

The Secretary of State's decision whether to refer the merger will be based on the advice received from the OFT and Ofcom, and must be made within the statutory deadline, which can be extended by 20 working days in a case where the merger has been notified by a merger notice.[21] If the Secretary of State determines that no intervention is necessary on the ground that media public interest considerations are not relevant, the case reverts to the OFT, with the decision being taken on competition considerations alone. In this case no reference can be made under the qualified threshold criteria. As with the general regime relating to public interest considerations, the Secretary of State is bound by

[17] S 42(2) EA 02.

[18] S 59(2) EA 02.

[19] DTI, above n 8, paras 4.11 and 4.14.

[20] The timescale at this point will be very tight, with the parties being given only a small number of days in which to respond. The DTI has indicated that a wide range of material may be relevant and considered at this stage.

[21] S 97(3)–(4) EA 02.

competition conclusions reached by the OFT, and must make a reference in a case where the OFT has identified that the merger may result in a SLC, unless this is outweighed by public interest considerations.[22] The DTI has stated that the approach to decisions to intervene will 'develop in the light of experience', and that 'this is not an area suited to generalisation'.[23] Clearly this is an area in which decisions will be extremely case sensitive, and given that decisions are made early on in the process it is likely that many relevant facts may not be known at the time of the making of the decision. It is possible that this may, at least for the first few years of the operation of this regime, encourage a conservative approach in which references are more likely to be made than not where concerns are raised.

The DTI has indicated that intervention is more likely in cases where a significant number of concerns are raised by third parties.[24] At the present only limited guidance is available in this area, in the form of broad 'rules of thumb' set out in *Enterprise Act 2002: Public Interest Intervention in Media Mergers*.[25] In the event that either a newspaper owner acquires a non-media business or a non-media business acquires a newspaper business it is unlikely that concerns will be raised.[26] Intervention in such cases is likely only when either in the first case the transaction as notified disguises the reality of the situation, or in the second case there are serious concerns about the identity of the acquirer. Quite reasonably, where the merger is between two newspaper businesses the decision to intervene will be determined primarily by the identity of the parties and the extent to which their activities overlap.[27] It would appear in this context that the main concern relates to concentration of ownership, which is also a factor that would be considered by the OFT in its competition assessment of the case. There may, however, be a difference between levels of concentration that raise concerns at the competitive level and at the public interest level.[28] Where a newspaper is acquired by a non-newspaper media business intervention is also unlikely under section 58(2A)–(2B),[29] although it may be considered under the public interest considerations set out in section 58(2C). In relation to interven-

[22] S 45(6) EA 02.

[23] DTI, above n 8, para 6.1.

[24] Ibid, para 6.6. Public outcry may be particularly important in determining if a reference is made in the case where a non-media business acquires a newspaper (see below).

[25] (2004). As of 4 June 2006, there had been no interventions made in respect of either newspaper or media mergers.

[26] Above n 23, paras 6.5, 6.10.

[27] Ibid, para 6.7.

[28] Ibid, para 7.3 of the DTI guidance states that 'there is a recognisable overlap between this competition assessment and at least the first of the broadcasting and cross-media public interest considerations'. Further, the DTI suggests that the Secretary of State 'may take the view that action to safeguard competition in a market will by itself be likely to provide a sufficient plurality of control'. However, 'such a view would be unlikely to be taken in cross-media mergers if the competition authorities considered that advertising in newspapers and in the broadcast media did not represent a sufficient competitive constraint on each other': ibid, para 7.4.

[29] Ibid, paras 6.8–6.9.

tion in broadcasting and cross-media public interest cases the DTI has indicated that intervention is likely to take place only in cases which would have fallen to be considered under the old media ownership rules which were repealed by the CA 03.[30]

The role of the CC in a media merger case referred to it is to consider both the general questions relating to jurisdiction and SLC, and it must also have regard to the relevant media public interest considerations which are set out in the reference. The CC maintains a specialist newspaper panel, and where the referred merger involves a newspaper public interest consideration, at least one member of this panel must sit on the appointed inquiry group. Section 104A EA 02[31] sets out additional obligations on the CC in relation to public consultation in the case of media mergers proceeding under section 50 which specify a media public interest consideration, or under section 65 on a reference which specifies a consideration set out in section 58(2A)–(2C), and where the CC is 'not under a duty to disregard the consideration concerned'.[32] Section 104A(2)–(3) states that:

> (2) The Commission shall have regard (among other things) to the need to consult the public so far as they might be affected by the creation of the relevant merger situation or special merger situation concerned and so far as such consultation is practicable.
> (3) Any consultation of the kind mentioned in subsection (2) may be undertaken by the Commission by consulting such representative sample of the public or section of the public concerned as the Commission considers appropriate.

Once the CC has completed its work its report goes to the Secretary of State and to Ofcom. The CC has 24 weeks within which to prepare its report, although if necessary this period may be extended by eight weeks.[33] The report must include recommendations on remedies where the CC believes that these are necessary.[34]

It then falls to the Secretary of State to determine whether, in light of the report from the CC, the merger is likely to act against the public interest.[35] If the Secretary of State finds that the merger is likely to act against the public interest he or she must also reach a conclusion on the appropriate remedy, if any, which would redress these concerns.[36] The Secretary of State has the power to adopt any of the remedies set out in Schedule 8 to the EA 02. These now include, in the case of media mergers, additional remedies inserted into Schedule 8 by section 387 CA 03. Schedule 8, paragraph 20A(4) provides that:

[30] The old rules created a complex set of restrictions on cross-media ownership. A summary is set out at para 8.2 of the DTI guidance, above n 23.
[31] Inserted by s 381 CA 03.
[32] S 104A(1)(b) EA 02.
[33] S 51 EA 02.
[34] S 50(2A) EA 02. Ofcom may also offer the Secretary of State advice as to the remedies to be adopted: s 106B EA 02.
[35] S 54(7)(a) EA 02.
[36] Ss 55 and 66 EA 02.

Provision made by virtue of this paragraph may, in particular, include provision—

(a) altering the constitution of a body corporate (whether in connection with the appointment of directors, the establishment of an editorial board or otherwise);
(b) requiring the agreement of the relevant authority or another person before the taking of particular action (including the appointment or dismissal of an editor, journalists or directors or acting as a shadow director);
(c) attaching conditions to the operation of a newspaper;
(d) prohibiting consultation or co-operation between subsidiaries.

As with the general merger regime, section 120 EA 02 applies, and any party affected by a decision of the Secretary of State may appeal to the CAT, which is to apply the general principles of judicial review in hearing the case.[37]

If no decision is made within the specified time limit the case reverts back to the CC, which makes a decision based purely on the competition concerns, ignoring the media public interest considerations.

Application of the media public interest considerations

There has, as of June 2006, been no application of the new rules,[38] although some guidance in relation to the 'newspaper public interest considerations'[39] may be found in decisions taken under the old regime.[40] The MMC and CC have considered in particular a substantial number of merger cases relating to newspapers, particularly at the local and regional levels, but also at the national level, over the last 30 years, and the DTI has indicated that section 58(2A)–(2B) will be interpreted consistently with cases determined under the FTA 73,[41] although MMC and CC reports do not have the status of binding precedent.[42] The considerations set out in section 58(2C) are new, and no guidance can be

[37] See further Chap 18, below.

[38] See however the response of the OFT in *Press Acquisitions Ltd/Hollinger International Inc (The Telegraph Group)*, 22 June 2004. See G Murphy, 'OFT Clears Sale of Telegraph Group to Barclay Brothers' [2005] *ECLR* 305.

[39] DTI, above n 8, para 1.4.

[40] The DTI notes that the number of relevant cases is small, and that they 'have generally been fairly easy identifiable from the outset'.

[41] The test set out in s 59(3) FTA 73 was only slightly different from the present considerations, requiring the MMC/CC to have regard to whether the merger might operate against the public interest, taking into account in particular the need for accurate presentation of news, and the free expression of opinion.

[42] In fact the CAT has, following the CFI, stressed the need for matters in competition investigations to be considered afresh each time, as markets and industries change over time and place. However, the practice of the MMC and CC has been to make frequent reference to earlier inquiries pertinent to a later inquiry, and this consistent approach creates principles which may be equated with 'precedent'.

obtained from earlier cases.[43] Further, in the case of broadcasting the situation is affected by a growth in dissemination technologies which are fundamentally influencing the way in which media are received by audiences, and these issues have not yet been considered in any detail by the CC, although in newspaper cases it has considered whether, for example, local advertising markets are altered by the existence of web-based advertising. Six main considerations may be identified within section 58(2A)–(2C): accurate presentation of news;[44] free expression of opinion;[45] plurality of views;[46] plurality of control;[47] range of broadcasting;[48] and commitment to attainment of broadcasting standards.[49]

Accurate presentation of news

The DTI guidance refers to *Bristol Evening Post/David Sullivan*.[50] David Sullivan held a 50 per cent stake in the publisher of the *Sunday Sport* and *The Sport* 'newspapers', and attempted to acquire control of the *Bristol Evening Post*. Mr Sullivan himself accepted that the *Sunday Sport* and *The Sport* for the most part did not deliver news, but argued that the publications satisfied a market niche. More importantly he argued that he had no intention of substantially changing the content of the *Bristol Evening Post*. Nevertheless the merger was blocked at the recommendation of the MMC, which argued that the credibility of the *Bristol Evening Post* would be damaged by an association with Mr Sullivan. The MMC found that Mr Sullivan's influence 'either in the shorter or the longer term, could be expected to harm both the accurate presentation of

43 There have, however, been merger inquiries in the broadcasting and related industries. See, eg, *Carlton Communications Plc/Granada Group PLC/United News and Media plc*, Cm 4781 (2000), in which the CC examined the three merger situations 'against the background of [a] desire to see two appropriately balanced companies within ITV': para 1.12; *Carlton Communications Plc/Granada plc*, Cm 5952 (2003), in which the CC found that the proposed merger would likely lead to 'benefits . . . in terms of broadcasting, programming and the competition for viewers', but concluded that other adverse effects, particularly on the market for advertising sales, outweighed these benefits: see para 1.11; *NTL Incorporated/Cable & Wireless Communications plc*, Cm 4666 (2000), in which the CC found that a merger in the cable pay-TV sector would not be expected to operate against the public interest; *Vivendi SA/British Sky Broadcasting Group plc*, Cm 4691 (2000), in which the CC cleared the merger, but noted that 'the pay-TV market is currently evolving rapidly as a result of technological and other developments, and would merit continued scrutiny': para 1.7; *Scottish Radio Holdings plc/GWR Group plc/Galaxy Radio Wales and the West Limited*, Cm 5811 (2003), in which the CC recommended divestiture remedies following a completed merger as a result of its adverse effects on the market for local radio advertising (this case did not raise issues relating to content, standards, or plurality, but does provide a substantial, and relatively recent, discussion of local radio markets).

44 S 58(2A)(a) EA 02.

45 S 58(2A)(b) EA 02.

46 S 58(2B) EA 02.

47 S 58(2C)(a) EA 02.

48 S 58(2C)(b) EA 02.

49 S 58(2C)(c) EA 02. The relevant broadcasting standards objectives are set out in s 319 CA 03.

50 Cm 1083 (1990). This case is briefly referred to in the DTI guidance, above n 23, at para 6.3, which describes Mr Sullivan as a 'contentious acquirer'.

news and the free expression of opinion'.[51] In practice, at least under the FTA 73 the MMC approach tended 'very much to be a "fit and proper" person test of the acquiring party', such that 'a purchaser with an impeccable record in this respect need have relatively little fear of the MMC advocating refusal of consent on this basis'.[52] The DTI guidance would appear to suggest that this approach is likely to continue under the new system. It has been noted that the CC may also consider whether a lack of financial viability, threatens the ability of a newspaper to present the news, such that this may lead to a recommendation to block a merger.[53] However, there have been no cases in which such a conclusion has been reached.

Free expression of opinion

The MMC and CC have in the past considered the extent to which editorial policy is independent of ownership, and have recognised that 'the situation in practice is often not as absolute and clear-cut as publishers sometimes imply'.[54] The MMC has cited with approval the recommendations of the Royal Commission on the Press 1974–7[55] which set out a view of the circumstances necessary to guarantee editorial independence. The Royal Commission accepted that proprietors might give advice relating to editorial policy, but stated that for true independence to exist the editor must be able to reject this advice, have the right to determine the editorial policy of the publication, and have the right to be critical of other parts of the same corporation. In the *George Outram & Company Ltd/The Observer*[56] merger the MMC raised concerns about the conduct of the Chief Executive who, it was argued, would impose very direct pressure on an editor to conform with the Group's stance. The MMC did not find that to be the case, but was concerned about the prospect that the coverage of the *Observer* could be distorted by its membership of a group with substantial commercial interests, particularly in Africa, that could reasonably be expected to form the subject of news stories. The MMC recommended that the merger be blocked unless the parties agreed a number of remedies, including the appointment of a number of independent directors with specified powers designed to ensure editorial independence. Concerns relating to editorial intervention and independence were also raised in *Bristol Evening Post/David Sullivan*.[57]

[51] Cm 1083 (1990), above n 50, para 6.12.

[52] Livingston, above n 10, para 33.124.

[53] A Scott, M Hviid and B Lyons, *Merger Control in the United Kingdom* (Oxford, OUP, 2006), para 21.51.

[54] See, eg, *Johnston Press/Trinity Mirror*, Cm 5495 (2002), para 2.126. The CC went on to note that '[e]ditors operate within the framework of commercial businesses and face financial and other constraints in consequence. They are likely to be mindful of their own career prospects, and of the desirability of their newspapers being profitable as well as respected for the quality of their journalism'.

[55] Cmnd 6810 (1977), above n 7.

[56] HC 378 (1981).

[57] Cm 1083 (1990), above n 50.

Plurality of views

The requirement that there be 'a sufficient plurality of views in newspapers in each market'[58] goes to the concentration of ownership. Necessarily, given that markets for newspapers may be very narrowly defined, it may not always be possible to achieve this plurality, and the CC is expected to take a realistic view in this respect. The MMC's view in respect of the threat to plurality flowing from ownership of local newspaper by national groups changed over time, and it may be unwise to rely upon results reached in older inquiries. As early as 1985 the MMC had held that it was not possible per se to conclude that concentrations in regional newspaper publications were against the public interest, and that it was necessary to look at each case on its specific facts.[59] In 1995 the MMC noted that 'the threat to diversity from increased concentration of ownership looks less severe today than it did [in 1977]'.[60] The MMC recognised on a number of occasions that commercial logic itself provides some protection from intervention at the local level, as local editors must respond to local opinions and concerns in order to maintain the viability of the publication in question. Thus, in *News Communications & Media and Newsquest Ltd/Johnston Press plc/Trinity Mirror plc* the CC stated that were a proprietor to attempt to control local editorial policy 'there would be sufficient competition from the rest of the industry, combined with an adverse reaction from readers and advertisers, to negate the ploy's effectiveness'.[61] In some instances it might be the case that a merger would result in a total change of editorial policy, as would be the case, for example, were a newspaper to switch its general political stance and orientation. The MMC considered this issue in *Trinity plc/Mirror Group plc*,[62] holding in that case that change in the orientation of the *Mirror* would be commercially unfeasible. It has however, considered that a change in ownership of the *News Letter*, a pro-Unionist newspaper published in Northern Ireland, might remove from the scene an important source of expression of these views.[63]

Plurality of control over media outlets

The only guidance relating to the operation of this media public interest consideration is that given by the DTI in Part 7 of *Enterprise Act 2002: Public Interest Intervention in Media Mergers*.[64] The central concern addressed by the first of the considerations set out in section 58(2C) of the EA 02 is that 'control

[58] S 58(2B) EA 02.
[59] *United Newspapers plc/Fleet Holdings plc*, Cmnd 9610 (1985).
[60] *Trinity International Holdings plc/Thomson Regional Newspapers Ltd*, Cm 3033 (1995), para 2.15.
[61] Cm 4680 (2000), para 2.39.
[62] Cm 4393 (1999).
[63] See, eg, *Trinity plc/Mirror Group plc*, Cm 4393 (1999).
[64] DTI, 2004, above n 23.

of media enterprises is not overly concentrated in the hands of a limited number of persons . . . because of their ability to influence opinions and control the agenda'.[65] A range of factors may be considered in determining the impact of the merger on plurality. First 'the number of persons controlling media interests serving relevant audiences in any given area of the UK'[66] would be of importance, although 'bare numbers may not tell the whole story'.[67] Audience shares may also be important, as 'what constitutes a sufficient number of owners controlling media enterprises in a given case may be affected by the relative audience shares that these enterprises hold'.[68] Wherever a merger situation involves two media enterprises serving the same audience there will be deemed to be a reduction in the number of enterprises serving that audience for the purposes of the plurality assessment.[69] The guidance states that all such mergers *may* be examined for the purposes of section 58(2C), but does not state that they *will* be so examined. The guidance emphasises the need to look not just at the core entities involved in the merger situation, but also at the extent to which these may, within the terms of section 26 EA 02, be treated as under common ownership or control.[70] Indeed, this view will be taken more widely, as:

> when looking across the spectrum to assess who has control of the remaining media enterprises, it is important to be able to look not just at the owners of those entities, but the controllers of those entities to get an accurate picture in relation to plurality in order to carry out the assessment relating to sufficiency of plurality.[71]

Range of broadcasting

The second of the considerations in section 58(2C) of the EA 02 relates to broadcasting content, and is 'concerned with safeguarding the quality and range of broadcasting when mergers take place in order to ensure a diversity of programming and protect the interests of viewers and listeners'.[72] A range of factors may be taken into account,[73] and 'the primary focus of the test will be

[65] DTI, 2004, above n 23, para 7.7.
[66] Ibid, para 7.9.
[67] Ibid, para 7.10.
[68] Ibid, para 7.10. The definition of 'audience' in this context is flexible. The Secretary of State 'can define an audience: as any one of the audiences served by that enterprise, taking them separately; as all of the audiences served by that enterprise taking them together; as a number of those audiences taken together in such group as the Secretary of State considers appropriate; or as any part of any of these audiences'.
[69] Ibid, para 7.13.
[70] Ibid, para 7.14.
[71] Ibid, para 7.14. The *Ofcom guidance for the public interest test for media mergers* (2004), above n 13, states that merging broadcasting enterprises should, if notifying their merger, provide full details of 'other media interests held by those controlling the merging parties, the duration and size of interest, both in the UK and overseas, and details of any plans to increase or decrease such media interests post-merger': app, para 76.
[72] Ibid, para 7.18.
[73] Ibid, para 7.19 states that this 'might involve an assessment of the impact of the merger on the availability of broadcasting services which secure programmes dealing with a wide range of subject matter; which are likely to meet the needs and satisfy the interests of as many different audiences as

on an assessment of future plans of the acquirer'.[74] The Secretary of State may also take into account the record of the owner in meeting broadcasting requirements in relation to other media enterprises under their control.

Commitment to attainment of broadcasting standards

Under the terms of the CA 03, Ofcom is charged with securing the application, in relation to all television and radio services, of standards providing adequate protection to the public. According to the DTI 'the intention behind this consideration is to assess whether persons controlling or carrying on media enterprises post-merger are likely to comply with the spirit as well as the letter of the broadcasting standards set down in the [CA 03]'.[75] As with the range of broadcasting considerations, attention may be paid in particular to the prior record of the owner in meeting standards. The guidance states that the Secretary of State 'will consider the likelihood that there will be a genuine commitment to broadcast standards',[76] and therefore 'comments, statements and any other plans' made by the acquiring owner may be pertinent.[77]

WATER MERGERS

Introduction

In almost all cases those to whom water is supplied are faced with little possibility of substituting that supplier, such that the industry is characterised by a lack of horizontal competition.[78] Prices are subject to regulatory control, and the usual concerns relating to monopoly power and concentration do not apply in this industry. However, the control of prices is determined substantially by a process of benchmarking, under which the Water Services Regulation Authority (WSRA) has regard to the costs of other water enterprises in assessing prices for the water enterprise in question. A central concern of the merger regime in this area has been to maintain the integrity of this benchmarking scheme by preventing mergers which might allow undertakers to distort the results of the process. Section 32 WIA 91 states that:

practicable; which are properly balanced in nature and subject matter for meeting the needs and satisfying the interests of the available audiences; and which maintain high general standards with respect to the contents of the programmes included in them, the quality of the programme making and the professional skill and editorial integrity applied in the making of the programmes'.

[74] Ibid, para 7.19.
[75] Ibid, para 7.22.
[76] Ibid, para 7.24.
[77] Ibid, para 7.25.
[78] The WIA 91 does make provision for limited competition by way of inset appointments, and bulk supply arrangements, but these have had only limited impact, and affect only a small number of customers.

> Subject to section 33 below, it shall be the duty of the OFT to make a merger reference to the Competition Commission if the OFT believes that it is or may be the case—
>
> (a) that arrangements are in progress which, if carried into effect, will result in a merger of any two or more water enterprises; or
>
> (b) that such a merger has taken place otherwise than as a result of the carrying into effect of arrangements that have been the subject of a reference by virtue of paragraph (a) above.

This means therefore that for this special regime to apply *both* of the merging entities must be water enterprises.[79] If they were not, there would be no reason to be concerned about the effect on the benchmarking process. Section 33 WIA 91 provides that in the case of certain 'small mergers' the duty to make a merger reference does not exist. This applies where the value of the turnover of the enterprise being taken over does not exceed £10m,[80] or that the only water enterprises belonging to the person making the takeover do not have a turnover value exceeding £10m.[81] Regulations have been made relating to the calculation of relevant turnover for the purpose of these provisions.[82] References to 'mergers' in this context are references to the relevant enterprises ceasing to be distinct businesses, within the terms of Part 3 of the EA 02, and are thus to be interpreted consistently with the general provisions relating to merger control (see Chapter 10, above).[83] The effect of these provisions therefore is to ensure that mergers between water enterprises when the turnover of either the acquired, or the acquiring, enterprise is in excess of £10m shall be referred to the Competition Commission by the OFT.[84] This strips the OFT of the discretion it enjoys in the operation of the general merger regime. The OFT does have discretion to make references in the case where a merger takes place which falls within the terms of section 33, by virtue of section 35(3).[85]

[79] A 'water enterprise' is an enterprise carried on by a company appointed under the WIA 91, s 6 or s 35(1) to be a water undertaker or a sewerage undertaker.

[80] S 33(1)(a) WIA 91.

[81] S 33(1)(b) WIA 91.

[82] Water Mergers (Determination of Turnover) Regulations 2004, SI 2004/3206.

[83] OFWAT has argued that the relevant law should make clear on its face that control in this respect included the gaining of a material influence, but it was not felt that it was necessary to make this an explicit provision.

[84] Where a merger takes place which includes within it a merger of water enterprises Part 3 of the EA 02 applies to the rest of the merger excluding the water enterprises: s 35(4) WIA 91. This means that for the purposes of determining turnover in the case of a wider merger the turnover of water enterprises is to be excluded.

[85] In its *Interim arrangements for informal advice and pre-notification contacts,* Apr 2006 (available at the OFT website), the OFT notes that 'the informal advice process is deemed unsuitable and inappropriate for the OFT to advise on the decisive legal question of whether the structure of a transaction, designed to fall outside the Water Act regime, is nonetheless caught by the relevant automatic reference provisions. Pre-notification is recommended in such a case': para 14.

The ECMR and water mergers

It may be the case that a merger between water enterprises is sufficiently large to reach the relevant thresholds for the operation of the ECMR, in which case the general principles governing the operation of the ECMR should mean that the EC Commission has exclusive competence to determine the legality of the merger. This was the case in the 1995 *Lyonnaise des Eaux SA/Northumbrian Water Group* merger[86] which was cleared by the EC Commission in December 1995.[87] However, in respect of the effect of the merger within the UK the OFT successfully argued that Article 21(4) ECMR (see Chapter 3, above) should be applicable, in that the control of the water industry in the UK was a 'legitimate interest', such that jurisdiction over that part of the merger should be transferred to the UK. Unless this policy changes, which is unlikely, it appears therefore that even the very largest of mergers involving water enterprises falls to be considered within the UK regime, at least in so far as it is consummated within the UK.[88] However, this principle is limited by the terms of the 1995 decision, paragraph 5 of which states:

> In order not to go beyond the interest pursued by the UK regulatory legislation other issues in relation to mergers between water companies can only be taken into account to the extent that they affect the control regime as set out above. These other issues would principally include the allocation of cost savings arising from the merger or the effect of the merger on the level of water charges and which would be used in the calculation of the pricing formula for the merged company. By contrast, the UK authorities are not entitled to consider other matters which the Commission must take into account in assessing concentrations that have a Community dimension and which do not directly relate to the operation of the regulatory regime.

Merger references

As with the general regime the procedures relating to mergers in the water industry involve, save in exceptional cases, only the OFT and the CC. Following a history of intervention in decisions in respect of this industry by the Secretary of State in the past,[89] this streamlining of the procedure is to be welcomed. Given that the OFT is *obliged* to make a reference in respect of mergers falling within section 32 WIA 91, it is unlikely that the OFT will conduct any

[86] Cm 2936 (1995).
[87] Case IV/M.567 (1995).
[88] The CC states at para 1.18 of the *Water Merger References: Competition Commission Guidelines*, CC9, Dec 2004, that '[w]hile the European Commission continues to recognize the maintenance of sufficient comparators as a legitimate interest for the purposes of Art 21, the Competition Commission will continue to receive references relating to mergers that have a community dimension'.
[89] See in particular *Vivendi Water UK plc/First Aqua (JVCo) Ltd*, DTI Press Release, 28 Apr 2003.

significant assessment of the merger prior to making the reference. It will, however, be expected to ensure that it has jurisdiction to make the reference, determining that the turnover thresholds are satisfied. Information in this respect will most likely be taken in the first place from both the parties and particularly from the WSRA, which in practice *is* likely to undertake an analysis of the anticipated effects of the merger, and will make its views known to the CC, although it has no privileged status in the proceedings.

The role of the Competition Commission

The role of the CC in relation to a merger between water enterprises is, as stated above, to determine first whether arrangements are in place which, if put into effect, would result in a water merger,[90] or whether such a merger has taken place.[91] If the answer is in the affirmative, the second question to be determined is whether the merger has prejudiced, or may prejudice, 'the ability of the Authority . . . to make comparisons between different water enterprises'.[92] This is a more limited function than is the case in general mergers. It has been argued that '[i]t is debatable, however, whether the experience of the water merger control regime will be much different on this ground in practice'.[93] It may be argued that in practice there are a number of different roles that the WSRA fulfils which require it to make comparison between water enterprises, and it is possible that this may require the CC to take a broad perspective when assessing a water merger referred to it. The main role, but not the exclusive one, is that of setting price caps, which are based on a determination of costs, and the WSRA will not rely exclusively on a water enterprise's statement of its own costs, but will make comparisons to others in the industry. However, the CC guidelines draw attention to the fact that:

> the advantages to the [WSRA] of comparisons go beyond the effects of setting price caps at periodic reviews. The [WSRA] publishes tables comparing companies' performance on various matters including quality of customer service and relative efficiency, and companies may be concerned about their position in these tables and stimulated to seek improvements. Second, comparative information is useful to the [WSRA] in appraising company proposals in a variety of areas, including tariffs, leakage and transfer pricing, and may enable the [WSRA] to negotiate improved proposals that better fulfil [its] functions.[94]

[90] WIA s 36(1)(a), as modified by The Water Mergers (Modification of Enactments) Regulations 2004, SI 2004/3202, reg 11.

[91] WIA s 35(1)(a), as modified by The Water Mergers (Modification of Enactments) Regulations 2004, SI 2004/3202, reg 11.

[92] WIA ss 35(1)(b), and 36(1)(b).

[93] Scott, Hviid and Lyons, above n 53, 404. Scott *et al* quote the DGWS as saying that although 'some commentators have suggested that . . . there has been a fundamental change in the tests the Competition Commission will apply when looking at water mergers . . . it doesn't look so fundamental to us': at 405.

[94] Note 88, above.

The CC has published guidance in relation to the way in which it performs its functions when determining a water merger, *Water Merger References: Competition Commission Guidelines*.[95] In this it works from the assumption that the more concentrated the industry becomes the more difficult it will be for the WSRA to make valid comparisons between water enterprises. Thus at paragraph 2.2 it states that:

> A water merger brings under common ownership or common control two or more water enterprises. The merging water enterprises must continue to operate under separate licences . . . unless their licences are modified, which would require the [WSRA's] approval. In the absence of licence changes, the [WSRA] will continue to receive separate information from each of the merging water companies and can continue to use this to make comparisons. This is because, in general, the Commission considers that companies under common ownership may be expected to behave in similar ways and hence that a water merger may be expected to affect the value of comparisons made by the [WSRA].[96]

In its 1995 *Lyonnaise des Eaux SA/Northumbrian Water Group* decision[97] the EC Commission inserted a qualification in paragraph 6, holding that:

> the implementation of this legislation must not be carried out in a discriminatory manner. The minimum number of independent water companies should not therefore be higher than necessary to ensure the effective operation of the regulatory regime in order to be appropriate and proportional to the objective in question.

In its guideline the CC recognises that the way in which it assesses water mergers may change if the use made by the WSRA of comparisons between water enterprises change.[98]

The CC sets out six factors that it will consider in assessing the impact of the merger on the ability of the WSRA to make comparisons. These are:

(a) the extent of common ownership or control;
(b) any other factors suggesting that the companies involved in the merger could remain to some extent under independent management after the merger;
(c) the extent to which the costs of one or all of the merging companies are, before the merger, not independent of the costs of other water companies;
(d) any particular similarities between the companies involved in the merger;
(e) whether the company or companies being taken over are among the most efficient, for example the loss of a frontier or price-setting company might mean that the [WSRA] would have to set softer price targets for the whole industry; and
(f) the number and quality of remaining independent contractors.[99]

[95] *Water Merger References: Competition Commission Guidelines*, CC9, Dec 2004, para 2.14.

[96] At ibid, para 2.15 the CC recognises that it may in the future be necessary for the WSRA 'to consider whether it would be practicable and cost-effective for [it] to use alternate methods of comparison to offset partially or wholly the effects of the merger on [its] comparisons through developing comparative methods which are less sensitive to the number of comparators than those currently used'.

[97] Case IV/M.567 (1995).

[98] Above n 95, para 1.3.

[99] Ibid, para 2.16.

The effect of these factors is further considered in the CC *Guidelines* at paragraphs 2.17–2.22. The CC further takes the view that there is no minimum number of comparators below which the WSRA will lose the ability to make valid comparisons, and that it 'will take into account all the factors set out above and not just the effect on the robustness of econometric modelling'.[100] The effect of this is that 'the impact depends on the circumstances of the merger under consideration'.[101]

Part 3 of the *Guideline* deals with the ability of the CC to impose remedies, and the question of what remedies may be appropriate. The CC can take action only if the reference to it was made within four months from the date of the merger or, if it is later, the day on which the material facts came to the attention of the OFT.[102] This limitation does not apply if the reference could not have been made earlier due to the application of the ECMR. The CC will consider the question of remedies as a two-stage process: first, could it either impose a remedy by way of making an Order, or accepting undertakings; secondly, should it recommend that remedial action be taken by others, such as the WSRA or any relevant minister. Sections 35(6) and 36(5) WIA[103] require the CC to 'in particular have regard to the need to achieve as comprehensive a solution as is reasonable and practicable to the prejudice to [the WSRA] and any adverse effects resulting from it'. The *Guideline* states that 'it is unlikely that the [CC] would take no remedial action if it has decided that a merger results or is expected to result in a prejudicial outcome'.[104] However, it may be the case in exceptional circumstances, such as where the costs of any remedy would be disproportionate to the harm identified, that no remedy would be advanced by the CC. Even in this case it may still recommend that others take action.[105] The CC may also, under sections 35(7) and 36(6) WIA 91, take into account any relevant customer benefits that arise from the merger. This would apply in two cases: first, where the consideration of those benefits would not prevent the application of a remedy; and, secondly, when the benefits are substantially more significant than the harm identified. The CC will have regard to the costs of proposed remedies, their efficacy, and the principle of proportionality.[106]

When considering the costs of any proposed remedy the CC 'will not require a remedy that it considers to be disproportionate in relation to the ability of the [WSRA] to make comparisons or any adverse effects resulting or which are expected to result from such prejudice'.[107] When choosing between two remedies which appear to be equally effective the CC will choose the one which

[100] Above n 95, para 2.23.
[101] Ibid, para 2.23.
[102] The Water Mergers (Modification of Enactments) Regulations 2004, SI 2004/3202, reg 4.
[103] As modified by The Water Mergers (Modification of Enactments) Regulations 2004, SI 2004/3202, reg 11.
[104] Para 3.6 of the guideline, above n 95.
[105] Ibid, para 3.6.
[106] Ibid, para 3.8.
[107] Ibid, para 3.9.

appears to bear the lesser cost, and will in particular endeavour to ensure that remedies are not disproportionate to the detriment when considering a merger to which the ECMR applies. In practice it should, as indicated above, endeavour in every case to ensure that remedies are not disproportionate. Although the CC will take into account the costs to the parties of implementing any remedy, it will not do so in relation to divestiture costs in the case of a completed merger, reasonably arguing that the parties would have had the opportunity to seek clearance of the merger before consummation. Further the CC argues that parties should have taken into account the risk of a divestiture being required, and that this should have been reflected in the purchase price.[108] Costs of forgone economies arising from the merger will be considered in the context of relevant customer benefits (it being assumed, therefore, that such savings would be passed on to the customers, which may be more likely to happen in a regulated market than is the case generally). The CC will *not* consider such factors as environmental or social costs of unemployment,[109] which does serve to place the focus more firmly on the ability of the WSRA to make comparisons, and the competitive environment, removing factors which are better left to other mechanisms to address. The CC will also take into account the extent of any continuing compliance and monitoring costs involved in the implementation of the remedy.[110]

At paragraph 3.17 of the Guideline the CC sets out the remedies which may be applied:

> The Commission will consider either of the following types of remedies:
>
> (a) structural remedies that are intended to restore all or part of the status quo ante, for example
>
> —prohibition of a proposed merger;
> —divestiture of a completed acquisition; and
> —partial prohibition or divestiture (ie covering part of one or more of the merging companies' business); and
>
> (b) behavioural remedies that are intended to decrease the prejudice to the [WSRA's] ability to make comparisons and any other adverse effect resulting from the prejudice, for example:
>
> —amendments to the company's licence, for instance regarding provision of information; and
> —a requirement to maintain separate management or separate accounting arrangements.

When determining which of these options may be the most appropriate, apart from a consideration of the costs involved, the CC will also have regard to the efficacy of the remedy. In this context it first notes that a key factor 'is whether

108 Ibid, para 3.10.
109 Ibid, para 3.11.
110 Ibid, para 3.12.

the remedy is clear to the person to whom it is directed and also to other relevant interested parties'.[111] Interested parties may include the OFT or WSRA if they are involved in continued monitoring of the remedy, or customers and competitors, who may be better placed to complain if they understand the obligations imposed by the remedy.[112] A second broad consideration is the likelihood of the remedy being properly implemented and complied with, and as with the general approach in the UK regime[113] one-off structural remedies are to be preferred, all else being equal, to conduct remedies. A third consideration is the timescale within which the remedy may be implemented, and the CC 'will tend to favour a remedy that can be expected to show results in a relatively short time period'.[114] This mitigates against choosing remedies which require action by another person, such as the WSRA or the relevant minister, and in particular those which may require a change in Government regulations.

As stated above, structural remedies are likely to be preferred to behavioural remedies generally. In the case of water mergers the structure of the market, and the regulatory choices made in relation to it, strengthens this preference. As the CC recognises, the harm in water mergers, given the remit set out in the WIA 91, flows from the prejudice to the ability of the WSRA to make comparisons in the benchmarking process. Although, as noted above, there is no 'magic number' of water enterprises which the CC or the WSRA believe to be optimal, it is clear that, unlike in other industries, *any* reduction in the numbers of water enterprises may have a prejudicial effect. In the case of a proposed merger the CC is clear that 'the most effective remedy will often be the prohibition of the merger'.[115] Where the purchaser has already acquired a shareholding in the target enterprise, the CC may require that this be reduced to a specified maximum level, such that there is no prospect of the holder of the shares exercising material influence on the target in the future. In the case of mergers which have already been completed the CC again believes that 'the most effective remedy may be divestiture of the acquired business'.[116] Any required divestiture would be expected to take place within a reasonable period of time, which would normally be a maximum of six months. The CC will 'generally insist on having the right to approve the prospective purchaser and the divestiture agreement before the parties may proceed with the divestiture'.[117] If the circumstances merit it the CC may consider requiring divestiture of the acquirer's holdings in other water enterprises, where this would restore the ability of the WSRA to make compar-

[111] Para 3.6 of the guideline, above n 95, para 3.14.

[112] It should be noted that third parties with locus standi may appeal the decision of the CC to the CAT. See Chap 18 below.

[113] See Chap 14, above.

[114] Para 3.16 of the guideline, above n 95.

[115] Ibid, para 3.20.

[116] Ibid, para 3.21.

[117] Ibid, para 3.21. See also Competition Commission, Application of divestiture remedies in merger inquiries: Competition Commission Guidelines, CC8, Dec 2004, discussed in more detail in Chapter 14, above and available at the CC website.

isons. In effect, an acquirer of a water enterprise who already holds controlling interests or ownership of other such enterprises may be faced with the choice of retaining the new acquisition, at the expense of the older holdings, or relinquishing control over the new target. Until such time as a divestiture was completed the CC would require that measures be put in place, including the appointment of a suitable trustee or other person to monitor the process, to maintain the competitiveness of the business to be divested.

In the case of a partial divestiture the CC will address two key questions:

> (a) whether the business or assets to be divested provide the basis of a viable business that can operate independently of the merging firms and, in a reasonably short time, say within one year, can be expected to provide an effective comparator to the [WSRA]; and
> (b) whether there is a suitable purchaser of the assets who will be capable of operating the assets and running a viable, independent and competitive business.[118]

The general factors to be considered in relation to partial divestitures and the conditions to be applied are the same as for full divestiture, outlined above.

The CC says little in relation to behavioural remedies in the *Guideline*, merely noting that these 'could include changes to the merging companies' price caps and licence conditions requiring the provision of information to the [WSRA]'.[119]

The discussion of relevant customer benefits is to a substantial degree, the same as that for the general UK merger regime, and this area is addressed in Chapters 11 and 14. However, there are some differences arising from the structure of the industry, with a strong recognition of the role played by price caps. For example, the CC notes that 'much more weight can be attached to anticipated cost savings which are supported by immediate proposed amendments to companies' price caps'.[120] The CC also recognises that customer benefits may accrue from factors such as an improved security of supply due to improved coordination between companies, or an improvement in standards. However, it 'would have to be satisfied that it would be unlikely to accrue without the merger or a similar prejudice to the [WSRA]; for example, that it would not be achieved through agreement between the parties'.[121] The CC recognises that it may be difficult to balance customer benefits against prejudice to the ability of the WSRA to make comparisons. The result is that 'in most cases, the [CC] will therefore make a qualitative comparison of that prejudice and the relevant customer benefits in deciding whether the latter is substantially more important than the former'.[122]

The procedure relating to undertakings and orders is discussed in Chapter 15.

[118] Para 3.24 of the Guideline, above n 95.
[119] Ibid, para 3.26.
[120] Ibid, para 3.34.
[121] Ibid, para 3.35.
[122] Ibid, para 3.36.

17

Public Interest Mergers and Special Merger Situations

INTRODUCTION

THE SECRETARY OF State has a residual power to intervene in the merger process by issuing public intervention notices in accordance with Chapter 2 of Part 3 of the EA 02 in respect of mergers which have 'public interest' implications. This has consequences for the powers and procedures employed by both the OFT and the CC. That this power exists attracted considerable comment at the time of the enactment of the legislation, and the Opposition was concerned about continued political involvement in the merger regime. As explained in Committee:

> the Secretary of State should have the power to refer a case that qualifies for investigation if he or she believes that the merger may operate against the public interest. The result will be that the Secretary of State will refer cases to the Competition Commission. The public interest test that the Secretary of State will apply under the regime will be more limited than that in the [FTA 1973]. The Secretary of State will be limited to taking into account of the relevant public interest considerations and any substantial lessening of competition.[1]

The OFT has a duty under section 57 EA 02 to bring to the attention of the Secretary of State any case which it is considering under section 22 or 33 that it believes raises any public interest considerations specified in section 58 (see below). The core power of the Secretary of State is set out in section 42(2) EA 02. This provides that:

> The Secretary of State may give a notice to the OFT (in this Part 'an intervention notice') if he believes that it is or may be the case that one or more than one public interest consideration is relevant to a consideration of the relevant merger situation.

A public interest consideration is one which is spelt out in section 58, or, in the opinion of the Secretary of State, should be so specified.[2] Where a public interest intervention is made the OFT will consider the competition issues and advise the Secretary of State accordingly, but the Secretary of State may decide that the

[1] Standing Committee B, HC, col 347, 30 Apr 2002.
[2] S 42(3) EA 02.

public interest concerns outweigh the competition considerations.[3] The Secretary of State also has a role in relation to media and water mergers, discussed in the previous chapter. Intervention on public interest grounds may also take place in respect of cases considered under the ECMR Article 21(3) (see Chapter 3).

SPECIFIED CONSIDERATIONS

The only public interest consideration to be specified at the time of the enactment of the EA 02 was that of 'national security'. Although the Act has been amended (as discussed in the previous chapter) to bring media mergers within section 58, at sections (2A)–(2C), nothing has been added to section 58(1). 'National security' is defined in the legislation and 'includes public security; and in this subsection "public security" has the same meaning as in article 21(4) of the EC Merger Regulation'.[4] However, the term 'public security' is not defined in Regulation 139/2004, but in the application of the Regulation, based on principles drawn in part from the EC Treaty. It has been explained elsewhere that '"public security" may overlap but is not synonymous with national defence and may be more restricted'.[5] The Commission and the ECJ have at various times recognised that there may be issues of public security that extend beyond national defence. Thus, for example, the ECJ held in *Campus Oil*[6] that the principle could extend to such matters as the securing of oil supplies in times of shortage.

There were a number of cases arising under the FTA 73 in which public security matters were found to be relevant. In *Finmeccanica SpA/Marconi Plc*[7] the OFT reported on a merger which fell originally within the terms of the ECMR, but where Article 21[4] applied. In this case the Ministry of Defence made

[3] At para 8.11 of *Mergers: Substantive assessment guidance* (London, OFT, May 2003), the OFT explains the position in the following terms:

> 'In public interest cases . . . which fall to the Secretary of State for decision, the OFT will consider whether the competition issues that arise are such that the OFT would recommend a reference if there were no public interest issues. If so, the OFT will consider whether or not these concerns could be resolved by undertakings and will advise the Secretary of State accordingly. The Secretary of State will have regard to the OFT's view on competition issues, but may decide that public interest issues require a different outcome to that which would occur if there were no such competition issues. This could include a decision to clear the merger, a decision to make a reference, or a decision to accept undertakings, which might be different from those proposed by the OFT to resolve any competition issues.'

[4] S 58(2) EA 02.

[5] CJ Cook and CS Kerse, *EC Merger Control* (3rd edn, London, Sweet and Maxwell, 2000), para 8.4.2.1.

[6] Case C–72/83, *Campus Oil Ltd v Minister of Industry and Energy* [1984] ECR I–2727, at 2764.

[7] See OFT report under s 125(4) of the Fair Trading Act 1973 on the advice of the Deputy Director General of Fair Trading, given on 5 Nov 2002 to the Secretary of State for Trade and Industry under s 76 of the Act.

representations to the effect that the merger might adversely affect the public interest on national security grounds, in that it could impact on the maintenance of strategic UK capabilities and the protection of classified information. In this case the Ministry of Defence itself obtained undertakings from the parties as to future conduct. The OFT noted that it was 'not expert in national security matters and must, therefore, rely heavily on the representations made by the [Ministry of Defence]'.[8]

The power exists for the Secretary of State to specify further considerations, and s/he may issue a notice in respect of such a consideration, but is then under an obligation to finalise this as soon as is practicable.[9] Such public interest considerations are finalised when an order is made and approved by Parliament, in accordance with section 124(6). At the time of the passage of the legislation there were no plans to introduce additional public interest considerations.[10]

PROCEDURE

Intervention notices may be issued only where the OFT has not yet made a decision in respect of a merger situation. However, a notice may be issued where the OFT has made a decision to accept undertakings under section 71 EA 02 as an alternative to making a reference. Only one notice may be issued in respect of any merger. The details that must be included in intervention notices are set out in section 43(1). These come into force when they are given, and cease to be in force at the point when the matter is finally decided.[11]

Where an intervention notice has been given, the OFT is required to give the Secretary of State a report containing its advice on the considerations relevant to the making of a standard reference under section 22 or section 33 EA 02, and the OFT performs its competition investigations in the usual way. In each case the time limit within which the report must be prepared is to be determined by the Secretary of State.[12] The Secretary of State will thus have had advice about the competition issues relating to the merger, and the OFT is obliged also to report back on any representations it has received in relation to the public interest consideration(s). In essence, the report is to be the summary of the position that the OFT would take in relation to the making of a merger reference, and

[8] Ibid. An identical formulation was used in the case of *Astrium NV/European Aeronautic Defence and space company* (A report under s 125(4) of the Fair Trading Act 1973 on the advice of the Chairman of the OFT given on 15 July 2003, to the Secretary of State for Trade and Industry under s 76 of the EA 02).

[9] S 41(7) EA 02. Where an intervention notice is made but the public interest consideration is not finalised within the required period, the notice will lapse. Likewise a reference shall be cancelled if more than 24 weeks have passed since the giving of the notice, and the public interest consideration has not been finalised: s 53(1) EA 02.

[10] Standing Committee B, HC, col 343, 30 Apr 2002.

[11] S 43(4) EA 02.

[12] S 44(2) EA 02.

may also 'include advice and recommendations on any public interest consideration mentioned in the intervention notice concerned'.[13] The OFT has indicated, however, that it 'will not usually make any recommendation on the public interest matter because comment on such issues lies outside its competition expertise'.[14] Both the OFT and the Secretary of State have the power, under section 46C EA 02, to require relevant persons to provide the OFT or the Secretary of State with such information as the Secretary of State needs in order to make a decision in respect of a reference.

Following the receipt of the OFT's report, it is for the Secretary of State to refer the matter to the CC if s/he is minded to do so. Section 45 EA 02 sets out the powers of the Secretary of State to make a reference in situations in which an intervention notice has been given. The provisions relating to completed or anticipated mergers are symmetrical. In both cases the Secretary of State may make a reference either where the OFT has indicated that an SLC is likely, or where it has not. In the case that an SLC is identified by the OFT the reference will ask the CC to determine whether:

> taking account only of the substantial lessening of competition and the relevant public interest consideration or considerations concerned, the creation of that situation operates or may be expected to operate against the public interest.[15]

Where there is no belief that the merger may lead to an SLC the CC's role will be limited to that of reporting:

> taking account only of the relevant public interest consideration or considerations concerned, the creation of that situation operates or may be expected to operate against the public interest.[16]

When determining whether to make a reference or not, the Secretary of State is bound by the views of the OFT as regards the competition matters,[17] but not as regards matters relating to the public interest consideration. Section 45(6) EA 02 therefore provides that *any* anti-competitive outcome identified by the OFT shall be treated as being against the public interest, unless it is outweighed by the relevant public interest consideration. Some qualifications on the power to refer are set out in section 46. These mirror those which limit the power of the OFT to make references under sections 22 and 33. Thus, references may not be made where an undertaking has been accepted by the OFT in respect of that merger situation, or where a merger notice is in force, or where Articles 22(1) or 4(5) of the ECMR is in play. Where, following the report made by the OFT, the Secretary of State decides not to make a reference under section 45 on the grounds that no relevant public interest consideration is applicable the matter is

[13] S 44(6) EA 02.
[14] Para 10(5) of OFT, above n 3.
[15] Ss 45(2)(d) EA 02 and 45(4)(d) EA 02.
[16] Ss 45(3)(d) EA 02 and 45(5)(d) EA 02.
[17] S 46(2) EA 02.

to revert to the OFT to deal with under the general merger regime, at which point the OFT will be free to determine the issue based exclusively on its approach to the SLC, any remedies advanced and the normal considerations governing references to the CC.[18] The powers of the Secretary of State to accept undertakings or to make orders in respect of relevant public or special public interest mergers are considered below.

The duties of the CC once a public or special public interest reference has been made are set out in sections 47–53, EA 02. First the CC is to determine, as for the general regime, whether a relevant merger situation has been created. Secondly it is to determine whether that situation leads, or may be expected to lead, to an SLC, and in addition:

> whether, taking account only of any substantial lessening of competition and the admissible public interest consideration or considerations concerned, the creation of that situation operates or may be expected to operate against the public interest.[19]

When a reference is made under section 45(3) EA 02 the CC's role is limited to considering the public interest considerations, and not the SLC considerations. Where the CC determines that the creation of the relevant merger situation operates, or may be expected to operate, against the public interest it is required to consider three further questions: (1) whether the Secretary of State should take any action under section 55 EA 02 to remedy, mitigate or prevent any of the adverse effects; (2) whether the CC should recommend that others take any action; and (3) 'in either case, if action should be taken, what action should be taken and what is to be remedied, mitigated or prevented'.[20] The CC is further to decide whether, in relation to any identified SLC, it should take action, or whether other persons should take action.[21] The CC's duty in determining these questions is to 'have regard to the need to achieve as comprehensive solution as is reasonable and practicable to—(a) the adverse effects to the public interest . . .'.[22] In the circumstances specified in sections 48 or 49 references may be abandoned or varied by the CC.

The report of the CC is to be addressed to the Secretary of State,[23] and is to be delivered within a period of 24 weeks beginning with the date of the reference, although this period may be extended by a further eight weeks if 'there are special reasons by the report cannot be prepared and given to the Secretary of State within that period'.[24] The time limit may also be extended where relevant persons have failed to provide the CC with required information.[25]

[18] S 56(1) EA 02.
[19] S 47(2)(b) EA 02.
[20] S 47(7)(c) EA 02.
[21] S 47(8) EA 02.
[22] S 47(9)(a) EA 02.
[23] S 50 EA 02.
[24] S 51(3) EA 02. Only one such extension may be made: s 52(4), EA 02.
[25] S 51(4) EA 02.

There is a lack of discussion in the OFT and CC guidelines relating to the assessment of mergers in which any of a public interest, special public interest, or European intervention notice (see below) has been issued. In the case of media and water mergers discussed in the previous chapter some guidance is available, and there are numbers of past decisions that may also shed light on the approach to be taken. However, in respect of other specified public interest considerations, including the special merger situations discussed below, there is little past practice to base conclusions on, and the cases should be treated as peculiar on their facts, such that it is difficult to give useful guidance ex ante on the approach to be taken.[26]

SPECIAL MERGER SITUATIONS

Sections 59–66 EA 02 make reference to 'special public interest cases'. The law relating to media mergers has been discussed in Chapter 16, and the discussion here excludes these cases. The most significant feature of the special public interest case regime is that it may be applied to mergers which *do not* qualify as relevant merger situations under the thresholds set out in the EA 02. This is to say that in these special categories merger control may be applied purely on the special interest grounds, irrespective of the size of the merger and without reference to any competition criteria or assessment whatsoever.

Where the Secretary of State has reasonable grounds for suspecting that a special merger situation has been created or is in contemplation s/he may give notice to the OFT ('a special intervention notice') where one or more of the considerations set out in section 58 EA 02 is relevant.[27] The conditions specified in section 59(3B) are that:

> (a) at least one of the enterprises concerned was carried on in the United Kingdom or by or under the control of a body incorporated in the United Kingdom; and
> (b) a person carrying on one or more of the enterprises concerned was a relevant government contractor.

'Government contractor' is defined in section 59(8) as:

> (a) a government contractor—
>   (i) who has been notified by or on behalf of the Secretary of State of information, documents or other articles relating to defence and of a confidential nature which the government contractor or an employee of his may hold or receive in connection with being such a contractor; and
>   (ii) whose notification has not been revoked by or on behalf of the Secretary of State; or

[26] The CC guidance, eg, is just over two pages long, and most of it restates the legislative provisions and tests: see *Merger References: Competition Commission Guidelines*, June 2003, Part 5.
[27] S 59(1)–(2) EA 02.

(b) a former government contractor who was so notified when he was a government contractor and whose notification has not been revoked by or on behalf of the Secretary of State.[28]

ENFORCEMENT

It falls to the Secretary of State to make final decisions, following the receipt of the report by the CC, in respect of public interest and special public interest merger situations. Section 54(2) EA 02 thus provides that:

> The Secretary of State shall decide whether to make an adverse public interest finding in relation to the relevant merger situation and whether to make no finding at all in the matter.

Where the Secretary of State determines that there is no public interest consideration relevant to the merger situation s/he shall 'make no finding at all'.[29] In this respect s/he is bound by any finding of the CC to the effect that there is no relevant public interest consideration.[30] The Secretary of State is also bound by any findings made by the CC in relation to the existence or otherwise of an SLC.[31] However, the Secretary of State is not bound by the findings of the CC on whether the merger may be expected to operate against the public interest in situations in which the CC has found that a relevant public interest consideration is applicable, although in determining what remedy, if any, to apply, the Secretary of State 'shall, in particular, have regard to the report of the [CC]'.[32]

A separate regime relating to enforcement in respect of public interest and special public interest merger cases is established under the terms of section 85 EA 02, which makes reference to Schedule 7. Although the regime established in Schedule 7 is similar to the generalised system, making provision for pre-emptive undertakings and orders,[33] undertakings in lieu of reference,[34] restrictions following a reference[35] and final undertakings and orders,[36] there are a number of technical differences which take into account the role of the Secretary of State in these cases. These provisions will be dealt with here in outline only, with the focus being on the differences from the generalised regime.

Where an intervention notice is in force, the Secretary of State may adopt any undertaking accepted by the OFT under section 71 where this remains in force at the time of the adoption, but the Secretary of State may also, for the purposes

[28] 'Defence' has here the same meaning as in the Official Secrets Act 1989, s 2.
[29] S 54(4) EA 02.
[30] S 54(6) EA 02.
[31] S 54(7) EA 02.
[32] S 55(3) EA 02.
[33] Sched 7, paras 1–2.
[34] Ibid, paras 3–6.
[35] Ibid, paras 7–8.
[36] Ibid, paras 9–11.

of preventing pre-emptive action, accept such undertakings as s/he considers appropriate. In this context '"pre-emptive action" means action which might prejudice the reference or possible reference . . . or impede the taking of any action under this Part which may be justified by the Secretary of State's decisions on the reference'.[37] Clearly, given that the considerations raised by public and special public interest merger cases go wider than pure competition concerns, undertakings sought under this paragraph may also be designed to address the wider considerations that prompt the public interest concerns. Similarly under paragraph 2 the Secretary of State (or the OFT) may, where an intervention notice or special intervention notice, is in force, make an order for the purpose of preventing pre-emptive action. Undertakings and orders falling within paragraph 1 or 2 shall cease to be in force when the intervention or special intervention notice ceases to be in force, if they have not already lapsed.

Under paragraph 3 of Schedule 7, the Secretary of State may accept an undertaking in lieu of making a reference:

> for the purpose of remedying, mitigating or preventing any of the effects adverse to the public interest which have or may have resulted, or which may be expected to result, from the creation of the relevant merger situation or (as the case may be) the special merger situation concerned.

The Secretary of State is bound to accept the decisions of the OFT included in its section 44 report[38] so far as they relate to the existence of the merger situation and any SLC, but is not so restricted in relation to the assessment of the relevant public interest consideration. Where any such undertaking has been accepted and remains in force no reference shall be made to the CC in respect of the merger situation.[39] Orders may also be made by the Secretary of State in circumstances in which s/he considers that an undertaking accepted by him under paragraph 3 is not being or will not be fulfilled.[40]

Paragraph 7 of Schedule 7 puts in place a number of statutory restrictions on the activities of relevant parties following the making of any reference under sections 45(2), (3) or 62(2) EA 02 where no undertakings or orders are in force. These standstill provisions prohibit any relevant person, without the Secretary of State's consent, from: completing any outstanding matters in connection with arrangements which have resulted in the relevant enterprises ceasing to be distinct; making further arrangements in consequence of that result, unless these reverse the result; and transferring the ownership or control of any enterprise to which the reference relates.

[37] Sched 7 para 1, EA 02.

[38] Sched 7 para 3(3)(a) EA 02.

[39] Sched 7 para 4(1). The same limitations apply as for the general regime, ie the undertaking must be based upon complete and accurate information.

[40] Sched 7, para 5(1). Para 6 further states that an order may be made to prevent any action which may prejudice the making of an order under para 5.

The Secretary of State may also accept final undertakings or make orders following the conclusion of a relevant merger reference. As with the general regime such undertakings or orders may contain wide terms, and these are widened further in respect of public and special public interest cases. Thus paragraph 10(4) provides that, in addition to anything permitted by Schedule 8,[41] any order may contain 'such supplementary, consequential or incidental provision as the Secretary of State considers appropriate'.

INTERACTION WITH THE ECMR—SECTIONS 67–68 EA 02

As discussed in Chapter 3, the ECMR makes provision for mergers affecting certain interests to be referred to relevant Member States, notwithstanding the fact that they meet the criteria set out in relation to a concentration having a Community dimension. The invocation of Article 21(4) ECMR is not dependent upon the consent of the EC Commission, such that the Member State concerned may act unilaterally, although the EC Commission may challenge the use of this power if it believes that intervention is not justified. Such action may be taken only in respect of the relevant considerations, and not on competition grounds.[42]

Section 67 EA 02 relates to the role of the Secretary of State in issuing 'European intervention notices'. These may be issued in relation to matters falling within Article 21(4) ECMR in the circumstances set out in sub-section (1). This specifies that:

> (1) Subsection (2) applies where—
>
> (a) the Secretary of State has reasonable grounds for suspecting that it is or may be the case that—
>
> (i) a relevant merger situation has been created or that arrangements are in progress or in contemplation which, if carried into effect, will result in the creation of a relevant merger situation; and
>
> (ii) a concentration with a Community dimension (within the meaning of the EC Merger Regulation, or a part of such a concentration, has thereby arisen or will thereby arise;
>
> (b) a reference is prevented from being made under section 22 or 33 in relation to the relevant merger situation concerned (whether or not there would otherwise have been a duty to make such a reference) by virtue of Community law or anything done under or in accordance with it; and
>
> (c) the Secretary of State is considering whether to take appropriate measures to protect legitimate interests as permitted by article 21(4) of the EC Merger Regulation.[43]

[41] See further Chap 16, above.

[42] See, eg, the Enterprise Act 2002 (Protection of legitimate interests) Order 2003, SI 2003/1592, reg 5.

[43] As amended by the EC Merger Control (Consequential Amendments) Regulations 2004, SI 2004/1079, and the Communications Act 2003.

European intervention notices are to be issued to the OFT in situations in which the Secretary of State believes that one or more public interest considerations are relevant to a European merger and that a relevant merger situation as defined within the EA 02 has been or is likely to be created.[44] The Secretary of State may, under section 68 EA 02, take such measures as are necessary to 'remedy, mitigate or prevent effects adverse to the public interest which have resulted from, or may be expected to result from, the creation of a European relevant merger situation'.[45] Further provision in relation to European intervention notices is made in the Enterprise Act 2002 (Protection of legitimate interests) Order 2003. In situations in which the Secretary of State has given a European intervention notice the OFT is required to report to the Secretary of State within a time limit specified by the Secretary of State.[46] Having received the report of the OFT the Secretary of State may make a reference to the CC if s/he believes that a European relevant merger situation has been created, one or more of the public interest considerations mentioned in the notice is relevant, and:

> taking account only of the relevant public interest consideration or considerations concerned, the creation of that situation operates or may be expected to operate against the public interest.[47]

Save for the omission of references to the determination of questions relating to any SLC, the provisions relating to European intervention notices are similar to those made under the public or special public interest notices set out above.

[44] S 67(2) EA 02.
[45] S 68(1) EA 02.
[46] SI 2003/1592 Reg 4. The requirements of the report are set out in the reg. Where the merger is a media merger a report may also be made by Ofcom.
[47] SI 2003/1592, above n 42, reg 5(3)(c).

18

Appeals and third party rights

INTRODUCTION

JUDICIAL INVOLVEMENT AND the assertion of third party rights are areas of merger control in the UK in respect of which the EA 02 made substantial strides when compared to the position that arose under the FTA 73. Judicial review was available under the FTA 73 and on rare occasions was resorted to,[1] but there were no other specific routes of appeal set out on the face of the legislation. In the EA 02 this position is remedied, and the CAT has been given the important role to hear appeals from those able to establish the necessary standing in respect of decisions made by the OFT, Secretary of State, or CC as the case may be. Clearly this includes the merging parties, but may also include customers, competitors and other interested bodies. At the time of writing only a small number of appeals have been dealt with—all of which are discussed in this chapter—but this is already a greater number than would have proceeded to judicial review in any equivalent period under the operation of the FTA 73. The EA 02 also gives explicit third party rights in relation to undertakings accepted by either the OFT or the CC, and orders made by those authorities. Such rights are enforceable before the civil courts. These are considered briefly at the end of this chapter.

APPEALS

Section 120 EA 2002 makes provision for the bringing forward of appeals in relation to relevant decisions:

> (1) Any person aggrieved by a decision of the OFT, the Secretary of State or the Commission may under this Part in connection with a reference or possible reference

[1] See, eg, *Interbrew SA v Competition Commission and the Secretary of State for Trade and Industry* [2001] EWHC Admin 367, [2001] UKCLR 954. In this case the applicant was successful in overturning a decision of the Secretary of State made on the basis of a report by the CC on the ground that it had not been given a proper opportunity during the course of the CC inquiry to comment on of the remedies proposed by the CC. For a critique of the approach adopted by the CC in this case see L Coppi and P Dobson, 'The Importance of Market Conduct in the Economic Analysis of Mergers—The Interbrew Saga' [2002] *ECLR* 386.

> in relation to a relevant merger situation or a special merger situation may apply to the Competition Appeal Tribunal for a review of that decision.

Section 120(4) provides that:

> In determining such an application the Competition Appeal Tribunal shall apply the same principles as would be applied by a court on an application for judicial review.

The CAT has the power under section 120(5) to: dismiss the application; quash the whole or part of the contested decision; and in the latter case may remit the matter to the decision-maker with a direction to reconsider the matter, and to make a new decision taking the ruling of the CAT into account. A further appeal, on a point of law only, may be made from the CAT to the appropriate court—the Court of Appeal or, in the case of Tribunal proceedings in Scotland, the Court of Session.

'Decision' does not include a decision relating to the imposition of penalties made as part of the enforcement process, but does expressly include 'a failure to take a decision permitted by this Part in connection with a reference or possible reference'.[2] In the case of a party to a merger the time limit within which to appeal is one month. In the case of a third party it is one month from the date of the publication of the decision.[3] Schedule 3 to the Act provides for Tribunal Rules that may, inter alia, permit the CAT to reject proceedings if it appears to it that the persons bringing them do not have sufficient interest in a decision, or where it believes that the appeal is vexatious. As of July 2006 the CAT has only once rejected an application to intervene in an appeal against a merger decision on the ground that the applicant had insufficient interest. This arose in the context of the *Somerfield* challenge.[4] In the course of its assessment of the competitive effects of the merger the CC had relied on 'diversion ratios'.[5] When the appeal was launched a third party, Vue Entertainment Holdings (UK) Ltd, was engaged in a merger that was also being reviewed by the CC, and Vue believed that the CC would employ the same techniques as it had in the Somerfield merger, and sought to participate in the *Somerfield* appeal.[6] Sir Christopher Bellamy, the Chairman of the CAT, rejected the application in a very short ruling, holding that Vue was not engaged in the grocery market, had played no part in the inquiry, did not represent any other companies and was not an association that represented general interests 'or anything of that kind'.[7] This implies therefore that appeals may come not only from those who are the subject of the inquiry, but also from those who participate in the inquiry, are

[2] S 120(2)(b) of the EA 02.

[3] CAT Rules 2003, SI 2003/1372, r 26.

[4] *Somerfield plc v Competition Commission* [2005] CAT 37, [2006] CompAR 266 (see below).

[5] See Chap 11, above.

[6] Concluded as *Vue Entertainment Holdings (UK) Ltd and A3 Cinema Limited: A report on the completed acquisition of A3 Cinema Limited by Vue Entertainment Holdings (UK) Ltd*, 24 Feb 2006.

[7] Ibid, at para 3.

involved to a significant degree in the relevant industry or market, and who represent more general interests.[8]

IBA v OFT[9]

The leading case at the time of writing relating to the rights of appeal, and the standard under which the review will be carried out, is *OFT v IBA*.[10] In this case the Court of Appeal dealt with an appeal from an earlier judgment of the CAT,[11] and 'took issue with the CAT's interpretation of the test under s 33(1) [EA 02] but largely agreed with the CAT's approach to review of the OFT's merger decisions'.[12] The *IBA* case has been discussed in Chapter 14 in so far as it deals with the test to be adopted by the OFT when determining whether or not to make a reference to the CC under section 22 or 33 EA 02. It will be recalled that the OFT declined to make a merger reference in respect of a merger arising in relation to the supply of IT systems to the healthcare industry. Following an appeal the CAT held that the OFT had erred in setting too high a standard, and that in 'grey areas' should refer. An important question considered in the case was that of the standard of review to be applied by the CAT under section 120 EA 02.

The CAT admitted in this respect that it did 'not find it entirely easy to interpret the duty imposed' under section 120(4). The CAT noted that judicial review principles vary depending on the context in which the judicial review is heard. In the present case the Tribunal held that the *Wednesbury* test,[13] which relates primarily to the way in which discretion is exercised, was not the appropriate one. Rather the issue was 'whether the OFT has complied with a duty, and in particular whether the OFT acted unlawfully in taking the view that the underlying circumstances giving rise to the duty were not present'.[14] The CAT found that the OFT did not apply the right test, could not reasonably have excluded the alternative view, and that the facts were not sufficiently found in the decision. The OFT and the merging parties applied for leave to appeal, and

[8] This approach would be consistent with the approach taken in respect of challenges to market investigation reference decisions under the Act. Eg, the CAT accepted an application in respect of the OFT decision (later rescinded) not to launch an investigation into the supermarket industry from a trade group representative, and Friends of the Earth: *Association of Convenience Stores, supported by Friends of the Earth v OFT* [2005] CAT 36, [2006] CompAR 183.

[9] See C Brown, 'IBA Health: The First Challenge Under the New UK Merger Regime' [2003] *Comp Law* 347.

[10] *OFT v IBA Health Ltd* [2004] EWCA Civ 142, [2004] UKCLR 683.

[11] *IBA Health Ltd v OFT, supported by iSOFT plc and Torex plc* [2003] CAT 27, [2004] CompAR 235.

[12] C Brown, 'IBA Health: The First Challenge Under the New UK Merger Regime' [2003] *Comp Law* 289 at 359. See also F Alese, 'UK Merger Review and S 33: Was the CAT Not Right?' [2004] *ECLR* 470.

[13] *Associated Provincial Picture Houses v Wednesbury Corporation* [1948] 1 KB 223, [1947] 2 All ER 680.

[14] Above n 11, at para 223.

although the CAT took the view that these 'had no reasonable prospects of success' permission was given 'on the basis only that this was the first case under the Act and that important issues had been raised'.[15]

The Court of Appeal dismissed the OFT's appeal, and the Vice Chancellor, in the leading judgment, found that the CAT had not erred in its determination of the role it had to play in reviewing OFT actions in relation to merger control. The Vice Chancellor held that the standard of review to be applied was that of the normal principles of judicial review, and noted that *if* the CAT had meant that its role was other than that it would have erred.[16] At paragraph 64 the Vice Chancellor held that:

> I do not consider that the Tribunal adopted the wrong standard of unreasonableness when seeking to apply the *Wednesbury* test. They were considering a different question; whether if there are two or more tenable views as to the likelihood of a SLC the OFT was reasonable to reject that which produced an affirmative answer.

Carnwarth LJ was less charitable in his view of the meaning to be attributed to the CAT's choice of words in its judgment.[17]

UniChem Limited v OFT[18]

In *UniChem* the OFT took the decision not to refer the *Phoenix Healthcare Distribution Ltd/East Anglian Pharmaceuticals Ltd* merger, in which the relevant market was that of full- and short-line wholesaling of pharmaceuticals to

[15] *IBA Health Ltd v OFT,* above n 11, para 66.

[16] At para 60 the V-C said, '[p]lainly, unreasonableness in the ordinary and natural meaning of the word is different from *Wednesbury* unreasonableness. If the Tribunal were seeking to apply the former meaning as the test of *Wednesbury* unreasonableness they were wrong to do so. But, once again, I do not think that a fair reading of their judgment leads to that conclusion'.

[17] At para 90, eg, he stated that:

> 'the Tribunal were right to observe that their approach should reflect the "specific context" in which it had been created as a specialised tribunal (at para [224]); but they wrong to suggest that this permitted them to discard established case-law relating to "reasonableness" in administrative law, in favour of the "ordinary and natural meaning" of that word.'

He concluded that:

> 'the Tribunal did not need to rely on some special dispensation from the ordinary principles of judicial review. Those principles, whether applied by a court or a specialised tribunal, are flexible enough to be adapted to the particular statutory context. No doubt the existence of such a special jurisdiction will help to ensure consistency from case to case; and the expertise of the Tribunal will better fit it to deal with such cases expeditiously and with a full understanding of the technical background. However, the essential question was no different from that which would have faced a court dealing with the same subject matter. That question was whether the material relied on by the OFT could reasonably be regarded as dispelling the uncertainties highlighted by the issues letter. That question was wholly suitable for evaluation by a court. It involved no policy or political judgment, such as would be regarded as inappropriate for review by the Administrative Court': ibid, at para 100.

[18] [2005] CAT 8. See M Lester, '*UniChem Limited v Office of Fair Trading*' [2005] *Comp Law* 99.

retail pharmacies and dispensing doctors. Although it had clearly been concerned about the effects of the merger during the procedure leading up to the issuing of its decision not to refer announced on 17 December 2004, the essence of the Decision taken was that competition was possible post-merger. UniChem, not a party to the merger, appealed on four grounds: (1) the decision was irrational and unjustified, and/or a misconstruction of the role of the OFT under section 33 EA 02; (2) the OFT's reasons not to refer were insufficient and did not dispel the serious likelihood of a substantial lessening of competition; (3) a number of unresolved issues of material fact were outstanding, and it was irrational or unreasonable of the OFT to purport to resolve those issues the way it did; (4) the OFT failed to take into account its previous decisions, and acted inconsistently. The OFT argued that it had a wide discretion as to the evaluation of the facts, and in forming a view about SLC.

The CAT held there was a limit to which the power of evaluation of facts might undermine the duty of the OFT, and that section 33(1) is concerned with a judgment of facts, not with policy or political issues.[19] The first question for the Tribunal was whether the OFT had properly evaluated the primary facts of the case; the second question was whether, on those facts, the OFT was entitled to draw the conclusion that there was an insufficient likelihood of SLC.[20] The issue in the present case turned on the first question, and the review carried out under section 120 EA 02 was to be limited to the legality of the decision within the framework in which it was taken. The CAT held that where an issues letter has been issued, as had been the case here, and then shortly afterwards the decision was taken not to refer, it must be shown that the requisite likelihood of SLC has been removed, and that the material relied on by the OFT can reasonably be regarded as dispelling the uncertainties highlighted in the issues letter. This is to say that the CAT felt bound to inquire whether the rejection of the hypotheses in the issues letter was justified.[21]

The OFT had, the CAT found, failed to give UniChem the opportunity to comment on information on which it intended to rely, and as a general principle the CAT held that where on an important issue the arguments advanced by merging party A depended on primary facts and matters that are within the knowledge of B it would normally be appropriate for the OFT to check with B the primary facts and to seek B's comments on the points raised, if they were to be relied upon.[22] The failure to do this in the particular circumstances of this case resulted in a fatal procedural failure, and the decision was in part quashed and remitted back to the OFT for reconsideration.[23]

[19] Above n 18, para 171.
[20] Ibid, para 173.
[21] Ibid, para 201.
[22] Ibid, para 268.
[23] The OFT made a second decision in June 2005 not to refer the case to the CC: *Anticipated acquisition by Phoenix Healthcare Distribution Limited of East Anglian Pharmaceuticals Limited*, 29 June 2005.

Somerfield plc v Competition Commission[24]

In *Somerfield plc and Wm Morrison Supermarkets plc*[25] the CC found the acquisition by Somerfield of 115 former Safeway stores to lead to SLC in 12 local markets, and ordered divestiture. This was the first case following the entry into force of the EA 02 in which a CC decision was challenged. The CAT applied the same reasoning as it had in *UniChem*,[26] and found that in making its report the CC had a great deal of evidence before it, and that Somerfield had advanced no detailed case to the effect that the CC's report was against the weight of, or unsupported by, the evidence.[27] The CAT held that in relation to merger control, where matters had to be determined within strict time limits, it would be extremely reluctant to entertain section 120 applications based on lack or misinterpretation of evidence unless the groundwork was properly laid out in the application before it.[28] There was no suggestion in the present case that the CC did not give Somerfield the proper opportunity to deal with its concerns or that it failed accurately to summarise the arguments it was putting forward.[29] The onus was on Somerfield to show that it was unreasonable for the CC to rely on the evidence before it in order to reach its conclusions, and in this respect Somerfield failed.[30]

Celesio AG v OFT, supported by Boots Group plc and Alliance UniChem plc[31]

In this case it was common ground that Celesio AG had the right to appeal in relation to a decision taken by the OFT not to refer to the CC a transaction under which Boots Group PLC would acquire some 958 pharmacies from UniChem. Celesio AG was active in the market, and was a participant in the investigation, in that it responded to a questionnaire sent to it by the OFT and also submitted further comments, both in writing and at a meeting. Celesio then argued that the OFT had erred in its competitive assessment, relying too heavily on a fascia reduction test to assess local competition. It also claimed that the undertakings that the OFT sought in lieu of a remedy were insufficient to address the competition concerns that were identified by the OFT. The appeal was rejected on the grounds that it was reasonable for the OFT to take the

[24] [2006] CAT 4.
[25] *Somerfield plc and Wm Morrison Supermarkets plc, a report on the acquisition by Somerfield plc of 115 stores from Wm Morrison Supermarkets plc*, Sept 2005.
[26] Above n 18.
[27] Ibid n 24, para 130.
[28] Ibid, para 131.
[29] Ibid, para 133.
[30] Ibid, para 140.
[31] [2006] CAT 9. An appeal from the OFT decision taken on 6 Feb 2006 in *Alliance UniChem Plc and Boots Group PLC.*

approach it had to the fascia reduction,[32] and that it was not unreasonable for the OFT to have arrived at its conclusions without considering the share of the market held by each outlet.[33]

THIRD PARTY RIGHTS

The right of third parties generally to challenge decisions taken in respect of the operation of the UK merger regime has been discussed above. Sections 94 and 95 EA 02 give specific rights to third parties to enforce respectively undertakings and orders,[34] and statutory restrictions.[35] Section 94(2) EA 02 provides that 'any person to whom such an undertaking or order relates shall have a duty to comply with it', and section 94(3) EA 02 that the duty 'is owed to any person who may be affected by a contravention'. The OFT, CC or Secretary of State has the power to bring civil proceedings in respect of undertakings accepted or orders made by them. These powers however do not prejudice the rights of any person to bring an action in respect of '[a]ny breach of the duty which causes such a person to sustain loss or damage'.[36] Section 95 EA 02 sets out a similar provision in respect of statutory restrictions on dealings arising under sections 77(2) (3) or 78(2) EA 02.[37] At the time of writing no such actions have been brought.

[32] Ibid, para 178.
[33] Ibid, para 179.
[34] See Chaps 14, 15 and 16, above.
[35] See Chap 15, above.
[36] S 94(4) EA 02.
[37] Or under Sched 7, para 8(2), EA 02.

Appendix 1

COUNCIL REGULATION (EC) No 139/2004 of 20 January 2004 on the control of concentrations between undertakings (the EC Merger Regulation)[1]

(Text with EEA relevance)

THE COUNCIL OF THE EUROPEAN UNION,

Having regard to the Treaty establishing the European Community, and in particular Articles 83 and 308 thereof,

Having regard to the proposal from the Commission,

Having regard to the opinion of the European Parliament,

Having regard to the opinion of the European Economic and Social Committee,

Whereas:

(1) Council Regulation (EEC) No 4064/89 of 21 December 1989 on the control of concentrations between undertakings (4) has been substantially amended. Since further amendments are to be made, it should be recast in the interest of clarity.

(2) For the achievement of the aims of the Treaty, Article 3(1)(g) gives the Community the objective of instituting a system ensuring that competition in the internal market is not distorted. Article 4(1) of the Treaty provides that the activities of the Member States and the Community are to be conducted in accordance with the principle of an open market economy with free competition. These principles are essential for the further development of the internal market.

(3) The completion of the internal market and of economic and monetary union, the enlargement of the European Union and the lowering of international barriers to trade and investment will continue to result in major corporate reorganisations, particularly in the form of concentrations.

(4) Such reorganisations are to be welcomed to the extent that they are in line with the requirements of dynamic competition and capable of increasing the competitiveness of European industry, improving the conditions of growth and raising the standard of living in the Community.

(5) However, it should be ensured that the process of reorganisation does not result in lasting damage to competition; Community law must therefore include provisions

[1] [2004] OJ L 24/1.

governing those concentrations which may significantly impede effective competition in the common market or in a substantial part of it.

(6) A specific legal instrument is therefore necessary to permit effective control of all concentrations in terms of their effect on the structure of competition in the Community and to be the only instrument applicable to such concentrations. Regulation (EEC) No 4064/89 has allowed a Community policy to develop in this field. In the light of experience, however, that Regulation should now be recast into legislation designed to meet the challenges of a more integrated market and the future enlargement of the European Union. In accordance with the principles of subsidiarity and of proportionality as set out in Article 5 of the Treaty, this Regulation does not go beyond what is necessary in order to achieve the objective of ensuring that competition in the common market is not distorted, in accordance with the principle of an open market economy with free competition.

(7) Articles 81 and 82, while applicable, according to the case-law of the Court of Justice, to certain concentrations, are not sufficient to control all operations which may prove to be incompatible with the system of undistorted competition envisaged in the Treaty. This Regulation should therefore be based not only on Article 83 but, principally, on Article 308 of the Treaty, under which the Community may give itself the additional powers of action necessary for the attainment of its objectives, and also powers of action with regard to concentrations on the markets for agricultural products listed in Annex I to the Treaty.

(8) The provisions to be adopted in this Regulation should apply to significant structural changes, the impact of which on the market goes beyond the national borders of any one Member State. Such concentrations should, as a general rule, be reviewed exclusively at Community level, in application of a 'one-stop shop' system and in compliance with the principle of subsidiarity. Concentrations not covered by this Regulation come, in principle, within the jurisdiction of the Member States.

(9) The scope of application of this Regulation should be defined according to the geographical area of activity of the undertakings concerned and be limited by quantitative thresholds in order to cover those concentrations which have a Community dimension. The Commission should report to the Council on the implementation of the applicable thresholds and criteria so that the Council, acting in accordance with Article 202 of the Treaty, is in a position to review them regularly, as well as the rules regarding prenotification referral, in the light of the experience gained; this requires statistical data to be provided by the Member States to the Commission to enable it to prepare such reports and possible proposals for amendments. The Commission's reports and proposals should be based on relevant information regularly provided by the Member States.

(10) A concentration with a Community dimension should be deemed to exist where the aggregate turnover of the undertakings concerned exceeds given thresholds; that is the case irrespective of whether or not the undertakings effecting the concentration have their seat or their principal fields of activity in the Community, provided they have substantial operations there.

(11) The rules governing the referral of concentrations from the Commission to Member States and from Member States to the Commission should operate as an effective corrective mechanism in the light of the principle of subsidiarity; these rules protect the

competition interests of the Member States in an adequate manner and take due account of legal certainty and the 'one-stop shop' principle.

(12) Concentrations may qualify for examination under a number of national merger control systems if they fall below the turnover thresholds referred to in this Regulation. Multiple notification of the same transaction increases legal uncertainty, effort and cost for undertakings and may lead to conflicting assessments. The system whereby concentrations may be referred to the Commission by the Member States concerned should therefore be further developed.

(13) The Commission should act in close and constant liaison with the competent authorities of the Member States from which it obtains comments and information.

(14) The Commission and the competent authorities of the Member States should together form a network of public authorities, applying their respective competences in close cooperation, using efficient arrangements for information- sharing and consultation, with a view to ensuring that a case is dealt with by the most appropriate authority, in the light of the principle of subsidiarity and with a view to ensuring that multiple notifications of a given concentration are avoided to the greatest extent possible. Referrals of concentrations from the Commission to Member States and from Member States to the Commission should be made in an efficient manner avoiding, to the greatest extent possible, situations where a concentration is subject to a referral both before and after its notification.

(15) The Commission should be able to refer to a Member State notified concentrations with a Community dimension which threaten significantly to affect competition in a market within that Member State presenting all the characteristics of a distinct market. Where the concentration affects competition on such a market, which does not constitute a substantial part of the common market, the Commission should be obliged, upon request, to refer the whole or part of the case to the Member State concerned. A Member State should be able to refer to the Commission a concentration which does not have a Community dimension but which affects trade between Member States and threatens to significantly affect competition within its territory. Other Member States which are also competent to review the concentration should be able to join the request. In such a situation, in order to ensure the efficiency and predictability of the system, national time limits should be suspended until a decision has been reached as to the referral of the case. The Commission should have the power to examine and deal with a concentration on behalf of a requesting Member State or requesting Member States.

(16) The undertakings concerned should be granted the possibility of requesting referrals to or from the Commission before a concentration is notified so as to further improve the efficiency of the system for the control of concentrations within the Community. In such situations, the Commission and national competition authorities should decide within short, clearly defined time limits whether a referral to or from the Commission ought to be made, thereby ensuring the efficiency of the system. Upon request by the undertakings concerned, the Commission should be able to refer to a Member State a concentration with a Community dimension which may significantly affect competition in a market within that Member State presenting all the characteristics of a distinct market; the undertakings concerned should not, however, be required to demonstrate that the effects of the concentration would be detrimental to competition. A concentration

should not be referred from the Commission to a Member State which has expressed its disagreement to such a referral. Before notification to national authorities, the undertakings concerned should also be able to request that a concentration without a Community dimension which is capable of being reviewed under the national competition laws of at least three Member States be referred to the Commission. Such requests for pre-notification referrals to the Commission would be particularly pertinent in situations where the concentration would affect competition beyond the territory of one Member State. Where a concentration capable of being reviewed under the competition laws of three or more Member States is referred to the Commission prior to any national notification, and no Member State competent to review the case expresses its disagreement, the Commission should acquire exclusive competence to review the concentration and such a concentration should be deemed to have a Community dimension. Such pre-notification referrals from Member States to the Commission should not, however, be made where at least one Member State competent to review the case has expressed its disagreement with such a referral.

(17) The Commission should be given exclusive competence to apply this Regulation, subject to review by the Court of Justice.

(18) The Member States should not be permitted to apply their national legislation on competition to concentrations with a Community dimension, unless this Regulation makes provision therefor. The relevant powers of national authorities should be limited to cases where, failing intervention by the Commission, effective competition is likely to be significantly impeded within the territory of a Member State and where the competition interests of that Member State cannot be sufficiently protected otherwise by this Regulation. The Member States concerned must act promptly in such cases; this Regulation cannot, because of the diversity of national law, fix a single time limit for the adoption of final decisions under national law.

(19) Furthermore, the exclusive application of this Regulation to concentrations with a Community dimension is without prejudice to Article 296 of the Treaty, and does not prevent the Member States from taking appropriate measures to protect legitimate interests other than those pursued by this Regulation, provided that such measures are compatible with the general principles and other provisions of Community law.

(20) It is expedient to define the concept of concentration in such a manner as to cover operations bringing about a lasting change in the control of the undertakings concerned and therefore in the structure of the market. It is therefore appropriate to include, within the scope of this Regulation, all joint ventures performing on a lasting basis all the functions of an autonomous economic entity. It is moreover appropriate to treat as a single concentration transactions that are closely connected in that they are linked by condition or take the form of a series of transactions in securities taking place within a reasonably short period of time.

(21) This Regulation should also apply where the undertakings concerned accept restrictions directly related to, and necessary for, the implementation of the concentration. Commission decisions declaring concentrations compatible with the common market in application of this Regulation should automatically cover such restrictions, without the Commission having to assess such restrictions in individual cases. At the request of the undertakings concerned, however, the Commission should, in cases presenting novel or

unresolved questions giving rise to genuine uncertainty, expressly assess whether or not any restriction is directly related to, and necessary for, the implementation of the concentration. A case presents a novel or unresolved question giving rise to genuine uncertainty if the question is not covered by the relevant Commission notice in force or a published Commission decision.

(22) The arrangements to be introduced for the control of concentrations should, without prejudice to Article 86(2) of the Treaty, respect the principle of non-discrimination between the public and the private sectors. In the public sector, calculation of the turnover of an undertaking concerned in a concentration needs, therefore, to take account of undertakings making up an economic unit with an independent power of decision, irrespective of the way in which their capital is held or of the rules of administrative supervision applicable to them.

(23) It is necessary to establish whether or not concentrations with a Community dimension are compatible with the common market in terms of the need to maintain and develop effective competition in the common market. In so doing, the Commission must place its appraisal within the general framework of the achievement of the fundamental objectives referred to in Article 2 of the Treaty establishing the European Community and Article 2 of the Treaty on European Union.

(24) In order to ensure a system of undistorted competition in the common market, in furtherance of a policy conducted in accordance with the principle of an open market economy with free competition, this Regulation must permit effective control of all concentrations from the point of view of their effect on competition in the Community. Accordingly, Regulation (EEC) No 4064/89 established the principle that a concentration with a Community dimension which creates or strengthens a dominant position as a result of which effective competition in the common market or in a substantial part of it would be significantly impeded should be declared incompatible with the common market.

(25) In view of the consequences that concentrations in oligopolistic market structures may have, it is all the more necessary to maintain effective competition in such markets. Many oligopolistic markets exhibit a healthy degree of competition. However, under certain circumstances, concentrations involving the elimination of important competitive constraints that the merging parties had exerted upon each other, as well as a reduction of competitive pressure on the remaining competitors, may, even in the absence of a likelihood of coordination between the members of the oligopoly, result in a significant impediment to effective competition. The Community courts have, however, not to date expressly interpreted Regulation (EEC) No 4064/89 as requiring concentrations giving rise to such non-coordinated effects to be declared incompatible with the common market. Therefore, in the interests of legal certainty, it should be made clear that this Regulation permits effective control of all such concentrations by providing that any concentration which would significantly impede effective competition, in the common market or in a substantial part of it, should be declared incompatible with the common market. The notion of 'significant impediment to effective competition' in Article 2(2) and (3) should be interpreted as extending, beyond the concept of dominance, only to the anti-competitive effects of a concentration resulting from the non-coordinated behaviour of undertakings which would not have a dominant position on the market concerned.

(26) A significant impediment to effective competition generally results from the creation or strengthening of a dominant position. With a view to preserving the guidance that may be drawn from past judgments of the European courts and Commission decisions pursuant to Regulation (EEC) No 4064/89, while at the same time maintaining consistency with the standards of competitive harm which have been applied by the Commission and the Community courts regarding the compatibility of a concentration with the common market, this Regulation should accordingly establish the principle that a concentration with a Community dimension which would significantly impede effective competition, in the common market or in a substantial part thereof, in particular as a result of the creation or strengthening of a dominant position, is to be declared incompatible with the common market.

(27) In addition, the criteria of Article 81(1) and (3) of the Treaty should be applied to joint ventures performing, on a lasting basis, all the functions of autonomous economic entities, to the extent that their creation has as its consequence an appreciable restriction of competition between undertakings that remain independent.

(28) In order to clarify and explain the Commission's appraisal of concentrations under this Regulation, it is appropriate for the Commission to publish guidance which should provide a sound economic framework for the assessment of concentrations with a view to determining whether or not they may be declared compatible with the common market.

(29) In order to determine the impact of a concentration on competition in the common market, it is appropriate to take account of any substantiated and likely efficiencies put forward by the undertakings concerned. It is possible that the efficiencies brought about by the concentration counteract the effects on competition, and in particular the potential harm to consumers, that it might otherwise have and that, as a consequence, the concentration would not significantly impede effective competition, in the common market or in a substantial part of it, in particular as a result of the creation or strengthening of a dominant position. The Commission should publish guidance on the conditions under which it may take efficiencies into account in the assessment of a concentration.

(30) Where the undertakings concerned modify a notified concentration, in particular by offering commitments with a view to rendering the concentration compatible with the common market, the Commission should be able to declare the concentration, as modified, compatible with the common market. Such commitments should be proportionate to the competition problem and entirely eliminate it. It is also appropriate to accept commitments before the initiation of proceedings where the competition problem is readily identifiable and can easily be remedied. It should be expressly provided that the Commission may attach to its decision conditions and obligations in order to ensure that the undertakings concerned comply with their commitments in a timely and effective manner so as to render the concentration compatible with the common market. Transparency and effective consultation of Member States as well as of interested third parties should be ensured throughout the procedure.

(31) The Commission should have at its disposal appropriate instruments to ensure the enforcement of commitments and to deal with situations where they are not fulfilled. In cases of failure to fulfil a condition attached to the decision declaring a concentration compatible with the common market, the situation rendering the concentration

compatible with the common market does not materialise and the concentration, as implemented, is therefore not authorised by the Commission. As a consequence, if the concentration is implemented, it should be treated in the same way as a non-notified concentration implemented without authorisation. Furthermore, where the Commission has already found that, in the absence of the condition, the concentration would be incompatible with the common market, it should have the power to directly order the dissolution of the concentration, so as to restore the situation prevailing prior to the implementation of the concentration. Where an obligation attached to a decision declaring the concentration compatible with the common market is not fulfilled, the Commission should be able to revoke its decision. Moreover, the Commission should be able to impose appropriate financial sanctions where conditions or obligations are not fulfilled.

(32) Concentrations which, by reason of the limited market share of the undertakings concerned, are not liable to impede effective competition may be presumed to be compatible with the common market. Without prejudice to Articles 81 and 82 of the Treaty, an indication to this effect exists, in particular, where the market share of the undertakings concerned does not exceed 25 % either in the common market or in a substantial part of it.

(33) The Commission should have the task of taking all the decisions necessary to establish whether or not concentrations with a Community dimension are compatible with the common market, as well as decisions designed to restore the situation prevailing prior to the implementation of a concentration which has been declared incompatible with the common market.

(34) To ensure effective control, undertakings should be obliged to give prior notification of concentrations with a Community dimension following the conclusion of the agreement, the announcement of the public bid or the acquisition of a controlling interest. Notification should also be possible where the undertakings concerned satisfy the Commission of their intention to enter into an agreement for a proposed concentration and demonstrate to the Commission that their plan for that proposed concentration is sufficiently concrete, for example on the basis of an agreement in principle, a memorandum of understanding, or a letter of intent signed by all undertakings concerned, or, in the case of a public bid, where they have publicly announced an intention to make such a bid, provided that the intended agreement or bid would result in a concentration with a Community dimension. The implementation of concentrations should be suspended until a final decision of the Commission has been taken. However, it should be possible to derogate from this suspension at the request of the undertakings concerned, where appropriate. In deciding whether or not to grant a derogation, the Commission should take account of all pertinent factors, such as the nature and gravity of damage to the undertakings concerned or to third parties, and the threat to competition posed by the concentration. In the interest of legal certainty, the validity of transactions must nevertheless be protected as much as necessary.

(35) A period within which the Commission must initiate proceedings in respect of a notified concentration and a period within which it must take a final decision on the compatibility or incompatibility with the common market of that concentration should be laid down. These periods should be extended whenever the undertakings concerned offer commitments with a view to rendering the concentration compatible with the common

market, in order to allow for sufficient time for the analysis and market testing of such commitment offers and for the consultation of Member States as well as interested third parties. A limited extension of the period within which the Commission must take a final decision should also be possible in order to allow sufficient time for the investigation of the case and the verification of the facts and arguments submitted to the Commission.

(36) The Community respects the fundamental rights and observes the principles recognised in particular by the Charter of Fundamental Rights of the European Union. Accordingly, this Regulation should be interpreted and applied with respect to those rights and principles.

(37) The undertakings concerned must be afforded the right to be heard by the Commission when proceedings have been initiated; the members of the management and supervisory bodies and the recognised representatives of the employees of the undertakings concerned, and interested third parties, must also be given the opportunity to be heard.

(38) In order properly to appraise concentrations, the Commission should have the right to request all necessary information and to conduct all necessary inspections throughout the Community. To that end, and with a view to protecting competition effectively, the Commission's powers of investigation need to be expanded. The Commission should, in particular, have the right to interview any persons who may be in possession of useful information and to record the statements made.

(39) In the course of an inspection, officials authorised by the Commission should have the right to ask for any information relevant to the subject matter and purpose of the inspection; they should also have the right to affix seals during inspections, particularly in circumstances where there are reasonable grounds to suspect that a concentration has been implemented without being notified; that incorrect, incomplete or misleading information has been supplied to the Commission; or that the undertakings or persons concerned have failed to comply with a condition or obligation imposed by decision of the Commission. In any event, seals should only be used in exceptional circumstances, for the period of time strictly necessary for the inspection, normally not for more than 48 hours.

(40) Without prejudice to the case-law of the Court of Justice, it is also useful to set out the scope of the control that the national judicial authority may exercise when it authorises, as provided by national law and as a precautionary measure, assistance from law enforcement authorities in order to overcome possible opposition on the part of the undertaking against an inspection, including the affixing of seals, ordered by Commission decision. It results from the case-law that the national judicial authority may in particular ask of the Commission further information which it needs to carry out its control and in the absence of which it could refuse the authorisation. The case-law also confirms the competence of the national courts to control the application of national rules governing the implementation of coercive measures. The competent authorities of the Member States should cooperate actively in the exercise of the Commission's investigative powers.

(41) When complying with decisions of the Commission, the undertakings and persons concerned cannot be forced to admit that they have committed infringements, but they are in any event obliged to answer factual questions and to provide documents, even if

this information may be used to establish against themselves or against others the existence of such infringements.

(42) For the sake of transparency, all decisions of the Commission which are not of a merely procedural nature should be widely publicised. While ensuring preservation of the rights of defence of the undertakings concerned, in particular the right of access to the file, it is essential that business secrets be protected. The confidentiality of information exchanged in the network and with the competent authorities of third countries should likewise be safeguarded.

(43) Compliance with this Regulation should be enforceable, as appropriate, by means of fines and periodic penalty payments. The Court of Justice should be given unlimited jurisdiction in that regard pursuant to Article 229 of the Treaty.

(44) The conditions in which concentrations, involving undertakings having their seat or their principal fields of activity in the Community, are carried out in third countries should be observed, and provision should be made for the possibility of the Council giving the Commission an appropriate mandate for negotiation with a view to obtaining non-discriminatory treatment for such undertakings.

(45) This Regulation in no way detracts from the collective rights of employees, as recognised in the undertakings concerned, notably with regard to any obligation to inform or consult their recognised representatives under Community and national law.

(46) The Commission should be able to lay down detailed rules concerning the implementation of this Regulation in accordance with the procedures for the exercise of implementing powers conferred on the Commission. For the adoption of such implementing provisions, the Commission should be assisted by an Advisory Committee composed of the representatives of the Member States as specified in Article 23,

HAS ADOPTED THIS REGULATION:

Article 1

Scope 1. Without prejudice to Article 4(5) and Article 22, this Regulation shall apply to all concentrations with a Community dimension as defined in this Article.

2. A concentration has a Community dimension where:

(a) the combined aggregate worldwide turnover of all the undertakings concerned is more than EUR 5 000 million; and

(b) the aggregate Community-wide turnover of each of at least two of the undertakings concerned is more than EUR 250 million,

unless each of the undertakings concerned achieves more than two-thirds of its aggregate Community-wide turnover within one and the same Member State.

3. A concentration that does not meet the thresholds laid down in paragraph 2 has a Community dimension where:

(a) the combined aggregate worldwide turnover of all the undertakings concerned is more than EUR 2 500 million;

(b) in each of at least three Member States, the combined aggregate turnover of all the undertakings concerned is more than EUR 100 million;

(c) in each of at least three Member States included for the purpose of point (b), the aggregate turnover of each of at least two of the undertakings concerned is more than EUR 25 million; and

(d) the aggregate Community-wide turnover of each of at least two of the undertakings concerned is more than EUR 100 million,

unless each of the undertakings concerned achieves more than two-thirds of its aggregate Community-wide turnover within one and the same Member State.

4. On the basis of statistical data that may be regularly provided by the Member States, the Commission shall report to the Council on the operation of the thresholds and criteria set out in paragraphs 2 and 3 by 1 July 2009 and may present proposals pursuant to paragraph 5.

5. Following the report referred to in paragraph 4 and on a proposal from the Commission, the Council, acting by a qualified majority, may revise the thresholds and criteria mentioned in paragraph 3.

Article 2

Appraisal of concentrations

1. Concentrations within the scope of this Regulation shall be appraised in accordance with the objectives of this Regulation and the following provisions with a view to establishing whether or not they are compatible with the common market. In making this appraisal, the Commission shall take into account:

(a) the need to maintain and develop effective competition within the common market in view of, among other things, the structure of all the markets concerned and the actual or potential competition from undertakings located either within or outwith the Community;

(b) the market position of the undertakings concerned and their economic and financial power, the alternatives available to suppliers and users, their access to supplies or markets, any legal or other barriers to entry, supply and demand trends for the relevant goods and services, the interests of the intermediate and ultimate consumers, and the development of technical and economic progress provided that it is to consumers' advantage and does not form an obstacle to competition.

2. A concentration which would not significantly impede effective competition in the common market or in a substantial part of it, in particular as a result of the creation or strengthening of a dominant position, shall be declared compatible with the common market.

3. A concentration which would significantly impede effective competition, in the common market or in a substantial part of it, in particular as a result of the creation or strengthening of a dominant position, shall be declared incompatible with the common market.

4. To the extent that the creation of a joint venture constituting a concentration pursuant to Article 3 has as its object or effect the coordination of the competitive behaviour of undertakings that remain independent, such coordination shall be appraised in accordance with the criteria of Article 81(1) and (3) of the Treaty, with a view to establishing whether or not the operation is compatible with the common market.

5. In making this appraisal, the Commission shall take into account in particular:

— whether two or more parent companies retain, to a significant extent, activities in the same market as the joint venture or in a market which is downstream or upstream from that of the joint venture or in a neighbouring market closely related to this market,

— whether the coordination which is the direct consequence of the creation of the joint venture affords the undertakings concerned the possibility of eliminating competition in respect of a substantial part of the products or services in question.

Article 3

Definition of concentration

1. A concentration shall be deemed to arise where a change of control on a lasting basis results from:

(a) the merger of two or more previously independent undertakings or parts of undertakings, or

(b) the acquisition, by one or more persons already controlling at least one undertaking, or by one or more undertakings, whether by purchase of securities or assets, by contract or by any other means, of direct or indirect control of the whole or parts of one or more other undertakings.

2. Control shall be constituted by rights, contracts or any other means which, either separately or in combination and having regard to the considerations of fact or law involved, confer the possibility of exercising decisive influence on an undertaking, in particular by:

(a) ownership or the right to use all or part of the assets of an undertaking;

(b) rights or contracts which confer decisive influence on the composition, voting or decisions of the organs of an undertaking.

3. Control is acquired by persons or undertakings which:

(a) are holders of the rights or entitled to rights under the contracts concerned; or

(b) while not being holders of such rights or entitled to rights under such contracts, have the power to exercise the rights deriving therefrom.

4. The creation of a joint venture performing on a lasting basis all the functions of an autonomous economic entity shall constitute a concentration within the meaning of paragraph 1(b).

5. A concentration shall not be deemed to arise where:

(a) credit institutions or other financial institutions or insurance companies, the normal activities of which include transactions and dealing in securities for their own account or for the account of others, hold on a temporary basis securities which they have acquired in an undertaking with a view to reselling them, provided that they do not exercise voting rights in respect of those securities with a view to determining the competitive behaviour of that undertaking or provided that they exercise such voting rights only with a view to preparing the disposal of all or part of that undertaking or of its assets or the disposal of those securities and that any such disposal takes place within one year of the date of acquisition; that period may be extended by the Commission on request where such institutions or companies can show that the disposal was not reasonably possible within the period set;

(b) control is acquired by an office-holder according to the law of a Member State relating to liquidation, winding up, insolvency, cessation of payments, compositions or analogous proceedings;

(c) the operations referred to in paragraph 1(b) are carried out by the financial holding companies referred to in Article 5(3) of Fourth Council Directive 78/660/EEC of 25 July 1978 based on Article 54(3)(g) of the Treaty on the annual accounts of certain types of companies (1) provided however that the voting rights in respect of the holding are exercised, in particular in relation to the appointment of members of the management and supervisory bodies of the undertakings in which they have holdings, only to maintain the full value of those investments and not to determine directly or indirectly the competitive conduct of those undertakings.

Article 4

Prior notification of concentrations and pre-notification referral at the request of the notifying parties

1. Concentrations with a Community dimension defined in this Regulation shall be notified to the Commission prior to their implementation and following the conclusion of the agreement, the announcement of the public bid, or the acquisition of a controlling interest.

Notification may also be made where the undertakings concerned demonstrate to the Commission a good faith intention to conclude an agreement or, in the case of a public bid, where they have publicly announced an intention to make such a bid, provided that the intended agreement or bid would result in a concentration with a Community dimension.

For the purposes of this Regulation, the term 'notified concentration' shall also cover intended concentrations notified pursuant to the second subparagraph. For the purposes of paragraphs 4 and 5 of this Article, the term 'concentration' includes intended concentrations within the meaning of the second subparagraph.

2. A concentration which consists of a merger within the meaning of Article 3(1)(a) or in the acquisition of joint control within the meaning of Article 3(1)(b) shall be notified jointly by the parties to the merger or by those acquiring joint control as the case may be. In all other cases, the notification shall be effected by the person or undertaking acquiring control of the whole or parts of one or more undertakings.

3. Where the Commission finds that a notified concentration falls within the scope of this Regulation, it shall publish the fact of the notification, at the same time indicating

the names of the undertakings concerned, their country of origin, the nature of the concentration and the economic sectors involved. The Commission shall take account of the legitimate interest of undertakings in the protection of their business secrets.

4. Prior to the notification of a concentration within the meaning of paragraph 1, the persons or undertakings referred to in paragraph 2 may inform the Commission, by means of a reasoned submission, that the concentration may significantly affect competition in a market within a Member State which presents all the characteristics of a distinct market and should therefore be examined, in whole or in part, by that Member State.

The Commission shall transmit this submission to all Member States without delay. The Member State referred to in the reasoned submission shall, within 15 working days of receiving the submission, express its agreement or disagreement as regards the request to refer the case. Where that Member State takes no such decision within this period, it shall be deemed to have agreed.

Unless that Member State disagrees, the Commission, where it considers that such a distinct market exists, and that competition in that market may be significantly affected by the concentration, may decide to refer the whole or part of the case to the competent authorities of that Member State with a view to the application of that State's national competition law.

The decision whether or not to refer the case in accordance with the third subparagraph shall be taken within 25 working days starting from the receipt of the reasoned submission by the Commission. The Commission shall inform the other Member States and the persons or undertakings concerned of its decision. If the Commission does not take a decision within this period, it shall be deemed to have adopted a decision to refer the case in accordance with the submission made by the persons or undertakings concerned.

If the Commission decides, or is deemed to have decided, pursuant to the third and fourth subparagraphs, to refer the whole of the case, no notification shall be made pursuant to paragraph 1 and national competition law shall apply. Article 9(6) to (9) shall apply *mutatis mutandis*.

5. With regard to a concentration as defined in Article 3 which does not have a Community dimension within the meaning of Article 1 and which is capable of being reviewed under the national competition laws of at least three Member States, the persons or undertakings referred to in paragraph 2 may, before any notification to the competent authorities, inform the Commission by means of a reasoned submission that the concentration should be examined by the Commission. The Commission shall transmit this submission to all Member States without delay.

Any Member State competent to examine the concentration under its national competition law may, within 15 working days of receiving the reasoned submission, express its disagreement as regards the request to refer the case.

Where at least one such Member State has expressed its disagreement in accordance with the third subparagraph within the period of 15 working days, the case shall not be referred. The Commission shall, without delay, inform all Member States and the persons or undertakings concerned of any such expression of disagreement.

Where no Member State has expressed its disagreement in accordance with the third subparagraph within the period of 15 working days, the concentration shall be deemed to have a Community dimension and shall be notified to the Commission in accordance with paragraphs 1 and 2. In such situations, no Member State shall apply its national competition law to the concentration.

6. The Commission shall report to the Council on the operation of paragraphs 4 and 5 by 1 July 2009. Following this report and on a proposal from the Commission, the Council, acting by a qualified majority, may revise paragraphs 4 and 5.

Article 5

Calculation of turnover

1. Aggregate turnover within the meaning of this Regulation shall comprise the amounts derived by the undertakings concerned in the preceding financial year from the sale of products and the provision of services falling within the undertakings' ordinary activities after deduction of sales rebates and of value added tax and other taxes directly related to turnover. The aggregate turnover of an undertaking concerned shall not include the sale of products or the provision of services between any of the undertakings referred to in paragraph 4. Turnover, in the Community or in a Member State, shall comprise products sold and services provided to undertakings or consumers, in the Community or in that Member State as the case may be.

2. By way of derogation from paragraph 1, where the concentration consists of the acquisition of parts, whether or not constituted as legal entities, of one or more undertakings, only the turnover relating to the parts which are the subject of the concentration shall be taken into account with regard to the seller or sellers.

However, two or more transactions within the meaning of the first subparagraph which take place within a two-year period between the same persons or undertakings shall be treated as one and the same concentration arising on the date of the last transaction.

3. In place of turnover the following shall be used: (a) for credit institutions and other financial institutions, the sum of the following income items as defined in Council Directive 86/635/EEC (1), after deduction of value added tax and other taxes directly related to those items, where appropriate:

(i) interest income and similar income;

(ii) income from securities:

— income from shares and other variable yield securities,

— income from participating interests,

— income from shares in affiliated undertakings;

(iii) commissions receivable;

(iv) net profit on financial operations;

(v) other operating income. The turnover of a credit or financial institution in the Community or in a Member State shall comprise the income items, as defined above, which are received by the branch or division of that institution established in the Community or in the Member State in question, as the case may be;

(b) for insurance undertakings, the value of gross premiums written which shall comprise all amounts received and receivable in respect of insurance contracts issued by or on behalf of the insurance undertakings, including also outgoing reinsurance premiums, and after deduction of taxes and parafiscal contributions or levies charged by reference to the amounts of individual premiums or the total volume of premiums; as regards Article 1(2)(b) and (3)(b), (c) and (d) and the final part of Article 1(2) and (3), gross premiums received from Community residents and from residents of one Member State respectively shall be taken into account.

4. Without prejudice to paragraph 2, the aggregate turnover of an undertaking concerned within the meaning of this Regulation shall be calculated by adding together the respective turnovers of the following:

(a) the undertaking concerned;

(b) those undertakings in which the undertaking concerned, directly or indirectly:

(i) owns more than half the capital or business assets, or

(ii) has the power to exercise more than half the voting rights, or

(iii) has the power to appoint more than half the members of the supervisory board, the administrative board or bodies legally representing the undertakings, or

(iv) has the right to manage the undertakings' affairs;

(c) those undertakings which have in the undertaking concerned the rights or powers listed in (b);

(d) those undertakings in which an undertaking as referred to in (c) has the rights or powers listed in (b);

(e) those undertakings in which two or more undertakings as referred to in (a) to (d) jointly have the rights or powers listed in (b).

5. Where undertakings concerned by the concentration jointly have the rights or powers listed in paragraph 4(b), in calculating the aggregate turnover of the undertakings concerned for the purposes of this Regulation:

(a) no account shall be taken of the turnover resulting from the sale of products or the provision of services between the joint undertaking and each of the undertakings concerned or any other undertaking connected with any one of them, as set out in paragraph 4(b) to (e);

(b) account shall be taken of the turnover resulting from the sale of products and the provision of services between the joint undertaking and any third undertakings. This turnover shall be apportioned equally amongst the undertakings concerned.

Article 6 **Examination of the notification and initiation of proceedings**

1. The Commission shall examine the notification as soon as it is received.

(a) Where it concludes that the concentration notified does not fall within the scope of this Regulation, it shall record that finding by means of a decision.

(b) Where it finds that the concentration notified, although falling within the scope of this Regulation, does not raise serious doubts as to its compatibility with the common market, it shall decide not to oppose it and shall declare that it is compatible with the common market.

A decision declaring a concentration compatible shall be deemed to cover restrictions directly related and necessary to the implementation of the concentration.

(c) Without prejudice to paragraph 2, where the Commission finds that the concentration notified falls within the scope of this Regulation and raises serious doubts as to its compatibility with the common market, it shall decide to initiate proceedings. Without prejudice to Article 9, such proceedings shall be closed by means of a decision as provided for in Article 8(1) to (4), unless the undertakings concerned have demonstrated to the satisfaction of the Commission that they have abandoned the concentration.

2. Where the Commission finds that, following modification by the undertakings concerned, a notified concentration no longer raises serious doubts within the meaning of paragraph 1(c), it shall declare the concentration compatible with the common market pursuant to paragraph 1(b).

The Commission may attach to its decision under paragraph 1(b) conditions and obligations intended to ensure that the undertakings concerned comply with the commitments they have entered into vis-à-vis the Commission with a view to rendering the concentration compatible with the common market.

3. The Commission may revoke the decision it took pursuant to paragraph 1(a) or (b) where:

(a) the decision is based on incorrect information for which one of the undertakings is responsible or where it has been obtained by deceit, or

(b) the undertakings concerned commit a breach of an obligation attached to the decision.

4. In the cases referred to in paragraph 3, the Commission may take a decision under paragraph 1, without being bound by the time limits referred to in Article 10(1).

5. The Commission shall notify its decision to the undertakings concerned and the competent authorities of the Member States without delay.

Article 7

Suspension of concentrations

1. A concentration with a Community dimension as defined in Article 1, or which is to be examined by the Commission pursuant to Article 4(5), shall not be implemented either before its notification or until it has been declared compatible with the common market pursuant to a decision under Articles 6(1)(b), 8(1) or 8(2), or on the basis of a presumption according to Article 10(6).

2. Paragraph 1 shall not prevent the implementation of a public bid or of a series of transactions in securities including those convertible into other securities admitted to

trading on a market such as a stock exchange, by which control within the meaning of Article 3 is acquired from various sellers, provided that:

(a) the concentration is notified to the Commission pursuant to Article 4 without delay; and

(b) the acquirer does not exercise the voting rights attached to the securities in question or does so only to maintain the full value of its investments based on a derogation granted by the Commission under paragraph 3.

3. The Commission may, on request, grant a derogation from the obligations imposed in paragraphs 1 or 2. The request to grant a derogation must be reasoned. In deciding on the request, the Commission shall take into account *inter alia* the effects of the suspension on one or more undertakings concerned by the concentration or on a third party and the threat to competition posed by the concentration. Such a derogation may be made subject to conditions and obligations in order to ensure conditions of effective competition. A derogation may be applied for and granted at any time, be it before notification or after the transaction.

4. The validity of any transaction carried out in contravention of paragraph 1 shall be dependent on a decision pursuant to Article 6(1)(b) or Article 8(1), (2) or (3) or on a presumption pursuant to Article 10(6).

This Article shall, however, have no effect on the validity of transactions in securities including those convertible into other securities admitted to trading on a market such as a stock exchange, unless the buyer and seller knew or ought to have known that the transaction was carried out in contravention of paragraph 1.

Article 8

Powers of decision of the Commission

1. Where the Commission finds that a notified concentration fulfils the criterion laid down in Article 2(2) and, in the cases referred to in Article 2(4), the criteria laid down in Article 81(3) of the Treaty, it shall issue a decision declaring the concentration compatible with the common market. A decision declaring a concentration compatible shall be deemed to cover restrictions directly related and necessary to the implementation of the concentration.

2. Where the Commission finds that, following modification by the undertakings concerned, a notified concentration fulfils the criterion laid down in Article 2(2) and, in the cases referred to in Article 2(4), the criteria laid down in Article 81(3) of the Treaty, it shall issue a decision declaring the concentration compatible with the common market.

The Commission may attach to its decision conditions and obligations intended to ensure that the undertakings concerned comply with the commitments they have entered into vis-à-vis the Commission with a view to rendering the concentration compatible with the common market.

A decision declaring a concentration compatible shall be deemed to cover restrictions directly related and necessary to the implementation of the concentration.

3. Where the Commission finds that a concentration fulfils the criterion defined in Article 2(3) or, in the cases referred to in Article 2(4), does not fulfil the criteria laid down in Article 81(3) of the Treaty, it shall issue a decision declaring that the concentration is incompatible with the common market.

4. Where the Commission finds that a concentration:

(a) has already been implemented and that concentration has been declared incompatible with the common market, or

(b) has been implemented in contravention of a condition attached to a decision taken under paragraph 2, which has found that, in the absence of the condition, the concentration would fulfil the criterion laid down in Article 2(3) or, in the cases referred to in Article 2(4), would not fulfil the criteria laid down in Article 81(3) of the Treaty, the Commission may:

—require the undertakings concerned to dissolve the concentration, in particular through the dissolution of the merger or the disposal of all the shares or assets acquired, so as to restore the situation prevailing prior to the implementation of the concentration; in circumstances where restoration of the situation prevailing before the implementation of the concentration is not possible through dissolution of the concentration, the Commission may take any other measure appropriate to achieve such restoration as far as possible,

—order any other appropriate measure to ensure that the undertakings concerned dissolve the concentration or take other restorative measures as required in its decision. In cases falling within point (a) of the first subparagraph, the measures referred to in that subparagraph may be imposed either in a decision pursuant to paragraph 3 or by separate decision.

5. The Commission may take interim measures appropriate to restore or maintain conditions of effective competition where a concentration:

(a) has been implemented in contravention of Article 7, and a decision as to the compatibility of the concentration with the common market has not yet been taken;

(b) has been implemented in contravention of a condition attached to a decision under Article 6(1)(b) or paragraph 2 of this Article;

(c) has already been implemented and is declared incompatible with the common market.

6. The Commission may revoke the decision it has taken pursuant to paragraphs 1 or 2 where:

(a) the declaration of compatibility is based on incorrect information for which one of the undertakings is responsible or where it has been obtained by deceit; or

(b) the undertakings concerned commit a breach of an obligation attached to the decision.

7. The Commission may take a decision pursuant to paragraphs 1 to 3 without being bound by the time limits referred to in Article 10(3), in cases where:

(a) it finds that a concentration has been implemented

(i) in contravention of a condition attached to a decision under Article 6(1)(b), or

(ii) in contravention of a condition attached to a decision taken under paragraph 2 and in accordance with Article 10(2), which has found that, in the absence of the condition, the concentration would raise serious doubts as to its compatibility with the common market; or

(b) a decision has been revoked pursuant to paragraph 6.

8. The Commission shall notify its decision to the undertakings concerned and the competent authorities of the Member States without delay.

Article 9

Referral to the competent authorities of the Member States

1. The Commission may, by means of a decision notified without delay to the undertakings concerned and the competent authorities of the other Member States, refer a notified concentration to the competent authorities of the Member State concerned in the following circumstances.

2. Within 15 working days of the date of receipt of the copy of the notification, a Member State, on its own initiative or upon the invitation of the Commission, may inform the Commission, which shall inform the undertakings concerned, that:

(a) a concentration threatens to affect significantly competition in a market within that Member State, which presents all the characteristics of a distinct market, or

(b) a concentration affects competition in a market within that Member State, which presents all the characteristics of a distinct market and which does not constitute a substantial part of the common market.

3. If the Commission considers that, having regard to the market for the products or services in question and the geographical reference market within the meaning of paragraph 7, there is such a distinct market and that such a threat exists, either:

(a) it shall itself deal with the case in accordance with this Regulation; or

(b) it shall refer the whole or part of the case to the competent authorities of the Member State concerned with a view to the application of that State's national competition law. If, however, the Commission considers that such a distinct market or threat does not exist, it shall adopt a decision to that effect which it shall address to the Member State concerned, and shall itself deal with the case in accordance with this Regulation. In cases where a Member State informs the Commission pursuant to paragraph 2(b) that a concentration affects competition in a distinct market within its territory that does not form a substantial part of the common market, the Commission shall refer the whole or part of the case relating to the distinct market concerned, if it considers that such a distinct market is affected.

4. A decision to refer or not to refer pursuant to paragraph 3 shall be taken:

(a) as a general rule within the period provided for in Article 10(1), second subparagraph, where the Commission, pursuant to Article 6(1)(b), has not initiated proceedings; or

(b) within 65 working days at most of the notification of the concentration concerned where the Commission has initiated proceedings under Article 6(1)(c), without taking the preparatory steps in order to adopt the necessary measures under Article 8(2), (3) or (4) to maintain or restore effective competition on the market concerned.

5. If within the 65 working days referred to in paragraph 4(b) the Commission, despite a reminder from the Member State concerned, has not taken a decision on referral in accordance with paragraph 3 nor has taken the preparatory steps referred to in paragraph 4(b), it shall be deemed to have taken a decision to refer the case to the Member State concerned in accordance with paragraph 3(b).

6. The competent authority of the Member State concerned shall decide upon the case without undue delay. Within 45 working days after the Commission's referral, the competent authority of the Member State concerned shall inform the undertakings concerned of the result of the preliminary competition assessment and what further action, if any, it proposes to take. The Member State concerned may exceptionally suspend this time limit where necessary information has not been provided to it by the undertakings concerned as provided for by its national competition law. Where a notification is requested under national law, the period of 45 working days shall begin on the working day following that of the receipt of a complete notification by the competent authority of that Member State.

7. The geographical reference market shall consist of the area in which the undertakings concerned are involved in the supply and demand of products or services, in which the conditions of competition are sufficiently homogeneous and which can be distinguished from neighbouring areas because, in particular, conditions of competition are appreciably different in those areas. This assessment should take account in particular of the nature and characteristics of the products or services concerned, of the existence of entry barriers or of consumer preferences, of appreciable differences of the undertakings' market shares between the area concerned and neighbouring areas or of substantial price differences.

8. In applying the provisions of this Article, the Member State concerned may take only the measures strictly necessary to safeguard or restore effective competition on the market concerned.

9. In accordance with the relevant provisions of the Treaty, any Member State may appeal to the Court of Justice, and in particular request the application of Article 243 of the Treaty, for the purpose of applying its national competition law.

Article 10

Time limits for initiating proceedings and for decisions

1. Without prejudice to Article 6(4), the decisions referred to in Article 6(1) shall be taken within 25 working days at most. That period shall begin on the working day following that of the receipt of a notification or, if the information to be supplied with the notification is incomplete, on the working day following that of the receipt of the complete information. That period shall be increased to 35 working days where the Commission receives a request from a Member State in accordance with Article 9(2)or where, the undertakings concerned offer commitments pursuant to Article 6(2) with a view to rendering the concentration compatible with the common market.

2. Decisions pursuant to Article 8(1) or (2) concerning notified concentrations shall be taken as soon as it appears that the serious doubts referred to in Article 6(1)(c) have been removed, particularly as a result of modifications made by the undertakings concerned, and at the latest by the time limit laid down in paragraph 3.

3. Without prejudice to Article 8(7), decisions pursuant to Article 8(1) to (3) concerning notified concentrations shall be taken within not more than 90 working days of the date on which the proceedings are initiated. That period shall be increased to 105 working days where the undertakings concerned offer commitments pursuant to Article 8(2), second subparagraph, with a view to rendering the concentration compatible with the common market, unless these commitments have been offered less than 55 working days after the initiation of proceedings.

The periods set by the first subparagraph shall likewise be extended if the notifying parties make a request to that effect not later than 15 working days after the initiation of proceedings pursuant to Article 6(1)(c). The notifying parties may make only one such request. Likewise, at any time following the initiation of proceedings, the periods set by the first subparagraph may be extended by the Commission with the agreement of the notifying parties. The total duration of any extension or extensions effected pursuant to this subparagraph shall not exceed 20 working days.

4. The periods set by paragraphs 1 and 3 shall exceptionally be suspended where, owing to circumstances for which one of the undertakings involved in the concentration is responsible, the Commission has had to request information by decision pursuant to Article 11 or to order an inspection by decision pursuant to Article 13.

The first subparagraph shall also apply to the period referred to in Article 9(4)(b).

5. Where the Court of Justice gives a judgment which annuls the whole or part of a Commission decision which is subject to a time limit set by this Article, the concentration shall be reexamined by the Commission with a view to adopting a decision pursuant to Article 6(1).

The concentration shall be re-examined in the light of current market conditions.

The notifying parties shall submit a new notification or supplement the original notification, without delay, where the original notification becomes incomplete by reason of intervening changes in market conditions or in the information provided. Where there are no such changes, the parties shall certify this fact without delay.

The periods laid down in paragraph 1 shall start on the working day following that of the receipt of complete information in a new notification, a supplemented notification, or a certification within the meaning of the third subparagraph. The second and third subparagraphs shall also apply in the cases referred to in Article 6(4) and Article 8(7).

6. Where the Commission has not taken a decision in accordance with Article 6(1)(b), (c), 8(1), (2) or (3) within the time limits set in paragraphs 1 and 3 respectively, the concentration shall be deemed to have been declared compatible with the common market, without prejudice to Article 9.

Article 11

Requests for information

1. In order to carry out the duties assigned to it by this Regulation, the Commission may, by simple request or by decision, require the persons referred to in Article 3(1)(b), as well as undertakings and associations of undertakings, to provide all necessary information.

2. When sending a simple request for information to a person, an undertaking or an association of undertakings, the Commission shall state the legal basis and the purpose of the request, specify what information is required and fix the time limit within which the information is to be provided, as well as the penalties provided for in Article 14 for supplying incorrect or misleading information.

3. Where the Commission requires a person, an undertaking or an association of undertakings to supply information by decision, it shall state the legal basis and the purpose of the request, specify what information is required and fix the time limit within which it is to be provided. It shall also indicate the penalties provided for in Article 14 and indicate or impose the penalties provided for in Article 15. It shall further indicate the right to have the decision reviewed by the Court of Justice.

4. The owners of the undertakings or their representatives and, in the case of legal persons, companies or firms, or associations having no legal personality, the persons authorised to represent them by law or by their constitution, shall supply the information requested on behalf of the undertaking concerned. Persons duly authorised to act may supply the information on behalf of their clients. The latter shall remain fully responsible if the information supplied is incomplete, incorrect or misleading.

5. The Commission shall without delay forward a copy of any decision taken pursuant to paragraph 3 to the competent authorities of the Member State in whose territory the residence of the person or the seat of the undertaking or association of undertakings is situated, and to the competent authority of the Member State whose territory is affected. At the specific request of the competent authority of a Member State, the Commission shall also forward to that authority copies of simple requests for information relating to a notified concentration.

6. At the request of the Commission, the governments and competent authorities of the Member States shall provide the Commission with all necessary information to carry out the duties assigned to it by this Regulation.

7. In order to carry out the duties assigned to it by this Regulation, the Commission may interview any natural or legal person who consents to be interviewed for the purpose of collecting information relating to the subject matter of an investigation. At the beginning of the interview, which may be conducted by telephone or other electronic means, the Commission shall state the legal basis and the purpose of the interview.

Where an interview is not conducted on the premises of the Commission or by telephone or other electronic means, the Commission shall inform in advance the competent authority of the Member State in whose territory the interview takes place. If the competent authority of that Member State so requests, officials of that authority may assist the officials and other persons authorised by the Commission to conduct the interview.

Article 12

Inspections by the authorities of the Member States

1. At the request of the Commission, the competent authorities of the Member States shall undertake the inspections which the Commission considers to be necessary under Article 13(1), or which it has ordered by decision pursuant to Article 13(4). The officials of the competent authorities of the Member States who are responsible for conducting these inspections as well as those authorised or appointed by them shall exercise their powers in accordance with their national law.

2. If so requested by the Commission or by the competent authority of the Member State within whose territory the inspection is to be conducted, officials and other accompanying persons authorised by the Commission may assist the officials of the authority concerned.

Article 13

The Commission's powers of inspection

1. In order to carry out the duties assigned to it by this Regulation, the Commission may conduct all necessary inspections of undertakings and associations of undertakings.

2. The officials and other accompanying persons authorised by the Commission to conduct an inspection shall have the power:

(a) to enter any premises, land and means of transport of undertakings and associations of undertakings;

(b) to examine the books and other records related to the business, irrespective of the medium on which they are stored;

(c) to take or obtain in any form copies of or extracts from such books or records;

(d) to seal any business premises and books or records for the period and to the extent necessary for the inspection;

(e) to ask any representative or member of staff of the undertaking or association of undertakings for explanations on facts or documents relating to the subject matter and purpose of the inspection and to record the answers.

3. Officials and other accompanying persons authorised by the Commission to conduct an inspection shall exercise their powers upon production of a written authorisation specifying the subject matter and purpose of the inspection and the penalties provided for in Article 14, in the production of the required books or other records related to the business which is incomplete or where answers to questions asked under paragraph 2 of this Article are incorrect or misleading. In good time before the inspection, the Commission shall give notice of the inspection to the competent authority of the Member State in whose territory the inspection is to be conducted.

4. Undertakings and associations of undertakings are required to submit to inspections ordered by decision of the Commission. The decision shall specify the subject matter and purpose of the inspection, appoint the date on which it is to begin and indicate the

penalties provided for in Articles 14 and 15 and the right to have the decision reviewed by the Court of Justice. The Commission shall take such decisions after consulting the competent authority of the Member State in whose territory the inspection is to be conducted.

5. Officials of, and those authorised or appointed by, the competent authority of the Member State in whose territory the inspection is to be conducted shall, at the request of that authority or of the Commission, actively assist the officials and other accompanying persons authorised by the Commission. To this end, they shall enjoy the powers specified in paragraph 2.

6. Where the officials and other accompanying persons authorised by the Commission find that an undertaking opposes an inspection, including the sealing of business premises, books or records, ordered pursuant to this Article, the Member State concerned shall afford them the necessary assistance, requesting where appropriate the assistance of the police or of an equivalent enforcement authority, so as to enable them to conduct their inspection.

7. If the assistance provided for in paragraph 6 requires authorisation from a judicial authority according to national rules, such authorisation shall be applied for. Such authorisation may also be applied for as a precautionary measure.

8. Where authorisation as referred to in paragraph 7 is applied for, the national judicial authority shall ensure that the Commission decision is authentic and that the coercive measures envisaged are neither arbitrary nor excessive having regard to the subject matter of the inspection. In its control of proportionality of the coercive measures, the national judicial authority may ask the Commission, directly or through the competent authority of that Member State, for detailed explanations relating to the subject matter of the inspection. However, the national judicial authority may not call into question the necessity for the inspection nor demand that it be provided with the information in the Commission's file. The lawfulness of the Commission's decision shall be subject to review only by the Court of Justice.

Article 14

Fines

1. The Commission may by decision impose on the persons referred to in Article 3(1)b, undertakings or associations of undertakings, fines not exceeding 1 % of the aggregate turnover of the undertaking or association of undertakings concerned within the meaning of Article 5 where, intentionally or negligently:

(a) they supply incorrect or misleading information in a submission, certification, notification or supplement thereto, pursuant to Article 4, Article 10(5) or Article 22(3);

(b) they supply incorrect or misleading information in response to a request made pursuant to Article 11(2);

(c) in response to a request made by decision adopted pursuant to Article 11(3), they supply incorrect, incomplete or misleading information or do not supply information within the required time limit;

(d) they produce the required books or other records related to the business in incomplete form during inspections under Article 13, or refuse to submit to an inspection ordered by decision taken pursuant to Article 13(4);

(e) in response to a question asked in accordance with Article 13(2)(e),

—they give an incorrect or misleading answer,

—they fail to rectify within a time limit set by the Commission an incorrect, incomplete or misleading answer given by a member of staff, or

—they fail or refuse to provide a complete answer on facts relating to the subject matter and purpose of an inspection ordered by a decision adopted pursuant to Article 13(4);

(f) seals affixed by officials or other accompanying persons authorised by the Commission in accordance with Article 13(2)(d) have been broken.

2. The Commission may by decision impose fines not exceeding 10 % of the aggregate turnover of the undertaking concerned within the meaning of Article 5 on the persons referred to in Article 3(1)b or the undertakings concerned where, either intentionally or negligently, they:

(a) fail to notify a concentration in accordance with Articles 4 or 22(3) prior to its implementation, unless they are expressly authorised to do so by Article 7(2) or by a decision taken pursuant to Article 7(3);

(b) implement a concentration in breach of Article 7;

(c) implement a concentration declared incompatible with the common market by decision pursuant to Article 8(3) or do not comply with any measure ordered by decision pursuant to Article 8(4) or (5);

(d) fail to comply with a condition or an obligation imposed by decision pursuant to Articles 6(1)(b), Article 7(3) or Article 8(2), second subparagraph.

3. In fixing the amount of the fine, regard shall be had to the nature, gravity and duration of the infringement.

4. Decisions taken pursuant to paragraphs 1, 2 and 3 shall not be of a criminal law nature.

Article 15

Periodic penalty payments

1. The Commission may by decision impose on the persons referred to in Article 3(1)b, undertakings or associations of undertakings, periodic penalty payments not exceeding 5 % of the average daily aggregate turnover of the undertaking or association of undertakings concerned within the meaning of Article 5 for each working day of delay, calculated from the date set in the decision, in order to compel them:

(a) to supply complete and correct information which it has requested by decision taken pursuant to Article 11(3);

(b) to submit to an inspection which it has ordered by decision taken pursuant to Article 13(4);

(c) to comply with an obligation imposed by decision pursuant to Article 6(1)(b), Article 7(3) or Article 8(2), second subparagraph; or;

(d) to comply with any measures ordered by decision pursuant to Article 8(4) or (5).

2. Where the persons referred to in Article 3(1)(b), undertakings or associations of undertakings have satisfied the obligation which the periodic penalty payment was intended to enforce, the Commission may fix the definitive amount of the periodic penalty payments at a figure lower than that which would arise under the original decision.

Article 16

Review by the Court of Justice

The Court of Justice shall have unlimited jurisdiction within the meaning of Article 229 of the Treaty to review decisions whereby the Commission has fixed a fine or periodic penalty payments; it may cancel, reduce or increase the fine or periodic penalty payment imposed.

Article 17

Professional secrecy

1. Information acquired as a result of the application of this Regulation shall be used only for the purposes of the relevant request, investigation or hearing.

2. Without prejudice to Article 4(3), Articles 18 and 20, the Commission and the competent authorities of the Member States, their officials and other servants and other persons working under the supervision of these authorities as well as officials and civil servants of other authorities of the Member States shall not disclose information they have acquired through the application of this Regulation of the kind covered by the obligation of professional secrecy.

3. Paragraphs 1 and 2 shall not prevent publication of general information or of surveys which do not contain information relating to particular undertakings or associations of undertakings.

Article 18

Hearing of the parties and of third persons

1. Before taking any decision provided for in Article 6(3), Article 7(3), Article 8(2) to (6), and Articles 14 and 15, the Commission shall give the persons, undertakings and associations of undertakings concerned the opportunity, at every stage of the procedure up to the consultation of the Advisory Committee, of making known their views on the objections against them.

2. By way of derogation from paragraph 1, a decision pursuant to Articles 7(3) and 8(5) may be taken provisionally, without the persons, undertakings or associations of undertakings concerned being given the opportunity to make known their views beforehand, provided that the Commission gives them that opportunity as soon as possible after having taken its decision.

3. The Commission shall base its decision only on objections on which the parties have been able to submit their observations. The rights of the defence shall be fully respected in the proceedings. Access to the file shall be open at least to the parties directly involved, subject to the legitimate interest of undertakings in the protection of their business secrets.

4. In so far as the Commission or the competent authorities of the Member States deem it necessary, they may also hear other natural or legal persons. Natural or legal persons showing a sufficient interest and especially members of the administrative or management bodies of the undertakings concerned or the recognised representatives of their employees shall be entitled, upon application, to be heard.

Article 19

Liaison with the authorities of the Member States

1. The Commission shall transmit to the competent authorities of the Member States copies of notifications within three working days and, as soon as possible, copies of the most important documents lodged with or issued by the Commission pursuant to this Regulation. Such documents shall include commitments offered by the undertakings concerned vis-à-vis the Commission with a view to rendering the concentration compatible with the common market pursuant to Article 6(2) or Article 8(2), second subparagraph.

2. The Commission shall carry out the procedures set out in this Regulation in close and constant liaison with the competent authorities of the Member States, which may express their views upon those procedures. For the purposes of Article 9 it shall obtain information from the competent authority of the Member State as referred to in paragraph 2 of that Article and give it the opportunity to make known its views at every stage of the procedure up to the adoption of a decision pursuant to paragraph 3 of that Article; to that end it shall give it access to the file.

3. An Advisory Committee on concentrations shall be consulted before any decision is taken pursuant to Article 8(1) to (6), Articles 14 or 15 with the exception of provisional decisions taken in accordance with Article 18(2).

4. The Advisory Committee shall consist of representatives of the competent authorities of the Member States. Each Member State shall appoint one or two representatives; if unable to attend, they may be replaced by other representatives. At least one of the representatives of a Member State shall be competent in matters of restrictive practices and dominant positions.

5. Consultation shall take place at a joint meeting convened at the invitation of and chaired by the Commission. A summary of the case, together with an indication of the most important documents and a preliminary draft of the decision to be taken for each case considered, shall be sent with the invitation. The meeting shall take place not less than 10 working days after the invitation has been sent. The Commission may in exceptional cases shorten that period as appropriate in order to avoid serious harm to one or more of the undertakings concerned by a concentration.

6. The Advisory Committee shall deliver an opinion on the Commission's draft decision, if necessary by taking a vote. The Advisory Committee may deliver an opinion even if

some members are absent and unrepresented. The opinion shall be delivered in writing and appended to the draft decision. The Commission shall take the utmost account of the opinion delivered by the Committee. It shall inform the Committee of the manner in which its opinion has been taken into account.

7. The Commission shall communicate the opinion of the Advisory Committee, together with the decision, to the addressees of the decision. It shall make the opinion public together with the decision, having regard to the legitimate interest of undertakings in the protection of their business secrets.

Article 20

Publication of decisions

1. The Commission shall publish the decisions which it takes pursuant to Article 8(1) to (6), Articles 14 and 15 with the exception of provisional decisions taken in accordance with Article 18(2) together with the opinion of the Advisory Committee in the *Official Journal of the European Union*. 2. The publication shall state the names of the parties and the main content of the decision; it shall have regard to the legitimate interest of undertakings in the protection of their business secrets.

Article 21

Application of the Regulation and jurisdiction

1. This Regulation alone shall apply to concentrations as defined in Article 3, and Council Regulations (EC) No 1/ 2003, (EEC) No 1017/68, (EEC) No 4056/86 and (EEC) No 3975/87 shall not apply, except in relation to joint ventures that do not have a Community dimension and which have as their object or effect the coordination of the competitive behaviour of undertakings that remain independent.

2. Subject to review by the Court of Justice, the Commission shall have sole jurisdiction to take the decisions provided for in this Regulation.

3. No Member State shall apply its national legislation on competition to any concentration that has a Community dimension.

The first subparagraph shall be without prejudice to any Member State's power to carry out any enquiries necessary for the application of Articles 4(4), 9(2) or after referral, pursuant to Article 9(3), first subparagraph, indent (b), or Article 9(5), to take the measures strictly necessary for the application of Article 9(8).

4. Notwithstanding paragraphs 2 and 3, Member States may take appropriate measures to protect legitimate interests other than those taken into consideration by this Regulation and compatible with the general principles and other provisions of Community law.

Public security, plurality of the media and prudential rules shall be regarded as legitimate interests within the meaning of the first subparagraph.

Any other public interest must be communicated to the Commission by the Member State concerned and shall be recognised by the Commission after an assessment of its compatibility with the general principles and other provisions of Community law before the measures referred to above may be taken. The Commission shall inform the Member State concerned of its decision within 25 working days of that communication.

Article 22

Referral to the Commission

1. One or more Member States may request the Commission to examine any concentration as defined in Article 3 that does not have a Community dimension within the meaning of Article 1 but affects trade between Member States and threatens to significantly affect competition within the territory of the Member State or States making the request.

Such a request shall be made at most within 15 working days of the date on which the concentration was notified, or if no notification is required, otherwise made known to the Member State concerned.

2. The Commission shall inform the competent authorities of the Member States and the undertakings concerned of any request received pursuant to paragraph 1 without delay. Any other Member State shall have the right to join the initial request within a period of 15 working days of being informed by the Commission of the initial request.

All national time limits relating to the concentration shall be suspended until, in accordance with the procedure set out in this Article, it has been decided where the concentration shall be examined. As soon as a Member State has informed the Commission and the undertakings concerned that it does not wish to join the request, the suspension of its national time limits shall end.

3. The Commission may, at the latest 10 working days after the expiry of the period set in paragraph 2, decide to examine, the concentration where it considers that it affects trade between Member States and threatens to significantly affect competition within the territory of the Member State or States making the request. If the Commission does not take a decision within this period, it shall be deemed to have adopted a decision to examine the concentration in accordance with the request.

The Commission shall inform all Member States and the undertakings concerned of its decision. It may request the submission of a notification pursuant to Article 4.

The Member State or States having made the request shall no longer apply their national legislation on competition to the concentration.

4. Article 2, Article 4(2) to (3), Articles 5, 6, and 8 to 21 shall apply where the Commission examines a concentration pursuant to paragraph 3. Article 7 shall apply to the extent that the concentration has not been implemented on the date on which the Commission informs the undertakings concerned that a request has been made.

Where a notification pursuant to Article 4 is not required, the period set in Article 10(1) within which proceedings may be initiated shall begin on the working day following that on which the Commission informs the undertakings concerned that it has decided to examine the concentration pursuant to paragraph 3.

5. The Commission may inform one or several Member States that it considers a concentration fulfils the criteria in paragraph 1. In such cases, the Commission may invite that Member State or those Member States to make a request pursuant to paragraph 1.

Article 23

Implementing provisions

1. The Commission shall have the power to lay down in accordance with the procedure referred to in paragraph 2:

(a) implementing provisions concerning the form, content and other details of notifications and submissions pursuant to Article 4;

(b) implementing provisions concerning time limits pursuant to Article 4(4), (5) Articles 7, 9, 10 and 22;

(c) the procedure and time limits for the submission and implementation of commitments pursuant to Article 6(2) and Article 8(2);

(d) implementing provisions concerning hearings pursuant to Article 18.

2. The Commission shall be assisted by an Advisory Committee, composed of representatives of the Member States.

(a) Before publishing draft implementing provisions and before adopting such provisions, the Commission shall consult the Advisory Committee.

(b) Consultation shall take place at a meeting convened at the invitation of and chaired by the Commission. A draft of the implementing provisions to be taken shall be sent with the invitation. The meeting shall take place not less than 10 working days after the invitation has been sent.

(c) The Advisory Committee shall deliver an opinion on the draft implementing provisions, if necessary by taking a vote. The Commission shall take the utmost account of the opinion delivered by the Committee.

Article 24

Relations with third countries

1. The Member States shall inform the Commission of any general difficulties encountered by their undertakings with concentrations as defined in Article 3 in a third country.

2. Initially not more than one year after the entry into force of this Regulation and, thereafter periodically, the Commission shall draw up a report examining the treatment accorded to undertakings having their seat or their principal fields of activity in the Community, in the terms referred to in paragraphs 3 and 4, as regards concentrations in third countries. The Commission shall submit those reports to the Council, together with any recommendations.

3. Whenever it appears to the Commission, either on the basis of the reports referred to in paragraph 2 or on the basis of other information, that a third country does not grant undertakings having their seat or their principal fields of activity in the Community, treatment comparable to that granted by the Community to undertakings from that country, the Commission may submit proposals to the Council for an appropriate mandate for negotiation with a view to obtaining comparable treatment for undertakings having their seat or their principal fields of activity in the Community.

4. Measures taken under this Article shall comply with the obligations of the Community or of the Member States, without prejudice to Article 307 of the Treaty, under international agreements, whether bilateral or multilateral.

Article 25

Repeal

1. Without prejudice to Article 26(2), Regulations (EEC) No 4064/89 and (EC) No 1310/97 shall be repealed with effect from 1 May 2004.

2. References to the repealed Regulations shall be construed as references to this Regulation and shall be read in accordance with the correlation table in the Annex.

Article 26

Entry into force and transitional provisions

1. This Regulation shall enter into force on the 20th day following that of its publication in the *Official Journal of the European Union*.

It shall apply from 1 May 2004.

2. Regulation (EEC) No 4064/89 shall continue to apply to any concentration which was the subject of an agreement or announcement or where control was acquired within the meaning of Article 4(1) of that Regulation before the date of application of this Regulation, subject, in particular, to the provisions governing applicability set out in Article 25(2) and (3) of Regulation (EEC) No 4064/89 and Article 2 of Regulation (EEC) No 1310/97.

3. As regards concentrations to which this Regulation applies by virtue of accession, the date of accession shall be substituted for the date of application of this Regulation.

This Regulation shall be binding in its entirety and directly applicable in all Member States.

Done at Brussels, 20 January 2004.

Appendix 2

COMMISSION REGULATION (EC) No 802/2004 of 7 April 2004[1]

implementing Council Regulation (EC) No 139/2004 on the control of concentrations between undertakings

(Text with EEA relevance)

THE COMMISSION OF THE EUROPEAN COMMUNITIES,

Having regard to the Treaty establishing the European Community,

Having regard to the Agreement on the European Economic Area,

Having regard to Council Regulation (EC) No 139/2004 of 20 January 2004 on the control of concentrations between undertakings (EC Merger Regulation), and in particular Article 23(1) thereof,

Having regard to Council Regulation (EEC) No 4064/89 of 21 December 1989 on the control of concentrations between undertakings, as last amended by Regulation (EC) No 1310/ 97, and in particular Article 23 thereof,

Having consulted the Advisory Committee,

Whereas:

(1) Council Regulation (EEC) No 4064/89 of 21 December 1989 on the control of concentrations between undertakings has been recast, with substantial amendments to various provisions of that Regulation.

(2) Commission Regulation (EC) No 447/98 of 1 March 1998 on the notifications, time-limits and hearings provided for in Council Regulation (EEC) No 4064/89 must be modified in order to take account of those amendments. For the sake of clarity it should therefore be repealed and replaced by a new regulation.

(3) The Commission has adopted measures concerning the terms of reference of hearing officers in certain competition proceedings.

(4) Regulation (EC) No 139/2004 is based on the principle of compulsory notification of concentrations before they are put into effect. On the one hand, a notification has important legal consequences which are favourable to the parties to the proposed concentration, while, on the other hand, failure to comply with the obligation to notify renders the

[1] [2004] OJ L 133/1.

parties liable to fines and may also entail civil law disadvantages for them. It is therefore necessary in the interests of legal certainty to define precisely the subject matter and content of the information to be provided in the notification.

(5) It is for the notifying parties to make a full and honest disclosure to the Commission of the facts and circumstances which are relevant for taking a decision on the notified concentration.

(6) Regulation (EC) No 139/2004 also allows the undertakings concerned to request, in a reasoned submission, prior to notification, that a concentration fulfilling the requirements of that Regulation be referred to the Commission by one or more Member States, or referred by the Commission to one or more Member States, as the case may be. It is important to provide the Commission and the competent authorities of the Member States concerned with sufficient information, in order to enable them to assess, within a short period of time, whether or not a referral ought to be made. To that end, the reasoned submission requesting the referral should contain certain specific information.

(7) In order to simplify and expedite examination of notifications and of reasoned submissions, it is desirable to prescribe that forms be used.

(8) Since notification sets in motion legal time-limits pursuant to Regulation (EC) No 139/2004, the conditions governing such time-limits and the time when they become effective should also be determined.

(9) Rules must be laid down in the interests of legal certainty for calculating the time-limits provided for in Regulation (EC) No 139/2004. In particular, the beginning and end of time periods and the circumstances suspending the running of such periods must be determined, with due regard to the requirements resulting from the exceptionally tight legal timeframe available for the proceedings.

(10) The provisions relating to the Commission's procedure must be framed in such a way as to safeguard fully the right to be heard and the rights of defence. For these purposes, the Commission should distinguish between the parties who notify the concentration, other parties involved in the proposed concentration, third parties and parties regarding whom the Commission intends to take a decision imposing a fine or periodic penalty payments.

(11) The Commission should give the notifying parties and other parties involved in the proposed concentration, if they so request, an opportunity before notification to discuss the intended concentration informally and in strict confidence. In addition, the Commission should, after notification, maintain close contact with those parties, to the extent necessary to discuss with them any practical or legal problems which it discovers on a first examination of the case, with a view, if possible, to resolving such problems by mutual agreement.

(12) In accordance with the principle of respect for the rights of defence, the notifying parties must be given the opportunity to submit their comments on all the objections which the Commission proposes to take into account in its decisions. The other parties involved in the proposed concentration should also be informed of the Commission's objections and should be granted the opportunity to express their views.

(13) Third parties demonstrating a sufficient interest must also be given the opportunity of expressing their views, if they make a written application to that effect.

(14) The various persons entitled to submit comments should do so in writing, both in their own interests and in the interests of sound administration, without prejudice to their right to request a formal oral hearing, where appropriate, to supplement the written procedure. In urgent cases, however, the Commission must be enabled to proceed immediately to formal oral hearings of the notifying parties, of other parties involved or of third parties.

(15) It is necessary to define the rights of persons who are to be heard, to what extent they should be granted access to the Commission's file and on what conditions they may be represented or assisted.

(16) When granting access to the file, the Commission should ensure the protection of business secrets and other confidential information. The Commission should be able to ask undertakings that have submitted documents or statements to identify confidential information.

(17) In order to enable the Commission to carry out a proper assessment of commitments offered by the notifying parties with a view to rendering the concentration compatible with the common market, and to ensure due consultation with other parties involved, with third parties and with the authorities of the Member States as provided for in Regulation (EC) No 139/2004, in particular Article 18(1), 18(4), Article 19(1), 19(2), 19(3) and 19(5) thereof, the procedure and time-limits for submitting the commitments referred to in Article 6(2) and Article 8(2) of that Regulation should be laid down.

(18) It is also necessary to define the rules applicable to certain time limits set by the Commission.

(19) The Advisory Committee on Concentrations must deliver its opinion on the basis of a preliminary draft decision. It must therefore be consulted on a case after the inquiry in to that case has been completed. Such consultation does not, however, prevent the Commission from reopening an inquiry if need be.

HAS ADOPTED THIS REGULATION:

CHAPTER I

SCOPE

Article 1

Scope This Regulation shall apply to the control of concentrations conducted pursuant to Regulation (EC) No 139/2004.

CHAPTER II

NOTIFICATIONS AND OTHER SUBMISSIONS

Article 2

Persons entitled to submit notifications

1. Notifications shall be submitted by the persons or undertakings referred to in Article 4(2) of Regulation (EC) No 139/ 2004.

2. Where notifications are signed by representatives of persons or of undertakings, such representatives shall produce written proof that they are authorised to act.

3. Joint notifications shall be submitted by a joint representative who is authorised to transmit and to receive documents on behalf of all notifying parties.

Article 3

Submission of notifications

1. Notifications shall be submitted in the manner prescribed by Form CO as set out in Annex I. Under the conditions set out in Annex II, notifications may be submitted in Short Form as defined therein. Joint notifications shall be submitted on a single form.

2. One original and 35 copies of the Form CO and the supporting documents shall be submitted to the Commission. The notification shall be delivered to the address referred to in Article 23(1) and in the format specified by the Commission.

3. The supporting documents shall be either originals or copies of the originals; in the latter case the notifying parties shall confirm that they are true and complete.

4. Notifications shall be in one of the official languages of the Community. For the notifying parties, this language shall also be the language of the proceeding, as well as that of any subsequent proceedings relating to the same concentration. Supporting documents shall be submitted in their original language. Where the original language is not one of the official languages of the Community, a translation into the language of the proceeding shall be attached.

5. Where notifications are made pursuant to Article 57 of the Agreement on the European Economic Area, they may also be submitted in one of the official languages of the EFTA States or the working language of the EFTA Surveillance Authority. If the language chosen for the notifications is not an official language of the Community, the notifying parties shall simultaneously supplement all documentation with a translation into an official language of the Community. The language which is chosen for the translation shall determine the language used by the Commission as the language of the proceeding for the notifying parties.

Article 4

Information and documents to be provided

1. Notifications shall contain the information, including documents, requested in the applicable forms set out in the Annexes. The information shall be correct and complete.

2. The Commission may dispense with the obligation to provide any particular information in the notification, including documents, or with any other requirement specified in Annexes I and II where the Commission considers that compliance with those obligations or requirements is not necessary for the examination of the case.

3. The Commission shall without delay acknowledge in writing to the notifying parties or their representatives receipt of the notification and of any reply to a letter sent by the Commission pursuant to Article 5(2) and 5(3).

Article 5

Effective date of notification

1. Subject to paragraphs 2, 3 and 4, notifications shall become effective on the date on which they are received by the Commission.

2. Where the information, including documents, contained in the notification is incomplete in any material respect, the Commission shall inform the notifying parties or their representatives in writing without delay. In such cases, the notification shall become effective on the date on which the complete information is received by the Commission.

3. Material changes in the facts contained in the notification coming to light subsequent to the notification which the notifying parties know or ought to know, or any new information coming to light subsequent to the notification which the parties know or ought to know and which would have had to be notified if known at the time of notification, shall be communicated to the Commission without delay. In such cases, when these material changes or new information could have a significant effect on the appraisal of the concentration, the notification may be considered by the Commission as becoming effective on the date on which the relevant information is received by the Commission; the Commission shall inform the notifying parties or their representatives of this in writing and without delay.

4. Incorrect or misleading information shall be considered to be incomplete information.

5. When the Commission publishes the fact of the notification pursuant to Article 4(3) of Regulation (EC) No 139/2004, it shall specify the date upon which the notification has been received. Where, further to the application of paragraphs 2, 3 and 4 of this Article, the effective date of notification is later than the date specified in that publication, the Commission shall issue a further publication in which it shall state the later date.

Article 6

Specific provisions relating to reasoned submissions, supplements and certifications

1. Reasoned submissions within the meaning of Article 4(4) and 4(5) of Regulation (EC) No 139/2004 shall contain the information, including documents, requested in accordance with Annex III to this Regulation.

2. Article 2, Article 3(1), third sentence, 3(2) to (5), Article 4, Article 5(1), 5 (2) first sentence, 5 (3), 5 (4), Article 21 and Article 23 of this Regulation shall apply *mutatis mutandis* to reasoned submissions within the meaning of Article 4(4) and 4(5) of Regulation (EC) No 139/2004.

Article 2, Article 3(1), third sentence, 3(2) to (5), Article 4, Article 5(1) to (4), Article 21 and Article 23 of this Regulation shall apply *mutatis mutandis* to supplements to notifications and certifications within the meaning of Article 10(5) of Regulation (EC) No 139/2004.

CHAPTER III

TIME-LIMITS

Article 7

Beginning of time periods

Time periods shall begin on the working day, as defined in Article 24 of this Regulation, following the event to which the relevant provision of Regulation (EC) No 139/2004 refers.

Article 8

Expiry of time periods

A time period calculated in working days shall expire at the end of its last working day.

A time period set by the Commission in terms of a calendar date shall expire at the end of that day.

Article 9

Suspension of time limit

1. The time limits referred to in Articles 9(4), Article 10(1) and 10(3) of Regulation (EC) No 139/2004 shall be suspended where the Commission has to take a decision pursuant to Article 11(3) or Article 13(4) of that Regulation, on any of the following grounds:

(a) information which the Commission has requested pursuant to Article 11(2) of Regulation (EC) No 139/2004 from one of the notifying parties or another involved party, as defined in Article 11 of this Regulation, is not provided or not provided in full within the time limit fixed by the Commission;

(b) information which the Commission has requested pursuant to Article 11(2) of Regulation (EC) No 139/2004 from a third party, as defined in Article 11 of this Regulation, is not provided or not provided in full within the time limit fixed by the Commission owing to circumstances for which one of the notifying parties or another involved party, as defined in Article 11 of this Regulation, is responsible;

(c) one of the notifying parties or another involved party, as defined in Article 11 of this Regulation, has refused to submit to an inspection deemed necessary by the Commission on the basis of Article 13(1) of Regulation (EC) No 139/2004 or to cooperate in the carrying out of such an inspection in accordance with Article 13(2) of that Regulation; (d) the notifying parties have failed to inform the Commission of material changes in the facts contained in the notification, or of any new information of the kind referred to in Article 5(3) of this Regulation.

2. The time limits referred to in Articles 9(4), Article 10(1) and 10(3) of Regulation (EC) No 139/2004 shall be suspended where the Commission has to take a decision pursuant to Article 11(3) of that Regulation, without proceeding first by way of simple request for information, owing to circumstances for which one of the undertakings involved in the concentration is responsible.

3. The time limits referred to in Articles 9(4), Article 10(1) and (3) of Regulation (EC) No 139/2004 shall be suspended:

(a) in the cases referred to in points (a) and (b) of paragraph 1, for the period between the expiry of the time limit set in the simple request for information, and the receipt of the complete and correct information required by decision;

(b) in the cases referred to in point (c) of paragraph 1, for the period between the unsuccessful attempt to carry out the inspection and the completion of the inspection ordered by decision;

(c) in the cases referred to in point (d) of paragraph 1, for the period between the occurrence of the change in the facts referred to therein and the receipt of the complete and correct information.

(d) in the cases referred to in paragraph 2 for the period between the expiry of the time limit set in the decision and the receipt of the complete and correct information required by decision.

4. The suspension of the time limit shall begin on the working day following the date on which the event causing the suspension occurred. It shall expire with the end of the day on which the reason for suspension is removed. Where such a day is not a working day, the suspension of the time-limit shall expire with the end of the following working day.

Article 10

Compliance with the time-limits

1. The time limits referred to in Article 4(4), fourth subparagraph, Article 9(4), Article 10(1) and (3), and Article 22(3) of Regulation (EC) No 139/2004 shall be met where the Commission has taken the relevant decision before the end of the period.

2. The time limits referred to in Article 4(4), second subparagraph, Article 4(5), third subparagraph, Article 9(2), Article 22(1), second subparagraph, and 22(2), second subparagraph, of Regulation (EC) No 139/2004 shall be met by a Member State concerned where that Member State, before the end of the period, informs the Commission in writing or makes or joins the request in writing, as the case may be.

3. The time limit referred to in Article 9(6) of Regulation (EC) No 139/2004 shall be met where the competent authority of a Member State concerned informs the undertakings concerned in the manner set out in that provision before the end of the period.

CHAPTER IV

EXERCISE OF THE RIGHT TO BE HEARD; HEARINGS

Article 11

Parties to be heard

For the purposes of the rights to be heard pursuant to Article 18 of Regulation (EC) No 139/2004, the following parties are distinguished:

(a) notifying parties, that is, persons or undertakings submitting a notification pursuant to Article 4(2) of Regulation (EC) No 139/2004;

(b) other involved parties, that is, parties to the proposed concentration other than the notifying parties, such as the seller and the undertaking which is the target of the concentration;

(c) third persons, that is natural or legal persons, including customers, suppliers and competitors, provided they demonstrate a sufficient interest within the meaning of Article 18(4), second sentence, of Regulation (EC) No 139/ 2004, which is the case in particular

—for members of the administrative or management bodies of the undertakings concerned or the recognised representatives of their employees;

—for consumer associations, where the proposed concentration concerns products or services used by final consumers.

(d) parties regarding whom the Commission intends to take a decision pursuant to Article 14 or Article 15 of Regulation (EC) No 139/2004.

Article 12

Decisions on the suspension of concentrations

1. Where the Commission intends to take a decision pursuant to Article 7(3) of Regulation (EC) No 139/2004 which adversely affects one or more of the parties, it shall, pursuant to Article 18(1) of that Regulation, inform the notifying parties and other involved parties in writing of its objections and shall set a time limit within which they may make known their views in writing.

2. Where the Commission, pursuant to Article 18(2) of Regulation (EC) No 139/2004, has taken a decision referred to in paragraph 1 of this Article provisionally without having given the notifying parties and other involved parties the opportunity to make known their views, it shall without delay send them the text of the provisional decision and shall set a time limit within which they may make known their views in writing.

Once the notifying parties and other involved parties have made known their views, the Commission shall take a final decision annulling, amending or confirming the provisional decision. Where they have not made known their views in writing within the time limit set, the Commission's provisional decision shall become final with the expiry of that period.

Article 13

Decisions on the substance of the case

1. Where the Commission intends to take a decision pursuant to Article 6(3) or Article 8(2) to (6) of Regulation (EC) No 139/2004, it shall, before consulting the Advisory Committee on Concentrations, hear the parties pursuant to Article 18(1) and (3) of that Regulation.

Article 12(2) of this Regulation shall apply *mutatis mutandis* where, in application of Article 18(2) of Regulation (EC) No 139/2004, the Commission has taken a decision pursuant to Article 8(5) of that Regulation provisionally.

2. The Commission shall address its objections in writing to the notifying parties.

The Commission shall, when giving notice of objections, set a time limit within which the notifying parties may inform the Commission of their comments in writing.

The Commission shall inform other involved parties in writing of these objections.

The Commission shall also set a time limit within which those other involved parties may inform the Commission of their comments in writing.

The Commission shall not be obliged to take into account comments received after the expiry of a time limit which it has set.

3. The parties to whom the Commission's objections have been addressed or who have been informed of those objections shall, within the time limit set, submit in writing their comments on the objections. In their written comments, they may set out all facts and matters known to them which are relevant to their defence, and shall attach any relevant documents as proof of the facts set out. They may also propose that the Commission hear persons who may corroborate those facts. They shall submit one original and 10 copies of their comments to the Commission to the address of the Commission's Directorate General for Competition. An electronic copy shall also be submitted at the same address and in the format specified by the Commission. The Commission shall forward copies of such written comments without delay to the competent authorities of the Member States.

4. Where the Commission intends to take a decision pursuant to Article 14 or Article 15 of Regulation (EC) No 139/2004, it shall, before consulting the Advisory Committee on Concentrations, hear pursuant to Article 18(1) and (3) of that Regulation the parties regarding whom the Commission intends to take such a decision.

The procedure provided for in paragraph 2, first and second subparagraphs, and paragraph 3 shall apply, *mutatis mutandis*.

Article 14

Oral hearings

1. Where the Commission intends to take a decision pursuant to Article 6(3) or Article 8(2) to (6) of Regulation (EC) No 139/2004, it shall afford the notifying parties who have so requested in their written comments the opportunity to develop their arguments in a formal oral hearing. It may also, at other stages in the proceedings, afford the notifying parties the opportunity of expressing their views orally. 30.4.2004 EN Official Journal of the European Union L 133/5

2. Where the Commission intends to take a decision pursuant to Article 6(3) or Article 8(2) to (6) of Regulation (EC) No 139/2004, it shall also afford other involved parties who have so requested in their written comments the opportunity to develop their arguments in a formal oral hearing. It may also, at other stages in the proceedings, afford other involved parties the opportunity of expressing their views orally.

3. Where the Commission intends to take a decision pursuant to Article 14 or Article 15 of Regulation (EC) No 139/2004, it shall afford parties on whom it proposes to impose a fine or periodic penalty payment the opportunity to develop their arguments in a formal

oral hearing, if so requested in their written comments. It may also, at other stages in the proceedings, afford such parties the opportunity of expressing their views orally.

Article 15

Conduct of formal oral hearings

1. Formal oral hearings shall be conducted by the Hearing Officer in full independence.

2. The Commission shall invite the persons to be heard to attend the formal oral hearing on such date as it shall determine.

3. The Commission shall invite the competent authorities of the Member States to take part in any formal oral hearing.

4. Persons invited to attend shall either appear in person or be represented by legal representatives or by representatives authorised by their constitution as appropriate. Undertakings and associations of undertakings may also be represented by a duly authorised agent appointed from among their permanent staff.

5. Persons heard by the Commission may be assisted by their lawyers or other qualified and duly authorised persons admitted by the Hearing Officer.

6. Formal oral hearings shall not be public. Each person may be heard separately or in the presence of other persons invited to attend, having regard to the legitimate interest of the undertakings in the protection of their business secrets and other confidential information.

7. The Hearing Officer may allow all parties within the meaning of Article 11, the Commission services and the competent authorities of the Member States to ask questions during the formal oral hearing. The Hearing Officer may hold a preparatory meeting with the parties and the Commission services, so as to facilitate the efficient organisation of the formal oral hearing.

8. The statements made by each person heard shall be recorded. Upon request, the recording of the formal oral hearing shall be made available to the persons who attended that hearing. Regard shall be had to the legitimate interest of the undertakings in the protection of their business secrets and other confidential information.

Article 16

Hearing of third persons

1. If third persons apply in writing to be heard pursuant to Article 18(4), second sentence, of Regulation (EC) No 139/ 2004, the Commission shall inform them in writing of the nature and subject matter of the procedure and shall set a time limit within which they may make known their views.

2. The third persons referred to in paragraph 1 shall make known their views in writing within the time limit set. The Commission may, where appropriate, afford such third parties who have so requested in their written comments the opportunity to participate in a formal hearing. It may also in other cases afford such third parties the opportunity of expressing their views orally.

3. The Commission may likewise invite any other natural or legal person to express its views, in writing as well as orally, including at a formal oral hearing.

CHAPTER V

ACCESS TO THE FILE AND TREATMENT OF CONFIDENTIAL INFORMATION

Article 17

Access to the file and use of documents

1. If so requested, the Commission shall grant access to the file to the parties to whom it has addressed a statement of objections, for the purpose of enabling them to exercise their rights of defence. Access shall be granted after the notification of the statement of objections.

2. The Commission shall, upon request, also give the other involved parties who have been informed of the objections access to the file in so far as this is necessary for the purposes of preparing their comments.

3. The right of access to the file shall not extend to confidential information, or to internal documents of the Commission or of the competent authorities of the Member States. The right of access to the file shall equally not extend to correspondence between the Commission and the competent authorities of the Member States or between the latter.

4. Documents obtained through access to the file pursuant to this Article may only be used for the purposes of the relevant proceeding pursuant to Regulation (EC) No 139/2004.

Article 18

Confidential information

1. Information, including documents, shall not be communicated or made accessible by the Commission in so far as it contains business secrets or other confidential information the disclosure of which is not considered necessary by the Commission for the purpose of the procedure.

2. Any person which makes known its views or comments pursuant to Articles 12, Article 13 and Article 16 of this Regulation, or supplies information pursuant to Article 11 of Regulation (EC) No 139/2004, or subsequently submits further information to the Commission in the course of the same procedure, shall clearly identify any material which it considers to be confidential, giving reasons, and provide a separate nonconfidential version by the date set by the Commission.

3. Without prejudice to paragraph 2, the Commission may require persons referred to in Article 3 of Regulation (EC) No 139/2004, undertakings and associations of undertakings in all cases where they produce or have produced documents or statements pursuant to Regulation (EC) No 139/2004 to identify the documents or parts of documents which they consider to contain business secrets or other confidential information belonging to them and to identify the undertakings with regard to which such documents are to be

considered confidential. The Commission may also require persons referred to in Article 3 of Regulation (EC) No 139/2004, undertakings or associations of undertakings to identify any part of a statement of objections, case summary or a decision adopted by the Commission which in their view contains business secrets. Where business secrets or other confidential information are identified, the persons, undertakings and associations of undertakings shall give reasons and provide a separate non-confidential version by the date set by the Commission.

CHAPTER VI

COMMITMENTS OFFERED BY THE UNDERTAKINGS CONCERNED

Article 19

Time limits for submission of commitments

1. Commitments offered by the undertakings concerned pursuant to Article 6(2) of Regulation (EC) No 139/2004 shall be submitted to the Commission within not more than 20 working days from the date of receipt of the notification.

2. Commitments offered by the undertakings concerned pursuant to Article 8(2) of Regulation (EC) No 139/2004 shall be submitted to the Commission within not more than 65 working days from the date on which proceedings were initiated.

Where pursuant to Article 10(3), second subparagraph, of Regulation (EC) No 139/2004 the period for the adoption of a decision pursuant to Article 8(1), (2) and (3) is extended, the period of 65 working days for the submission of commitments shall automatically be extended by the same number of working days.

In exceptional circumstances, the Commission may accept commitments offered after the expiry of the time limit for their submission within the meaning of this paragraph provided that the procedure provided for in Article 19(5) of Regulation (EC) No 139/2004 is complied with.

3. Articles 7, 8 and 9 shall apply *mutatis mutandis*.

Article 20

Procedure for the submission of commitments

1. One original and 10 copies of commitments offered by the undertakings concerned pursuant to Article 6(2) or Article 8(2) of Regulation (EC) No 139/2004 shall be submitted to the Commission at the address of the Commission's Directorate General for Competition. An electronic copy shall also be submitted at the same address and in the format specified by the Commission. The Commission shall forward copies of such commitments without delay to the competent authorities of the Member States.

2. When offering commitments pursuant to Articles 6(2) or Article 8(2) of Regulation (EC) No 139/2004, the undertakings concerned shall at the same time clearly identify any information which they consider to be confidential, giving reasons, and shall provide a separate non-confidential version.

CHAPTER VII

MISCELLANEOUS PROVISIONS

Article 21

Transmission of documents

1. Transmission of documents and invitations from the Commission to the addressees may be effected in any of the following ways:

(a) delivery by hand against receipt;

(b) registered letter with acknowledgement of receipt;

(c) fax with a request for acknowledgement of receipt;

(d) telex;

(e) electronic mail with a request for acknowledgement of receipt.

2. Unless otherwise provided in this Regulation, paragraph 1 also applies to the transmission of documents from the notifying parties, from other involved parties or from third parties to the Commission.

3. Where a document is sent by telex, by fax or by electronic mail, it shall be presumed that it has been received by the addressee on the day on which it was sent.

Article 22

Setting of time limits In setting the time limits provided for pursuant to Article 12(1) and (2), Article 13(2) and Article 16(1), the Commission shall have regard to the time required for the preparation of statements and to the urgency of the case. It shall also take account of working days as well as public holidays in the country of receipt of the Commission's communication.

Time limits shall be set in terms of a precise calendar date.

Article 23

Receipt of documents by the Commission

1. In accordance with the provisions of Article 5(1) of this Regulation, notifications shall be delivered to the Commission at the address of the Commission's Directorate General for Competition as published by the Commission in the *Official Journal of the European Union.*

2. Additional information requested to complete notifications must reach the Commission at the address referred to in paragraph 1.

3. Written comments on Commission communications pursuant to Article 12(1) and (2), Article 13(2) and Article 16(1) of this Regulation must have reached the Commission at the address referred to in paragraph 1 before the expiry of the time limit set in each case.

Article 24

Definition of working days

The expression working days in Regulation (EC) No 139/2004 and in this Regulation means all days other than Saturdays, Sundays, and Commission holidays as published in the *Official Journal of the European Union* before the beginning of each year.

Article 25

Repeal and transitional provision

1. Without prejudice to paragraphs 2 and 3, Regulation (EC) No 447/98 is repealed with effect from 1 May 2004. References to the repealed Regulation shall be construed as references to this Regulation.

2. Regulation (EC) No 447/98 shall continue to apply to any concentration falling within the scope of Regulation (EEC) No 4064/89.

3. For the purposes of paragraph 2, Sections 1 to 12 of the Annex to Regulation (EC) No 447/98 shall be replaced by Sections 1 to 11 of Annex I to this Regulation. In such cases references in those sections to the 'EC Merger Regulation' and to the 'Implementing Regulation' shall be read as referring to the corresponding provisions of Regulation (EEC) No 4064/89 and Regulation (EC) No 447/98, respectively.

Article 26

Entry into force

This Regulation shall enter into force on 1 May 2004.

This Regulation shall be binding in its entirety and directly applicable in all Member States.

Done at Brussels, 7 April 2004.

For the Commission

Franz FISCHLER

Member of the Commission

Note—the annexes to this regulation, which include the notification forms, are not included here

Enterprise Act 2002[1]

PART 3 MERGERS

CHAPTER 1 DUTY TO MAKE REFERENCES

Duty to make references: completed mergers

22 Duty to make references in relation to completed mergers

(1) The OFT shall, subject to subsections (2) and (3), make a reference to the Commission if the OFT believes that it is or may be the case that—

(a) a relevant merger situation has been created; and
(b) the creation of that situation has resulted, or may be expected to result, in a substantial lessening of competition within any market or markets in the United Kingdom for goods or services.

(2) The OFT may decide not to make a reference under this section if it believes that—

(a) the market concerned is not, or the markets concerned are not, of sufficient importance to justify the making of a reference to the Commission; or
(b) any relevant customer benefits in relation to the creation of the relevant merger situation concerned outweigh the substantial lessening of competition concerned and any adverse effects of the substantial lessening of competition concerned.

(3) No reference shall be made under this section if—

(a) the making of the reference is prevented by section 74(1) or 96(3) or paragraph 4 of Schedule 7;
(b) the OFT is considering whether to accept undertakings under section 73 instead of making such a reference;
(c) the relevant merger situation concerned is being, or has been, dealt with in connection with a reference made under section 33;
(d) a notice under section 42(2) is in force in relation to the matter or the matter to which such a notice relates has been finally determined under Chapter 2 otherwise than in circumstances in which a notice is then given to the OFT under section 56(1);
(e) the European Commission is considering a request made, in relation to the matter concerned, by the United Kingdom (whether alone or with others) under article

[1] This includes, in s 70 and Sched 6, the material to be inserted into the Water Industry Act 1991 relating to water mergers. The text set out here is up to date as at 1 Aug 2006. For the sake of simplicity amendments and deletions have not been annotated.

22(1) of the EC Merger Regulation, is proceeding with the matter in pursuance of such a request or has dealt with the matter in pursuance of such a request; or
(f) subject to subsection (3A), a reasoned submission requesting referral to the European Commission has been submitted to the European Commission under article 4(5) of the EC Merger Regulation.

(4) A reference under this section shall, in particular, specify—

(a) the enactment under which it is made; and
(b) the date on which it is made.

(5) The references in this section to the creation of a relevant merger situation shall be construed in accordance with section 23, the reference in subsection (2) of this section to relevant customer benefits shall be construed in accordance with section 30 and the reference in subsection (3) of this section to a matter to which a notice under section 42(2) relates being finally determined under Chapter 2 shall be construed in accordance with section 43(4) and (5).

(6) In this Part "market in the United Kingdom" includes—

(a) so far as it operates in the United Kingdom or a part of the United Kingdom, any market which operates there and in another country or territory or in a part of another country or territory; and
(b) any market which operates only in a part of the United Kingdom;

and references to a market for goods or services include references to a market for goods and services.

(7) In this Part "the decision-making authority" means—

(a) in the case of a reference or possible reference under this section or section 33, the OFT or (as the case may be) the Commission; and
(b) in the case of a notice or possible notice under section 42(2) or 59(2) or a reference or possible reference under section 45 or 62, the OFT, the Commission or (as the case may be) the Secretary of State.

23 Relevant merger situations

(1) For the purposes of this Part, a relevant merger situation has been created if—

(a) two or more enterprises have ceased to be distinct enterprises at a time or in circumstances falling within section 24; and
(b) the value of the turnover in the United Kingdom of the enterprise being taken over exceeds £70 million.

(2) For the purposes of this Part, a relevant merger situation has also been created if—

(a) two or more enterprises have ceased to be distinct enterprises at a time or in circumstances falling within section 24; and
(b) as a result, one or both of the conditions mentioned in subsections (3) and (4) below prevails or prevails to a greater extent.

(3) The condition mentioned in this subsection is that, in relation to the supply of goods of any description, at least one-quarter of all the goods of that description which are supplied in the United Kingdom, or in a substantial part of the United Kingdom—

(a) are supplied by one and the same person or are supplied to one and the same person; or

(b) are supplied by the persons by whom the enterprises concerned are carried on, or are supplied to those persons.

(4) The condition mentioned in this subsection is that, in relation to the supply of services of any description, the supply of services of that description in the United Kingdom, or in a substantial part of the United Kingdom, is to the extent of at least one-quarter—

(a) supply by one and the same person, or supply for one and the same person;

(b) supply by the persons by whom the enterprises concerned are carried on, or supply for those persons.

(5) For the purpose of deciding whether the proportion of one-quarter mentioned in subsection (3) or (4) is fulfilled with respect to goods or (as the case may be) services of any description, the decision-making authority shall apply such criterion (whether value, cost, price, quantity, capacity, number of workers employed or some other criterion, of whatever nature), or such combination of criteria, as the decision-making authority considers appropriate.

(6) References in subsections (3) and (4) to the supply of goods or (as the case may be) services shall, in relation to goods or services of any description which are the subject of different forms of supply, be construed in whichever of the following ways the decision-making authority considers appropriate—

(a) as references to any of those forms of supply taken separately;

(b) as references to all those forms of supply taken together; or

(c) as references to any of those forms of supply taken in groups.

(7) For the purposes of subsection (6) the decision-making authority may treat goods or services as being the subject of different forms of supply whenever—

(a) the transactions concerned differ as to their nature, their parties, their terms or their surrounding circumstances; and

(b) the difference is one which, in the opinion of the decision-making authority, ought for the purposes of that subsection to be treated as a material difference.

(8) The criteria for deciding when goods or services can be treated, for the purposes of this section, as goods or services of a separate description shall be such as in any particular case the decision-making authority considers appropriate in the circumstances of that case.

(9) For the purposes of this Chapter, the question whether a relevant merger situation has been created shall be determined as at—

(a) in the case of a reference which is treated as having been made under section 22 by virtue of section 37(2), such time as the Commission may determine; and

(b) in any other case, immediately before the time when the reference has been, or is to be, made.

24 Time-limits and prior notice

(1) For the purposes of section 23 two or more enterprises have ceased to be distinct enterprises at a time or in circumstances falling within this section if—

(a) the two or more enterprises ceased to be distinct enterprises before the day on which the reference relating to them is to be made and did so not more than four months before that day; or
(b) notice of material facts about the arrangements or transactions under or in consequence of which the enterprises have ceased to be distinct enterprises has not been given in accordance with subsection (2).

(2) Notice of material facts is given in accordance with this subsection if—

(a) it is given to the OFT prior to the entering into of the arrangements or transactions concerned or the facts are made public prior to the entering into of those arrangements or transactions; or
(b) it is given to the OFT, or the facts are made public, more than four months before the day on which the reference is to be made.

(3) In this section—
'made public' means so publicised as to be generally known or readily ascertainable; and 'notice' includes notice which is not in writing.

25 Extension of time-limits

(1) The OFT and the persons carrying on the enterprises which have or may have ceased to be distinct enterprises may agree to extend by no more than 20 days the four month period mentioned in section 24(1)(a) or (2)(b).

(2) The OFT may by notice to the persons carrying on the enterprises which have or may have ceased to be distinct enterprises extend the four month period mentioned in section 24(1)(a) or (2)(b) if it considers that any of those persons has failed to provide, within the period stated in a notice under section 31 and in the manner authorised or required, information requested of him in that notice.

(3) An extension under subsection (2) shall be for the period beginning with the end of the period within which the information is to be provided and which is stated in the notice under section 31 and ending with—

(a) the provision of the information to the satisfaction of the OFT; or
(b) if earlier, the cancellation by the OFT of the extension.

(4) The OFT may by notice to the persons carrying on the enterprises which have or may have ceased to be distinct enterprises extend the four month period mentioned in section 24(1)(a) or (2)(b) if it is seeking undertakings from any of those persons under section 73.

(5) An extension under subsection (4) shall be for the period beginning with the receipt of the notice under that subsection and ending with the earliest of the following events—

(a) the giving of the undertakings concerned;
(b) the expiry of the period of 10 days beginning with the first day after the receipt by the OFT of a notice from the person who has been given a notice under subsection (4) and from whom the undertakings are being sought stating that he does not intend to give the undertakings; or
(c) the cancellation by the OFT of the extension.

(6) The OFT may by notice to the persons carrying on the enterprises which have or may have ceased to be distinct enterprises extend the four month period mentioned in section 24(1)(a) or (2)(b) if the European Commission is considering a request made, in relation to the matter concerned, by the United Kingdom (whether alone or with others) under article 22(1) of the EC Merger Regulation (but is not yet proceeding with the matter in pursuance of such a request).

(7) An extension under subsection (6) shall be for the period beginning with the receipt of the notice under that subsection and ending with the receipt of a notice under subsection (8).

(8) The OFT shall, in connection with any notice given by it under subsection (6), by notice inform the persons carrying on the enterprises which have or may have ceased to be distinct enterprises of the completion by the European Commission of its consideration of the request of the United Kingdom.

(9) Subject to subsections (10) and (11), where the four month period mentioned in section 24(1)(a) or (2)(b) is extended or further extended by virtue of this section in relation to a particular case, any reference to that period in section 24 or the preceding provisions of this section shall have effect in relation to that case as if it were a reference to a period equivalent to the aggregate of the period being extended and the period of the extension (whether or not those periods overlap in time).

(10) Subsection (11) applies where—

- (a) the four month period mentioned in section 24(1)(a) or (2)(b) is further extended;
- (b) the further extension and at least one previous extension is made under one or more of subsections (2), (4) and (6); and
- (c) the same days or fractions of days are included in or comprise the further extension and are included in or comprise at least one such previous extension.

(11) In calculating the period of the further extension, any days or fractions of days of the kind mentioned in subsection (10)(c) shall be disregarded.

(12) No more than one extension is possible under subsection (1).

26 Enterprises ceasing to be distinct enterprises

(1) For the purposes of this Part any two enterprises cease to be distinct enterprises if they are brought under common ownership or common control (whether or not the business to which either of them formerly belonged continues to be carried on under the same or different ownership or control).

(2) Enterprises shall, in particular, be treated as being under common control if they are—

- (a) enterprises of interconnected bodies corporate;
- (b) enterprises carried on by two or more bodies corporate of which one and the same person or group of persons has control; or
- (c) an enterprise carried on by a body corporate and an enterprise carried on by a person or group of persons having control of that body corporate.

(3) A person or group of persons able, directly or indirectly, to control or materially to influence the policy of a body corporate, or the policy of any person in carrying on an enterprise but without having a controlling interest in that body corporate or in that enterprise, may, for the purposes of subsections (1) and (2), be treated as having control of it.

(4) For the purposes of subsection (1), in so far as it relates to bringing two or more enterprises under common control, a person or group of persons may be treated as bringing an enterprise under his or their control if—

(a) being already able to control or materially to influence the policy of the person carrying on the enterprise, that person or group of persons acquires a controlling interest in the enterprise or, in the case of an enterprise carried on by a body corporate, acquires a controlling interest in that body corporate; or
(b) being already able materially to influence the policy of the person carrying on the enterprise, that person or group of persons becomes able to control that policy.

27 Time when enterprises cease to be distinct

(1) Subsection (2) applies in relation to any arrangements or transaction—

(a) not having immediate effect or having immediate effect only in part; but
(b) under or in consequence of which any two enterprises cease to be distinct enterprises.

(2) The time when the parties to any such arrangements or transaction become bound to such extent as will result, on effect being given to their obligations, in the enterprises ceasing to be distinct enterprises shall be taken to be the time at which the two enterprises cease to be distinct enterprises.

(3) In accordance with subsections (1) and (2) (but without prejudice to the generality of those subsections) for the purpose of determining the time at which any two enterprises cease to be distinct enterprises no account shall be taken of any option or other conditional right until the option is exercised or the condition is satisfied.

(4) Subsections (1) to (3) are subject to subsections (5) to (8) and section 29.

(5) The decision-making authority may, for the purposes of a reference, treat successive events to which this subsection applies as having occurred simultaneously on the date on which the latest of them occurred.

(6) Subsection (5) applies to successive events—

(a) which occur within a period of two years under or in consequence of the same arrangements or transaction, or successive arrangements or transactions between the same parties or interests; and
(b) by virtue of each of which, under or in consequence of the arrangements or the transaction or transactions concerned, any enterprises cease as between themselves to be distinct enterprises.

(7) The decision-making authority may, for the purposes of subsections (5) and (6), treat such arrangements or transactions as the decision-making authority considers appropriate as arrangements or transactions between the same interests.

(8) In deciding whether it is appropriate to treat arrangements or transactions as arrangements or transactions between the same interests the decision-making authority shall, in particular, have regard to the persons substantially concerned in the arrangements or transactions concerned.

28 Turnover test

(1) For the purposes of section 23 the value of the turnover in the United Kingdom of the enterprise being taken over shall be determined by taking the total value of the turnover in the United Kingdom of the enterprises which cease to be distinct enterprises and deducting—

(a) the turnover in the United Kingdom of any enterprise which continues to be carried on under the same ownership and control; or
(b) if no enterprise continues to be carried on under the same ownership and control, the turnover in the United Kingdom which, of all the turnovers concerned, is the turnover of the highest value.

(2) For the purposes of this Part (other than section 121(4)(c)(ii)) the turnover in the United Kingdom of an enterprise shall be determined in accordance with such provisions as may be specified in an order made by the Secretary of State.

(3) An order under subsection (2) may, in particular, make provision as to—

(a) the amounts which are, or which are not, to be treated as comprising an enterprise's turnover;
(b) the date or dates by reference to which an enterprise's turnover is to be determined;
(c) the connection with the United Kingdom by virtue of which an enterprise's turnover is turnover in the United Kingdom.

(4) An order under subsection (2) may, in particular, make provision enabling the decision-making authority to determine matters of a description specified in the order (including any of the matters mentioned in paragraphs (a) to (c) of subsection (3)).

(5) The OFT shall—

(a) keep under review the sum for the time being mentioned in section 23(1)(b); and
(b) from time to time advise the Secretary of State as to whether the sum is still appropriate.

(6) The Secretary of State may by order amend section 23(1)(b) so as to alter the sum for the time being mentioned there.

29 Obtaining control by stages

(1) Where an enterprise is brought under the control of a person or group of persons in the course of two or more transactions (in this section a 'series of transactions') to which subsection (2) applies, those transactions may, if the decision-making authority considers it appropriate, be treated for the purposes of a reference as having occurred simultaneously on the date on which the latest of them occurred.

(2) This subsection applies to—

(a) any transaction which—
(i) enables that person or group of persons directly or indirectly to control or materially to influence the policy of any person carrying on the enterprise;
(ii) enables that person or group of persons to do so to a greater degree; or
(iii) is a step (whether direct or indirect) towards enabling that person or group of persons to do so; and
(b) any transaction by virtue of which that person or group of persons acquires a controlling interest in the enterprise or, where the enterprise is carried on by a body corporate, in that body corporate.

(3) Where a series of transactions includes a transaction falling within subsection (2)(b), any transaction occurring after the occurrence of that transaction is to be disregarded for the purposes of subsection (1).

(4) Where the period within which a series of transactions occurs exceeds two years, the transactions that may be treated as mentioned in subsection (1) are any of those transactions that occur within a period of two years.

(5) Sections 26(2) to (4) and 127(1), (2) and (4) to (6) shall apply for the purposes of this section to determine—

(a) whether an enterprise is brought under the control of a person or group of persons; and
(b) whether a transaction is one to which subsection (2) applies;

as they apply for the purposes of section 26 to determine whether enterprises are brought under common control.

(6) In determining for the purposes of this section the time at which any transaction occurs, no account shall be taken of any option or other conditional right until the option is exercised or the condition is satisfied.

30 Relevant customer benefits

(1) For the purposes of this Part a benefit is a relevant customer benefit if—

(a) it is a benefit to relevant customers in the form of—
(i) lower prices, higher quality or greater choice of goods or services in any market in the United Kingdom (whether or not the market or markets in which the substantial lessening of competition concerned has, or may have, occurred or (as the case may be) may occur); or
(ii) greater innovation in relation to such goods or services; and
(b) the decision-making authority believes—
(i) in the case of a reference or possible reference under section 22 or 45(2), as mentioned in subsection (2); and
(ii) in the case of a reference or possible reference under section 33 or 45(4), as mentioned in subsection (3).

(2) The belief, in the case of a reference or possible reference under section 22 or section 45(2), is that—

(a) the benefit has accrued as a result of the creation of the relevant merger situation concerned or may be expected to accrue within a reasonable period as a result of the creation of that situation; and
(b) the benefit was, or is, unlikely to accrue without the creation of that situation or a similar lessening of competition.

(3) The belief, in the case of a reference or possible reference under section 33 or 45(4), is that—

(a) the benefit may be expected to accrue within a reasonable period as a result of the creation of the relevant merger situation concerned; and
(b) the benefit is unlikely to accrue without the creation of that situation or a similar lessening of competition.

(4) In subsection (1) "relevant customers" means—

(a) customers of any person carrying on an enterprise which, in the creation of the relevant merger situation concerned, has ceased to be, or (as the case may be) will cease to be, a distinct enterprise;
(b) customers of such customers; and
(c) any other customers in a chain of customers beginning with the customers mentioned in paragraph (a);

and in this subsection "customers" includes future customers.

31 Information powers in relation to completed mergers

(1) The OFT may by notice to any of the persons carrying on the enterprises which have or may have ceased to be distinct enterprises request him to provide the OFT with such information as the OFT may require for the purpose of deciding whether to make a reference under section 22.

(2) The notice shall state—

(a) the information required;
(b) the period within which the information is to be provided; and
(c) the possible consequences of not providing the information within the stated period and in the authorised or required manner.

32 Supplementary provision for purposes of sections 25 and 31

(1) The Secretary of State may make regulations for the purposes of sections 25 and 31.(2) The regulations may, in particular—

(a) provide for the manner in which any information requested by the OFT under section 31 is authorised or required to be provided, and the time at which such information is to be treated as provided (including the time at which it is to be treated as provided to the satisfaction of the OFT for the purposes of section 25(3));
(b) provide for the persons carrying on the enterprises which have or may have ceased to be distinct enterprises to be informed, in circumstances in which section 25(3) applies—
(i) of the fact that the OFT is satisfied as to the provision of the information

requested by it or (as the case may be) of the OFT's decision to cancel the extension; and

(ii) of the time at which the OFT is to be treated as so satisfied or (as the case may be) of the time at which the cancellation is to be treated as having effect;

(c) provide for the persons carrying on the enterprises which have or may have ceased to be distinct enterprises to be informed, in circumstances in which section 25(5) applies—

(i) of the OFT's decision to cancel the extension; and

(ii) of the time at which the cancellation is to be treated as having effect;

(d) provide for the time at which any notice under section 25(4), (5)(b), (6) or (8) is to be treated as received;

(e) provide that a person is, or is not, to be treated, in such circumstances as may be specified in the regulations, as acting on behalf of a person carrying on an enterprise which has or may have ceased to be a distinct enterprise.

(3) A notice under section 25(2)—

(a) shall be given within 5 days of the end of the period within which the information is to be provided and which is stated in the notice under section 31; and(b) shall inform the person to whom it is addressed of—

(i) the OFT's opinion as mentioned in section 25(2); and

(ii) the OFT's intention to extend the period for considering whether to make a reference.

(4) In determining for the purposes of section 25(1) or (5)(b) or subsection (3)(a) above any period which is expressed in the enactment concerned as a period of days or number of days no account shall be taken of—

(a) Saturday, Sunday, Good Friday and Christmas Day; and

(b) any day which is a bank holiday in England and Wales.

Duty to make references: anticipated mergers

33 Duty to make references in relation to anticipated mergers

(1) The OFT shall, subject to subsections (2) and (3), make a reference to the Commission if the OFT believes that it is or may be the case that—

(a) arrangements are in progress or in contemplation which, if carried into effect, will result in the creation of a relevant merger situation; and

(b) the creation of that situation may be expected to result in a substantial lessening of competition within any market or markets in the United Kingdom for goods or services.

(2) The OFT may decide not to make a reference under this section if it believes that—

(a) the market concerned is not, or the markets concerned are not, of sufficient importance to justify the making of a reference to the Commission;

(b) the arrangements concerned are not sufficiently far advanced, or are not sufficiently likely to proceed, to justify the making of a reference to the Commission; or

(c) any relevant customer benefits in relation to the creation of the relevant merger situation concerned outweigh the substantial lessening of competition concerned and any adverse effects of the substantial lessening of competition concerned.

(3) No reference shall be made under this section if—

(a) the making of the reference is prevented by section 74(1) or 96(3) or paragraph 4 of Schedule 7;
(b) the OFT is considering whether to accept undertakings under section 73 instead of making such a reference;
(c) the arrangements concerned are being, or have been, dealt with in connection with a reference made under section 22;
(d) a notice under section 42(2) is in force in relation to the matter or the matter to which such a notice relates has been finally determined under Chapter 2 otherwise than in circumstances in which a notice is then given to the OFT under section 56(1);
(e) the European Commission is considering a request made, in relation to the matter concerned, by the United Kingdom (whether alone or with others) under article 22(1) of the EC Merger Regulation, is proceeding with the matter in pursuance of such a request or has dealt with the matter in pursuance of such a request; or
(f) subject to subsection (3A), a reasoned submission requesting referral to the European Commission has been submitted to the European Commission under article 4(5) of the EC Merger Regulation.

(3A) Section 33(3)(f) shall cease to apply if the OFT is informed that a Member State competent to examine the concentration under its national competition law has, within the time permitted by Article 4(5) of the EC Merger Regulation, expressed its disagreement as regards the request to refer the case to the European Commission; and this subsection shall be construed in accordance with that Regulation.

(4) A reference under this section shall, in particular, specify—

(a) the enactment under which it is made; and
(b) the date on which it is made.

34 Supplementary provision in relation to anticipated mergers

(1) The Secretary of State may by order make such provision as he considers appropriate about the operation of sections 27 and 29 in relation to—

(a) references under this Part which relate to arrangements which are in progress or in contemplation; or
(b) notices under section 42(2), 59(2) or 67(2) which relate to such arrangements.

(2) An order under subsection (1) may, in particular—

(a) provide for sections 27(5) to (8) and 29 to apply with modifications in relation to such references or notices or in relation to particular descriptions of such references or notices;
(b) enable particular descriptions of events, arrangements or transactions which have already occurred—
  (i) to be taken into account for the purposes of deciding whether to make such references or such references of a particular description or whether to give such notices or such notices of a particular description;

(ii) to be dealt with under such references or such references of a particular description or under such notices or such notices of a particular description.

Cases referred by European Commission under EC Merger Regulation

34A Duty of OFT where case referred by the European Commission

(1) Subsection (2) applies if the European Commission has by a decision referred the whole or part of a case to the OFT under Article 4(4) or 9 of the EC Merger Regulation, or is deemed to have taken such a decision, unless an intervention notice is in force in relation to that case.

(2) Before the end of the preliminary assessment period, the OFT shall—

(a) decide whether to make a reference to the Commission under section 22 or 33; and
(b) inform the persons carrying on the enterprises concerned by notice of that decision and of the reasons for it.

(3) The OFT may, for the purposes of subsection (2), decide not to make a reference on the basis that it is considering whether to seek or accept undertakings under section 73 instead of making a reference; but a decision taken on that basis does not prevent the OFT from making a reference under section 22 or 33 in the event of no such undertakings being offered or accepted.

(4) In this section—
'the preliminary assessment period' means, subject to subsection (5), the period of 45 working days beginning with the day after the day on which the decision of the European Commission to refer the case is taken (or is deemed to have been taken); and "working day" means any day which is not—
(a) a Saturday;
(b) a Sunday; or
(c) a day which is a European Commission holiday (as published in the Official Journal of the European Communities before the beginning of the year in which it occurs).

(5) If the OFT has imposed a requirement under section 34B and it considers that the person on whom that requirement was imposed has failed to comply with it, the OFT may, by notice to the persons carrying on the enterprises concerned, extend the preliminary assessment period.(6) The period of an extension under subsection (5) shall—

(a) begin with the end of the period within which the requirement under section 34B could be complied with; and
(b) end with the earlier of either compliance with the requirement to the satisfaction of the OFT or cancellation by the OFT of the extension.

(7) A notice under subsection (6) shall—

(a) be given within 5 working days of the end of the period mentioned in paragraph
(a) of that subsection; and
(b) inform the person to whom it is addressed that the OFT is of the opinion mentioned in subsection (5) and that it intends to extend the preliminary assessment period.

34B Power to request information in referred cases

(1) In a case mentioned in section 34A(1), the OFT may by notice to any of the persons carrying on the enterprises concerned request him to provide the OFT with such information as the OFT may require for the purpose of making a decision for the purposes of section 34A(2).

(2) The notice shall state—

(a) the information required;
(b) the period within which the information is to be provided;
(c) the manner (if any) in which the information is required to be provided; and
(d) the possible consequences—
(i) of not providing the information within the stated period; and
(ii) if a manner for its provision is stated in the notice, of not providing it in that manner.

Determination of references

35 Questions to be decided in relation to completed mergers

(1) Subject to subsections (6) and (7) and section 127(3), the Commission shall, on a reference under section 22, decide the following questions—

(a) whether a relevant merger situation has been created; and
(b) if so, whether the creation of that situation has resulted, or may be expected to result, in a substantial lessening of competition within any market or markets in the United Kingdom for goods or services.

(2) For the purposes of this Part there is an anti-competitive outcome if—

(a) a relevant merger situation has been created and the creation of that situation has resulted, or may be expected to result, in a substantial lessening of competition within any market or markets in the United Kingdom for goods or services; or
(b) arrangements are in progress or in contemplation which, if carried into effect, will result in the creation of a relevant merger situation and the creation of that situation may be expected to result in a substantial lessening of competition within any market or markets in the United Kingdom for goods or services.

(3) The Commission shall, if it has decided on a reference under section 22 that there is an anti-competitive outcome (within the meaning given by subsection (2)(a)), decide the following additional questions—

(a) whether action should be taken by it under section 41(2) for the purpose of remedying, mitigating or preventing the substantial lessening of competition concerned or any adverse effect which has resulted from, or may be expected to result from, the substantial lessening of competition;
(b) whether it should recommend the taking of action by others for the purpose of remedying, mitigating or preventing the substantial lessening of competition concerned or any adverse effect which has resulted from, or may be expected to result from, the substantial lessening of competition; and

(c) in either case, if action should be taken, what action should be taken and what is to be remedied, mitigated or prevented.

(4) In deciding the questions mentioned in subsection (3) the Commission shall, in particular, have regard to the need to achieve as comprehensive a solution as is reasonable and practicable to the substantial lessening of competition and any adverse effects resulting from it.

(5) In deciding the questions mentioned in subsection (3) the Commission may, in particular, have regard to the effect of any action on any relevant customer benefits in relation to the creation of the relevant merger situation concerned.

(6) In relation to the question whether a relevant merger situation has been created, a reference under section 22 may be framed so as to require the Commission to exclude from consideration—

(a) subsection (1) of section 23;
(b) subsection (2) of that section; or
(c) one of those subsections if the Commission finds that the other is satisfied.

(7) In relation to the question whether any such result as is mentioned in section 23(2)(b) has arisen, a reference under section 22 may be framed so as to require the Commission to confine its investigation to the supply of goods or services in a part of the United Kingdom specified in the reference.

36 Questions to be decided in relation to anticipated mergers

(1) Subject to subsections (5) and (6) and section 127(3), the Commission shall, on a reference under section 33, decide the following questions—

(a) whether arrangements are in progress or in contemplation which, if carried into effect, will result in the creation of a relevant merger situation; and
(b) if so, whether the creation of that situation may be expected to result in a substantial lessening of competition within any market or markets in the United Kingdom for goods or services.

(2) The Commission shall, if it has decided on a reference under section 33 that there is an anti-competitive outcome (within the meaning given by section 35(2)(b)), decide the following additional questions—

(a) whether action should be taken by it under section 41(2) for the purpose of remedying, mitigating or preventing the substantial lessening of competition concerned or any adverse effect which may be expected to result from the substantial lessening of competition;
(b) whether it should recommend the taking of action by others for the purpose of remedying, mitigating or preventing the substantial lessening of competition concerned or any adverse effect which may be expected to result from the substantial lessening of competition; and
(c) in either case, if action should be taken, what action should be taken and what is to be remedied, mitigated or prevented.

(3) In deciding the questions mentioned in subsection (2) the Commission shall, in particular, have regard to the need to achieve as comprehensive a solution as is reasonable

and practicable to the substantial lessening of competition and any adverse effects resulting from it.

(4) In deciding the questions mentioned in subsection (2) the Commission may, in particular, have regard to the effect of any action on any relevant customer benefits in relation to the creation of the relevant merger situation concerned.

(5) In relation to the question whether a relevant merger situation will be created, a reference under section 33 may be framed so as to require the Commission to exclude from consideration—

- (a) subsection (1) of section 23;
- (b) subsection (2) of that section; or
- (c) one of those subsections if the Commission finds that the other is satisfied.

(6) In relation to the question whether any such result as is mentioned in section 23(2)(b) will arise, a reference under section 33 may be framed so as to require the Commission to confine its investigation to the supply of goods or services in a part of the United Kingdom specified in the reference.

37 Cancellation and variation of references under section 22 or 33

(1) The Commission shall cancel a reference under section 33 if it considers that the proposal to make arrangements of the kind mentioned in the reference has been abandoned.

(2) The Commission may, if it considers that doing so is justified by the facts (including events occurring on or after the making of the reference concerned), treat a reference made under section 22 or 33 as if it had been made under section 33 or (as the case may be) 22; and, in such cases, references in this Part to references under those sections shall, so far as may be necessary, be construed accordingly.

(3) Where, by virtue of subsection (2), the Commission treats a reference made under section 22 or 33 as if it had been made under section 33 or (as the case may be) 22, sections 77 to 81 shall, in particular, apply as if the reference had been made under section 33 or (as the case may be) 22 instead of under section 22 or 33.

(4) Subsection (5) applies in relation to any undertaking accepted under section 80, or any order made under section 81, which is in force immediately before the Commission, by virtue of subsection (2), treats a reference made under section 22 or 33 as if it had been made under section 33 or (as the case may be) 22.(5) The undertaking or order shall, so far as applicable, continue in force as if—

(a) in the case of an undertaking or order which relates to a reference made under section 22, accepted or made in relation to a reference made under section 33; and
(b) in the case of an undertaking or order which relates to a reference made under section 33, accepted or made in relation to a reference made under section 22;

and the undertaking or order concerned may be varied, superseded, released or revoked accordingly.

(6) The OFT may at any time vary a reference under section 22 or 33.

(7) The OFT shall consult the Commission before varying any such reference.

(8) Subsection (7) shall not apply if the Commission has requested the variation concerned.

(9) No variation by the OFT under this section shall be capable of altering the period permitted by section 39 within which the report of the Commission under section 38 is to be prepared and published.

38 Investigations and reports on references under section 22 or 33

(1) The Commission shall prepare and publish a report on a reference under section 22 or 33 within the period permitted by section 39.

(2) The report shall, in particular, contain—

(a) the decisions of the Commission on the questions which it is required to answer by virtue of section 35 or (as the case may be) 36;
(b) its reasons for its decisions; and
(c) such information as the Commission considers appropriate for facilitating a proper understanding of those questions and of its reasons for its decisions.

(3) The Commission shall carry out such investigations as it considers appropriate for the purposes of preparing a report under this section.

(4) The Commission shall, at the same time as a report prepared under this section is published, give it to the OFT.

39 Time-limits for investigations and reports

(1) The Commission shall prepare and publish its report under section 38 within the period of 24 weeks beginning with the date of the reference concerned.

. . .

(3) The Commission may extend, by no more than 8 weeks, the period within which a report under section 38 is to be prepared and published if it considers that there are special reasons why the report cannot be prepared and published within that period.

(4) The Commission may extend the period within which a report under section 38 is to be prepared and published if it considers that a relevant person has failed (whether with or without a reasonable excuse) to comply with any requirement of a notice under section 109.

(5) In subsection (4) "relevant person" means—

(a) any person carrying on any of the enterprises concerned;
(b) any person who (whether alone or as a member of a group) owns or has control of any such person; or
(c) any officer, employee or agent of any person mentioned in paragraph (a) or (b).

(6) For the purposes of subsection (5) a person or group of persons able, directly or indirectly, to control or materially to influence the policy of a body of persons corporate or unincorporate, but without having a controlling interest in that body of persons, may be treated as having control of it.

(7) An extension under subsection (3) or (4) shall come into force when published under section 107.

(8) An extension under subsection (4) shall continue in force until—

(a) the person concerned provides the information or documents to the satisfaction of the Commission or (as the case may be) appears as a witness in accordance with the requirements of the Commission; or
(b) the Commission publishes its decision to cancel the extension.

(9) References in this Part to the date of a reference shall be construed as references to the date specified in the reference as the date on which it is made.

(10) This section is subject to section 40.

40 Section 39: supplementary

. . .

(3) A period extended under subsection (3) of section 39 may also be extended under subsection (4) of that section and a period extended under subsection (4) of that section may also be extended under subsection (3) of that section.

(4) No more than one extension is possible under section 39(3).

(5) Where a period within which a report under section 38 is to be prepared and published is extended or further extended under section 39(3) or (4), the period as extended or (as the case may be) further extended shall, subject to subsections (6) and (7), be calculated by taking the period being extended and adding to it the period of the extension (whether or not those periods overlap in time).

(6) Subsection (7) applies where—

(a) the period within which the report under section 38 is to be prepared and published is further extended;
(b) the further extension and at least one previous extension is made under section 39(4); and
(c) the same days or fractions of days are included in or comprise the further extension and are included in or comprise at least one such previous extension.

(7) In calculating the period of the further extension, any days or fractions of days of the kind mentioned in subsection (6)(c) shall be disregarded.

(8) The Secretary of State may by order amend section 39 so as to alter any one or more of the following periods—

(a) the period of 24 weeks mentioned in subsection (1) of that section or any period for the time being mentioned in that subsection in substitution for that period;
. . .
(c) the period of 8 weeks mentioned in subsection (3) of that section or any period for the time being mentioned in that subsection in substitution for that period.

(9) No alteration shall be made by virtue of subsection (8) which results in the period for the time being mentioned in subsection (1) of section 39 exceeding 24 weeks or the period for the time being mentioned in subsection (3) of that section exceeding 8 weeks.

(10) An order under subsection (8) shall not affect any period of time within which the Commission is under a duty to prepare and publish its report under section 38 in relation

to a reference under section 22 or 33 if the Commission is already under that duty in relation to that reference when the order is made.

(11) Before making an order under subsection (8) the Secretary of State shall consult the Commission and such other persons as he considers appropriate.

(12) The Secretary of State may make regulations for the purposes of section 39(8).

(13) The regulations may, in particular—

(a) provide for the time at which information or documents are to be treated as provided (including the time at which they are to be treated as provided to the satisfaction of the Commission for the purposes of section 39(8));
(b) provide for the time at which a person is to be treated as appearing as a witness (including the time at which he is to be treated as appearing as a witness in accordance with the requirements of the Commission for the purposes of section 39(8));
(c) provide for the persons carrying on the enterprises which have or may have ceased to be, or may cease to be, distinct enterprises to be informed, in circumstances in which section 39(8) applies, of the fact that—
(i) the Commission is satisfied as to the provision of the information or documents required by it; or
(ii) the person concerned has appeared as a witness in accordance with the requirements of the Commission;
(d) provide for the persons carrying on the enterprises which have or may have ceased to be, or may cease to be, distinct enterprises to be informed, in circumstances in which section 39(8) applies, of the time at which the Commission is to be treated as satisfied as mentioned in paragraph (c)(i) above or the person concerned is to be treated as having appeared as mentioned in paragraph (c)(ii) above.

41 Duty to remedy effects of completed or anticipated mergers

(1) Subsection (2) applies where a report of the Commission has been prepared and published under section 38 within the period permitted by section 39 and contains the decision that there is an anti-competitive outcome.

(2) The Commission shall take such action under section 82 or 84 as it considers to be reasonable and practicable—

(a) to remedy, mitigate or prevent the substantial lessening of competition concerned; and
(b) to remedy, mitigate or prevent any adverse effects which have resulted from, or may be expected to result from, the substantial lessening of competition.

(3) The decision of the Commission under subsection (2) shall be consistent with its decisions as included in its report by virtue of section 35(3) or (as the case may be) 36(2) unless there has been a material change of circumstances since the preparation of the report or the Commission otherwise has a special reason for deciding differently.

(4) In making a decision under subsection (2), the Commission shall, in particular, have regard to the need to achieve as comprehensive a solution as is reasonable and practicable to the substantial lessening of competition and any adverse effects resulting from it.

(5) In making a decision under subsection (2), the Commission may, in particular, have regard to the effect of any action on any relevant customer benefits in relation to the creation of the relevant merger situation concerned.

CHAPTER 2
PUBLIC INTEREST CASES

Power to make references

42 Intervention by Secretary of State in certain public interest cases

(1) Subsection (2) applies where—

(a) the Secretary of State has reasonable grounds for suspecting that it is or may be the case that a relevant merger situation has been created or that arrangements are in progress or in contemplation which, if carried into effect, will result in the creation of a relevant merger situation;
(b) no reference under section 22 or 33 has been made in relation to the relevant merger situation concerned;
(c) no decision has been made not to make such a reference (other than a decision made by virtue of subsection (2)(b) of section 33 or a decision to accept undertakings under section 73 instead of making such a reference); and
(d) no reference is prevented from being made under section 22 or 33 by virtue of—
(i) section 22(3)(a) or (e) or (as the case may be) 33(3)(a) or (e); or
(ii) Community law or anything done under or in accordance with it.

(2) The Secretary of State may give a notice to the OFT (in this Part 'an intervention notice') if he believes that it is or may be the case that one or more than one public interest consideration is relevant to a consideration of the relevant merger situation concerned.

(3) For the purposes of this Part a public interest consideration is a consideration which, at the time of the giving of the intervention notice concerned, is specified in section 58 or is not so specified but, in the opinion of the Secretary of State, ought to be so specified.

(4) No more than one intervention notice shall be given under subsection (2) in relation to the same relevant merger situation.

(5) For the purposes of deciding whether a relevant merger situation has been created or whether arrangements are in progress or in contemplation which, if carried into effect, will result in the creation of a relevant merger situation, sections 23 to 32 (read together with section 34) shall apply for the purposes of this Chapter as they do for the purposes of Chapter 1 but subject to subsection (6).

(6) In their application by virtue of subsection (5) sections 23 to 32 shall have effect as if—

(a) for paragraph (a) of section 23(9) there were substituted—
'(a) in relation to the giving of an intervention notice, the time when the notice is given; (aa) in relation to the making of a report by the OFT under section 44, the time of the making of the report; (ab) in the case of a reference which is treated

as having been made under section 45(2) or (3) by virtue of section 49(1), such time as the Commission may determine; and';

(b) the references to the OFT in sections 25(1) to (3), (6) and (8) and 31 included references to the Secretary of State;

(c) the references to the OFT in section 25(4) and (5) were references to the Secretary of State;

(d) the reference in section 25(4) to section 73 were a reference to paragraph 3 of Schedule 7;

(e) after section 25(5) there were inserted—

'(5A) The Secretary of State may by notice to the persons carrying on the enterprises which have or may have ceased to be distinct enterprises extend the four month period mentioned in section 24(1)(a) or (2)(b) if, by virtue of section 46(5) or paragraph 3(6) of Schedule 7, he decides to delay a decision as to whether to make a reference under section 45.(5B) An extension under subsection (5A) shall be for the period of the delay.';

(f) in section 25(10)(b) after the word '(4)' there were inserted ', (5A)';

(g) the reference in section 25(12) to one extension were a reference to one extension by the OFT and one extension by the Secretary of State;

(h) the powers to extend time-limits under section 25 as applied by subsection (5) above, and the power to request information under section 31(1) as so applied, were not exercisable by the OFT or the Secretary of State before the giving of an intervention notice but the existing time-limits in relation to possible references under section 22 or 33 were applicable for the purposes of the giving of that notice;

(i) the existing time-limits in relation to possible references under section 22 or 33 (except for extensions under section 25(4)) remained applicable on and after the giving of an intervention notice as if any extensions were made under section 25 as applied by subsection (5) above but subject to further alteration by the OFT or the Secretary of State under section 25 as so applied;

(j) in subsection (1) of section 31 for the words 'section 22' there were substituted 'section 45(2) or (3)' and, in the application of that subsection to the OFT, for the word 'deciding' there were substituted 'enabling the Secretary of State to decide';

(k) in the case of the giving of intervention notices, the references in sections 23 to 32 to the making of a reference or a reference were, so far as necessary, references to the giving of an intervention notice or an intervention notice; and

(l) the references to the OFT in section 32(2)(a) to (c) and (3) were construed in accordance with the above modifications.

(7) Where the Secretary of State has given an intervention notice mentioning a public interest consideration which, at that time, is not finalised, he shall, as soon as practicable, take such action as is within his power to ensure that it is finalised.(8) For the purposes of this Part a public interest consideration is finalised if—

(a) it is specified in section 58 otherwise than by virtue of an order under subsection (3) of that section; or

(b) it is specified in that section by virtue of an order under subsection (3) of that section and the order providing for it to be so specified has been laid before, and approved by, Parliament in accordance with subsection (7) of section 124 and within the period mentioned in that subsection.

43 Intervention notices under section 42

(1) An intervention notice shall state—

(a) the relevant merger situation concerned;
(b) the public interest consideration or considerations which are, or may be, relevant to a consideration of the relevant merger situation concerned; and
(c) where any public interest consideration concerned is not finalised, the proposed timetable for finalising it.

(2) Where the Secretary of State believes that it is or may be the case that two or more public interest considerations are relevant to a consideration of the relevant merger situation concerned, he may decide not to mention in the intervention notice such of those considerations as he considers appropriate.

(3) An intervention notice shall come into force when it is given and shall cease to be in force when the matter to which it relates is finally determined under this Chapter.(4) For the purposes of this Part, a matter to which an intervention notice relates is finally determined under this Chapter if—

(a) the time within which the OFT or (if relevant) OFCOM is to report to the Secretary of State under section 44 or (as the case may be) 44A has expired and no such report has been made;
(b) the Secretary of State decides to accept an undertaking or group of undertakings under paragraph 3 of Schedule 7 instead of making a reference under section 45;
(c) the Secretary of State otherwise decides not to make a reference under that section;
(d) the Commission cancels such a reference under section 48(1) or 53(1);
(e) the time within which the Commission is to prepare a report under section 50 and give it to the Secretary of State has expired and no such report has been prepared and given to the Secretary of State;
(f) the time within which the Secretary of State is to make and publish a decision under section 54(2) has expired and no such decision has been made and published;
(g) the Secretary of State decides under section 54(2) to make no finding at all in the matter;
(h) the Secretary of State otherwise decides under section 54(2) not to make an adverse public interest finding;
(i) the Secretary of State decides under section 54(2) to make an adverse public interest finding but decides neither to accept an undertaking under paragraph 9 of Schedule 7 nor to make an order under paragraph 11 of that Schedule; or
(j) the Secretary of State decides under section 54(2) to make an adverse public interest finding and accepts an undertaking under paragraph 9 of Schedule 7 or makes an order under paragraph 11 of that Schedule.

(5) For the purposes of this Part the time when a matter to which an intervention notice relates is finally determined under this Chapter is—

(a) in a case falling within subsection (4)(a), (e) or (f), the expiry of the time concerned;
(b) in a case falling within subsection (4)(b), the acceptance of the undertaking or group of undertakings concerned;

(c) in a case falling within subsection (4)(c), (d), (g) or (h), the making of the decision concerned;
(d) in a case falling within subsection (4)(i), the making of the decision neither to accept an undertaking under paragraph 9 of Schedule 7 nor to make an order under paragraph 11 of that Schedule; and
(e) in a case falling within subsection (4)(j), the acceptance of the undertaking concerned or (as the case may be) the making of the order concerned.

(6) In this Part "OFCOM" means the Office of Communications.

44 Investigation and report by OFT

(1) Subsection (2) applies where the Secretary of State has given an intervention notice in relation to a relevant merger situation.

(2) The OFT shall, within such period as the Secretary of State may require, give a report to the Secretary of State in relation to the case.

(3) The report shall contain—

(a) advice from the OFT on the considerations relevant to the making of a reference under section 22 or 33 which are also relevant to the Secretary of State's decision as to whether to make a reference under section 45; and
(b) a summary of any representations about the case which have been received by the OFT and which relate to any public interest consideration mentioned in the intervention notice concerned (other than a media public interest consideration) and which is or may be relevant to the Secretary of State's decision as to whether to make a reference under section 45.

(4) The report shall, in particular, include decisions as to whether the OFT believes that it is, or may be, the case that—

(a) a relevant merger situation has been created or arrangements are in progress or in contemplation which, if carried into effect, will result in the creation of a relevant merger situation;
(b) the creation of that situation has resulted, or may be expected to result, in a substantial lessening of competition within any market or markets in the United Kingdom for goods or services;
(c) the market or markets concerned would not be of sufficient importance to justify the making of a reference to the Commission under section 22 or 33;
(d) in the case of arrangements which are in progress or in contemplation, the arrangements are not sufficiently far advanced, or not sufficiently likely to proceed, to justify the making of such a reference;
(e) any relevant customer benefits in relation to the creation of the relevant merger situation concerned outweigh the substantial lessening of competition and any adverse effects of the substantial lessening of competition; or
(f) it would be appropriate to deal with the matter (disregarding any public interest considerations mentioned in the intervention notice concerned) by way of undertakings under paragraph 3 of Schedule 7.

(5) If the OFT believes that it is or may be the case that it would be appropriate to deal with the matter (disregarding any public interest considerations mentioned in the inter-

vention notice concerned) by way of undertakings under paragraph 3 of Schedule 7, the report shall contain descriptions of the undertakings which the OFT believes are, or may be, appropriate.

(5A) The report may, in particular, contain a summary of any representations about the case which have been received by the OFT and which relate to any media public interest consideration mentioned in the intervention notice concerned and which is or may be relevant to the Secretary of State's decision as to whether to make a reference under section 45.

(6) The report may, in particular, include advice and recommendations on any public interest consideration mentioned in the intervention notice concerned and which is or may be relevant to the Secretary of State's decision as to whether to make a reference under section 45.

(7) The OFT shall carry out such investigations as it considers appropriate for the purposes of producing a report under this section.

(8) In this Part 'media public interest consideration' means any consideration which, at the time of the giving of the intervention notice concerned—

(a) is specified in section 58(2A) to (2C); or
(b) in the opinion of the Secretary of State, is concerned with broadcasting or newspapers and ought to be specified in section 58.

(9) In this Part 'broadcasting' means the provision of services the provision of which—

(a) is required to be licensed under Part 1 or 3 of the Broadcasting Act 1990 or Part 1 or 2 of the Broadcasting Act 1996; or
(b) would be required to be so licensed if provided by a person subject to licensing under the Part in question.

(10) In this Part 'newspaper' means a daily, Sunday or local (other than daily or Sunday) newspaper circulating wholly or mainly in the United Kingdom or in a part of the United Kingdom.

(11) The Secretary of State may by order amend subsections (9) and (10).

44A Additional investigation and report by OFCOM: media mergers

(1) Subsection (2) applies where—

(a) the Secretary of State has given an intervention notice in relation to a relevant merger situation; and
(b) the intervention notice mentions any media public interest consideration.

(2) OFCOM shall, within such period as the Secretary of State may require, give a report to the Secretary of State on the effect of the consideration or considerations concerned on the case.

(3) The report shall contain—

(a) advice and recommendations on any media public interest consideration mentioned in the intervention notice concerned and which is or may be relevant to the

Secretary of State's decision as to whether to make a reference under section 45; and

(b) a summary of any representations about the case which have been received by OFCOM and which relate to any such consideration.

(4) OFCOM shall carry out such investigations as they consider appropriate for the purposes of producing a report under this section.

45 Power of Secretary of State to refer matter to Commission

(1) Subsections (2) to (5) apply where the Secretary of State—

(a) has given an intervention notice in relation to a relevant merger situation; and
(b) has received a report of the OFT under section 44, and any report of OFCOM which is required by virtue of section 44A, in relation to the matter.

(2) The Secretary of State may make a reference to the Commission if he believes that it is or may be the case that—

(a) a relevant merger situation has been created;
(b) the creation of that situation has resulted, or may be expected to result, in a substantial lessening of competition within any market or markets in the United Kingdom for goods or services;
(c) one or more than one public interest consideration mentioned in the intervention notice is relevant to a consideration of the relevant merger situation concerned; and
(d) taking account only of the substantial lessening of competition and the relevant public interest consideration or considerations concerned, the creation of that situation operates or may be expected to operate against the public interest.

(3) The Secretary of State may make a reference to the Commission if he believes that it is or may be the case that—

(a) a relevant merger situation has been created;
(b) the creation of that situation has not resulted, and may be expected not to result, in a substantial lessening of competition within any market or markets in the United Kingdom for goods or services;
(c) one or more than one public interest consideration mentioned in the intervention notice is relevant to a consideration of the relevant merger situation concerned; and
(d) taking account only of the relevant public interest consideration or considerations concerned, the creation of that situation operates or may be expected to operate against the public interest.

(4) The Secretary of State may make a reference to the Commission if he believes that it is or may be the case that—

(a) arrangements are in progress or in contemplation which, if carried into effect, will result in the creation of a relevant merger situation;
(b) the creation of that situation may be expected to result in a substantial lessening of competition within any market or markets in the United Kingdom for goods or services;
(c) one or more than one public interest consideration mentioned in the intervention notice is relevant to a consideration of the relevant merger situation concerned; and

(d) taking account only of the substantial lessening of competition and the relevant public interest consideration or considerations concerned, the creation of the relevant merger situation may be expected to operate against the public interest.

(5) The Secretary of State may make a reference to the Commission if he believes that it is or may be the case that—

(a) arrangements are in progress or in contemplation which, if carried into effect, will result in the creation of a relevant merger situation;
(b) the creation of that situation may be expected not to result in a substantial lessening of competition within any market or markets in the United Kingdom for goods or services;
(c) one or more than one public interest consideration mentioned in the intervention notice is relevant to a consideration of the relevant merger situation concerned; and
(d) taking account only of the relevant public interest consideration or considerations concerned, the creation of the relevant merger situation may be expected to operate against the public interest.

(6) For the purposes of this Chapter any anti-competitive outcome shall be treated as being adverse to the public interest unless it is justified by one or more than one public interest consideration which is relevant.

(7) This section is subject to section 46.

46 References under section 45: supplementary

(1) No reference shall be made under section 45 if—

(a) the making of the reference is prevented by section 74(1) or 96(3) or paragraph 4 of Schedule 7;
(b) the European Commission is considering a request made, in relation to the matter concerned, by the United Kingdom (whether alone or with others) under article 22(1) of the EC Merger Regulation, is proceeding with the matter in pursuance of such a request or has dealt with the matter in pursuance of such a request; or
(c) subject to subsection (1A), a reasoned submission requesting referral to the European Commission has been submitted to the European Commission under article 4(5) of the EC Merger Regulation..

(1A) Subsection (1)(c) shall cease to apply if the Secretary of State is informed that a Member State competent to examine the concentration under its national competition law has, within the time permitted by Article 4(5) of the EC Merger Regulation, expressed its disagreement as regards the request to refer the case to the European Commission; and this subsection shall be construed in accordance with that Regulation.

(2) The Secretary of State, in deciding whether to make a reference under section 45, shall accept the decisions of the OFT included in its report by virtue of subsection (4) of section 44 and any descriptions of undertakings as mentioned in subsection (5) of that section.

(3) Where the decision to make a reference under section 45 is made at any time on or after the end of the period of 24 weeks beginning with the giving of the intervention notice concerned, the Secretary of State shall, in deciding whether to make such a

reference, disregard any public interest consideration which is mentioned in the intervention notice but which has not been finalised before the end of that period.

(4) Subject to subsection (5), where the decision to make a reference under section 45(2) or (4) is made at any time before the end of the period of 24 weeks beginning with the giving of the intervention notice concerned, the Secretary of State shall, in deciding whether to make such a reference, disregard any public interest consideration which is mentioned in the intervention notice but which has not been finalised if its effect would be to prevent, or to help to prevent, an anti-competitive outcome from being adverse to the public interest.

(5) The Secretary of State may, if he believes that there is a realistic prospect of the public interest consideration mentioned in subsection (4) being finalised within the period of 24 weeks beginning with the giving of the intervention notice concerned, delay deciding whether to make the reference concerned until the public interest consideration is finalised or, if earlier, the period expires.

(6) A reference under section 45 shall, in particular, specify—

(a) the subsection of that section under which it is made;
(b) the date on which it is made; and
(c) the public interest consideration or considerations mentioned in the intervention notice concerned which the Secretary of State is not under a duty to disregard by virtue of subsection (3) above and which he believes are or may be relevant to a consideration of the relevant merger situation concerned.

Cases referred by European Commission under the EC Merger Regulation

46A Cases referred by the European Commission where intervention notice is in force

(1) Subsection (2) applies if the European Commission has by a decision referred the whole or part of a case to the OFT under Article 4(4) or 9 of the EC Merger Regulation, or is deemed to have taken such a decision, and an intervention notice is in force in relation to that case.

(2) Before the end of the preliminary assessment period, the Secretary of State shall—

(a) decide whether to make a reference to the Commission under section 45; and
(b) inform the persons carrying on the enterprises concerned by notice of that decision and of the reasons for it.

(3) The Secretary of State may, for the purposes of subsection (2), decide not to make a reference on the basis that he is considering whether to seek or accept undertakings under paragraph 3 of Schedule 7 instead of making a reference; but a decision taken on that basis does not prevent the Secretary of State from making a reference under section 45 in the event of no such undertakings being offered or accepted.

(4) In this section—
'the preliminary assessment period' means, subject to section 46B, the period of 45 working days beginning with the day after the day on which the decision of the European Commission to refer the case is taken (or is deemed to have been taken); and 'working day' means any day which is not—

(a) a Saturday;
(b) a Sunday; or
(c) a day which is a European Commission holiday (as published in the Official Journal of the European Communities before the beginning of the year in which it occurs).

46B Extension of preliminary assessment period

(1) If the OFT has imposed a requirement under section 46C and it considers that the person on whom that requirement was imposed has failed to comply with it, the OFT may, by notice to the persons carrying on the enterprises concerned, extend the preliminary assessment period.

(2) If the Secretary of State has imposed a requirement under section 46C and he considers that the person on whom that requirement was imposed has failed to comply with it, he may, by notice to the persons carrying on the enterprises concerned, extend the preliminary assessment period.(3) The period of an extension under this section shall—

(a) begin with the end of the period within which the requirement under section 46C could be complied with; and
(b) end with—
(i) in the case of a notice under subsection (1), the earlier of either compliance with the requirement to the satisfaction of the OFT or cancellation by the OFT of the extension.
(ii) in the case of a notice under subsection (2), the earlier of either compliance with the requirement to the satisfaction of the Secretary of State or cancellation by him of the extension.

(4) A notice under this section shall—

(a) be given within 5 working days of the end of the period mentioned in subsection (3)(a); and
(b) inform the person to whom it is addressed—
(i) in the case of a notice under subsection (1), that the OFT is of the opinion mentioned in that subsection and that it intends to extend the preliminary assessment period.
(ii) in the case of a notice under subsection (2), that the Secretary of State is of the opinion mentioned in that subsection and that he intends to extend the preliminary assessment period.

46C Power to request information in referred cases

(1) In a case mentioned in section 46A(1), the OFT may by notice to any of the persons carrying on the enterprises concerned request him to provide the OFT with such information as the OFT may require for the purpose of enabling the Secretary of State to make a decision for the purposes of section 46A(2).

(2) In such a case, the Secretary of State may by notice to any of the persons carrying on the enterprises concerned request him to provide the Secretary of State with such information as he may require for the purpose of enabling him to make a decision for the purposes of section 46A(2).

(3) A notice under subsection (1) or (2) shall state—

(a) the information required;
(b) the period within which the information is to be provided; and
(c) the manner (if any) in which the information is required to be provided; and
(d) the possible consequences—
(i) of not providing the information within the stated period; and
(ii) if a manner for its provision is stated in the notice, of not providing it in that manner.

Reports on references

47 Questions to be decided on references under section 45

(1) The Commission shall, on a reference under section 45(2) or (3), decide whether a relevant merger situation has been created.

(2) If the Commission decides that such a situation has been created, it shall, on a reference under section 45(2), decide the following additional questions—

(a) whether the creation of that situation has resulted, or may be expected to result, in a substantial lessening of competition within any market or markets in the United Kingdom for goods or services; and
(b) whether, taking account only of any substantial lessening of competition and the admissible public interest consideration or considerations concerned, the creation of that situation operates or may be expected to operate against the public interest.

(3) If the Commission decides that a relevant merger situation has been created, it shall, on a reference under section 45(3), decide whether, taking account only of the admissible public interest consideration or considerations concerned, the creation of that situation operates or may be expected to operate against the public interest.

(4) The Commission shall, on a reference under section 45(4) or (5), decide whether arrangements are in progress or in contemplation which, if carried into effect, will result in the creation of a relevant merger situation.

(5) If the Commission decides that such arrangements are in progress or in contemplation, it shall, on a reference under section 45(4), decide the following additional questions—

(a) whether the creation of that situation may be expected to result in a substantial lessening of competition within any market or markets in the United Kingdom for goods or services; and
(b) whether, taking account only of any substantial lessening of competition and the admissible public interest consideration or considerations concerned, the creation of that situation may be expected to operate against the public interest.

(6) If the Commission decides that arrangements are in progress or in contemplation which, if carried into effect, will result in the creation of a relevant merger situation, it shall, on a reference under section 45(5), decide whether, taking account only of the admissible public interest consideration or considerations concerned, the creation of that situation may be expected to operate against the public interest.

(7) The Commission shall, if it has decided on a reference under section 45 that the creation of a relevant merger situation operates or may be expected to operate against the public interest, decide the following additional questions—

(a) whether action should be taken by the Secretary of State under section 55 for the purpose of remedying, mitigating or preventing any of the effects adverse to the public interest which have resulted from, or may be expected to result from, the creation of the relevant merger situation;
(b) whether the Commission should recommend the taking of other action by the Secretary of State or action by persons other than itself and the Secretary of State for the purpose of remedying, mitigating or preventing any of the effects adverse to the public interest which have resulted from, or may be expected to result from, the creation of the relevant merger situation; and
(c) in either case, if action should be taken, what action should be taken and what is to be remedied, mitigated or prevented.

(8) Where the Commission has decided by virtue of subsection (2)(a) or (5)(a) that there is or will be a substantial lessening of competition within any market or markets in the United Kingdom for goods or services, it shall also decide separately the following questions (on the assumption that it is proceeding as mentioned in section 56(6))—

(a) whether action should be taken by it under section 41 for the purpose of remedying, mitigating or preventing the substantial lessening of competition concerned or any adverse effect which has resulted from, or may be expected to result from, the substantial lessening of competition;
(b) whether the Commission should recommend the taking of action by other persons for the purpose of remedying, mitigating or preventing the substantial lessening of competition concerned or any adverse effect which has resulted from, or may be expected to result from, the substantial lessening of competition; and
(c) in either case, if action should be taken, what action should be taken and what is to be remedied, mitigated or prevented.

(9) In deciding the questions mentioned in subsections (7) and (8) the Commission shall, in particular, have regard to the need to achieve as comprehensive a solution as is reasonable and practicable to—

(a) the adverse effects to the public interest; or
(b) (as the case may be) the substantial lessening of competition and any adverse effects resulting from it.

(10) In deciding the questions mentioned in subsections (7) and (8) in a case where it has decided by virtue of subsection (2)(a) or (5)(a) that there is or will be a substantial lessening of competition, the Commission may, in particular, have regard to the effect of any action on any relevant customer benefits in relation to the creation of the relevant merger situation concerned.

(11) In this section 'admissible public interest consideration' means any public interest consideration which is specified in the reference under section 45 and which the Commission is not under a duty to disregard.

48 Cases where references or certain questions need not be decided

(1) The Commission shall cancel a reference under section 45(4) or (5) if it considers that the proposal to make arrangements of the kind mentioned in that reference has been abandoned.(2) In relation to the question whether a relevant merger situation has been created or the question whether a relevant merger situation will be created, a reference under section 45 may be framed so as to require the Commission to exclude from consideration—

(a) subsection (1) of section 23;
(b) subsection (2) of that section; or
(c) one of those subsections if the Commission finds that the other is satisfied.

(3) In relation to the question whether any such result as is mentioned in section 23(2)(b) has arisen or the question whether any such result will arise, a reference under section 45 may be framed so as to require the Commission to confine its investigation to the supply of goods or services in a part of the United Kingdom specified in the reference.

49 Variation of references under section 45

(1) The Commission may, if it considers that doing so is justified by the facts (including events occurring on or after the making of the reference concerned), treat—

(a) a reference made under subsection (2) or (3) of section 45 as if it had been made under subsection (4) or (as the case may be) (5) of that section; or
(b) a reference made under subsection (4) or (5) of section 45 as if it had been made under subsection (2) or (as the case may be) (3) of that section;
and, in such cases, references in this Part to references under those enactments shall, so far as may be necessary, be construed accordingly.

(2) Where, by virtue of subsection (1), the Commission treats a reference made under subsection (2) or (3) of section 45 as if it had been made under subsection (4) or (as the case may be) (5) of that section, paragraphs 1, 2, 7 and 8 of Schedule 7 shall, in particular, apply as if the reference had been made under subsection (4) or (as the case may be) (5) of that section instead of under subsection (2) or (3) of that section.

(3) Where, by virtue of subsection (1), the Commission treats a reference made under subsection (4) or (5) of section 45 as if it had been made under subsection (2) or (as the case may be) (3) of that section, paragraphs 1, 2, 7 and 8 of Schedule 7 shall, in particular, apply as if the reference had been made under subsection (2) or (as the case may be) (3) of that section instead of under subsection (4) or (5) of that section.

(4) Subsection (5) applies in relation to any undertaking accepted under paragraph 1 of Schedule 7, or any order made under paragraph 2 of that Schedule, which is in force immediately before the Commission, by virtue of subsection (1), treats a reference as mentioned in subsection (1).

(5) The undertaking or order shall, so far as applicable, continue in force as if—

(a) in the case of an undertaking or order which relates to a reference under subsection (2) or (3) of section 45, accepted or made in relation to a reference made under subsection (4) or (as the case may be) (5) of that section; and

(b) in the case of an undertaking or order which relates to a reference made under subsection (4) or (5) of that section, accepted or made in relation to a reference made under subsection (2) or (as the case may be) (3) of that section;

and the undertaking or order concerned may be varied, superseded, released or revoked accordingly.

(6) The Secretary of State may at any time vary a reference under section 45.

(7) The Secretary of State shall consult the Commission before varying any such reference.

(8) Subsection (7) shall not apply if the Commission has requested the variation concerned.

(9) No variation by the Secretary of State under this section shall be capable of altering the public interest consideration or considerations specified in the reference or the period permitted by section 51 within which the report of the Commission under section 50 is to be prepared and given to the Secretary of State.

50 Investigations and reports on references under section 45

(1) The Commission shall prepare a report on a reference under section 45 and give it to the Secretary of State within the period permitted by section 51.

(2) The report shall, in particular, contain—

(a) the decisions of the Commission on the questions which it is required to answer by virtue of section 47;
(b) its reasons for its decisions; and
(c) such information as the Commission considers appropriate for facilitating a proper understanding of those questions and of its reasons for its decisions.

(2A) Where the report relates to a reference under section 45 which has been made after a report of OFCOM under section 44A, the Commission shall give a copy of its report (whether or not published) to OFCOM.

(3) The Commission shall carry out such investigations as it considers appropriate for the purpose of producing a report under this section.

51 Time-limits for investigations and reports by Commission

(1) The Commission shall prepare its report under section 50 and give it to the Secretary of State under that section within the period of 24 weeks beginning with the date of the reference concerned.

(3) The Commission may extend, by no more than 8 weeks, the period within which a report under section 50 is to be prepared and given to the Secretary of State if it considers that there are special reasons why the report cannot be prepared and given to the Secretary of State within that period.

(4) The Commission may extend the period within which a report under section 50 is to be prepared and given to the Secretary of State if it considers that a relevant person has

failed (whether with or without a reasonable excuse) to comply with any requirement of a notice under section 109.

(5) In subsection (4) "relevant person" means—

(a) any person carrying on any of the enterprises concerned;
(b) any person who (whether alone or as a member of a group) owns or has control of any such person; or
(c) any officer, employee or agent of any person mentioned in paragraph (a) or (b).

(6) For the purposes of subsection (5) a person or group of persons able, directly or indirectly, to control or materially to influence the policy of a body of persons corporate or unincorporate, but without having a controlling interest in that body of persons, may be treated as having control of it.

(7) An extension under subsection (3) or (4) shall come into force when published under section 107.

(8) An extension under subsection (4) shall continue in force until—

(a) the person concerned provides the information or documents to the satisfaction of the Commission or (as the case may be) appears as a witness in accordance with the requirements of the Commission; or
(b) the Commission publishes its decision to cancel the extension.

(9) This section is subject to sections 52 and 53.

52 Section 51: supplementary

. . .

(3) A period extended under subsection (3) of section 51 may also be extended under subsection (4) of that section and a period extended under subsection (4) of that section may also be extended under subsection (3) of that section.

(4) No more than one extension is possible under section 51(3).

(5) Where a period within which a report under section 50 is to be prepared and given to the Secretary of State is extended or further extended under section 51(3) or (4), the period as extended or (as the case may be) further extended shall, subject to subsections (6) and (7), be calculated by taking the period being extended and adding to it the period of the extension (whether or not those periods overlap in time).

(6) Subsection (7) applies where—

(a) the period within which the report under section 50 is to be prepared and given to the Secretary of State is further extended;
(b) the further extension and at least one previous extension is made under section 51(4); and
(c) the same days or fractions of days are included in or comprise the further extension and are included in or comprise at least one such previous extension.

(7) In calculating the period of the further extension, any days or fractions of days of the kind mentioned in subsection (6)(c) shall be disregarded.

(8) The Secretary of State may by order amend section 51 so as to alter any one or more of the following periods—

(a) the period of 24 weeks mentioned in subsection (1) of that section or any period for the time being mentioned in that subsection in substitution for that period;

. . .

(c) the period of 8 weeks mentioned in subsection (3) of that section or any period for the time being mentioned in that subsection in substitution for that period.

(9) No alteration shall be made by virtue of subsection (8) which results in the period for the time being mentioned in subsection (1) of section 51 exceeding 24 weeks or the period for the time being mentioned in subsection (3) of that section exceeding 8 weeks.

(10) An order under subsection (8) shall not affect any period of time within which the Commission is under a duty to prepare and give to the Secretary of State its report under section 50 in relation to a reference under section 45 if the Commission is already under that duty in relation to that reference when the order is made.

(11) Before making an order under subsection (8) the Secretary of State shall consult the Commission and such other persons as he considers appropriate.

(12) The Secretary of State may make regulations for the purposes of section 51(8).(13) The regulations may, in particular—

(a) provide for the time at which information or documents are to be treated as provided (including the time at which they are to be treated as provided to the satisfaction of the Commission for the purposes of section 51(8));
(b) provide for the time at which a person is to be treated as appearing as a witness (including the time at which he is to be treated as appearing as a witness in accordance with the requirements of the Commission for the purposes of section 51(8));
(c) provide for the persons carrying on the enterprises which have or may have ceased to be, or may cease to be, distinct enterprises to be informed, in circumstances in which section 51(8) applies, of the fact that—
  (i) the Commission is satisfied as to the provision of the information or documents required by it; or
  (ii) the person concerned has appeared as a witness in accordance with the requirements of the Commission;
(d) provide for the persons carrying on the enterprises which have or may have ceased to be, or may cease to be, distinct enterprises to be informed, in circumstances in which section 51(8) applies, of the time at which the Commission is to be treated as satisfied as mentioned in paragraph (c)(i) above or the person concerned is to be treated as having appeared as mentioned in paragraph (c)(ii) above.

53 Restrictions on action where public interest considerations not finalised

(1) The Commission shall cancel a reference under section 45 if—

(a) the intervention notice concerned mentions a public interest consideration which was not finalised on the giving of that notice or public interest considerations which, at that time, were not finalised;
(b) no other public interest consideration is mentioned in the notice;

(c) at least 24 weeks has elapsed since the giving of the notice; and(d) the public interest consideration mentioned in the notice has not been finalised within that period of 24 weeks or (as the case may be) none of the public interest considerations mentioned in the notice has been finalised within that period of 24 weeks.

(2) Where a reference to the Commission under section 45 specifies a public interest consideration which has not been finalised before the making of the reference, the Commission shall not give its report to the Secretary of State under section 50 in relation to that reference unless—

(a) the period of 24 weeks beginning with the giving of the intervention notice concerned has expired; or
(b) the public interest consideration concerned has been finalised;

(3) The Commission shall, in reporting on any of the questions mentioned in section 47(2)(b), (3), (5)(b), (6) and (7), disregard any public interest consideration which has not been finalised before the giving of the report.

(4) The Commission shall, in reporting on any of the questions mentioned in section 47(2)(b), (3), (5)(b), (6) and (7), disregard any public interest consideration which was not finalised on the giving of the intervention notice concerned and has not been finalised within the period of 24 weeks beginning with the giving of the notice concerned.

(5) Subsections (1) to (4) are without prejudice to the power of the Commission to carry out investigations in relation to any public interest consideration to which it might be able to have regard in its report.

Decisions of the Secretary of State

54 Decision of Secretary of State in public interest cases

(1) Subsection (2) applies where the Secretary of State has received a report of the Commission under section 50 in relation to a relevant merger situation.

(2) The Secretary of State shall decide whether to make an adverse public interest finding in relation to the relevant merger situation and whether to make no finding at all in the matter.

(3) For the purposes of this Part the Secretary of State makes an adverse public interest finding in relation to a relevant merger situation if, in relation to that situation, he decides—

(a) in connection with a reference to the Commission under subsection (2) of section 45, that it is the case as mentioned in paragraphs (a) to (d) of that subsection or subsection (3) of that section;
(b) in connection with a reference to the Commission under subsection (3) of that section, that it is the case as mentioned in paragraphs (a) to (d) of that subsection;
(c) in connection with a reference to the Commission under subsection (4) of that section, that it is the case as mentioned in paragraphs (a) to (d) of that subsection or subsection (5) of that section; and
(d) in connection with a reference to the Commission under subsection (5) of that section, that it is the case as mentioned in paragraphs (a) to (d) of that subsection.

(4) The Secretary of State may make no finding at all in the matter only if he decides that there is no public interest consideration which is relevant to a consideration of the relevant merger situation concerned.

(5) The Secretary of State shall make and publish his decision under subsection (2) within the period of 30 days beginning with the receipt of the report of the Commission under section 50.

(6) In making a decision under subsections (2) to (4), the Secretary of State shall disregard any public interest consideration not specified in the reference under section 45 and any public interest consideration disregarded by the Commission for the purposes of its report.

(7) In deciding whether to make an adverse public interest finding under subsection (2), the Secretary of State shall accept—

- (a) in connection with a reference to the Commission under section 45(2) or (4), the decision of the report of the Commission under section 50 as to whether there is an anti-competitive outcome; and
- (b) in connection with a reference to the Commission under section 45(3) or (5)—
  - (i) the decision of the report of the Commission under section 50 as to whether a relevant merger situation has been created or (as the case may be) arrangements are in progress or in contemplation which, if carried into effect, will result in the creation of a relevant merger situation; and
  - (ii) the decision of the report of the OFT under section 44 as to the absence of a substantial lessening of competition.

(8) In determining for the purposes of subsection (5) the period of 30 days no account shall be taken of—

- (a) Saturday, Sunday, Good Friday and Christmas Day; and
- (b) any day which is a bank holiday in England and Wales.

55 Enforcement action by Secretary of State

(1) Subsection (2) applies where the Secretary of State has decided under subsection (2) of section 54 within the period required by subsection (5) of that section to make an adverse public interest finding in relation to a relevant merger situation and has published his decision within the period so required.

(2) The Secretary of State may take such action under paragraph 9 or 11 of Schedule 7 as he considers to be reasonable and practicable to remedy, mitigate or prevent any of the effects adverse to the public interest which have resulted from, or may be expected to result from, the creation of the relevant merger situation concerned.

(3) In making a decision under subsection (2) the Secretary of State shall, in particular, have regard to the report of the Commission under section 50.

(4) In making a decision under subsection (2) in any case of a substantial lessening of competition, the Secretary of State may, in particular, have regard to the effect of any action on any relevant customer benefits in relation to the creation of the relevant merger situation concerned.

Other

56 Competition cases where intervention on public interest grounds ceases

(1) Where the Secretary of State decides not to make a reference under section 45 on the ground that no public interest consideration to which he is able to have regard is relevant to a consideration of the relevant merger situation concerned, he shall by notice require the OFT to deal with the matter otherwise than under this Chapter.

(2) Where a notice is given to the OFT in the circumstances mentioned in subsection (1), the OFT shall decide whether to make a reference under section 22 or 33; and any time-limits in relation to the Secretary of State's decision whether to make a reference under section 45 (including any remaining powers of extension) shall apply in relation to the decision of the OFT whether to make a reference under section 22 or 33.

(3) Where the Commission cancels under section 53(1) a reference under section 45 and the report of the OFT under section 44 contains the decision that it is or may be the case that there is an anti-competitive outcome in relation to the relevant merger situation concerned, the Commission shall proceed under this Part as if a reference under section 22 or (as the case may be) 33 had been made to it by the OFT.

(4) In proceeding by virtue of subsection (3) to prepare and publish a report under section 38, the Commission shall proceed as if—

(a) the reference under section 22 or 33 had been made at the same time as the reference under section 45;
(b) the timetable for preparing and giving its report under section 50 (including any remaining powers of extension and as extended by an additional period of 20 days) were the timetable for preparing and publishing its report under section 38; and
(c) in relation to the question whether a relevant merger situation has been created or the question whether arrangements are in progress or in contemplation which, if carried into effect, will result in the creation of a relevant merger situation, the Commission were confined to the questions on the subject to be investigated by it under section 47.

(5) In determining the period of 20 days mentioned in subsection (4) no account shall be taken of—

(a) Saturday, Sunday, Good Friday and Christmas Day; and
(b) any day which is a bank holiday in England and Wales.

(6) Where the Secretary of State decides under section 54(2) to make no finding at all in the matter in connection with a reference under section 45(2) or (4), the Commission shall proceed under this Part as if a reference under section 22 or (as the case may be) 33 had been made to it instead of a reference under section 45 and as if its report to the Secretary of State under section 50 had been prepared and published by it under section 38 within the period permitted by section 39.

(7) In relation to proceedings by virtue of subsection (6), the reference in section 41(3) to decisions of the Commission as included in its report by virtue of section 35(3) or 36(2) shall be construed as a reference to decisions which were included in the report of the Commission by virtue of section 47(8).

(8) Where the Commission becomes under a duty to proceed as mentioned in subsection (3) or (6), references in this Part to references under sections 22 and 33 shall, so far as may be necessary, be construed accordingly; and, in particular, sections 77 to 81 shall apply as if a reference has been made to the Commission by the OFT under section 22 or (as the case may be) 33.

57 Duties of OFT and Commission to inform Secretary of State

(1) The OFT shall, in considering whether to make a reference under section 22 or 33, bring to the attention of the Secretary of State any case which it believes raises any consideration specified in section 58 unless it believes that the Secretary of State would consider any such consideration immaterial in the context of the particular case.

(2) The OFT, OFCOM and the Commission shall bring to the attention of the Secretary of State any representations about exercising his powers under section 58(3) which have been made to the OFT, OFCOM or (as the case may be) the Commission.

58 Specified considerations

(1) The interests of national security are specified in this section.

(2) In subsection (1) 'national security' includes public security; and in this subsection 'public security' has the same meaning as in article 21(4) of the EC Merger Regulation.

(2A) The need for—

(a) accurate presentation of news; and
(b) free expression of opinion;

in newspapers is specified in this section.

(2B) The need for, to the extent that it is reasonable and practicable, a sufficient plurality of views in newspapers in each market for newspapers in the United Kingdom or a part of the United Kingdom is specified in this section.

(2C) The following are specified in this section—

(a) the need, in relation to every different audience in the United Kingdom or in a particular area or locality of the United Kingdom, for there to be a sufficient plurality of persons with control of the media enterprises serving that audience;
(b) the need for the availability throughout the United Kingdom of a wide range of broadcasting which (taken as a whole) is both of high quality and calculated to appeal to a wide variety of tastes and interests; and
(c) the need for persons carrying on media enterprises, and for those with control of such enterprises, to have a genuine commitment to the attainment in relation to broadcasting of the standards objectives set out in section 319 of the Communications Act 2003.

(3) The Secretary of State may by order modify this section for the purpose of specifying in this section a new consideration or removing or amending any consideration which is for the time being specified in this section.

(4) An order under this section may, in particular—

(a) provide for a consideration to be specified in this section for a particular purpose or purposes or for all purposes;
(b) apply in relation to cases under consideration by the OFT, OFCOM, the Commission or the Secretary of State before the making of the order as well as cases under consideration on or after the making of the order.

58A Construction of consideration specified in section 58(2C)

(1) For the purposes of section 58 and this section an enterprise is a media enterprise if it consists in or involves broadcasting.

(2) In the case of a merger situation in which at least one of the enterprises ceasing to be distinct consists in or involves broadcasting, the references in section 58(2C)(a) or this section to media enterprises include references to newspaper enterprises.

(3) In this Part 'newspaper enterprise' means an enterprise consisting in or involving the supply of newspapers.

(4) Wherever in a merger situation two media enterprises serving the same audience cease to be distinct, the number of such enterprises serving that audience shall be assumed to be more immediately before they cease to be distinct than it is afterwards.

(5) For the purposes of section 58, where two or more media enterprises—

(a) would fall to be treated as under common ownership or common control for the purposes of section 26, or
(b) are otherwise in the same ownership or under the same control,
they shall be treated (subject to subsection (4)) as all under the control of only one person.

(6) A reference in section 58 or this section to an audience shall be construed in relation to a media enterprise in whichever of the following ways the decision-making authority considers appropriate—

(a) as a reference to any one of the audiences served by that enterprise, taking them separately;
(b) as a reference to all the audiences served by that enterprise, taking them together;
(c) as a reference to a number of those audiences taken together in such group as the decision-making authority considers appropriate; or
(d) as a reference to a part of anything that could be taken to be an audience under any of paragraphs (a) to (c) above.

(7) The criteria for deciding who can be treated for the purposes of this section as comprised in an audience, or as comprised in an audience served by a particular service—

(a) shall be such as the decision-making authority considers appropriate in the circumstances of the case; and
(b) may allow for persons to be treated as members of an audience if they are only potentially members of it.

(8) In this section 'audience' includes readership.

(9) The power under subsection (3) of section 58 to modify that section includes power to modify this section.

CHAPTER 3
OTHER SPECIAL CASES

Special public interest cases

59 Intervention by Secretary of State in special public interest cases

(1) Subsection (2) applies where the Secretary of State has reasonable grounds for suspecting that it is or may be the case that a special merger situation has been created or arrangements are in progress or in contemplation which, if carried into effect, will result in the creation of a special merger situation.

(2) The Secretary of State may give a notice to the OFT (in this Part "a special intervention notice") if he believes that it is or may be the case that one or more than one consideration specified in section 58 is relevant to a consideration of the special merger situation concerned.

(3) For the purposes of this Part a special merger situation has been created if—

(a) the condition mentioned in subsection (3A) is satisfied; and
(b) immediately before the enterprises concerned ceased to be distinct—
(i) the conditions mentioned in subsection (3B) were satisfied;
(ii) the condition mentioned in subsection (3C) was satisfied; or
(iii) the condition mentioned in subsection (3D) was satisfied.

(3A) The condition mentioned in this subsection is that—

(a) no relevant merger situation has been created because of section 23(1)(b) and (2)(b); but
(b) a relevant merger situation would have been created if those enactments were disregarded.

(3B) The conditions mentioned in this subsection are that—

(a) at least one of the enterprises concerned was carried on in the United Kingdom or by or under the control of a body corporate incorporated in the United Kingdom; and
(b) a person carrying on one or more of the enterprises concerned was a relevant government contractor.

(3C) The condition mentioned in this subsection is that, in relation to the supply of newspapers of any description, at least one-quarter of all the newspapers of that description which were supplied in the United Kingdom, or in a substantial part of the United Kingdom, were supplied by the person or persons by whom one of the enterprises concerned was carried on.

(3D) The condition mentioned in this subsection is that, in relation to the provision of broadcasting of any description, at least one-quarter of all broadcasting of that description provided in the United Kingdom, or in a substantial part of the United Kingdom, was provided by the person or persons by whom one of the enterprises concerned was carried on.

(5) For the purposes of deciding whether a relevant merger situation has been created or whether arrangements are in progress or in contemplation which, if carried into effect,

will result in the creation of a relevant merger situation, sections 23 to 32 (read together with section 34) shall apply for the purposes of this Chapter as they do for the purposes of Chapter 1 but subject to subsection (6).

(6) In their application by virtue of subsection (5) sections 23 to 32 shall have effect as if—

(a) for paragraph (a) of section 23(9) there were substituted—
'(a) in relation to the giving of a special intervention notice, the time when the notice is given; (aa) in relation to the making of a report by the OFT under section 61, the time of the making of the report; (ab) in the case of a reference which is treated as having been made under section 62(2) by virtue of section 64(2), such time as the Commission may determine; and';
(b) the references to the OFT in section 24(2)(a) and (b) included references to the Secretary of State;
(c) the references to the OFT in sections 25(1) to (3), (6) and (8) and 31 included references to the Secretary of State;
(d) the references to the OFT in section 25(4) and (5) were references to the Secretary of State;
(e) the reference in section 25(4) to section 73 were a reference to paragraph 3 of Schedule 7;
(f) the reference in section 25(12) to one extension were a reference to one extension by the OFT and one extension by the Secretary of State;
(g) the powers to extend time-limits under section 25 as applied by subsection (5) above, and the power to request information under section 31(1) as so applied, were not exercisable by the OFT or the Secretary of State before the giving of a special intervention notice;
(h) in subsection (1) of section 31 for the words 'section 22' there were substituted 'section 62(2)' and, in the application of that subsection to the OFT, for the word 'deciding' there were substituted 'enabling the Secretary of State to decide';
(i) in the case of the giving of special intervention notices, the references in sections 23 to 32 to the making of a reference or a reference were, so far as necessary, references to the giving of a special intervention notice or a special intervention notice; and
(j) the references to the OFT in section 32(2)(a) to (c) and (3) were construed in accordance with the above modifications.

(6A) The Secretary of State may by order amend the conditions mentioned in subsection (3)(b)(ii) and (iii).

(7) No more than one special intervention notice shall be given under subsection (2) in relation to the same special merger situation.

(8) In this section "relevant government contractor" means—

(a) a government contractor—
(i) who has been notified by or on behalf of the Secretary of State of information, documents or other articles relating to defence and of a confidential nature which the government contractor or an employee of his may hold or receive in connection with being such a contractor; and
(ii) whose notification has not been revoked by or on behalf of the Secretary of State; or

(b) a former government contractor who was so notified when he was a government contractor and whose notification has not been revoked by or on behalf of the Secretary of State.

(9) In this section—
'defence' has the same meaning as in section 2 of the Official Secrets Act 1989 (c 6); and 'government contractor' has the same meaning as in the Act of 1989 and includes any sub-contractor of a government contractor, any sub-contractor of that sub-contractor and any other sub-contractor in a chain of sub-contractors which begins with the sub-contractor of the government contractor.

59A Construction of conditions in section 59(3C) and (3D)

(1) For the purpose of deciding whether the proportion of one-quarter mentioned in section 59(3C) or (3D) is fulfilled with respect to—

(a) newspapers of any description, or
(b) broadcasting of any description,
the decision-making authority shall apply such criterion (whether value, cost, price, quantity, capacity, number of workers employed or some other criterion, of whatever nature), or such combination of criteria, as the decision-making authority considers appropriate.

(2) References in section 59(3C) to the supply of newspapers shall, in relation to newspapers of any description which are the subject of different forms of supply, be construed in whichever of the following ways the decision-making authority considers appropriate—

(a) as references to any of those forms of supply taken separately;
(b) as references to all those forms of supply taken together; or
(c) as references to any of those forms of supply taken in groups.

(3) For the purposes of subsection (2) the decision-making authority may treat newspapers as being the subject of different forms of supply whenever—

(a) the transactions concerned differ as to their nature, their parties, their terms or their surrounding circumstances; and
(b) the difference is one which, in the opinion of the decision-making authority, ought for the purposes of that subsection to be treated as a material difference.

(4) References in section 59(3D) to the provision of broadcasting shall, in relation to broadcasting of any description which is the subject of different forms of provision, be construed in whichever of the following ways the decision-making authority considers appropriate—

(a) as references to any of those forms of provision taken separately;
(b) as references to all those forms of provision taken together; or
(c) as references to any of those forms of provision taken in groups.

(5) For the purposes of subsection (4) the decision-making authority may treat broadcasting as being the subject of different forms of provision whenever—

(a) the transactions concerned differ as to their nature, their parties, their terms or their surrounding circumstances; and

(b) the difference is one which, in the opinion of the decision-making authority, ought for the purposes of that subsection to be treated as a material difference.

(6) The criteria for deciding when newspapers or broadcasting can be treated, for the purposes of section 59, as newspapers or broadcasting of a separate description shall be such as in any particular case the decision-making authority considers appropriate in the circumstances of that case.

(7) In section 59 and this section "provision" and cognate expressions have the same meaning in relation to broadcasting as in Part 3 of the Communications Act 2003; but this subsection is subject to subsections (4) and (5) of this section.

60 Special intervention notices under section 59

(1) A special intervention notice shall state—

(a) the special merger situation concerned; and
(b) the consideration specified in section 58 or considerations so specified which are, or may be, relevant to the special merger situation concerned.

(2) Where the Secretary of State believes that it is or may be the case that two or more considerations specified in section 58 are relevant to a consideration of the special merger situation concerned, he may decide not to mention in the special intervention notice such of those considerations as he considers appropriate.

(3) A special intervention notice shall come into force when it is given and shall cease to be in force when the matter to which it relates is finally determined under this Chapter.

(4) For the purposes of this Part, a matter to which a special intervention notice relates is finally determined under this Chapter if—

(a) the time within which the OFT or (if relevant) OFCOM is to report to the Secretary of State under section 61 or (as the case may be) 61A has expired and no such report has been made;
(b) the Secretary of State decides to accept an undertaking or group of undertakings under paragraph 3 of Schedule 7 instead of making a reference under section 62;
(c) the Secretary of State otherwise decides not to make a reference under that section;
(d) the Commission cancels such a reference under section 64(1);
(e) the time within which the Commission is to prepare a report under section 65 and give it to the Secretary of State has expired and no such report has been prepared and given to the Secretary of State;
(f) the time within which the Secretary of State is to make and publish a decision under section 66(2) has expired and no such decision has been made and published;
(g) the Secretary of State decides under subsection (2) of section 66 otherwise than as mentioned in subsection (5) of that section;
(h) the Secretary of State decides under subsection (2) of section 66 as mentioned in subsection (5) of that section but decides neither to accept an undertaking under paragraph 9 of Schedule 7 nor to make an order under paragraph 11 of that Schedule; or

(i) the Secretary of State decides under subsection (2) of section 66 as mentioned in subsection (5) of that section and accepts an undertaking under paragraph 9 of Schedule 7 or makes an order under paragraph 11 of that Schedule.

(5) For the purposes of this Part the time when a matter to which a special intervention notice relates is finally determined under this Chapter is—

(a) in a case falling within subsection (4)(a), (e) or (f), the expiry of the time concerned;
(b) in a case falling within subsection (4)(b), the acceptance of the undertaking or group of undertakings concerned;
(c) in a case falling within subsection (4)(c), (d) or (g), the making of the decision concerned;
(d) in a case falling within subsection (4)(h), the making of the decision neither to accept an undertaking under paragraph 9 of Schedule 7 nor to make an order under paragraph 11 of that Schedule; and
(e) in a case falling within subsection (4)(i), the acceptance of the undertaking concerned or (as the case may be) the making of the order concerned.

61 Initial investigation and report by OFT

(1) Subsection (2) applies where the Secretary of State has given a special intervention notice in relation to a special merger situation.

(2) The OFT shall, within such period as the Secretary of State may require, give a report to the Secretary of State in relation to the case.

(3) The report shall contain—

(a) advice from the OFT on the considerations relevant to the making of a reference under section 22 or 33 which are also relevant to the Secretary of State's decision as to whether to make a reference under section 62; and
(b) a summary of any representations about the case which have been received by the OFT and which relate to any consideration mentioned in the special intervention notice concerned (other than a consideration which, at the time of the giving of the notice, was specified in section 58(2A) to (2C)) and which is or may be relevant to the Secretary of State's decision as to whether to make a reference under section 62.

(4) The report shall include a decision as to whether the OFT believes (disregarding section 59(3B)(b)) that it is, or may be, the case that a special merger situation has been created or (as the case may be) arrangements are in progress or in contemplation which, if carried into effect, will result in the creation of a special merger situation.

(4A) The report may, in particular, contain a summary of any representations about the case which have been received by the OFT and which relate to any consideration which—

(a) is mentioned in the special intervention notice concerned and, at the time of the giving of that notice, was specified in section 58(2A) to (2C); and
(b) is or may be relevant to the Secretary of State's decision as to whether to make a reference under section 62.

(5) The report may, in particular, include advice and recommendations on any consideration mentioned in the special intervention notice concerned and which is or may be

relevant to the Secretary of State's decision as to whether to make a reference under section 62.

(6) The OFT shall carry out such investigations as it considers appropriate for the purposes of producing a report under this section.

61A Additional investigation and report by OFCOM: certain media mergers

(1) Subsection (2) applies where—

(a) the Secretary of State has given a special intervention notice in relation to a special merger situation; and
(b) the special intervention notice mentions any consideration which, at the time of the giving of the notice, was specified in section 58(2A) to (2C).

(2) OFCOM shall, within such period as the Secretary of State may require, give a report to the Secretary of State on the effect of the consideration or considerations concerned on the case.(3) The report shall contain—

(a) advice and recommendations on any consideration which—
(i) is mentioned in the special intervention notice concerned and, at the time of the giving of that notice, was specified in section 58(2A) to (2C); and
(ii) is or may be relevant to the Secretary of State's decision as to whether to make a reference under section 62; and
(b) a summary of any representations about the case which have been received by OFCOM and which relate to any such consideration.

(4) OFCOM shall carry out such investigations as they consider appropriate for the purposes of producing a report under this section.

62 Power of Secretary of State to refer the matter

(1) Subsection (2) applies where the Secretary of State—

(a) has given a special intervention notice in relation to a special merger situation; and
(b) has received a report of the OFT under section 61, and any report of OFCOM which is required by virtue of section 61A, in relation to the matter.

(2) The Secretary of State may make a reference to the Commission if he believes that it is or may be the case that—

(a) a special merger situation has been created;
(b) one or more than one consideration mentioned in the special intervention notice is relevant to a consideration of the special merger situation concerned; and
(c) taking account only of the relevant consideration or considerations concerned, the creation of that situation operates or may be expected to operate against the public interest.

(3) The Secretary of State may make a reference to the Commission if he believes that it is or may be the case that—

(a) arrangements are in progress or in contemplation which, if carried into effect, will result in the creation of a special merger situation;

(b) one or more than one consideration mentioned in the special intervention notice is relevant to a consideration of the special merger situation concerned; and
(c) taking account only of the relevant consideration or considerations concerned, the creation of that situation may be expected to operate against the public interest.

(4) No reference shall be made under this section if the making of the reference is prevented by paragraph 4 of Schedule 7.

(5) The Secretary of State, in deciding whether to make a reference under this section, shall accept the decision of the OFT included in its report under section 61 by virtue of subsection (4) of that section.

(6) A reference under this section shall, in particular, specify—

(a) the subsection of this section under which it is made;
(b) the date on which it is made; and
(c) the consideration or considerations mentioned in the special intervention notice which the Secretary of State believes are, or may be, relevant to a consideration of the special merger situation concerned.

63 Questions to be decided on references under section 62

(1) The Commission shall, on a reference under section 62(2), decide whether a special merger situation has been created.

(2) The Commission shall, on a reference under section 62(3), decide whether arrangements are in progress or in contemplation which, if carried into effect, will result in the creation of a special merger situation.

(3) If the Commission decides that a special merger situation has been created or that arrangements are in progress or in contemplation which, if carried into effect, will result in the creation of a special merger situation, it shall, on a reference under section 62, decide whether, taking account only of the consideration or considerations mentioned in the reference, the creation of that situation operates or may be expected to operate against the public interest.

(4) The Commission shall, if it has decided on a reference under section 62 that the creation of a special merger situation operates or may be expected to operate against the public interest, decide the following additional questions—

(a) whether action should be taken by the Secretary of State under section 66 for the purpose of remedying, mitigating or preventing any of the effects adverse to the public interest which have resulted from, or may be expected to result from, the creation of the special merger situation concerned;
(b) whether the Commission should recommend the taking of other action by the Secretary of State or action by persons other than itself and the Secretary of State for the purpose of remedying, mitigating or preventing any of the effects adverse to the public interest which have resulted from, or may be expected to result from, the creation of the special merger situation concerned; and
(c) in either case, if action should be taken, what action should be taken and what is to be remedied, mitigated or prevented.

64 Cancellation and variation of references under section 62

(1) The Commission shall cancel a reference under section 62(3) if it considers that the proposal to make arrangements of the kind mentioned in that reference has been abandoned.

(2) The Commission may, if it considers that doing so is justified by the facts (including events occurring on or after the making of the reference concerned), treat a reference made under subsection (2) or (3) of section 62 as if it had been made under subsection (3) or (as the case may be) (2) of that section; and, in such cases, references in this Part to references under those enactments shall, so far as may be necessary, be construed accordingly.

(3) Where, by virtue of subsection (2), the Commission treats a reference made under subsection (2) or (3) of section 62 as if it had been made under subsection (3) or (as the case may be) (2) of that section, paragraphs 1, 2, 7 and 8 of Schedule 7 shall, in particular, apply as if the reference had been made under subsection (3) or (as the case may be) (2) of that section instead of under subsection (2) or (3) of that section.

(4) Subsection (5) applies in relation to any undertaking accepted under paragraph 1 of Schedule 7, or any order made under paragraph 2 of that Schedule, which is in force immediately before the Commission, by virtue of subsection (2), treats a reference made under subsection (2) or (3) of section 62 as if it had been made under subsection (3) or (as the case may be) (2) of that section.

(5) The undertaking or order shall, so far as applicable, continue in force as if—

(a) in the case of an undertaking or order which relates to a reference under subsection (2) of section 62, accepted or made in relation to a reference made under subsection (3) of that section; and
(b) in the case of an undertaking or order which relates to a reference made under subsection (3) of that section, accepted or made in relation to a reference made under subsection (2) of that section;

and the undertaking or order concerned may be varied, superseded, released or revoked accordingly.

(6) The Secretary of State may at any time vary a reference under section 62.

(7) The Secretary of State shall consult the Commission before varying any such reference.

(8) Subsection (7) shall not apply if the Commission has requested the variation concerned.

(9) No variation by the Secretary of State under this section shall be capable of altering the consideration or considerations specified in the reference or the period permitted by virtue of section 65 within which the report of the Commission under that section is to be prepared and given to the Secretary of State.

65 Investigations and reports on references under section 62

(1) The Commission shall prepare a report on a reference under section 62 and give it to the Secretary of State within the period permitted by virtue of this section.

(2) The report shall, in particular, contain—

(a) the decisions of the Commission on the questions which it is required to answer by virtue of section 63;
(b) its reasons for its decisions; and
(c) such information as the Commission considers appropriate for facilitating a proper understanding of those questions and of its reasons for its decisions.

(2A) Where the report relates to a reference under section 62 which has been made after a report of OFCOM under section 61A, the Commission shall give a copy of its report (whether or not published) to OFCOM.

(3) Sections 51 and 52 (but not section 53) shall apply for the purposes of a report under this section as they apply for the purposes of a report under section 50.

(4) The Commission shall carry out such investigations as it considers appropriate for the purpose of producing a report under this section.

66 Decision and enforcement action by Secretary of State

(1) Subsection (2) applies where the Secretary of State has received a report of the Commission under section 65 in relation to a special merger situation.

(2) The Secretary of State shall, in connection with a reference under section 62(2) or (3), decide the questions which the Commission is required to decide by virtue of section 63(1) to (3).

(3) The Secretary of State shall make and publish his decision under subsection (2) within the period of 30 days beginning with the receipt of the report of the Commission under section 65; and subsection (8) of section 54 shall apply for the purposes of this subsection as it applies for the purposes of subsection (5) of that section.

(4) In making his decisions under subsection (2), the Secretary of State shall accept the decisions of the report of the Commission under section 65 as to whether a special merger situation has been created or whether arrangements are in progress or in contemplation which, if carried into effect, will result in the creation of a special merger situation.

(5) Subsection (6) applies where the Secretary of State has decided under subsection (2) that—

(a) a special merger situation has been created or arrangements are in progress or in contemplation which, if carried into effect, will result in the creation of a special merger situation;
(b) at least one consideration which is mentioned in the special intervention notice concerned is relevant to a consideration of the special merger situation concerned; and
(c) taking account only of the relevant consideration or considerations concerned, the creation of that situation operates or may be expected to operate against the public interest;

and has so decided, and published his decision, within the period required by subsection (3).

(6) The Secretary of State may take such action under paragraph 9 or 11 of Schedule 7 as he considers to be reasonable and practicable to remedy, mitigate or prevent any of the

effects adverse to the public interest which have resulted from, or may be expected to result from, the creation of the special merger situation concerned.

(7) In making a decision under subsection (6), the Secretary of State shall, in particular, have regard to the report of the Commission under section 65.

European mergers

67 Intervention to protect legitimate interests

(1) Subsection (2) applies where—

(a) the Secretary of State has reasonable grounds for suspecting that it is or may be the case that—

(i) a relevant merger situation has been created or that arrangements are in progress or in contemplation which, if carried into effect, will result in the creation of a relevant merger situation; and

(ii) a concentration with a Community dimension (within the meaning of the EC Merger Regulation), or a part of such a concentration, has thereby arisen or will thereby arise;

(b) a reference is prevented from being made under section 22 or 33 in relation to the relevant merger situation concerned (whether or not there would otherwise have been a duty to make such a reference) by virtue of Community law or anything done under or in accordance with it; and

(c) the Secretary of State is considering whether to take appropriate measures to protect legitimate interests as permitted by article 21(4) of the EC Merger Regulation.

(2) The Secretary of State may give a notice to the OFT (in this section 'a European intervention notice') if he believes that it is or may be the case that one or more than one public interest consideration is relevant to a consideration of the relevant merger situation concerned.

(3) A European intervention notice shall state—

(a) the relevant merger situation concerned;

(b) the public interest consideration or considerations which are, or may be, relevant to a consideration of the relevant merger situation concerned; and

(c) where any public interest consideration concerned is not finalised, the proposed timetable for finalising it.

(4) Where the Secretary of State believes that it is or may be the case that two or more public interest considerations are relevant to a consideration of the relevant merger situation concerned, he may decide not to mention in the intervention notice such of those considerations as he considers appropriate.

(5) No more than one European intervention notice shall be given under subsection (2) in relation to the same relevant merger situation.

(6) Where the Secretary of State has given a European intervention notice mentioning a public interest consideration which, at that time, is not finalised, he shall, as soon as practicable, take such action as is within his power to ensure that it is finalised.

(7) For the purposes of deciding whether a relevant merger situation has been created or whether arrangements are in progress or in contemplation which, if carried into effect, will result in the creation of a relevant merger situation, sections 23 to 32 (read together with section 34) shall apply for the purposes of this section as they do for the purposes of Chapter 1 but subject to subsection (8).

(8) In their application by virtue of subsection (7) sections 23 to 32 shall have effect as if—

(a) references in those sections to the decision-making authority were references to the Secretary of State;
(b) for paragraphs (a) and (b) of section 23(9) there were substituted ', in relation to the giving of a European intervention notice, the time when the notice is given';
(c) the references to the OFT in section 24(2)(a) and (b) included references to the Secretary of State;
(d) sections 25, 31 and 32 were omitted; and
(e) the references in sections 23 to 29 to the making of a reference or a reference were, so far as necessary, references to the giving of a European intervention notice or a European intervention notice.

(9) Section 42(3) shall, in its application to this section and section 68, have effect as if for the words 'intervention notice' there were substituted 'European intervention notice'.

68 Scheme for protecting legitimate interests

(1) The Secretary of State may by order provide for the taking of action, where a European intervention notice has been given, to remedy, mitigate or prevent effects adverse to the public interest which have resulted from, or may be expected to result from, the creation of a European relevant merger situation.

(2) In subsection (1) 'European relevant merger situation' means a relevant merger situation—

(a) which has been created or will be created if arrangements which are in progress or in contemplation are carried into effect;
(b) by virtue of which a concentration with a Community dimension (within the meaning of the EC Merger Regulation), or a part of such a concentration, has arisen or will arise; and
(c) in relation to which a reference was prevented from being made under section 22 or 33 (whether or not there would otherwise have been a duty to make such a reference) by virtue of Community law or anything done under or in accordance with it.

(3) Provision made under subsection (1) shall include provision ensuring that considerations which are not public interest considerations mentioned in the European intervention notice concerned may not be taken into account in determining whether anything operates, or may be expected to operate, against the public interest.

(4) Provision made under subsection (1) shall include provision—

(a) applying with modifications sections 23 to 32 for the purposes of deciding for the purposes of this section whether a relevant merger situation has been created or whether arrangements are in progress or in contemplation which, if carried into effect, will result in the creation of a relevant merger situation;

(b) requiring the OFT to make a report to the Secretary of State before a reference is made;
(c) enabling the Secretary of State to make a reference to the Commission;
(d) requiring the Commission to investigate and report to the Secretary of State on such a reference;
(e) enabling the taking of interim and final enforcement action.

(5) An order under this section may include provision (including provision for the creation of offences and penalties, the payment of fees and the delegation of functions) corresponding to any provision made in, or in connection with, this Part in relation to intervention notices or special intervention notices and the cases to which they relate.

(6) In this section 'European intervention notice' has the same meaning as in section 67.

69 . . .

Other
70 Water mergers

(1) For sections 32 to 35 of the Water Industry Act 1991 (c 56) (special provision for water merger references) there shall be substituted—

'32 Duty to refer merger of water or sewerage undertaking
Subject to section 33 below, it shall be the duty of the OFT to make a merger reference to the Competition Commission if the OFT believes that it is or may be the case—

(a) that arrangements are in progress which, if carried into effect, will result in a merger of any two or more water enterprises; or
(b) that such a merger has taken place otherwise than as a result of the carrying into effect of arrangements that have been the subject of a reference by virtue of paragraph (a) above.

33 Exclusion of small mergers from duty to make reference
(1) The OFT shall not make a merger reference under section 32 above in respect of any actual or prospective merger of two or more water enterprises if it appears to the OFT—

(a) that the value of the turnover of the water enterprise being taken over does not exceed or, as the case may be, would not exceed £10 million; or
(b) that the only water enterprises already belonging to the person making the take over are enterprises each of which has a turnover the value of which does not exceed or, as the case may be, would not exceed £10 million.

(2) For the purposes of subsection (1)(a) above, the value of the turnover of the water enterprise being taken over shall be determined by taking the total value of the turnover of the water enterprises ceasing to be distinct enterprises and deducting—

(a) the turnover of any water enterprise continuing to be carried on under the same ownership and control; or
(b) if there is no water enterprise continuing to be carried on under the same ownership and control, the turnover which, of all the turnovers concerned, is the turnover of the highest value.

(3) For the purposes of subsection (1)(b) above—

(a) every water enterprise ceasing to be a distinct enterprise and whose turnover is to be deducted by virtue of subsection (2)(a) or (b) above shall be treated as a water enterprise belonging to the person making the take over; and
(b) water enterprises shall be treated as separate enterprises so far as they are carried on by different companies holding appointments under Chapter 1 of this Part.

(4) For the purposes of this section the turnover of a water enterprise shall be determined in accordance with such provisions as may be specified in regulations made by the Secretary of State.

(5) Regulations under subsection (4) above may, in particular, make provision as to—

(a) the amounts which are, or which are not, to be treated as comprising an enterprise's turnover; and
(b) the date or dates by reference to which an enterprise's turnover is to be determined.

(6) Regulations under subsection (4) above may, in particular, make provision enabling the Secretary of State or the OFT to determine matters of a description specified in the regulations (including any of the matters mentioned in paragraphs (a) and (b) of subsection (5) above).

(7) The Secretary of State may by regulations amend subsection (1) above so as—

(a) to alter the sum for the time being mentioned in paragraph (a) of that subsection or otherwise to modify the condition set out in that paragraph; or
(b) to alter the sum for the time being mentioned in paragraph (b) of that subsection or otherwise to modify the condition set out in that paragraph.

(8) Regulations under subsection (7) above—

(a) shall not make any modifications in relation to mergers on or before the coming into force of the regulations; and
(b) may, in particular, include supplemental, consequential or transitional provision amending or repealing any provision of this section.

(9) References in this section to enterprises being carried on under the same ownership and control shall be construed in accordance with Part 3 of the 2002 Act.

34 Application of provisions of Enterprise Act 2002

The provisions of Schedule 4ZA to this Act shall have effect with respect to mergers of water enterprises.

35 Construction of merger provisions

(1) In this Chapter (including Schedule 4ZA)—
'enterprise' has the same meaning as in Part 3 of the 2002 Act; and 'water enterprise' means an enterprise carried on by a water undertaker.

(2) References in this Chapter (including Schedule 4ZA), in relation to any two or more enterprises, to the merger of those enterprises are references to those

enterprises ceasing, within the meaning of Part 3 of the 2002 Act, to be distinct enterprises; and sections 27 and 29 of that Act and any provision made under section 34 of that Act (time at which enterprises cease to be distinct) shall have effect for the purposes of this Chapter (including Schedule 4ZA) as they have effect for the purposes of that Part.

(3) Nothing in sections 32 to 34 above (including Schedule 4ZA) shall prejudice any power of the OFT or the Secretary of State, in a case in which, or to any extent to which, the OFT is not required to make a reference under section 32 above, to make a reference under Part 3 of the 2002 Act in respect of any actual or prospective merger of two or more water enterprises.

(4) Where two or more enterprises have merged or will merge as part of transactions or arrangements which also involve an actual or prospective merger of two or more water enterprises, Part 3 of the 2002 Act shall apply in relation to the actual or prospective merger of the enterprises concerned excluding the water enterprises; and references in that Part to the creation of a relevant merger situation shall be construed accordingly.

(5) Subject to subsections (3) and (4), Part 3 of the 2002 Act shall not apply in a case in which the OFT is required to make a reference under section 32 above except as applied by virtue of Schedule 4ZA.'

(2) Before Schedule 4A to the Act of 1991 there shall be inserted, as Schedule 4ZA, the Schedule set out in Schedule 6 to this Act.

CHAPTER 4
ENFORCEMENT

Powers exercisable before references under section 22 or 33

71 Initial undertakings: completed mergers

(1) Subsection (2) applies where the OFT is considering whether to make a reference under section 22.

(2) The OFT may, for the purpose of preventing pre-emptive action, accept from such of the parties concerned as it considers appropriate undertakings to take such action as it considers appropriate.

(3) No undertaking shall be accepted under subsection (2) unless the OFT has reasonable grounds for suspecting that it is or may be the case that a relevant merger situation has been created.(4) An undertaking under this section—

(a) shall come into force when accepted;
(b) may be varied or superseded by another undertaking; and
(c) may be released by the OFT.

(5) An undertaking which—

(a) is in force under this section in relation to a possible reference or reference under section 22; and

(b) has not been adopted under section 80 or paragraph 1 of Schedule 7;

shall cease to be in force if an order under section 72 or 81 comes into force in relation to that reference or an order under paragraph 2 of that Schedule comes into force in relation to the matter.

(6) An undertaking under this section shall, if it has not previously ceased to be in force and if it has not been adopted under section 80 or paragraph 1 of Schedule 7, cease to be in force—

(a) where the OFT has decided to make the reference concerned under section 22, at the end of the period of 7 days beginning with the making of the reference;
(b) where the OFT has decided to accept an undertaking under section 73 instead of making that reference, on the acceptance of that undertaking;
(c) where an intervention notice is in force, at the end of the period of 7 days beginning with the giving of that notice; and
(d) where the OFT has otherwise decided not to make the reference concerned under section 22, on the making of that decision.

(7) The OFT shall, as soon as reasonably practicable, consider any representations received by it in relation to varying or releasing an undertaking under this section.

(8) In this section and section 72 'pre-emptive action' means action which might prejudice the reference concerned or impede the taking of any action under this Part which may be justified by the Commission's decisions on the reference.

72 Initial enforcement orders: completed mergers

(1) Subsection (2) applies where the OFT is considering whether to make a reference under section 22.

(2) The OFT may by order, for the purpose of preventing pre-emptive action—

(a) prohibit or restrict the doing of things which the OFT considers would constitute pre-emptive action;
(b) impose on any person concerned obligations as to the carrying on of any activities or the safeguarding of any assets;
(c) provide for the carrying on of any activities or the safeguarding of any assets either by the appointment of a person to conduct or supervise the conduct of any activities (on such terms and with such powers as may be specified or described in the order) or in any other manner;
(d) do anything which may be done by virtue of paragraph 19 of Schedule 8.

(3) No order shall be made under subsection (2) unless the OFT has reasonable grounds for suspecting that it is or may be the case that—

(a) a relevant merger situation has been created; and
(b) pre-emptive action is in progress or in contemplation.

(4) An order under this section—

(a) shall come into force at such time as is determined by or under the order; and
(b) may be varied or revoked by another order.

(5) An order which—

(a) is in force under this section in relation to a possible reference or a reference under section 22; and

(b) has not been adopted under section 81 or paragraph 2 of Schedule 7;

shall cease to be in force if an undertaking under section 71 or 80 comes into force in relation to that reference or an undertaking under paragraph 1 of that Schedule comes into force in relation to the matter.

(6) An order under this section shall, if it has not previously ceased to be in force and if it is not adopted under section 81 or paragraph 2 of Schedule 7, cease to be in force—

(a) where the OFT has decided to make the reference concerned under section 22, at the end of the period of 7 days beginning with the making of the reference;

(b) where the OFT has decided to accept an undertaking under section 73 instead of making that reference, on the acceptance of that undertaking;

(c) where an intervention notice is in force, at the end of the period of 7 days beginning with the giving of that notice; and

(d) where the OFT has otherwise decided not to make the reference concerned under section 22, on the making of that decision.

(7) The OFT shall, as soon as reasonably practicable, consider any representations received by it in relation to varying or revoking an order under this section.

73 Undertakings in lieu of references under section 22 or 33

(1) Subsection (2) applies if the OFT considers that it is under a duty to make a reference under section 22 or 33 (disregarding the operation of section 22(3)(b) or (as the case may be) 33(3)(b) but taking account of the power of the OFT under section 22(2) or (as the case may be) 33(2) to decide not to make such a reference).

(2) The OFT may, instead of making such a reference and for the purpose of remedying, mitigating or preventing the substantial lessening of competition concerned or any adverse effect which has or may have resulted from it or may be expected to result from it, accept from such of the parties concerned as it considers appropriate undertakings to take such action as it considers appropriate.

(3) In proceeding under subsection (2), the OFT shall, in particular, have regard to the need to achieve as comprehensive a solution as is reasonable and practicable to the substantial lessening of competition and any adverse effects resulting from it.

(4) In proceeding under subsection (2), the OFT may, in particular, have regard to the effect of any action on any relevant customer benefits in relation to the creation of the relevant merger situation concerned.

(5) An undertaking under this section—

(a) shall come into force when accepted;

(b) may be varied or superseded by another undertaking; and

(c) may be released by the OFT.

(6) An undertaking under this section which is in force in relation to a relevant merger situation shall cease to be in force if an order comes into force under section 75 or 76 in relation to that undertaking.

(7) The OFT shall, as soon as reasonably practicable, consider any representations received by it in relation to varying or releasing an undertaking under this section.

74 Effect of undertakings under section 73

(1) The relevant authority shall not make a reference under section 22, 33 or 45 in relation to the creation of a relevant merger situation if—

(a) the OFT has accepted an undertaking or group of undertakings under section 73; and
(b) the relevant merger situation is the situation by reference to which the undertaking or group of undertakings was accepted.

(2) Subsection (1) does not prevent the making of a reference if material facts about relevant arrangements or transactions, or relevant proposed arrangements or transactions, were not notified (whether in writing or otherwise) to the OFT or made public before any undertaking concerned was accepted.

(3) For the purposes of subsection (2) arrangements or transactions, or proposed arrangements or transactions, are relevant if they are the ones in consequence of which the enterprises concerned ceased or may have ceased, or may cease, to be distinct enterprises.

(4) In subsection (2) 'made public' means so publicised as to be generally known or readily ascertainable.

(5) In this section 'relevant authority' means—

(a) in relation to a possible reference under section 22 or 33, the OFT; and(b) in relation to a possible reference under section 45, the Secretary of State.

75 Order-making power where undertakings under section 73 not fulfilled etc

(1) Subsection (2) applies where the OFT considers that—

(a) an undertaking accepted by it under section 73 has not been, is not being or will not be fulfilled; or
(b) in relation to an undertaking accepted by it under that section, information which was false or misleading in a material respect was given to the OFT by the person giving the undertaking before the OFT decided to accept the undertaking.

(2) The OFT may, for any of the purposes mentioned in section 73(2), make an order under this section.

(3) Subsections (3) and (4) of section 73 shall apply for the purposes of subsection (2) above as they apply for the purposes of subsection (2) of that section.

(4) An order under this section may contain—

(a) anything permitted by Schedule 8; and
(b) such supplementary, consequential or incidental provision as the OFT considers appropriate.

(5) An order under this section—

(a) shall come into force at such time as is determined by or under the order;
(b) may contain provision which is different from the provision contained in the undertaking concerned; and
(c) may be varied or revoked by another order.

(6) The OFT shall, as soon as reasonably practicable, consider any representations received by it in relation to varying or revoking an order under this section.

76 Supplementary interim order-making power

(1) Subsection (2) applies where—

(a) the OFT has the power to make an order under section 75 in relation to a particular undertaking and intends to make such an order; or
(b) the Commission has the power to make an order under section 83 in relation to a particular undertaking and intends to make such an order.

(2) The OFT or (as the case may be) the Commission may, for the purpose of preventing any action which might prejudice the making of that order, make an order under this section.

(3) No order shall be made under subsection (2) unless the OFT or (as the case may be) the Commission has reasonable grounds for suspecting that it is or may be the case that action which might prejudice the making of the order under section 75 or (as the case may be) 83 is in progress or in contemplation.

(4) An order under subsection (2) may—

(a) prohibit or restrict the doing of things which the OFT or (as the case may be) the Commission considers would prejudice the making of the order under section 75 or (as the case may be) 83;
(b) impose on any person concerned obligations as to the carrying on of any activities or the safeguarding of any assets;
(c) provide for the carrying on of any activities or the safeguarding of any assets either by the appointment of a person to conduct or supervise the conduct of any activities (on such terms and with such powers as may be specified or described in the order) or in any other manner;
(d) do anything which may be done by virtue of paragraph 19 of Schedule 8.

(5) An order under this section—

(a) shall come into force at such time as is determined by or under the order; and
(b) may be varied or revoked by another order.

(6) An order under this section shall, if it has not previously ceased to be in force, cease to be in force on—

(a) the coming into force of an order under section 75 or (as the case may be) 83 in relation to the undertaking concerned; or
(b) the making of the decision not to proceed with such an order.

(7) The OFT or (as the case may be) the Commission shall, as soon as reasonably practicable, consider any representations received by it in relation to varying or revoking an order under this section.

Interim restrictions and powers

77 Restrictions on certain dealings: completed mergers

(1) Subsections (2) and (3) apply where—

(a) a reference has been made under section 22 but not finally determined; and
(b) no undertakings under section 71 or 80 are in force in relation to the relevant merger situation concerned and no orders under section 72 or 81 are in force in relation to that situation.

(2) No relevant person shall, without the consent of the Commission—

(a) complete any outstanding matters in connection with any arrangements which have resulted in the enterprises concerned ceasing to be distinct enterprises;
(b) make any further arrangements in consequence of that result (other than arrangements which reverse that result); or
(c) transfer the ownership or control of any enterprises to which the reference relates.

(3) No relevant person shall, without the consent of the Commission, assist in any of the activities mentioned in paragraphs (a) to (c) of subsection (2).

(4) The prohibitions in subsections (2) and (3) do not apply in relation to anything which the person concerned is required to do by virtue of any enactment.

(5) The consent of the Commission under subsection (2) or (3)—

(a) may be general or special;
(b) may be revoked by the Commission; and
(c) shall be published in such manner as the Commission considers appropriate for the purpose of bringing it to the attention of any person entitled to the benefit of it.

(6) Paragraph (c) of subsection (5) shall not apply if the Commission considers that publication is not necessary for the purpose mentioned in that paragraph.

(7) Subsections (2) and (3) shall apply to a person's conduct outside the United Kingdom if (and only if) he is—

(a) a United Kingdom national;
(b) a body incorporated under the law of the United Kingdom or of any part of the United Kingdom; or
(c) a person carrying on business in the United Kingdom.

(8) In this section 'relevant person' means—

(a) any person who carries on any enterprise to which the reference relates or who has control of any such enterprise;
(b) any subsidiary of any person falling within paragraph (a); or
(c) any person associated with any person falling within paragraph (a) or any subsidiary of any person so associated.

78 Restrictions on certain share dealings: anticipated mergers

(1) Subsection (2) applies where—

(a) a reference has been made under section 33; and
(b) no undertakings under section 80 are in force in relation to the relevant merger situation concerned and no orders under section 81 are in force in relation to that situation.

(2) No relevant person shall, without the consent of the Commission, directly or indirectly acquire during the relevant period an interest in shares in a company if any enterprise to which the reference relates is carried on by or under the control of that company.

(3) The consent of the Commission under subsection (2)—

(a) may be general or special;
(b) may be revoked by the Commission; and
(c) shall be published in such manner as the Commission considers appropriate for bringing it to the attention of any person entitled to the benefit of it.

(4) Paragraph (c) of subsection (3) shall not apply if the Commission considers that publication is not necessary for the purpose mentioned in that paragraph.

(5) Subsection (2) shall apply to a person's conduct outside the United Kingdom if (and only if) he is—

(a) a United Kingdom national;
(b) a body incorporated under the law of the United Kingdom or of any part of the United Kingdom; or
(c) a person carrying on business in the United Kingdom.

(6) In this section and section 79—
'company' includes any body corporate; 'relevant period' means the period beginning with the making of the reference concerned and ending when the reference is finally determined; 'relevant person' means—

(a) any person who carries on any enterprise to which the reference relates or who has control of any such enterprise;
(b) any subsidiary of any person falling within paragraph (a); or
(c) any person associated with any person falling within paragraph (a) or any subsidiary of any person so associated; and
'share' means share in the capital of a company, and includes stock.

79 Sections 77 and 78: further interpretation provisions

(1) For the purposes of this Part a reference under section 22 or 33 is finally determined if—

(a) the reference is cancelled under section 37(1);
(b) the time within which the Commission is to prepare and publish a report under section 38 in relation to the reference has expired and no such report has been prepared and published;

(c) the report of the Commission under section 38 contains the decision that there is not an anti-competitive outcome;

(d) the report of the Commission under section 38 contains the decision that there is an anti-competitive outcome and the Commission has decided under section 41(2) neither to accept an undertaking under section 82 nor to make an order under section 84; or

(e) the report of the Commission under section 38 contains the decision that there is an anti-competitive outcome and the Commission has decided under section 41(2) to accept an undertaking under section 82 or to make an order under section 84.

(2) For the purposes of this Part the time when a reference under section 22 or 33 is finally determined is—

(a) in a case falling within subsection (1)(a), the making of the decision concerned;

(b) in a case falling within subsection (1)(b), the expiry of the time concerned;

(c) in a case falling within subsection (1)(c), the publication of the report;

(d) in a case falling within subsection (1)(d), the making of the decision under section 41(2); and

(e) in a case falling within subsection (1)(e), the acceptance of the undertaking concerned or (as the case may be) the making of the order concerned.

(3) For the purposes of section 78 and subject to subsection (4) below, the circumstances in which a person acquires an interest in shares include those where—

(a) he enters into a contract to acquire the shares (whether or not for cash);

(b) he is not the registered holder but acquires the right to exercise, or to control the exercise of, any right conferred by the holding of the shares; or

(c) he—

(i) acquires a right to call for delivery of the shares to himself or to his order or to acquire an interest in the shares; or

(ii) assumes an obligation to acquire such an interest.

(4) The circumstances in which a person acquires an interest in shares for the purposes of section 78 do not include those where he acquires an interest in pursuance of an obligation assumed before the publication by the OFT of the reference concerned.

(5) The circumstances in which a person acquires a right mentioned in subsection (3)—

(a) include those where he acquires a right, or assumes an obligation, whose exercise or fulfilment would give him that right; but

(b) do not include those where he is appointed as proxy to vote at a specified meeting of a company or of any class of its members or at any adjournment of the meeting or he is appointed by a corporation to act as its representative at any meeting of the company or of any class of its members.

(6) References to rights and obligations in subsections (3) to (5) include conditional rights and conditional obligations.

(7) References in sections 77 and 78 to a person carrying on or having control of any enterprise includes a group of persons carrying on or having control of an enterprise and any member of such a group.

(8) Sections 26(2) to (4) and 127(1), (2) and (4) to (6) shall apply for the purposes of sections 77 and 78 to determine whether any person or group of persons has control of any enterprise and whether persons are associated as they apply for the purposes of section 26 to determine whether enterprises are brought under common control.

(9) Sections 736 and 736A of the Companies Act 1985 (c 6) shall apply for the purposes of sections 77 and 78 to determine whether a company is a subsidiary of an individual or of a group of persons as they apply to determine whether it is a subsidiary of a company; and references to a subsidiary in subsections (8) and (9) of section 736A as so applied shall be construed accordingly.

80 Interim undertakings

(1) Subsections (2) and (3) apply where a reference under section 22 or 33 has been made but is not finally determined.

(2) The Commission may, for the purpose of preventing pre-emptive action, accept from such of the parties concerned as it considers appropriate undertakings to take such action as it considers appropriate.

(3) The Commission may, for the purpose of preventing pre-emptive action, adopt an undertaking accepted by the OFT under section 71 if the undertaking is still in force when the Commission adopts it.

(4) An undertaking adopted under subsection (3)—

- (a) shall continue in force, in accordance with its terms, when adopted;
- (b) may be varied or superseded by an undertaking under this section; and
- (c) may be released by the Commission.

(5) Any other undertaking under this section—

- (a) shall come into force when accepted;
- (b) may be varied or superseded by another undertaking; and(c) may be released by the Commission.

(6) References in this Part to undertakings under this section shall, unless the context otherwise requires, include references to undertakings adopted under this section; and references to the acceptance or giving of undertakings under this section shall be construed accordingly.

(7) An undertaking which is in force under this section in relation to a reference under section 22 or 33 shall cease to be in force if an order under section 81 comes into force in relation to that reference.

(8) An undertaking under this section shall, if it has not previously ceased to be in force, cease to be in force when the reference under section 22 or 33 is finally determined.

(9) The Commission shall, as soon as reasonably practicable, consider any representations received by it in relation to varying or releasing an undertaking under this section.

(10) In this section and section 81 ‘pre-emptive action’ means action which might prejudice the reference concerned or impede the taking of any action under this Part which may be justified by the Commission’s decisions on the reference.

81 Interim orders

(1) Subsections (2) and (3) apply where a reference has been made under section 22 or 33 but is not finally determined.

(2) The Commission may by order, for the purpose of preventing pre-emptive action—

(a) prohibit or restrict the doing of things which the Commission considers would constitute pre-emptive action;
(b) impose on any person concerned obligations as to the carrying on of any activities or the safeguarding of any assets;
(c) provide for the carrying on of any activities or the safeguarding of any assets either by the appointment of a person to conduct or supervise the conduct of any activities (on such terms and with such powers as may be specified or described in the order) or in any other manner;
(d) do anything which may be done by virtue of paragraph 19 of Schedule 8.

(3) The Commission may, for the purpose of preventing pre-emptive action, adopt an order made by the OFT under section 72 if the order is still in force when the Commission adopts it.

(4) An order adopted under subsection (3)—

(a) shall continue in force, in accordance with its terms, when adopted; and
(b) may be varied or revoked by an order under this section.

(5) Any other order under this section—

(a) shall come into force at such time as is determined by or under the order; and
(b) may be varied or revoked by another order.

(6) References in this Part to orders under this section shall, unless the context otherwise requires, include references to orders adopted under this section; and references to the making of orders under this section shall be construed accordingly.

(7) An order which is in force under this section in relation to a reference under section 22 or 33 shall cease to be in force if an undertaking under section 80 comes into force in relation to that reference.

(8) An order under this section shall, if it has not previously ceased to be in force, cease to be in force when the reference under section 22 or 33 is finally determined.

(9) The Commission shall, as soon as reasonably practicable, consider any representations received by it in relation to varying or revoking an order under this section.

Final powers

82 Final undertakings

(1) The Commission may, in accordance with section 41, accept, from such persons as it considers appropriate, undertakings to take action specified or described in the undertakings.

(2) An undertaking under this section—

(a) shall come into force when accepted;
(b) may be varied or superseded by another undertaking; and(c) may be released by the Commission.

(3) An undertaking which is in force under this section in relation to a reference under section 22 or 33 shall cease to be in force if an order under section 76(1)(b) or 83 comes into force in relation to the subject-matter of the undertaking.

(4) No undertaking shall be accepted under this section in relation to a reference under section 22 or 33 if an order has been made under—

(a) section 76(1)(b) or 83 in relation to the subject-matter of the undertaking; or
(b) section 84 in relation to that reference.

(5) The Commission shall, as soon as reasonably practicable, consider any representations received by it in relation to varying or releasing an undertaking under this section.

83 Order-making power where final undertakings not fulfilled

(1) Subsection (2) applies where the Commission considers that—

(a) an undertaking accepted by it under section 82 has not been, is not being or will not be fulfilled; or
(b) in relation to an undertaking accepted by it under that section, information which was false or misleading in a material respect was given to the Commission or the OFT by the person giving the undertaking before the Commission decided to accept the undertaking.

(2) The Commission may, for any of the purposes mentioned in section 41(2), make an order under this section.

(3) Subsections (3) to (5) of section 41 shall apply for the purposes of subsection (2) above as they apply for the purposes of subsection (2) of that section.

(4) An order under this section may contain—

(a) anything permitted by Schedule 8; and
(b) such supplementary, consequential or incidental provision as the Commission considers appropriate.

(5) An order under this section—

(a) shall come into force at such time as is determined by or under the order;
(b) may contain provision which is different from the provision contained in the undertaking concerned; and
(c) may be varied or revoked by another order.

(6) No order shall be varied or revoked under this section unless the OFT advises that such a variation or revocation is appropriate by reason of a change of circumstances.

84 Final orders

(1) The Commission may, in accordance with section 41, make an order under this section.

(2) An order under this section may contain—

(a) anything permitted by Schedule 8; and
(b) such supplementary, consequential or incidental provision as the Commission considers appropriate.

(3) An order under this section—

(a) shall come into force at such time as is determined by or under the order; and
(b) may be varied or revoked by another order.

(4) No order shall be varied or revoked under this section unless the OFT advises that such a variation or revocation is appropriate by reason of a change of circumstances.

(5) No order shall be made under this section in relation to a reference under section 22 or 33 if an undertaking has been accepted under section 82 in relation to that reference.

Public interest and special public interest cases

85 Enforcement regime for public interest and special public interest cases

(1) Schedule 7 (which provides for the enforcement regime in public interest and special public interest cases) shall have effect.

(2) The OFT may advise the Secretary of State in relation to the taking by him of enforcement action under Schedule 7.

Undertakings and orders: general provisions

86 Enforcement orders: general provisions

(1) An enforcement order may extend to a person's conduct outside the United Kingdom if (and only if) he is—

(a) a United Kingdom national;
(b) a body incorporated under the law of the United Kingdom or of any part of the United Kingdom; or
(c) a person carrying on business in the United Kingdom.

(2) Nothing in an enforcement order shall have effect so as to—

(a) cancel or modify conditions in licences granted—
(i) under a patent granted under the Patents Act 1977 (c 37) or a European patent (UK) (within the meaning of the Act of 1977); or
(ii) in respect of a design registered under the Registered Designs Act 1949 (c 88);
by the proprietor of the patent or design; or
(b) require an entry to be made in the register of patents or the register of designs to the effect that licences under such a patent or such a design are to be available as of right.

(3) An enforcement order may prohibit the performance of an agreement already in existence when the order is made.

(4) Schedule 8 (which provides for the contents of certain enforcement orders) shall have effect.

(5) Part 1 of Schedule 9 (which enables certain enforcement orders to modify licence conditions etc in regulated markets) shall have effect.

(6) In this Part 'enforcement order' means an order made under section 72, 75, 76, 81, 83 or 84 or under paragraph 2, 5, 6, 10 or 11 of Schedule 7.

87 Delegated power of directions

(1) An enforcement order may authorise the person making the order to give directions falling within subsection (2) to—

(a) a person specified in the directions; or
(b) the holder for the time being of an office so specified in any body of persons corporate or unincorporate.

(2) Directions fall within this subsection if they are directions—

(a) to take such action as may be specified or described in the directions for the purpose of carrying out, or ensuring compliance with, the enforcement order concerned; or
(b) to do, or refrain from doing, anything so specified or described which the person might be required by that order to do or refrain from doing.

(3) An enforcement order may authorise the person making the order to vary or revoke any directions so given.

(4) The court may by order require any person who has failed to comply with directions given by virtue of this section to comply with them, or otherwise remedy his failure, within such time as may be specified in the order.

(5) Where the directions related to anything done in the management or administration of a body of persons corporate or unincorporate, the court may by order require the body of persons concerned or any officer of it to comply with the directions, or otherwise remedy the failure to comply with them, within such time as may be specified in the order.

(6) An order under subsection (4) or (5) shall be made on the application of the person authorised by virtue of this section to give the directions concerned.

(7) An order under subsection (4) or (5) may provide for all the costs or expenses of, or incidental to, the application for the order to be met by any person in default or by any officers of a body of persons corporate or unincorporate who are responsible for its default.

(8) In this section 'the court' means—

(a) in relation to England and Wales or Northern Ireland, the High Court; and
(b) in relation to Scotland, the Court of Session.

88 Contents of certain enforcement orders

(1) This section applies in relation to any order under section 75, 83 or 84 or under paragraph 5, 10 or 11 of Schedule 7.

(2) The order or any explanatory material accompanying the order shall state—

(a) the actions that the persons or description of persons to whom the order is addressed must do or (as the case may be) refrain from doing;
(b) the date on which the order comes into force;
(c) the possible consequences of not complying with the order; and
(d) the section of this Part under which a review can be sought in relation to the order.

89 Subject-matter of undertakings

(1) The provision which may be contained in an enforcement undertaking is not limited to the provision which is permitted by Schedule 8.

(2) In this Part 'enforcement undertaking' means an undertaking under section 71, 73, 80 or 82 or under paragraph 1, 3 or 9 of Schedule 7.

90 Procedural requirements for certain undertakings and orders

Schedule 10 (which provides for the procedure for accepting certain enforcement undertakings and making certain enforcement orders and for their termination) shall have effect.

91 Register of undertakings and orders

(1) The OFT shall compile and maintain a register for the purposes of this Part.

(2) The register shall be kept in such form as the OFT considers appropriate.

(3) The OFT shall ensure that the following matters are entered in the register—

(a) the provisions of any enforcement undertaking accepted under this Part;
(b) the provisions of any enforcement order made under this Part;
(c) the details of any variation, release or revocation of such an undertaking or order; and
(d) the details of any consent given by the Commission under section 77(2) or (3) or 78(2) or by the Secretary of State under paragraph 7(2) or (3) or 8(2) of Schedule 7.

(4) The duty in subsection (3) does not extend to anything of which the OFT is unaware.

(5) The Commission and the Secretary of State shall inform the OFT of any matters which are to be included in the register by virtue of subsection (3) and which relate to enforcement undertakings accepted by them, enforcement orders made by them or consents given by them.

(6) The OFT shall ensure that the contents of the register are available to the public—

(a) during (as a minimum) such hours as may be specified in an order made by the Secretary of State; and
(b) subject to such reasonable fees (if any) as the OFT may determine.

(7) If requested by any person to do so and subject to such reasonable fees (if any) as the OFT may determine, the OFT shall supply the person concerned with a copy (certified to be true) of the register or of an extract from it.

Enforcement functions of OFT

92 Duty of OFT to monitor undertakings and orders

(1) The OFT shall keep under review—

(a) the carrying out of any enforcement undertaking or any enforcement order; and
(b) compliance with the prohibitions in sections 77(2) and (3) and 78(2) and in paragraphs 7(2) and (3) and 8(2) of Schedule 7.

(2) The OFT shall, in particular, from time to time consider—

(a) whether an enforcement undertaking or enforcement order has been or is being complied with;
(b) whether, by reason of any change of circumstances, an enforcement undertaking is no longer appropriate and—
(i) one or more of the parties to it can be released from it; or
(ii) it needs to be varied or to be superseded by a new enforcement undertaking; and
(c) whether, by reason of any change of circumstances, an enforcement order is no longer appropriate and needs to be varied or revoked.

(3) The OFT shall give the Commission or (as the case may be) the Secretary of State such advice as it considers appropriate in relation to—

(a) any possible variation or release by the Commission or (as the case may be) the Secretary of State of an enforcement undertaking accepted by it or (as the case may be) him;
(b) any possible new enforcement undertaking to be accepted by the Commission or (as the case may be) the Secretary of State so as to supersede another enforcement undertaking given to the Commission or (as the case may be) the Secretary of State;
(c) any possible variation or revocation by the Commission or (as the case may be) the Secretary of State of an enforcement order made by the Commission or (as the case may be) the Secretary of State;
(d) any possible enforcement undertaking to be accepted by the Commission or (as the case may be) the Secretary of State instead of an enforcement order or any possible enforcement order to be made by the Commission or (as the case may be) the Secretary of State instead of an enforcement undertaking;
(e) the enforcement by virtue of section 94(6) to (8) of any enforcement undertaking or enforcement order; or
(f) the enforcement by virtue of section 95(4) and (5) of the prohibitions in sections 77(2) and (3) and 78(2) and in paragraphs 7(2) and (3) and 8(2) of Schedule 7.

(4) The OFT shall take such action as it considers appropriate in relation to—

(a) any possible variation or release by it of an enforcement undertaking accepted by it;
(b) any possible new enforcement undertaking to be accepted by it so as to supersede another enforcement undertaking given to it;
(c) any possible variation or revocation by it of an enforcement order made by it;

(d) any possible enforcement undertaking to be accepted by it instead of an enforcement order or any possible enforcement order to be made by it instead of an enforcement undertaking;
(e) the enforcement by it by virtue of section 94(6) of any enforcement undertaking or enforcement order; or
(f) the enforcement by it by virtue of section 95(4) and (5) of the prohibitions in sections 77(2) and (3) and 78(2) and in paragraphs 7(2) and (3) and 8(2) of Schedule 7.

(5) The OFT shall keep under review the effectiveness of enforcement undertakings accepted under this Part and enforcement orders made under this Part.

(6) The OFT shall, whenever requested to do so by the Secretary of State and otherwise from time to time, prepare a report of its findings under subsection (5).

(7) The OFT shall—

(a) give any report prepared by it under subsection (6) to the Commission;
(b) give a copy of the report to the Secretary of State; and
(c) publish the report.

93 Further role of OFT in relation to undertakings and orders

(1) Subsections (2) and (3) apply where—

(a) the Commission is considering whether to accept undertakings under section 80 or 82; or
(b) the Secretary of State is considering whether to accept undertakings under paragraph 1, 3 or 9 of Schedule 7.

(2) The Commission or (as the case may be) the Secretary of State (in this section 'the relevant authority') may require the OFT to consult with such persons as the relevant authority considers appropriate with a view to discovering whether they will offer undertakings which the relevant authority would be prepared to accept under section 80 or 82 or (as the case may be) paragraph 1, 3 or 9 of Schedule 7.

(3) The relevant authority may require the OFT to report to the relevant authority on the outcome of the OFT's consultations within such period as the relevant authority may require.

(4) A report under subsection (3) shall, in particular, contain advice from the OFT as to whether any undertakings offered should be accepted by the relevant authority under section 80 or 82 or (as the case may be) paragraph 1, 3 or 9 of Schedule 7.

(5) The powers conferred on the relevant authority by subsections (1) to (4) are without prejudice to the power of the relevant authority to consult the persons concerned itself.

(6) If asked by the relevant authority for advice in relation to the taking of enforcement action (whether or not by way of undertaking) in a particular case, the OFT shall give such advice as it considers appropriate.

Other

94 Rights to enforce undertakings and orders

(1) This section applies to any enforcement undertaking or enforcement order.

(2) Any person to whom such an undertaking or order relates shall have a duty to comply with it.

(3) The duty shall be owed to any person who may be affected by a contravention of the undertaking or (as the case may be) order.

(4) Any breach of the duty which causes such a person to sustain loss or damage shall be actionable by him.

(5) In any proceedings brought under subsection (4) against a person to whom an enforcement undertaking or an enforcement order relates it shall be a defence for that person to show that he took all reasonable steps and exercised all due diligence to avoid contravening the undertaking or (as the case may be) order.

(6) Compliance with an enforcement undertaking or an enforcement order shall also be enforceable by civil proceedings brought by the OFT for an injunction or for interdict or for any other appropriate relief or remedy.

(7) Compliance with an undertaking under section 80 or 82, an order made by the Commission under section 76 or an order under section 81, 83 or 84, shall also be enforceable by civil proceedings brought by the Commission for an injunction or for interdict or for any other appropriate relief or remedy.

(8) Compliance with an undertaking under paragraph 1, 3 or 9 of Schedule 7, an order made by the Secretary of State under paragraph 2 of that Schedule or an order under paragraph 5, 6, 10 or 11 of that Schedule, shall also be enforceable by civil proceedings brought by the Secretary of State for an injunction or for interdict or for any other appropriate relief or remedy.

(9) Subsections (6) to (8) shall not prejudice any right that a person may have by virtue of subsection (4) to bring civil proceedings for contravention or apprehended contravention of an enforcement undertaking or an enforcement order.

95 Rights to enforce statutory restrictions

(1) The obligation to comply with section 77(2) or (3) or 78(2) or paragraph 7(2) or (3) or 8(2) of Schedule 7 shall be a duty owed to any person who may be affected by a contravention of the enactment concerned.

(2) Any breach of the duty which causes such a person to sustain loss or damage shall be actionable by him.

(3) In any proceedings brought under subsection (2) against a person who has an obligation to comply with section 77(2) or (3) or 78(2) or paragraph 7(2) or (3) or 8(2) of Schedule 7 it shall be a defence for that person to show that he took all reasonable steps and exercised all due diligence to avoid contravening the enactment concerned.

(4) Compliance with section 77(2) or (3) or 78(2) shall also be enforceable by civil proceedings brought by the OFT or the Commission for an injunction or for interdict or for any other appropriate relief or remedy.

(5) Compliance with paragraph 7(2) or (3) or 8(2) of Schedule 7 shall also be enforceable by civil proceedings brought by the OFT or the Secretary of State for an injunction or for interdict or for any other appropriate relief or remedy.

(6) Subsections (4) and (5) shall not prejudice any right that a person may have by virtue of subsection (2) to bring civil proceedings for contravention or apprehended contravention of section 77(2) or (3) or 78(2) or paragraph 7(2) or (3) or 8(2) of Schedule 7.

CHAPTER 5
SUPPLEMENTARY

Merger notices

96 Merger notices

(1) A person authorised to do so by regulations under section 101 may give notice to the OFT of proposed arrangements which might result in the creation of a relevant merger situation.

(2) Any such notice (in this Part a 'merger notice')—

(a) shall be in the prescribed form; and
(b) shall state that the existence of the proposal has been made public.

(3) No reference shall be made under section 22, 33 or 45 in relation to—

(a) arrangements of which notice is given under subsection (1) above or arrangements which do not differ from them in any material respect; or
(b) the creation of any relevant merger situation which is, or may be, created in consequence of carrying such arrangements into effect;

if the period for considering the merger notice has expired without a reference being made under that section in relation to those arrangements.

(4) Subsection (3) is subject to section 100.

(5) In this section and sections 99(5)(c) and 100(1)(c) 'prescribed' means prescribed by the OFT by notice having effect for the time being and published in the London, Edinburgh and Belfast Gazettes.

(6) In this Part 'notified arrangements' means arrangements of which notice is given under subsection (1) above or arrangements not differing from them in any material respect.

97 Period for considering merger notices

(1) The period for considering a merger notice is, subject as follows, the period of 20 days beginning with the first day after—

(a) the notice has been received by the OFT; and
(b) any fee payable by virtue of section 121 to the OFT in respect of the notice has been paid.

(2) Where no intervention notice is in force in relation to the matter concerned, the OFT may by notice to the person who gave the merger notice extend by a further 10 days the period for considering the merger notice.

(3) Where an intervention notice is in force in relation to the matter concerned and there has been no extension under subsection (2), the OFT may by notice to the person who gave the merger notice extend by a further 20 days the period for considering the merger notice.

(4) Where an intervention notice is in force in relation to the matter concerned and there has been an extension under subsection (2), the OFT may by notice to the person who gave the merger notice extend the period for considering the merger notice by a further number of days which, including any extension already made under subsection (2), does not exceed 20 days.

(5) The OFT may by notice to the person who gave the merger notice extend the period for considering a merger notice if the OFT considers that the person has failed to provide, within the period stated in a notice under section 99(2) and in the authorised or required manner, information requested of him in that notice.

(6) An extension under subsection (5) shall be for the period until the person concerned provides the information to the satisfaction of the OFT or, if earlier, the cancellation by the OFT of the extension.

(7) The OFT may by notice to the person who gave the merger notice extend the period for considering a merger notice if the OFT is seeking undertakings under section 73 or (as the case may be) the Secretary of State is seeking undertakings under paragraph 3 of Schedule 7.

(8) An extension under subsection (7) shall be for the period beginning with the receipt of the notice under that subsection and ending with the earliest of the following events—

(a) the giving of the undertakings concerned;
(b) the expiry of the period of 10 days beginning with the first day after the receipt by the OFT of a notice from the person from whom the undertakings are being sought stating that he does not intend to give the undertakings; or
(c) the cancellation by the OFT of the extension.

(9) The Secretary of State may by notice to the person who gave the merger notice extend the period for considering a merger notice if, by virtue of paragraph 3(6) of Schedule 7, he decides to delay a decision as to whether to make a reference under section 45.

(10) An extension under subsection (9) shall be for the period of the delay.

(11) The OFT may by notice to the person who gave the merger notice extend the period for considering a merger notice if the European Commission is considering a request made, in relation to the matter concerned, by the United Kingdom (whether alone or with others) under article 22(1) of the EC Merger Regulation (but is not yet proceeding with the matter in pursuance of such a request).

(12) An extension under subsection (11) shall be for the period beginning with the receipt of the notice under that subsection and ending with the receipt of a notice under subsection (13).

(13) The OFT shall, in connection with any notice given by it under subsection (11), by notice inform the person who gave the merger notice of the completion by the European Commission of its consideration of the request of the United Kingdom.

98 Section 97: supplementary

(1) A notice under section 97(2), (3), (4), (5), (7), (9) or (11) shall be given, before the end of the period for considering the merger notice, to the person who gave the merger notice.

(2) A notice under section 97(5)—

(a) shall also be given within 5 days of the end of the period within which the information is to be provided and which is stated in the notice under section 99(2); and
(b) shall also inform the person who gave the merger notice of—
  (i) the OFT's opinion as mentioned in section 97(5); and
  (ii) the OFT's intention to extend the period for considering a merger notice.

(3) In determining for the purposes of section 97(1), (2), (3), (4) or (8)(b) or subsection (2)(a) above any period which is expressed in the enactment concerned as a period of days or number of days no account shall be taken of—

(a) Saturday, Sunday, Good Friday and Christmas Day; and
(b) any day which is a bank holiday in England and Wales.

(4) Any reference in this Part (apart from in section 97(1) and section 99(1)) to the period for considering a merger notice shall, if that period is extended by virtue of any one or more of subsections (2), (3), (4) (5), (7), (9) and (11) of section 97 in relation to a particular case, be construed in relation to that case as a reference to that period as so extended; but only one extension is possible under section 97(2), (3) or (4).

(5) Where the period for considering a merger notice is extended or further extended by virtue of section 97, the period as extended or (as the case may be) further extended shall, subject to subsections (6) and (7), be calculated by taking the period being extended and adding to it the period of the extension (whether or not those periods overlap in time).

(6) Subsection (7) applies where—

(a) the period for considering a merger notice is further extended;
(b) the further extension and at least one previous extension is made under one or more of subsections (5), (7), (9) and (11) of section 97; and

(c) the same days or fractions of days are included in or comprise the further extension and are included in or comprise at least one such previous extension.

(7) In calculating the period of the further extension, any days or fractions of days of the kind mentioned in subsection (6)(c) shall be disregarded.

99 Certain functions of OFT and Secretary of State in relation to merger notices

(1) The OFT shall, so far as practicable and when the period for considering any merger notice begins, take such action as the OFT considers appropriate to bring—

(a) the existence of the proposal;
(b) the fact that the merger notice has been given; and
(c) the date on which the period for considering the notice may expire;

to the attention of those whom the OFT considers would be affected if the arrangements were carried into effect.

(2) The OFT may by notice to the person who gave the merger notice request him to provide the OFT with such information as the OFT or (as the case may be) the Secretary of State may require for the purpose of carrying out its or (as the case may be) his functions in relation to the merger notice.

(3) A notice under subsection (2) shall state—

(a) the information required;
(b) the period within which the information is to be provided; and
(c) the possible consequences of not providing the information within the stated period and in the authorised or required manner.

(4) A notice by the OFT under subsection (2) shall be given, before the end of the period for considering the merger notice, to the person who gave the merger notice.

(5) The OFT may, at any time before the end of the period for considering any merger notice, reject the notice if—

(a) the OFT suspects that any information given in respect of the notified arrangements (whether in the merger notice or otherwise) by the person who gave the notice or any connected person is in any material respect false or misleading;
(b) the OFT suspects that it is not proposed to carry the notified arrangements into effect;
(c) any prescribed information is not given in the merger notice or any information requested by notice under subsection (2) is not provided as required; or
(d) the OFT considers that the notified arrangements are, or if carried into effect would result in, a concentration with a Community dimension within the meaning of the EC Merger Regulation.

(6) In this section and section 100 'connected person', in relation to the person who gave a merger notice, means—

(a) any person who, for the purposes of section 127, is associated with him; or
(b) any subsidiary of the person who gave the merger notice or of any person so associated with him.

100 Exceptions to protection given by merger notices

(1) Section 96(3) does not prevent any reference being made to the Commission if—

(a) before the end of the period for considering the merger notice, the OFT rejects the notice under section 99(5);

(b) before the end of that period, any of the enterprises to which the notified arrangements relate cease to be distinct from each other;

(c) any information (whether prescribed information or not) that—

(i) is, or ought to be, known to the person who gave the merger notice or any connected person; and

(ii) is material to the notified arrangements;

is not disclosed to the OFT by such time before the end of that period as may be specified in regulations under section 101;

(d) at any time after the merger notice is given but before the enterprises to which the notified arrangements relate cease to be distinct from each other, any of those enterprises ceases to be distinct from any enterprise other than an enterprise to which those arrangements relate;

(e) the six months beginning with the end of the period for considering the merger notice expires without the enterprises to which the notified arrangements relate ceasing to be distinct from each other;

(f) the merger notice is withdrawn; or

(g) any information given in respect of the notified arrangements (whether in the merger notice or otherwise) by the person who gave the notice or any connected person is in any material respect false or misleading.

(2) Subsection (3) applies where—

(a) two or more transactions which have occurred, or, if any arrangements are carried into effect, will occur, may be treated for the purposes of a reference under section 22, 33 or 45 as having occurred simultaneously on a particular date; and

(b) section 96(3) does not prevent such a reference in relation to the last of those transactions.

(3) Section 96(3) does not prevent such a reference in relation to any of those transactions which actually occurred less than six months before—

(a) that date; or

(b) the actual occurrence of another of those transactions in relation to which such a reference may be made (whether or not by virtue of this subsection).

(4) In determining for the purposes of subsections (2) and (3) the time at which any transaction actually occurred, no account shall be taken of any option or other conditional right until the option is exercised or the condition is satisfied.

(5) In this section references to the enterprises to which the notified arrangements relate are references to those enterprises that would have ceased to be distinct from one another if the arrangements mentioned in the merger notice concerned had been carried into effect at the time when the notice was given.

101 Merger notices: regulations

(1) The Secretary of State may make regulations for the purposes of sections 96 to 100.

(2) The regulations may, in particular—

(a) provide for section 97(1), (2), (3) or (4) or section 100(1)(e) to apply as if any reference to a period of days or months were a reference to a period specified in the regulations for the purposes of the enactment concerned;

(b) provide for the manner in which any merger notice is authorised or required to be rejected or withdrawn, and the time at which any merger notice is to be treated as received or rejected;

(c) provide for the time at which any notice under section 97(7), (8)(b), (11) or (13) is to be treated as received;

(d) provide for the manner in which any information requested by the OFT or any other material information is authorised or required to be provided or disclosed, and the time at which such information is to be treated as provided or disclosed (including the time at which it is to be treated as provided to the satisfaction of the OFT for the purposes of section 97(6));

(e) provide for the person who gave the merger notice to be informed, in circumstances in which section 97(6) applies—

(i) of the fact that the OFT is satisfied as to the provision of the information requested by the OFT or (as the case may be) of the OFT's decision to cancel the extension; and

(ii) of the time at which the OFT is to be treated as so satisfied or (as the case may be) of the time at which the cancellation is to be treated as having effect;

(f) provide for the person who gave the merger notice to be informed, in circumstances in which section 97(8) applies—

(i) of any decision by the OFT to cancel the extension; and

(ii) of the time at which such a cancellation is to be treated as having effect;

(g) provide for the time at which any fee is to be treated as paid;

(h) provide that a person is, or is not, to be treated, in such circumstances as may be specified in the regulations, as acting on behalf of a person authorised by regulations under this section to give a merger notice or a person who has given such a notice.

102 Power to modify sections 97 to 101

The Secretary of State may, for the purposes of determining the effect of giving a merger notice and the action which may be or is to be taken by any person in connection with such a notice, by order modify sections 97 to 101.

General duties in relation to references

103 Duty of expedition in relation to references

(1) In deciding whether to make a reference under section 22 or 33 the OFT shall have regard, with a view to the prevention or removal of uncertainty, to the need for making a decision as soon as reasonably practicable.

(2) In deciding whether to make a reference under section 45 or 62 the Secretary of State shall have regard, with a view to the prevention or removal of uncertainty, to the need for making a decision as soon as reasonably practicable.

104 Certain duties of relevant authorities to consult

(1) Subsection (2) applies where the relevant authority is proposing to make a relevant decision in a way which the relevant authority considers is likely to be adverse to the interests of a relevant party.

(2) The relevant authority shall, so far as practicable, consult that party about what is proposed before making that decision.

(3) In consulting the party concerned, the relevant authority shall, so far as practicable, give the reasons of the relevant authority for the proposed decision.

(4) In considering what is practicable for the purposes of this section the relevant authority shall, in particular, have regard to—

(a) any restrictions imposed by any timetable for making the decision; and
(b) any need to keep what is proposed, or the reasons for it, confidential.

(5) The duty under this section shall not apply in relation to the making of any decision so far as particular provision is made elsewhere by virtue of this Part for consultation before the making of that decision.

(6) In this section—

'the relevant authority' means the OFT, the Commission or the Secretary of State;
'relevant decision' means—
(a) in the case of the OFT, any decision by the OFT—
(i) as to whether to make a reference under section 22 or 33 or accept undertakings under section 73 instead of making such a reference; or
(ii) to vary under section 37 such a reference;
(b) in the case of the Commission, any decision on the questions mentioned in section 35(1) or (3), 36(1) or (2), 47 or 63; and
(c) in the case of the Secretary of State, any decision by the Secretary of State—
(i) as to whether to make a reference under section 45 or 62; or
(ii) to vary under section 49 or (as the case may be) 64 such a reference; and
'relevant party' means any person who appears to the relevant authority to control enterprises which are the subject of the reference or possible reference concerned.

104A Public consultation in relation to media mergers

(1) Subsection (2) applies where the Commission—

(a) is preparing—
(i) a report under section 50 on a reference which specifies a media public interest consideration; or
(ii) a report under section 65 on a reference which specifies a consideration specified in section 58(2A) to (2C); and
(b) is not under a duty to disregard the consideration concerned.

(2) The Commission shall have regard (among other things) to the need to consult the public so far as they might be affected by the creation of the relevant merger situation or special merger situation concerned and so far as such consultation is practicable.

(3) Any consultation of the kind mentioned in subsection (2) may be undertaken by the Commission by consulting such representative sample of the public or section of the public concerned as the Commission considers appropriate.

Information and publicity requirements

105 General information duties of OFT and Commission

(1) Where the OFT decides to investigate a matter so as to enable it to decide whether to make a reference under section 22 or 33, or so as to make a report under section 44 or 61, it shall, so far as practicable, take such action as it considers appropriate to bring information about the investigation to the attention of those whom it considers might be affected by the creation of the relevant merger situation concerned or (as the case may be) the special merger situation concerned.

(1A) Where OFCOM decide to investigate a matter so as to make a report under section 44A or 61A, they shall, so far as practicable, take such action as they consider appropriate to bring information about the investigation to the attention of those who they consider might be affected by the creation of the relevant merger situation concerned or (as the case may be) the special merger situation concerned.

(2) Subsections (1) and (1A) do not apply in relation to arrangements which might result in the creation of a relevant merger situation if a merger notice has been given in relation to those arrangements under section 96.

(3) The OFT shall give the Commission or OFCOM—

(a) such information in its possession as the Commission or (as the case may be) OFCOM may reasonably require to enable the Commission or (as the case may be) OFCOM to carry out its functions under this Part; and
(b) any other assistance which the Commission or (as the case may be) OFCOM may reasonably require for the purpose of assisting it in carrying out its functions under this Part and which it is within the power of the OFT to give.

(3A) OFCOM shall give the Commission or the OFT—

(a) such information in their possession as the Commission or (as the case may be) the OFT may reasonably require to enable the Commission or (as the case may be) the OFT to carry out its functions under this Part; and
(b) any other assistance which the Commission or (as the case may be) the OFT may reasonably require for the purpose of assisting it in carrying out its functions under this Part and which it is within the power of OFCOM to give.

(4) The OFT shall give the Commission or OFCOM any information in its possession which has not been requested by the Commission or (as the case may be) OFCOM but which, in the opinion of the OFT, would be appropriate to give to the Commission or (as the case may be) OFCOM for the purpose of assisting it in carrying out its functions under this Part.

(4A) OFCOM shall give the Commission or the OFT any information in their possession which has not been requested by the Commission or (as the case may be) the OFT but which, in the opinion of OFCOM, would be appropriate to give to the Commission or (as the case may be) the OFT for the purpose of assisting it in carrying out its functions under this Part.

(5) The OFT, OFCOM and the Commission shall give the Secretary of State—

(a) such information in their possession as the Secretary of State may by direction reasonably require to enable him to carry out his functions under this Part; and
(b) any other assistance which the Secretary of State may by direction reasonably require for the purpose of assisting him in carrying out his functions under this Part and which it is within the power of the OFT, OFCOM or (as the case may be) the Commission to give.

(6) The OFT and OFCOM shall give the Secretary of State any information in their possession which has not been requested by the Secretary of State but which, in the opinion of the OFT or (as the case may be) OFCOM, would be appropriate to give to the Secretary of State for the purpose of assisting him in carrying out his functions under this Part.

(7) The Commission shall have regard to any information given to it under subsection (3), (3A), (4) or (4A); and the Secretary of State shall have regard to any information given to him under subsection (5) or (6).

(7A) OFCOM shall have regard to any information given to them under subsection (3) or (4); and the OFT shall have regard to any information given to it under subsection (3A) or (4A).

(8) Any direction given under subsection (5)—

(a) shall be in writing; and
(b) may be varied or revoked by a subsequent direction.

106 Advice and information about references under sections 22 and 33

(1) As soon as reasonably practicable after the passing of this Act, the OFT shall prepare and publish general advice and information about the making of references by it under section 22 or 33.

(2) The OFT may at any time publish revised, or new, advice or information.

(3) As soon as reasonably practicable after the passing of this Act, the Commission shall prepare and publish general advice and information about the consideration by it of references under section 22 or 33 and the way in which relevant customer benefits may affect the taking of enforcement action in relation to such references.

(4) The Commission may at any time publish revised, or new, advice or information.

(5) Advice and information published under this section shall be prepared with a view to—

(a) explaining relevant provisions of this Part to persons who are likely to be affected by them; and
(b) indicating how the OFT or (as the case may be) the Commission expects such provisions to operate.

(6) Advice (or information) published by virtue of subsection (1) or (3) may include advice (or information) about the factors which the OFT or (as the case may be) the Commission may take into account in considering whether, and if so how, to exercise a function conferred by this Part.

(7) Any advice or information published by the OFT or the Commission under this section shall be published in such manner as the OFT or (as the case may be) the Commission considers appropriate.

(8) In preparing any advice or information under this section, the OFT shall consult the Commission and such other persons as it considers appropriate.

(9) In preparing any advice or information under this section, the Commission shall consult the OFT and such other persons as it considers appropriate.

106A Advice and information in relation to media mergers

(1) The Secretary of State may prepare and publish general advice and information about the considerations specified in section 58(2A) to (2C).

(2) The Secretary of State may at any time publish revised, or new, advice or information.

(3) Advice or information published under this section shall be prepared with a view to—

(a) explaining the considerations specified in section 58(2A) to (2C) to persons who are likely to be affected by them; and
(b) indicating how the Secretary of State expects this Part to operate in relation to such considerations.

(4) Any advice or information published by the Secretary of State under this section shall be published in such manner as the Secretary of State considers appropriate.

(5) In preparing any advice or information under this section, the Secretary of State shall consult the OFT, OFCOM, the Commission and such other persons as he considers appropriate.

106B General advisory functions of OFCOM

(1) OFCOM may, in connection with any case on which they are required to give a report by virtue of section 44A or 61A, give such advice as they consider appropriate to the Secretary of State in relation to—

(a) any report made in such a case by the Commission under section 50 or 65; and
(b) the taking by the Secretary of State of enforcement action under Schedule 7.

(2) OFCOM may, if requested to do so by the Secretary of State, give such other advice as they consider appropriate to the Secretary of State in connection with any case on which they are required to give a report by virtue of section 44A or 61A.

(3) OFCOM shall publish any advice given by them under this section but advice given by them in relation to a report of the Commission under section 50 or 65 or related enforcement action shall not be published before the report itself is published.

107 Further publicity requirements

(1) The OFT shall publish—

(a) any reference made by it under section 22 or 33 or any decision made by it not to make such a reference (other than a decision made by virtue of subsection (2)(b) of section 33);
(b) any variation made by it under section 37 of a reference under section 22 or 33;
(c) such information as it considers appropriate about any decision made by it under section 57(1) to bring a case to the attention of the Secretary of State;
(d) any enforcement undertaking accepted by it under section 71;
(e) any enforcement order made by it under section 72 or 76 or paragraph 2 of Schedule 7;
(f) any variation, release or revocation of such an undertaking or order;
(g) any decision made by it as mentioned in section 76(6)(b); and
(h) any decision made by it to dispense with the requirements of Schedule 10.

(2) The Commission shall publish—

(a) any cancellation by it under section 37(1) of a reference under section 33;
(b) any decision made by it under section 37(2) to treat a reference made under section 22 or 33 as if it had been made under section 33 or (as the case may be) 22;
(c) any extension by it under section 39 of the period within which a report under section 38 is to be prepared and published;
(d) any decision made by it to cancel an extension as mentioned in section 39(8)(b);
(e) any decision made by it under section 41(2) neither to accept an undertaking under section 82 nor to make an order under section 84;
(f) any decision made by it that there has been a material change of circumstances as mentioned in subsection (3) of section 41 or there is another special reason as mentioned in that subsection of that section;
(g) any cancellation by it under section 48(1) or 53(1) of a reference under section 45 or any cancellation by it under section 64(1) of a reference under section 62;
(h) any decision made by it under section 49(1) to treat—
 (i) a reference made under subsection (2) or (3) of section 45 as if it had been made under subsection (4) or (as the case may be) (5) of that section; or
 (ii) a reference made under subsection (4) or (5) of section 45 as if it had been made under subsection (2) or (as the case may be) (3) of that section;
(i) any extension by it under section 51 of the period within which a report under section 50 is to be prepared and published;
(j) any decision made by it under section 51(8)(b) to cancel such an extension;
(k) any extension by it under section 51 as applied by section 65(3) of the period within which a report under section 65 is to be prepared and published;
(l) any decision made by it under section 51(8)(b) as applied by section 65(3) to cancel such an extension;
(m) any decision made by it under section 64(2) to treat a reference made under subsection (2) or (3) of section 62 as if it had been made under subsection (3) or (as the case may be) (2) of that section;
(n) any decision made by it as mentioned in section 76(6)(b);
(o) any enforcement order made by it under section 76 or 81;
(p) any enforcement undertaking accepted by it under section 80;
(q) any variation, release or revocation of such an order or undertaking; and
(r) any decision made by it to dispense with the requirements of Schedule 10.

(3) The Secretary of State shall publish—

(a) any intervention notice or special intervention notice given by him;
(b) any report of the OFT under section 44 or 61 which has been received by him;
(ba) any report of OFCOM under section 44A or 61A which has been received by him;
(c) any reference made by him under section 45 or 62 or any decision made by him not to make such a reference;
(d) any variation made by him under section 49 of a reference under section 45 or under section 64 of a reference under section 62;
(e) any report of the Commission under section 50 or 65 which has been received by him;
(f) any decision made by him neither to accept an undertaking under paragraph 9 of Schedule 7 nor to make an order under paragraph 11 of that Schedule;
(g) any notice given by him under section 56(1);
(h) any enforcement undertaking accepted by him under paragraph 1 of Schedule 7;
(i) any variation or release of such an undertaking;
(j) any decision made by him as mentioned in paragraph 6(6)(b) of Schedule 7; and
(k) any decision made by him to dispense with the requirements of Schedule 10.

(4) Where any person is under a duty by virtue of subsection (1), (2) or (3) to publish the result of any action taken by that person or any decision made by that person, the person concerned shall, subject to subsections (5) and (6), also publish that person's reasons for the action concerned or (as the case may be) the decision concerned.

(5) Such reasons need not, if it is not reasonably practicable to do so, be published at the same time as the result of the action concerned or (as the case may be) as the decision concerned.

(6) Subsections (4) and (5) shall not apply in relation to any information published under subsection (1)(c).(7) The Secretary of State shall publish his reasons for—

(a) any decision made by him under section 54(2) or 66(2); or
(b) any decision to make an order under section 58(3) or vary or revoke such an order.

(8) Such reasons may be published after—

(a) in the case of subsection (7)(a), the publication of the decision concerned; and
(b) in the case of subsection (7)(b), the making of the order or of the variation or revocation;
if it is not reasonably practicable to publish them at the same time as the publication of the decision or (as the case may be) the making of the order or variation or revocation.

(9) The Secretary of State shall publish—

(a) the report of the OFT under section 44, and any report of OFCOM under section 44A, in relation to a matter no later than publication of his decision as to whether to make a reference under section 45 in relation to that matter; and
(b) the report of the Commission under section 50 in relation to a matter no later than publication of his decision under section 54(2) in relation to that matter.

(10) The Secretary of State shall publish—

(a) the report of the OFT under section 61, and any report of OFCOM under section 61A, in relation to a matter no later than publication of his decision as to whether to make a reference under section 62 in relation to that matter; and
(b) the report of the Commission under section 65 in relation to a matter no later than publication of his decision under section 66(2) in relation to that matter.

(11) Where the Secretary of State has decided under section 55(2) or 66(6) to accept an undertaking under paragraph 9 of Schedule 7 or to make an order under paragraph 11 of that Schedule, he shall (after the acceptance of the undertaking or (as the case may be) the making of the order) lay details of his decision and his reasons for it, and the Commission's report under section 50 or (as the case may be) 65, before each House of Parliament.

108 Defamation

For the purposes of the law relating to defamation, absolute privilege attaches to any advice, guidance, notice or direction given, or decision or report made, by the OFT, OFCOM, the Commission or the Secretary of State in the exercise of any of their functions under this Part.

Investigation powers

109 Attendance of witnesses and production of documents etc

(1) The Commission may, for the purpose of any investigation on a reference made to it under this Part, give notice to any person requiring him—

(a) to attend at a time and place specified in the notice; and
(b) to give evidence to the Commission or a person nominated by the Commission for the purpose.

(2) The Commission may, for the purpose of any investigation on a reference made to it under this Part, give notice to any person requiring him—

(a) to produce any documents which—
  (i) are specified or described in the notice, or fall within a category of document which is specified or described in the notice; and
  (ii) are in that person's custody or under his control; and
(b) to produce them at a time and place so specified and to a person so specified.

(3) The Commission may, for the purpose of any investigation on a reference made to it under this Part, give notice to any person who carries on any business requiring him—

(a) to supply to the Commission such estimates, forecasts, returns or other information as may be specified or described in the notice; and
(b) to supply it at a time and place, and in a form and manner, so specified and to a person so specified.

(4) A notice under this section shall include information about the possible consequences of not complying with the notice.

(5) The Commission or any person nominated by it for the purpose may, for the purpose of any investigation on a reference made to it under this Part, take evidence on oath, and for that purpose may administer oaths.

(6) The person to whom any document is produced in accordance with a notice under this section may, for the purpose of any investigation on a reference made to the Commission under this Part, copy the document so produced.

(7) No person shall be required under this section—

(a) to give any evidence or produce any documents which he could not be compelled to give or produce in civil proceedings before the court; or
(b) to supply any information which he could not be compelled to supply in evidence in such proceedings.

(8) No person shall be required, in compliance with a notice under this section, to go more than 10 miles from his place of residence unless his necessary travelling expenses are paid or offered to him.

(9) Any reference in this section to the production of a document includes a reference to the production of a legible and intelligible copy of information recorded otherwise than in legible form.

(10) In this section 'the court' means—

(a) in relation to England and Wales or Northern Ireland, the High Court; and
(b) in relation to Scotland, the Court of Session.

110 Enforcement of powers under section 109: general

(1) Where the Commission considers that a person has, without reasonable excuse, failed to comply with any requirement of a notice under section 109, it may impose a penalty in accordance with section 111.

(2) The Commission may proceed (whether at the same time or at different times) under subsection (1) and section 39(4) or (as the case may be) 51(4) (including that enactment as applied by section 65(3)) in relation to the same failure.

(3) Where the Commission considers that a person has intentionally obstructed or delayed another person in the exercise of his powers under section 109(6), it may impose a penalty in accordance with section 111.

(4) No penalty shall be imposed by virtue of subsection (1) or (3) if more than 4 weeks have passed since the publication of the report of the Commission on the reference concerned; but this subsection shall not apply in relation to any variation or substitution of the penalty which is permitted by virtue of this Part.

(5) A person, subject to subsection (6), commits an offence if he intentionally alters, suppresses or destroys any document which he has been required to produce by a notice under section 109.

(6) A person does not commit an offence under subsection (5) in relation to any act which constitutes a failure to comply with a notice under section 109 if the Commission has proceeded against that person under subsection (1) above in relation to that failure.

(7) A person who commits an offence under subsection (5) shall be liable—

(a) on summary conviction, to a fine not exceeding the statutory maximum;
(b) on conviction on indictment, to imprisonment for a term not exceeding two years or to a fine or to both.

(8) The Commission shall not proceed against a person under subsection (1) in relation to an act which constitutes an offence under subsection (5) if that person has been found guilty of that offence.

(9) In deciding whether and, if so, how to proceed under subsection (1) or (3) or section 39(4) or 51(4) (including that enactment as applied by section 65(3)), the Commission shall have regard to the statement of policy which was most recently published under section 116 at the time when the failure concerned or (as the case may be) the obstruction or delay concerned occurred.

(10) The reference in this section to the production of a document includes a reference to the production of a legible and intelligible copy of information recorded otherwise than in legible form; and the reference to suppressing a document includes a reference to destroying the means of reproducing information recorded otherwise than in legible form.

111 Penalties

(1) A penalty imposed under section 110(1) or (3) shall be of such amount as the Commission considers appropriate.

(2) The amount may, in the case of a penalty imposed under section 110(1), be a fixed amount, an amount calculated by reference to a daily rate or a combination of a fixed amount and an amount calculated by reference to a daily rate.

(3) The amount shall, in the case of a penalty imposed under section 110(3), be a fixed amount.

(4) No penalty imposed under section 110(1) shall—

(a) in the case of a fixed amount, exceed such amount as the Secretary of State may by order specify;
(b) in the case of an amount calculated by reference to a daily rate, exceed such amount per day as the Secretary of State may so specify; and
(c) in the case of a fixed amount and an amount calculated by reference to a daily rate, exceed such fixed amount and such amount per day as the Secretary of State may so specify.

(5) In imposing a penalty by reference to a daily rate—

(a) no account shall be taken of any days before the service of the notice under section 112 on the person concerned; and
(b) unless the Commission determines an earlier date (whether before or after the penalty is imposed), the amount payable shall cease to accumulate at the beginning of—
(i) the day on which the requirement of the notice concerned under section 109 is satisfied or (as the case may be) the obstruction or delay is removed; or

(ii) if earlier, the day on which the report of the Commission on the reference concerned is published (or, in the case of a report under section 50 or 65, given) or, if no such report is published (or given) within the period permitted for that purpose by this Part, the latest day on which the report may be published (or given) within the permitted period.

(6) No penalty imposed under section 110(3) shall exceed such amount as the Secretary of State may by order specify.

(7) An order under subsection (4) or (6) shall not specify—

(a) in the case of a fixed amount, an amount exceeding £30,000;
(b) in the case of an amount calculated by reference to a daily rate, an amount per day exceeding £15,000; and
(c) in the case of a fixed amount and an amount calculated by reference to a daily rate, a fixed amount exceeding £30,000 and an amount per day exceeding £15,000.

(8) Before making an order under subsection (4) or (6) the Secretary of State shall consult the Commission and such other persons as he considers appropriate.

112 Penalties: main procedural requirements

(1) As soon as practicable after imposing a penalty under section 110(1) or (3), the Commission shall give notice of the penalty.

(2) The notice shall state—

(a) that the Commission has imposed a penalty on the person concerned;
(b) whether the penalty is of a fixed amount, of an amount calculated by reference to a daily rate or of both a fixed amount and an amount calculated by reference to a daily rate;
(c) the amount or amounts concerned and, in the case of an amount calculated by reference to a daily rate, the day on which the amount first starts to accumulate and the day or days on which it might cease to accumulate;
(d) the failure or (as the case may be) the obstruction or delay which the Commission considers gave it the power to impose the penalty;
(e) any other facts which the Commission considers justify the imposition of a penalty and the amount or amounts of the penalty;
(f) the manner in which, and place at which, the penalty is required to be paid to the Commission;
(g) the date or dates, no earlier than the end of the relevant period beginning with the date of service of the notice on the person concerned, by which the penalty or (as the case may be) different portions of it are required to be paid;
(h) that the penalty or (as the case may be) different portions of it may be paid earlier than the date or dates by which it or they are required to be paid; and
(i) that the person concerned has the right to apply under subsection (3) below or to appeal under section 114 and the main details of those rights.

(3) The person against whom the penalty was imposed may, within 14 days of the date of service on him of a notice under subsection (1), apply to the Commission for it to specify a different date or (as the case may be) different dates by which the penalty or (as the case may be) different portions of it are to be paid.

(4) A notice under this section shall be given by—

(a) serving a copy of the notice on the person on whom the penalty was imposed; and
(b) publishing the notice.

(5) In this section 'relevant period' means the period of 28 days mentioned in subsection (3) of section 114 or, if another period is specified by the Secretary of State under that subsection, that period.

113 Payments and interest by instalments

(1) If the whole or any portion of a penalty is not paid by the date by which it is required to be paid, the unpaid balance from time to time shall carry interest at the rate for the time being specified in section 17 of the Judgments Act 1838 (c 110).

(2) Where an application has been made under section 112(3), the penalty shall not be required to be paid until the application has been determined, withdrawn or otherwise dealt with.

(3) If a portion of a penalty has not been paid by the date required for it, the Commission may, where it considers it appropriate to do so, require so much of the penalty as has not already been paid (and is capable of being paid immediately) to be paid immediately.

(4) Any sums received by the Commission in or towards the payment of a penalty, or interest on a penalty, shall be paid into the Consolidated Fund.

114 Appeals in relation to penalties

(1) This section applies if a person on whom a penalty is imposed under section 110(1) or (3) is aggrieved by—

(a) the imposition or nature of the penalty;
(b) the amount or amounts of the penalty; or
(c) the date by which the penalty is required to be paid or (as the case may be) the different dates by which portions of the penalty are required to be paid.

(2) The person aggrieved may apply to the Competition Appeal Tribunal.

(3) If a copy of the notice under section 112(1) was served on the person on whom the penalty was imposed, the application to the Competition Appeal Tribunal shall, subject to subsection (4), be made within—

(a) the period of 28 days starting with the day on which the copy was served on the person concerned; or
(b) such other period as the Secretary of State may by order specify.

(4) If the application relates to a decision of the Commission on an application by the person on whom the penalty was imposed under section 112(3), the application to the Competition Appeal Tribunal shall be made within—

(a) the period of 28 days starting with the day on which the person concerned is notified of the decision; or
(b) such other period as the Secretary of State may by order specify.

(5) On an application under this section, the Competition Appeal Tribunal may—

(a) quash the penalty;
(b) substitute a penalty of a different nature or of such lesser amount or amounts as the Competition Appeal Tribunal considers appropriate; or
(c) in a case falling within subsection (1)(c), substitute for the date or dates imposed by the Commission an alternative date or dates;
if it considers it appropriate to do so.

(6) The Competition Appeal Tribunal shall not substitute a penalty of a different nature under subsection (5)(b) unless it considers that the person on whom the penalty is imposed will, or is likely to, pay less under the substituted penalty than he would have paid under the original penalty.

(7) Where an application has been made under this section—

(a) the penalty shall not be required to be paid until the application has been determined, withdrawn or otherwise dealt with; and
(b) the Commission may agree to reduce the amount or amounts of the penalty in settlement of the application.

(8) Where the Competition Appeal Tribunal substitutes a penalty of a different nature or of a lesser amount or amounts it may require the payment of interest on the substituted penalty at such rate or rates, and from such date or dates, as it considers appropriate.

(9) Where the Competition Appeal Tribunal specifies as a date by which the penalty, or a portion of the penalty, is to be paid a date before the determination of the application under this section it may require the payment of interest on the penalty, or portion, from that date at such rate as it considers appropriate.

(10) An appeal lies to the appropriate court—

(a) on a point of law arising from a decision of the Tribunal in proceedings under this section; or
(b) from a decision of the Tribunal in such proceedings as to the amount or amounts of a penalty.

(11) An appeal under subsection (10)—

(a) may be brought by a party to the proceedings before the Tribunal; and
(b) requires the permission of the Tribunal or the appropriate court.

(12) In this section 'the appropriate court' means the Court of Appeal or, in the case of Tribunal proceedings in Scotland, the Court of Session.

115 Recovery of penalties

Where a penalty imposed under section 110(1) or (3), or any portion of such a penalty, has not been paid by the date on which it is required to be paid and—

(a) no application relating to the penalty has been made under section 114 during the period within which such an application may be made, or
(b) any such application which has been made has been determined, withdrawn or otherwise dealt with,

the Commission may recover from the person on whom the penalty was imposed any of the penalty and any interest which has not been paid; and in England and Wales and Northern Ireland such penalty and interest may be recovered as a civil debt due to the Commission.

116 Statement of policy

(1) The Commission shall prepare and publish a statement of policy in relation to the enforcement of notices under section 109.

(2) The statement shall, in particular, include a statement about the considerations relevant to the determination of the nature and amount of any penalty imposed under section 110(1) or (3).

(3) The Commission may revise its statement of policy and, where it does so, it shall publish the revised statement.

(4) The Commission shall consult such persons as it considers appropriate when preparing or revising its statement of policy.

117 False or misleading information

(1) A person commits an offence if—

(a) he supplies any information to the OFT, OFCOM, the Commission or the Secretary of State in connection with any of their functions under this Part;
(b) the information is false or misleading in a material respect; and
(c) he knows that it is false or misleading in a material respect or is reckless as to whether it is false or misleading in a material respect.

(2) A person commits an offence if he—

(a) supplies any information to another person which he knows to be false or misleading in a material respect; or
(b) recklessly supplies any information to another person which is false or misleading in a material respect;

knowing that the information is to be used for the purpose of supplying information to the OFT, OFCOM, the Commission or the Secretary of State in connection with any of their functions under this Part.

(3) A person who commits an offence under subsection (1) or (2) shall be liable—

(a) on summary conviction, to a fine not exceeding the statutory maximum;
(b) on conviction on indictment, to imprisonment for a term not exceeding two years or to a fine or to both.

Reports

118 Excisions from reports

(1) Subsection (2) applies where the Secretary of State is under a duty to publish—

(a) a report of the OFT under section 44 or 61;
(aa) a report of OFCOM under section 44A or 61A; or
(b) a report of the Commission under section 50 or 65.

(2) The Secretary of State may exclude a matter from the report concerned if he considers that publication of the matter would be inappropriate.

(3) In deciding what is inappropriate for the purposes of subsection (2) the Secretary of State shall have regard to the considerations mentioned in section 244.

(4) The body which has prepared the report shall advise the Secretary of State as to the matters (if any) which it considers should be excluded by him under subsection (2).

(5) References in sections 38(4) and 107(11) to the giving or laying of a report of the Commission shall be construed as references to the giving or laying of the report as published.

119 Minority reports of Commission

(1) Subsection (2) applies where, on a reference to the Commission under this Part, a member of a group constituted in connection with the reference in pursuance of paragraph 15 of Schedule 7 to the Competition Act 1998 (c 41), disagrees with any decisions contained in the report of the Commission under this Part as the decisions of the Commission.

(2) The report shall, if the member so wishes, include a statement of his disagreement and of his reasons for disagreeing.

Further provision about media mergers

119A Other general functions of OFCOM in relation to this Part

(1) OFCOM have the function of obtaining, compiling and keeping under review information about matters relating to the carrying out of their functions under this Part.

(2) That function is to be carried out with a view to (among other things) ensuring that OFCOM have sufficient information to take informed decisions and to carry out their other functions effectively.

(3) In carrying out that function OFCOM may carry out, commission or support (financially or otherwise) research.

(4) Section 3 of the Communications Act 2003 (general duties of OFCOM) shall not apply in relation to functions of OFCOM under this Part.

119B Monitoring role for OFT in relation to media mergers

(1) The OFT has the function of obtaining, compiling and keeping under review information about matters which may be relevant to the Secretary of State in deciding whether to give a special intervention notice mentioning a consideration specified in section 58(2A) to (2C).

(2) That function is to be carried out with a view to (among other things) ensuring that the Secretary of State is aware of cases where, in the opinion of the OFT, he might wish to consider giving such a notice.

(3) That function does not extend to obtaining, compiling or keeping under review information with a view to carrying out a detailed analysis in each case of the operation in relation to that case of the consideration specified in section 58(2A) to (2C).

Miscellaneous

120 Review of decisions under Part 3

(1) Any person aggrieved by a decision of the OFT, OFCOM, the Secretary of State or the Commission under this Part in connection with a reference or possible reference in relation to a relevant merger situation or a special merger situation may apply to the Competition Appeal Tribunal for a review of that decision.

(2) For this purpose 'decision'—

(a) does not include a decision to impose a penalty under section 110(1) or (3); but
(b) includes a failure to take a decision permitted or required by this Part in connection with a reference or possible reference.

(3) Except in so far as a direction to the contrary is given by the Competition Appeal Tribunal, the effect of the decision is not suspended by reason of the making of the application.

(4) In determining such an application the Competition Appeal Tribunal shall apply the same principles as would be applied by a court on an application for judicial review.

(5) The Competition Appeal Tribunal may—

(a) dismiss the application or quash the whole or part of the decision to which it relates; and
(b) where it quashes the whole or part of that decision, refer the matter back to the original decision maker with a direction to reconsider and make a new decision in accordance with the ruling of the Competition Appeal Tribunal.

(6) An appeal lies on any point of law arising from a decision of the Competition Appeal Tribunal under this section to the appropriate court.

(7) An appeal under subsection (6) requires the permission of the Tribunal or the appropriate court.

(8) In this section—

'the appropriate court' means the Court of Appeal or, in the case of Tribunal proceedings in Scotland, the Court of Session; and 'Tribunal rules' has the meaning given by section 15(1).

121 Fees

(1) The Secretary of State may by order require the payment to him or the OFT of such fees as may be prescribed by the order in connection with the exercise by the Secretary of

State, the OFT, OFCOM and the Commission of their functions under or by virtue of this Part and sections 32 to 34 of, and Schedule 4ZA to, the Water Industry Act 1991 (c 56).

(2) An order under this section may, in particular, provide for fees to be payable—

(a) in respect of a merger notice; or
(c) on the occurrence of any event specified in the order.

(3) The events that may be specified in an order under this section by virtue of subsection (2)(c) include, in particular—

(a) the decision by the OFT in relation to a possible reference under section 22 or 33 that it is or may be the case that a relevant merger situation has been created or (as the case may be) that arrangements are in progress or in contemplation which, if carried into effect, will result in the creation of a relevant merger situation;
(b) the decision by the Secretary of State in relation to a possible reference under section 45 that it is or may be the case that a relevant merger situation has been created or (as the case may be) that arrangements are in progress or in contemplation which, if carried into effect, will result in the creation of a relevant merger situation;
(c) the decision by the Secretary of State in relation to a possible reference under section 62 that—
(i) it is or may be the case that a special merger situation has been created or (as the case may be) that arrangements are in progress or in contemplation which, if carried into effect, will result in the creation of a special merger situation; and
(ii) one or more than one consideration mentioned in the special intervention notice is relevant to a consideration of the special merger situation concerned; and
(d) the decision by the OFT in relation to a possible reference under section 32 of the Act of 1991 that it is or may be the case that arrangements are in progress which, if carried into effect, will result in a merger of any two or more water enterprises or that such a merger has taken place otherwise than as a result of the carrying into effect of arrangements that have been the subject of a reference by virtue of paragraph (a) of that section.

(4) An order under this section may, in particular, contain provision—

(a) for ascertaining the persons by whom fees are payable;
(b) specifying whether any fee is payable to the Secretary of State or the OFT;
(c) for the amount of any fee to be calculated by reference to matters which may include—
(ii) the value of the turnover of the enterprises concerned;
(d) as to the time when any fee is to be paid; and
(e) for the repayment by the Secretary of State or the OFT of the whole or part of any fee in specified circumstances.

(5) For the purposes of subsection (4)(c)(ii) the turnover of an enterprise shall be determined in accordance with such provisions as may be specified in an order under this section.

(6) Provision made by virtue of subsection (5) may, in particular, include provision—

(a) as to the amounts which are, or which are not, to be treated as comprising an enterprise's turnover;

(b) as to the date or dates by reference to which an enterprise's turnover is to be determined;

(c) restricting the turnover to be taken into consideration to turnover which has a connection of a particular description with the United Kingdom.

(7) An order under this section may, in particular, in connection with provisions of the kind mentioned in subsection (5) make provision enabling the Secretary of State or the OFT to determine matters of a description specified in the order (including any of the matters mentioned in paragraphs (a) to (c) of subsection (6)).

(8) In determining the amount of any fees to be prescribed by an order under this section, the Secretary of State may take into account all costs incurred by him and by the OFT in respect of the exercise by him, the OFT, OFCOM and the Commission of their respective functions under or by virtue of this Part and sections 32 to 34 of, and Schedule 4ZA to, the Act of 1991.

(9) Fees paid to the Secretary of State or the OFT under this section shall be paid into the Consolidated Fund.

122 Primacy of Community law

(1) Advice and information published by virtue of section 106(1) or (3) shall include such advice and information about the effect of Community law, and anything done under or in accordance with it, on the provisions of this Part as the OFT or (as the case may be) the Commission considers appropriate.

(2) Advice and information published by the OFT by virtue of section 106(1) shall, in particular, include advice and information about the circumstances in which the duties of the OFT under sections 22 and 33 do not apply as a result of the EC Merger Regulation or anything done under or in accordance with them.

(3) The duty or power to make a reference under section 22 or 45(2) or (3), and the power to give an intervention notice under section 42, shall apply in a case in which the relevant enterprises ceased to be distinct enterprises at a time or in circumstances not falling within section 24 if the condition mentioned in subsection (4) is satisfied.

(4) The condition mentioned in this subsection is that, because of the EC Merger Regulation or anything done under or in accordance with them, the reference, or (as the case may be) the reference under section 22 to which the intervention notice relates, could not have been made earlier than 4 months before the date on which it is to be made.

(5) Where the duty or power to make a reference under section 22 or 45(2) or (3), or the power to give an intervention notice under section 42, applies as mentioned in subsection (3), references in this Part to the creation of a relevant merger situation shall be construed accordingly.

123 Power to alter share of supply test

(1) The Secretary of State may by order amend or replace the conditions which determine for the purposes of this Part whether a relevant merger situation has been created.

(2) The Secretary of State shall not exercise his power under subsection (1)—

(a) to amend or replace the conditions mentioned in paragraphs (a) and (b) of subsection (1) of section 23;

(b) to amend or replace the condition mentioned in paragraph (a) of subsection (2) of that section.

(3) In exercising his power under subsection (1) to amend or replace the condition mentioned in paragraph (b) of subsection (2) of section 23 or any condition which for the time being applies instead of it, the Secretary of State shall, in particular, have regard to the desirability of ensuring that any amended or new condition continues to operate by reference to the degree of commercial strength which results from the enterprises concerned having ceased to be distinct.

(4) Before making an order under this section the Secretary of State shall consult the OFT and the Commission.

(5) An order under this section may provide for the delegation of functions to the decision-making authority.

Other

124 Orders and regulations under Part 3

(1) Any power of the Secretary of State to make an order or regulations under this Part shall be exercisable by statutory instrument.

(2) Any power of the Secretary of State to make an order or regulations under this Part—

(a) may be exercised so as to make different provision for different cases or different purposes; and

(b) includes power to make such incidental, supplementary, consequential, transitory, transitional or saving provision as the Secretary of State considers appropriate.

(3) The power of the Secretary of State under section 34, 59(6A) or 123 (including that power as extended by subsection (2) above) may be exercised by modifying any enactment comprised in or made under this Act, or any other enactment.

(4) The power of the Secretary of State under section 40(8), 44(11), 52(8) (including that enactment as applied by section 65(3)), 58(3), 68 or 102 as extended by subsection (2) above may be exercised by modifying any enactment comprised in or made under this Act, or any other enactment.

(5) An order made by the Secretary of State under section 28 (including that enactment as applied by section 42(5), 59(5) and 67(7)), 40(8), 52(8) (including that enactment as applied by section 65(3)), 111(4) or (6), 114(3)(b) or (4)(b) or 121 or Schedule 7 shall be subject to annulment in pursuance of a resolution of either House of Parliament.

(6) No order shall be made by the Secretary of State under section 34, 44(11), 59(6A), 68, 102, 123 or 128(6) unless a draft of it has been laid before, and approved by a resolution of, each House of Parliament.

(7) An order made by the Secretary of State under section 58(3) shall be laid before Parliament after being made and shall cease to have effect unless approved, within the period of 28 days beginning with the day on which it is made, by a resolution of each House of Parliament.

(8) In calculating the period of 28 days mentioned in subsection (7), no account shall be taken of any time during which Parliament is dissolved or prorogued or during which both Houses are adjourned for more than four days.

(9) If an order made by the Secretary of State ceases to have effect by virtue of subsection (7), any modification made by it of an enactment is repealed (and the previous enactment revived) but without prejudice to the validity of anything done in connection with that modification before the order ceased to have effect and without prejudice to the making of a new order.

(10) If, apart from this subsection, an order made by the Secretary of State under section 58(3) would be treated for the purposes of the standing orders of either House of Parliament as a hybrid instrument, it shall proceed in that House as if it were not such an instrument.

125 Offences by bodies corporate

(1) Where an offence under this Part committed by a body corporate is proved to have been committed with the consent or connivance of, or to be attributable to any neglect on the part of—

(a) a director, manager, secretary or other similar officer of the body corporate, or
(b) a person purporting to act in such a capacity,

he as well as the body corporate commits the offence and shall be liable to be proceeded against and punished accordingly.

(2) Where the affairs of a body corporate are managed by its members, subsection (1) applies in relation to the acts and defaults of a member in connection with his functions of management as if he were a director of the body corporate.

(3) Where an offence under this Part is committed by a Scottish partnership and is proved to have been committed with the consent or connivance of a partner, or to be attributable to any neglect on the part of a partner, he as well as the partnership commits the offence and shall be liable to be proceeded against and punished accordingly.

(4) In subsection (3) 'partner' includes a person purporting to act as a partner.

126 Service of documents

(1) Any document required or authorised by virtue of this Part to be served on any person may be served—

(a) by delivering it to him or by leaving it at his proper address or by sending it by post to him at that address;
(b) if the person is a body corporate other than a limited liability partnership, by serving it in accordance with paragraph (a) on the secretary of the body;
(c) if the person is a limited liability partnership, by serving it in accordance with paragraph (a) on a member of the partnership; or
(d) if the person is a partnership, by serving it in accordance with paragraph (a) on a partner or a person having the control or management of the partnership business.

(2) For the purposes of this section and section 7 of the Interpretation Act 1978 (c 30) (service of documents by post) in its application to this section, the proper address of any person on whom a document is to be served shall be his last known address, except that—

(a) in the case of service on a body corporate (other than a limited liability partnership) or its secretary, it shall be the address of the registered or principal office of the body;
(b) in the case of service on a limited liability partnership or a member of the partnership, it shall be the address of the registered or principal office of the partnership;
(c) in the case of service on a partnership or a partner or a person having the control or management of a partnership business, it shall be the address of the principal office of the partnership.

(3) For the purposes of subsection (2) the principal office of a company constituted under the law of a country or territory outside the United Kingdom or of a partnership carrying on business outside the United Kingdom is its principal office within the United Kingdom.

(4) Subsection (5) applies if a person to be served under this Part with any document by another has specified to that other an address within the United Kingdom other than his proper address (as determined under subsection (2)) as the one at which he or someone on his behalf will accept documents of the same description as that document.

(5) In relation to that document, that address shall be treated as his proper address for the purposes of this section and section 7 of the Interpretation Act 1978 in its application to this section, instead of that determined under subsection (2).

(6) Any notice in writing or other document required or authorised by virtue of this Part to be served on any person may be served on that person by transmitting the text of the notice or other document to him by means of an electronic communications network or by other means but while in electronic form provided the text is received by that person in legible form and is capable of being used for subsequent reference.

(7) This section does not apply to any document if rules of court make provision about its service.

(8) In this section references to serving include references to similar expressions (such as giving or sending).

127 Associated persons

(1) Associated persons, and any bodies corporate which they or any of them control, shall be treated as one person—

(a) for the purpose of deciding under section 26 whether any two enterprises have been brought under common ownership or common control;
(aa) for the purposes of section 58(2C); and
(b) for the purpose of determining what activities are carried on by way of business by any one person so far as that question arises in connection with paragraph 13(2) of Schedule 8.

(2) Subsection (1) shall not exclude from section 26 any case which would otherwise fall within that section.

(3) A reference under section 22, 33, 45 or 62 (whether or not made by virtue of this section) may be framed so as to exclude from consideration, either altogether or for a specified purpose or to a specified extent, any matter which, apart from this section, would not have been taken into account on that reference.

(4) For the purposes of this section—

(a) any individual and that individual's spouse, civil partner or partner and any relative, or spouse, civil partner or partner of a relative, of that individual or of that individual's spouse, civil partner or partner;
(b) any person in his capacity as trustee of a settlement and the settlor or grantor and any person associated with the settlor or grantor;
(c) persons carrying on business in partnership and the spouse, civil partner or partner and relatives of any of them; or
(d) two or more persons acting together to secure or exercise control of a body of persons corporate or unincorporate or to secure control of any enterprise or assets,
shall be regarded as associated with one another.

(5) The reference in subsection (1) to bodies corporate which associated persons control shall be construed in accordance with section 26(3) and (4).

(6) In this section 'relative' means a brother, sister, uncle, aunt, nephew, niece, lineal ancestor or descendant (the stepchild of any person, or anyone adopted by a person, whether legally or otherwise, as his child being regarded as a relative or taken into account to trace a relationship in the same way as that person's child); and references to a spouse, civil partner or partner shall include a former spouse, civil partner or partner.

128 Supply of services and market for services etc

(1) References in this Part to the supply of services shall be construed in accordance with this section; and references in this Part to a market for services and other related expressions shall be construed accordingly.

(2) The supply of services does not include the provision of services under a contract of service or of apprenticeship whether it is express or implied and (if it is express) whether it is oral or in writing.

(3) The supply of services includes—

(a) performing for gain or reward any activity other than the supply of goods;
(b) rendering services to order;
(c) the provision of services by making them available to potential users.

(4) The supply of services includes making arrangements for the use of computer software or for granting access to data stored in any form which is not readily accessible.

(5) The supply of services includes making arrangements by means of a relevant agreement (within the meaning of paragraph 29 of Schedule 2 to the Telecommunications Act 1984) for sharing the use of telecommunications apparatus.

(6) The supply of services includes permitting or making arrangements to permit the use of land in such circumstances as the Secretary of State may by order specify.

129 Other interpretation provisions

(1) In this Part, unless the context otherwise requires—

'action' includes omission; and references to the taking of action include references to refraining from action;

'agreement' means any agreement or arrangement, in whatever way and whatever form it is made, and whether it is, or is intended to be, legally enforceable or not;

'business' includes a professional practice and includes any other undertaking which is carried on for gain or reward or which is an undertaking in the course of which goods or services are supplied otherwise than free of charge;

'change of circumstances' includes any discovery that information has been supplied which is false or misleading in a material respect;

'Community law' means—

(a) all the rights, powers, liabilities, obligations and restrictions from time to time created or arising by or under the Community Treaties; and

(b) all the remedies and procedures from time to time provided for by or under the Community Treaties;

'consumer' means any person who is—

(a) a person to whom goods are or are sought to be supplied (whether by way of sale or otherwise) in the course of a business carried on by the person supplying or seeking to supply them; or

(b) a person for whom services are or are sought to be supplied in the course of a business carried on by the person supplying or seeking to supply them;

and who does not receive or seek to receive the goods or services in the course of a business carried on by him;

'customer' includes a customer who is not a consumer;"the EC Merger Regulation" means Council Regulation (EC) No 139/2004 of 20th January 2004 on the control of concentrations between undertakings;

'enactment' includes an Act of the Scottish Parliament, Northern Ireland legislation and an enactment comprised in subordinate legislation, and includes an enactment whenever passed or made;

'enterprise' means the activities, or part of the activities, of a business;

'goods' includes buildings and other structures, and also includes ships, aircraft and hovercraft;

'modify' includes amend or repeal;

'notice' means notice in writing;

'price' includes any charge or fee (however described);

'subordinate legislation' has the same meaning as in the Interpretation Act 1978 (c 30) and also includes an instrument made under an Act of the Scottish Parliament and an instrument made under Northern Ireland legislation;

'subsidiary' has the meaning given by section 736 of the Companies Act 1985 (c 6);

'supply', in relation to the supply of goods, includes supply by way of sale, lease, hire or hire-purchase, and, in relation to buildings or other structures, includes the construction of them by a person for another person; and

'United Kingdom national' means an individual who is—

(a) a British citizen, a British overseas territories citizen, a British National (Overseas) or a British Overseas citizen;

(b) a person who under the British Nationality Act 1981 (c 61) is a British subject; or

(c) a British protected person within the meaning of that Act.

(2) For the purposes of this Part any two bodies corporate are interconnected if—

(a) one of them is a body corporate of which the other is a subsidiary; or

(b) both of them are subsidiaries of one and the same body corporate;

and in this Part 'interconnected bodies corporate' shall be construed accordingly and 'group of interconnected bodies corporate' means a group consisting of two or more bodies corporate all of whom are interconnected with each other.

(3) References in this Part to a person carrying on business include references to a person carrying on business in partnership with one or more other persons.

(4) Any duty to publish which is imposed on a person by this Part shall, unless the context otherwise requires, be construed as a duty on that person to publish in such manner as he considers appropriate for the purpose of bringing the matter concerned to the attention of those likely to be affected by it.

130 Index of defined expressions

In this Part, the expressions listed in the left-hand column have the meaning given by, or are to be interpreted in accordance with, the provisions listed in the right-hand column.

Expression	*Provision of this Act*
Action (and the taking of action)	Section 129(1)
Adverse public interest finding	Section 54(3)
Agreement	Section 129(1)
Anti-competitive outcome	Section 35(2)
Broadcasting	Section 44(9)
Business (and carrying on business)	Section 129(1) and (3)
Change of circumstances	Section 129(1)
The Commission	Section 273
Community law	Section 129(1)
Consumer	Section 129(1)
Customer	Section 129(1)
Date of reference	Section 39(9)
The decision-making authority	Section 22(7)
EC Merger Regulation	Section 129(1)
Enactment	Section 129(1)
Enforcement order	Section 86(6)
Enforcement undertaking	Section 89(2)
Enterprise	Section 129(1)
Enterprises ceasing to be distinct	Section 26(1)

Expression	*Provision of this Act*
Final determination of matter to which intervention notice relates	Section 43(4) and (5)
Final determination of matter to which special intervention notice relates	Section 60(4) and (5)
Final determination of reference under ection 22 or 33	Section 79(1) and (2)
Goods	Section 129(1)
Interconnected bodies corporate (and a group of interconnected bodies corporate)	Section 129(2)
Intervention notice	Section 42(2)
Market for goods or services	Section 22(6)
Market in the United Kingdom	Section 22(6)
Media public interest consideration	Section 44(8)
Merger notice	Section 96(2)
Modify	Section 129(1)
Newspaper	Section 44(10)
Newspaper enterprise	Section 58A(3)
Notice	Section 129(1)
Notified arrangements	Section 96(6)
OFCOM	Section 43(6)
The OFT	Section 273
Orders under section 81	Section 81(6)
Orders under paragraph 2 of Schedule 7	Paragraph 2(7) of Schedule 7
The period for considering a merger notice	Sections 97 and 98
Price	Section 129(1)
Public interest consideration	Sections 42(3) and 67(9)
Public interest consideration being finalised	Section 42(8)
Publish	Section 129(4)
References under section 22, 33, 45 or 62	Sections 37(2), 49(1), 56(8) and 64(2)
Relevant customer benefit	Section 30
Relevant merger situation	Section 23 (as read with other enactments)
Reports of the Commission	Section 118(5)
Special intervention notice	Section 59(2)
Special merger situation	Section 59(3)
Subordinate legislation	Section 129(1)
Subsidiary	Section 129(1)
Supply (in relation to the supply of goods)	Section 129(1)
The supply of services (and a market for services etc)	Section 128
The turnover in the United Kingdom of an enterprise	Section 28(2)
Undertakings under section 80	Section 80(6)
Undertakings under paragraph 1 of Schedule 7	Paragraph 1(7) of Schedule 7
United Kingdom national	Section 129(1)

SCHEDULE 6
SCHEDULE TO BE INSERTED INTO THE WATER INDUSTRY ACT 1991

Section 70

SCHEDULE 4ZA

Application of Provisions of Enterprise Act 2002 to Mergers of Water Enterprises

Section 34

1
Part 3 of the 2002 Act (and any other provisions of that Act so far as relating to that Part) shall apply, with such prescribed modifications as the Secretary of State considers to be necessary or expedient, in relation to water mergers and merger references under section 32 of this Act as it applies in relation to relevant merger situations and references under Part 3 of that Act.

2
The modifications made by virtue of paragraph 1 above shall include modifications to give effect to paragraphs 3 to 6 below.

3
(1) The first questions to be decided by the Competition Commission on a merger reference under section 32(a) of this Act shall be—

(a) whether arrangements are in progress which, if carried into effect, will result in a water merger; and
(b) if so, whether that merger may be expected to prejudice the ability of the Director, in carrying out his functions by virtue of this Act, to make comparisons between different water enterprises.

(2) The first questions to be decided by the Competition Commission on a merger reference under section 32(b) of this Act shall be—

(a) whether a water merger has taken place; and
(b) if so, whether that merger has prejudiced, or may be expected to prejudice, the ability of the Director, in carrying out his functions by virtue of this Act, to make comparisons between different water enterprises.

(3) Any decision of the Competition Commission on a merger reference under section 32(a) of this Act that arrangements are in progress which, if carried into effect, will result in a water merger shall be treated as a decision that no arrangements are in progress which, if carried into effect, will result in a water merger if the decision is not that of at least two-thirds of the members of the group constituted in connection with the reference in pursuance of paragraph 15 of Schedule 7 to the Competition Act 1998 (c 41).

(4) Any decision of the Competition Commission on a merger reference under section 32(a) of this Act that a water merger may be expected to prejudice the ability of the Director, in carrying out his functions by virtue of this Act, to make comparisons

between different water enterprises shall be treated as a decision that the water merger may be expected not to prejudice that ability of the Director if the decision is not that of at least two-thirds of the members of the group constituted in connection with the reference in pursuance of paragraph 15 of Schedule 7 to the Competition Act 1998.

(5) Any decision of the Competition Commission on a merger reference under section 32(b) of this Act that a water merger has taken place shall be treated as a decision that no water merger has taken place if the decision is not that of at least two-thirds of the members of the group constituted in connection with the reference in pursuance of paragraph 15 of Schedule 7 to the Competition Act 1998.

(6) Any decision of the Competition Commission on a merger reference under section 32(b) of this Act that a water merger has prejudiced, or may be expected to prejudice, the ability of the Director, in carrying out his functions by virtue of this Act, to make comparisons between different water enterprises shall be treated as a decision that the water merger has not prejudiced, or may be expected not to prejudice, that ability of the Director if the decision is not that of at least two-thirds of the members of the group constituted in connection with the reference in pursuance of paragraph 15 of Schedule 7 to the Competition Act 1998.

4

(1) In deciding, on a merger reference under section 32(a) of this Act whether to take action for the purpose of remedying, mitigating or preventing the prejudice to the Director or any adverse effect which may be expected to result from the prejudice to the Director and, if so, what action should be taken, the Competition Commission may, in particular, have regard to the effect of any such action on any relevant customer benefits in relation to the merger concerned provided that—

(a) a consideration of those benefits would not prevent a solution to the prejudice concerned; or
(b) the benefits which may be expected to accrue are substantially more important than the prejudice concerned.

(2) In deciding, on a merger reference under section 32(b) of this Act whether to take action for the purpose of remedying, mitigating or preventing the prejudice to the Director or any adverse effect which has resulted from, or may be expected to result from, the prejudice to the Director and, if so, what action should be taken, the Competition Commission may, in particular, have regard to the effect of any such action on any relevant customer benefits in relation to the merger concerned provided that—

(a) a consideration of those benefits would not prevent a solution to the prejudice concerned; or
(b) the benefits which have accrued, or may be expected to accrue, are substantially more important than the prejudice concerned.

(3) This paragraph is without prejudice to the power of the Secretary of State to provide in regulations made under paragraph 1 above for other matters to which the Competition Commission may or must have regard in deciding the questions as mentioned in sub-paragraph (1) or (2) above (including matters which are to take priority over the effect of action on relevant customer benefits).

5
(1) No enforcement action shall be taken on a merger reference under section 32(b) of this Act in respect of an actual merger unless the reference was made within the period of four months beginning with whichever is the later of—

(a) the day on which the merger took place; and
(b) the day on which the material facts about the transactions which resulted in the merger first came to the attention of the OFT or were made public (within the meaning given by section 24(3) of the 2002 Act).

(2) This paragraph is without prejudice to the power of the Secretary of State to provide in regulations made under paragraph 1 above for extensions of the four month period; and, if any such provision is made in such regulations, the provision which is to be made in regulations under paragraph 1 above by virtue of sub-paragraph (1) above or paragraph 6 below may be adjusted accordingly.

6
If, on a merger reference under section 32(b) of this Act, the Competition Commission are satisfied that the reference was not made within the period of four months mentioned in paragraph 5 above, its report on the reference shall state that fact.

7
(1) For the purposes of this Schedule a benefit is a relevant customer benefit if—

(a) it is a benefit to relevant customers in the form of—
(i) lower prices, higher quality or greater choice of goods or services in any market in the United Kingdom; or
(ii) greater innovation in relation to such goods or services; and
(b) the Competition Commission believes—
(i) in the case of a merger reference under section 32(a) of this Act, as mentioned in sub-paragraph (2) below; and
(ii) in the case of a merger reference under section 32(b) of this Act, as mentioned in sub-paragraph (3) below.

(2) The belief, in the case of a merger reference under section 32(a) of this Act, is that—

(a) the benefit may be expected to accrue within a reasonable period as a result of the merger concerned; and
(b) the benefit is unlikely to accrue without the merger concerned or a similar prejudice to the Director.

(3) The belief, in the case of a merger reference under section 32(b) of this Act is that—

(a) the benefit has accrued as a result of the merger concerned or may be expected to accrue within a reasonable period as a result of the merger concerned; and
(b) the benefit was, or is, unlikely to accrue without the merger concerned or a similar prejudice to the Director.

(4) In sub-paragraph (1) above "relevant customers" means—

(a) customers of any person carrying on an enterprise which, in the merger concerned, has ceased to be, or (as the case may be) will cease to be, a distinct enterprise;

(b) customers of such customers; and

(c) any other customers in a chain of customers beginning with the customers mentioned in paragraph (a);

and in this sub-paragraph "customers" includes future customers.

8

In this Schedule—

'customers', 'goods', 'market in the United Kingdom', 'services' and 'relevant merger situation' have the same meanings as in Part 3 of the 2002 Act; and 'water merger' means a merger of any two or more water enterprises.

SCHEDULE 7
ENFORCEMENT REGIME FOR PUBLIC INTEREST AND SPECIAL PUBLIC INTEREST CASES

Section 85

Pre-emptive undertakings and orders

1

(1) Sub-paragraph (2) applies where an intervention notice or special intervention notice is in force.

(2) The Secretary of State may, for the purpose of preventing pre-emptive action, accept from such of the parties concerned as he considers appropriate undertakings to take such action as he considers appropriate.

(3) Sub-paragraph (4) applies where an intervention notice is in force.

(4) The Secretary of State may, for the purpose of preventing pre-emptive action, adopt an undertaking accepted by the OFT under section 71 if the undertaking is still in force when the Secretary of State adopts it.

(5) An undertaking adopted under sub-paragraph (4)—

(a) shall continue in force, in accordance with its terms, when adopted;

(b) may be varied or superseded by an undertaking under this paragraph; and

(c) may be released by the Secretary of State.

(6) Any other undertaking under this paragraph—

(a) shall come into force when accepted;

(b) may be varied or superseded by another undertaking; and

(c) may be released by the Secretary of State.

(7) References in this Part to undertakings under this paragraph shall, unless the context otherwise requires, include references to undertakings adopted under this paragraph; and references to the acceptance or giving of undertakings under this paragraph shall be construed accordingly.

(8) An undertaking which is in force under this paragraph in relation to a reference or possible reference under section 45 or (as the case may be) 62 shall cease to be in force if

an order under paragraph 2 or an undertaking under paragraph 3 comes into force in relation to that reference.

(9) An undertaking under this paragraph shall, if it has not previously ceased to be in force, cease to be in force when the intervention notice concerned or (as the case may be) special intervention notice concerned ceases to be in force.

(10) No undertaking shall be accepted by the Secretary of State under this paragraph before the making of a reference under section 45 or (as the case may be) 62 unless the undertaking relates to a relevant merger situation which has been, or may have been, created or (as the case may be) a special merger situation which has been, or may have been, created.

(11) The Secretary of State shall, as soon as reasonably practicable, consider any representations received by him in relation to varying or releasing an undertaking under this paragraph.

(12) In this paragraph and paragraph 2 "pre-emptive action" means action which might prejudice the reference or possible reference concerned under section 45 or (as the case may be) 62 or impede the taking of any action under this Part which may be justified by the Secretary of State's decisions on the reference.

2

(1) Sub-paragraph (2) applies where an intervention notice or special intervention notice is in force.(2) The Secretary of State or the OFT may by order, for the purpose of preventing pre-emptive action—

(a) prohibit or restrict the doing of things which the Secretary of State or (as the case may be) the OFT considers would constitute pre-emptive action;
(b) impose on any person concerned obligations as to the carrying on of any activities or the safeguarding of any assets;
(c) provide for the carrying on of any activities or the safeguarding of any assets either by the appointment of a person to conduct or supervise the conduct of any activities (on such terms and with such powers as may be specified or described in the order) or in any other manner;
(d) do anything which may be done by virtue of paragraph 19 of Schedule 8.

(3) Sub-paragraph (4) applies where an intervention notice is in force.

(4) The Secretary of State or the OFT may, for the purpose of preventing pre-emptive action, adopt an order made by the OFT under section 72 if the order is still in force when the Secretary of State or (as the case may be) the OFT adopts it.(5) An order adopted under sub-paragraph (4)—

(a) shall continue in force, in accordance with its terms, when adopted; and
(b) may be varied or revoked by an order under this paragraph.

(6) Any other order under this paragraph—

(a) shall come into force at such time as is determined by or under the order; and
(b) may be varied or revoked by another order.

(7) References in this Part to orders under this paragraph shall, unless the context other-

wise requires, include references to orders adopted under this paragraph; and references to the making of orders under this paragraph shall be construed accordingly.

(8) An order which is in force under this paragraph in relation to a reference or possible reference under section 45 or (as the case may be) 62 shall cease to be in force if an undertaking under paragraph 1 or 3 comes into force in relation to that reference.

(9) An order under this paragraph shall, if it has not previously ceased to be in force, cease to be in force when the intervention notice concerned or (as the case may be) special intervention notice concerned ceases to be in force.

(10) No order shall be made by the Secretary of State or the OFT under this paragraph before the making of a reference under section 45 or (as the case may be) 62 unless the order relates to a relevant merger situation which has been, or may have been, created or (as the case may be) a special merger situation which has been, or may have been, created.

(11) The Secretary of State or (as the case may be) the OFT shall, as soon as reasonably practicable, consider any representations received by that person in relation to varying or revoking an order under this paragraph.

Undertakings in lieu of reference under section 45 or 62

3

(1) Sub-paragraph (2) applies if the Secretary of State has power to make a reference to the Commission under section 45 or 62 and otherwise intends to make such a reference.

(2) The Secretary of State may, instead of making such a reference and for the purpose of remedying, mitigating or preventing any of the effects adverse to the public interest which have or may have resulted, or which may be expected to result, from the creation of the relevant merger situation concerned or (as the case may be) the special merger situation concerned, accept from such of the parties concerned as he considers appropriate undertakings to take such action as he considers appropriate.

(3) In proceeding under sub-paragraph (2), the Secretary of State shall, in particular—
- (a) accept the decisions of the OFT included in its report under section 44 so far as they relate to the matters mentioned in subsections (4) and (5) of that section; or
- (b) (as the case may be) accept the decisions of the OFT included in its report under section 61 so far as they relate to the matters mentioned in subsections (3)(a) and (4) of that section.

(4) In proceeding under sub-paragraph (2) in relation to an anti-competitive outcome, the Secretary of State may, in particular, have regard to the effect of any action on any relevant customer benefits in relation to the creation of the relevant merger situation concerned.

(5) No undertaking shall be accepted by the Secretary of State under this paragraph in connection with a possible reference under section 45 if a public interest consideration mentioned in the intervention notice concerned has not been finalised and the period of 24 weeks beginning with the giving of that notice has not expired.

(6) The Secretary of State may delay making a decision as to whether to accept any such undertaking (and any related decision as to whether to make a reference under section

45) if he considers that there is a realistic prospect of the public interest consideration being finalised within the period of 24 weeks beginning with the giving of the intervention notice concerned.

(7) A delay under sub-paragraph (6) shall not extend beyond—

(a) the time when the public interest consideration is finalised; or

(b) if earlier, the expiry of the period of 24 weeks mentioned in that sub-paragraph.

(8) An undertaking under this paragraph—

(a) shall come into force when accepted;

(b) may be varied or superseded by another undertaking; or(c) may be released by the Secretary of State.

(9) An undertaking under this paragraph which is in force in relation to a relevant merger situation or (as the case may be) a special merger situation shall cease to be in force if an order comes into force under paragraph 5 or 6 in relation to that undertaking.

(10) The Secretary of State shall, as soon as reasonably practicable, consider any representations received by him in relation to varying or releasing an undertaking under this section.

4

(1) The relevant authority shall not make a reference under section 22, 33 or 45 in relation to the creation of a relevant merger situation or (as the case may be) a reference under section 62 in relation to the creation of a special merger situation if—

(a) the Secretary of State has accepted an undertaking or group of undertakings under paragraph 3; and

(b) the relevant merger situation or (as the case may be) the special merger situation is the situation by reference to which the undertaking or group of undertakings was accepted.

(2) In sub-paragraph (1) 'the relevant authority' means—

(a) in relation to a possible reference under section 22 or 33, the OFT; and

(b) in relation to a possible reference under section 45 or 62, the Secretary of State.

(3) Sub-paragraph (1) does not prevent the making of a reference if material facts about relevant arrangements or transactions, or relevant proposed arrangements or transactions, were not notified (whether in writing or otherwise) to the Secretary of State or the OFT or made public before any undertaking concerned was accepted.

(4) For the purposes of sub-paragraph (3) arrangements or transactions, or proposed arrangements or transactions, are relevant if they are the ones in consequence of which the enterprises concerned ceased or may have ceased, or may cease, to be distinct enterprises.

(5) In sub-paragraph (3) 'made public' means so publicised as to be generally known or readily ascertainable.

5

(1) Sub-paragraph (2) applies where the Secretary of State considers that—

(a) an undertaking accepted by him under paragraph 3 has not been, is not being or will not be fulfilled; or

(b) in relation to an undertaking accepted by him under that paragraph, information which was false or misleading in a material respect was given to him or the OFT by the person giving the undertaking before he decided to accept the undertaking.

(2) The Secretary of State may, for any of the purposes mentioned in paragraph 3(2), make an order under this paragraph.

(3) Sub-paragraphs (3) and (4) of paragraph 3 shall apply for the purposes of sub-paragraph (2) above as they apply for the purposes of sub-paragraph (2) of that paragraph.

(4) An order under this paragraph may contain—

(a) anything permitted by Schedule 8; and

(b) such supplementary, consequential or incidental provision as the Secretary of State considers appropriate.

(5) An order under this paragraph

(a) hall come into force at such time as is determined by or under the order; and

(b) may contain provision which is different from the provision contained in the undertaking concerned.

(6) No order shall be varied or revoked under this paragraph unless the OFT advises that such a variation or revocation is appropriate by reason of a change of circumstances.

6

(1) Sub-paragraph (2) applies where—

(a) the Secretary of State has the power to make an order under paragraph 5 in relation to a particular undertaking and intends to make such an order; or

(b) the Secretary of State has the power to make an order under paragraph 10 in relation to a particular undertaking and intends to make such an order.

(2) The Secretary of State may, for the purpose of preventing any action which might prejudice the making of that order, make an order under this paragraph.

(3) No order shall be made under sub-paragraph (2) unless the Secretary of State has reasonable grounds for suspecting that it is or may be the case that action which might prejudice the making of the order under paragraph 5 or (as the case may be) 10 is in progress or in contemplation.

(4) An order under sub-paragraph (2) may—

(a) prohibit or restrict the doing of things which the Secretary of State considers would prejudice the making of the order under paragraph 5 or 10;

(b) impose on any person concerned obligations as to the carrying on of any activities or the safeguarding of any assets;

(c) provide for the carrying on of any activities or the safeguarding of any assets either by the appointment of a person to conduct or supervise the conduct of any activities (on such terms and with such powers as may be specified or described in the order) or in any other manner;

(d) do anything which may be done by virtue of paragraph 19 of Schedule 8.

(5) An order under this paragraph shall come into force at such time as is determined by or under the order.

(6) An order under this paragraph shall, if it has not previously ceased to be in force, cease to be in force on—

(a) the coming into force of an order under paragraph 5 or (as the case may be) 10 in relation to the undertaking concerned; or

(b) The making of the decision not to proceed with such an order.

(7) The Secretary of State shall, as soon as reasonably practicable, consider any representations received by him in relation to varying or revoking an order under this paragraph.

7

Statutory restrictions following reference under section 45 or 62

(1) Sub-paragraphs (2) and (3) apply where—

(a) a reference has been made under section 45(2) or (3) or 62(2) but not finally determined; and

(b) no undertakings under paragraph 1 are in force in relation to the relevant merger situation concerned or (as the case may be) the special merger situation concerned and no orders under paragraph 2 are in force in relation to that situation.

(2) No relevant person shall, without the consent of the Secretary of State—

(a) complete any outstanding matters in connection with any arrangements which have resulted in the enterprises concerned ceasing to be distinct enterprises;

(b) make any further arrangements in consequence of that result (other than arrangements which reverse that result); or

(c) transfer the ownership or control of any enterprises to which the reference relates.

(3) No relevant person shall, without the consent of the Secretary of State, assist in any of the activities mentioned in paragraphs (a) to (c) of sub-paragraph (2).

(4) The prohibitions in sub-paragraphs (2) and (3) do not apply in relation to anything which the person concerned is required to do by virtue of any enactment.

(5) The consent of the Secretary of State under sub-paragraph (2) or (3)—

(a) may be general or specific;

(b) may be revoked by the Secretary of State; and

(c) shall be published in such manner as the Secretary of State considers appropriate for bringing it to the attention of any person entitled to the benefit of it.

(6) Paragraph (c) of sub-paragraph (5) shall not apply if the Secretary of State considers that publication is not necessary for the purpose mentioned in that paragraph.

(7) Sub-paragraphs (2) and (3) shall apply to a person's conduct outside the United Kingdom if (and only if) he is—

(a) a United Kingdom national;

(b) a body incorporated under the law of the United Kingdom or of any part of the United Kingdom; or

(c) a person carrying on business in the United Kingdom.

(8) For the purpose of this paragraph a reference under section 45(2) or (3) is finally determined if—

(a) the time within which the Commission is to prepare a report under section 50 in relation to the reference and give it to the Secretary of State has expired and no such report has been so prepared and given;

(b) the Commission decides to cancel the reference under section 53(1);

(c) the time within which the Secretary of State is to make and publish a decision under section 54(2) has expired and no such decision has been made and published;

(d) the Secretary of State decides under section 54(2) to make no finding at all in the matter;

(e) the Secretary of State otherwise decides under section 54(2) not to make an adverse public interest finding;

(f) the Secretary of State decides under section 54(2) to make an adverse public interest finding but decides neither to accept an undertaking under paragraph 9 of this Schedule nor to make an order under paragraph 11 of this Schedule; or

(g) the Secretary of State decides under section 54(2) to make an adverse public interest finding and accepts an undertaking under paragraph 9 of this Schedule or makes an order under paragraph 11 of this Schedule.

(9) For the purpose of this paragraph a reference under section 62(2) is finally determined if—

(a) the time within which the Commission is to prepare a report under section 65 in relation to the reference and give it to the Secretary of State has expired and no such report has been so prepared and given;

(b) the time within which the Secretary of State is to make and publish a decision under section 66(2) has expired and no such decision has been made and published;

(c) the Secretary of State decides under subsection (2) of section 66 otherwise than as mentioned in subsection (5) of that section;

(d) the Secretary of State decides under subsection (2) of section 66 as mentioned in subsection (5) of that section but decides neither to accept an undertaking under paragraph 9 of this Schedule nor to make an order under paragraph 11 of this Schedule; or

(e) the Secretary of State decides under subsection (2) of section 66 as mentioned in subsection (5) of that section and accepts an undertaking under paragraph 9 of this Schedule or makes an order under paragraph 11 of this Schedule.

(10) For the purposes of this paragraph the time when a reference under section 45(2) or (3) or (as the case may be) 62(2) is finally determined is—

(a) in a case falling within sub-paragraph (8)(a) or (c) or (as the case may be) (9)(a) or (b), the expiry of the time concerned;

(b) in a case falling within sub-paragraph (8)(b), (d) or (e) or (as the case may be) (9)(c), the making of the decision concerned;

(c) in a case falling within sub-paragraph (8)(f) or (as the case may be) (9)(d), the making of the decision neither to accept an undertaking under paragraph 9 of this Schedule nor to make an order under paragraph 11 of this Schedule; and

(d) in a case falling within sub-paragraph (8)(g) or (as the case may be) (9)(e), the acceptance of the undertaking concerned or (as the case may be) the making of the order concerned.

(11) In this paragraph 'relevant person' means—

(a) any person who carries on any enterprise to which the reference relates or who has control of any such enterprise;

(b) any subsidiary of any person falling within paragraph (a); or

(c) any person associated with any person falling within paragraph (a) or any subsidiary of any person so associated.

8

(1) Sub-paragraph (2) applies where—

(a) a reference has been made under section 45(4) or (5) or 62(3); and

(b) no undertakings under paragraph 1 are in force in relation to the relevant merger situation concerned or (as the case may be) special merger situation concerned and no orders under paragraph 2 are in force in relation to that situation.

(2) No relevant person shall, without the consent of the Secretary of State, directly or indirectly acquire during the relevant period an interest in shares in a company if any enterprise to which the reference relates is carried on by or under the control of that company.

(3) The consent of the Secretary of State under sub-paragraph (2)—

(a) may be general or specific;

(b) may be revoked by the Secretary of State; and

(c) shall be published in such manner as the Secretary of State considers appropriate for bringing it to the attention of any person entitled to the benefit of it.

(4) Paragraph (c) of sub-paragraph (3) shall not apply if the Secretary of State considers that publication is not necessary for the purpose mentioned in that paragraph.

(5) Sub-paragraph (2) shall apply to a person's conduct outside the United Kingdom if (and only if) he is—

(a) a United Kingdom national;

(b) a body incorporated under the law of the United Kingdom or of any part of the United Kingdom; or

(c) a person carrying on business in the United Kingdom.

(6) In this paragraph—

'company' includes any body corporate;

'relevant period' means the period beginning with the publication of the decision of the Secretary of State to make the reference concerned and ending when the reference is finally determined;

'relevant person' means—

(a) any person who carries on any enterprise to which the reference relates or who has control of any such enterprise;

(b) any subsidiary of any person falling within paragraph (a); or

(c) any person associated with any person falling within paragraph (a) or any subsidiary of any person so associated; and

'share' means share in the capital of a company, and includes stock.

(7) For the purposes of the definition of 'relevant period' in sub-paragraph (6), a reference under section 45(4) or (5) is finally determined if—

(a) the Commission cancels the reference under section 48(1) or 53(1);

(b) the time within which the Commission is to prepare a report under section 50 in relation to the reference and give it to the Secretary of State has expired and no such report has been so prepared and given;

(c) the time within which the Secretary of State is to make and publish a decision under section 54(2) has expired and no such decision has been made and published;
(d) the Secretary of State decides under section 54(2) to make no finding at all in the matter;
(e) the Secretary of State otherwise decides under section 54(2) not to make an adverse public interest finding;
(f) the Secretary of State decides under section 54(2) to make an adverse public interest finding but decides neither to accept an undertaking under paragraph 9 of this Schedule nor to make an order under paragraph 11 of this Schedule; or
(g) the Secretary of State decides under section 54(2) to make an adverse public interest finding and accepts an undertaking under paragraph 9 of this Schedule or makes an order under paragraph 11 of this Schedule.

(8) For the purposes of the definition of 'relevant period' in sub-paragraph (6), a reference under section 62(3) is finally determined if—
(a) the Commission cancels the reference under section 64(1);
(b) the time within which the Commission is to prepare a report under section 65 in relation to the reference and give it to the Secretary of State has expired and no such report has been so prepared and given;
(c) the time within which the Secretary of State is to make and publish a decision under section 66(2) has expired and no such decision has been made and published;
(d) the Secretary of State decides under subsection (2) of section 66 otherwise than as mentioned in subsection (5) of that section;
(e) the Secretary of State decides under subsection (2) of section 66 as mentioned in subsection (5) of that section but decides neither to accept an undertaking under paragraph 9 of this Schedule nor to make an order under paragraph 11 of this Schedule; or(f) the Secretary of State decides under subsection (2) of section 66 as mentioned in subsection (5) of that section and accepts an undertaking under paragraph 9 of this Schedule or makes an order under paragraph 11 of this Schedule.

(9) For the purposes of the definition of "relevant period" in sub-paragraph (6) above, the time when a reference under section 45(4) or (5) or (as the case may be) 62(3) is finally determined is—
(a) in a case falling within sub-paragraph (7)(a), (d) or (e) or (as the case may be) (8)(a) or (d), the making of the decision concerned;
(b) in a case falling within sub-paragraph (7)(b) or (c) or (as the case may be) (8)(b) or (c), the expiry of the time concerned;
(c) in a case falling within sub-paragraph (7)(f) or (as the case may be) (8)(e), the making of the decision neither to accept an undertaking under paragraph 9 of this Schedule nor to make an order under paragraph 11 of this Schedule; and
(d) in a case falling within sub-paragraph (7)(g) or (as the case may be) (8)(f), the acceptance of the undertaking concerned or (as the case may be) the making of the order concerned.

(10) Section 79 shall apply for the purposes of paragraph 7 and this paragraph in relation to a reference under section 45 or 62 as it applies for the purposes of sections 77 and 78 in relation to a reference under section 22 or 33.

(11) In its application by virtue of sub-paragraph (10) section 79 shall have effect as if—
(a) subsections (1) and (2) were omitted; and

(b) for the reference in subsection (4) to the OFT there were substituted a reference to the Secretary of State.

Final undertakings and orders

9

(1) The Secretary of State may, in accordance with section 55 or (as the case may be) 66(5) to (7), accept, from such persons as he considers appropriate, undertakings to take action specified or described in the undertakings.

(2) An undertaking under this paragraph—

(a) shall come into force when accepted;

(b) may be varied or superseded by another undertaking; and

(c) may be released by the Secretary of State.

(3) An undertaking which is in force under this paragraph in relation to a reference under section 45 or 62 shall cease to be in force if an order under paragraph 6(1)(b) or 10 comes into force in relation to the subject-matter of the undertaking.

(4) No undertaking shall be accepted under this paragraph in relation to a reference under section 45 or 62 if an order has been made under—

(a) paragraph 6(1)(b) or 10 in relation to the subject-matter of the undertaking; or

(b) paragraph 11 in relation to that reference.

(5) The Secretary of State shall, as soon as reasonably practicable, consider any representations received by him in relation to varying or releasing an undertaking under this section.

10

(1) Sub-paragraph (2) applies where the Secretary of State considers that—

(a) an undertaking accepted by him under paragraph 9 has not been, is not being or will not be fulfilled; or

(b) in relation to an undertaking accepted by him under that paragraph, information which was false or misleading in a material respect was given to him or the OFT by the person giving the undertaking before he decided to accept the undertaking.

(2) The Secretary of State may, for any purpose mentioned in section 55(2) or (as the case may be) 66(6), make an order under this paragraph.

(3) Subsections (3) and (4) of section 55 or (as the case may be) subsection (7) of section 66 shall apply for the purposes of sub-paragraph (2) above as they or it applies for the purposes of section 55(2) or (as the case may be) 66(6).(4) An order under this paragraph may contain—

(a) anything permitted by Schedule 8; and

(b) such supplementary, consequential or incidental provision as the Secretary of State considers appropriate.

(5) An order under this paragraph—

(a) shall come into force at such time as is determined by or under the order; and

(b) may contain provision which is different from the provision contained in the undertaking concerned.

(6) No order shall be varied or revoked under this paragraph unless the OFT advises that such a variation or revocation is appropriate by reason of a change of circumstances.

11

(1) The Secretary of State may, in accordance with section 55 or (as the case may be) 66(5) to (7), make an order under this paragraph.

(2) An order under this paragraph may contain—

(a) anything permitted by Schedule 8; and

(b) such supplementary, consequential or incidental provision as the Secretary of State considers appropriate.

(3) An order under this paragraph shall come into force at such time as is determined by or under the order.

(4) No order shall be made under this paragraph in relation to a reference under section 45 or (as the case may be) 62 if an undertaking has been accepted under paragraph 9 in relation to that reference.

(5) No order shall be varied or revoked under this paragraph unless the OFT advises that such a variation or revocation is appropriate by reason of a change of circumstances.

SCHEDULE 8
PROVISION THAT MAY BE CONTAINED IN CERTAIN ENFORCEMENT ORDERS

Section 86(4)

Introductory

1

This Schedule applies in relation to such orders, and to such extent, as is provided by this Part and Part 4 and any other enactment; and references in this Schedule to an order shall be construed accordingly.

General restrictions on conduct

2

(1) An order may—

(a) prohibit the making or performance of an agreement;

(b) require any party to an agreement to terminate the agreement.

(2) An order made by virtue of sub-paragraph (1) shall not—

(a) prohibit the making or performance of; or

(b) require any person to terminate,

an agreement so far as, if made, the agreement would relate, or (as the case may be) so far as the agreement relates, to the terms and conditions of employment of any workers or to the physical conditions in which any workers are required to work.

3

(1) An order may prohibit the withholding from any person of—

(a) any goods or services;

(b) any orders for any such goods or services.

(2) References in sub-paragraph (1) to withholding include references to—

(a) agreeing or threatening to withhold; and

(b) procuring others to withhold or to agree or threaten to withhold.

4

An order may prohibit requiring as a condition of the supply of goods or services to any person—

(a) the buying of any goods;

(b) the making of any payment in respect of services other than the goods or services supplied;

(c) the doing of any other such matter or the refraining from doing anything mentioned in paragraph (a) or (b) or any other such matter.

5

An order may prohibit—

(a) discrimination between persons in the prices charged for goods or services;

(b) anything which the relevant authority considers to be such discrimination;

(c) procuring others to do anything which is such discrimination or which the relevant authority considers to be such discrimination.

6

An order may prohibit—

(a) giving, or agreeing to give in other ways, any preference in respect of the supply of goods or services or in respect of the giving of orders for goods or services;

(b) giving, or agreeing to give in other ways, anything which the relevant authority considers to be a preference in respect of the supply of goods or services or in respect of the giving of orders for goods or services;

(c) procuring others to do anything mentioned in paragraph (a) or (b).

7

An order may prohibit—

(a) charging, for goods or services supplied, prices differing from those in any published list or notification;

(b) doing anything which the relevant authority considers to be charging such prices.

8

(1) An order may regulate the prices to be charged for any goods or services.

(2) No order shall be made by virtue of sub-paragraph (1) unless the relevant report in relation to the matter concerned identifies the prices charged for the goods or services as requiring remedial action.

(3) In this paragraph 'the relevant report' means the report of the Commission which is required by the enactment concerned before an order can be made under this Schedule.

9

An order may prohibit the exercise of any right to vote exercisable by virtue of the holding of any shares, stock or securities.

General obligations to be performed

10

(1) An order may require a person to supply goods or services or to do anything which the relevant authority considers appropriate to facilitate the provision of goods or services.

(2) An order may require a person who is supplying, or is to supply, goods or services to supply such goods or services to a particular standard or in a particular manner or to do anything which the relevant authority considers appropriate to facilitate the provision of such goods or services to that standard or in that manner.

11

An order may require any activities to be carried on separately from any other activities.
Acquisitions and divisions

12

(1) An order may prohibit or restrict—
 (a) the acquisition by any person of the whole or part of the undertaking or assets of another person's business;
 (b) the doing of anything which will or may result in two or more bodies corporate becoming interconnected bodies corporate.

(2) An order may require that if—
 (a) an acquisition of the kind mentioned in sub-paragraph (1)(a) is made; or
 (b) anything is done which results in two or more bodies corporate becoming interconnected bodies corporate;
the persons concerned or any of them shall observe any prohibitions or restrictions imposed by or under the order.

(3) This paragraph shall also apply to any result consisting in two or more enterprises ceasing to be distinct enterprises (other than any result consisting in two or more bodies corporate becoming interconnected bodies corporate).

13

(1) An order may provide for—
 (a) the division of any business (whether by the sale of any part of the undertaking or assets or otherwise);
 (b) the division of any group of interconnected bodies corporate.

(2) For the purposes of sub-paragraph (1)(a) all the activities carried on by way of business by any one person or by any two or more interconnected bodies corporate may be treated as a single business.

(3) An order made by virtue of this paragraph may contain such provision as the relevant authority considers appropriate to effect or take account of the division, including, in particular, provision as to—

(a) the transfer or creation of property, rights, liabilities or obligations;
(b) the number of persons to whom the property, rights, liabilities or obligations are to be transferred or in whom they are to be vested;
(c) the time within which the property, rights, liabilities or obligations are to be transferred or vested;
(d) the adjustment of contracts (whether by discharge or reduction of any liability or obligation or otherwise);
(e) the creation, allotment, surrender or cancellation of any shares, stock or securities;
(f) the formation or winding up of any company or other body of persons corporate or unincorporate;
(g) the amendment of the memorandum and articles or other instruments regulating any such company or other body of persons;
(h) the extent to which, and the circumstances in which, provisions of the order affecting a company or other body of persons corporate or unincorporate in its share capital, constitution or other matters may be altered by the company or other body of persons concerned;
(i) the registration of the order under any enactment by a company or other body of persons corporate or unincorporate which is affected by it as mentioned in paragraph (h);
(j) the continuation, with any necessary change of parties, of any legal proceedings;
(k) the approval by the relevant authority or another person of anything required by virtue of the order to be done or of any person to whom anything is to be transferred, or in whom anything is to be vested, by virtue of the order; or
(l) the appointment of trustees or other persons to do anything on behalf of another person which is required of that person by virtue of the order or to monitor the doing by that person of any such thing.

14
The references in paragraph 13 to the division of a business as mentioned in sub-paragraph (1)(a) of that paragraph shall, in the case of an order under section 75, 83, 84, 160 or 161, or an order under paragraph 5, 10 or 11 of Schedule 7, be construed as including references to the separation, by the sale of any part of any undertaking or assets concerned or other means, of enterprises which are under common control (within the meaning of section 26) otherwise than by reason of their being enterprises of interconnected bodies corporate.

Supply and publication of information

15
(1) An order may require a person supplying goods or services to publish a list of prices or otherwise notify prices.

(2) An order made by virtue of this paragraph may also require or prohibit the publication or other notification of further information.

16
An order may prohibit any person from notifying (whether by publication or otherwise) to persons supplying goods or services prices recommended or suggested as appropriate to be charged by those persons for those goods or services.

17

(1) An order may require a person supplying goods or services to publish—

(a) accounting information in relation to the supply of the goods or services;

(b) information in relation to the quantities of goods or services supplied;

(c) information in relation to the geographical areas in which they are supplied.

(2) In sub-paragraph (1) 'accounting information', in relation to a supply of goods or services, means information as to—

(a) the costs of the supply, including fixed costs and overheads;

(b) the manner in which fixed costs and overheads are calculated and apportioned for accounting purposes of the supplier; and

(c) the income attributable to the supply.

18

An order made by virtue of paragraph 15 or 17 may provide for the manner in which information is to be published or otherwise notified.

19

An order may—

(a) require any person to supply information to the relevant authority;

(b) where the OFT is not the relevant authority, require any person to supply information to the OFT;

(c) provide for the publication, by the person who has received information by virtue of paragraph (a) or (b), of that information.

National security

20

(1) An order may make such provision as the person making the order considers to be appropriate in the interests of national security (within the meaning of section 58(1)).

(2) Such provision may, in particular, include provision requiring a person to do, or not to do, particular things.

Newspaper mergers

20A

(1) This paragraph applies in relation to any order—

(a) which is to be made following the giving of—

(i) an intervention notice which mentions a newspaper public interest consideration;

(ii) an intervention notice which mentions any other media public interest consideration in relation to a relevant merger situation in which one of the enterprises ceasing to be distinct is a newspaper enterprise;

(iii) a special intervention notice which mentions a consideration specified in section 58(2A) or (2B); or(iv) a special intervention notice which, in relation to a special merger situation in which one of the enterprises ceasing to be distinct is a newspaper enterprise, mentions a consideration specified in section 58(2C); and

(b) to which the consideration concerned is still relevant.

(2) The order may make such provision as the person making the order considers to be appropriate in all circumstances of the case.

(3) Such provision may, in particular, include provision requiring a person to do, or not to do, particular things.

(4) Provision made by virtue of this paragraph may, in particular, include provision—

(a) altering the constitution of a body corporate (whether in connection with the appointment of directors, the establishment of an editorial board or otherwise);

(b) requiring the agreement of the relevant authority or another person before the taking of particular action (including the appointment or dismissal of an editor, journalists or directors or acting as a shadow director);

(c) attaching conditions to the operation of a newspaper;

(d) prohibiting consultation or co-operation between subsidiaries.

(5) In this paragraph 'newspaper public interest consideration' means a media public interest consideration other than one which is such a consideration—

(a) by virtue of section 58(2C); or

(b) by virtue of having been, in the opinion of the Secretary of State, concerned with broadcasting and a consideration that ought to have been specified in section 58.

(6) This paragraph is without prejudice to the operation of the other paragraphs of this Schedule in relation to the order concerned.

Supplementary

21

(1) An order, as well as making provision in relation to all cases to which it may extend, may make provision in relation to—

(a) those cases subject to specified exceptions; or

(b) any particular case or class of case.

(2) An order may, in relation to the cases in relation to which it applies, make the full provision which may be made by it or any less provision (whether by way of exception or otherwise).

(3) An order may make provision for matters to be determined under the order.

(4) An order may—

(a) make different provision for different cases or classes of case or different purposes;

(b) make such transitional, transitory or saving provision as the person making it considers appropriate.

22

(1) An order which may prohibit the doing of anything (or the refraining from doing anything) may in particular by virtue of paragraph 21(2) prohibit the doing of that thing (or the refraining from doing of it) except to such extent and in such circumstances as may be provided by or under the order.

(2) Any such order may, in particular, prohibit the doing of that thing (or the refraining from doing of it)—

(a) without the agreement of the relevant authority or another person; or

(b) by or in relation to a person who has not been approved by the relevant authority or another person.

Interpretation

23

References in this Schedule to the notification of prices or other information are not limited to the notification in writing of prices or other information.

24

In this Schedule 'the relevant authority' means—

(a) in the case of an order to be made by the OFT, the OFT;

(b) in the case of an order to be made by the Commission, the Commission; and

(c) in the case of an order to be made by the Secretary of State, the Secretary of State.

SCHEDULE 10

PROCEDURAL REQUIREMENTS FOR CERTAIN ENFORCEMENT UNDERTAKINGS AND ORDERS

Section 90

Requirements for accepting undertakings and making orders

1

Paragraph 2 applies in relation to—

(a) any undertaking under section 73 or 82 or paragraph 3 or 9 of Schedule 7 (other than an undertaking under the enactment concerned which varies an undertaking under that enactment but not in any material respect); and

(b) any order under section 75, 83 or 84 or paragraph 5, 10 or 11 of Schedule 7 (other than an order under the enactment concerned which is a revoking order of the kind dealt with by paragraphs 6 to 8 below).

2

(1) Before accepting an undertaking to which this paragraph applies or making an order to which this paragraph applies, the OFT, the Commission or (as the case may be) the Secretary of State (in this Schedule 'the relevant authority') shall—

(a) give notice of the proposed undertaking or (as the case may be) order; and

(b) consider any representations made in accordance with the notice and not withdrawn.

(2) A notice under sub-paragraph (1) shall state—

(a) that the relevant authority proposes to accept the undertaking or (as the case may be) make the order;

(b) the purpose and effect of the undertaking or (as the case may be) order;

(c) the situation that the undertaking or (as the case may be) order is seeking to deal with;

(d) any other facts which the relevant authority considers justify the acceptance of the undertaking or (as the case may be) the making of the order;

(e) a means of gaining access to an accurate version of the proposed undertaking or (as the case may be) order at all reasonable times; and

(f) the period (not less than 15 days starting with the date of publication of the notice in the case of an undertaking and not less than 30 days starting with that date in the case of an order) within which representations may be made in relation to the proposed undertaking or (as the case may be) order.

(3) A notice under sub-paragraph (1) shall be given by—

(a) in the case of a proposed order, serving on any person identified in the order as a person on whom a copy of the order should be served a copy of the notice and a copy of the proposed order; and

(b) in every case, publishing the notice.

(4) The relevant authority shall not accept the undertaking with modifications or (as the case may be) make the order with modifications unless the relevant authority—

(a) gives notice of the proposed modifications; and

(b) considers any representations made in accordance with the notice and not withdrawn.

(5) A notice under sub-paragraph (4) shall state—

(a) the proposed modifications;

(b) the reasons for them; and

(c) the period (not less than 7 days starting with the date of the publication of the notice under sub-paragraph (4)) within which representations may be made in relation to the proposed modifications.

(6) A notice under sub-paragraph (4) shall be given by—

(a) in the case of a proposed order, serving a copy of the notice on any person identified in the order as a person on whom a copy of the order should be served; and

(b) in every case, publishing the notice.

3

(1) If, after giving notice under paragraph 2(1) or (4), the relevant authority decides—

(a) not to accept the undertaking concerned or (as the case may be) make the order concerned; and

(b) not to proceed by virtue of paragraph 5;

the relevant authority shall give notice of that decision.

(2) A notice under sub-paragraph (1) shall be given by—

(a) in the case of a proposed order, serving a copy of the notice on any person identified in the order as a person on whom a copy of the order should be served; and

(b) in every case, publishing the notice.

4

As soon as practicable after accepting an undertaking to which paragraph 2 applies or (as the case may be) making an order to which that paragraph applies, the relevant authority shall (except in the case of an order which is a statutory instrument)—

(a) serve a copy of the undertaking on any person by whom it is given or (as the case may be) serve a copy of the order on any person identified in the order as a person on whom a copy of the order should be served; and

(b) publish the undertaking or (as the case may be) the order.

5

(1) The requirements of paragraph 2(4) (and those of paragraph 2(1)) shall not apply if the relevant authority—

(a) has already given notice under paragraph 2(1) but not paragraph 2(4) in relation to the proposed undertaking or order; and

(b) considers that the modifications which are now being proposed are not material in any respect.

(2) The requirements of paragraph 2(4) (and those of paragraph 2(1)) shall not apply if the relevant authority—

(a) has already given notice under paragraphs 2(1) and (4) in relation to the matter concerned; and

(b) considers that the further modifications which are now being proposed do not differ in any material respect from the modifications in relation to which notice was last given under paragraph 2(4).

Termination of undertakings and orders

6

Paragraph 7 applies where the relevant authority is proposing to—

(a) release any undertaking under section 73 or 82 or paragraph 3 or 9 of Schedule 7 (other than in connection with accepting an undertaking under the enactment concerned which varies or supersedes an undertaking under that enactment); or

(b) revoke any order under section 75, 83 or 84 or paragraph 5, 10 or 11 of Schedule 7 (other than in connection with making an order under the enactment concerned which varies or supersedes an order under that enactment).

7

(1) Before releasing an undertaking to which this paragraph applies or (as the case may be) revoking an order to which this paragraph applies, the relevant authority shall—

(a) give notice of the proposed release or (as the case may be) revocation; and

(b) consider any representations made in accordance with the notice and not withdrawn.

(2) A notice under sub-paragraph (1) shall state—

(a) the fact that a release or (as the case may be) revocation is proposed;

(b) the reasons for it; and

(c) the period (not less than 15 days starting with the date of publication of the notice in the case of an undertaking and not less than 30 days starting with that date in the case of an order) within which representations may be made in relation to the proposed release or (as the case may be) revocation.

(3) If after giving notice under sub-paragraph (1) the relevant authority decides not to proceed with the release or (as the case may be) the revocation, the relevant authority shall give notice of that decision.

(4) A notice under sub-paragraph (1) or (3) shall be given by—

(a) serving a copy of the notice on the person who gave the undertaking which is being released or (as the case may be) on any person identified in the order being revoked as a person on whom a copy of the order should be served; and
(b) publishing the notice.

8
As soon as practicable after releasing the undertaking or making the revoking order, the relevant authority shall (except in the case of an order which is a statutory instrument)—

(a) serve a copy of the release of the undertaking on the person who gave the undertaking or (as the case may be) serve a copy of the revoking order on any person identified in the order being revoked as a person on whom a copy of that order should be served; and
(b) publish the release or (as the case may be) the revoking order.

Power to dispense with the requirements of the Schedule

9
The relevant authority may dispense with any or all of the requirements of this Schedule if the relevant authority considers that the relevant authority has special reasons for doing so.

Bibliography[1]

BOOKS

BERGEIJK, PAG VAN, AND KLOOSTERHUIS, E, (eds), *Modelling European Mergers: Theory, Competition Policy and Case Studies* (Cheltenham, Edward Elgar, 2005).

BESANKO, D, DRANOVE, D , SHANLEY, M, AND SCHAEFER, S *Economics of Strategy* (3rd edn Hoboken, NJ, John Wiley & Sons, 2003).

BISHOP, S, AND WALKER, M, *The Economics of EC Competition Law: Concepts, Application and Measurement* (London, Sweet & Maxwell, 1999).

— *The Economics of EC Competition Law: Concepts, Application and Measurement* (2nd edn, London, Sweet & Maxwell, 2002).

BROBERG, MP, *The European Commission's Jurisdiction to Scrutinise Mergers* (2nd edn, The Hague, Kluwer Law International 2003).

CARLTON, DW, and PERLOFF, JM, *Modern Industrial Orgnanization* (4th edn Boston, Mass, Addison Wesley, 2005).

CHURCH, J, and WARE, R, *Industrial Organization: A Strategic Approach* (Boston, Mass, Irwin McGraw Hill, 2000).

COOK CJ, and KERSE, CS, *EC Merger Control* (3rd edn, London, Sweet & Maxwell, 2000).

— *EC Merger Control* 4th edn, London, Sweet & Maxwell, 2005).

CUNNINGHAM, JP, *The Fair Trading Act 1973: Consumer Protection and Competition Law* (London, Sweet & Maxwell, 1974).

DIXIT, A, and SKEATH, S, *Games of Strategy* (2nd edn, New York, WW Norton and Company, 2004).

DRAUZ, G, and REYNOLDS, M, (eds), *EC Merger Control: A Major Reform in Progress*, (Richmond, Surrey, Richmond Law and Tax, 2003).

FAULL, J, and A NIKPAY (eds), *The EC Law of Competition* (Oxford, Oxford University Press, 1999).

FURSE, M, *Competition and the Enterprise Act 2002* (Bristol, Jordans, 2003).

GERBER, DJ, *Law and Competition in Twentieth Century Europe: Protecting Prometheus* (Oxford, Clarendon Press 1998).

GOYDER, DG, *EC Competition Law*, (4th edn, Oxford, OUP, 2003).

HILDEBRAND, D, *The Role of Economic Analysis in the EC Competition Rules*, (2nd edn, The Hague, Kluwer Law International, 2002).

ILZKOVITZ, F, and MEIKELJOHN, R, (eds) *European Merger Control: Do we need an efficiency defence?* (Cheltenham, Edward Elgar, 2006).

[1] This bibliography lists works consulted in the preparation of this book or referred to in the text, and is not a comprehensive bibliography of the literature relating to merger control in the EC and UK. Where material is available on the Internet specific web addresses have not been given, as these change. However, the main web location is indicated in respect of materials which are not available in hard-copy format.

KERSE, CS, and KHAN, N, *EC Antitrust Procedure*, (5th edn, London, Sweet & Maxwell, 2005).

KWOKA, JE, Jr and WHITE, LJ, (eds), *The Antitrust Revolution: Economics, Competition and Policy*, (4th edn, New York, OUP, 2004).

LEVEQUE, F, and SHELANSKI, H, *Merger Remedies in American and European Union Competition Law*, (Cheltenham, Edward Elgar , 2003).

LINDSAY, A, *The EC Merger Regulation: Substantive Issues*, (London, Sweet & Maxwell, 2003).

— *The EC Merger Regulation: Substantive Issues*, (2nd edn, London, Sweet & Maxwell, 2006).

LINDRUP, G, *Butterworths Competition Law Handbook*, (10th edn, London, LexisNexis, 2005).

LIVINGSTON, D, *Competition Law and Practice*, (London, FT Law and Tax, 1995).

MOTTA, M, *Competition Policy: Theory and Practice*, (Cambridge, Cambridge University Press, 2004).

NAVARRO, E, FONT, E, FOLGUERA, J, and BRIONES, J, *Merger Control in the EU*, (2nd edn, Oxford, OUP, 2005).

PARR, N, FINBOW, R, and HUGHES, M, *UK Merger Control: Law and Practice*, (2nd edn, London, Sweet & Maxwell, 2005).

PEPALL, L, RICHARDS, DJ, and NORMAN, G, *Industrial Organization: Contemporary Theory and Practice*, (2nd edn, Mason Ohio, South-Western, 2002).

PORTER, MP, *Competitive Strategy: Techniques for Analyzing Industries and Competitors*, (New York, The Free Press, 1980).

SCHLOSSBERG, RS, (ed), *Mergers and Acquisitions: Understanding the Antitrust Issues*, (2nd edn, Chicago, American Bar Association, 2004).

SCOTT, A, HVIID, M, LYONS, B, *Merger Control in the United Kingdom*, (Oxford, OUP 2006).

STROUX, S, *US and EC Oligopoly Control*, (The Hague, Kluwer Law International, 2004).

UTTON, MA, *Market Dominance and Antitrust Policy*, (2nd edn, Cheltenham, Edward Elgar, 2003).

VISCUSI, WK, HARRINGTON, JE, and VERNON, JM, *Economics of Regulation and Antitrust*, (4th edn, Cambridge Mass, The MIT Press, 2005).

Zanettin, B, *Cooperation Between Antitrust Agencies at the International Level*, (Oxford, Hart Publishing, 2002).

ARTICLES, ETC

ABBAMONTE, AG, and RABASSA, V, 'Foreclosure and Vertical Mergers—The Commission's Review of Vertical Effects in the Last Wave of Media and Internet Mergers: AOL/Time Warner, Vivendi/Seagram, MCI Worldcom/Sprint' [2001] *ECLR* 214.

AHIMUD, Y, and LEV, B, 'Risk Reduction as a Managerial Motive for Conglomerate Mergers' (1981) 12 *Bell Journal of Economics* 605.

AHLBORN, C, and YSEWYN, J, 'EC Merger Control Regulation—Problems and Solutions', [2002] *Comp Law* 301.

ALESE, F, 'UK Merger Review and Section 33: Was the CAT Not Right? ' [2004] *ECLR* 470.

ALPA, G, 'Mergers: Remedies and Freedom of Contract' [2004] *European Business Law Review* 129.
ANDREANGELI, A, 'Fairness and Timing in Merger Control Proceedings: will the "Stop-the-Clock" Clause Work?' [2005] *ECLR* 403.
BACCARO, V, 'Failing Firm Defence and Lack of Causality: Doctrine and Practice in Europe of Two Closely Related Concepts' [2004] *ECLR* 11.
BAILEY, D, 'Standard of Proof in EC Merger Proceedings: a Common Law Perspective' (2003) 40 *CML Rev* 845.
BAKER, J, 'The Problem with *Baker Hughes* and *Syufy*: On the Role of Entry in Merger Analysis' (1997) 65 *Antitrust Law Journal* 353.
BAKER, S, COSCELLI, A, and DIJK, TV, 'Unilateral Effects in Retail Chain Mergers: An Application to Supermarkets' [2002] *ECLR* 180.
—— and LOFARO, A, 'Buyer Power and the Enso/Stora Decision' [2000] *ECLR* 187.
BANKS, D, 'Non-Competition Factors and their Future Relevance under European Merger Law' [1997] *ECLR* 182.
BANKS, JD, 'The Development of the Concept of Extraterritoriality under European Merger Law and its Effectiveness under the Merger Regulation following the Boeing/McDonnell Douglas Decision' [1998] *ECLR* 306.
BARROS, PP, BRITO D, and LUCENA, D DE, 'Mergers in the Food Retailing Sector: An Empirical Investigation' (2006) 50 *European Economic Review* 447.
BAVASSO, AF, 'Boeing/McDonnell Douglas: Did the Commission Fly Too High?' [1998] *ECLR* 243.
BAXTER, S, and DETHMERS, F, 'Unilateral Effects Under the European Merger Regulation: How Big is the Gap?' [2005] *ECLR* 380.
BEALE, N, 'The *Somerfield* Decisions of the Competition Commission and Competition Appeal Tribunal and the Economics of Divestment Remedies' [2006] *Comp Law* 45.
BERG, W, and OSTENDORF, P, 'The Reform of EC Merger Control: Substance and Impact of the Proposed New Procedural Rules' [2003] *ECLR* 594.
BIRO, Z, and PARKER, D, 'A New EC Merger Test? Dominance v Substantial Lessening of Competition' [2002] *Comp Law* 157.
BISHOP, S, 'Power and Responsibility: The ECJ's Kali-Salz Judgment' [1999] *ECLR* 37.
—— LOFARO, A, ROSATI, F, and YOUNG, J, *The Efficiency-Enhancing Effects of Non-Horizontal Mergers*, (Luxembourg, Office for Official Publications of the European Communities, 2005).
—— and RIDYARD, D, 'Prometheus Unbound: Increasing the Scope for Intervention in EC Merger Control' [2003] *ECLR* 357.
BJORVATN, K, 'Economic Integration and the Profitability of Cross-border Mergers and Acquisitions' (2004) 48 *European Economic Review* 1211.
BLACK, O, 'The Fair Trading Act's Market Share Test: A Heresy' [1996] *ECLR* 414.
—— 'Collusion and Co-ordination in EC Merger Control' [2003] *ECLR* 408.
BÖGE, U, and MÜLLER, E, 'From the Market Dominance Test to the SLC Test: Are There Any Reasons for a Change?' [2002] *ECLR* 495.
BOK, DC, 'Section 7 of the Clayton Act and the Merging of Law and Economics' (1960) 74 *Harvard Law Review* 226.
BORGES, CM, 'The Legitimate Interests of Member States in EC Merger Law' (2003) 9 *European Public Law* 345.
BRIGHT, C, and PERSSON, M, 'Article 22 of the EC Merger Regulation: An Opportunity Not to be Missed?' [2003] *ECLR* 490.

BROBERG, MP, 'Commitments in Phase One Merger Proceedings: the Commission's Power to Accept and Enforce Phase One Commitments' (1997) 34 *CML Rev* 845.
—— 'The Geographic Allocation of Turnover under the Merger Regulation' [1997] *ECLR* 103.
—— 'The Concept of Control in the Merger Control Regulation' [2004] *ECLR* 741.
BROWN, C, 'IBA Health: The First Challenge Under the New UK Merger Regime' [2003] *Comp Law* 347.
BURNLEY, R, 'The EC Merger Regulation and the Meaning of "Community Dimension"' [2003] *European Business Law Review* 819.
BURNSIDE, A, 'GE, Honey, I Sunk the Merger' [2002] *ECLR* 107.
CAFFARRA, C, and KÜHN, K-U, 'Joint Dominance: The CFI Judgment on Gencor/Lonrho' [1999] *ECLR* 355.
CAFFARRA, C, and COSCELLI, A, 'Merger to Monopoly: *NewsCorp/Telepiù*' [2003] *ECLR* 625.
CAMESASCA, PD, 'The Explicit Efficiency Defence in Merger Control: Does it Make the Difference' [1999] *ECLR* 14.
—— 'Mayday or Heyday? Dynamic Competition Meets Media Ownership Rules after Premiere' [2000] *ECLR* 76.
CANENBLEY, C, and ROSENTHAL, M, 'Cooperation between Antitrust Authorities in and outside the EU: What does it Mean for Multinational Corporations? (Part 2)', [2005] *ECLR* 178.
CHIBNALL, C, 'Expedited Treatment of Appeals against EC Commission Decisions under the EC Merger Regulation' [2002] *Comp Law* 327.
CHURCH, J, 'The Impact of Vertical and Conglomerate Mergers on Competition: Final Report' (2004) (DG Comp website).
COLLEY, L, 'From "Defence" to "Attack"? Quantifying Efficiency Arguments in Mergers' [2004] *ECLR* 342.
Competition Commission, *Annual Report and Accounts 2005/2006* (2006) (DG Comp website)
COMPTE, O, JENNY, F, and REY, P, 'Capacity Constraints, Mergers and Collusion' (2002) 46 *European Economic Review* 1.
COPPI, L, and DOBSON, P, 'The Importance of Market Conduct in the Economic Analysis of Mergers—The Interbrew Saga' [2002] *ECLR* 386.
DABBAH, MM, 'Opinion: *Tetra Laval v European Commission*' [2004] *Comp Law* 234.
DAUGHETY, AF, 'Beneficial Concentration' (1990) 80:1 *American Economic Review* 231.
DAVISON, LM, 'The GE/Honeywell Merger Controversy and the Path to Analytical Convergence in International Merger Assessment: A Critical Commentary' (2002) 24 *Liverpool Law Review* 89.
—— 'EU Merger Control and the Compatibility Test: A Review of Recent Developments' (2004) 25 *Liverpool Law Review* 195.
—— 'The New EC Merger Control Regulation: Guaranteeing the Effectiveness of the Architecture of Separate Jurisdictional Zones?' [2005] *Intereconomics* (May/June) 148.
Department of Trade and Industry, *A World Class Competition Regime*, Cm 5233, July 2001 (DTI website)
—— *Enterprise Act 2002: Public Interest Intervention in Media Mergers: Guidance on the operation of the public interest merger provisions relating to newspaper and other media mergers* (2004) (DTI website)

DERMINE, J, 'Bank Mergers in Europe: The Public Policy Issues' (2000) 28 *Journal of Common Market Studies* 409.

DUBOW, B, ELLIOTT, D, and MORRISON, E, 'Unilateral Effects and Merger Simulation Models' [2004] *ECLR* 114.

Editorial, 'The Next Step in Reform of EC Competition Law: Merger Control' (2003) 40 *CML Rev* 1.

ELLIOTT, GP, 'The Gencor Judgment: Collective Dominance, Remedies and Extraterritoriality under the Merger Regulation' [1999] *EL Rev* 638.

EPSTEIN, RJ, RUBINFELD, DL, 'Merger Simulation: A Simplified Approach with new Applications' (2001) 69 *Antitrust Law Journal* 883.

—— 'Technical Report: Effects of Mergers Involving Differentiated Products', (2003) COMP/B1/2003/07 (DG Comp website)

ERSBØLL, NC, 'Commitments under the Merger Regulation' [2001] *ECLR* 357.

EZRACHI, A, 'Limitations on the Extraterritorial Reach of the European Merger Regulation' [2001] *ECLR* 137.

FARRELL, L, 'Airtours plc v Commission' [2002] *Comp Law* 207.

FIEBIG, AR, 'International Law Limits on the Extraterritorial Application of the European Merger Control Regulation and Suggestions for Reform' [1998] *ECLR* 323.

FOUNTOUKAKOS, K, and RYAN, S, 'A New Substantive Test for EU Merger Control' [2005] *ECLR* 277.

FOX, EM, 'The Merger Regulation and its Territorial Reach: Gencor Ltd v Commission' [1999] *ECLR* 334.

FRAZER, T, 'NTL Communications Corp/Newcastle United plc', case note [1999] UKCLR 252.

GERARD, D, 'Merger Control Policy: how to Give Meaningful Consideration to Efficiency Claims?' (2003) 40 *CML Rev* 1367.

GIOTAKOS, D, 'GE/Honeywell: A Theoretic Bundle Assessing Conglomerate Mergers Across the Atlantic', (2002) 23 *University of Pennsylvania Journal of International Economic Law* 469.

GOLDBERG, AH, 'Merger Control: A Complex Trade-off' [2005] *Comp Law* 171.

GOODMAN, S, 'Steady As She Goes: The Enterprise Act 2002 Charts a Familiar Course for UK Merger Control' [2003] *ECLR* 331.

GRANT, J, and NEVEN, DJ, 'The Attempted Merger between General Electric and Honeywell: A Case Study of Transatlantic Conflict' [2005] 1 *Journal of Competition Law and Economics* 595.

GRIFFIN, JP, 'Antitrust Aspects of Cross-border Mergers and Acquisitions' [1998] *ECLR* 12.

HARBERGER, AC, 'Monopoly and Resource Allocation' (1954) 44 *American Economic Review* 77.

HARRIS, BC, and VELJANOVSKI, CG, 'Critical Loss Analysis: Its Growing Use in Competition Law' [2003] *ECLR* 212.

HAUPT, H, 'Collective Dominance Under Article 82 EC and EC Merger Control in the Light of the *Airtours* Judgment' [2002] *ECLR* 434.

HAY, GA, and WERDEN, GJ, 'Horizontal Mergers: Law Policy and Economics' (1993) 83 *American Economic Review* 173.

HOCHSTADT, ES, 'The *Brown Shoe* of European Union Competition Law' [2002] *Cardozo Law Review* 287.

HOFMANN, HCH, 'Good Governance in European Merger Control: Due Process and Checks and Balances under Review' [2003] *ECLR* 114.

HOLMES, S, and TURNBULL, S, 'Remedies in Merger Cases: Recent Developments' [2002] *ECLR* 499.

HOWARTH, D, '*Tetra Laval/Sidel*: Microeconomics or Microlaw?' [2005] *ECLR* 369.

HUGHES, M, and BEALE, N, 'Customer Surveys in UK Merger Cases—the Art and Science of Asking the Right People the Right Questions' [2005] *ECLR* 297.

ICN Working Group: Analytical Framework Subgroup, 'Project on Merger Guidelines: Report for the Third ICN Annual Conference in Seoul', April 2004 (ICN website)

IVALDI, M, JULLIEN, B, REY, P, SEABRIGHT, P, and TIROLE, J, 'The Economics of Unilateral Effects: Interim Report for DG Competition, European Commission' (2003) (DG Comp website)

—— 'The Economics of Tacit Collusion: Final Report for DG Competition, European Commission', (2003) (DG Comp website)

JEPHCOTT, M, and MAHTANI, MR, 'The *Somerfield* Judgment: A Damp Squib?' [2006] *Comp Law* 56.

KARACAN, P, 'Differences in Merger Analysis Between the United States and the European Union, Highlighted in the Context of the Boeing/McDonnell Douglas and GE/Honeywell Mergers' (2004) 17 *Transnational Law* 209.

KÄSERBERG, T, 'Are Merger Control and Article 82 EC in the Same Market?—The Assessment of Mergers which Facilitate Exclusionary Conduct under EC Merger Control' [2006] *ECLR* 409.

KASSAMALI, RA, 'From Fiction to Fallacy: Reviewing the EC Merger Regulation's Community-Dimension Thresholds in the Light of Economics and Experience in Merger Control' (1996) 21 *EL Rev* Supp (Competition).

KATTAN, J, 'Efficiencies and Merger Analysis' (1994) 62 *Antitrust Law Journal* 513.

KEKELEKIS, M, 'The Rights of Notifying Parties and Third Parties During the Preliminary Investigation Procedures under the ECMR' [2003] *European Business Law Review* 429.

—— 'The "Statement of Objections" as an Inherent Part of the Right to be Heard in EC Merger Proceedings: Issues of Concern' [2004] *ECLR* 518.

KIRCHGAESSNER, S, 'Merging Companies "should make the case for efficiencies"', *Financial Times*, 20 June 2006.

KOKKORIS, I, 'The Reform of the European Control Merger Regulation in the Aftermath of the *Airtours* Case—the Eagerly Expected Debate: SLC v Dominance Test' [2005] *ECLR* 37.

—— 'The Concept of Market Definition and the SSNIP Test in the Merger Appraisal' [2005] *ECLR* 209.

KOPKE, A, 'Merger Remedies Study' [2005] *Competition Policy Newsletter*, Autumn, 3.

KORAH, V, 'Gencor v Commission: Collective Dominance' [1999] *ECLR* 337.

LANGER, J, 'The *Airtours* Judgment: a Welcome Lecture on Oligopolies, Economics and Joint Dominance' (2003) 10 *Columbia Journal of European Law* 105.

LESTER, M, '*UniChem Limited v Office of Fair Trading*' [2005] *Comp Law* 99.

LEVY, N, 'Kimberly-Clark/Scott and the Power of Brands' [1996] *ECLR* 403.

LOMMERUD, KE, STRAUME, OR, and SØRGARD, L, 'Downstream Merger with Upstream Market Power' (2005) 49 *European Economic Review* 717.

LOFARO, A, and RIDYARD, D, 'Switching Costs and Merger Assessment—Don't Move the Goalposts' [2003] *ECLR* 268.

LOWE, P, 'The Future of EU Merger Control' [2002] *Comp Law* 310.

LUESCHER, C, 'Efficiency Considerations in European Merger Control—Just Another

Battle Ground for the European Commission, Economists and Competition Lawyers?' [2004] *ECLR* 72.

Lyons, BR, 'Could Politicians be more Right than Economists? A Theory of Merger Standards', Centre for Competition and Regulation, Working paper CCR 02-1 (2002), available at www.competition-regulation.org.uk

Mano, M de la, *For the Customer's Sake: The Competitive Effects of Efficiencies in European Merger Control*, (Luxembourg, Office for Official Publications of the European Communities, 2002) (DG Comp website)

Megregian, S, and Garrod, D, 'EU and US Merger Control: Transatlantic Convergence Rolls On' [2005] *Comp Law* 124.

Metaxas, G, and Armengod, H, 'EC Merger Regulation and the Status of Ancillary Restrictions: Evolution of the European Commission's Policy' [2005] *ECLR* 500.

Modrall, JR, and Ciullo, S, 'Gun-Jumping and EU Merger Control' [2003] *ECLR* 424.

Mohamed, S, 'National Interests Limiting EU Cross-Border Bank Mergers' [2000] *ECLR* 248.

Monti, M, 'The Commission Notice on Merger Remedies—One Year After', Speech, Paris, 18 January 2002 (DG Comp website)

Motta, M, 'EC Merger Policy and the Airtours Case' [2000] *ECLR* 199.

Mueller, DC, 'A Theory of Conglomerate Mergers' (1982) 82 *Quarterly Journal of Economics* 643.

Murphy, G, 'OFT Clears Sale of Telegraph Group to Barclay Brothers' [2005] *ECLR* 305.

National Economic Research Associates (NERA), 'Merger Appraisal in Oligopolistic Markets', OFT Research Paper 19 (1999) (now removed from website)

Neven, DJ, and Röller, L-H, 'The Allocation of Jurisdiction in International Antitrust' (2000) 44 *European Economic Review* 845.

Niels, G. 'The SSNIP Test: Some Common Misconceptions' [2004] *Comp Law* 267.

Nikolinakos, N, 'The Importance of Maintaining Competition in the Internet Market: the WorldCom/MCI Case' [2000] *ECLR* 393.

—— 'Mergers and Strategic Alliances in the Emerging Multi-Media Sector: The EU Competition Policy', [2004] *ECLR* 625.

Nikpay, A, and Houwen, F, 'Tour de Force or a Little Local Turbulence? A Heretical View on the *Airtours* Judgment' [2003] *ECLR* 193.

Noël, P-E, 'Efficiency Considerations in the Assessment of Horizontal Mergers under European and US Antitrust Law' [1997] *ECLR* 498.

Nucara, A, '*Schneider/Legrand* and *Tetra Laval/Sidel*: Fast Track Towards Merger Reform?' [2003] *European Business Law Review* 193.

O'Donoghue, R, and Feddersen, C, 'Case T-342/99, *Airtours plc v Commission*' (2002) 39 *CML Rev* 1171.

Office of Fair Trading, *Office of Fair Trading Annual Report 2005–06* (2006) (OFT website)

Organisation for Economic Cooperation and Development Council, 'Council Recommendation on Merger Review' (2005), available at 7:3 *OECD Journal of Competition Law and Policy* 7 www.oecd.org/competition.

Overd, A, 'After the Airtours Appeal' [2002] *ECLR* 375.

Papandropoulos, P, and Tajana, A, 'The Merger Remedies Study—In Divestiture We Trust?', [2006] *ECLR* 443.

Parker, D, 'A Screening Device for Tacit Collusion Concerns' [2006] *ECLR* 424.

PARKER, J, 'Air France/KLM: an Assessment of the Commission's Approach to Consolidation in the Air Transport Sector' [2005] *ECLR* 128.

PÉREZ, MGP, 'Collective Dominance Under the Merger Regulation' [1998] *EL Rev* 475.

PÉREZ, M, and BURNLEY, R, 'The Article 9 Referral Back Procedure: A Solution to the Jurisdictional Dilemma of the European Merger Regulation?' [2003] *ECLR* 364.

PERRY, M, and PORTER, R, 'Oligopoly and the Incentive for Horizontal Merger' (1985) 75 *American Economic Review* 219.

PERSSON, L, 'Predation and Mergers: Is Merger Law Counterproductive?' (2004) 48 *European Economic Review* 239.

PFLANZ, M, and CAFFARRA, C,'The Economics of GE/Honeywell' [2002] *ECLR* 115.

PICKERING, JF, 'Competition Policy and Vertical Relationships: The Approach of the UK Monopolies and Mergers Commission' [1999] *ECLR* 225.

PINSKE, J, and SLADE, ME, 'Mergers, Brand Competition, and the Price of a Pint' (2004) 48 *European Economic Review* 617.

PITOFSKY, R, 'New Definitions of Relevant Market and the Assault on Antitrust' (1990) 90 *Columbia Law Review* 1805.

PricewaterhouseCoopers LLP, 'Ex post evaluation of mergers' (2005) (OFT website)

PRYOR, A, 'The New Regime for the Regulation of Newspaper Mergers' [2004] *Comp Law* 63.

RADICATI DI BROZOLO, LG, and GUSTAFSSON, M, 'Full-function Joint Ventures Under the Merger Regulation: The Need for Clarification' [2003] *ECLR* 574.

RAGOLLE, F, '*Schneider Electric v Commission*: The CFI's Response to the Green Paper on Merger Review' [2003] *ECLR* 176.

RAVENSCRAFT, DJ, and SCHERER, FM, 'The Profitability of Mergers', (1989) *International Journal of Industrial Organization Special Issue* 101.

RBB Economics, 'A Bridge Too Far?—Complements, Substitutes and Theories of Exclusion in EC Merger Control', RBB Brief 1, May 2002.

—— 'Airtours/First Choice: CFI Holds Commission to Account', RBB Brief 2, July 2002.

—— 'Switching Costs and Merger Assessment—don't Move the Goalposts', RBB Brief 6, November 2002.

—— 'Full Marks? The Draft EC Notice on the Appraisal of Horizontal Mergers', RBB Brief 7, January 2003.

—— 'Goldilocks and the Three Bears—the Story of Market Definition and the Cruise Mergers', RBB Brief 11, October 2003.

—— 'The Emperor's New Clothes?—the Role of Merger Simulation Models', RBB Brief 12, January 2004.

—— 'Turning the Tables: Why Vertical and Conglomerate Mergers are Different', RBB Brief 18, March 2006.

—— 'Lost in Translation: The Use and Abuse of Diversion Ratios in Unilateral Effects Analysis', RBB Brief 19, June 2006.

ROBERT, G, and HUDSON, C, 'Past Co-ordination and the Commission Notice on the Appraisal of Horizontal Mergers' [2004] *ECLR* 163.

RODGER, BJ, 'UK Merger Control: Politics, the Public Interest and Reform' [2000] *ECLR* 24.

ROUSSEVA, E, and MONTI, G, 'Failing Firms in the Framework of the EC Merger Control Regulation' [1999] *EL Rev* 38.

Royal Commission on the Press, *Report of the Royal Commission on the Press 1961–1962*, Cmnd 1811 (London, HMSO, 1962).

SALANT, SW, SWITZER, S, and REYNOLDS, RJ, 'Losses from Horizontal Merger: The Effects of an Exogenous Change in Industry Structure on Cournot-Nash Equilibrium' (1983) 98 *Quarterly Journal of Economics* 185.

SALINGER, MA, 'Vertical Mergers and Market Foreclosure' (1988) 103 *Quarterly Journal of Economics* 345.

SCHMIDT, J, 'The New ECMR: "Significant Impediment" or "Significant Improvement"?' (2004) 41 *CML Rev* 1555.

SCHMITZ, S, 'How Dare They? European Merger Control and the European Commission's blocking of the General Electric/Honeywell Merger', (2002) 23 *University of Pennsylvania Journal of International Economic Law L* 325.

SCHNELL, DK, 'All Bundled Up: Bringing the Failed GE/Honeywell Merger in from the Cold' 37 *Cornell International Law Journal* 217.

SINAN, I, and LOMAX, J, 'Transatlantic Mergers and Merger Control' (2001) 20(7) *International Financial Law Review* Supp, 71.

SINCLAIR, D, 'Ancillary Restraints Under the Merger Regulation: The Commission's Approach Case into Doubt by the Court of First Instance' [2003] *ECLR* 315.

SLOT, PJ, 'Case T–102/96, *Gencor Ltd v Commission*' (2001) 38 *CML Rev* 1573.

SOAMES, T, and MAUDHUIT, S, 'Changes in EU Merger Control: Part 1' [2005] *ECLR* 57.

—— 'Changes in EU Merger Control: Part 2' [2005] *ECLR* 75.

—— 'Changes in EU Merger Control: Part 3' [2005] *ECLR* 144.

STEHMANN, O, and AGUADO, JR, 'The Air France—KLM Merger: a First Step Towards the Consolidation of the European Aviation Industry' [2005] *ECLR* 258.

STROUX, S, 'Collective Dominance under the Merger Regulation: A Serious Evidentiary Reprimand for the Commission' [2002] *EL Rev* 736.

TASSANO, F, 'Are Vertical Mergers Harmful?' [1999] *ECLR* 395.

TEMPLE LANG, J, 'Two Important Merger Regulation Judgments: The Implications of *Schneider-Legrand* and *Tetra Laval-Sidel*' [2003] *EL Rev* 259.

THOMPSON, R, 'Goodbye to "the Dominance Test"? Substantive Appraisal Under the New UK and EC Merger Regimes' [2003] *Comp Law* 332.

USHER, T, 'EU Mergers and Strategic Alliances in the Broadcasting Industry' [2002] *Comp Law* 15.

Vanderelest Wijckmans Everaert Witters & Vennoten, *European Law Update*, February/March 2001, available at www.vwew.be

VAN DEN BERGH, R, 'Modern Industrial Organisation versus Old-fashioned European Competition Law' [1996] *ECLR* 75.

NAVARRO VARONA, E, and GONZALEZ DURANTEZ, H, 'Interim Measures in Competition Cases Before the European Commission and Courts' [2002] *ECLR* 512.

VENIT, JS, 'Two Steps Forward and No Steps Back: Economic Analysis and Oligopolistic Dominance after *Kali&Salz*' (1998) 35 *CML Rev* 1101.

VICKERS, J, 'How to Reform the EC Merger Test', 8 November 2002, www.oft.gov.

—— 'Competition Economics and Policy' [2003] *ECLR* 95.

VOIGT, S, and SCHMIDT, A, 'The Commission's Guidelines on Horizontal Mergers: Improvement or Deterioration?' (2004) 41 *CML Rev* 1583.

VÖLCKER, SB, 'Leveraging as a Theory of Competitive Harm in EU Merger Control' (2003) 40 *CML Rev* 581.

—— 'Mind the Gap: Unilateral Effects Analysis Arrives in EC Merger Control' [2004] *ECLR* 395.

WEITBRECHT, A, 'EU Merger Control in 2004—An Overview' [2005] *ECLR* 67.

WENT, D, 'The Acceptability of Remedies Under the EC Merger Regulation: Structural Versus Behavioural' [2006] *ECLR* 455.

WILLIAMSON, O, 'Economies as an Antitrust Defense: the Welfare Trade-offs' (1968) 58 *American Economic Review* 18.

YAO, D, and DAHDOUH, T, 'Information Problems in Merger Decision Making and Their Impact on Development of an Efficiencies Defense' (1993) 62 *Antitrust Law Journal* 23.

YSEWYN, J, and CAFFARRA, C, 'Two's Company, Three's a Crowd: The Future of Collective Dominance After the Kali & Salz Judgment' [1998] *ECLR* 468.

Index